A New

GREEK-ENGLISH LEXICON

to the

NEW TESTAMENT

SUPPLEMENTED BY A CHAPTER ELUCIDATING THE SYNONYMS
OF THE NEW TESTAMENT WITH A COMPLETE INDEX TO
THE SYNONYMS

GEORGE RICKER BERRY, PH.D.

Wilcox & Follett Company
Chicago, 1944

PRINTED IN THE U. S. A.

INTRODUCTION TO NEW TESTAMENT LEXICON.

A S a result of their wide experience as sellers of text-books of all kinds, extending over many years, the publishers have become aware that clergymen, theological students, and New Testament students generally, possess the conviction that none of the smaller New Testament Lexicons is entirely satisfactory. There are several essential and entirely practical features, not embodied in any of the smaller New Testament Lexicons, which should be incorporated in a work intended to fulfill all necessary require-ments. It is with the definite intention of supplying this need that the publishers nave undertaken the preparation of this new Lexicon. It aims to retain all the desirable features of the best small Lexicons in use, and also to present the several additional points demanded, while keeping within the compass of a volume of convenient size.

This Lexicon endeavors to put into a brief and compact form as much as possible of the material found in the larger New Testament Lexicons. The fact has been remembered that in nine cases out of ten the object in consulting a Lexicon is to refer quickly to the standard meanings of a word, rather than to study an exhaustive treatment of it. Hence, while every clergyman would like to possess one of the larger New Testament Lexicons, he still needs the small one for convenience in ordinary use. So it is assumed that this small New Testament Lexicon will be needed both for use independently, and also by those who have one of the larger Lexicons. It is hoped that in this volume the publishers' intention has been realized of producing a volume that better than any other so far published will serve this purpose quickly and well.

It may be desirable to point out a few features which have been made prominent. It will be at once apparent that some of these are not ordinarily found in the smaller New Testament Lexicons :

The inflection of nouns, adjectives, and verbs has been indicated with all the fullness which was considered practically necessary. In nouns, the ending of the genitive case has regularly been given, being omitted only with indeclinable nouns. The article indicating the gender regularly follows the genitive ending. Other cases have been given only rarely, when they are irregular or peculiar. In adjectives, the endings of the nominative have been given. In verbs, a different form for the present tense, such as a contracted form, has regularly been given, and ordinarily the ending of the future. The endings of the other tenses have only been given in some special cases when they are peculiar, or irregular. Of course the inflection in general has considered only the forms occurring in the New Testament; it is only rarely that classical forms not occurring in the New Testament have been given, since they would be of little practical value in ordinary New Testament study.

The hyphen, to separate the parts of compound words, has been used with considerable freedom, but in general accordance with the following principles. It has been used of course to separate the parts of words which are actually compounded of the two or more portions which appear in the word. Words derived from a compound word would not usually have the hyphen, but sometimes it has been inserted, especially when otherwise the derivation would not be obvious. So, too, the hyphen has been used with derivatives of a compound word, in cases where the original compound word does not occur in the New Testament, as otherwise the character of the word would not appear. The hyphen has also been used in many cases where the compound word is slightly changed in form from the parts of which it is composed, where this variation is not very great. Such a wide use of the hyphen has been for the purpose of increasing the practical value of this feature.

The original plan in reference to Synonyms was to give in the Lexicon itself definitions of a few of the most important ones. After most of the Lexicon was in type, however, it was decided, in view of the importance of the subject, that a very helpful feature would be a special section devoted to Synonyms. This has accordingly been prepared. The result is, of course, that a few words already treated in the Lexicon have here been given a fuller treatment.

The Index to the Synonyms includes all the nouns treated in the Lexicon proper, as well as those in the Synonyms, and this double treatment will always be found to be expressly indicated by its appropriate sign.

Some indications of the history of a word will surely be serviceable to the average student. Consequently, the words whose first known occurrence is in the Septuagint, in the Apocrypha, and in the New Testament, are indicated by the respective abbreviations at the end of the articles. Where the usage is in doubt, no indication has been given. The material for this has been drawn chiefly from Thayer. The other classifications which Thayer gives, it was thought would not be of sufficient practical use to the average student to be incorporated.

In the case of words from foreign languages, the language has been indicated in every instance, except with a part of the proper names, chiefly from the Hebrew, where the origin would be readily inferred. It has been the aim to make this feature accurate and up to date. In this matter, considerable help has been received from E. Kautzsch, *Grammatik des Biblisch-Aramäischen.*

The grammatical references given are to the three grammars which are probably in the most common use, viz.: S. G. Green, *Handbook to the Grammar of the Greek Testament,* Revised and Improved Edition; G. B. Winer, *A Grammar of the Idiom of the New Testament,* Seventh Edition, Translated by J. H. Thayer; and Alexander Buttman, *A Grammar of the New Testament Greek,* Translated by J. H. Thayer. These have been indicated respectively by the abbreviations Gr., Wi., and Bu., the references in the first two being by sections, in the last, for convenience, by pages.

The usual custom has been followed of making the received text, the so-called *Textus Receptus,* the basis of this Lexicon, except that sometimes another accentuation has been adopted, which seemed preferable. All the variations of any importance of the text of Westcott and Hort have been given. This does not include all the minor variations in spelling and accentuation. It was thought that to indicate the variants of other editors would occupy more space than it would be profitable to give. For the same reason no mention has been made of variant readings of the *Textus Receptus* itself.

The asterisk * at the end of many articles indicates that all the passages in which the word occurs in the New Testament have been given.

Besides other works which have already been mentioned, much material has been drawn from R. C. Trench, *Synonyms of the New Testament,* and from the New Testament Lexicons of Thayer and Cremer, as well as from the small ones of Green and Hickie.

The New Testament books have been indicated by the shortest abbreviations that would be easily intelligible. It is thought that they will be understood without explanation. The list of other abbreviations which is here added includes only those which might not be recognized without express indication.

ABBREVIATIONS.

Ap.	= Apocrypha (of the Old Testament).	O. T.	= Old Testament.
A. V.	= Authorized Version.	Rec.	= Textus Receptus.
Bu.	= Alexander Buttman (*Grammar of New Testament Greek*).	R. V.	= Revised Version.
		S.	= Septuagint.
dim.	= diminutive.	sc.	= namely, to wit.
fig.	= figurative.	sq.	= following.
Gr.	= S. G. Green (*Handbook to the Grammar of the Greek Testament*).	W. H.	= Westcott and Hort (*The New Testament in the Original Greek*).
i.e.	= that is.	Wi.	= G. B. Winer (*Grammar of the Idiom of the New Testament*).
lit.	= literally.		
met.	= metaphorically.	-	hyphen, see Introduction.
mrg.	= margin.	*	indicates that all the passages in which a word occurs in the New Testament have been given.
N. T.	= New Testament.		
orig.	= originally.		

Concerning the abbreviations for the Books of the New Testament, see last paragraph of Introduction.

GREEK-ENGLISH NEW TESTAMENT LEXICON.

Α, α, ἄλφα, *alpha,* *a,* the first
letter. Numerally, α' = 1;
,α = 1000. For α in com-
position, see Gr. § 147*b, c.*
Fig., τὸ Α, or τὸ Ἄλφα (W.
H.), *the first principle of all
things;* of the Father, Rev.
i. 8, xxi. 6; the Son, i. 11
(W. H. omit), xxii. 13.*

Ἀαρών (Heb.), *Aaron,* Lu. i. 5;
Ac. vii. 40; Heb. v. 4, vii.
11, ix. 4.*

Ἀβαδδών, ὁ (Heb. "destruction"), *Abaddon,* Rev. ix. 11.
(S.)*

ἀ-βαρής, *ές* (from βάρος), *without weight;* hence, *not burdensome,* 2 Cor. xi. 9.*

Ἀββᾶ, or Ἀββά (W. H.),
(Aram.), *Father!* only as an
invocation, Mar. xiv. 36;
Ro. viii. 15; Gal. iv. 6. (N.
T.)*

Ἄβελ, ὁ (W. H. Ἅβελ), (Heb.),
Abel, Mat. xxiii. 35; Lu. xi.
51; Heb. xi. 4, xii. 24.*

Ἀβιά, ὁ (Heb.), *Abia* or *Abijah,*
the king, Mat. i. 7; the priest,
Lu. i. 5.*

Ἀβιάθαρ, ὁ (Heb.), *Abiathar,*
Mar. ii. 26.*

Ἀβιληνή, ῆς, ἡ, *Abilene,* a district between Lebanon and
Hermon towards Phœnicia,
named from Abila, its chief
city, Lu. iii. 1.*

Ἀβιούδ, ὁ (Heb.), *Abiud,* Mat.
i. 13.*

Ἀβραάμ, ὁ (Heb.), *Abraham,*
Mat. i. 1, 2; Ro. iv. 1, 2, 3.*

ἄ-βυσσος, ον, ἡ (originally adj.
bottomless), *abyss,* Lu. viii. 31;
Ro. x. 7; Rev. ix. 1, 2, 11,
xi. 7, xvii. 8, xx. 1, 3.*

Ἄγαβος, ον, ὁ, *Agabus,* Ac. xi.
28, xxi. 10.*

ἀγαθο-εργέω, ῶ (or ἀγαθουργέω),
to be beneficent, 1 Tim. vi. 18;
Ac. xiv. 17 (W. H.). (N. T.)*

ἀγαθο-ποιέω, ῶ, (1) *to do good to,*
acc. of pers., Lu. vi. 33; (2)
to act well, 1 Pet. ii. 15, 20.
(S.)

ἀγαθο-ποιΐα, ας, ἡ, *well-doing,*
in sense (2) of preceding, 1
Pet. iv. 19. (N. T.)*

ἀγαθο-ποιός, οῦ, ὁ (originally
adj.), *well-doer,* 1 Pet. ii. 14.*

ἀγαθός, ή, όν (κρείσσων, κράτιστος), *good* in general, in
various senses, in itself or
its effects, physically or morally, used of both persons
and things, Mat. vii. 18; Lu.
vi. 45; 1 Pet. ii. 18; Phil. i.
6. τὸ ἀγαθόν, *the Good,* Mat.
xix. 17 (W. H.); τὰ ἀγαθά,
goods, wealth, blessings, Lu.
i. 53; Ro. x. 15.

ἀγαθωσύνη, ης, ἡ, *goodness,* 2
Th. i. 11. (S.) *Syn.:* ἀγαθωσύνη emphasizes the *zeal for
goodness;* χρηστότης, *kindness, benignity.*

ἀγαλλίασις, εως, ἡ, *exultation,
gladness,* Lu. i. 14, 44. (S.)

ἀγαλλιάω, ῶ, ασω, *to leap for
joy;* hence, *exult, rejoice;*
generally deponent. Fol-
lowed by ἵνα (subj.), Jn. viii.
56; ἐπί (dat.), Lu. i. 47; or
ἐν (dat.), Jn. v. 35. (S.)

ἄ-γαμος, ον, adj., *unmarried,* 1
Cor. vii. 8, 11, 32, 34.*

ἀγανακτέω, ῶ, ήσω, *to be indignant, angry.* With περί (gen.),
Mat. xx. 24; or ὅτι, Lu. xiii.
14.

ἀγανάκτησις, εως, ἡ, *indignation,* 2 Cor. vii. 11.*

ἀγαπάω, ῶ, ήσω, *to love,* Lu. vii.
47; *to wish well to,* Mat. v.

43, xix. 19; *to take pleasure
in,* Heb. i. 9; *to long for,* 2
Tim. iv. 8. *Syn.:* ἀγαπάω
denotes the love of the reason, esteem; φιλέω, the love
of the feelings, warm in-
stinctive affection.

ἀγάπη, ης, ἡ, *love, benevolence.*
Object with εἰς, ἐν, or genitive, Gr. § 269, Wi. § 30*a,*
Bu. 329. ἀγάπαι (Ju. 12),
love-feasts. (S.)

ἀγαπητός, ή, όν, *beloved,* Mat.
iii. 17.

Ἄγαρ, ἡ (W. H. Ἅγαρ), (Heb.),
Hagar, Gal. iv. 24, 25 (W.
H.).*

ἀγγαρεύω, σω (from the Persian), *to impress* into the
public service; hence, *to compel to perform any service,*
Mat. v. 41, xxvii. 32; Mar.
xv. 21.*

ἀγγεῖον, ον, τό, *vessel, utensil,*
Mat. xiii. 48 (Rec.), xxv. 4.*

ἀγγελία, ας, ἡ, *message,* 1 Jn. i.
5 (W. H.), iii. 11.*

ἄγγελος, ον, ὁ, *messenger,* Mat.
xi. 10; spec. of God's messengers to men, *angel,* Mat.
iv. 6. So of fallen spirits,
Ju. 6. "Angel of a church"
(Rev. i. 20, ii., iii.), either
messenger, or *elder,* or *an
angel* who watches over the
church.

ἄγγος, εος, τό, *vessel,* Mat. xiii.
48 (W. H.).*

ἄγε, interj. (properly impv. of
ἄγω), *come now!* Ja. iv. 13,
v. 1.*

ἀγέλη, ης, ἡ, *a flock* or *herd,*
Mat. viii. 30.

ἀ-γενεα-λόγητος, ον, adj., *of un-
recorded genealogy,* Heb. vii.
3. (N. T.)*

ἀ-γενής, ἐς (from γένος), low-born, base, 1 Cor. i. 28.*

ἁγιάζω, σω (from ἅγιος), to set apart from common use. Hence, to hallow, or regard with religious reverence, Mat. vi. 9; to consecrate to religious service, whether persons or things, Mat. xxiii. 17; Jn. xvii. 19; to cleanse for such consecration, Heb. ix. 13; so to purify, sanctify, 1 Cor. vi. 11. οἱ ἁγιαζόμενοι, those who are being sanctified; οἱ ἡγιασμένοι, those who are sanctified, Ac. xx. 32.

ἁγιασμός, οῦ, ὁ, sanctification, holiness, 1 Cor. i. 30; 1 Th. iv. 7. (S.)

ἅγιος, α, ον, hallowed, worthy of veneration, holy, consecrated, whether persons, places, or things. οἱ ἅγιοι, "the Saints"; τὸ ἅγιον, the Temple; τὰ ἅγια, the Sanctuary; ἅγια ἁγίων, the Holy of Holies; πνεῦμα ἅγιον, the Holy Spirit. Syn.: see Trench, § lxxxviii.

ἁγιότης, τητος, ἡ, holiness, Heb. xii. 10; 2 Cor. i. 12 (W. H.). (Ap.)*

ἁγιωσύνη, ης, ἡ, holiness, Ro. i. 4; 2 Cor. vii. 1; 1 Th. iii. 13. (S.)*

ἀγκάλη, ης, ἡ, the (curve of the) arm, Lu. ii. 28.*

ἄγκιστρον, ου, τό, fishhook, Mat. xvii. 27.*

ἄγκυρα, ας, ἡ, an anchor, Ac. xxvii. 29, 30, 40; Heb. vi. 19.

ἄ-γναφος, ον, adj., unfulled, undressed, Mat. ix. 16; Mar. ii. 21. (N. T.)*

ἁγνεία, ας, ἡ, purity, 1 Tim. iv. 12, v. 2.*

ἁγνίζω, σω, to cleanse, purify, ceremonially, Jn. xi. 55; morally, Ja. iv. 8.

ἁγνισμός, οῦ, ὁ, ceremonial purification, Ac. xxi. 26.*

ἀ-γνοέω, ῶ, ἥσω (see γιγνώσκω), (1) not to know, to be ignorant, 1 Tim. i. 13; ἀγνοῶν, ignorant; ἀγνοούμενος, unknown, Gal. i. 22; ignored, disregarded, 1 Cor. xiv. 38 (W. H.); (2) not to understand, Mar. ix. 32; Lu. ix. 45.

ἀγνόημα, ατος, τό, a sin of ignorance, error, Heb. ix. 7.* Syn.: see Trench, § lxvi.

ἄγνοια, ας, ἡ, ignorance, Ac. iii.

17, xvii. 30; Ep. iv. 18; 1 Pet. i. 14.*

ἁγνός, ή, όν, pure, 2 Cor. vii. 11; chaste, Tit. ii. 5. Syn.: see ἅγιος.

ἁγνότης, τητος, ἡ, purity, 2 Cor. vi. 6, xi. 3 (W. H.).*

ἁγνῶς, adv., purely, sincerely, Phil. i. 17.*

ἀγνωσία, ας, ἡ, ignorance, spec. willful ignorance, 1 Cor. xv. 34; 1 Pet. ii. 15.*

ἄγνωστος, ον, unknown, Ac. xvii. 23.*

ἀγορά, ᾶς, ἡ (ἀγείρω), a place of public resort, forum, market place, Ac. xvii. 17; used for the market, Mar. vii. 4; as the place of public assemblies, trials, etc., Ac. xvi. 19.

ἀγοράζω, σω, to purchase, buy, with gen. of price, Mar. vi. 37, or ἐκ, Mat. xxvii. 7, once ἐν, Rev. v. 9; fig., to redeem, ransom, Rev. v. 9, xiv. 3.

ἀγοραῖος, ον, belonging to the forum; hence (sc. ἡμέραι) court days, Ac. xix. 38; (sc. ἄνθρωποι) idlers, xvii. 5.*

ἄγρα, ας, ἡ, a catching, Lu. v. 4; the thing caught, a catch of fish, v. 9.*

ἀ-γράμματος, ον, unlearned, i.e., in Rabbinical lore, Ac. iv. 13.* Syn.: ἀγράμματος means illiterate, without knowledge gained by study; ἰδιώτης, not a specialist, or without knowledge gained by mingling in public life.

ἀγρ-αυλέω, ῶ, to live in the fields, Lu. ii. 8.*

ἀγρεύω, σω (to take in hunting), fig., to ensnare, Mar. xii. 13.*

ἀγρι-έλαιος, ου, ἡ, wild olive, Ro. xi. 17, 24.*

ἄγριος, ία, ιον, wild, of honey, Mat. iii. 4; Mar. i. 6; fierce, of waves, Ju. 13.*

Ἀγρίππας, α, ὁ, Agrippa, i.e., Herod Agrippa II. See Ἡρῴδης.

ἀγρός, οῦ, ὁ, field, spec. the country, Mat. vi. 28; plur., country districts, hamlets, Mar. v. 14.

ἀγρυπνέω, ῶ (ὕπνος), to be sleepless; hence, met., to watch, to be vigilant, Mar. xiii. 33; Lu. xxi. 36; Ep. vi. 18; Heb. xiii. 17.*

ἀγρυπνία, ας, ἡ, sleeplessness,

watching, 2 Cor. vi. 5, xi. 27.*

ἄγω, ξω, 2 a., ἤγαγον, trans., to lead, bring; with πρός (acc.), ἕως, εἰς, of destination; with ἐπί (acc.), of purpose, as Ac. viii. 32; to bring before, for trial, Ac. xxv. 17. Also to spend, as of time; to keep, as a particular day, Mat. xiv. 6 (not W. H.); Lu. xxiv. 21 (impers.). Fig., to lead the inclination, induce, Lu. iv. 1. Mid., to go, depart; subj., ἄγωμεν, let us go! Mat. xxvi. 46.

ἀγωγή, ῆς, ἡ (ἄγω), a leading, course of life, 2 Tim. iii. 10.*

ἀγών, ῶνος, ὁ, contest, conflict; fig., of the Christian life, as Heb. xii. 1; solicitude, anxiety, Col. ii. 1.

ἀγωνία, ας, ἡ, contest, agony, Lu. xxii. 44 (not W. H.).*

ἀγωνίζομαι, to strive, as in the public games, 1 Cor. ix. 25; to contend with an adversary, Jn. xviii. 36; fig., of Christian effort and endurance, Col. i. 29.

Ἀδάμ, ὁ (Heb.), Adam.

ἀ-δάπανος, ον, free of charge, gratuitous, 1 Cor. ix. 18.*

Ἀδδί, ὁ, Addi, Lu. iii. 28 (not mentioned in O. T.).*

ἀδελφή, ῆς, ἡ, a sister, (1) lit., Mat. xix. 29; (2) fig. of Christian friendship, 1 Cor. vii. 15.

ἀδελφός, οῦ, ὁ, a brother, (1) lit. (see Gr. § 256), Mat. i. 2; (2) of more general relations, a fellow-countryman, Mat. v. 47; a fellow-Christian, Mat. xxiii. 8; a fellow-man, Mat. v. 22–24; also expressing the relation between Christ and believers, Mat. xxv. 40. The "brethren of Jesus" (Mat. xiii. 55; Jn. vii. 3; Ac. i. 14; Gal. i. 19) are probably to be understood literally.

ἀδελφότης, τητος, ἡ, the brotherhood, i.e., the Christian community, 1 Pet. ii. 17, v. 9. (Ap.)*

ἄ-δηλος, ον, not manifest, uncertain, Lu. xi. 44; 1 Cor. xiv. 8.*

ἀ-δηλότης, τητος, uncertainty, 1 Tim. vi. 17.*

ἀδήλως, adv., uncertainly, 1 Cor. ix. 26.*

ἀδημονέω, ῶ, to be troubled, distressed, Mar. xiv. 33.

ᾅδης, ου, ὁ (ἀ priv. and ἰδεῖν), the invisible world, Hades, Lu. xvi. 23; fig., of deep degradation, Mat. xi. 23. See πύλη.

ἀ-διά-κριτος, ον, without uncertainty, unambiguous, Ja. iii. 17.*

ἀ-διά-λειπτος, ον, without intermission, unceasing, Ro. ix. 2; 2 Tim. i. 3.*

ἀδιαλείπτως, adv., without intermission, incessantly, Ro. i. 9; 1 Th. i. 2, ii. 13, v. 17.*

ἀ-δια-φθορία, ας, ἡ, incorruptibility, soundness, Tit. ii. 7 (not W. H.). (N. T.)*

ἀδικέω, ῶ, ἡσω (ἄδικος), intrans., to act unjustly, commit a crime, Ac. xxv. 11; trans., to wrong, injure, Mat. xx. 13; hence, to hurt, without any notion of wrong, Lu. x. 19, and Rev. often; pass., to be wronged, 2 Cor. vii. 12; mid., to suffer wrong, 1 Cor. vi. 7.

ἀδίκημα, ατος, τό, a wrong, misdeed, Ac. xviii. 14, xxiv. 20; Rev. xviii. 5.*

ἀδικία, ας, ἡ, wrong (towards man or God); hence, injustice, Lu. xviii. 6; Ro. ix. 14; unrighteousness, Ro. i. 18, 29; act of unrighteousness, 1 Jn. v. 17; Heb. viii. 12.

ἄ-δικος, ον, unjust, unrighteous, generally, opposed to δίκαιος, as Mat. v. 45, to εὐσεβής, as 2 Pet. ii. 9, or to πιστός, as Lu. xvi. 10.

ἀδίκως, adv., unjustly, undeservedly, 1 Pet. ii. 19.*

ἀ-δόκιμος, ον (tested, but not approved), reprobate, rejected, Ro. i. 28; 1 Cor. ix. 27; 2 Cor. xiii. 5, 6, 7; 2 Tim. iii. 8; Tit. i. 16; Heb. vi. 8.*

ἄ-δολος, ον, without fraud, unadulterated, 1 Pet. ii. 2.* Syn.: see Trench, § lvi.

Ἀδραμυττηνός, ή, όν, of Adramyttium, a seaport of Mysia, Ac. xxvii. 2.*

Ἀδρίας, ου, ὁ, the Adriatic, the sea between Greece and Italy, Ac. xxvii. 27.*

ἀδρότης, τητος, ἡ, abundance, liberality, 2 Cor. viii. 20.*

ἀδυνατέω, ῶ, ἡσω, to be impossible, with dat. of pers., Mat. xvii. 20; or παρά (dat., W. H. gen.), Lu. i. 37.*

ἀ-δύνατος, ον, (1) of persons, act., powerless, Ac. xiv. 8; (2) of things, pass., impossible, Ro. viii. 3.

ᾄδω, ᾄσω (contr. from ἀείδω), to sing, with cognate acc., ᾠδήν, a song, Rev. v. 9, xiv. 3, xv. 3; with dat., to sing (praise) to, Ep. v. 19; Col. iii. 16.*

ἀεί, adv., always; of continuous time, unceasingly, Ac. vii. 51; of successive intervals, from time to time, on every occasion, 1 Pet. iii. 15.

ἀετός, οῦ, ὁ, an eagle, Rev. iv. 7; gen. bird of prey, as Mat. xxiv. 28.

ἄ-ζυμος, ον, unleavened, only in plur., sc. λάγανα, cakes, or ἄρτοι, loaves; met., the paschal feast, Lu. xxii. 1; fig., uncorrupted, sincere, 1 Cor. v. 7, 8.

Ἀζώρ, indecl. (Heb.), Azor, Mat. i. 13, 14; not mentioned in O. T.*

Ἄζωτος, ου, ἡ, Azotus or Ashdod, Ac. viii. 40.*

ἀήρ, ἀέρος, ὁ, the air, atmosphere, Ac. xxii. 23; Ep. ii. 2.

ἀ-θανασία, ας, ἡ (see θάνατος), immortality, 1 Cor. xv. 53, 54; 1 Tim. vi. 16.*

ἀ-θέμιτος, ον (θέμις, law), unlawful, criminal, Ac. x. 28; 1 Pet. iv. 3.*

ἄ-θεος, ον, without God, Ep. ii. 12.*

ἄ-θεσμος, ον (θεσμός, statute), lawless, 2 Pet. ii. 7, iii. 17.*

ἀ-θετέω, ῶ, ἡσω (θε- as in τίθημι), to make void, invalid; of things, to nullify, Lu. vii. 30; chiefly of persons, to slight, reject, Lu. x. 16.

ἀ-θέτησις, εως, ἡ, nullification, abrogation, Heb. vii. 18, ix. 26.*

Ἀθῆναι, ῶν, αἱ, Athens, Ac. xvii. 15.

Ἀθηναῖος, α, ον, Athenian, Ac. xvii. 21, 22.*

ἀθλέω, ῶ (ἄθλος, a contest), to contend in the public games, 2 Tim. ii. 5.*

ἄθλησις, εως, ἡ, contest, as in the public games; only fig. Heb. x. 32.*

ἀθροίζω, to gather together, Lu. xxiv. 33 (W. H.).*

ἀ-θυμέω, ω, to lose heart, despond, Col. iii. 21.*

ἀθῶος, ον, unpunished, innocent, Mat. xxvii. 4 (not W. H.); with ἀπό, of the crime, ver. 24.*

αἴγειος, η, ον (αἴξ, goat), of or belonging to a goat, Heb. xi. 37.*

αἰγιαλός, οῦ, ὁ, the shore, beach; used of Gennesaret, Mat. xiii. 2, 48; Jn. xxi. 4; of the Mediterranean, Ac. xxi. 5, xxvii. 39, 40.*

Αἰγύπτιος, α, ον, Egyptian, Ac. vii. 22.

Αἴγυπτος, ου, ἡ, Egypt, Mat. ii. 13.

ἀΐδιος, ον, adj. (ἀεί), eternal, everlasting, Ro. i. 20; Ju. 6.*

αἰδώς, οῦς, ἡ, modesty, 1 Tim. ii. 9; reverence, Heb. xii. 28 (not W. H.).* Syn.: see Trench, § xix; Thayer, p. 14.

Αἰθίοψ, οπος, ὁ, an Ethiopian, Ac. viii. 27.*

αἷμα, ατος, τό, blood, (1) in general, Jn. xix. 34; (2) natural life, which was believed to reside in the blood, especially with σάρξ, 1 Cor. xv. 20; so human nature generally; hence, (3) natural relationship, Jn. i. 13; (4) blood shed of sacrificial victims, Heb. ix. 7, 12; (5) hence, the blood of Christ, his atoning death, 1 Cor. x. 16; Rev. vii. 14; (6) violent death, bloodshed, murder, Lu. xiii. 1; Mat. xxiii. 30, 35; (7) in Ac. ii. 20, etc., the reference is to the color of blood.

αἱματ-εκ-χυσία, ας, ἡ, shedding of blood, Heb. ix. 22. (N. T.)*

αἱμορροέω, ῶ, to suffer from a flow of blood, Mat. ix. 20.*

Αἰνέας, α, ὁ, Aeneas, Ac. ix. 33, 34.*

αἴνεσις, εως, ἡ, praise, Heb. xiii. 15. (S.)*

αἰνέω, ῶ, έσω and ήσω, to praise, only of praise to God, Lu. ii. 13, 20.

αἴνιγμα, ατος, τό, an enigma, an obscure thing, 1 Cor. xiii. 12.*

αἶνος, ου, ὁ, praise to God, Mat. xxi. 16; Lu. xviii. 43.*

Αἰνών, ἡ (Heb.), Aenon, Jn. iii. 23.*

αἵρεσις, εως, ἡ (αἱρέω), choice, its act or result; hence, a

tenet, heresy, 2 Pet. ii. 1;
a sect, Ac. v. 17; *dissension*,
Gal. v. 20.

αἱρετίζω, σω, *to choose*, Mat. xii.
18.*

αἱρετικός, ή, όν, *schismatic, factious*, Tit. iii. 10.*

αἱρέω (irreg., Gr. § 103, 1, Wi.
§ 15, Bu. 53), *to take*, only in
mid. in N. T., *to choose, prefer*, Phil. i. 22; 2 Th. ii. 13;
Heb. xi. 25.*

αἴρω (Gr. § 92), (1) *to raise,
lift up*, Mar. xvi. 18; Jn. xi.
41; (2) *to bear, carry*, Mat.
iv. 6; Lu. ix. 23; (3) *to bear
away, carry off*, in general,
Mat. xxi. 21; Jn. xix. 31; *to
take away* sin, of the redeeming work of Christ, Jn. i. 29;
1 Jn. iii. 5; *to remove by
death*, Jn. xvii. 15; Mat. xxiv.
39.

αἰσθάνομαι, 2 a. ᾐσθόμην, dep.,
to perceive, understand, Lu.
ix. 45.*

αἴσθησις, εως, ἡ, *perception, discernment*, Phil. i. 9.*

αἰσθητήριον, ου, τό, *organ of
perception, faculty of judgment*, Heb. v. 14.*

αἰσχρο-κερδής, ες, *eager for
base gain, sordid*, 1 Tim. iii.
3 (not W. H.), 8; Tit. i.
7.*

αἰσχροκερδῶς, *from eagerness
for base gain*, 1 Pet. v. 2.
(N. T.)*

αἰσχρο-λογία, ας, ἡ, *foul language, scurrility*, Col. iii. 8.*

αἰσχρός, ά, όν, *base, disgraceful*, 1 Cor. xi. 6.

αἰσχρότης, τητος, ἡ, *baseness,
dishonor*, Ep. v. 4.*

αἰσχύνη, ης, ἡ, *shame*, in personal feeling, Lu. xiv. 9; or
in the estimation of others,
Heb. xii. 2; *a shameful thing*,
Ju. 13. *Syn.:* see αἰδώς.

αἰσχύνομαι, οῦμαι, in N. T. only
pass., *to be put to shame, made
ashamed*, 2 Cor. x. 8; Phil.
i. 20.

αἰτέω, ῶ, ήσω, *to ask, pray, require*, Ja. i. 6; usually with
two accs., or acc. of thing
and ἀπό or παρά (gen.) of
person; mid., *to ask for one's
self, beg*, Jn. xvi. 26. *Syn.:*
αἰτέω is to ask a favor, as a
suppliant; ἐρωτάω, to ask a
question, or as an equal;
πυνθάνομαι, to ask for infor-

mation. But see Thayer, p.
18.

αἴτημα, ατος, τό, *petition, request*, Lu. xxiii. 24; Phil. iv.
6; 1 Jn. v. 15. *Syn.:* see
Trench, § li.

αἰτία, ας, ἡ, *cause*, (1) as the
reason or *ground* of anything, Ac. x. 21; (2) in Mat.
xix. 10, *the state of the case;*
(3) forensically, *a crime*, Ac.
xiii. 28; *a charge of crime,
accusation*, Ac. xxv. 18, 27.

αἰτίαμα, ατος, τό, *accusation,
charge*, Ac. xxv. 7 (W. H.
read αἰτίωμα).*

αἴτιος, ία, ιον, *causative of*, used
as subst., in masc., *the cause,
author*, only Heb. v. 9; in
neut., *a cause, reason*, espec.
of punishment, Ac. xix. 40;
a fault, crime, like αἰτία, Lu.
xxiii. 4, 14, 22.*

αἰτίωμα. See αἰτίαμα. (N.T.)*

αἰφνίδιος, ον, *unexpected, sudden*, Lu. xxi. 34 (W. H. ἐφνίδιος); 1 Th. v. 3.*

αἰχμ-αλωσία, ας, ἡ, *captivity*,
Rev. xiii. 10; abstract for
concrete, Ep. iv. 8.*

αἰχμ-αλωτεύω, σω, *to make prisoners of, to take captive*, Ep.
iv. 8; 2 Tim. iii. 6 (W. H.
read the following). (S.)*

αἰχμ-αλωτίζω, σω, *to lead captive*, Lu. xxi. 24.

αἰχμ-άλωτος, ου, ὁ, ἡ, *captive*,
Lu. iv. 18 (from Is. lxi. 1).*

αἰών, ῶνος, ὁ (ἀεί), originally
*an indefinitely long period of
time, an age;* hence, (1) *an
unbroken age, eternity*, past,
as Ac. xv. 18; future, 2 Pet.
iii. 18, especially in the following phrases: εἰς τὸν αἰῶ-
να, *for ever*, with negative
adv. *never;* εἰς τοὺς αἰῶνας, a
stronger expression, *for evermore;* εἰς τοὺς αἰῶνας τῶν
αἰώνων, stronger still (see Gr.
§ 327, ii, Wi. § 36, 2), *for
ever and ever.* Phrase slightly varied, Ep. iii. 21; Heb.
i. 8; 2 Pet. iii. 18; Ju. 25;
Rev. xiv. 11; (2) in plur., *the
worlds, the universe*, Heb. i.
2, xi. 3; (3) *the present age*
(ὁ αἰὼν οὗτος, ὁ ἐνεστὼς αἰών,
ὁ νῦν αἰών), Gal. i. 4; 1 Tim.
vi. 17, in contrast with the
time after the second coming
of Christ, *the coming age* (ὁ
αἰὼν ἐκεῖνος, αἰὼν μέλλων, ὁ

αἰὼν ὁ ἐρχόμενος, οἱ αἰῶνες
οἱ ἐπερχόμενοι), Lu. xx. 35,
xviii. 30; Ep. ii. 7; Mat. xii.
32. *Syn.:* αἰών is the world
under the aspect of *time;*
κόσμος, under that of *space.*
See Thayer, p. 19.

αἰώνιος (ία, only in 2 Th. ii.
16; Heb. ix. 12; or ιος), ιον,
(1) *without beginning or end,
eternal*, Ro. xvi. 26; Heb. ix.
14; (2) *without beginning*,
Ro. xvi. 25; 2 Tim. i. 9;
(3) *without end, everlasting;*
often with ζωή, *eternal life*,
denoting life which in its
character is essentially eternal, see Jn. v. 24, vi. 47,
xvii. 3. Neut., used as adv.,
for ever, Philem. 15.

ἀ-καθαρσία, ας, ἡ (καθαίρω), *uncleanness, impurity*, usually
in a moral sense, Ro. i. 24;
2 Cor. xii. 21.

ἀ-καθάρτης, τητος, ἡ, *impurity*,
Rev. xvii. 4 (W. H. read the
following). (N. T.)*

ἀ-κάθαρτος, ον, *unclean, impure*, (1) of ceremonial defilement, Ac. x. 14; 1 Cor.
vii. 14; (2) of evil spirits,
with πνεῦμα, Gospels, Acts,
Rev.; (3) of human beings,
impure, lewd, Ep. v. 5.

ἀ-καιρέομαι, οῦμαι, dep., *to lack
opportunity*, Phil. iv. 10.*

ἀ-καίρως, adv., *unseasonably*, 2
Tim. iv. 2, opp. to εὐκαίρως.*

ἄ-κακος, ον, *guileless*, Ro. xvi.
18; Heb. vii. 26.*

ἄκανθα, ης, ἡ, *thorn, briar*, Mat.
vii. 16.

ἀκάνθινος, ον, *made of thorns*,
Mar. xv. 17; Jn. xix. 5.*

ἄ-καρπος, ον, *unfruitful, barren*, generally fig., Mat. xiii.
22; Tit. iii. 14.

ἀ-κατά-γνωστος, ον, *not to be
condemned*, Tit. ii. 8.*

ἀ-κατά-κάλυπτος, ον, *unveiled*,
1 Cor. xi. 5, 13.*

ἀ-κατά-κριτος, ον, *uncondemned*,
Ac. xvi. 37, xxii. 25. (N.T.)*

ἀ-κατά-λυτος, ον, *indissoluble*,
Heb. vii. 16.*

ἀ-κατά-παστος, ον, *unfed, hungry for* (gen.), 2 Pet. ii. 14
(W. H. for the following).
(N. T.)*

ἀ-κατά-παυστος, ον, *not to be
restrained*, with gen., 2 Pet.
ii. 14 (see preceding).*

ἀ-κατα-στασία, ας, ἡ, *instabil-*

4

ity; hence, sedition, tumult, disorder, Ja. iii. 16, 2 Cor. vi. 5.

ἀ-κατά-στατος, ον, *inconstant, unstable,* Ja. i. 8, iii. 8 (W. H.).*

ἀ-κατά-σχετος, ον, *that cannot be restrained,* Ja. iii. 8 (W. H. read preceding). (S.)*

Ἀκελ-δαμά (Aram., *field of blood*), *Aceldama,* Ac. i. 19 (W. H. read Ἀκελδαμάχ). (N. T.)*

ἀ-κέραιος, ον (κεράννυμι), *unmixed;* hence, fig., *simple, innocent, guileless,* Mat. x. 16; Ro. xvi. 19; Phil. ii. 15.*

ἀ-κλινής, ές, *unbending;* hence, *firm, steadfast,* Heb. x. 23.*

ἀκμάζω, σω, *to reach the point of perfection;* so, of fruit, *to be fully ripe,* Rev. xiv. 18.*

ἀκμήν, acc. of ἀκμή as adv., *even now, even yet,* Mat. xv. 16.*

ἀκοή, ῆς, ἡ (ἀκούω), *hearing,* (1) *the sense of hearing,* 2 Pet. ii. 8; (2) *the organ of hearing, the ear,* 2 Tim. iv. 3, 4; (3) *the thing heard, a report, speech, doctrine,* Jn. xii. 38; Mar. i. 28. ἀκοῇ ἀκούειν, "to hear with hearing," *i.e, attentively* (a Hebraism), Mat. xiii. 14.

ἀκολουθέω, ῶ, ήσω, (1) *to accompany, follow,* or *attend,* with dat., or μετά (gen.), or ὀπίσω (gen.), espec. of the disciples of Christ; so, met., *to obey* and *imitate,* Mat. iv. 25; Mar. ix. 38.

ἀκούω, σω or σομαι, pf., ἀκήκοα, *to hear,* (1) without object, Mar. iv. 3, vii. 37; (2) with object (acc. or gen., Gr. § 249*a*, 1, Wi. § 30, 7*c*, Bu. 165 sq., 301), *to hear, listen to, heed, understand,* Mat. xii. 19; Lu. i. 41. οἱ ἀκούοντες, *hearers* or *disciples.* In pass., *to be noised abroad,* Ac. xi. 22.

ἀ-κρασία, ας, ἡ, *intemperance, incontinence,* Mat. xxiii. 25; 1 Cor. vii. 5.*

ἀ-κρατής, ές (κράτος), *powerless, without self-control,* 2 Tim. iii. 3.*

ἄ-κρατος, ον (κεράννυμι), *unmixed, undiluted* (of strong wine), Rev. xiv. 10.*

ἀκρίβεια, ας, ἡ, *exactness, strictness,* Ac. xxii. 3.*

ἀκριβής, ές, *exact, strict,* Ac. xxvi. 5.

ἀκριβόω, ῶ, ώσω, *to inquire closely, learn carefully* (R. V.), Mat. ii. 7, 16.*

ἀκριβῶς, adv., *exactly, diligently,* Ac. xviii. 25.

ἀκρίς, ίδος, ἡ, *a locust,* Mat. iii. 4.

ἀκροατήριον, ίου, τό (ἀκροάομαι, *to hear*), *the place of* (judicial) *hearing,* Ac. xxv. 23.*

ἀκροατής, οῦ, ὁ, *a hearer,* Ro. ii. 13; Ja. i. 22, 23, 25.*

ἀκροβυστία, ας, ἡ, *the foreskin,* Ac. xi. 3; *uncircumcision,* Ro. iv. 10; met., *an uncircumcised Gentile,* Ep. ii. 11. (S.)

ἀκρο-γωνιαῖος, α, ον (with λίθος expressed or understood), *a corner foundation stone,* ref. to Christ, Ep. ii. 20; 1 Pet. ii. 6. (S.)*

ἀκρο-θίνιον, ίου, τό, *first-fruits, i.e.,* the best of the produce, applied (plur.) to spoils taken in battle, Heb. vii. 4.*

ἄκρος, α, ον, *outermost, pointed;* neut., τὸ ἄκρον, *the end, extremity,* Lu. xvi. 24.

Ἀκύλας, ου, ὁ (Latin), *Aquila,* Ac. xviii. 2.

ἀ-κυρόω, ῶ, *to deprive of power, set aside* (a law), Mat. xv. 6; Mar. vii. 13; Gal. iii. 17.

ἀ-κωλύτως, adv., *freely, without hindrance,* Ac. xxviii. 31.*

ἄκων, ουσα, ον (ἀ, ἕκων), *unwilling,* 1 Cor. ix. 17.*

ἀλάβαστρον, ου, τό, *a box made of alabaster, a vessel for perfume,* Mat. xxvi. 7; Mar. xiv. 3; Lu. vii. 37.*

ἀλαζονία, ας, ἡ, *boasting, show, ostentation,* Ja. iv. 16; 1 Jn. ii. 16.*

ἀλαζών, όνος, ὁ, *a boaster,* Ro. i. 30; 2 Tim. iii. 2.*

ἀλαλάζω, άσω, *to raise a cry* or loud sound; *in mourning,* Mar. v. 38; of cymbals, 1 Cor. xiii. 1.*

ἀ-λάλητος, ον, *not to be uttered in words,* Ro. viii. 26.*

ἄ-λαλος, ον, *dumb, making dumb,* Mar. vii. 37, ix. 17, 25.*

ἅλας, ατος, τό, *salt,* lit. and fig., as Mat. v. 13.

ἀλείφω, ψω, *to anoint,* festally, or in homage, also medicinally, or in embalming the dead, Mar. xvi. 1, Lu. vii. 46. *Syn.:* χρίω has always a religious and symbolical force, which is absent in ἀλείφω.

ἀλεκτορο-φωνία, ας, ἡ, *the cock-crowing,* the third watch of the night, between midnight and dawn, Mar. xiii. 35.*

ἀλέκτωρ, ορος, ὁ, *a cock,* Mat. xxvi. 34; Jn. xiii. 38.

Ἀλεξανδρεύς, έως, ὁ, *an Alexandrian,* Ac. vi. 9, xviii. 24.*

Ἀλεξανδρινός, ή, όν, *Alexandrian,* Ac. xxvii. 6, xxviii. 11.*

Ἀλέξανδρος, ου, ὁ, *Alexander.* Four of this name are mentioned, Mar. xv. 21; Ac. iv. 6; Ac. xix. 33; 1 Tim. i. 20; 2 Tim. iv. 14.*

ἄλευρον, ου, τό, *wheaten flour,* Mat. xiii. 33; Lu. xiii. 21.*

ἀλήθεια, ας, ἡ, *truth;* generally, as Mar. v. 33; espec., (1) *freedom from error, exactness,* as (2) the Truth, or *Word of God;* Jesus is called *the Truth,* Jn. xiv. 6; (3) *truthfulness, veracity, sincerity, integrity,* opposed to ἀδικία, Ro. ii. 8; 1 Cor. xiii. 6.

ἀληθεύω, *to speak the truth,* Gal. iv. 16; Ep. iv. 15.*

ἀληθής, ές (ἀ, λαθ- in λανθάνω), *unconcealed, true,* Ac. xii. 9; Jn. iv. 18; *truthful,* Mat. xxii. 16; Mar. xii. 14. *Syn.:* ἀληθής means true *morally,* faithful; ἀληθινός, *genuine,* in contrast either with the *false* or the *imperfect.*

ἀληθινός, ή, όν, *real, genuine,* contrasted with the fictitious, as Lu. xvi. 11; Jn. i. 9; with the typical, as Jn. vi. 32; Heb. viii. 2, ix. 24. *Syn.:* see ἀληθής.

ἀλήθω, ήσω, *to grind* with a handmill, Mat. xxiv. 41; Lu. xvii. 35.*

ἀληθῶς, adv., *truly, really, certainly,* Ac. xii. 11.

ἁλιεύς (W. H. ἁλεεύς), έως, ὁ, *a fisherman,* Mat. iv. 18.

ἁλιεύω, εύσω, *to fish,* Jn. xxi. 3. (S.)*

ἁλίζω, ίσω, *to salt, season with salt,* Mat. v. 13; Mar. ix. 49

ἀλίσγημα, ατος, τό, *pollution,* Ac. xv. 20. (N. T.)*

ἀλλά (prop. n. plur. of ἄλλος), *but,* an adversative particle.

See Gr. § 404, Wi. § 53, 7, Bu. 369 sq.

ἀλλάσσω, άξω, *to change*, Ac. vi. 14; *to exchange*, Ro. i. 23; *to transform*, I Cor. xv. 51.

ἀλλαχόθεν, adv., *from elsewhere*, Jn. x. 1.*

ἀλλαχοῦ, adv., *elsewhere*, Mar. i. 38 (W. H.).*

ἀλλ-ηγορέω, ῶ, *to speak allegorically;* pass. part., Gal. iv. 24.*

Ἀλληλούϊα (W. H. ᾽Αλ-), (Heb.), Hallelujah, *Praise ye Jehovah*, Rev. xix, 1, 3, 4, 6. (S.)*

ἀλλήλων, reciprocal pron., gen. plur. (Gr. § 61c), *one another, each other*, Ro. i. 12.

ἀλλο-γενής, ές, *of another nation, a foreigner*, Lu. xvii. 18. (S.)*

ἅλλομαι (dep.), ἀλοῦμαι, ἡλάμην, *to leap*, Ac. iii. 8, xiv. 10; *to bubble up*, as water, Jn. iv. 14.*

ἄλλος, η, ο, *other, another*, Mar. vi. 15; ὁ ἄλλος, *the other*, Mat. v. 39; οἱ ἄλλοι, *the others, the rest. Syn.:* ἄλλος indicates that which is simply *numerically* distinct; ἕτερος, that which is generically distinct, *different*.

ἀλλοτριο-επίσκοπος, ου, ὁ, *one who looks at* or *busies himself in the things of another, a busybody*, 1 Pet. iv. 15 (W. H. ἀλλοτριεπίσκοπος). (N. T.)*

ἀλλότριος, ία, ιον, *belonging to another*, Heb. ix. 25; *foreign, strange*, Ac. vii. 6; *not of one's own family*, Mat. xvii. 25; *hostile*, Heb. xi. 34.

ἀλλό-φυλος, ου, adj., *foreign, of another tribe* or *race*, Ac. x. 28.*

ἄλλως, adv., *otherwise*, 1 Tim. v. 25.*

ἀλοάω, ῶ, ήσω, *to beat* or *thresh*, as grain, 1 Cor. ix. 9, 10; 1 Tim. v. 18.*

ἄ-λογος, ον, (1) *without speech* or *reason, irrational*, 2 Pet. ii. 12, Ju. 10; (2) *unreasonable, absurd*, Ac. xxv. 27.*

ἀλόη, ης, ἡ, *the aloe*, Jn. xix. 39. (S.)*

ἅλς, ἁλός, ὁ, *salt*. Rec. only in Mar. ix. 49 (dat.), W. H. only in ix. 50 (acc.). See ἅλας.

ἁλυκός, ή, όν (ἅλς), *salt, brackish*, Ja. iii. 12.*

ἄ-λυπος, ον, *free from sorrow*, Phil. ii. 28.*

ἅλυσις, εως, ἡ, *a chain* or *manacle*, Mar. v. 3; Ac. xxi. 33.

ἀ-λυσιτελής, ές, *without gain, unprofitable*, Heb. xiii. 17.*

ἄλφα, το, see A.

Ἀλφαῖος, ου, ὁ, *Alphæus*. Two of the name are mentioned, Mar. ii. 14, iii. 18 (the latter being called Κλωπάς, Jn. xix. 25; another form of the orig. Hebrew name).

ἅλων, ωνος, ὁ, ἡ, *a threshing-floor;* met., *the grain of the threshing-floor*, Mat. iii. 12; Lu. iii. 17.

ἀλώπηξ, εκος, ἡ, *a fox*, Mat. viii. 20; Lu. ix. 58; applied to Herod, Lu. xiii. 32.*

ἅλωσις, εως, ἡ, *a taking* or *catching*, 2 Pet. ii. 12.*

ἅμα, adv., *at the same time*, Ac. xxiv. 26; prep., *with* or *together with* (dat.), Mat. xiii. 29; ἅμα πρωΐ, *with the dawn*, Mat. xx. 1.

ἀ-μαθής, ές, *unlearned, ignorant*, 2 Pet. iii. 16.*

ἀμαράντινος, ου, adj., *composed of amaranth, i.e., everlasting*, 1 Pet. v. 4.*

ἀ-μάραντος, ου, adj. (μαραίνομαι), *unfading*, 1 Pet. i. 4.*

ἁμαρτάνω, τήσω, *to miss a mark, to err, to sin*, Mat. xxvii. 4; Jn. v. 14; with cogn. acc., ἁμαρτίαν, *to sin a sin*, 1 Jn. v. 16; with εἰς, *to sin against*, Lu. xv. 18, 21.

ἁμάρτημα, ατος, τό, *a sin, evil deed. Syn.:* see ἁγνόημα.

ἁμαρτία, ας, ἡ, (1) *a sinning* (= τὸ ἁμαρτάνειν), Ro. v. 12, 13; 2 Cor. v. 21; (2) *a sin*, sing., as Ac. vii. 60; plur. (more freq.), spec. in the phrase ἀφιέναι τὰς ἁμαρτίας, *to forgive sins*, Mat. ix. 2, 5, 6. In Heb. x. 6, 8, 18, περὶ ἁμαρτίας is *sin-offering. Syn.:* see ἁγνόημα.

ἀ-μάρτυρος, ου, *without witness*, Ac. xiv. 17.*

ἁμαρτωλός, ον, *sinful*, or substantively, *a sinner*, espec. habitually and notoriously, 1 Tim. i. 19; Lu. xv. 2. The Jews used the word for

idolaters, i.e., Gentiles, Mar. xiv. 41.

ἄ-μαχος, ον, *not quarrelsome*, 1 Tim. iii. 3; Tit. iii. 2.*

ἀμάω, ῶ, ήσω, *to reap*, Ja. v. 4.*

ἀμέθυστος, ου, ἡ, *an amethyst* (supposed to be an antidote against drunkenness. Hence the name, from ἀ, μεθύω), Rev. xxi. 20.*

ἀμελέω, ῶ, ήσω, *not to care for, to disregard, neglect*, with gen. or inf., Heb. ii. 3; 2 Pet. i. 12 (not W. H.).

ἄ-μεμπτος, ον, *blameless*, Phil. ii. 15; Heb. viii. 7.

ἀ-μέμπτως, adv., *blamelessly*, 1 Th. ii. 10, iii. 13 (W. H. mrg.).

ἀ-μέριμνος, ον, *free from solicitude* or *anxiety*, Mat. xxviii. 14; 1 Cor. vii. 32.*

ἀ-μετά-θετος, ον, *unchangeable*, Heb. vi. 18; τὸ ἀμετάθετον, *immutability*, Heb. vi. 17.*

ἀ-μετα-κίνητος, ου, adj., *immovable, firm*, 1 Cor. xv. 58.*

ἀ-μετα-μέλητος, ον, *not to be regretted* or *repented of*, Ro. xi. 29; hence, *unchangeable*, 2 Cor. vii. 10.*

ἀ-μετα-νόητος, ου, adj., *unrepentant, impenitent*, Ro. ii. 5.*

ἄ-μετρος, ον, *beyond measure, immoderate* 2 Cor. x. 13, 15.*

ἀμήν, Amen, a Hebrew adjective, *true, faithful*, used (1) as an adverb, at the beginning of a sentence, *verily, truly, indeed;* (2) at the end of ascriptions of praise, etc., optatively, as γένοιτο, *so be it;* (3) substantively, 2 Cor. i. 20, as a name of Christ, *the Amen, the faithful witness*, Rev. iii. 14. (S.)

ἀ-μήτωρ, ορος, ὁ, ἡ (μήτηρ), *without mother, i.e.*, in the genealogies, Heb. vii. 3.*

ἀ-μίαντος, ον (μιαίνω), *undefiled, sincere, pure*, Heb. vii. 26, xiii. 4; 1 Pet. i. 4; Ja. i. 27.*

Ἀμιναδάβ, ὁ (Heb.), *Aminadab*, Mat. i. 4; Lu. iii. 33 (not W. H.).*

ἄμμος, ου, ἡ, *sand*, Ro. ix. 27; Heb. xi. 12.

ἀμνός, οῦ, ὁ, *a lamb;* fig., of Christ, Jn. i. 29, 36; Ac. viii. 32; 1 Pet. i. 19.*

6

ἐμοιβή, ῆς, ἡ (ἀμείβω), requital, 1 Tim. v. 4.*

ἔμπελος, ου, ἡ, a vine, (1) lit., Mat. xxvi. 29; (2) fig., as Jn. xv. 1.

ἀμπελ-ουργός, οῦ, ὁ, ἡ, a vine-dresser, Lu. xiii. 7.*

ἀμπελών, ῶνος, ὁ, a vineyard, Lu. xx. 9; 1 Cor. ix. 7.

Ἀμπλίας, ίου, ὁ, Amplias, Ro. xvi. 8.*

ἀμύνω, ῶ, in N. T. only in mid., to defend from, take vengeance on, Ac. vii. 24.*

ἀμφιάζω, to clothe, Lu. xii. 28 (W. H.).*

ἀμφιβάλλω, to cast around, Mar. i. 16 (W. H.).*

ἀμφί-βληστρον, ου, τό, a fishing net, Mat. iv. 18; Mar. i. 16 (not W. H.).* Syn.: σαγήνη is the drag-net, much larger than ἀμφίβληστρον, the casting net; δίκτυον is general, a net of any kind.

ἀμφι-έννυμι, ἔσω, to put on, to clothe, Lu. vii. 25.

Ἀμφίπολις, εως, ἡ, Amphipolis, a city in the S. of Macedonia, Ac. xvii. 1.*

ἔμφ-οδον, ου, τό, a street, Mar. xi. 4.*

ἀμφότεροι, αι, α, both, Ac. xxiii. 8.

ἀ-μώμητος, ον, without blame or fault, Phil. ii. 15 (W. H. ἄμεμπτοι); 2 Pet. iii. 14.*

ἄμωμον, ον, τό, amomum, a spice plant, Rev. xviii. 13 (not Rec.).*

ἄ-μωμος, ον, without blemish, 1 Pet. i. 19; Heb. ix. 14; fig., blameless, Eph. i. 4; Ju. 24.

Ἀμών, ὁ (Heb.), Amon, Mat. i. 10 (W. H. Ἀμώς).*

Ἀμώς, ὁ (Heb.), Amos, Lu. iii. 25.*

ἄν, a particle, expressing possibility, uncertainty, or conditionality. At the beginning of a sentence it is a contraction of ἐάν. See Gr. §§ 378b, 380, 383δ, Wi. § 42, Bu. 216 sq.

ἀνά, prep., lit., upon (acc.); in composition, up, again; used in many phrases. See Gr. §§ 297 and 147a, Wi. §§ 49b, 52, 4, 2), Bu. 331, 332.

ἀνα-βαθμός, οῦ, ὁ (βαίνω), means of ascent, steps, stairs, Ac. xxi. 35, 40.*

ἀνα-βαίνω, βήσομαι, 2 a. ἀνέβην, (1) to ascend, espec. to Jerusalem, Mat. xx. 17; on board ship, Mar. vi. 51; to heaven, Ro. x. 6; (2) to spring up, as plants, etc., used of a rumor, Ac. xxi. 31; of thoughts coming into mind, Lu. xxiv. 38.

ἀνα-βάλλω, mid., to postpone, defer, Ac. xxiv. 22.*

ἀνα-βιβάζω, to draw up, as a net to shore, Mat. xiii. 48.*

ἀνα-βλέπω, (1) to look up, as Mar. viii. 24; (2) to look again, to recover sight, as Mat. xi. 5.

ἀνά-βλεψις, εως, ἡ, recovery of sight, Lu. iv. 18.*

ἀνα-βοάω, ῶ, to exclaim, cry aloud (not in W. H.), Mat. xxvii. 46, Mar. xv. 8, Lu. ix. 38.*

ἀνα-βολή, ῆς, ἡ, putting off, delay, Ac. xxv. 17.*

ἀνάγαιον, ου, τό, upper room, W. H. in Mar. xiv. 15; Lu. xxii. 12, for Rec. ἀνώγεον.*

ἀν-αγγέλλω, to announce, make known, Ac. xiv. 27, xix. 18; to report, 2 Cor. vii. 7.

ἀνα-γεννάω, ῶ, to beget again, 1 Pet. i. 3, 23.*

ἀνα-γινώσκω, to know again, to know well. N. T., to read, Jn. xix. 20; 2 Cor. iii. 15.

ἀναγκάζω, άσω, to force, to compel by force or persuasion, Ac. xxvi. 11; 2 Cor. xii. 11.

ἀναγκαῖος, αία, αῖον, necessary, fit, Tit. iii. 14; Phil. i. 24; also close or near, as friends, Ac. x. 24.

ἀναγκαστῶς, adv., necessarily or by constraint, 1 Pet. v. 2.*

ἀνάγκη, ης, ἡ, (1) necessity, Philem. 14; 1 Cor. vii. 37; followed by inf. (with ἐστι understood), there is need to, Mat. xviii. 7; (2) distress, Lu. xxi. 23.

ἀνα-γνωρίζω, to make known, aor. pass., Ac. vii. 13 (Rec.).*

ἀνά-γνωσις, εως, ἡ, reading, Ac. xiii. 15; 2 Cor. iii. 14; 1 Tim. iv. 13.*

ἀν-άγω, to bring, lead, or take up, Lu. ii. 22; Ac. ix. 39; to offer up, as sacrifices, Ac. vii. 41; pass., to put to sea, to set sail, Lu. viii. 22; Ac. xiii. 13.

ἀνα-δείκνυμι, to show, as by uplifting, to show plainly, Ac.

i. 24; to appoint, announce, Lu. x. 1.*

ἀνά-δειξις, εως, ἡ, a showing or public announcing, Lu. i. 80.*

ἀνα-δέχομαι, dep., to receive with a welcome, guests, Ac. xxviii. 7; promises, Heb. xi. 17.*

ἀνα-δίδωμι, to give up, deliver, as by messengers, Ac. xxiii. 33.*

ἀνα-ζάω, ῶ, to live again, revive (W. H. only in Ro. vii. 9, and doubtfully Lu. xv. 24).

ἀνα-ζητέω, ῶ, to seek with diligence, Lu. ii. 44, 45 (W. H.); Ac. xi. 25.*

ἀνα-ζώννυμι, to gird or bind up, as a loose dress is girded about the loins; mid. fig., 1 Pet. i. 13. (S.)*

ἀνα-ζωπυρέω, ῶ (πῦρ), to rekindle or rouse up; fig., 2 Tim. i. 6.*

ἀνα-θάλλω, to thrive or flourish again, Phil. iv. 10.*

ἀνά-θεμα, ατος, τό, a person or thing accursed, Gal. i. 8; 1 Cor. xvi. 22; an execration or curse, Ac. xxiii. 14. Syn.: ἀνάθημα is a thing devoted in honor of God, consecrated; ἀνάθεμα, simply a later form of ἀνάθημα, has come to mean a thing devoted to destruction.

ἀναθεματίζω, ίσω, to bind (one's self) by a curse, Ac. xxiii. 12, 14, 21; to affirm with curses, Mar. xiv. 71.*

ἀνα-θεωρέω, ῶ, to look at attentively, to consider, Ac. xvi. 23; Heb. xiii. 7.*

ἀνά-θημα, ατος, τό, anything consecrated and laid by, a votive offering, Lu. xxi. 5 (W. H.).* Syn.: see ἀνάθεμα.

ἀν-αιδεία, ας, ἡ, shamelessness, impudence, Lu. xi. 8.*

ἀναιρέσις, εως, ἡ, a taking away. i.e., by a violent death, Ac. viii. 1, xxii. 20 (Rec.).*

ἀν-αιρέω, ῶ (see Gr. § 103, 1, Wi. § 15, Bu. 53), to take away, to abolish, Heb. x. 9; to take off, to kill, Mat. ii. 16; mid., to take up, Ac. vii. 21.

ἀν-αίτιος, ον, guiltless, Mat. xii. 5, 7.*

ἀνα-καθίζω, to sit up (properly trans. with ἑαυτόν under

stooá), Lu. vii. 15; Ac. ix. 40.*

ἀνα-καινίζω, to renew, restore to a former condition, Heb. vi. 6.*

ἀνα-καινόω, ῶ, to renew, amend, to change the life, 2 Cor. iv. 16; Col. iii. 10. (N. T.)*

ἀνα-καίνωσις, εως, ἡ, a renewal or change of heart and life, Ro. xii. 2: Tit. iii. 5. (N. T.)* Syn.: see Trench, § xviii.

ἀνα-καλύπτω, to unveil, make manifest; pass., 2 Cor. iii. 14, 18.*

ἀνα-κάμπτω, to bend or turn back, return, Heb. xi. 15.

ἀνά-κειμαι, dep., to recline at a meal, Mat. ix. 10; ὁ ἀνακείμενος, one who reclines at table, a guest, Mat. xxii. 10, 11 (W. H. omit in Mar. v. 40).

ἀνα-κεφαλαιόω, ῶ, to gather together into one, to sum up under one head; pass., Ro. xiii. 9; mid., Ep. i. 10.*

ἀνα-κλίνω, to lay down an infant, Lu. ii. 7; to make to recline at table, Mar. vi. 39; pass., to recline, as at a feast, like ἀνάκειμαι, Lu. xiii. 29.

ἀνα-κόπτω, to check (lit., beat back), Gal. v. 7 (W. H. ἐγκόπτω).*

ἀνα-κράζω, to cry out, to shout aloud, Mar. i. 23, vi. 49.

ἀνα-κρίνω, to investigate, inquire, examine (judicially), to judge of. Only in Lu., Ac., and 1 Cor.

ἀνά-κρισις, εως, ἡ, judicial examination, Ac. xxv. 26.*

ἀνα-κυλίω, to roll back, Mar. xvi. 4 (W. H. for ἀποκ-).*

ἀνα-κύπτω, to raise one's self up, Lu. xiii. 11; Jn. viii. 7, 10; fig., to be elated, Lu. xxi. 28.*

ἀνα-λαμβάνω, to take up, Ac. vii. 43; pass., of Christ's being taken up to heaven, Mar. xvi. 19.

ἀνά-ληψις (W. H. -λημψις), εως, ἡ, a being taken up, i.e., into heaven, Lu. ix. 51.*

ἀν-αλίσκω, λώσω, to consume, destroy, Lu. ix. 54; Gal. v. 15; 2 Th. ii. 8 (not W. H.).*

ἀνα-λογία, as, ἡ, proportion, analogy, Ro. xii. 6.*

ἀνα-λογίζομαι, to think upon, consider attentively, Heb. xii. 3.*

ἄν-αλος, ον, without saltness, insipid, Mar. ix. 50.*

ἀνά-λυσις, εως, ἡ, a loosening of a ship from her moorings, departure, 2 Tim. iv. 6.*

ἀνα-λύω, to depart, Phil. i. 23; to return, Lu. xii. 36.*

ἀν-αμάρτητος, ον, without blame, faultless, Jn. viii. 7 (W. H. omit).*

ἀνα-μένω, to await, 1 Th. i. 10.*

ἀνα-μιμνήσκω, to remind, admonish, two accs., or acc. and inf., 1 Cor. iv. 17; pass., to remember, to call to mind, gen. or acc., 2 Cor. vii. 15.

ἀνά-μνησις, εως, ἡ, remembrance, a memorial, Heb. x. 3.

ἀνα-νεόω, ῶ, to renew; mid., to renew one's self, to be renewed, Ep. iv. 23.*

ἀνα-νήφω, to recover soberness, 2 Tim. ii. 26.*

Ἀνανίας, α, ὁ (from Heb.), Ananias. Three of the name are mentioned, Ac. v. 1–5, ix. 10, xxiii. 2.

ἀν-αντι-ρρήτος, ον, indisputable, not to be contradicted, Ac. xix. 36.*

ἀναντιρρήτως, adv., without contradiction, Ac. x. 29.*

ἀν-άξιος, ον, unworthy, inadequate, 1 Cor. vi. 2.*

ἀναξίως, adv., unworthily, unbecomingly, 1 Cor. xi. 27 (not in ver. 29, W. H.).*

ἀνά-παυσις, εως, ἡ, rest, cessation from labor, refreshment, Rev. iv. 8; Mat. xii. 43.

ἀνα-παύω, to give rest or refreshment, Mat. xi. 28; mid., to take rest, Mar. vi. 31 (W. H. read in Rev. xiv. 13, ἀναπαήσονται, 2 fut. pass.).

ἀνα-πείθω, σω, to persuade, in a bad sense, seduce, mislead, Ac. xviii. 13.*

ἀνα-πέμπω, to remit, send back, Lu. xxiii. 11.

ἀνα-πηδάω, leap up (W. H., in Mar. x. 50, for Rec. ἀνίστημι).*

ἀνά-πηρος, ον, maimed, having lost a member, Lu. xiv. 13, 21 (W. H. ἀνάπειρος).*

ἀνα-πίπτω, to fall down, lie down, Mat. xv. 35; N. T., to recline at table, Lu. xi. 37, xiv. 10.

ἀνα-πληρόω, ῶ, to fill up, 1 Th. ii. 16; to fulfill, as a prophecy,

Mat. xiii. 14; to perform, as a precept, Gal. vi. 2; to occupy or fill a place, 1 Cor. xiv. 16; to supply a deficiency, Phil. ii. 30.

ἀν-απο-λόγητος, ον, adj., inexcusable, Ro. i. 20, ii. 1.*

ἀνα-πτύσσω, to unroll, as a volume, Lu. iv. 17 (not W. H.).*

ἀν-άπτω, to kindle, set on fire, Lu. xii. 49; Ac. xxviii. 2 (not W. H.); Ja. iii. 5.*

ἀν-αρίθμητος, ον, innumerable, Heb. xi. 12.*

ἀνα-σείω, to stir up, move, instigate, Mar. xv. 11; Lu. xxiii. 5.*

ἀνα-σκευάζω, to pervert, unsettle, destroy, Ac. xv. 24.*

ἀνα-σπάω, to draw up, Lu. xiv. 5; Ac. xi. 10.*

ἀνά-στασις, εως, ἡ, a rising up, as opposed to falling, Lu. ii. 34; rising, as from death or the grave, resurrection, the future state, Ro. i. 4, vi. 5.

ἀνα-στατόω, ῶ, to unsettle, put in commotion, Ac. xvii. 6, xxi. 38; Gal. v. 12.*

ἀνα-σταυρόω, ῶ, to crucify afresh, Heb. vi. 6.*

ἀνα-στενάζω, to groan or sigh deeply, Mar. viii. 12.*

ἀνα-στρέφω, to turn up, overturn, Jn. ii. 15; intrans., to return, Ac. v. 22; mid. (as Lat. versari), to be or to live in a place or state, to move among, to pass one's time or be conversant with persons; generally, to conduct one's self, 2 Cor. i. 12; 1 Tim. iii. 15.

ἀνα-στροφή, ῆς, ἡ, behavior, manner of life, Gal. i. 13; Ep. iv. 22.

ἀνα-τάσσομαι, to arrange, compose a narrative, Lu. i. 1.*

ἀνα-τέλλω, to spring up or rise, as the sun, a star, a cloud, Mat. xiii. 6; Lu. xii. 54; of the Messiah, Heb. vii. 14; trans., to cause to rise, Mat v. 45.

ἀνα-τίθημι, mid., to set forth, declare, Ac. xxv. 14; Gal. ii. 2.*

ἀνατολή, ῆς, ἡ, the dawn, dayspring, Lu. i. 78; generally, the east, where the sun rises, Mat. ii. 2, 9; sing. and plur., see Gr. § 240a.

8

ἀνα-τρέπω, *to subvert, overthrow*, 2 Tim. ii. 18; Tit. i. 11.*

ἀνα-τρέφω, *to nurse, bring up, educate*, Lu. iv. 16 (W. H. mrg.); Ac. vii. 20, 21, xxii. 3.*

ἀνα-φαίνω, mid., *to appear*, Lu. xix. 11; pass., *to be shown a thing* (acc.), Ac. xxi. 3 (W. H. read act., in sense *to come in sight of*).*

ἀνα-φέρω, οἴσω, *to bear* or *lead, to offer*, as sacrifice, Heb. vii. 27; *to bear*, as sin, 1 Pet. ii. 24.

ἀνα-φωνέω, ῶ, *to cry out aloud*, Lu. i. 42.*

ἀνά-χυσις, εως, ἡ, *a pouring out;* hence, *excess*, 1 Pet. iv. 4.*

ἀνα-χωρέω, ῶ, *to depart, withdraw*, Mat. ix. 24; Mar. iii. 7.

ἀνά-ψυξις, εως, ἡ, *a refreshing*, Ac. iii. 20.*

ἀνα-ψύχω, *to refresh, to revive*, 2 Tim. i. 16.*

ἀνδραποδιστής, οῦ, ὁ, *a manstealer*, 1 Tim. i. 10.*

Ἀνδρέας, ου, ὁ, *Andrew*, Jn. i. 40.

ἀνδρίζω, ίσω, mid., *to act like a man, to be brave*, 1 Cor. xvi. 13.*

Ἀνδρόνικος, ου, ὁ, *Andronicus*, Ro. xvi. 7.*

ἀνδρό-φονος, ου, ὁ, *a manslayer*, 1 Tim. i. 9.*

ἀν-έγκλητος, ον, *not open to accusation, unblamable*, 1 Cor. i. 8; Col. i. 22.

ἀν-εκ-διήγητος, ον, *not to be spoken, inexpressible*, 2 Cor. ix. 15. (N. T.)*

ἀν-εκ-λάλητος, *unspeakable*, 1 Pet. i. 8. (N. T.)*

ἀν-έκ-λειπτος, ον, *unfailing*, Lu. xii. 33.*

ἀνεκτός, ή, όν, *tolerable, supportable;* only in comp., Mat. x. 15, xi. 22, 24.

ἀν-ελεήμων, ον, *without compassion, cruel*, Ro. i. 31.*

ἀνεμίζω, *to agitate* or *drive with wind;* pass., Ja. i. 6. (N. T.)*

ἄνεμος, ου, ὁ, *the wind*, Mat. xi. 7; fig., applied to empty doctrines, Ep. iv. 14.

ἀν-ένδεκτος, ον (ἐνδέχομαι), adj., *impossible*, Lu. xvii. 1. (N. T.)*

ἀν-εξ-ερεύνητος (W. H. -ραύ-), ον, adj., *unsearchable*, Ro. xi. 33.*

ἀνεξί-κακος, ον, *patient of injury*, 2 Tim. ii. 24. (N. T.)*

ἀν-εξ-ιχνίαστος, ον, *that cannot be explored, incomprehensible*, Ro. xi. 33; Ep. iii. 8. (S.)*

ἀν-επ-αίσχυντος, ον, *having no cause to be ashamed*, 2 Tim. ii. 15.*

ἀν-επί-ληπτος (W. H. -λημπ-), ον, adj., *never caught doing wrong, irreproachable*, 1 Tim. iii. 2, v. 7, vi. 14.*

ἀν-έρχομαι, *to come* or *go up*, Jn. vi. 3; Gal. i. 17, 18.*

ἄνεσις, εως, ἡ (ἀνίημι), *relaxation, remission*, as from bonds, burden, etc., Ac. xxiv. 23; 2 Th. i. 7.

ἀν-ετάζω, *to examine judicially*, Ac. xxii. 24, 29. (S.)*

ἄνευ, adv. as prep., with gen., *without*, 1 Pet. iii. 1.

ἀν-εύθετος, ον, *inconvenient*, Ac. xxvii. 12. (N. T.)*

ἀν-ευρίσκω, *to find by searching for*, Lu. ii. 16; Ac. xxi. 4.*

ἀν-έχω, mid., *to bear with, forbear, have patience with, endure*, Mat. xvii. 17; Lu. ix. 41; gen. of pers. or thing.

ἀνεψιός, οῦ, ὁ, *a cousin*, Col. iv. 10.*

ἄνηθον, ου, τό, *anise, dill*, Mat. xxiii. 23.*

ἀνήκει, impers., *it is fit* or *proper;* part., τὸ ἀνῆκον, τὰ ἀνήκοντα, *the becoming*, Philem. 8.

ἀν-ήμερος, ον, adj., *not tame, fierce*, 2 Tim. iii. 3.*

ἀνήρ, ἀνδρός, ὁ, (1) *a man*, in sex and age (Lat. *vir*), Ac. viii. 12; hence, (2) *a husband*, Ro. vii. 2, 3; (3) *a person* generally, Lu. vii. 41; plur. voc., ἄνδρες, *Sirs!;* often in apposition with adjectives and nouns, as ἀνὴρ ἁμαρτωλός, ἀνὴρ προφήτης, Lu. v. 8, xxiv. 19.

ἀνθ-ίστημι, *to oppose, withstand, resist*, with dat., Ro. ix. 19, Mat. v. 39.

ἀνθ-ομολογέομαι, οῦμαι, *to confess, give thanks to*, dat., Lu. ii. 38.*

ἄνθος, ους, τό, *a flower*, Ja. i. 10, 11; 1 Pet. i. 24.*

ἀνθρακιά, ᾶς, ἡ, *a heap of burning coals*, Jn. xviii. 18, xxi. 9.*

ἄνθραξ, ακος, ὁ, *a coal*, Ro. xii. 20.*

ἀνθρωπ-άρεσκος, ον, *desirous of pleasing men*, Ep. vi. 6; Col. iii. 22. (S.)*

ἀνθρώπινος, ίνη, ινον, *human, belonging to man*, Ja. iii. 7; 1 Cor. x. 13.

ἀνθρωπο-κτόνος, ον, ὁ, ἡ, *a homicide, a manslayer*, Jn. viii. 44; 1 Jn. iii. 15.*

ἄνθρωπος, ου, ὁ, *a man, one of the human race* (Lat. *homo*). Like ἀνήρ, joined in apposition with substantives, as Mat. xviii. 23, xxi. 33.

ἀνθ-υπατεύω, *to be proconsul*, Ac. xviii. 12 (not W. H.).*

ἀνθ-ύπατος, ου, ὁ, *a proconsul*, Ac. xiii. 7, 8, 12.

ἀν-ίημι, *to unloose, let go*, Ac. xvi. 26, xxvii. 40; *to give up*, Ep. vi. 9; *to leave, neglect*, Heb. xiii. 5.*

ἀν-ίλεως, ων, *without mercy*, Ja. ii. 13 (W. H. read ἀνέλεος). (N. T.)*

ἄ-νιπτος, ον, adj., *unwashed*, Mat. xv. 20; Mar. vii. 2, 5 (Rec.).*

ἀν-ίστημι, *to raise up* one lying or dead, Ac. ix. 41; Jn. vi. 39, 40; intrans. (in 2 a., pf. and mid.), *to rise* from a recumbent posture, Mar. i. 35; *to rise again* from the dead, Lu. xvi. 31; aor. part., often combined with other verbs, as "rising (ἀναστάς) he went."

Ἄννα, ας, ἡ, *Anna*, Lu. ii. 36.*

Ἄννας, α, ὁ, *Annas*, Lu. iii. 2; Jn. xviii. 13, 24; Ac. iv. 6.*

ἀ-νόητος, ον, *foolish, thoughtless*, Ro. i. 14; 1 Tim. vi. 9.

ἄνοια, ας, ἡ, *folly, madness*, Lu. vi. 11; 2 Tim. iii. 9.*

ἀνοίγω, ξω, *to open*, Ac. v. 19, xii. 10, 14; intrans. in 2 perf., ἀνέῳγα, to *be open*, 2 Cor. vi. 11; 1 Cor. xvi. 9.

ἀν-οικο-δομέω, ῶ, *to build up again*, Ac. xv. 16.*

ἄνοιξις, εως, ἡ, *opening* (the act of), Ep. vi. 19.*

ἀ-νομία, ας, ἡ, *lawlessness, iniquity*, Mat. xxiii. 28; Tit. ii. 14; al ἀνομίαι, *iniquities, evil deeds*, Ro. iv. 7. *Syn.:* see ἀγνόημα.

ἄ-νομος, ον, (1) *without law*, not subject to the law, used of Gentiles, 1 Cor. ix. 21; (2) *'awless;* as subst., *a male-*

factor; ὁ ἄνομος, the lawless one, 2 Th. ii. 8.

ἀνόμως, adv., without law, Ro. ii. 12.

ἀν-ορθόω, ῶ, to make upright or straight again, to rebuild, make strong, Lu. xiii. 13; Ac. xv. 16; Heb. xii. 12.*

ἀν-όσιος, ον, unholy, 1 Tim. i. 9; 2 Tim. iii. 2.*

ἀνοχή, ῆς, ἡ, forbearance, toleration, Ro. ii. 4, iii. 25.* Syn.: ὑπομονή is patience under trials, referring to things; μακροθυμία, patience under provocation, referring to persons; ἀνοχή is a forbearance temporary in its nature.

ἀντ-αγωνίζομαι, to resist, strive against, Heb. xii. 4.*

ἀντ-άλλαγμα, ατος, τό, an equivalent, price, Mat. xvi. 26; Mar. viii. 37.*

ἀντ-ανα-πληρόω, ῶ, to fill up in turn, Col. i. 24.*

ἀντ-απο-δίδωμι, to recompense, requite, Lu. xiv. 14; Ro. xii. 19.

ἀντ-από-δομα, ατος, τό, a recompense, requital, Lu. xiv. 12; Ro. xi. 9. (S.)*

ἀντ-από-δοσις, εως, ἡ, a reward, recompense, Col. iii. 24.*

ἀντ-απο-κρίνομαι, to reply against, contradict, Lu. xiv. 6; Ro. ix. 20.*

ἀντ-εῖπον (used as 2 aor. of ἀντιλέγω, see φημί), to contradict, to gainsay, Lu. xxi. 15; Ac. iv. 14.*

ἀντ-έχω, mid., to hold fast, to adhere to (gen.), Mat. vi. 24; Lu. xvi. 13; 1 Th. v. 14; Tit. i. 9.*

ἀντί, prep., gen., instead of, for. See Gr. §§ 291, 147 a, Wi. §§ 47 a, 52, 4, 3), Bu. 321.

ἀντι-βάλλω, to throw in turn, exchange words, Lu. xxiv. 17.*

ἀντι-δια-τίθημι, mid., to set one's self against, oppose, 2 Tim. ii. 25.*

ἀντί-δικος, ου, ὁ (orig. adj.), an opponent at law, Mat. v. 25; Lu. xii. 58, xviii. 3; an adversary, 1 Pet. v. 8.*

ἀντί-θεσις, εως, ἡ, opposition, 1 Tim. vi. 20.*

ἀντι-καθ-ίστημι, to resist, Heb. xii. 4.*

ἀντι-καλέω, to call or invite in turn, Lu. xiv. 12.*

ἀντί-κειμαι, to oppose. resist

(dat.), Lu. xiii. 17, xxi. 15; ὁ ἀντικείμενος, an adversary, 1 Cor. xvi. 9; Phil. i. 28.

ἀντικρύ (W. H. ἄντικρυς), adv., over against, Ac. xx. 15.*

ἀντι-λαμβάνω, mid., to take hold of, help, share in (gen.), Lu. i. 54; Ac. xx. 35; 1 Tim. vi. 2.

ἀντι-λέγω, to speak against, contradict (dat.), Ac. xiii. 45; to oppose, deny, Jn. xix. 12.

ἀντί-ληψις (W. H. -λημψ-), εως, help, ministration, 1 Cor. xii. 28.*

ἀντι-λογία, ας, ἡ, contradiction, contention, rebellion, Heb. vi. 16, vii. 7, xii. 3; Ju. 11.*

ἀντι-λοιδορέω, to revile or reproach again, 1 Pet. ii. 23.*

ἀντί-λυτρον, ου, τό, a ransomprice, 1 Tim. ii. 16.*

ἀντι-μετρέω, ῶ, to measure in return, Mat. vii. 2 (not W. H.); Lu. vi. 38. (N. T.)*

ἀντι-μισθία, ας, ἡ, recompense, Ro. 1. 27; 2 Cor. vi. 13. (N. T.)*

Ἀντιόχεια, ας, ἡ, Antioch. Two places of the name are mentioned, Ac. xi. 26, xiii. 14.

Ἀντιοχεύς, έως, ὁ, a citizen of Antioch, Ac. vi. 5.*

ἀντι-παρ-έρχομαι, to pass by opposite to, Lu. x. 31, 32.*

Ἀντίπας, α, ὁ, Antipas, Rev. ii. 13.*

Ἀντιπατρίς, ίδος, ἡ, Antipatris, Ac. xxiii. 31.*

ἀντι-πέραν (W. H. ἀντίπερα), adv., on the opposite side or shore, Lu. viii. 26.*

ἀντι-πίπτω, to fall against, resist, Ac. vii. 51.*

ἀντι-στρατεύομαι, dep., to make war against, Ro. vii. 23.*

ἀντι-τάσσω, mid., to set one's self against, resist (dat.), Ro. xiii. 2; Ja. iv. 6, v. 6; 1 Pet. v. 5; Ac. xviii. 6.*

ἀντί-τυπος, ον, like in pattern, Heb. ix. 24; τὸ ἀντίτυπον, corresponding in form, as wax to the seal, antitype, 1 Pet. iii. 21.*

Ἀντί-χριστος, ου, ὁ, opposer of Christ, Antichrist, 1 Jn. ii. 18, 22, iv. 3; 2 Jn. 7. (N. T.)*

ἀντλέω, ῶ, to draw from a vessel, Jn. ii. 8, 9, iv. 7, 15.*

ἄντλημα, ατος, τό, a bucket, Jn. iv. 11.*

ἀντ-οφθαλμέω, ῶ, to look in the face; so to meet the wind, Ac. xxvii. 15.*

ἄν-υδρος, ον, without water, dry, Mat. xii. 43; Lu. xi. 24.

ἀν-υπό-κριτος, ον, adj., without hypocrisy, unfeigned, Ro. xii. 9; 2 Cor. vi. 6. (Ap.)

ἀν-υπό-τακτος, ον, not subject to rule, of things, Heb. ii. 8; unruly, of persons, 1 Tim. i. 9; Tit. i. 6, 10.*

ἄνω, adv. (ἀνά), up, above, upwards; τὰ ἄνω, heaven or heavenly things, as Jn. viii. 23.

ἀνώγεον, ου, τό, an upper chamber. See ἀνάγαιον.*

ἄνωθεν, adv. (ἄνω), (1) of place, from above, as Jn. iii. 31, xix. 11; with prepp. ἀπό, ἐκ, from the top, as Mar. xv. 38; Jn. xix. 23; (2) of time, from the first, only Lu. i. 3; Ac. xxvi. 5. In Jn. iii. 4, 7, again (see Gal. iv. 9); or, perhaps here also, from above.

ἀνωτερικός, ή, όν, upper, higher, Ac. xix. 1.*

ἀνώτερος, α, ον (compar. of ἄνω; only neut. as adv.), higher, to a higher place, Lu. xiv. 10; above, before, Heb. x. 8.*

ἀν-ωφελής, ές, unprofitable, Tit iii. 9; Heb. vii. 18.*

ἀξίνη, ης, ἡ, an axe, Mat. iii 10; Lu. iii. 9.*

ἄξιος, ία, ιον, adj., worthy, deserving of, suitable to (gen.), Heb. xi. 38; Lu. xii. 48; Ac. xxvi. 20.

ἀξιόω, ῶ, to deem worthy (acc. and gen., or inf.), Lu. vii. 7; 2 Th. i. 11; think fit, Ac. xv. 38, xxviii. 22.

ἀξίως, adv., worthily, suitably (with gen.), Ro. xvi. 2; Phil. i. 27.

ἀ-όρατος, ον invisible, unseen, Col. i. 16; 1 Tim. i. 17.

ἀπ-αγγέλλω, to report, relate, make known, declare, Ac. iv. 23; 1 Th. i. 9.

ἀπ-άγχω, mid., to hang or strangle one's self, Mat. xxvii. 5.*

ἀπ-άγω, to lead, carry, or take away, Lu. xiii. 15; to lead away to execution, Mat. xxvi. 57; Mar. xiv. 44, 53; to lead or tend, as a way, Mat. vii. 13, 14.

ἀ-παίδευτος, ον, adj., uninstructed, ignorant, 2 Tim. ii. 23.*

ἀπ-αίρω, *to take away;* in N.T. only 1 a. pass., Mat. ix. 15; Mar. ii. 20; Lu. v. 35.*

ἀπ-αιτέω, *to ask back, require, reclaim,* Lu. vi. 30, xii. 20.*

ἀπ-αλγέω, *to be past feeling,* Ep. iv. 19.*

ἀπ-αλλάσσω, pass., *to be removed from, to depart,* Ac. xix. 12; pass., *to be set free* (with ἀπό), Lu. xii. 58; *to deliver,* Heb. ii. 15.*

ἀπ-αλλοτριόω, *to estrange, alienate* (gen.), Ep. ii. 12, iv. 18; Col. i. 21.*

ἀπαλός, ή, όν, *tender,* as a shoot of a tree, Mat. xxiv. 32; Mar. xiii. 28.*

ἀπ-αντάω, ῶ, *to meet, to encounter* (dat.), Mar. xiv. 13.

ἀπ-άντησις, εως, ή, *a meeting, an encountering;* εἰς ἀπάντησιν (gen. or dat.), *to meet* any one, Ac. xxviii. 15.

ἅπαξ, adv., of time, *once,* 1 Th. ii. 18; *once for all,* Heb. vi. 4, x. 2.

ἀ-παρά-βατος, ον, *inviolable, unchangeable,* Heb. vii. 24.*

ἀ-παρα-σκεύαστος, ον, adj., *unprepared,* 2 Cor. ix. 4.*

ἀπ-αρνέομαι, οῦμαι, *to deny, disown,* Mat. xxvi. 34, 35; *to disregard,* Mar. viii. 34.

ἀπ-άρτι, adv., of time (see ἄρτι), *henceforth,* Rev. xiv. 13. (W. H. read ἀπ' ἄρτι.)*

ἀπ-αρτισμός, οῦ, ὁ, *completion,* Lu. xiv. 28.*

ἀπ-αρχή, ῆς, ή, *the first-fruits,* consecrated to God (see W. H., 2 Th. ii. 13).

ἅ-πας, ασα, αν (like πᾶς, Gr. § 37), *all, all together, the whole.*

ἀπασπάζομαι, see ἀσπάζομαι. (N. T.)

ἀπατάω, ῶ, ήσω, *to deceive, lead into error,* Ja. i. 26; Ep. v. 6; 1 Tim. ii. 14 (W. H. ἐξαπ-).* (The stronger form ἐξαπατάω is more freq.)

ἀπάτη, ης, ή, *deceit, deceitfulness,* Col. ii. 8; Heb. iii. 13.

ἀ-πάτωρ, ορος, ὁ, ή (πατήρ), *without father, i.e.,* in the genealogies, Heb. vii. 3.*

ἀπ-αύγασμα, ατος, τό, *reflected brightness,* Heb. i. 3.*

ἀτ-εῖδον (W. H. ἀφεῖδον), 2 aor. οἱ ἀφοράω, which see.

ἀ-πείθεια, ας, ή, *willful unbelief,*

obstinacy, disobedience, Heb. iv. 6, 11.

ἀ-πειθέω ῶ, *to refuse belief, be disobedient,* Jn. iii. 36; Ro. ii. 8.

ἀ-πειθής, ές, *unbelieving, disobedient,* Lu. i. 17; 2 Tim. iii. 2.

ἀπειλέω, ῶ, ήσω, *to threaten, forbid by threatening,* Ac. iv. 17; 1 Pet. ii. 23.*

ἀπειλή, ῆς, ή, *a threatening, threat,* Ac. iv. 17 (W. H. omit), 29, ix. 1; Ep. vi. 9.*

ἄπ-ειμι (εἰμί, *to be*), *to be absent,* as 1 Cor. v. 3.

ἄπ-ειμι (εἶμι, *to go*), *to go away, to depart,* Ac. xvii. 10.*

ἀπ-εῖπον (see εἶπον), mid., *to renounce, disown,* 2 Cor. iv. 2.*

ἀ-πείραστος, ον, adj., *incapable of being tempted,* Ja. i. 13.*

ἄ-πειρος, ον, adj., *inexperienced, unskillful* in (gen.), Heb. v. 13.*

ἀπ-εκ-δέχομαι, *to wait for, expect earnestly* or *patiently,* Ro. viii. 19, 23, 25; Heb. ix. 28. (N. T.)

ἀπ-εκ-δύομαι, *to strip, divest, renounce,* Col. ii. 15, iii. 9.*

ἀπέκδυσις, εως, ή, *a putting* or *stripping off, renouncing,* Col. ii. 11. (N. T.)*

ἀπ-ελαύνω, *to drive away,* Ac. xviii. 16.*

ἀπ-ελεγμός, οῦ, ὁ (ἐλέγχω), *repudiation, censure, disrepute,* Ac. xix. 27. (N. T.)*

ἀπ-ελεύθερος, ον, ὁ, ή, *a freedman,* 1 Cor. vii. 22.*

Ἀπελλῆς, οῦ, ὁ, *Apelles,* Ro. xvi. 10.*

ἀπ-ελπίζω, σω, *to despair,* Lu. vi. 35; R.V. "never despairing" (see R. V. mrg.).*

ἀπ-έναντι, adv. (gen.), *over against, in the presence of, in opposition to.*

ἀ-πέραντος, ον (περαίνω), *interminable,* 1 Tim. i. 4.*

ἀ-περισπάστως, adv. (περισπάω), *without distraction,* 1 Cor. vii. 35.*

ἀ-περί-τμητος, ον, *uncircumcised;* fig., Ac. vii. 51. (S.)*

ἀπ-έρχομαι, *to go* or *come from* one place to another, *to go away, depart; to go apart; to go back, to return; to go forth,* as a rumor.

ἀπ-έχω, *to have in full,* Mat.

vi. 2; *to be far* (abs., or ἀπό), Lu. vii. 6; impers., ἀπέχει, *it is enough,* Mar. xiv. 41; mid., *to abstain from* (gen., or ἀπό), 1 Th. iv. 3.

ἀπιστέω, ῶ, *to disbelieve* (dat.), Mar. xvi. 11; *to be unfaithful,* Ro. iii. 3.

ἀπιστία, ας, ή, *unbelief, distrust, a state of unbelief,* 1 Tim. i. 13; Heb. iii. 12, 19; *unfaithfulness,* Ro. iii. 3.

ἄ-πιστος, ον, *not believing, incredulous,* Jn. xx. 27; hence, *an unbeliever* or *infidel,* 2 Cor. iv. 4; *unfaithful,* Lu. xii. 46; Rev. xxi. 8; pass., *incredible,* only Ac. xxvi. 8.

ἁπλόος, οῦς, ῆ, οῦν, *simple, sound,* Mat. vi. 22; Lu. xi. 34.*

ἁπλότης, τητος, ή, *simplicity, sincerity, purity,* 2 Cor. i. 12; Col. iii. 22.

ἁπλῶς, adv., *simply, sincerely,* Ja. i. 5.*

ἀπό, prep. gen., *from.* See Gr. § 292, Wi. § 47 b, Bu. 321 sq.; and for the force of the prep. in composition, Gr. § 147 a, Wi. § 52, 4, Bu. 344.

ἀπο-βαίνω (for βαίνω, see Gr. § 94, I., 6 d; fut., -βήσομαι), *to go* or *come out of,* as from a ship, Lu. v. 2; Jn. xxi. 9; *to turn out, result,* Lu. xxi. 13; Phil. i. 19.*

ἀπο-βάλλω, *to throw away,* Mar. x. 50; Heb. x. 35.*

ἀπο-βλέπω, *to look away from* all besides; hence, *to look earnestly at* (εἰς), Heb. xi. 26.*

ἀπό-βλητος, ον, verbal adj., *to be thrown away, rejected,* 1 Tim. iv. 4.*

ἀπο-βολή, ῆς, ή, *a casting away, rejection, loss,* Ac. xxvii. 22; Ro. xi. 15.*

ἀπο-γίνομαι, *to die,* 1 Pet. ii. 24.*

ἀπο-γραφή, ῆς, ή, *a record, register, enrolment,* Lu. ii. 2; Ac. v. 37.*

ἀπο-γράφω, *to enrol, inscribe in a register,* Lu. ii. 1, 3, 5; Heb. xii. 23.*

ἀπο-δείκνυμι, *to show by proof, demonstrate, set forth,* Ac. ii. 22, xxv. 7; 1 Cor. iv. 9; 2 Th. ii. 4.*

ἀπό-δειξις, εως, ή, *demonstration, proof,* 1 Cor. ii. 4.*

ἀπο-δεκατόω, ῶ, (1) to pay the tenth or tithe, Mat. xxiii. 23; (2) to levy tithes on, acc., Heb. vii. 5. (S.)

ἀπό-δεκτος, ον, verbal adj., acceptable, 1 Tim. ii. 3, v. 4.*

ἀπο-δέχομαι, to receive with pleasure, to welcome, Ac. xviii. 27, xxviii. 30.

ἀπο-δημέω, ῶ, to go from one's own people, to go into another country; only in the parables of our Lord, as Mat. xxi. 33; Lu. xv. 13.

ἀπό-δημος, ον, gone abroad, sojourning in another country (R. V.), Mar. xiii. 34.*

ἀπο-δίδωμι, to give from one's self, to deliver, Mat. xxvii. 58; in mid., to sell, Ac. v. 8; to pay off, discharge what is due, Mat. v. 26; Lu. xvi. 2; to restore, Lu. iv. 20; to requite, recompense, Ro. ii. 6; Rev. xviii. 6.

ἀπο-δι-ορίζω, to separate off, i.e., into parties, Ju. 19.*

ἀπο-δοκιμάζω, to reject, as disapproved or worthless, Mar. viii. 31; Heb. xii. 17.

ἀπο-δοχή, ῆς, ἡ, acceptance, approbation, 1 Tim. i. 15, iv. 9.*

ἀπό-θεσις, εως, ἡ, a putting away, 1 Pet. iii. 21; 2 Pet. i. 14.*

ἀπο-θήκη, ης, ἡ, a repository, granary, storehouse, Mat. iii. 12; Lu. iii. 17.

ἀπο-θησαυρίζω, to treasure up, lay by in store, 1 Tim. vi. 19.*

ἀπο-θλίβω, to press closely, Lu. viii. 45.*

ἀπο-θνήσκω (ἀπό, intensive; the simple θνήσκω is rare), to die, (1) of natural death, human, animal, or vegetable, Mat. ix. 24; (2) of spiritual death, Ro. vii. 10; Rev. iii. 2; (3) in Epp. of Paul, to die to (dat.), as Ro. vi. 2; also in other shades of meaning. For tenses see θνήσκω.

ἀπο-καθ-ίστημι, ἀποκαταστήσω (also -καθιστάω and -άνω, see Mar. ix. 12; Ac. i. 6), to restore, e.g., to health, or as a state or kingdom, Lu. vi. 10, Ac. i. 6.

ἀπο-καλύπτω, to uncover, bring to light, reveal, Mat. x. 26; Lu. x. 21; 1 Cor. ii. 10. See Thayer, p. 62.

ἀπο-κάλυψις, εως, ἡ, revelation, manifestation, enlightenment, 1 Cor. xiv. 26; Ep. iii. 3; 2 Th. i. 7. (S.) Syn.: see Trench, § xciv.

ἀπο-καρα-δοκία, ας, ἡ (κάρα, head; ἀπό, intensive), earnest expectation, as if looking for with the head outstretched, Ro. viii. 19; Phil. i. 20.*

ἀπο-κατ-αλλάσσω, to reconcile, change from one state of feeling to another, Ep. ii. 16; Col. i. 20, 22. (N. T.)*

ἀπο-κατά-στασις, εως, ἡ, restitution, restoration, Ac. iii. 21.*

ἀπό-κειμαι, to be laid away, to be reserved for (dat.), Lu. xix. 20; Col. i. 5; 2 Tim. iv. 8; Heb. ix. 27.*

ἀπο-κεφαλίζω (κεφαλή), to behead, Mat. xiv. 10; Mar. vi. 16, 27; Lu. ix. 9. (S.)*

ἀπο-κλείω, to shut close, as a door, Lu. xiii. 25.*

ἀπο-κόπτω, to smite or cut off, Mar. ix. 43, 45; Jn. xviii. 10, 26; Ac. xxvii. 32; mid., Gal. v. 12 (see R. V.).*

ἀπό-κριμα, ατος, τό, an answer, 2 Cor. i. 9.*

ἀπο-κρίνομαι (for aor., see Gr. § 100, Wi. § 39, 2), to answer, Mar. xii. 28; Col. iv. 6; often used (like the corresponding Hebrew verb) where the "answer" is not to a distinct question, but to some suggestion of the accompanying circumstances; so especially in the phrase ἀποκριθεὶς εἶπεν, answered and said, as Mat. xi. 25; Lu. i. 60.

ἀπό-κρισις, εως, ἡ, an answer, reply, Lu. ii. 47.

ἀπο-κρύπτω, to hide, conceal, 1 Cor. ii. 7; Ep. iii. 9.

ἀπό-κρυφος, ον, hidden, concealed, Mar. iv. 22; Lu. viii. 17; stored up, Col. ii. 3.

ἀπο-κτείνω, ενῶ, to put to death, kill, Mat. xvi. 21; Rev. ii. 13; fig., to abolish, Ep. ii. 16.

ἀπο-κυέω, ῶ, to bring forth; fig., Ja. i. 15, 18.*

ἀπο-κυλίω, ίσω, to roll away, Mat. xxviii. 2; Mar. xvi. 3; Lu. xxiv. 2. (S.)*

ἀπο-λαμβάνω, to receive from any one, Gal. iv. 5· to receive back, recover, Lu. xv. 27;

mid., to take aside with one's self, Mar. vii. 33.

ἀπό-λαυσις, εως, ἡ (λαύω, to enjoy), enjoyment, 1 Tim. vi. 17; Heb. xi. 25.*

ἀπο-λείπω, to leave, to leave behind, 2 Tim. iv. 13, 20; to desert, Ju. 6; pass., to be reserved, Heb. iv. 9.

ἀπο-λείχω, to lick, as a dog, Lu. xvi. 21 (W. H. ἐπιλείχω).*

ἀπ-όλλυμι (see Gr. § 116, 2, Wi. § 15, Bu. 64), to destroy, to bring to nought, to put to death, Mar. i. 24; Ro. xiv. 15; to lose, Mat. x. 42; Jn. vi. 39; mid., pass. (and 2d perf.), to perish, die, Mat. viii. 25; to be lost, Lu. xxi. 18.

Ἀπολλύων, οντος, ὁ (prop. part of ἀπολλύω, Destroyer), Apollyon, Rev. ix. 11. (N. T.)*

Ἀπολλωνία, ας, ἡ, Apollonia, a city of Macedonia, Ac. xvii. 1.*

Ἀπολλώς, ώ, ὁ, Apollos, Ac. xviii. 24.

ἀπο-λογέομαι, οῦμαι (λόγος), to defend one's self by speech, Lu. xxi. 14; Ac. xxvi. 24; to defend, excuse, Ro. ii. 15.

ἀπο-λογία, ας, ἡ, a verbal defense, "apology," Ac. xxv. 16; 1 Cor. ix. 3.

ἀπο-λούω, mid., to wash away, as sins, Ac. xxii. 16; 1 Cor. vi. 11.*

ἀπο-λύτρωσις, εως, ἡ, redemption, deliverance, Ro. iii. 24; Heb. ix. 15, xi. 35. Syn.: see Trench, § lxxvii.

ἀπο-λύω, to release, let go, to send away, Ac. xxviii. 18; Mat. xv. 23; spec., to put away a wife, divorce, Mat. i. 19; Lu. xvi. 18; mid., to depart, Ac. xxviii. 25.

ἀπο-μάσσω, ξω, to wipe off, as dust from the feet; mid., Lu. x. 11.*

ἀπο-νέμω, to assign to, apportion, 1 Pet. iii. 7.*

ἀπο-νίπτω, mid., to wash one's self, Mat. xxvii. 24.*

ἀπο-πίπτω, to fall from, Ac. ix. 18.*

ἀπο-πλανάω, ῶ, to lead astray, Mar. xiii. 22; 1 Tim. vi. 10.*

ἀπο-πλέω, εύσω, to sail away, Ac. xiii. 4, xiv. 26, xx. 15, xxvii. 1.*

ἀπο-πλύνω, *to wash* or *rinse*, as nets, Lu. v. 2 (W. H. πλύνω).*

ἰπο-πνίγω, *to suffocate, choke,* Mat. xiii. 7; Lu. viii. 7, 33.*

ἰ-πορέω, ῶ (πόρος, *resource*), except Mar. vi. 20 (W. H.), only mid. in N. T., *to be in doubt, to be perplexed,* Jn. xiii. 22; 2 Cor. iv. 8.

ἀπορία, ας, ἡ, *perplexity, disquiet,* Lu. xxi. 25.*

ἀπο-ρρίπτω, *to throw* or *cast down* or *off,* Ac. xxvii. 43; ἑαυτούς understood.*

ἀπ-ορφανίζω (ὀρφανος), "to make orphans of"; *to bereave,* pass., 1 Th. ii. 17.*

ἀπο-σκευάζομαι, *to pack away, pack up,* Ac. xxi. 15 (W. H. ἐπισκευάζομαι).*

ἀπο-σκίασμα, ατος, τό (σκίαζω), *a shade, a shadow,* Ja. i. 17. (N. T.)*

ἀπο-σπάω, ῶ, άσω, *to draw out, unsheathe,* Mat. xxvi. 51; *to withdraw, to draw away,* Ac. xxi. 1.

ἀπο-στασία, ας, ἡ, *defection, apostasy,* Ac. xxi. 21; 2 Th. ii. 3.*

ἀπο-στάσιον, ου, τό, *repudiation, divorce,* Mat. xix. 7; Mar. x. 4; met., *bill of divorce,* as Mat. v. 31.*

ἀπο-στεγάζω (στέγη), *to unroof,* Mar. ii. 4.*

ἀπο-στέλλω, *to send forth, send,* as a messenger, commission, etc., spoken of prophets, teachers, and other messengers, Mat. x. 40; Lu. vii. 3; Ac. x. 36; *to send away, dismiss,* Lu. iv. 18; Mar. v. 10, viii. 26.

ἀπο-στερέω, ῶ, ήσω, *to defraud,* abs., as Mar. x. 19; *deprive of* by fraud, acc. and gen., 1 Tim. vi. 5.

ἀπο-στολή, ῆς, ἡ, *apostleship,* Ac. i. 25; Ro. i. 5; 1 Cor. ix. 2; Gal. ii. 8.*

ἀπό-στολος, ου, ὁ, (1) *a messenger,* 2 Cor. viii. 23; Heb. iii. 1; (2) *an apostle, i.e.,* a messenger of Christ to the world, Lu. vi. 13; Gal. i. 1; used of others besides Paul and the Twelve, Ac. xiv. 14; 1 Th. ii. 6; 2 Cor. viii. 23.

ἀπο-στοματίζω (στόμα), *to entice to speak off-hand,* Lu. xi. 53.*

ἀπο-στρέφω, *to turn away, trans.*

(with ἀπό, as Ac. iii. 26); *restore, replace,* Mat. xxvi. 52; mid., *to desert, reject,* acc., Mat. v. 42.

ἀπο-στυγέω, ῶ, *to detest, to abhor,* Ro. xii. 9.*

ἀπο-συνάγωγος, ον, *excluded from the synagogue, excommunicated,* Jn. ix. 22, xii. 42, xvi. 2. (N. T.)*

ἀπο-τάσσω, ξω, mid., *to separate one's self from, withdraw from* (dat.), Mar. vi. 46; *to take leave of, renounce, send away* (dat.), Lu. xiv. 33.

ἀπο-τελέω, ῶ, έσω, *to perfect,* Ja. i. 15; Lu. xiii. 32 (W. H.).*

ἀπο-τίθημι, mid., *to lay off* or *aside,* Ac. vii. 58; *to renounce,* Ro. xiii. 12.

ἀπο-τίνασσω, *to shake off,* Lu. ix. 5; Ac. xxviii. 5.*

ἀπο-τίνω (or -τίω), τίσω, *to repay,* Philem. 19.*

ἀπο-τολμάω, ῶ, *to assume boldness,* Ro. x. 20.*

ἀπο-τομία, ας, ἡ (τέμνω, *to cut*), *severity,* Ro. xi. 22.*

ἀπο-τόμως, adv., *severely, sharply,* 2 Cor. xiii. 10; Tit. i. 13.*

ἀπο-τρέπω, mid., *to turn away from, shun,* acc., 2 Tim. iii. 5.*

ἀπ-ουσία, ας (ἄπειμι), *absence,* Phil. ii. 12.*

ἀπο-φέρω, *to bear away* from one place to another, Mar. xv. 1; Rev. xvii. 3.

ἀπο-φεύγω, *to escape,* 2 Pet. i. 4, ii. 18, 20.*

ἀπο-φθέγγομαι, *to speak out, declare,* Ac. ii. 4, 14, xxvi. 25. (S.)*

ἀπο-φορτίζομαι (φόρτος, *a burden*), *to unload, discharge,* Ac. xxi. 3.*

ἀπό-χρησις, εως, ἡ (ἀπό, intens.), *abuse, misuse,* Col. ii. 22.*

ἀπο-χωρέω, ῶ, *to go away, depart,* Mat. vii. 23; Lu. ix. 39; Ac. xiii. 13.*

ἀπο-χωρίζω, *to part asunder,* Ac. xv. 39; Rev. vi. 14.*

ἀπο-ψύχω, *to breathe out life, to faint,* Lu. xxi. 26.*

Ἄππιος, ου, ὁ, *Appius;* Ἀππίου φόρον, *the Forum of Appius,* a town in Italy, situated on the Appian Way, Ac. xxviii. 15.*

ἀ-πρός-ιτος, ον (προς, εἶμι), *not to be approached,* 1 Tim. vi. 16.*

ἀ-πρός-κοπος, ον (κόπτω), act., *not causing to stumble,* 1 Cor. x. 32; pass., *not caused to stumble, blameless, without offense,* Ac. xxiv. 16; Phil. i. 10. (Ap.)*

ἀ-προσωπο-λήπτως (W. H. -λήμπτ-), adv., *without respect of persons, impartially,* 1 Pet. i. 17. (N. T.)*

ἄ-πταιστος, ον (πταίω, *to fall*), *without stumbling* or *falling,* Ju. 24.*

ἅπτω, ψω, *to kindle,* as light or fire, Lu. viii. 16, xi. 33; mid., *to touch,* Mat viii. 3; 1 Cor. vii. 1. *Syn.:* ἅπτομαι is to touch or handle; θιγγάνω, a lighter touch; ψηλαφάω, to feel or feel after.

Ἀπφία, ας, ἡ, *Apphia,* Philem. 2.*

ἀπ-ωθέω, ῶ, ἀπώσω, mid., *to repulse, to reject,* Ac. vii. 27, 39.

ἀπώλεια, ας, ἡ (ἀπόλλυμι), *destroying, waste,* of things, Ro. ix. 22; Mar. xiv. 4; *destruction,* in general, Ac. viii. 20; *perdition,* 2 Th. ii. 3; Rev. xvii. 8, 11.

ἀρά, ᾶς, ἡ, *curse, imprecation,* Ro. iii. 14.*

ἄρα, conj., illative, *therefore, thence, since.* See Gr. § 406, Wi. § 53, 8, Bu. 371.

ἆρα, adv. interrogative, usually where the answer is negative, Lu. xviii. 8; Ac. viii. 30; Gal. ii. 17.*

Ἀραβία, ας, ἡ, *Arabia,* Gal. i. 17, iv. 25.*

Ἀράμ, ὁ (Heb.), *Aram,* Mat. i. 3, 4; Lu. iii. 33 (not W. H.).*

Ἄραψ, αβος, ὁ, *an Arabian,* Ac. ii. 11.*

ἀργέω, ῶ, *to linger, to delay,* 2 Pet. ii. 3.*

ἀργός, όν (ἀ, ἔργον), *idle, lazy,* Mat. xx. 3; Tit. i. 12.

ἀργύρεος, οῦς, ᾶ, οῦν, *made of silver,* Ac. xix. 24; 2 Tim. ii. 20; Rev. ix. 20.*

ἀργύριον, ου, τό, *silver,* Ac. iii. 6; *a piece of silver, a shekel,* Mat. xvi. 15; *money* in general, Mar. xiv. 11.

ἀργυρο-κόπος, ου, ὁ, *a silversmith,* Ac. xix. 24.*

ἄργυρος, ου, ὁ, *silver,* Ac. xvii. 29; Ja. v. 3.

Ἄρειος πάγος, ου, ὁ, *Areopagus,* or *Mars' Hill,* an open space on a hill in Athens, where

the supreme court was held,
Ac. xvii. 19, 22.* ("Αρειος
is an adj. from "Αρης, *Mars.*)
'Αρεοπαγίτης, ου, ὁ, *a judge of
the Areopagite court*, Ac. xvii.
34.*
ἀρέσκεια, as, ἡ, *a pleasing, a
desire of pleasing*, Col. i. 10.*
ἀρέσκω, ἀρέσω, *to be pleasing to*,
Mat. xiv. 6; Gal. i. 10; *to
seek to please* or *gratify, to
accommodate one's self to*
(dat.), 1 Cor. x. 33; 1 Th.
ii. 4.
ἀρεστός, ἡ, όν, *acceptable, pleasing to*, Jn. viii. 29; Ac. xii. 3.
'Αρέτας, a, ὁ, *Aretas*, a king of
Arabia Petræa, 2 Cor. xi.
32.*
ἀρετή, ἧς, ἡ, *virtue*, 2 Pet. i. 5;
*any moral excellence, perfec-
tion*, Phil. iv. 8; 1 Pet. ii. 9;
2 Pet. i. 3.*
(ἄρην), gen. ἀρνός, *a lamb*, Lu.
x. 3.*
ἀριθμέω, ῶ, *to number*, Mat. x.
30; Lu. xii. 7; Rev. vii. 9.*
ἀριθμός, οῦ, ὁ, *a number*, Jn. vi.
10; Ac. vi. 7.
'Αριμαθαία, as, ἡ, *Arimathæa,*
a city of Palestine, Mat.
xxvii. 57; Mar. xv. 43.
'Αρίσταρχος, ου, ὁ, *Aristarchus*,
Ac. xix. 29; Col. iv. 10.
ἀριστάω, ῶ, ἤσω (ἄριστον), *to
breakfast*, Jn. xxi. 12, 15;
to dine, Lu. xi. 37.
ἀριστερός, ά, όν, *left;* ἡ ἀριστερά
(χείρ), *the left hand*, Mat. vi.
3; ἐξ ἀριστερῶν, *on the left*,
Mar. x. 37 (W. H.); Lu. xxiii.
33, *without* ἐξ; 2 Cor. vi. 7.
(The more common word is
εὐώνυμος.)*
'Αριστόβουλος, ου, ὁ, *Aristo-
bulus*, Ro. xvi. 10.*
ἄριστον, ου, τό, *dinner*, Mat.
xxii. 4; Lu. xi. 38, xiv. 12.*
See δεῖπνον.
ἀρκετός, ἡ, όν, *sufficient*, Mat.
vi. 34, x. 25; 1 Pet. iv. 3.*
ἀρκέω, ῶ, *to be sufficient for*,
Mat. xxv. 9; 2 Cor. xii. 9;
pass., *to be satisfied with*, Lu.
iii. 14; Heb. xiii. 5.
ἄρκτος (W. H. ἄρκος), ου, ὁ, ἡ,
a bear, Rev. xiii. 2.*
ἅρμα, ατος, τό, *a chariot*, Ac.
viii. 28, 29, 38; Rev. ix. 9.*
'Αρμαγεδδών (Heb. or Aram.,
der. disputed), (W. H. "Αρ
Μαγεδών), *Harmageddon*,
Rev. xvi. 16. (N. T.)*

ἁρμόζω, σω, *to fit together;* mid.,
to espouse, to betroth, 2 Cor.
xi. 2.*
ἁρμός, οῦ, ὁ, *a joint, i.e.*, of
limbs in a body, Heb. iv.
12.*
ἀρνέομαι, οῦμαι, *to deny*, Mat.
xxvi. 70; Jn. i. 20; 2 Tim.
ii. 12; *to renounce*, Tit. ii.
12; *to reject*, Ac. iii. 14.*
ἀρνίον, ου, τό (dimin. of ἀρήν),
a little lamb, Jn. xxi. 15;
freq. in Rev., of Christ.
ἀροτριάω, ῶ, άσω, *to plow*, Lu.
xvii. 7; 1 Cor. ix. 10.*
ἄροτρον, ου, τό, *a plow*, Lu. ix.
62.*
ἁρπαγή, ῆς, ἡ (ἁρπάζω), *the act
of plundering*, Heb. x. 34;
plunder, spoil, Mat. xxiii. 25;
Lu. xi. 39.*
ἁρπαγμός, οῦ, ὁ, *spoil, an object
of eager desire, a prize*, Phil.
ii. 6.*
ἁρπάζω, άσω (2 aor. pass.,
ἡρπάγην), *to snatch, seize
violently, take by force*, Jn.
x. 12; *to carry off suddenly*,
Jn. vi. 15; Ac. xxiii. 10.
ἅρπαξ, αγος, adj., *rapacious,
ravenous*, Mat. vii. 15; Lu.
xviii. 11; *a robber, an extor-
tioner*, 1 Cor. v. 10, 11, vi.
10.*
ἀρραβών, ῶνος, ὁ (from Heb.),
a pledge, an earnest, ratify-
ing a contract, 2 Cor. i. 22,
v. 5; Ep. i. 14.*
ἄρραφος (W. H. ἄραφος), ον,
not seamed or *sewn*, Jn. xix.
23. (N. T.)*
ἄρρην, εν (W. H. ἄρσην, εν), *of
the male sex*, Ro. i. 27; Rev.
xii. 5, 13.*
ἄρρητος, ον, adj., *unspoken, unspeakable*, 2 Cor. xii. 4.*
ἄρρωστος, ον, adj. (ῥώννυμι), *infirm, sick*, Mat. xiv. 14; 1
Cor. xi. 30.
ἀρσενο-κοίτης, ου, ὁ (ἄρσην κοίτη), *a sodomite*, 1 Cor. vi. 9;
1 Tim. i. 10.*
ἄρσην, εν, *male*, Mat. xix. 4;
Gal. iii. 28.
'Αρτεμᾶς, ᾶ, ὁ, *Artemas*, Tit.
iii. 12.*
"Αρτεμις, ιδος or ιος, ἡ, *Artemis,*
the Persian or Ephesian Artemis, to be distinguished
from the Artemis of the
Greeks, the sister of Apollo,
Ac. xix. 24, 27, 28, 34, 35.*
ἀρτέμων, ονος, ὁ (ἀρτάω, *to sus-*

pend), prob. *the foresail*, Ac.
xxvii. 40.*
ἄρτι, adv. of time, *now, just
now, at this moment;* with
other particles, as ἕως ἄρτι,
till now; ἀπ' ἄρτι, *from now*
or *henceforward.*
ἀρτι-γέννητος, ον, *newly* or *recently born*, 1 Pet. ii. 2. (N.
T.)*
ἄρτιος, ου, adj., *perfect, complete*, wanting in nothing, 2
Tim. iii. 17.* Syn.: ἄρτιος
means fully adapted for its
purpose; ὁλόκληρος, entire,
having lost nothing; τέλειος,
fully developed, complete.
ἄρτος, ου, ὁ, *bread, loaf, food;*
fig., *spiritual nutriment;* ἄρτοι τῆς προθέσεως, *show-bread*,
Mat. xii. 4; Mar. ii. 26.
ἀρτύω (ἄρω, *to fit*), *to season, to
flavor*, as with salt, Mar. ix.
50; Lu. xiv. 34; fig., Col.
iv. 6.*
'Αρφαξάδ, ὁ (Heb.), *Arphaxad*,
Lu. iii. 36.*
ἀρχ-άγγελος, ου, ὁ, *an arch-* or
chief-angel, 1 Th. iv. 16; Ju.
9. (N. T.)*
ἀρχαῖος, a, ον, *old, ancient*, Lu.
ix. 8, 19; 2 Pet. ii. 5.
'Αρχέλαος, ου, ὁ, *Archelaus*,
Mat. ii. 22.*
ἀρχή, ῆς, ἡ, (1) *a beginning*, of
time, space, or series, Jn. i.
1; 2 Pet. iii. 4; *the outermost
point*, Ac. x. 11. Used of
Christ, *the leader*, Col. i. 18;
Rev. iii. 14, xxi. 6, xxii. 13.
Adv. phrases: ἀπ' ἀρχῆς,
from the beginning; ἐν ἀρχῇ
in the beginning; ἐξ ἀρχῆς,
from the beginning or *from
the first;* κατ' ἀρχάς, *at
the beginning;* τὴν ἀρχήν,
originally. (2) *rule, pre-
eminence, principality* (see
ἄρχω): espec. in pl., ἀρχαι,
rulers, magistrates, as Lu.
xii. 11; of supramundane
powers, *principalities*, as Ep.
iii. 10.
ἀρχ-ηγός, οῦ, ὁ (ἀρχή, ἄγω), *the
beginner, author, prince*, Ac.
iii. 15, v. 31; Heb. ii. 10,
xii. 2.*
ἀρχ-ιερατικός, ἡ, όν, *belonging
to the office of the high-priest,
pontifical*, Ac. iv. 6.*
ἀρχ-ιερεύς, έως, ὁ, (1) *the high-
priest*, Mat. xxvi. 3; Heb. ix.
7, 25; so of Christ only in

Heb., as ii. 17, iii. 1, etc.;
(2) in pl. used more widely to include high-priestly
families and deposed high-
priests, Mat. ii. 4; Lu. xix.
47; Ac. iv. 23.

ἀρχι-ποίμην, ενος, ὁ, *the chief
shepherd*, a title of Christ,
1 Pet. v. 4. (N. T.)*

Ἄρχιππος, ου, ὁ, *Archippus*,
Col. iv. 17; Philem. 2.*

ἀρχι-συνάγωγος, ου, ὁ, *presid-
ing officer* or *ruler of a synagogue*, Lu. viii. 49; Ac. xiii.
15.

ἀρχι-τέκτων, ονος, ὁ, *a master-
builder, an architect*, 1 Cor.
iii. 10.*

ἀρχι-τελώνης, ου, ὁ, *a chief collector of taxes, a chief publican*, Lu. xix. 2. (N. T.)*

ἀρχι-τρίκλινος, ου, ὁ, *a superintendent of a dining room*,
Jn. ii. 8, 9. (N. T.)*

ἄρχω, *to reign, to rule* (gen.),
only Mar. x. 42; Ro. xv. 12;
mid., *to begin*, often with
infin.; ἀρξάμενος ἀπό, *beginning from* (see Gr. § 287).

ἄρχων, οντος, ὁ, prop. particip.,
ruler, prince, leader, Ac. xvi.
19; Ro. xiii. 3.

ἄρωμα, ατος, τό, *spice, perfume*,
Mar. xvi. 1; Lu. xxiii. 56,
xxiv. 1; Jn. xix. 40.*

Ἀσά, ὁ (Heb.), *Asa*, Mat. i. 7, 8.*

ἀ-σάλευτος, ον, *unshaken, immovable*, Ac. xxvii. 41; Heb.
xii. 28.*

ἄ-σβεστος, ον, adj. (σβέννυμι),
*not to be quenched, inextin-
guishable*, Mat. iii. 12; Lu.
iii. 17; Mar. ix. 43, 45 (W.
H. omit).*

ἀσέβεια, ας, ἡ, *impiety, ungodliness, wickedness*, Ro. i. 18;
Ju. 15, 18. Syn.: see ἀγνόημα.

ἀσεβέω, ῶ, ήσω, *to be ungodly,
act impiously*, 2 Pet. ii. 6;
Ju. 15.*

ἀ-σεβής, ές (σέβομαι), *impious,
ungodly, wicked*, Ro. iv. 5;
Ju. 4, 15.

ἀ-σέλγεια, ας, ἡ, *excess, wanton-
ness, lasciviousness*, Mar. vii.
22; Ep. iv. 19.

ἄ-σημος, ον, *not remarkable, obscure, ignoble*, Ac. xxi. 39.*

Ἀσήρ, ὁ, *Asher*, Lu. ii. 36;
Rev. vii. 6.*

ἀσθένεια, ας, ἡ, *weakness, bodily
infirmity, sickness*, 1 Cor. xv.
43; Heb. xi. 34; fig., *mental

weakness, distress*, Ro. vi. 19;
Heb. v. 2.

ἀσθενέω, ῶ, *to be weak*, Ro. viii.
3; 2 Cor. xiii. 4; *to be sick*,
Lu. iv. 40; Ac. ix. 37.

ἀσθένημα, ατος, τό, *weakness,
infirmity;* fig., Ro. xv. 1.*

ἀ-σθενής, ές (σθένος, strength),
"without strength," *weak,
infirm*, Mat. xxvi. 41; Ro.
v. 6; 1 Cor. iv. 10; *sick*, Lu.
x. 9; Ac. iv. 9; 1 Cor. xi.
30.

Ἀσία, ας, ἡ, *Asia proper* or
Proconsular Asia, a district
in the west of Asia Minor,
Ac. vi. 9; 1 Pet. i. 1; Rev. i.
4; *a part of Proconsular Asia*,
Ac. ii. 9.

Ἀσιανός, οῦ, ὁ, *belonging to
Asia*, Ac. xx. 4.*

Ἀσιάρχης, ου, ὁ, *an Asiarch,
a president of Asia*, a citizen
appointed annually to preside over the worship and
celebrations in honor of the
gods, Ac. xix. 31.*

ἀσιτία, ας, ἡ (σῖτος, corn), *ab-
stinence, a fast*, Ac. xxvii.
21.*

ἄ-σιτος, ον, *fasting*, Ac. xxvii.
33.*

ἀσκέω, ῶ, ήσω, *to exercise one's
self, use diligence in*, Ac.
xxiv. 16.*

ἀσκός, οῦ, ὁ, *a bottle* of skin,
Mat. ix. 17; Mar. ii. 22; Lu.
v. 37, 38.*

ἀσμένως, adv. (from part. of
ἥδομαι), *with joy, gladly*, Ac.
ii. 41 (W. H. omit); Ac. xxi.
17.*

ἄ-σοφος, ον, *not wise*, Ep. v.
15.*

ἀσπάζομαι, dep., *to embrace,
salute, to greet* (actually or
by letter), Mat. x. 2; 1 Cor.
xvi. 19, 20; always of persons, except Heb. xi. 13,
"having embraced (R. V.
greeted) the promises"; *to
take leave of* (only Ac. xx. 1;
in xxi. 6, W. H. read ἀπασπάζομαι).

ἀσπασμός, οῦ, ὁ, *salutation,
greeting*, Mat. xxiii. 7; Col.
iv. 18.

ἄ-σπιλος, ον (σπῖλος), *without
spot, unblemished*, 1 Tim. vi.
14; 1 Pet. i. 19.

ἀσπίς, ίδος, ἡ, *an asp, a venom-
ous serpent*, Ro. iii. 13.*

ἄ-σπονδος, ον (σπονδή), "not

to be bound by truce," *implacable*, 2 Tim. iii. 3; Ro. i.
31 (not W. H.).*

ἀσσάριον, ιου, τό, *a small coin*
equal to the tenth part of a
drachma, *an assarium*, Mat.
x. 29; Lu. xii. 6. See Gr.
§ 154 a.

ἄσσον, adv. (compar. of ἄγχι),
nearer, close by, Ac. xxvii. 13.*

Ἄσσος, ου, ἡ, *Assos*, Ac. xx.
13, 14.*

ἀ-στατέω, ῶ, ήσω, *to be un-
settled, to have no fixed abode*,
1 Cor. iv. 11.*

ἀστεῖος, ον (ἄστυ, city, see urbane), *fair, beautiful*, Ac.
vii. 20; Heb. xi. 23.*

ἀστήρ, έρος, ὁ, *a star*, Mar. xiii.
25; 1 Cor. xv. 41; Rev. vi.
13.

ἀ-στήρικτος, ον (στηρίζω), *un-
settled, unstable*, 2 Pet. ii. 14,
iii. 16.*

ἄ-στοργος, ον (στοργή), *without
natural affection*, Ro. i. 31;
2 Tim. iii. 3.*

ἀ-στοχέω, ῶ (στόχος), *to miss
in aim, swerve from*, 1 Tim.
i. 6, vi. 21; 2 Tim. ii. 18.*

ἀστραπή, ῆς, ἡ, *lightning*, Lu.
x. 18; Rev. iv. 5; vivid
brightness, lustre, Lu. xi. 36.

ἀστράπτω, *to flash*, as lightning, Lu. xvii. 24; *to be lus-
trous*, xxiv. 4.*

ἄστρον, ου, τό, *a star* (orig. con-
stellation), Lu. xxi. 25; Ac.
vii. 43, xxvii. 20; Heb. xi.
12.*

Ἀσύγκριτος, ου, ὁ, *Asyncritus*,
Ro. xvi. 14.*

ἀ-σύμφωνος, ον, *dissonant, dis-
cordant*, Ac. xxviii. 25.*

ἀ-σύνετος, ον, *without understanding, foolish*, Mat. xv.
16; Ro. x. 19.

ἀ-σύνθετος, ον, *covenant-break-
ing, treacherous*, Ro. i. 31.*

ἀσφάλεια, ας, ἡ, *security*, Ac.
v. 23; 1 Th. v. 3; *certainty*,
Lu. i. 4.*

ἀ-σφαλής, ές (σφάλλω, fallo),
safe, Phil. iii. 1; *secure, firm*,
Heb. vi. 19; *certain*, Ac. xxv.
26; τὸ ἀσφαλές, *the certainty*,
Ac. xxi. 34, xxii. 30.*

ἀσφαλίζω, σω (mid.), *to make
fast, to secure*, Mat. xxvii.
65, 66; Ac. xvi. 24; pass., *to
be made secure*, Mat. xxvii.
64.*

ἀσφαλῶς, adv., *safely*, Mar. xiv.

44; Ac. xvi. 23; *assuredly*, Ac. ii. 36.*

ἀσχημονέω, ῶ, *to act improperly* or *unseemly*, 1 Cor. vii. 36, xiii. 5.*

ἀσχημοσύνη, ης, ἡ, *unseemliness*, Ro. i. 27; *shame, nakedness*, Rev. xvi. 15.*

ἀ-σχήμων, ον (σχῆμα), *uncomely, unseemly*, 1 Cor. xii. 23.*

ἀ-σωτία, ας, ἡ (σώζω), *an abandoned course, profligacy*, Ep. v. 18; Tit. i. 6; 1 Pet. iv. 4.*

ἀ-σώτως, adv., *profligately, dissolutely*, Lu. xv. 13.*

ἀτακτέω, ῶ, *to behave disorderly*, 2 Th. iii. 7.*

ἄ-τακτος, ον (τάσσω), *irregular, disorderly*, 1 Th. v. 14.*

ἀτάκτως, adv., *disorderly, irregularly*, 2 Th. iii. 6, 11.*

ἄ-τεκνος, ου, ὁ, ἡ (τέκνον), *childless*, Lu. xx. 28, 29.*

ἀτενίζω, σω, *to look intently upon* (dat. or εἰς), Lu. iv. 20; Ac. i. 10; 2 Cor. iii. 7, 13.

ἄτερ, adv., as prep. with gen., *without, in the absence of*, Lu. xxii. 6, 35.*

ἀτιμάζω, σω, *to dishonor, contemn*, whether persons or things, by word or by deed, Lu. xx. 11; Jn. viii. 49; Ja. ii. 6.

ἀτιμία, ας, ἡ, *dishonor, ignominy, disgrace, ignoble use*, 1 Cor. xi. 14; Ro. i. 26, ix. 21.

ἄ-τιμος, ον (τιμή), *without honor, despised*, Mat. xiii. 57; Mar. vi. 4; 1 Cor. iv. 10, xii. 23.*

ἀτιμόω, ῶ, *to dishonor, treat with indignity*, Mar. xii. 4 (not W. H.).*

ἀτμίς, ίδος, ἡ, *a vapor*, Ac. ii. 19; Ja. iv. 14.

ἄ-τομον, ου, τό (τέμνω), *an atom* of time, *moment*, 1 Cor. xv. 52.*

ἄ-τοπος, ον (τόπος), *misplaced, unbecoming, mischievous*, Lu. xxiii. 41; Ac. xxviii. 6.

Ἀττάλεια, ας, ἡ, *Attalia*, Ac. xiv. 25.*

αὐγάζω, *to shine forth*, 2 Cor. iv. 4.*

αὐγή, ῆς, ἡ, *brightness, daylight*, Ac. xx. 11.*

Αὔγουστος, ου, ὁ (Lat.), *Augustus*, Lu. ii. 1.* Compare Σεβαστός.

αὐθάδης, ες (αὐτός, ἥδομαι), *self-*

pleasing, arrogant, Tit. i. 7; 2 Pet. ii. 10.*

αὐθαίρετος, ον (αὐτός, αἱρέομαι), *of one's own accord*, 2 Cor. viii. 3, 17.*

αὐθεντέω, ῶ, *to exercise authority over* (gen.), 1 Tim. ii. 12. (N. T.)*

αὐλέω, ῶ, ήσω, *to play on a flute, to pipe*, Mat. xi. 17; Lu. vii. 32; 1 Cor. xiv. 7.

αὐλή, ῆς, ἡ (ἄω, *to blow*), *an open space, uncovered court* or *hall* of a house, as Lu. xi. 21, xxii. 55; *a sheepfold*, Jn. x. 1, 16.

αὐλητής, οῦ, ὁ, *a flute-player*, Mat. ix. 23; Rev. xviii. 22.*

αὐλίζομαι (to lodge in the open air), *to lodge, pass the night*, Mat. xxi. 17; Lu. xxi. 37.*

αὐλός, οῦ, ὁ (ἄω), *a flute, pipe*, 1 Cor. xiv. 7.*

αὐξάνω (also αὔξω), αὐξήσω, trans., *to make to grow*, as 1 Cor. iii. 6, 7; pass., *to grow, increase, become greater*, Mat. xiii. 32; Col. i. 10; generally intrans., *to grow, increase*, as Mat. vi. 28.

αὔξησις, εως, ἡ, *growth, increase*, Ep. iv. 16; Col. ii. 19.*

αὔριον, adv. (αὔρα, *morning breeze*, ἄω), *to-morrow*, Mat. vi. 30; Lu. xiii. 32, 33; ἡ (sc. ἡμέρα) αὔριον, *the morrow*, Mat. vi. 34; Ac. iv. 3.

αὐστηρός, ά, όν (dry), *harsh, austere*, Lu. xix. 21, 22.*

αὐτάρκεια, ας, ἡ, *sufficiency*, 2 Cor. ix. 8; *contentment*, 1 Tim. vi. 6.*

αὐτ-άρκης, ες (ἀρκέω, sufficient for self), *content, satisfied*, Phil. iv. 11.*

αὐτο-κατά-κριτος, ον, *self-condemned*, Tit. iii. 11. (N. T.)*

αὐτόματος, ον, *spontaneous, of its own accord*, Mar. iv. 28; Ac. xii. 10.*

αὐτ-όπτης, ου, ὁ, *an eye-witness*, Lu. i. 2.*

αὐτός, ή, ό, pron., *he, she, it*; in nom. nearly always emphatic. Properly demonstrative, *self, very*; joined with each of the persons of the verb, with or without a pers. pron., *I myself, thou thyself*, etc.; with the article, *the same; the same* with (dat.), 1 Cor. xi. 5; ἐπὶ τὸ αὐτό, *at the same place* or *time, together;*

κατὰ τὸ αὐτό, *together*, only Ac. xiv. 1. See Gr. § 335, Wi. § 22, 3, 4, Bu. 105 sq.

αὐτοῦ, adv. of place, *here, there*, Mat. xxvi. 36; Ac. xviii. 19, xxi. 4.

αὑτοῦ, ῆς, οῦ, pron. reflex. (contr. for ἑαυτοῦ), *of himself, herself*, etc. (W. H. in the majority of cases read αὐτοῦ, αὐτῷ, etc., but retain αὑτοῦ, etc., in some, as Mat. vi. 34; Jn. ii. 24; Ac. xiv. 17, etc.).

αὐτό-φωρος, ον (φώρ, *a thief*), *in the very act*, Jn. viii. 4, neut. dat. with ἐπί (W. H. omit).*

αὐτό-χειρ, ρος, ὁ, *with one's own hand*, Ac. xxvii. 19.*

αὐχμηρός, ά, όν, *dark, dismal*, 2 Pet. i. 19.*

ἀφ-αιρέω, ῶ, *to take away*, as Lu. x. 42; *to take away* sin, only Ro. xi. 27; Heb. x. 4; *to smite off*, as Mat. xxvi. 51, and parallel passages.

ἀ-φανής, ές (φαίνω), *not appearing, hidden*, Heb. iv. 13.*

ἀ-φανίζω, *to put out of sight, destroy*, Mat. vi. 19, 20; *to disfigure*, Mat. vi. 16; pass., *to vanish, perish*, Ac. xiii. 41; Ja. iv. 14.*

ἀ-φανισμός, οῦ, ὁ, *a disappearing, destruction*, Heb. viii. 13.*

ἄ-φαντος, ον, *disappearing, not seen*, Lu. xxiv. 31.*

ἀφεδρών, ῶνος, ὁ, *draught, privy*, Mat. xv. 17 · Mar. vii. 19. (N. T.)*

ἀ-φειδία, ας, ἡ (φείδομαι), *severity*, Col. ii. 23.*

ἀφελότης, τητος, *simplicity, sincerity*, Ac. ii. 46. (N. T.)*

ἄφ-εσις, εως, ἡ (ἀφίημι), *deliverance*; lit., only Lu. iv. 18; elsewhere always of *deliverance* from sin, *remission, forgiveness*, Mat. xxvi. 28; Lu. i. 77; Ep. i. 7. *Syn.:* πάρεσις is a simple *suspension of punishment* for sin, in contrast with ἄφεσις, *complete forgiveness.*

ἀφή, ῆς, ἡ (ἅπτω, *to fit*), *that which connects, a joint*, Ep. iv. 16; Col. ii. 19.*

ἀφθαρσία, ας, ἡ, *incorruption, immortality*, 1 Cor. xv.; Ro. ii. 7; 2 Tim. i. 10; Ep. vi. 24; *incorruptness*, Tit. ii. 7 (W. H. ἀφθορία).*

ἄ-φθαρτος, ον (φθείρω), *incorruptible, imperishable,* Ro. i. 23; 1 Cor. ix. 25, xv. 52; 1 Tim. i. 17; 1 Pet. i. 4, 23, iii. 4.*

ἀ-φθορία, ας, ἡ, *incorruptness,* Tit. ii. 7 (W. H.). (N. T.)*

ἀφ-ίημι (see Gr. § 112, Wi. § 14, 3), *to send away,* as (1) *to let go, emit,* Mat. xxvii. 50; Mar. xv. 37; *dismiss,* in senses varying according to the obj.; spec., *to disregard, pass by, send away, divorce,* Mat. xv. 14; Heb. vi. 1; 1 Cor. vii. 11, 12, 13; hence, (2) *to forgive* (dat. pers.), very often, Mat. xviii. 27; Mar. ii. 5, 7; (3) *to permit, concede,* abs., or with inf., as Mar. x. 14; or acc., as Mat. iii. 15 (dat., Mat. v. 40); or ἵνα, subj., Mar. xi. 6; or subj. alone, Lu. vi. 42; (4) *to leave, depart from, abandon, leave behind,* Mat. xxii. 22; Mar. i. 31; Lu. v. 11, xvii. 34, 35.

ἀφικνέομαι, οῦμαι (2 aor., ἀφικόμην), *to arrive at, to reach,* Ro. xvi. 19.*

ἀ-φιλ-άγαθος, ον, *not loving goodness and good men,* 2 Tim. iii. 3. (N. T.)*

ἀ-φιλ-άργυρος, ον, *not loving money, not avaricious,* 1 Tim. iii. 3; Heb. xiii. 5. (N. T.)*

ἄφιξις, εως, ἡ, orig. arrival; *departure,* Ac. xx. 29.*

ἀφ-ίστημι, ἀποστήσω, trans. in pres., imperf., 1 aor., fut., *to lead away, to seduce;* intrans. in perf., plup., 2 aor., *to go away, depart, avoid, withdraw from* (often with ἀπό); mid., *to fail, abstain from, absent one's self.*

ἄφνω, adv., *suddenly,* Ac. ii. 2, xvi. 26, xxviii. 6.*

ἀ-φόβως, adv., *without fear,* Lu. i. 74; Phil. i. 14; 1 Cor. xvi. 10; Ju. 12.*

ἀφ-ομοιόω, ῶ, *to make like,* in pass., Heb. vii. 3.*

ἀφ-οράω, ῶ (2 a., ἀπ- or ἀφ-εῖδον), *to look away from others at* (εἰς) one, *to regard earnestly,* Heb. xii. 2; *to see,* Phil. ii. 23.*

ἀφ-ορίζω, fut. ιῶ, trans., *to separate from* (ἐκ or ἀπό), Mat. xiii. 49, xxv. 32; *to separate* for a purpose (εἰς, Ac. xiii. 2; Ro. i. 1; or inf.,

Gal. i. 15); *to excommunicate,* Lu. vi. 22.

ἀφ-ορμή, ῆς, ἡ, *an occasion, opportunity,* Ro. vii. 8, 11; 2 Cor. v. 12.

ἀφρίζω, *to foam at the mouth,* Mar. ix. 18, 20.*

ἀφρός, οῦ, ὁ, *foam, froth,* Lu. ix. 39.*

ἀ-φροσύνη, ης, ἡ, *foolishness,* Mar. vii. 22; 2 Cor. xi. 1, 17, 22.*

ἄ-φρων, ονος, ὁ, ἡ (φρήν), *inconsiderate, foolish, rash,* Lu. xi. 40; Ro. ii. 20.

ἀφ-υπνόω, ῶ (ἀπό, intensive), *to fall asleep,* Lu. viii. 23.*

ἀφυστερέω, ῶ, *to keep back by fraud,* Ja. v. 4 (W. H.).*

ἄ-φωνος, ον, *dumb, without the faculty of speech:* of animals, Ac. viii. 32; 2 Pet. ii. 16; of idols, 1 Cor. xii. 2. In 1 Cor. xiv. 10 the R. V. mrg. is probably the correct rendering.*

Ἄχαζ, ὁ (Heb.), *Ahaz,* Mat. i. 9.*

Ἀχαΐα, ας, ἡ, *Achaia,* a Roman province including all Greece except Thessaly, Ac. xix. 21; 1 Cor. xvi. 15.

Ἀχαϊκός, οῦ, ὁ, *Achaicus,* 1 Cor. xvi. 17.*

ἀ-χάριστος, ον, *unthankful,* Lu. vi. 35; 2 Tim. iii. 2.*

Ἀχείμ, ὁ (Heb.), *Achim,* Mat. i. 14.*

ἀ-χειρο-ποίητος, ον, *not made with hands,* Mar. xiv. 58; 2 Cor. v. 1; Col. ii. 11. (N. T.)*

ἀχλύς, ύος, ἡ, *a mist, dimness,* Ac. xiii. 11.*

ἀ-χρεῖος, ον, *useless, good for nothing, unprofitable,* Mat. xxv. 30; Lu. xvii. 10.*

ἀ-χρειόω (W. H. ἀχρεόω), pass., *to be made useless,* Ro. iii. 12.*

ἄ-χρηστος, ον, *useless, unprofitable,* Philem. 11.*

ἄχρι and ἄχρις, adv. as prep., with gen., *even to, until, as far as,* whether of place, time, or degree; ἄχρις οὗ or ἄχρις alone, with the force of a conjunction, *until.* See μέχρι.

ἄχυρον, ου, τό, *chaff,* Mat. iii. 12; Lu. iii. 17.*

ἀ-ψευδής, ές, *free from falsehood, truthful,* Tit. i. 2.*

ἄψινθος, ου, ὁ and ἡ, *wormwood,* Rev. viii. 11.*

ἄ-ψυχος, ον, *without life, inanimate,* 1 Cor. xiv. 7.*

B

B, β, βῆτα, *beta, b,* the second letter. Numerally, β′ = 2; β = 2000.

Βαάλ (W. H. Βάαλ), ὁ, ἡ (Heb. *Master*), *Baal,* chief deity of the Phœnicians and other Semitic nations, Ro. xi. 4 (fem.), from 1 Kings xix. 18 (S.)*

Βαβυλών, ῶνος, ἡ, *Babylon,* lit., Mat. i. 11, 12, 17; Ac. vii. 43, and prob. 1 Pet. v. 13; mystically, in Rev. xiv. 8, xvi. 19, xvii. 5, xviii. 2, 10, 21.*

βαθμός, οῦ, ὁ (βαίνω, *to step*), *a step* or *degree* in dignity, 1 Tim. iii. 13. (S.)*

βάθος, ους, τό, *depth,* lit. or fig., Mat. xiii. 5; 1 Cor. ii. 10; 2 Cor. viii. 2 (ἡ κατὰ βάθους πτωχεία, *their deep poverty*).

βαθύνω, υνῶ, *to make deep,* Lu. vi. 48.*

βαθύς, εῖα, ύ, *deep,* Jn. iv. 11; in Lu. xxiv. 1, ὄρθρου βαθέος, in the early dawn (W. H. βαθέως, probably a genit. form).

βαΐον, ου, τό (Egyptian), *a palm branch,* Jn. xii. 13.*

Βαλαάμ, ὁ (Heb.), *Balaam.* A name emblematic of seducing teachers, 2 Pet. ii. 15; Ju. 11; Rev. ii. 14.*

Βαλάκ, ὁ (Heb.), *Balak,* Rev. ii. 14.*

βαλάντιον (W. H. -λλ-), ου, τό, *a money-bag, purse,* Lu. x. 4, xii. 33, xxii. 35, 36.*

βάλλω, βαλῶ, βέβληκα, ἔβαλον, *to throw, cast, put* (with more or less force, as modified by the context); of liquids, *to pour.* Pass. perf., with intrans. force, as Mat. viii. 6 ("has been cast"), *lies.* The verb is intrans., Ac. xxvii. 14, *rushed.* In Mar. xiv. 65 the true reading is prob. ἔλαβον. Generally trans. with acc. and dat., or ἐπί (acc., sometimes gen.), εἰς, ἀπό, ἐκ, and other prepp. or advv.

βαπτίζω, σω (in form a frequentative of βάπτω, see G.

§ 144 *b*), (1) mid. or pass., reflex., *to bathe* one's self, only in Mar. vii. 4; Lu. xi. 38; (2) of the Christian ordinance, *to immerse, submerge, to baptize.* The material (water, fire, the Holy Spirit) is expressed by dat., εἰς or ἐν; the purpose or result by εἰς. Pass. or. mid., *to be baptized, to receive baptism;* (3) fig., of overwhelming woe, Mar. x. 38, 39; Lu. xii. 50.

βάπτισμα, ατος, τό, *the rite* or *ceremony of baptism*, Mat. iii. 7; Ep. iv. 5; fig., for overwhelming afflictions, Mar. x. 38, 39; Lu. xii. 50. (N. T.)

βαπτισμός, οῦ, ὁ, *the act of cleansing*, as vessels, Mar. vii. 4, 8 (W. H. omit); of Jewish lustrations, *washings* (pl.), Heb. ix. 10. For Heb. vi. 2, see Gr. § 260 *b*, 2 (*b*).*

βαπτιστής, οῦ, ὁ, *one who baptizes;* the surname of John, Christ's forerunner, Mat. iii. 1; Mar. viii. 28.

βάπτω, βάψω, *to dip*, Lu. xvi. 24; Jn. xiii. 26; *to dye, color*, Rev. xix. 13.*

βάρ (Aram.), *son*, only Mat. xvi. 17 (βὰρ Ἰωνᾶ, W. H. βαριωνᾶ). Also prefix to many surnames, meaning *son of.* (N. T.)

Βαρ-αββᾶς, ᾶ, ὁ, *Barabbas*, Mat. xxvii. 16, 17; Jn. xviii. 40.

Βαράκ, ὁ, *Barak*, Heb. xi. 32.*

Βαραχίας, ου, ὁ, *Barachiah*, Mat. xxiii. 35.*

βάρβαρος, ου, ὁ (prob. onomatop., descriptive of unintelligible sounds), properly adj., *a foreigner, barbarian*, as 1 Cor. xiv. 11; used of all foreigners not Greeks, Ac. xxviii. 2, 4; Col. iii. 11; Ro. i. 14.*

βαρέω, ῶ (see βάρος), in N. T. only pass. βαρέομαι, οῦμαι, *to be weighed down, to be oppressed*, as by sleep, Lu. ix. 32; mental troubles, 2 Cor. i. 8, v. 4.

βαρέως, adv., *heavily, with difficulty*, Mat. xiii. 15; Ac. xxviii. 27.*

Βαρ-θολομαῖος, ου, ὁ, *Bartholomew*, surname (prob.) of Nathanael, Mat. x. 3.

Βαρ-ιησοῦς, οῦ, ὁ, *Bar-Jesus*, Ac. xiii. 6.*

Βαρ-ιωνᾶς, ᾶ, ὁ, *Bar-Jonas*, surname of Peter, Mat. xvi. 17 (W. H.).*

Βαρ-νάβας, α, ὁ, *Barnabas* (perhaps "son of comfort," see παράκλησις), Ac. ix. 27; Col. iv. 10.

βάρος, ους, τό, *weight, burden*, only fig., Ac. xv. 28; Rev. ii. 24.

Βαρ-σαβᾶς, ᾶ, ὁ, *Barsabas.* Two are mentioned, Ac. i. 23, xv. 22.*

Βαρ-τίμαιος, ου, ὁ, *Bartimæus*, Mar. x. 46.*

βαρύνω, *to weigh down*, Lu. xxi. 34 (Rec.).*

βαρύς, εῖα, ύ (see βάρος), (1) *heavy*, Mat. xxiii. 4; (2) *weighty, important*, Mat. xxiii. 23; Ac. xxv. 7; 2 Cor. x. 10; (3) *oppressive* or *grievous*, Ac. xx. 29; 1 Jn. v. 3.*

βαρύ-τιμος, ον, *of great price*, Mat. xxvi. 7.*

βασανίζω (see βάσανος), *to examine*, as by torture; hence, *to torment, vex*, Mar. v. 7; Rev. xi. 10, xii. 2; of waves, *to buffet*, Mat. xiv. 24; Mar. vi. 48.

βασανισμός, οῦ, ὁ, *torture, torment*, Rev. ix. 5, xiv. 11, xviii. 7, 10, 15.*

βασανιστής, οῦ, ὁ, *one who tortures, a tormentor, jailer*, Mat. xviii. 34.*

βάσανος, ου, ἡ (lit., *a touchstone*), *torture, torment*, Mat. iv. 24; Lu. xvi. 23, 28.*

βασιλεία, ας, ἡ, *a kingdom, royal power* or *dignity, reign;* ἡ βασιλεία τοῦ Θεοῦ, τοῦ χριστοῦ, τῶν οὐρανῶν (the last form only in Mat.), *the divine, spiritual kingdom*, or *reign* of Messiah, in the world, in the individual, or in the future state; υἱοὶ τῆς βασιλείας, *sons of the kingdom*, Jews, its original possessors, Mat. viii. 12; true believers, Mat. xiii. 38. In Rev. i. 6, v. 10, for βασιλεῖς καί, W. H. read βασιλείαν, *a kingdom* consisting of priests (R. V.).

βασίλειος, ον, *royal, regal*, 1 Pet. ii. 9, from Exod. xix. 6; τὰ βασίλεια, as subst., *a regal mansion, palace*, Lu. vii. 25.*

βασιλεύς, έως, ὁ, *a leader, ruler,*

king, sometimes subordinate to higher authority, as the Herods. Applied to God, always with distinguishing epithets, Mat. v. 35; 1 Tim. i. 17, vi. 15; Rev. xv. 3; to Christ, Mat. ii. 2; Jn. i. 49, etc.; to Christians, Rev. i. 6, v. 10 (Rec., but see under βασιλεία).

βασιλεύω, εύσω, *to have authority, to reign*, or *to possess* or *exercise dominion; to be* βασιλεύς generally. With gen. or ἐπί (gen.), of the kingdom; ἐπί (acc.), of the persons governed.

βασιλικός, ή, όν, *belonging to a king, royal*, Jn. iv. 46, 49; Ac. xii. 20, 21; Ja. ii. 8.*

βασίλισσα, ης, ἡ, *a queen*, Mat. xii. 42; Lu. xi. 31; Ac. viii. 27; Rev. xviii. 7.*

βάσις, εως, ἡ (βαίνω), prop. *a going*, hence, *the foot*, Ac. iii. 7.*

βασκαίνω, ανῶ, *to bewitch, bring under malign influence*, Gal. iii. 1.*

βαστάζω, άσω, *to lift, lift up;* often with the sense of bearing away. Thus, (1) *to carry*, a burden, as Lu. xiv. 27; tidings, as Ac. ix. 15; (2) *to take on one's self*, as disease or weaknesses, Ro. xv. 1; condemnation, Gal. v. 10; reproach, Gal. vi. 17; (3) *to bear with* or *endure*, Rev. ii. 2; (4) *to take away*, Mat. viii. 17; Jn. xii. 6.

βάτος, ου, ἡ, *a thorn-bush* or *bramble*, Lu. vi. 44; Ac. vii. 30, 35. "The Bush," Mar. xii. 26; Lu. xx. 37 denotes the section of the O. T. so called (Exod. iii.).*

βάτος, ου, ὁ (Heb.), *a bath*, or Jewish measure for liquids containing 8 or 9 gallons, Lu. xvi. 6. (Ap.)*

βάτραχος, ου, ὁ, *a frog*, Rev. xvi. 13.*

βαττο-λογέω, ῶ (prob. from βατ, an unmeaning sound; see βάρβαρος), *to babble, talk to no purpose*, Mat. vi. 7. (N. T.)*

βδέλυγμα, ατος, τό (see βδελύσσω), *something unclean and abominable, an object of moral repugnance*, Lu. xvi. 15; spec. (as often in O.T.) idol-

atry, Rev. xvii. 4, 5, xxi. 27.
" Abomination of desola-
tion," Mat. xxiv. 15; Mar.
xiii. 14 (from Dan. ix. 27)
refers to the pollution of
the temple by some idola-
trous symbol. (S.)*

βδελυκτός, ή, όν, *disgusting,*
abominable, Tit. i. 16. (S.)*

βδελύσσω, ξω, to *defile,* only
mid.; to *loathe,* Ro. ii. 22;
and pass. perf. part., *defiled,*
Rev. xxi. 8.*

βέβαιος, α, ον, *steadfast, constant,*
firm, Heb. vi. 19; Ro. iv. 16.

βεβαιόω, ῶ, to *confirm,* to *estab-*
lish, whether of persons or
things, Mar. xvi. 20; Ro.
xv. 8; Heb. xiii. 9.

βεβαίωσις, εως, ή, *confirmation,*
Phil. i. 7; Heb. vi. 16.*

βέβηλος, ον (βα- in βαίνω,
"that on which any one
may step"), *common, un-*
sanctified, profane, of things
or persons, 1 Tim. iv. 7;
Heb. xii. 16.

βεβηλόω, ῶ, to *make common,*
to *profane,* the Sabbath, Mat.
xii. 5; the temple, Ac. xxiv.
6. (S.)*

Βεελ-ζεβούλ (W. H. Βεεζεβούλ),
ὁ (Heb.), *Beelzebul,* a name
of *Satan,* Mat. x. 25; Lu. xi.
15, 18, 19. (N. T.)

Βελίαλ, ὁ (Heb. *worthlessness*),
or Βελίαρ (W. H.), derivation
doubtful, a name for *Satan,*
2 Cor. vi. 15. (N. T.)*

βελόνη, ης, ή, a *needle,* Lu.
xviii. 25 (W. H.).*

βέλος, ους, τό (βάλλω), a *missile,*
such as a *javelin* or *dart,* Ep.
vi. 16.*

βελτίων, ον, ονος (a compar. of
ἀγαθός), *better;* neut. as adv.,
2 Tim. i. 18.*

Βεν-ιαμίν, ὁ (Heb. *Ben* = son),
Benjamin, Ac. xiii. 21; Rev.
vii. 8.

Βερνίκη, ης, ή, *Bernice,* Ac.
xxv. 13, 23, xxvi. 30.*

Βέροια, ας, ή, *Beroea,* Ac. xvii.
10, 13.*

Βεροιαῖος, α, ον, *Beroean,* Ac.
xx. 4.*

Βηθ-, a Hebrew and Aramaic
prefix to many local names,
meaning *house* or *abode of.*

Βηθ-αβαρά, ᾶς, ἡ, *Bethabara,*
"house of the ford," Jn. i.
28 (W. H. read Βηθανία).*

Βηθ-ανία, ας, ή, *Bethany,* "house

of misery." There were two
places of the name: (1) Jn.
xi. 1, etc.; (2) on the Jordan,
Jn. i. 28 (W. H.). See Βηθα-
βαρά.

Βηθ-εσδά, ἡ, *Bethesda,* "house
of compassion," Jn. v. 2 (W.
H. Βηθζαθά).*

Βηθ-λεέμ, ή, *Bethlehem,* "house
of bread," Lu. ii. 4, 15.

Βηθ-σαϊδά, ἡ, *Bethsaida,* "house
of hunting " or " fishing."
There were two places of
the name: one in Galilee,
Jn. xii. 21; the other on the
east of the Jordan, Lu. ix.
10.

Βηθ-φαγή, ἡ, *Bethphage,* "house
of figs," Mat. xxi. 1; Mar.
xi. 1; Lu. xix. 29.*

βῆμα, ατος, τό (βα- in βαίνω), a
step, a *space;* βῆμα ποδός, a
space for the foot, Ac. vii. 5;
a *raised space* or *bench, tri-*
bunal, judgment-seat, Jn. xix.
13; 2 Cor. v. 10.

βήρυλλος, ου, ὁ, ή, a *beryl,* a
gem of greenish hue, Rev.
xxi. 20.*

βία, ας, ή, *force, violence,* Ac.
v. 26, xxi. 35, xxiv. 7 (W. H.
omit), xxvii. 41.*

βιάζω, to *use violence;* mid., to
enter forcibly, with εἰς, Lu.
xvi. 16; pass., to *suffer vio-*
lence, to *be assaulted,* Mat. xi.
12.*

βίαιος, α, ον, *violent,* Ac. ii. 2.*

βιαστής, οῦ, ὁ, *one who employs*
force, a *man of violence,* Mat.
xi. 12.*

βιβλαρίδιον, ου, τό, a *little book,*
Rev. x. 2, 8 (not W. H.), 9,
10. (N. T.)*

βιβλίον, ου, τό (dim. of following), a *small book,* a *scroll,*
as Lu. iv. 17; Rev. v. 1;
βιβλίον ἀποστασίου, a bill of
divorcement, Mat. xix. 7;
Mar. x. 4.

βίβλος, ου, ὁ, a *written book,*
roll or *volume,* Mat. i. 1;
Phil. iv. 3. The word means
papyrus, from which ancient
books were made.

βιβρώσκω (βρο-), perf. βέβρωκα,
to *eat,* Jn. vi. 13.*

Βιθυνία, ας, ή, *Bithynia,* Ac.
xvi. 7; 1 Pet. i. 1.*

βίος, ου, ὁ, (1) *life,* as Lu. viii.
14; (2) *means of life, liveli-*
hood, as Lu. viii. 43; (3)
goods or *property,* as Lu. xv.

12; 1 Jn. iii. 17. *Syn.:* ζωή
is life in its *principle,* and
used for spiritual and im-
mortal life; βίος is life in its
manifestations, denoting the
manner of life.

βιόω, ῶ, to *pass one's life,* 1 Pet.
iv. 2.*

βίωσις, εως, ή, *manner* or *habit*
of life, Ac. xxvi. 4. (Ap.)*

βιωτικός, ή, όν, *of* or *belonging*
to (this) *life,* Lu. xxi. 34;
1 Cor. vi. 3, 4.*

βλαβερός, ά, όν, *hurtful,* 1 Tim.
vi. 9.*

βλάπτω (βλαβ-), βλάψω, to *hurt*
or *injure,* Mar. xvi. 18 (W.
H. omit); Lu. iv. 35.*

βλαστάνω (or βλαστάω, Mar.
iv. 27, W. H.), βλαστήσω,
intrans., to *sprout,* to *spring*
up, to *put forth buds,* Mat.
xiii. 26; Mar. iv. 27; Heb.
ix. 4; trans., to *bring forth*
(καρπόν), Ja. v. 18.*

Βλάστος, ου, ὁ, *Blastus,* Ac.
xii. 20.*

βλασφημέω, ῶ, to *speak abusive-*
ly, to *rail,* abs., as Ac. xiii.
45; to *calumniate, speak evil*
of, blaspheme, with acc., rarely εἰς; often of men or things.
Spec. of God, Rev. xvi. 11;
the Holy Spirit, Lu. xii. 10;
the divine name or doctrine,
1 Tim. vi. 1.

βλασφημία, ας, ή, *evil-speaking,*
reviling, blasphemy, Mat. xii.
31; Mar. xiv. 64.

βλάσφημος, ον, *slanderous,* Ac.
vi. 11; subst., a *blasphemer,*
1 Tim. i. 13; 2 Tim. iii. 2.

βλέμμα, ατος, τό, a *look, glance,*
2 Pet. ii. 8.*

βλέπω, ψω, to *see,* to *have the*
power of seeing, to *look at,*
behold; with εἰς, to *look to,*
Mat. xxii. 16; Mar. xii. 14;
with ἵνα or μή, to *take care*
(once without, Mar. xiii. 9);
with ἀπό, to *beware of;* once
with κατά (acc.), geograph-
ically, to *look towards,* Ac.
xxvii. 12.

βλητέος, έα, έον, a verbal adj.
(βάλλω), *that ought to be put,*
Mar. ii. 22 (W. H. omit);
Lu. v. 38. (N. T.)*

Βοανεργές (W. H. -ηρ-), (Heb.),
Boanerges, "sons of thunder," Mar. iii. 17. (N. T.)*

βοάω, ῶ (βοή), to *shout* for joy,
Gal. iv. 27; to *cry* for grief,

Ac. viii. 7; *to publish openly, to cry aloud*, Mar. xv. 34; Ac. xvii. 6; with πρός (acc.), *to appeal to*, Lu. xviii. 7, 38.

βοή, ῆς, ἡ, *a loud cry*, Ja. v. 4.*

βοήθεια, as, ἡ, *help*, Ac. xxvii. 17; Heb. iv. 16.*

βοηθέω, ῶ, *to go to the help of, to succor* (dat.), Mat. xv. 25; Rev. xii. 16.

βοηθός, οῦ, ὁ, ἡ (properly adj.), *a helper*, Heb. xiii. 6.*

βόθυνος, ου, ὁ, *a pit, ditch*, Mat. xii. 11, xv. 14; Lu. vi. 39.*

βολή, ῆς, ἡ, *a throwing;* λίθου βολή, *a stone's throw*, Lu. xxii. 41.*

βολίζω, σω, *to heave the lead, take soundings*, Ac. xxvii. 28. (N. T.)*

βολίς, ίδος, ἡ, *a weapon thrown, as a dart or javelin*, Heb. xii. 20 (W. H. omit).*

Βοόζ, ὁ (Heb.), *Booz* or *Boaz*, Mat. i. 5 (W. H. Βοές); Lu. iii. 32 (W. H. Βοός).*

βόρβορος, ου, ὁ, *mire, filth*, 2 Pet. ii. 22.*

Βορρᾶς, ᾶ, ὁ (*Boreas*, the north wind), *the North*, Lu. xiii. 29; Rev. xxi. 13.*

βόσκω, ήσω, *to feed*, as Mat. viii. 33; Jn. xxi. 15, 17; mid., *to feed, graze*, as Mar. v. 11. *Syn.:* ποιμαίνω is the broader word, to act as shepherd, literally or spiritually; βόσκω, simply to *feed* the flock.

Βοσόρ, ὁ (Heb. *Beor*), *Bosor*, 2 Pet. ii. 15 (W. H. Βεώρ).*

βοτάνη, ης, ἡ (βόσκω), *herbage, pasturage*, Heb. vi. 7.*

βότρυς, υος, ὁ, *a cluster of grapes*, Rev. xiv. 18.*

βουλευτής, οῦ, ὁ, *a councilor, a senator*, Mar. xv. 43; Lu. xxiii. 50.*

βουλεύω, σω, *to advise*, N. T. mid. only; (1) *to consult, to deliberate*, with εἰ, Lu. xiv. 31; (2) *to resolve on* or *purpose*, with inf., Ac. v. 33, xv. 37 (W. H. in both passages read βούλομαι), xxvii. 39; ἵνα, Jn. xi. 53 (W. H.), xii. 10; acc., 2 Cor. i. 17.*

βουλή, ῆς, ἡ, *a design, purpose, plan*, Lu. xxiii. 51; Ac. v. 38; Ep. i. 11.

βούλημα, ατος, τό (βούλομαι), *will, counsel, purpose*, Ac. xxvii. 43; Ro. ix. 19; 1 Pet. iv. 3 (W. H.).*

βούλομαι, 2d pers. sing. βούλει, aug. with ἐ or ἠ, *to will*, as (1) *to be willing, to incline to*, Mar. xv. 15; (2) *to intend*, Mat. i. 19; (3) *to desire*, 1 Tim. vi. 9. Generally with inf., sometimes understood, as Ja. i. 18; with subj., Jn. xviii. 39.

βουνός, οῦ, ὁ, *a hill, rising ground*, Lu. iii. 5; xxiii. 30.*

βοῦς, βοός, ὁ, ἡ, *an animal of the ox kind*, male or female, Lu. xiii. 15; 1 Tim. v. 18.

βραβεῖον, ου, τό, *the prize*, in the games, 1 Cor. ix. 24; Phil. iii. 14.*

βραβεύω (lit., to act as arbiter in the games), *to rule, arbitrate*, Col. iii. 15.*

βραδύνω, νῶ (βραδύς), *to be slow, to linger*, 1 Tim. iii. 15; 2 Pet. iii. 9 (gen.).*

βραδυ-πλοέω, ῶ, *to sail slowly*, Ac. xxvii. 7. (N. T.)*

βραδύς, εῖα, ύ, *slow;* dat. of sphere, Lu. xxiv. 25; εἰς, Ja. i. 19.*

βραδυτής, ῆτος, ἡ, *slowness*, 2 Pet. iii. 9.*

βραχίων, ονος, ὁ, *the arm;* met., *strength*, Lu. i. 51; Jn. xii. 38; Ac. xiii. 17.*

βραχύς, εῖα, ύ, *short, little*, only neut.; of time, Lu. xxii. 58; Ac. v. 34; Heb. ii. 7, 9; place, Ac. xxvii. 28; διὰ βραχέων, Heb. xiii. 22, *in few words;* βραχύ τι, Jn. vi. 7, of quantity, *a little.*

βρέφος, ους, τό, *a child unborn*, Lu. i. 41, 44; *a babe*, as Lu. ii. 12, 16; 2 Tim. iii. 15.

βρέχω, ξω, *to moisten*, Lu. vii. 38, 44; *to rain, to send rain*, Mat. v. 45; Lu. xvii. 29; impers., Ja. v. 17; intrans., Rev. xi. 6.*

βροντή, ῆς, ἡ, *thunder*, Jn. xii. 29; Rev. iv. 5.

βροχή, ῆς, ἡ (βρέχω), *a heavy rain*, Mat. vii. 25, 27. (S.)*

βρόχος, ου, ὁ, *a noose* or *snare*, 1 Cor. vii. 35.*

βρυγμός, οῦ, ὁ, *a grinding* or *gnashing*, as Mat. viii. 12.

βρύχω, ξω, *to grind* or *gnash*, as the teeth, for rage or pain, Ac. vii. 54.*

βρύω, σω, *to send forth abundantly*, as a fountain, Ja. iii. 11.*

βρῶμα, ατος, τό (see βιβρώσκω), *food* of any kind, Mat. xiv. 15; Jn. iv. 34; 1 Cor. viii. 8, 13.

βρώσιμος, ον, *eatable*, Lu. xxiv. 41.*

βρῶσις, εως, ἡ, (1) *the act of eating*, as 1 Cor. viii. 4; (2) *corrosion*, Mat. vi. 19, 20; (3) *food*, Jn. iv. 32; Heb. xii. 16.

βυθίζω, σω, *to cause to sink*, fig., 1 Tim. vi. 9; mid., *to sink*, Lu. v. 7.*

βυθός, οῦ, ὁ, *the deep, the sea*, 2 Cor. xi. 25.*

βυρσεύς, έως, ὁ, *a tanner*, Ac. ix. 43, x. 6, 32.*

βύσσινος, η, ον, *made of byssus, fine linen*, Rev. xviii. 12 (W. H.), 16, xix. 8, 14.*

βύσσος, ου, ἡ, *byssus*, a species of flax, and of linen manufactured from it, highly prized for its softness, whiteness, and delicacy, Lu. xvi. 19; Rev. xviii. 12 (Rec.).*

βωμός, οῦ, ὁ, *an altar*, Ac. xvii. 23.* *Syn.:* βωμός is a heathen altar; θυσιαστήριον, the altar of the true God.

Γ

Γ, γ, γάμμα, *gamma*, *g* hard, the third letter of the Greek alphabet. In numeral value, γ´ = 3; ‚γ = 3000.

Γαββαθᾶ (W. H.-θά), ἡ (Aram.), *Gabbatha; an elevated place* or *tribunal*, Jn. xix. 13. See λιθόστρωτον. (N. T.)*

Γαβριήλ, ὁ (Heb. *man of God*), the archangel *Gabriel*, Lu. i. 19, 26.*

γάγγραινα, ης, ἡ, *a gangrene, mortification*, 2 Tim. ii. 17.*

Γάδ, ὁ (Heb.), *Gad*, Rev. vii. 5.*

Γαδαρηνός, ή, όν, *belonging to Gadara*, Mar. v. 1 (Rec.); Mat. viii. 28 (W. H.). See Γεργεσηνός.

γάζα, ης, ἡ (Persian), *treasure*, as of a government, Ac. viii. 27.*

Γάζα, ης, ἡ (Heb.), *Gaza*, a strong city of the ancient Philistines in the W. of Palestine, Ac. viii. 26. (The adj., ἔρημος, *desert*, refers to ὁδός.)*

γαζο-φυλάκιον, ου, τό, *a place*

for the guardianship of treasure, treasury; a part of the temple so called, Mar. xii. 41, 43; Lu. xxi. 1; Jn. viii. 20. (S.)*

Γάϊος, ου, ὁ (Lat.), *Gaius,* or *Caius.* There are four of the name in N. T., Ac. xix. 29, xx. 4; 1 Cor. i. 14, and Ro. xvi. 23; 3 Jn. 1.*

γάλα, ακτος, τό, *milk,* lit., 1 Cor. ix. 7; fig., for the elements of Christian knowledge, 1 Cor. iii. 2; Heb. v. 12, 13; 1 Pet. ii. 2.*

Γαλάτης, ου, ὁ, *a Galatian,* Gal. iii. 1.*

Γαλατία, ας, ἡ, *Galatia,* or *Gallogræcia,* a province of Asia Minor, Gal. i. 2; 1 Cor. xvi. 1; 2 Tim. iv. 10; 1 Pet. i. 1.*

Γαλατικός, ή, όν, *belonging to Galatia,* Ac. xvi. 6, xviii. 23.*

γαλήνη, ης, ἡ, *a calm,* Mat. viii. 26; Mar. iv. 39; Lu. viii. 24.*

Γαλιλαία, ας, ἡ (from Heb.), *Galilee,* the N. division of Palestine, Mat. iv. 15.

Γαλιλαῖος, αία, αῖον, *of or belonging to Galilee,* Mat. xxvi. 69; Ac. i. 11.

Γαλλίων, ωνος, ὁ, *Gallio,* a proconsul of Achaia, Ac. xviii. 12, 14, 17.*

Γαμαλιήλ, ὁ (Heb.), *Gamaliel,* Ac. v. 34, xxii. 3.*

γαμέω, ῶ, ήσω, 1st aor. ἐγάμησα and ἔγημα, abs. or trans. (with acc.), *to marry;* active properly of the man; pass. and mid. of the woman, with dat., 1 Cor. vii. 39; Mar. x. 12 (W. H. ἄλλον for Rec. ἄλλῳ); but in N. T. the act. also is used of the woman, as 1 Cor. vii. 28, 34.

γαμίζω, *to give in marriage* (a daughter), Rec. only Mar. xii. 25; Lu. xvii. 27, xx. 35; W. H. add Mat. xxii. 30, xxiv. 38; 1 Cor. vii. 38. (N. T.)*

γαμίσκω = γαμίζω, Mar. xii. 25 (Rec.); Lu. xx. 34 (W. H.).*

γάμος, ου, ὁ, *marriage,* spec. *a marriage feast,* sing. or plur., Heb. xiii. 4; Rev. xix. 7. See Gr. § 240, Wi. § 27, 3, Bu. 23.

γάρ (γε ἄρα), "truly then," a causal postpositive particle

or conjunction, *for,* introducing a reason for the thing previously said. Used in questions to intensify the inquiry; often with other particles. For the special uses of γάρ, see Gr. § 407, Wi. § 53, 8, Bu. 370.

γαστήρ, τρός (sync.), **ἡ,** (1) *the womb,* as Mat. i. 18; (2) *the stomach,* only Tit. i. 12, from Epimenides, "idle bellies," *gluttons.*

γέ, an enclitic particle indicating emphasis, *at least, indeed.* Sometimes used alone, as Ro. viii. 32; 1 Cor. iv. 8; generally in connection with other particles, as ἀλλά, ἄρα, εἴ; εἰ δὲ μήγε, stronger than εἰ δὲ μή, *if otherwise indeed;* καίγε, *and at least, and even;* καίτοιγε, *though indeed;* μενοῦνγε, *yea, indeed;* μήτιγε, *"to say nothing of,"* 1 Cor. vi. 3.

Γεδεών, ὁ (Heb.), *Gideon,* Heb. xi. 32.*

γέ-εννα, ης, ἡ (Heb. *valley of Hinnom*), met., *Gehenna, place of punishment* in the future world, Mat. x. 28, etc. Sometimes with τοῦ πυρός, as Mat. v. 22. Compare 2 Kings xxiii. 10. (S.)

Γεθ-σημανῆ, or *-νεί* (W. H.), **ἡ** (Heb. *oil-press*), *Gethsemane,* a small field at the foot of the Mount of Olives, over the brook Kidron, Mat. xxvi. 36; Mar. xiv. 32.*

γείτων, ονος, ὁ, ἡ, *a neighbor,* Lu. xiv. 12, xv. 6, 9; Jn. ix. 8.*

γελάω, ῶ, άσω, *to laugh,* Lu. vi. 21, 25.*

γέλως, ωτος, ὁ, *laughter,* Ja. iv. 9.*

γεμίζω, σω, *to fill,* with acc. and gen. (also ἀπό or ἐκ), Mar. xv. 36; Rev. viii. 5; pass. abs., *to be full,* Mar. iv. 37; Lu. xiv. 23.

γέμω, *to be full of,* with gen. (ἐκ, Mat. xxiii. 25; perhaps acc., Rev. xvii. 3).

γενεά, ᾶς, ἡ, *generation,* as (1) *offspring, race, descent,* Mat. i. 17; Lu. ix. 41; (2) *the people of any given time;* (3) *an age of the world's duration,* Mat. xxiv. 34; Ac. xiii. 36; εἰς γενεὰς καὶ γενεάς (W.

H.), *unto generations and generations* (R. V.), Lu. i. 50.

γενεα-λογέω, ῶ, *to reckon a genealogy* or *pedigree,* pass. with ἐκ, Heb. vii. 6.*

γενεα-λογία, ας, ἡ, *genealogy,* N. T. plur., 1 Tim. i. 4; Tit. iii. 9; prob. of Gnostic speculations on the origin of being.*

γενέσια, ων, τά, *a birthday celebration,* Mat. xiv. 6; Mar. vi. 21.*

γένεσις, εως, ἡ, *birth, lineage,* Mat. i. 1 (W. H. add Mat. i. 18; Lu. i. 14, for Rec. γέννησις); Ja. i. 23, τὸ πρόσωπον τῆς γενέσεως αὐτοῦ, *the countenance of his birth,* or, as A. V., R. V., "his natural face"; Ja. iii. 6, τὸν τροχὸν τῆς γενέσεως, *the wheel of nature* (R. V.).*

γενετή, ῆς, ἡ, *birth,* Jn. ix. 1.*

γένημα, ατος, τό. See γέννημα.

γεννάω, ῶ, ήσω, *to beget, give birth to, produce, effect,* Mat. i. 3, 5, 6; Lu. i. 13, 57; Ac. vii. 8, 29; pass., *to be begotten, born* (often in John, of spiritual renewal), Mat. i. 20; Jn. i. 13; 1 Jn. v. 1.

γέννημα, ατος, τό, (1) *progeny, generation,* as Mat. iii. 7; (2) *produce* generally, as Mat. xxvi. 29; fig., *fruit, result,* as 2 Cor. ix. 10. In sense (2) W. H. always read γένημα, and sometimes elsewhere.

Γεννησαρέτ (Aram.), *Gennesaret* (*Chinnereth* or *Chinneroth,* in O. T.), a region of Galilee, with village or town of the same name, Mat. xiv. 34. Used of the adjacent lake, as Lu. v. 1.

γέννησις, εως, ἡ. See γένεσις.*

γεννητός, ή, όν, verb. adj., *begotten, born,* Mat. xi. 11; Lu. vii. 28.*

γένος, ους, τό, (1) *offspring,* Ac. xvii. 28, 29; (2) *family,* Ac. xiii. 26; (3) *stock, race,* Ac. vii. 19; Gal. i. 14; (4) *nation,* Mar. vii. 26; (5) *kind* or *species,* Mar. ix. 29; 1 Cor. xiv. 10.

Γεργεσηνός, ή, όν, or **Γερασηνός,** *Gergesene, belonging to Gergesa* or *Gerasa.* The copies vary between these forms and Γαδαρηνός, Mat. viii. 28; Mar. v. 1; Lu. viii. 26, 37.*

γερουσία, ας, ἡ (γέρων), an assembly of elders, senate, Ac.
v. 21.*

γέρων, οντος, ὁ, an old man, Jn.
iii. 4.*

γεύω, to make to taste, only mid.
in N. T.; to taste, as abs., to
take food, Ac. x. 10; or with
obj. gen., or acc. See Gr.
§ 249a, (2), Wi. §§ 3, p. 33,
30, 7c, Bu. 167. Fig., to experience, as Mat. xvi. 28;
once with ὅτι, 1 Pet. ii. 3.

γεωργέω, ῶ, to cultivate or till
the earth, Heb. vi. 7.*

γεώργιον, ου, τό, a tilled field,
fig., 1 Cor. iii. 9. (S.)*

γεωργός, οῦ, ὁ, one who tills the
ground, a husbandman, 2
Tim. ii. 6; Ja. v. 7; a vine-
dresser, Lu. xx. 9, 10, 14, 16.

γῆ, γῆς, ἡ, contr. for γέα or
γαῖα, land or earth, as (1) the
material soil; (2) the producing soil, the ground; (3) land,
as opposed to sea; (4) earth,
as opposed to heaven, often
involving suggestions of human weakness and sin; (5)
region or territory.

γῆρας, (αος) ως, τό, old age, Lu.
i. 36 (dat., Rec. γήρᾳ, W. H.
γήρει).*

γηράσκω, or γηράω, άσω, to become old, Jn. xxi. 18; Heb.
viii. 13.*

γίνομαι, for γίγνομαι. See Gr.
§ 94, 8a. γενήσομαι, ἐγενό-
μην and ἐγενήθην, γέγονα
(with pres. force) and γεγέ-
νημαι, to become, as (1) to begin to be, used of persons, to
be born, Jn. viii. 58; of the
works of creation, to be made,
Jn. i. 3, 10; and of other
works, to be wrought or per-
formed; so, to pass out of
one state into another, to
grow into, to be changed into,
Jn. ii. 9; often with εἰς, Lu.
xiii. 19; (2) of ordinary or
extraordinary occurrences, to
happen, to take place, to be
done; of the day, the night,
Mar. vi. 2; of thunder, earthquake, calm, etc.; of feasts
or public solemnities, to be
held or celebrated; frequently
in the phrase καὶ ἐγένετο, and
it came to pass (with καί, or
following verb, or inf.); also,
μὴ γένοιτο, let it never happen! or God forbid!; (3) with

adj. or predicative subst., to
become, where quality, character, or condition is speci-
fied; often in prohibitions,
μὴ γίνου, μὴ γίνεσθε, become
not, as Mat vi. 16; (4) with
the cases of substantives and
the prepositions, the verb
forms many phrases, to be
interpreted according to the
meaning of the case or prep.

γινώσκω, or γιγνώσκω (see Gr.
§ 94, 8b, Wi. § 39, 3, note 2,
Bu. 55), γνώσομαι, 2d aor.
ἔγνων (imper. γνῶθι), perf.
ἔγνωκα, (1) to become aware
of, to perceive, know; (2)
to know, to perceive, understand, with acc. or ὅτι, or
acc. and inf., or τί interrog.;
Ἑλληνιστὶ γ., to understand
Greek, Ac. xxi. 37; to be conscious of, by experience, as
2 Cor. v. 21; (3) to know
carnally (a Hebraistic euphe-
mism), Mat. i. 25; Lu. i. 34;
(4) specially of the fellowship between Christians and
God or Christ, 1 Cor. viii. 3;
Mat. vii. 23 (negatively); Jn.
xvii. 3; Heb. viii. 11; Phil.
iii. 10, etc.

γλεῦκος, ους, τό, sweet or new
wine, Ac. ii. 13.*

γλυκύς, εῖα, ύ, sweet, Ja. iii. 11,
12; Rev. x. 9, 10.*

γλῶσσα, ης, ἡ, (1) the tongue,
Mar. vii. 33, 35; 1 Jn. iii. 18
(2) a language, Ac. ii. 11;
(3) a nation or people distinguished by their language,
Rev. v. 9, vii. 9.

γλωσσό-κομον, ου, τό, a little
box or case for money, Jn.
xii. 6, xiii. 29 (orig. from
holding the "tongue-pieces"
of flutes, etc.).*

γναφεύς, έως, ὁ, a fuller, cloth-
dresser, Mar. ix. 3.*

γνήσιος, α, ον (sync. from γενή-
σιος), legitimate, genuine, true,
1 Tim. i. 2; Tit. i. 4; Phil.
iv. 3; τὸ γνήσιον, sincerity,
2 Cor. viii. 8.*

γνησίως, adv., genuinely, sincerely, Phil. ii. 20.*

γνόφος, ου, ὁ, darkness, gloom,
Heb. xii. 18.*

γνώμη, ης, ἡ, (γνο- in γινώσκω),
opinion, judgment, intention,
1 Cor. i. 10; 2 Cor. viii. 10.

γνωρίζω, ίσω, or ιῶ, (1) to make
known, to declare (with acc.

and dat., ὅτι or τί, interrog.,
Col. i. 27); (2) intrans., to
know, only Phil. i. 22.

γνῶσις, εως, ἡ, (1) subj., knowledge, with gen. of obj. (gen.
subj., Ro. xi. 33); (2) obj.,
science, doctrine, wisdom, as
Lu. xi. 52. Syn.: see Trench,
§ lxxv.

γνώστης, ου, ὁ, one who knows,
an expert, Ac. xxvi. 3. (S.)*

γνωστός, ή, όν, verb. adj.,
known, as Ac. ii. 14, iv. 10;
knowable, Ro. i. 19; notable,
Ac. iv. 16; οἱ γνωστοί, one's
acquaintance, Lu. ii. 44.

γογγύζω, ύσω, to murmur in a
low voice, Jn. vii. 32; dis-
contentedly, to grumble, as
1 Cor. x. 10, with acc., or
περί, gen., πρός, acc., κατά,
gen. (S.)

γογγυσμός, οῦ, ὁ, muttering, Jn.
vii. 12; murmuring, Ac. vi.
1; Phil. ii. 14; 1 Pet. iv. 9.
(S.)*

γογγυστής, οῦ, ὁ, a murmurer,
complainer, Ju. 16. (N. T.)*

γόης, ητος, ὁ (γοάω, to moan),
an enchanter, an impostor, 2
Tim. iii. 13.*

Γολγοθά (W. H., some -θᾶ),
(Aram.), Golgotha, "the place
of a skull" (prob. from its
shape), Calvary, Mat. xxvii.
33; Mar. xv. 22; Jn. xix. 17.
See κρανίον. (N. T.)*

Γόμορρα, ας, ἡ, and ων, τά, Go-
morrha, Ro. ix. 29.

γόμος, ου, ὁ (γέμω), (1) a burden, e.g., of a ship, Ac. xxi.
3; (2) wares or merchandise,
Rev. xviii. 11, 12.*

γονεύς, έως, ὁ (γεν- in γίγνομαι),
a parent, only in plural, Lu.
ii. 41; Ep. vi. 1.

γόνυ, ατος, τό, the knee; often
in plur. after τιθέναι or κάμπ-
τειν, to put or bend the knees,
to kneel, in devotion, Lu. xxii.
41; Ro. xi. 4.

γονυ-πετέω, ῶ (πίπτω), to fall
on the knees, to kneel to (acc.),
Mar. x. 17.

γράμμα, ατος, τό (γράφω), (1) a
letter of the alphabet, Gal.
vi. 11, in what large letters,
perhaps noting emphasis;
letter, as opposed to spirit,
Ro. ii. 29, etc.; (2) a writing,
such as a bill or an epistle,
as Lu. xvi. 6, 7; Ac. xxviii.
21; τὰ ἱερὰ γράμματα, 2 Tim.

:ii. 15, *the holy writings,* or
the Scriptures; (3) plur., *literature, learning* generally,
Jn. vii. 15.
γραμματεύς, *έως, ὁ,* (1) *a clerk,
secretary, a scribe,* Ac. xix.
35; (2) one of that class
among the Jews who copied
and interpreted the O. T.
Scriptures (see *νομικός*), Mat.
xxiii. 34; (3) met., *a man of
learning generally,* Mat. xiii.
52.
γραπτός, *ή, όν,* verb. adj., *written,* Ro. ii. 15.*
γραφή, *ῆς, ἡ,* (1) *a writing;*
(2) spec., *ἡ γραφή* or *αἱ γρα-
φαί, the Scriptures, writings*
of the O. T., 2 Pet. iii. 16;
(3) a particular *passage,* Mar.
xii. 10.
γράφω, *ψω, γέγραφα, to grave,
write, inscribe; ἐγράφη, γέ-
γραπται,* or *γεγραμμένον ἐστί,*
a formula of quotation, *It is
written;* often with dat. of
pers., as Mar. x. 5.
γραώδης, *ες (γραῦς, εἶδος), old-
womanish, foolish,* 1 Tim.
iv. 7.*
γρηγορέω, *ῶ* (from *ἐγρήγορα,*
perf. of *ἐγείρω), to keep awake,
watch, be vigilant,* Mar. xiii.
35, 37; Rev. xvi. 15.
γυμνάζω (*γυμνός), to exercise,
train,* 1 Tim. iv. 7; Heb. v.
14, xii. 11; 2 Pet. ii. 14.*
γυμνασία, *as, ἡ, exercise, training,* 1 Tim. iv. 8.*
γυμνητεύω, or *ιτεύω* (W. H.), *to
be naked* or *poorly clad,* 1 Cor.
iv. 11.*
γυμνός, *ή, όν,* (1) *naked,* Mar.
xiv. 52; Rev. iii. 17; *ill-clad,*
Mat. xxv. 36, 48; *having
only an inner garment,* Jn.
xxi. 7; (2) *bare, i.e., open* or
manifest, Heb. iv. 13; (3)
mere, 1 Cor. xv. 37.
γυμνότης, *τητος, ἡ,* (1) *nakedness,* Rev. iii. 18; (2) *scanty
clothing,* Ro. viii. 35; 2 Cor.
xi. 27. (N. T.)*
γυναικάριον, *ου, τό* (dim.), *a
silly woman,* 2 Tim. iii. 6.*
γυναικεῖος, *a, ον, womanish,
female;* 1 Pet. iii. 7, the
weaker vessel.*
γυνή, *γυναικός,* voc. *γύναι, ἡ,*
(1) *a woman,* Mat. ix. 20;
Ro. vii. 2; (2) *a wife,* Ac. v.
1, 7; Ep. v. 28. The voc. is
the form of ordinary address,

often used in reverence and
honor; compare Jn. ii. 4 and
xix. 26.
Γώγ, *ὁ,* a proper name, *Gog.*
In Ezek. xxxviii. 2, king of
Magog, a land of the remote
north; hence, in Rev. xx. 8,
of a people far remote from
Palestine.*
γωνία, *as, ἡ, a corner,* as Mat.
vi. 5, xxi. 42 (from S.); met.,
a secret place, Ac. xxvi. 26.

Δ

Δ, δ, δέλτα, *delta, d,* the fourth
letter of the Greek alphabet.
As a numeral, *δ′* = 4; *,δ* =
4000.
Δαβίδ, also **Δαυΐδ, Δαυείδ** (W.
H.), *ὁ* (Heb.), *David,* king of
Israel; *ὁ υἱὸς Δ., the Son of
David,* an appellation of the
Messiah; *ἐν Δ., in David,
i.e.,* in the Psalms, Heb.
iv. 7.
δαιμονίζομαι (see *δαίμων*), 1st
aor. part., *δαιμονισθείς, to be
possessed by a demon,* Mat.
iv. 24; Mar. i. 32.
δαιμόνιον, *ου, τό* (orig. adj.),
a deity, Ac. xvii. 18; *a demon*
or *evil spirit; δαιμόνιον ἔχειν,
to have a demon* or *to be a
demoniac,* Lu. iv. 33; Jn. vii.
20.
δαιμονιώδης, *ες, resembling a
demon, demoniacal,* Ja. iii.
15. (N. T.)*
δαίμων, *ονος, ὁ, ἡ,* in classic
Greek, any spirit superior
to man; hence often of the
inferior deities; in N. T., *an
evil spirit, a demon* (W. H.
have the word only in one
passage, Mat. viii. 31); *δαιμόνιον* is generally used.
δάκνω, *to bite,* met., Gal. v.
15.*
δάκρυ, *νος,* or *δάκρυον, ου, τό,
a tear,* Ac. xx. 19, 31: Heb.
v. 7.
δακρύω, *σω, to weep,* Jn. xi. 35.*
δακτύλιος, *ου, ὁ (δάκτυλος), a
ring,* Lu. xv. 22.*
δάκτυλος, *ου, ὁ, a finger; ἐν
δακτύλῳ θεοῦ,* met., *by the
power of God,* Lu. xi. 20,
comp. Mat. xii. 28.
Δαλμανουθά, *ἡ, Dalmanutha,*
a town or village near Magdala, Mar. viii. 10.*
Δαλματία, *as, ἡ, Dalmatia,* a

part of Illyricum near Macedonia, 2 Tim. iv. 10.*
δαμάζω, *σω, to subdue, tame,*
Mar. v. 4; Ja. iii. 7, 8.*
δάμαλις, *εως, ἡ, a heifer,* Heb.
ix. 13.*
Δάμαρις, *ιδος, ἡ, Damaris,* Ac.
xvii. 34.*
Δαμασκηνός, *ή, όν, belonging
to Damascus,* 2 Cor. xi. 32.*
Δαμασκός, *οῦ, ἡ, Damascus,* Ac.
ix. 2, 3.
δανείζω, *to lend* money, Lu. vi.
34, 35; mid., *to borrow,* Mat.
v. 42.*
δάνειον, *ου, τό, a loan, a debt,*
Mat. xviii. 27.*
δανειστής, *οῦ, ὁ, a money-lender,
a creditor,* Lu. vii. 41.*
Δανιήλ, *ὁ* (Heb.), *Daniel,* Mat.
xxiv. 15; Mar. xiii. 14 (not
W. H.).*
δαπανάω, *ῶ, ήσω, to spend,* Mar.
v. 26; trans., *to bear expense*
for (*ἐπί,* dat.), Ac. xxi. 24;
(*ὑπέρ,* gen.), 2 Cor. xii. 15;
*to consume in luxury, to
waste,* Lu. xv. 14; Ja. iv. 3.*
δαπάνη, *ης, ἡ, expense, cost,*
Lu. xiv. 28.*
δέ, an adversative and distinctive particle, *but, now, moreover,* etc. See Gr. § 404, ii,
Wi. § 53, 7, Bu. 364 sq., and
μέν.
δέησις, *εως, ἡ, supplication,
prayer,* Ep. vi. 18; Ja. v. 16.
Syn.: see *αἴτημα.*
δεῖ, impers., see Gr. § 101, Wi.
§ 58, 9b, Bu. 147, 164, *it is
necessary, one must, it ought,
it is right* or *proper,* with
inf. (expressed or implied),
as Mat. xvi. 21; Ac. iv. ν·
Mar. xiii. 14.
δεῖγμα, *ατος, τό (δείκνυμι), an
example, a specimen,* Ju. 7.*
δειγματίζω, *σω, to make an example* or *spectacle of* (as disgrace), Col. ii. 15; Mat. i. 19
(W. H.). (N. T.)*
δείκνυμι and **δεικνύω** (see Gr.
§ 114, Bu. 45), (1) *to present
to sight, to show, to teach* (acc
and dat.), Mat. iv. 18; 1 Cor
xii. 31; Rev. xvii. 1; (2) *to
prove* (acc. and *ἐκ*), Ja. ii. 18,
iii. 13; *to show by words (ὅτι),*
Mat. xvi. 21; inf., Ac. x. 28.
δειλία, *as, ἡ, timidity, cowardice,*
2 Tim. i. 7.* *Syn.: δειλία* is
always used in a bad sense;
εὐλάβεια, regularly in a good

sense, *pious* fear; φόβος is general, denoting either bad or good.

δειλιάω, ῶ, *to be timid, fearful*, Jn. xiv. 27. (S.)*

δειλός, ή, όν, *timid, cowardly*, Mat. viii. 26; Mar. iv. 40; Rev. xxi. 8.*

δεῖνα, ὁ, ἡ, τό, gen. δεῖνος, pron., *a certain person, such a one*, Mat. xxvi. 18.*

δεινῶς, adv. (δεινός, *vehement*), *vehemently, terribly*, Mat. viii. 6; Lu. xi. 53.*

δειπνέω, ῶ, *to take the* δεῖπνον, *to sup*, Lu. xvii. 8, xxii. 20; 1 Cor. xi. 25; met., of familiar intercourse, Rev. iii. 20.*

δεῖπνον, ου, τό, *the chief or evening meal, supper* (see ἄριστον), Lu. xiv. 17, 24; Jn. xiii. 2, 4; κυριακὸν δεῖπνον, *the Lord's Supper*, 1 Cor. xi. 20.

δεισιδαιμονία, ας, ἡ, *religion*, in general, Ac. xxv. 19.*

δεισι-δαίμων, ον (δείδω, *to fear*), *devoutly disposed, addicted to worship*, Ac. xvii. 22. See Gr. § 323 c.* *Syn.*: see Trench, § xlviii.

δέκα, οἱ, αἱ, τά, *ten;* in Rev. ii. 10, *a ten days' tribulation, i.e.*, brief.

δεκα-δύο (W. H. δώδεκα), *twelve*, Ac. xix. 7, xxiv. 11. (S.)*

δεκα-πέντε, *fifteen*, Jn. xi. 18; Ac. xxvii. 28, Gal. i. 18.*

Δεκά-πολις, εως, ἡ, *Decapolis*, a district E. of Jordan comprising ten towns. It is uncertain what they all were, but they included Gadara, Hippo, Pella, and Scythopolis, Mat. iv. 25; Mar. v. 20, vii. 31.*

δεκα-τέσσαρες, ων, οἱ, αἱ, -σαρα, τά, *fourteen*, Mat. i. 17; 2 Cor. xii. 2; Gal. ii. 1.*

δεκάτη, ης, ἡ, *a tenth part, a tithe*, Heb. vii. 2, 4, 8, 9.*

δέκατος, η, ον, ordinal, *tenth*, Jn. i. 39; Rev. xxi. 20; τὸ δέκατον, Rev. xi. 13, *the tenth part.*

δεκατόω. ῶ, *to receive tithe of*, acc., Heb. vii. 6; pass., *to pay tithe*, Heb. vii. 9. (S.)*

δεκτός, ή, όν (verbal adj. from δέχομαι), *accepted, acceptable*, Lu. iv. 19, 24; Ac. x. 35; 2 Cor. vi. 2; Phil. iv. 18. (S.)*

δελεάζω (δέλεαρ, *a bait*), *to take*

or *entice*, as with a bait, Ja. i. 14; 2 Pet. ii. 14, 18.*

δένδρον, ου, τό, *a tree*, Mat. vii. 17; Lu. xiii. 19.

δεξιό-λαβος, ου, ὁ, "holding in the right hand"; plur., *spearmen*, Ac. xxiii. 23. (N. T.)*

δεξιός, ά, όν, *the right*, opp. to ἀριστερός, *the left; ἡ δεξιά, the right hand; τὰ δεξιά, the right-hand side; ἐκ δεξιῶν, on the right* (see Gr. § 293, 1, Wi. § 19, 1 a); δεξιὰς διδόναι, *to give the right hand, i.e., to receive to friendship* or *fellowship.*

δέομαι, 1st aor. ἐδεήθην, *to have need of* (gen.), as mid. of δέω (see δεῖ); *to make request of* (gen.); *to beseech, pray*, abs., or with εἰ, ἵνα, or ὅπως, of purpose.

δέον, οντος, τό (particip. of δεῖ, as subst.), *the becoming* or *needful;* with ἐστί = δεῖ, 1 Pet. i. 6; Ac. xix. 36; plur., 1 Tim. v. 13.*

δέος, ους, τό (W. H.), *fear, awe*, Heb. xii. 28.*

Δερβαῖος, ου, ὁ, *of Derbe*, Ac. xx. 4.*

Δέρβη, ης, ἡ, *Derbe*, a city of Lycaonia, Ac. xiv. 6, 20, xvi. 1.*

δέρμα, ατος, τό (δέρω), *an animal's skin*, Heb. xi. 37.*

δερμάτινος, η, ον, *made of skin, leathern*, Mat. iii. 4; Mar. i. 6.*

δέρω, 1st aor. ἔδειρα, 2d fut. pass. δαρήσομαι, *to scourge, to beat*, so as to flay off the skin; ἀέρα δέρων, 1 Cor. ix. 26, *beating air.*

δεσμεύω, σω, *to bind, put in chains* as a prisoner, Lu. viii. 29 (W. H.); Ac. xxii. 4; *to bind* as a bundle, Mat. xxiii. 4.*

δεσμέω, ῶ, *to bind*, Lu. viii. 29 (Rec.).*

δέσμη, ης, ἡ, *a bundle*, Mat. xiii. 30.*

δέσμιος, ίου, ὁ, *one bound, a prisoner*, Ac. xvi. 25, 27; Ep. iii. 1.

δεσμός, οῦ, ὁ (δέω), *a bond*, sing. only in Mar. vii. 35, ὁ δεσμὸς τῆς γλώσσης, and Lu. xiii. 16; plur., δεσμοὶ or (τὰ) δεσμά, *bonds* or *imprisonment*, Lu. viii. 29; Phil. i. 13.

δεσμο-φύλαξ, ακος, ὁ, *a jailer*, Ac. xvi. 23, 27, 36.*

δεσμωτήριον, ίου, τό, *a prison*, Mat. xi. 2; Ac. v. 21, 23, xvi. 26.*

δεσμώτης, ου, ὁ, *a prisoner*, Ac. xxvii. 1, 42.

δεσπότης, ου, ὁ, *a lord* or *prince, a master*, as 1 Tim. vi. 1; applied to God, Lu. ii. 29; Ac. iv. 24; Ju. 4; to Christ, 2 Pet. ii. 1; Rev. vi. 10. *Syn.:* δεσπότης indicates more absolute and unlimited authority than κύριος.

δεῦρο, adv., (1) of place, *here, hither;* used only as an imperative, *come hither*, as Mat. xix. 21; (2) of time, *hitherto*, only Ro. i. 13.

δεῦτε, adv., as if plur. of δεῦρο (or contr. from δεῦρ' ἴτε), *come, come hither*, as Mat iv. 19, xi. 28.

δευτεραῖος, αία, αῖον, *on the second day*, Ac. xxviii. 13. See Gr. § 319.*

δευτερό-πρωτος, ον, *the second-first*, Lu. vi. 1 (W. H. omit). See Gr. § 148, Wi. § 16, 4, and note. (N. T.)*

δεύτερος, α, ον, ordinal, *second* in number, as Mat. xxii. 26; in order, Mat. xxii. 39; τὸ δεύτερον or δεύτερον, adverbially, *the second time, again*, as 2 Cor. xiii. 2; so ἐκ δευτέρου, as Mar. xiv. 72; ἐν τῷ δευτέρῳ, Ac. vii. 13.

δέχομαι, 1st aor. ἐδεξάμην, dep., *to take, receive, accept, to receive* kindly, *to welcome*, persons, as Mar. vi. 11; things (a doctrine, the kingdom of heaven), as Mar. x. 15; 2 Cor. xi. 4.

δέω, *to want.* See δεῖ and δέομαι.

δέω, 1st aor., ἐδησα; perf., δέδεκα; pass., δέδεμαι; 1st aor. pass. inf., δεθῆναι, *to bind together*, bundles, as Ac. x. 11; *to swathe* dead bodies for burial, as Jn. xi. 44; *to bind* persons in bondage, as Mat. xxii. 13; Mar. vi. 17; 2 Tim. ii. 9; fig., Mat. xviii. 18; δεδεμένος τῷ πνεύματι, Ac. xx. 22, *bound in the spirit*, under an irresistible impulse.

δή, a particle indicating *certainty* or *reality*, and so augmenting the vivacity of a clause or sentence; *truly, indeed, by all means, therefore.* Used with other particles, δήποτε, δήπου, which see.

δῆλος, η, ον, *manifest, evident,* Mat. xxvi. 73; neut., sc. ἐστί, *it is evident,* with ὅτι, 1 Cor. xv. 27; Gal. iii. 11; 1 Tim. vi. 7 (W. H., R. V. omit).*

δηλόω, ῶ, *to manifest, to reveal, to bring to light, to imply* or *signify,* 1 Cor. i.' 11, iii. 13; Col. i. 8; Heb. ix. 8, xii. 27; 1 Pet. i. 11; 2 Pet. i. 14.*

Δημᾶς, ᾶ, ὁ, *Demas,* Col. iv. 14; Philem. 24; 2 Tim. iv. 10.*

δημ-ηγορέω, ῶ, *to deliver a public oration;* with πρός, Ac. xii. 21.*

Δημήτριος, ου, ὁ, *Demetrius.* Two of the name are mentioned, Ac. xix. 24, 38; 3 Jn. 12.*

δημι-ουργός, οῦ, ὁ ("a public worker"), *an artisan, a builder,* Heb. xi. 10.* *Syn.:* δημιουργός emphasizes more the idea of *power;* τεχνίτης, that of *wisdom.*

δῆμος, ου, ὁ, *the people,* an organized multitude publicly convened, Ac. xii. 22, xvii. 5, xix. 30, 33.*

δημόσιος, α, ον, *belonging to the people, public,* Ac. v. 18; dat. fem., as adv., δημοσίᾳ, *publicly,* Ac. xvi. 37, xviii. 28, xx. 20.*

δηνάριον, ίου, τό, properly a Latin word (see Gr. § 154 *a*), *denarius,* Mat. xviii. 28; Rev. vi. 6.

δή-ποτε, adv. with ᾧ, *whatsoever,* giving a generalizing force, Jn. v. 4 (W. H. omit).*

δή-που, adv., *indeed, perhaps, verily,* Heb. ii. 16.*

διά, prep. (cognate with δύο, *two*; δίς, *twice*), *through;* (1) with gen., *through, during, by means of;* (2) with acc., *through, on account of, for the sake of.* See Gr. §§ 147 *a*, 299, Wi. § 47 *i*, Bu. 182, 183, 187.

δια-βαίνω, *to pass through,* trans., Heb. xi. 29; or intrans., with πρός (person), Lu. xvi. 26; εἰς (place), Ac. xvi. 9.*

δια-βάλλω, *to slander, accuse,* Lu. xvi. 1.*

δια-βεβαιόω, ῶ, in mid., *to affirm, assert strongly,* 1 Tim. i. 7; Tit. iii. 8.*

δια-βλέπω, *to see through, to see clearly,* Mat. vii. 5; Lu. vi. 42; Mar. viii. 25 (W. H.).*

διάβολος, ον (διαβάλλω), *prone to slander, slanderous,* 1 Tim. iii. 11; 2 Tim. iii. 3; Tit. ii. 3; ὁ διάβολος, *the accuser, the devil,* equivalent to the Hebrew *Satan,* Mat. iv. 1, 5; 2 Tim. ii. 26.

δι-αγγέλλω, *to announce everywhere, publish abroad,* Lu. ix. 60; Ac. xxi. 26; Ro. ix. 17.*

διά-γε, or διά γε (W. H.), *yet on account of,* Lu. xi. 8.*

δια-γίνομαι, *to pass, elapse,* of time; in N. T. only 2d aor. part., gen. abs., *having elapsed,* Mar. xvi. 1; Ac. xxv. 13, xxvii. 9.*

δια-γινώσκω, *to distinguish, know accurately,* Ac. xxiii. 15; *to examine, decide,* Ac. xxiv. 22.*

δια-γνωρίζω, *to publish abroad,* Lu. ii. 17 (W. H. γνωρίζω).*

διά-γνωσις, εως, ἡ, *judicial examination, decision,* Ac. xxv. 21.*

δια-γογγύζω, *to murmur greatly,* Lu. xv. 2, xix. 7. (S.)*

δια-γρηγορέω, ῶ, *to remain awake* or *to be fully awake,* Lu. ix. 32. (N. T.)*

δι-άγω, *to lead* or *pass,* as time, life, 1 Tim. ii. 2 (βίον); Tit. iii. 3 (βίον omitted).*

δια-δέχομαι, *to succeed to,* Ac. vii. 45.*

διά-δημα, ατος, τό (δέω), *a diadem, crown,* Rev. xii. 3, xiii. 1, xix. 12.* *Syn.:* διάδημα always indicates the fillet, the symbol of royalty; στέφανος is the festal *garland* of victory.

δια-δίδωμι, *to distribute, divide,* Lu. xi. 22, xviii. 22; Jn. vi. 11; Ac. iv. 35; Rev. xvii. 13 (W. H. δίδωμι).*

διά-δοχος, ου, ὁ, ἡ, *a successor,* Ac. xxiv. 27.*

δια-ζώννυμι, *to gird,* Jn. xiii. 4, 5, xxi. 7.*

δια-θήκη, ης, ἡ (διατίθημι), (1) *a will* or *testament, a disposition,* as of property, Gal. iii. 15; Heb. ix. 16, 17; (2) *a compact* or *covenant* between God and man (see Gen. vi,

ix, xv, xvii; Exod. xxiv; Deut. v, xxviii). The two covenants mentioned, Gal. iv. 24; that of the O. T. is termed ἡ πρώτη δ., Heb. ix. 15; that of the N. T., ἡ καινὴ δ., Lu. xxii. 20. The O. T. itself (ἡ παλαιὰ δ., 2 Cor. iii. 14) as containing the first, and the N. T. as containing the second, are each called διαθήκη.

δι-αίρεσις, εως, ἡ, *difference, distinction,* as the result of distribution, 1 Cor. xii. 4, 5, 6.*

δι-αιρέω, ῶ, *to divide, distribute,* Lu. xv. 12; 1 Cor. xii. 11.*

δια-καθαρίζω, ιῶ, *to cleanse thoroughly,* Mat. iii. 12; Lu. iii. 17 (W. H. διακαθαίρω). (N. T.)*

δια-κατ-ελέγχομαι, *to confute entirely,* Ac. xviii. 28. (N. T.)*

διακονέω, ῶ, *to serve* or *wait upon,* especially at table, Jn. xii. 26; Lu. iv. 39; *to supply wants, to administer* or *distribute alms,* etc. (dat., person; acc., thing; occasionally abs.), Mat. xxv. 44; Ro. xv. 25; specially, *to serve as a deacon,* 1 Tim. iii. 10, 13, of prophets and apostles who ministered the divine will, 1 Pet. i. 12; 2 Cor. iii. 3.

διακονία, ας, ἡ, *service, ministry,* in various senses, especially for Christ, 2 Cor. iii. 7; Ro. xi. 13; Ac. vi. 4; *relief,* Ac xi. 29; *a serving,* Lu. x. 40, *the office of deacon,* Ro. xii 7.

διάκονος, ου, ὁ, ἡ, *a servant,* viewed in relation to his *work,* specially at table, as Mat. xxiii. 11; Mar. x. 43; one in God's service, *a minister,* as Ro. xiii. 4, xv. 8; *one who serves in the church, deacon* or *deaconess,* Phil. i. 1; 1 Tim. iii. 8, 12; Ro. xvi. 1.

διακόσιοι, αι, α, card. num., *two hundred,* Mar. vi. 37; Jn. vi. 7.

δι-ακούω, *to hear thoroughly,* Ac. xxiii. 35.*

δια-κρίνω, *to discern, to distinguish, make a distinction,* as Ac. xv. 9; 1 Cor. xi. 29. Mid. (aor. pass.), (1) *to doubt, to*

hesitate, as Mat. xxi. 21; Ja.
i. 6; (2) *to dispute with,* Ac.
xi. 2; Ju. 9.

διά-κρισις, εως, ἡ, *the act of distinction, discrimination,* Ro.
xiv. 1; 1 Cor. xii. 10; Heb.
v. 14.*

δια-κωλύω, *to hinder,* Mat. iii.
14.*

δια-λαλέω, ῶ, *to converse together,* Lu. vi. 11; *to talk of,*
Lu. i. 65.*

δια-λέγω, in mid., *to reason, to
discuss, to dispute,* as Mar.
ix. 34; Ac. xx. 7; Ju. 9.

δια-λείπω, *to leave off, to cease,*
Lu. vii. 45.*

διά-λεκτος, ου, ἡ, *speech, dialect,
language,* Ac. i. 19, ii. 6, 8,
xxi. 40, xxii. 2, xxvi. 14.*

δι-αλλάσσω, *to change,* as the
disposition; pass., *to be reconciled to,* Mat. v. 24.*

δια-λογίζομαι, *to reason, to deliberate, to debate,* as Mar. ii.
6, 8, viii. 16, ix. 33.

διαλογισμός, οῦ, ὁ, *reflection,
thought,* as Lu. ii. 35; *reasoning, opinion,* as Ro. i. 21;
hesitation, doubt, Lu. xxiv.
38; *dispute, debate,* as Phil.
ii. 14; 1 Tim. ii. 8.

δια-λύω, *to disperse, to break up,*
Ac. v. 36.*

δια-μαρτύρομαι, dep. mid., *to
testify, solemnly charge,* as
Ac. ii. 40; 1 Tim. v. 21; *to
testify to, solemnly affirm,* Ac.
viii. 25; Heb. ii. 6.

δια-μάχομαι, dep. mid., *to contend* or *dispute fiercely,* Ac.
xxiii. 9.*

δια-μένω, *to remain, continue,*
Lu. i. 22, xxii. 28; Gal. ii.
5; Heb. i. 11; 2 Pet. iii.
4.*

δια-μερίζω, (1) *to divide* or *separate into parts,* as Mat. xxvii.
35, etc.; *to distribute,* as Lu.
xxii. 17; (2) pass. with ἐπί,
to be divided against, *be at
discord* with; acc., Lu. xi. 17;
dat., xii. 52.

δια-μερισμός, οῦ, ὁ, *dissension,*
Lu. xii. 51.*

δια-νέμω, *to disseminate, to
spread abroad,* Ac. iv. 17.*

δια-νεύω, *to make signs,* prob.
by nodding, Lu. i. 22.*

δια-νόημα, ατος, τό, *a thought,*
Lu. xi. 17.*

διά-νοια, ας, ἡ, *the mind, the
intellect,* or *thinking faculty,*

as Mar. xii. 30; *the understanding,* 1 Jn. v. 20; *the
feelings, disposition, affections,* as Col. i. 21; plur., *the
thoughts,* as willful, depraved,
Ep. ii. 3 (in Ep. i. 18, A. V.,
the eyes of your understanding (διανοίας), W. H. and R.
V. read καρδίας, *the eyes of
your heart*).

δι-αν-οίγω, *to open fully, i.e.,*
the ears, Mar. vii. 34; the
eyes, Lu. xxiv. 31; the heart,
Ac. xvi. 14; the Scriptures,
Lu. xxiv. 32.

δια-νυκτερεύω, *to pass the whole
night,* Lu. vi. 12.*

δι-ανύω, *to perform to the end,
complete,* Ac. xxi. 7.*

δια-παντός, adv., *always, continually* (W. H. always read
διὰ παντός).

δια-παρα-τριβή, ῆς, ἡ, *contention, incessant wrangling,* 1
Tim. vi. 5 (W. H., Rec. has
παραδιατριβή). (N. T.)*

δια-περάω, ῶ, ἄσω, *to cross over,*
as Mat. ix. 1.

δια-πλέω, εύσω, *to sail across,*
Ac. xxvii. 5.*

δια-πονέω, ῶ, mid., aor. pass.,
to grieve one's self, to be vexed,
Ac. iv. 2, xvi. 18.*

δια-πορεύομαι, pass., *to go* or
pass through, as Lu. xiii. 22.

δι-απορέω, ῶ, *to be in great
doubt* or *perplexity,* Lu. ix. 7,
xxiv. 4 (W. H. ἀπορέω); Ac.
ii. 12, v. 24, x. 17.*

δια-πραγματεύομαι, *to gain bv
business* or *trading,* Lu. xix.
15.*

δια-πρίω (πρίω, *to saw*), in pass.,
to be sawn through; fig., *to be
greatly moved with anger,* Ac.
v. 33, vii. 54.*

δι-αρπάζω, ἄσω, *to plunder,* Mat.
xii. 29; Mar. iii. 27.*

δια-ρρήγνυμι and διαρρήσσω,
ξω, *to tear,* as garments, in
grief or indignation, Mat.
xxvi. 65; Mar. xiv. 63; Ac.
xiv. 14; *to break asunder,* as
a net, Lu. v. 6; as bonds,
Lu. viii. 29.*

δια-σαφέω, ῶ, *to make clear, to
declare,* Mat. xiii. 36 (W. H.),
xviii. 31.

δια-σείω, *to treat with violence,*
so as to extort anything, Lu.
iii. 14.*

δια-σκορπίζω, *to scatter, to winnow,* as Mat. xxv. 24; *to dis-*

perse in conquest, as Lu. i.
51; *to waste* or *squander,* Lu.
xv. 13, xvi. 1.

δια-σπάω, 1st aor. pass. διεσπάσθην, *to break asunder,* Mar.
v. 4; *to tear in pieces,* Ac.
xxiii. 10.*

δια-σπείρω, 2d aor. pass. διεσπάρην, *to scatter abroad, disperse,*
Ac. viii. 1, 4, xi. 19.*

δια-σπορά, ᾶς, ἡ, *dispersion, state
of being dispersed;* used of
the Jews as scattered among
the Gentiles, Jn. vii. 35; Ja.
i. 1; 1 Pet. i. 1. (Ap.)*

δια-στέλλω, in mid., *to give a
command* or *injunction,* Mar.
viii. 15; Ac. xv. 24; foll. by
ἵνα, Mat. xvi. 20 (W. H.
mrg.); Mar. v. 43, vii. 36,
ix. 9; pass. part., τὸ διαστελλόμενον, Heb. xii. 20, *the
command.*

διά-στημα, ατος, τό, *an interval* of time, Ac. v. 7.*

δια-στολή, ῆς, ἡ, *distinction,
difference,* Ro. iii. 22, x. 12;
1 Cor. xiv. 7.*

δια-στρέφω, *to seduce, turn away,* Lu. xxiii. 2; Ac. xiii. 8;
to pervert, oppose, Ac. xiii.
10; perf. part. pass., διεστραμμένος, *perverse, corrupt,*
Mat. xvii. 17; Lu. ix. 41;
Ac. xx. 30; Phil. ii. 15.*

διασώζω, σω, *to save, to convey
safe through,* Ac. xxiii. 24;
xxvii. 43; 1 Pet. iii. 20; pass.,
to reach a place in safety, Ac.
xxvii. 44, xxviii. 1, 4; *to heal
perfectly,* Mat. xiv. 36; Lu.
vii. 3.*

δια-ταγή, ῆς, ἡ, *a disposition,
arrangement, ordinance,* Ac.
vii. 53; Ro. xiii. 2.*

διά-ταγμα, ατος, τό, *a mandate,
a decree,* Heb. xi. 23.*

δια-ταράσσω, *to trouble greatly,
to agitate,* Lu. i. 29.*

δια-τάσσω, *to give orders to*
(dat.), *arrange, prescribe,*
Mat. xi. 1; Lu. viii. 55; 1
Cor. xvi. 1; mid., *to appoint,
to ordain,* as 1 Cor. vii. 17
(also with dat. person; acc.,
thing).

δια-τελέω, ῶ, *to continue,* Ac.
xxvii. 33.*

δια-τηρέω, ῶ, *to guard* or *keep
with care,* Lu. ii. 51; with
ἑαυτόν, etc., *to guard one's
self from, to abstain* (ἐκ or
ἀπό), Ac. xv. 29.*

δια-τί or διὰ τί (W. H.), *where-fore?*

δια-τίθημι, only mid. in N. T., *to dispose,* as (1) *to assign,* Lu. xxii. 29; (2) with cog. acc., διαθήκην, *make* a covenant with (dat. or πρός, acc.), Ac. iii. 25; Heb. viii. 10, x. 16; *make* a will, Heb. ix. 16, 17. See διαθήκη.*

δια-τρίβω, *to spend* or *pass* (χρόνον or ἡμέρας), as Ac. xiv. 3, 28; abs., *to stay,* as Jn. iii. 22.

δια-τροφή, ῆς, ἡ, *food, nourishment,* 1 Tim. vi. 8.*

δι-αυγάζω, *to shine through, to dawn,* 2 Pet. i. 19.*

δια-φανής, ές, *transparent,* Rev. xxi. 21 (W. H. διαυγής in same signif.).*

δια-φέρω, (1) *to carry through,* Mar. xi. 16; (2) *to spread abroad,* Ac. xiii. 49; (3) *to carry hither and thither,* Ac. xxvii. 27; (4) *to differ from* (gen.), 1 Cor. xv. 41; Gal. iv. 1; hence, (5) *to excel, surpass,* as Mat. vi. 26; (6) impers., διαφέρει, with οὐδέν, *it makes no difference* to (dat.), *matters nothing* to, Gal. ii. 6.

δια-φεύγω, *to escape by flight,* Ac. xxvii. 42.*

δια-φημίζω, *to report, publish abroad,* Mat. ix. 31, xxviii. 15; Mar. i. 45.*

δια-φθείρω, *to corrupt,* 1 Tim. vi. 5; Rev. xi. 18; *to destroy utterly,* Lu. xii. 33; Rev. viii. 9, xi. 18; pass., *to decay. to perish,* 2 Cor. iv. 16; opp. to ἀνακαινόω, *to renew.*

δια-φθορά, ᾶς, ἡ, *decay, corruption, i.e.,* of the grave, Ac. ii. 27, 31, xiii. 34–37 (from S.).*

διά-φορος, ον, (1) *diverse, of different kinds,* Ro. xii. 6; Heb. ix. 10; (2) compar., *more excellent* than, Heb. i. 4, viii. 6.*

δια-φυλάσσω, *to guard carefully, protect, defend,* Lu. iv. 10 (from S.).*

δια-χειρίζω, mid. N. T., *to lay hands on, put to death,* Ac. v. 30, xxvi. 21.*

δια-χλευάζω, see χλευάζω.

δια-χωρίζω, pass. N. T., "to be separated," *to depart from* (ἀπό), Lu. ix. 33.*

διδακτικός, ή, όν, *apt in teach-*

ing, 1 Tim. iii. 2; 2 Tim. ii. 24.*

διδακτός, ή, όν, *taught, instructed,* Jn. vi. 45; 1 Cor. ii. 13.*

διδασκαλία, ας, ἡ, *instruction, teaching,* as Ro. xii. 7; *the doctrine taught, precept, instruction,* as Mat. xv. 9, etc.

διδάσκαλος, ου, ὁ, *a teacher,* especially of the Jewish law, *master, doctor,* as Lu. ii. 46; often in voc. as a title of address to Christ, *Master, Teacher.*

διδάσκω, διδάξω, *to teach, to be a teacher,* abs., Ro. xii. 7; *to teach,* with acc. of person, generally also acc. of thing; also with inf. or ὅτι, Mat. v. 2; Ac. iv. 2.

διδαχή, ῆς, ἡ, *the act of teaching,* Ac. ii. 42; 2 Tim. iv. 2; *that which is taught,* doctrine, Mar. i. 27; Ac. xvii. 19; Rev. ii. 24; with obj. gen., perhaps in Heb. vi. 2, see Gr. § 260 b, note, Wi. § 30, 1 a.

δί-δραχμον, ου, τό (prop. adj., sc. νόμισμα, *coin*), *a double drachma,* or silver half-shekel (in S. often *the shekel*), Mat. xvii. 24. (S.)*

Δίδυμος, η, ον, *double,* or *twin; a surname of Thomas* the apostle, Jn. xi. 16, xx. 24, xxi. 2.*

δίδωμι, *to give* (acc. and dat.); hence, in various connections, *to yield, deliver, supply, commit,* etc. When used in a general sense, the dat. of person may be omitted, as Mat. xiii. 8. The thing given may be expressed by ἐκ or ἀπό, with gen. in a partitive sense instead of acc.; so Mat. xxv. 8; Lu. xx. 10. The purpose of a gift may be expressed by inf., as Mat. xiv. 16; Jn. iv. 7; Lu. i. 73.

δι-εγείρω, *to wake up thoroughly,* as Lu. viii. 24; *to excite,* Jn. vi. 18; fig., *to stir up, arouse,* 2 Pet. i. 13.

δι-ενθυμέομαι, οῦμαι (W. H.), *to reflect,* Ac. x. 19. (N. T.)*

δι-έξ-οδος, ου, ἡ, *a meeting-place of roads, a public spot* in a city, Mat. xxii. 9.*

δι-ερμηνευτής, οῦ, ὁ, *an interpreter,* 1 Cor. xiv. 28. (N. T.)*

δι-ερμηνεύω, *to interpret,* Lu. xxiv. 27; 1 Cor. xii. 30, xiv. 5, 13, 27; *to translate,* Ac. ix. 36.*

δι-έρχομαι, *to pass through,* acc. or διά (gen.), destination expressed by εἰς or ἕως; *to pass over* or *travel,* abs., Ac. viii. 4; *to spread,* as a report, Lu. v. 15.

δι-ερωτάω, ῶ, *to find by inquiry,* Ac. x. 17.*

δι-ετής, ές (δίς), *of two years,* Mat. ii. 16.*

διετία, ας, ἡ, *the space of two years,* Ac. xxiv. 27, xxviii. 30.*

δι-ηγέομαι, οῦμαι, *to relate in full, describe,* Mar. v. 16; Ac. viii. 33, ix. 27.

διήγησις, εως, ἡ, *a narrative,* Lu. i. 1.*

δι-ηνεκής, ές, *continuous; εἰς τὸ διηνεκές, continually,* Heb. vii. 3, x. 1, 12, 14.*

δι-θάλασσος, ον (δίς), *lying between two seas,* Ac. xxvii. 41.*

δι-ϊκνέομαι, οῦμαι, *to pass through, pierce,* Heb. iv. 12.*

δι-ΐστημι, *to put apart, proceed,* Ac. xxvii. 28; 2 aor., intrans., Lu. xxii. 59, *one hour having intervened;* xxiv. 51, *he parted* from them.*

δι-ϊσχυρίζομαι, *to affirm con fidently,* Lu. xxii. 59; Ac. xii. 15.*

δικαιο-κρισία, ας, ἡ, *just judgment,* Ro. ii. 5. (S.)*

δίκαιος, α, ον, *just, right, upright, righteous, impartial;* applied to things, to persons, to Christ, to God, Mat. i. 19; Heb. xi. 4; Ac. x. 22.

δικαιοσύνη, ης, ἡ, *righteousness, justice, rectitude,* Mat. iii. 15; Jn. xvi. 8, 10; Ro. v. 17, 21.

δικαιόω, ῶ, *to show to be righteous,* 1 Tim. iii. 16; Ro. iii. 4; usually in N. T. in the declarative sense, *to hold guiltless, to justify, to pronounce* or *treat as righteous,* as Mat. xii. 37; 1 Cor. iv. 4.

δικαίωμα, ατος, τό, *a righteous statute, an ordinance,* Lu. i. 6; Ro. i. 32, ii. 26; Heb. ix. 1, 10; especially *a judicial decree, of acquittal* (opp. to κατάκριμα, *condemnation*), Ro. v. 16; *of condemnation,*

3

Rev. xv. 4; *a righteous act*,
Ro. v. 18; Rev. xix. 8.*

δικαίως, adv., *justly*, 1 Pet. ii.
23; Lu. xxiii. 41; *properly*,
1 Cor. xv. 34; *uprightly*, 1 Th.
ii. 10; Tit. ii. 12.*

δικαίωσις, εως, ἡ, *acquittal, jus-
tification*, Ro. iv. 25, v. 18.*

δικαστής, οῦ, ὁ, *a judge*, Lu.
xii. 14 (W. H. κριτής); Ac.
vii. 27, 35.*

δίκη, ης, ἡ, *a judicial sentence*,
Ac. xxv. 15 (W. H. καταδίκη);
τίνω or ὑπέχω δίκην, *to suffer
punishment*, 2 Th. i. 9; Ju. 7;
*Justice, the name of a heathen
deity*, Ac. xxviii. 4.*

δίκτυον, ου, τό, *a fishing-net*, Jn.
xxi. 6, 8, 11. *Syn.*: see ἀμφί-
βληστρον.

δι-λόγος, ον (δίς), *double-tongued,
deceitful*, 1 Tim. iii. 8. (N.T.)*

διό, conj. (διά and ὅ), *on which
account, wherefore.*

δι-οδεύω, *to journey through*,
Ac. xvii. 1; *to go about*, Lu.
viii. 1.*

Διονύσιος, ου, ὁ, *Dionysius*, Ac.
xvii. 34.*

διό-περ, conj., *for which very
reason*, 1 Cor. viii. 13, x. 14,
xiv. 13 (W. H. διό).*

Διο-πετής, ές, *fallen from Zeus,
i.e.*, from heaven, Ac. xix. 35.*

δι-όρθωμα, see κατόρθωμα.

δι-όρθωσις, εως, ἡ, *reformation*,
Heb. ix. 10.*

δι-ορύσσω, ξω, *to dig through*,
Mat. vi. 19, 20, xxiv. 43; Lu.
xii. 39.*

Διόσ-κουροι, ων, οἱ (children of
Zeus), *Castor* and *Pollux*, Ac.
xxviii. 11.*

δι-ότι, conj. (= διὰ τοῦτο, ὅτι),
on this account, because, for.

Διο-τρεφής, οῦς, ὁ, *Diotrephes*,
3 Jn. 9.*

διπλόος, οῦς, ῆ, οῦν, *double, twofold*, 1 Tim. v. 17; Rev. xviii.
6; comp., διπλότερος with
gen., *twofold more than*, Mat.
xxiii. 15.*

διπλόω, ῶ, *to double*, Rev. xviii.
6.*

δίς, adv., *twice*, Lu. xviii. 12.

(Δίς), obsolete nom. for Ζεύς,
gen. Διός, acc. Δία, *Zeus* or
Jupiter, see Ζεύς.

διστάζω, σω (δίς), *to waver, to
doubt*, Mat. xiv. 31, xxviii.
17.*

δί-στομος, ον (δίς), *two-edged*,
Heb. iv. 12; Rev. i. 16, ii. 12.*

δισ-χίλιοι, αι, α, num., *two
thousand*, Mar. v. 13.

δι-υλίζω, *to strain off, filter
through*, Mat. xxiii. 24.*

διχάζω, σω, *to set at variance,
divide*, Mat. x. 35.*

διχο-στασία, ας, ἡ, *division,
dissension*, Ro. xvi. 17; 1 Cor.
iii. 3 (not W. H.); Gal. v. 20.*

διχο-τομέω, ῶ, ήσω, *to cut in two*,
perhaps meaning *to scourge
severely*, Mat. xxiv. 51; Lu.
xii. 46.*

διψάω, ῶ, ήσω, *to thirst for, to
desire earnestly*, acc., Mat. v.
6; or abs., *to thirst*, Jn. iv. 15;
1 Cor. iv. 11.

δίψος, ους, τό, *thirst*, 2 Cor. xi.
27.*

δί-ψυχος, ον (δίς), *double-mind-
ed*, Ja. i. 8, iv. 8.*

διωγμός, οῦ, ὁ, *persecution*, Mat.
xiii. 21; Ro. viii. 35.

διώκτης, ου, ὁ, *a persecutor*, 1
Tim. i. 13. (N. T.)*

διώκω, ξω, *to pursue*, in various
senses according to context;
*to follow, follow after, press
forward, to persecute.*

δόγμα, ατος, τό (δοκέω), *a decree,
edict, ordinance*, Lu. ii. 1;
Ac. xvi. 4, xvii. 7; Ep. ii. 15;
Col. ii. 14.*

δογματίζω, σω, *to impose an
ordinance;* mid., *to submit to
ordinances*, Col. ii. 20.*

δοκέω, ῶ, δόξω, (1) *to think*, acc.
and inf., Lu. viii. 18; 2 Cor.
xi. 16; (2) *to seem, appear*,
Lu. x. 36; Ac. xvii. 18; (3)
δοκεῖ, impers., *it seems*, Mat.
xvii. 25; *it seems good to or
pleases*, dat., Lu. i. 3; Ac.
xv. 22. *Syn.*: φαίνομαι means
to appear *on the outside*;
δοκέω, to appear *to an individual* to be true.

δοκιμάζω, σω, *to try, scrutinize,
prove*, as 2 Cor. viii. 22; Lu.
xii. 56; *to judge fit, approve*,
as 1 Cor. xvi. 3. *Syn.*: δοκιμάζω means to test anything
with the expectation of finding it good; πειράζω, either
with no expectation, or of
finding it bad.

δοκιμασία, ας, ἡ, the act of *proving*, Heb. iii. 9 (W. H.).*

δοκιμή, ῆς, ἡ, *a trial*, 2 Cor.
viii. 2; *a proof*, 2 Cor. xiii.
3; *tried, approved character*,
Ro. v. 4; 2 Cor. ix. 13. (N.
T.)

δοκίμιον, ου, τό, *a test, trial*,
1 Pet. i. 7; Ja. i. 3.*

δόκιμος, ον (δέχομαι), *approved,
acceptable*, as Ro. xiv. 18,
xvi. 10.

δοκός, οῦ, ἡ, *a beam*, Mat. vii.
3, 4, 5; Lu. vi. 41, 42.*

δόλιος, ία, ιον, *deceitful*, 2 Cor.
xi. 13.*

δολιόω, ῶ, *to deceive*, impf., 3d
pers. plur., ἐδολιοῦσαν, an
Alexandrian form from S.,
Ro. iii. 13. (S.)*

δόλος, ου, ὁ, *fraud, deceit, craft*,
Mat. xxvi. 4; 2 Cor. xii. 16.

δολόω, ῶ, *to adulterate, corrupt*,
2 Cor. iv. 2.*

δόμα, ατος, τό (δίδωμι), *a gift*,
Mat. vii. 11; Lu. xi. 13; Ep.
iv. 8; Phil. iv. 17.*

δόξα, ης, ἡ, from δοκέω, in two
main significations: (1) *favorable recognition* or *estimation, honor, renown*, as Jn.
v. 41, 44; 2 Cor. vi. 8; Lu.
xvii. 18; and very frequently (2) *the appearance, the
manifestation of that which
calls forth praise;* so especially in the freq. phrase ἡ
δόξα τοῦ θεοῦ, *glory, splendor.*
Concrete plur. δόξαι, in 2 Pet.
ii. 10; Ju. 8, *dignities*, an-
gelic powers.

δοξάζω, σω, *to ascribe glory to,
to honor, glorify*, Ro. xi. 13;
1 Cor. vi. 20.

Δορκάς, άδος, ἡ, *Dorcas*, Ac. i·
36, 39.*

δόσις, εως, ἡ, *a giving*, Phil. iv·
15; *a gift*, Ja. i. 17.*

δότης, ου, ὁ, *a giver*, 2 Cor. ix·
7. (S.)*

δουλ-αγωγέω, ῶ, *to bring into
subjection*, 1 Cor. ix. 27.*

δουλεία, ας, ἡ, *slavery, bondage*,
Ro. viii. 15, 21; Heb. ii. 15.

δουλεύω, σω, (1) *to be a slave*,
absolutely, Ep. vi. 7; Ro.
ix. 12; (2) *to be subject to, to
obey*, dat., Ro. vii. 6; Gal
iv. 8.

δοῦλος, η, ον, adj. only Ro. vi.
19; as subst. ἡ δούλη, *a female slave*, Lu. i. 38, 48;
ὁ δοῦλος, *a slave, bondman*,
the lowest word for this
idea (opp. to ἐλεύθερος); *a
servant* (opp. to κύριος, δεσπότης), so in the freq. phrases
δοῦλος τοῦ θεοῦ, δοῦλος Χριστοῦ.

δουλόω, ῶ, ώσω, *to reduce to*

bondage (acc. and dat.), Ac.
vii. 6; 1 Cor. ix. 19; pass.,
*to be held subject to, be in
bondage*, 1 Cor. vii. 15.

δοχή, ῆς, ἡ (δέχομαι), *a receiving* of guests, *a banquet*, Lu.
v. 29, xiv. 13.*

δράκων, οντος, ὁ, *a dragon* or
huge serpent; symb. for Satan, Rev.

δράμω, obs., *to run*, see τρέχω.

δράσσομαι, dep., *to grasp, take;*
acc., 1 Cor. iii. 19.*

δραχμή, ῆς, ἡ, *a drachma,*
an Attic silver coin nearly
equal to the Roman dena-
rius, or worth about sixteen
cents of our money, Lu. xv.
8, 9.*

δρέπανον, ου, τό, *a sickle* or
pruning-hook, Mar. iv. 29;
Rev. xiv. 14–19.*

δρόμος, ου, ὁ, *a running;* fig.,
course, career, Ac. xiii. 25,
xx. 24; 2 Tim. iv. 7.*

Δρουσίλλα, ης, ἡ, *Drusilla*, Ac.
xxiv. 24.*

δύναμαι, dep. (see Gr. § 109*b*,
1), *to be able,* abs., or with
inf. (sometimes omitted) or
acc.: *to have a capacity for;
to be strong,* as 1 Cor. iii. 2 ;
to have power to do, whether
through ability, disposition,
permission, or opportunity.

δύναμις, εως, ἡ, (1) *power, might,*
absolutely or as an attribute,
Lu. i. 17; Ac. iii. 12 ; (2)
power over, expressed by εἰς
or ἐπί (acc.), *ability to do;*
(3) *exercise of power, mighty
work, miracle*, as Mat. xi. 20;
(4) *forces,* as of an army,
spoken of the heavenly hosts,
as Mat. xxiv. 29; (5) *force,*
as of a word, *i.e., significance,*
1 Cor. xiv. 11. *Syn.:* τέρας
indicates a miracle as a
wonderful portent or prod-
igy ; σημεῖον, as a sign, au-
thenticating the divine mission of the doer; δύναμις,
as an exhibition of divine
power.

δυναμόω, ῶ, *to strengthen, confirm*, Col. i. 11; Heb. xi. 34
(W. H.). (S.)*

δυνάστης, ου, ὁ, (1) *a potentate,
prince*, Lu. i. 52; 1 Tim. vi.
15; (2) *one in authority*, Ac.
viii. 27.*

δυνατέω, ῶ, *to be powerful, have
power*, 2 Cor. xiii. 3; (inf.),

Ro. xiv. 4 (W. H.); 2 Cor. ix.
8 (W. H.). (N. T.)*

δυνατός, ή, όν, *able, having
power, mighty*, Lu. xiv. 31 ;
1 Cor. i. 26; ὁ δυνατός, *the
Almighty*, Lu. i. 49; δυνατόν,
possible, Ro. xii. 18; Gal. iv.
15.

δύνω or δύω, 2d aor. ἔδυν, *to
sink; to set,* as the sun, Mar.
i. 32; Lu. iv. 40.*

δύο, indecl. num., except dat.
δυσί, *two.*

δυς-, an inseparable prefix, implying *adverse, difficult,* or
grievous.

δυσ-βάστακτος, ον, *hard to be
borne*, Mat. xxiii. 4 (not W.
H.); Lu. xi. 46. (S.)*

δυσ-εντερία, ας, ἡ (W. H. ιον,
τό), *dysentery*, Ac. xxviii.
8.*

δυσ-ερμήνευτος, ον, *hard to explain*, Heb. v. 11.*

δύσ-κολος, ον (lit., " difficult
about food "), *difficult*, Mar.
x. 24.*

δυσκόλως, adv., *with difficulty,
hardly*, Mat. xix. 23; Mar. x.
23; Lu. xviii. 24.*

δυσμή, ῆς, ἡ (only plur., δυσμαί),
the setting of the sun, the west,
Rev. xxi. 13; Mat. viii. 11.

δυσ-νόητος, ον, *hard* or *difficult
to be understood*, 2 Pet. iii.
16.*

δυσ-φημέω, ῶ, *to speak evil, de-
fame*, 1 Cor. iv. 13 (W. H.).*

δυσ-φημία, ας, ἡ, *evil report,
defamation*, 2 Cor. vi. 8.*

δώδεκα, indecl. num., *twelve ;*
οἱ δώδεκα, *the twelve, i.e., the
Apostles.*

δωδέκατος, η, ον, ord. num.,
twelfth, Rev. xxi. 20.*

δωδεκά-φυλον, ου, τό, *the twelve
tribes, Israel*, Ac. xxvi. 7.*

δῶμα, ατος, τό, *a house, a house-
top*, Mat. xxiv. 17; Ac. x.
9.

δωρεά, ᾶς, ἡ, *a gift*, Jn. iv. 10;
Ro. v. 15; Ep. iv. 7.

δωρεάν, accus. of preced., as an
adv., *freely,* as 2 Cor. xi. 7;
without cause, groundlessly,
Jn. xv. 25; Gal. ii. 21.

δωρέομαι, οῦμαι, *to present, bestow*, Mar. xv. 45; pass., 2
Pet. i. 3, 4.*

δώρημα, ατος, τό, *a gift, bounty*,
Ro. v. 16; Ja. i. 17.*

δῶρον, ου, τό, *a gift, present*,
Ep. ii. 8; Rev. xi. 10.

E

E, ε, ἐψῖλον, *epsilon, e,* the fifth
letter. As a numeral, ε΄ = 5;
,ε = 5000.

ἔα, interj., expressing surprise
or indignation, *ha! ah!* Mar.
i. 24 (W. H. omit); Lu. iv.
34.*

ἐάν or ἄν, conj. (for εἰ ἄν), *if,*
usually construed with sub-
junctive verb. See Gr. § 383,
Wi. § 41 *b*, 2, Bu. 221 sq.
W. H. have the indic. fut.
in Lu. xix. 40; Ac. viii. 31 ;
pres. in 1 Th. iii. 8; 1 Jn. v.
15 (Rec. also). Sometimes
equivalent to a particle of
time, *when*, Jn. xii. 32; after
the relative, with an indefinite force, ὃς ἐάν, who*soever*,
as Mat. v. 19, viii. 19; 1 Cor.
xvi. 6; ἐὰν δὲ καί, *and if also;*
ἐὰν μή, *except, unless*, Mat.
v. 20; *but that*, Mar. iv. 22 ;
ἐὰν πέρ, *if indeed*, Heb. vi. 3.

ἑαυτοῦ, ῆς, οῦ, pron., reflex., 3d
pers., *of one's self;* used also
in 1st and 2d persons. See
Gr. § 335, Wi. §§ 22, 5, 38, 6,
Bu. 111 sq. Genitive often
for possess. pron. λέγειν or
εἰπεῖν ἐν ἑαυτῷ, *to say within
one's self ;* γίνεσθαι or ἔρ-
χεσθαι ἐν ἑαυτῷ, *to come to
one's self ;* πρὸς ἑαυτόν, *to
one's home*, Jn. xx. 10, or
privately, as Lu. xviii. 11; ἐν
ἑαυτοῖς, *among yourselves,
i.e.,* one with another; καθ'
ἑαυτόν, *apart;* παρ' ἑαυτόν,
at home.

ἐάω, ῶ, ἐάσω; impf., εἴων; 1st
aor., εἴασα, (1) *to permit,* inf.,
or acc. and inf., Mat. xxiv.
33; Lu. iv. 41 ; (2) *to leave,*
Ac. xxvii. 40.

ἑβδομήκοντα, indecl. num., *sev-
enty;* οἱ ἑβδομήκοντα, *the sev-
enty* disciples, Lu. x. 1, 17.

ἑβδομηκοντάκις, num. adv., *sev-
enty times*, Mat. xviii. 22.
(S.)*

ἕβδομος, η, ον, ord. num., *seventh*,
Jn. iv. 52; Heb. iv. 4.

Ἔβερ, ὁ, *Eber* or *Heber*, Lu. iii.
35.*

Ἑβραϊκός, ή, όν (from Heb.),
Hebrew, Lu. xxiii. 38 (W. H.
omit). (N. T.)*

Ἑβραῖος (W. H. 'E-), αία, αῖον
(from Heb.), also subst., ὁ, ἡ, *a
Hebrew;* designating (1) any

Jew, 2 Cor. xi. 22; Phil. iii. 5; (2) a Jew of Palestine, in distinction from οἱ Ἑλληνισταί, or Jews born out of Palestine, and using the Greek language, Ac. vi. 1; (3) any Jewish Christian, Heb. (heading). (S.)* *Syn.:* Ἑβραῖος denotes a Jew who spoke Aramaic or Hebrew, in distinction from Ἑλληνιστής, a Greek-speaking Jew; Ἰουδαῖος, a Jew in distinction from other nations; Ἰσραηλίτης, one of the chosen people.

Ἑβραΐς (W. H. 'E-), (from Heb.), ἴδος, ἡ, *Hebrew, i.e., the Aramaic language,* vernacular in the time of Christ and the Apostles, Ac. xxi. 40, xxii. 2, xxvi. 14. See Gr. § 150, Wi. § 3a. (Ap.)*

Ἑβραϊστί (W. H. 'E-), (from Heb.), adv., *in the Hebrew language, i.e., in Aramaic,* Jn. v. 2; Rev. ix. 11. (Ap.)

ἐγγίζω, fut. att., ἐγγιῶ; pf., ἤγγικα, *to approach, to draw near, to be near,* abs., or with dat. or εἰς, or ἐπί (acc.), Lu. xviii. 40; Ac. ix. 3; Mar. xi. 1.

ἐγ-γράφω (W. H. ἐνγ-), *to inscribe, engrave,* 2 Cor. iii. 2; Lu. x. 20 (W. H.).*

ἔγγυος, ου, ὁ, ἡ, *a surety,* Heb. vii. 22.*

ἐγγύς, adv., *near;* used of both place and time, with gen. or dat.

ἐγγύτερον, comp. of preceding, *nearer,* Ro. xiii. 11.*

ἐγείρω, ἐγερῶ, pass. perf., ἐγήγερμαι, *to arouse, to awaken,* Ac. xii. 7; *to raise up,* as a Savior, Ac. xiii. 23 (Rec.); *to erect,* as a building, Jn. ii. 19, 20; mid., *to rise up,* as from sleep, or from a recumbent posture, as at table, Jn. xi. 29, xiii. 4; applied to raising the dead, Jn. v. 21; used also of *rising up against,* as an adversary, or in judgment, Mat. xxiv. 7.

ἔγερσις, εως, ἡ, *a rousing up;* of the resurrection, Mat. xxvii. 53.*

ἐγκ-. In words beginning thus, W. H. generally write ἐνκ-.

ἐγ-κάθ-ετος, ου, ὁ, ἡ (ἐγκαθίημι), *a spy,* Lu. xx. 20.*

ἐγκαίνια, ίων, τά, *a dedication,*

Jn. x. 22; of the feast commemorating the dedicating or purifying of the temple, after its pollution by Antiochus Epiphanes, 25 Chisleu, answering to mid-December. (S.)*

ἐγ-καινίζω, *to dedicate,* Heb. ix. 18, x. 20. (S.)*

ἐγ-κακέω, ῶ, and ἐνκακέω, *to grow weary, to faint* (W. H. in many passages for Rec. ἐκκακέω).

ἐγ-καλέω, ῶ, ἔσω, impf., ἐνεκάλουν, *to bring a charge against, accuse,* pers. dat., or κατά (gen.), crime in gen., Ac. xix. 38, 40; Ro. viii. 33.

ἐγ-κατα-λείπω, ψω, (1) *to desert, to abandon,* Mat. xxvii. 46; 2 Tim. iv. 10, 16; (2) *to leave remaining,* Ro. ix. 29.

ἐγ-κατ-οικέω, ῶ, *to dwell among* (ἐν), 2 Pet. ii. 8.*

ἐγ-καυχάομαι, *to boast in,* 2 Th. i. 4 (W. H.).*

ἐγ-κεντρίζω, *to insert,* as a bud or graft, *to graft in;* fig., Ro. xi. 17, 19, 23, 24.*

ἐγ-κλημα, ατος, τό, *a charge* or *accusation,* Ac. xxiii. 29, xxv. 16.*

ἐγ-κομβόομαι, οῦμαι, *to gird on,* as an outer garment, the badge of slavery, 1 Pet. v. 5. (N. T.)*

ἐγ-κοπή, ῆς, ἡ (W. H. ἐνκ-), *a hindrance,* 1 Cor. ix. 12.*

ἐγ-κόπτω, ψω, *to impede, to hinder* (acc., or inf. with τοῦ), Ro. xv. 22; 1 Th. ii. 18.

ἐγκράτεια, ας, ἡ, *self-control, continence,* Ac. xxiv. 25; Gal. v. 23; 2 Pet. i. 6.*

ἐγκρατεύομαι, dep., *to be self-controlled, continent,* especially in sensual pleasures, 1 Cor. vii. 9, ix. 25.*

ἐγ-κρατής, ές, *self-controlled, continent,* Tit. i. 8.*

ἐγ-κρίνω, *to adjudge* or *reckon,* to a particular rank (acc. and dat.), 2 Cor. x. 12.*

ἐγ-κρύπτω, *to hide in, to mix with,* Mat. xiii. 33; Lu. xiii. 21 (W. H. κρύπτω).*

ἔγ-κυος, ον, *pregnant,* Lu. ii. 5.*

ἐγ-χρίω, *to rub in, anoint,* Rev. iii. 18.*

ἐγώ, pers. pron., *I;* plur., ἡμεῖς, *we.* See Gr. § 53.

ἐδαφίζω, fut. (attic), ιῶ, *to throw to the ground, to raze,* Lu. xix. 44.*

ἔδαφος, ους, τό, *the base, the ground,* Ac xxii. 7.*

Ἑδραῖος, αία, αῖον, *steadfast, firm,* 1 Cor. vii. 37, xv. 58; Col. i. 23.*

ἑδραίωμα, ατος, τό, *a stay, support,* 1 Tim. iii. 15. (N. T.)*

Ἐζεκίας, ου, ὁ, *Hezekiah,* Mat. i. 9, 10.*

ἐθελο-θρησκεία, ας, ἡ, *voluntary, arbitrary worship,* Col. ii. 23. (N. T.)*

ἐθέλω, see θέλω.

ἐθίζω, *to accustom;* pass., perf. part., neut., τὸ εἰθισμένον, *the custom,* Lu. ii. 27.*

ἐθνάρχης, ου, ὁ, *a prefect, ethnarch,* 2 Cor. xi. 32.*

ἐθνικός, ή, όν, *of Gentile race, heathen,* as subst. ὁ ἐθνικός, *the pagan, the Gentile,* Mat. v. 47 (W. H.), vi. 7, xviii. 17; 3 Jn. 7 (W. H.).*

ἐθνικῶς, adv., *like the Gentiles,* Gal. ii. 14. (N. T.)*

ἔθνος, ους, τό, *a race, a nation,* Lu. xxii. 25; Ac. x. 35; τὰ ἔθνη, *the nations, the heathen world, the Gentiles,* Mat. iv. 15; Ro. iii. 29; by Paul, even *Gentile Christians,* Ro. xi. 13; Gal. ii. 12.

ἔθος, ους, τό, *a usage, custom,* Lu. i. 9; Ac. xxv. 16.

ἔθω, obs., pf. εἴωθα in pres. signif., *to be accustomed,* Mat. xxvii. 15; Mar. x. 1; τὸ εἰωθὸς αὐτῷ, *his custom,* Lu. iv. 16; Ac. xvii. 2.*

εἰ, a conditional conjunction (see Gr. § 383), *if, since, though.* After verbs indicating emotion, εἰ is equivalent to ὅτι, Mar. xv. 44. As an interrogative particle, εἰ occurs in both indirect and direct questions, Mar. xv. 45; Ac. i. 6. In oaths and solemn assertions, it may be rendered by *that ... not.* εἰ μή and εἰ μήτι, *unless, except;* εἰ δὲ μή, *but if not, otherwise,* Jn. xiv. 2; εἴ περ, *if so be;* εἴ πως, *if possibly;* εἴτε ... εἴτε, *whether ... or.*

εἶδον, see ὁράω, οἶδα.

εἶδος, ους, τό, *outward appearance, form,* Lu. iii. 22, ix. 29; Jn. v. 37; 2 Cor. v. 7; *species, kind,* 1 Th. v. 22.*

εἰδωλεῖον, ου, τό, an idol-temple, 1 Cor. viii. 10. (Ap.)*

εἰδωλό-θυτος, ον, sacrificed to idols ; used of meats, as Ac. xv. 29. (Ap.)

εἰδωλο-λατρεία, ας, ἡ, idolatry, 1 Cor. x. 14; Gal. v. 20; Col. iii. 5; 1 Pet. iv. 3. (N. T.)*

εἰδωλο-λάτρης, ου, ὁ, an idolater, 1 Cor. x. 7; Rev. xxi. 8. (N. T.)

εἴδωλον, ου, τό, an idol, a false god worshipped in an image, Ac. vii. 41; Ro. ii. 22.

εἰκῆ or εἰκῇ (W. H.), adv., without purpose, as Ro. xiii. 4; in vain, 1 Cor. xv. 2 (W. H. and R. V. omit in Mat. v. 22).

εἴκοσι, indecl. num., twenty.

εἴκω, to give way, to yield, Gal. ii. 5.*

εἴκω, obs., whence 2d perf. ἔοικα, to be like; with dat., Ja. i. 6, 23.*

εἰκών, όνος, ἡ, an image, likeness, Mar. xii. 16; 1 Cor. xi. 7. Syn. : see Trench, § xv.

εἰλικρίνεια, ας, ἡ, clearness, sincerity, 1 Cor. v. 8; 2 Cor. i. 12, ii. 17.*

εἰλικρινής, ές (derivation doubtful), sincere, pure, Phil. i. 10; 2 Pet. iii. 1.*

εἰλίσσω (W. H. ἑλίσσω), to roll together, as a scroll, Rev. vi. 14.*

εἰμί (see Gr. § 110, Wi. § 14, 2, Bu. 49, 50), a verb of existence, (1) used as a predicate, to be, to exist, to happen, to come to pass ; with an infin. following, ἔστι, it is convenient, proper, etc., as Heb. ix. 5; (2) as the copula of subject and predicate, simply to be, or in the sense of to be like, to represent, Jn. vi. 35; Mat. xxvi. 26; 1 Cor. x. 4. With participles, it is used to form the periphrastic tenses, as Lu. i. 22, iv. 16; Mat. xvi. 19, etc. With gen., as predicate, it marks quality, possession, participation, etc.; with dat., property, possession, destination, etc. The verb, when copula, is often omitted. Participle, ὤν, being; τὸ ὄν, that which is ; οἱ ὄντες, τὰ ὄντα, persons or things that are.

εἶμι, to go, in some copies for

εἰμί, in Jn. vii. 34, 36 (not W. H.).*

εἵνεκα, εν, see ἕνεκα, εν.

εἴπερ, εἴπως, see under εἰ.

εἶπον (see Gr. § 103, 7, Wi. § 15, Bu. 57), (W. H. εἶπα), from obs. ἔπω, or εἴπω, to say ; in reply, to answer ; in narration, to tell ; in authoritative directions, to bid or command, as Lu. vii. 7.

εἰρηνεύω, to have peace, to be at peace, Mar. ix. 50; Ro. xii. 18; 2 Cor. xiii. 11; 1 Th. v. 13.*

εἰρήνη, ης, ἡ, peace, the opposite of strife; peace of mind, arising from reconciliation with God. In N. T. (like the corresponding Heb. word in O. T.), εἰρήνη generally denotes a perfect well-being. Often employed in salutations, as in Hebrew.

εἰρηνικός, ἡ, όν, peaceable, Ja. iii. 17; peaceful, Heb. xii. 11.*

εἰρηνο-ποιέω, ῶ, to make peace, reconcile, Col. i. 20. (S.)*

εἰρηνο-ποιός, όν, pacific, loving peace, Mat. v. 9.*

εἰς, prep. governing acc., into, to (the interior). See Gr. §§ 124, 298. In composition, it implies motion into or towards.

εἷς, μία, ἕν, a card. num., one ; used distributively, as Mat. xx. 21; by way of emphasis, as Mar. ii. 7; and indefinitely, as Mat. viii. 19; Mar. xii. 42. As an ordinal, the first, Mat. xxviii. 1; Rev. ix. 12.

εἰσ-άγω, 2d aor. εἰσήγαγον, to lead in, bring in, Lu. xxii. 54; Ac. viii. 45.

εἰσ-ακούω, to listen to, to hear prayer, Mat. vi. 7; Lu. i. 13; Ac. x. 31; Heb. v. 7; to hear so as to obey (gen.), 1 Cor. xiv. 21.*

εἰσ-δέχομαι, ἔξομαι, to receive with favor (acc.), 2 Cor. vi. 17, from S.*

εἴσ-ειμι, impf. εἰσήειν, inf. εἰσιέναι (εἶμι), to go in, to enter (with εἰς), Ac. iii. 3, xxi. 18, 26; Heb. ix. 6.*

εἰσ-έρχομαι, 2d aor. εἰσῆλθον, to come in, to enter (chiefly with εἰς), Ac. xxiii. 16, 33; εἰσέρχομαι καὶ ἐξέρχομαι, to come and go in and out,

spoken of daily life and intercourse, Ac. i. 21; fig., of entrance into any state or condition, Mat. xix. 17; Heb. iii. 11, 18.

εἰσ-καλέω, ῶ, only mid. in N.T., to call or invite in, Ac. x. 23.*

εἴσ-οδος, ου, ἡ, an entrance, the act of entering, Heb. x. 19; 2 Pet. i. 11.

εἰσ-πηδάω, ῶ, to spring in, Ac xiv. 14 (W. H. ἐκπ-), xvi. 29.*

εἰσ-πορεύομαι, dep., to go in, to enter ; spoken of persons, as Mar. i. 21; of things, as Mat. xv. 17; εἰσπορεύομαι καὶ ἐκπορεύομαι, to go in and out in daily duties, Ac. ix. 28.

εἰσ-τρέχω, 2d aor. εἰσέδραμον, to run in, Ac. xii. 14.*

εἰσ-φέρω (see Gr. § 103, 6, Wi. § 15, Bu. 68), to lead into (with εἰς), e.g., temptation, as Lu. xi. 4; to bring in, Ac. xvii. 20; 1 Tim. vi. 7.

εἶτα, adv., then, afterwards.

εἴτε, conj., see εἰ.

ἐκ, or, before a vowel, ἐξ, a prep. gov. gen., from, out of (the interior), used of place, time, and source. See Gr. § 293, Wi. § 47 b, Bu. 326 sq. In composition, ἐκ implies egress, removal, origin, publicity, unfolding, or is of intensive force.

ἕκαστος, η, ον, each, every one (with partitive gen.); εἷς ἕκαστος, every one.

ἑκάστοτε, adv., at every time, always, 2 Pet. i. 15.*

ἑκατόν, card. num., a hundred, Mat. xiii. 8, xviii. 12.

ἑκατοντα-έτης, ες, a hundred years old, Ro. iv. 9.*

ἑκατονταπλασίων, ον, acc. ονα, a hundredfold, Mat. xix. 29 (not W. H.); Mar. x. 30; Lu. viii. 8.*

ἑκατοντάρχης, ου, ὁ, captain over a hundred men, a centurion, Ac. x. 1, 22, xxiv. 23.

ἑκατόνταρχος, ου, ὁ = preceding, Mat. viii. 5, 8, 13. In many passages a variant for preceding.

ἐκ-βαίνω, 2d aor. ἐξέβην, to go out, Heb. xi. 15 (W. H.).*

ἐκ-βάλλω, βαλῶ, to cast out, Jn. vi. 37; to drive out, Mat. xxi. 12; to expel, Gal. iv. 30; to send away, dismiss, reject,

Mar. i. 43; Lu. vi. 22; *to ex-tract, draw out,* Lu. vi. 42; Mat. xii. 35.

ἔκ-βασις, εως, ἡ, *a way of es-cape,* 1 Cor. x. 13; *end, issue,* Heb. xiii. 7.*

ἐκ-βολή, ῆς, ἡ, *a throwing out,* Ac. xxvii. 18.*

ἐκ-γαμίζω (W. H. γαμίζω), *to give in marriage,* Mat. xxiv. 38 (Rec.); 1 Cor. vii. 38 (Rec.). (N. T.)

ἐκ-γαμίσκω = preceding, Lu. xx. 34, 35 (Rec.). (N. T.)*

ἔκ-γονος, ον, *sprung from;* neut. plur., *descendants,* 1 Tim. v. 4.*

ἐκ-δαπανάω, ῶ, *to spend entire-ly;* pass. reflex., *to expend one's energies* for (ὑπέρ), 2 Cor. xii. 15.*

ἐκ-δέχομαι, *to expect* (ἕως), *to wait for* (acc. or ἕως), Ja. v. 7; Heb. x. 13.

ἔκ-δηλος, ον, *conspicuous, mani-fest,* 2 Tim. iii. 9.*

ἐκ-δημέω, ῶ, *to go abroad, to be absent,* 2 Cor. v. 6, 8, 9.*

ἐκ-δίδωμι, N. T. mid., *to let out for one's advantage,* Mat. xxi. 33, 41; Mar. xii. 1; Lu. xx. 9.*

ἐκ-δι-ηγέομαι, οῦμαι, dep. mid., *to narrate at length, to de-clare,* Ac. xiii. 41, xv. 3.*

ἐκ-δικέω, ῶ, *to do justice to, de-fend, avenge* a person (acc. and ἀπό), Lu. xviii. 3, 5; Ro. xii. 19; *to demand re-quital for, avenge* a deed (acc.), 2 Cor. x. 6; Rev. vi. 10, xix. 2.*

ἐκ-δίκησις, εως, ἡ, *an avenging, vindication, punishment,* Ac. vii. 24; Ro. xii. 19; 1 Pet. ii. 14.

ἔκ-δικος, ον, ὁ, ἡ, *an avenger,* one who *adjudges* a culprit (dat.) *to punishment* for (περί) a crime, Ro. xiii. 4; 1 Th. iv. 6.*

ἐκ-διώκω, ὤξω, *to persecute, to expel by persecuting,* Lu. xi. 49 (not W. H.); 1 Th. ii. 15.*

ἔκ-δοτος, ον, *delivered up,* Ac. ii. 23.*

ἐκ-δοχή, ῆς, ἡ, *a waiting for, expectation,* Heb. x. 27.*

ἐκ-δύω, *to unclothe, to strip off* (two accs.), Mat. xxvii. 31; 2 Cor. v. 4.

ἐκεῖ, adv., *there, thither.*

ἐκεῖθεν, adv., *from that place, thence.*

ἐκεῖνος, η, ο, pron., demonst., *that, that one there;* used antithetically, Mar. xvi. 20; and by way of emphasis, Mat. xxii. 23. See Gr. §§ 338, 340, Wi. §§ 18, 4, 23, 1, Bu. 104, 120.

ἐκεῖσε, adv., *thither,* Ac. xxi. 3; in const. præg., Ac. xxii. 5.*

ἐκ-ζητέω, ῶ, *to seek out* with diligence, Heb. xii. 17; 1 Pet. i. 10; *to seek after* God, Ac. xv. 17; Ro. iii. 11; Heb. xi. 6; *to require,* judicially, Lu. xi. 50, 51. (S.)*

ἐκ-ζήτησις, εως, ἡ, *a subject of inquiry,* 1 Tim. i. 4 (W. H.).*

ἐκ-θαμβέω, ῶ, N. T. pass., *to be amazed, greatly astonished,* Mar. ix. 15, xiv. 33, xvi. 5, 6.*

ἔκ-θαμβος, ον, *greatly astonished, amazed,* Ac. iii. 11.*

ἐκ-θαυμάζω, *to wonder greatly,* Mar. xii. 17 (W. H.).*

ἔκ-θετος, ον, *cast out, exposed* to perish, Ac. vii. 19.*

ἐκ-καθαίρω, 1st aor. ἐξεκάθαρα, *to cleanse thoroughly,* 1 Cor. v. 7; 2 Tim. ii. 4.*

ἐκ-καίω, N. T. pass., *to burn vehemently,* as with lust, Ro. i. 27.*

ἐκ-κακέω, ῶ, *to faint, to despond through fear* (Rec., for which W. H. have ἐγκ- and ἐνκ-).

ἐκ-κεντέω, ῶ, *to pierce through, to transfix,* Jn. xix. 37; Rev. i. 7.*

ἐκ-κλάω, *to break off,* Ro. xi. 17, 19, 20 (W. H.).*

ἐκ-κλείω, σω, *to shut out,* Gal. iv. 17; *to exclude,* Ro. iii. 27.*

ἐκκλησία, ας, ἡ (ἐκκαλέω), *an assembly,* Ac. xix. 32, 39, 41; usually legally, sometimes tumultuously gathered. Es-pec. in N. T., *an assembly of Christian believers, a church* in one place, Ac. xi. 26; often plural, as Ac. xv. 41; *the whole body of believers* on earth, 1 Cor. xii. 28; Ep. i. 22; or in heaven, Heb. xii. 23. *Syn.:* see Trench, § 1.

ἐκ-κλίνω, *to turn away from* (ἀπό), Ro. iii. 12, xvi. 17; 1 Pet. iii. 11.*

ἐκ-κολυμβάω, ῶ, *to swim out,* Ac. xxvii. 42.*

ἐκ-κομίζω, *to carry out* for bu-rial, Lu. vii. 12.*

ἐκ-κόπτω, κόψω, *to cut off,* Mat. iii. 10, v. 30; 2 Cor. xi. 12 (in 1 Pet. iii. 7, W. H. read ἐνκόπτω, *to hinder*).

ἐκ-κρέμαμαι (mid. of ἐκκρεμάν-νυμι), *to hang upon,* of earnest attention, Lu. xix. 48.*

ἐκ-λαλέω, ῶ, *to speak out, to disclose,* Ac. xxiii. 22.*

ἐκ-λάμπω, *to shine forth,* Mat. xiii. 43.*

ἐκ-λανθάνω, in mid., *to forget entirely,* Heb. xii. 5.*

ἐκ-λέγω, mid. in N. T., 1st aor. ἐξελεξάμην, *to choose out* for one's self, *to elect,* Lu. x. 42; Ac. vi. 5, xiii. 17; 1 Cor. i. 27, 28.

ἐκ-λείπω, 2d aor. ἐξέλιπον, *to fail, to cease, to die,* Lu. xvi. 9, xxii. 32, xxiii. 45 (W. H.); Heb. i. 12.*

ἐκλεκτός, ή, όν, (1) *chosen, elect,* Lu. xviii. 7, xxiii. 35; 1 Tim. v. 21; Ro. viii. 33; Rev. xvii. 14; (2) *choice, select,* 2 Jn. i. 13; 1 Pet. ii. 4.

ἐκλογή, ῆς, ἡ, *a choice, selection,* Ro. ix. 11; 1 Th. i. 4; Ac. ix. 15 (*a vessel of choice, i.e., a chosen vessel*); concr., *the chosen ones,* Ro. xi. 7

ἐκ-λύω, in pass., *to become weary* in body, or *despondent* in mind, Mar. viii. 3; Gal. vi. 9; Heb. xii. 5.

ἐκ-μάσσω, ξω, *to wipe, to wipe off,* Lu. vii. 38, 44; Jn. xi. 2, xii. 3, xiii. 5.*

ἐκ-μυκτηρίζω, *to deride, scoff at* (acc.), Lu. xvi. 14, xxiii. 35. (S.)*

ἐκ-νέω (lit., swim out), or ἐκνεύω (lit., turn by a side motion), *to withdraw,* Jn. v. 13.*

ἐκ-νήφω, *to return to soberness* of mind, 1 Cor. xv. 34.*

ἑκούσιος, ον (ἑκών), *voluntary, spontaneous,* Philem. 14.*

ἑκουσίως, adv., *voluntarily, of one's own accord,* Heb. x. 26; 1 Pet. v. 2.*

ἔκ-παλαι, adv., *from of old,* 2 Pet. ii. 3, iii. 5.*

ἐκ-πειράζω, σω, *to put to the test, to make trial of, to tempt,* Mat. iv. 7; Lu. iv. 12, x. 25; 1 Cor. x. 9. (S.)*

ἐκ-πέμπω, to send forth, Ac. xiii. 4, xvii. 10.*

ἐκ-περισσῶς, adv., exceedingly, Mar. xiv. 31 (W. H.). (N.T.)*

ἐκ-πετάννυμι, 1st aor. ἐξεπέτασα, to stretch forth, Ro. x. 21.*

ἐκ-πηδάω, ῶ, 1st aor. ἐξεπήδησα (W. H.), to spring forth, Ac. xiv. 14.*

ἐκ-πίπτω, to fall from (ἐκ), Ac. xii. 7; abs., to fall, Ja. i. 11; of a ship driven from its course, Ac. xxvii. 17; of love, to fail, 1 Cor. xiii. 8; of moral lapse, Gal. v. 4.

ἐκ-πλέω, εύσω, to sail away, Ac. xv. 39, xviii. 18, xx. 6.*

ἐκ-πληρόω, ῶ, to fill entirely, fulfill, Ac. xiii. 32.*

ἐκ-πλήρωσις, εως, ἡ, fulfillment, Ac. xxi. 26.*

ἐκ-πλήσσω, 2d aor. pass. ἐξεπλάγην, to strike with astonishment, Mat. xiii. 54; Ac. xiii. 12.

ἐκ-πνέω, εύσω, to breathe out, to expire, Mar. xv. 37, 39; Lu. xxiii. 46.*

ἐκ-πορεύομαι, dep., to go out (ἀπό, ἐκ, παρά, and εἰς, ἐπί, πρός); to proceed from, as from the heart; or as a river from its source, etc.

ἐκ-πορνεύω, to be given up to fornication, Ju. 7. (S.)*

ἐκ-πτύω, to reject, to loathe, Gal. iv. 14.*

ἐκ-ριζόω, ῶ, to root out, root up, Mat. xiii. 29, xv. 13; Lu. xvii. 6; Ju. 12.*

ἐκ-στασις, εως, ἡ, trance, Ac. x. 10; amazement, Mar. v. 42.

ἐκ-στρέφω, perf. pass. ἐξέστραμμαι, to change for the worse, to corrupt, Tit. iii. 11.*

ἐκ-ταράσσω, ξω, to agitate greatly, Ac. xvi. 20.*

ἐκ-τείνω, νῶ, 1st aor. ἐξέτεινα, to stretch out the hand, as Lu. v. 13; to cast out, as anchors, Ac. xxvii. 30.

ἐκ-τελέω, ῶ, έσω, to complete, Lu. xiv. 29, 30.*

ἐκτένεια, ας, ἡ, intentness, Ac. xxvi. 7.*

ἐκ-τενής, ές, intense, fervent, intent, 1 Pet. iv. 8; Ac. xii. 5 (W. H. -ῶς) ; ἐκτενέστερον, comp. as adv., more earnestly, Lu. xxii. 44 (W.H. omit).*

ἐκτενῶς, adv., intently, earnest-

ly, 1 Pet. i. 22; Ac. xii. 5 (W. H.).*

ἐκ-τίθημι (see Gr. § 107, Wi. § 14, 1 b, Bu. 45 sq.), (1) to put out, expose an infant, Ac. vii. 21; (2) to expound, Ac. xi. 4, xviii. 26, xxviii. 23.*

ἐκ-τινάσσω, ξω, to shake off, Mat. x. 14; Mar. vi. 11; Ac. xiii. 51; to shake out, Ac. xviii. 6.*

ἕκτος, η, ον, ord. num., sixth.

ἐκτός, adv., generally as prep., with gen., without, besides, except, 1 Cor. vi. 18; Ac. xxvi. 22; ἐκτὸς εἰ μή, except, 1 Cor. xiv. 5; τὸ ἐκτός, the outside, Mat. xxiii. 26.

ἐκ-τρέπω, pass. in mid. sense, to turn from, to forsake, 1 Tim. i. 6, v. 15, vi. 20; 2 Tim. iv. 4; Heb. xii. 13.*

ἐκ-τρέφω, to nourish, Ep. v. 29; to bring up, Ep. vi. 4.*

ἔκ-τρωμα, ατος, τό, an abortive birth, an abortion, 1 Cor. xv. 8.*

ἐκ-φέρω, ἐξοίσω, to bring forth, carry out; espec. to burial, Ac. v. 6, 9; to produce, of the earth, Heb. vi. 8.

ἐκ-φεύγω, to flee out (abs., or with ἐκ), Ac. xvi. 27, xix. 16; to escape, 1 Th. v. 3; Ro. ii. 3.

ἐκ-φοβέω, ῶ, to terrify greatly, 2 Cor. x. 9.*

ἔκ-φοβος, ον, greatly terrified, Mar. ix. 6; Heb. xii. 21.*

ἐκ-φύω, 2d aor. pass. ἐξεφύην, to put forth, as a tree its leaves, Mat. xxiv. 32; Mar. xiii. 28.*

ἐκ-χέω, also ἐκχύνω; fut. ἐκχεῶ, 1st aor. ἐξέχεα (see Gr. § 96 c, Wi. § 13, 3 a, Bu. 68), to pour out, as Rev. xvi. 1-17; money, Jn. ii. 15; to shed blood, Lu. xi. 50; fig., to shed abroad, love, Ro. v. 5; pass., to be wholly given up to, Ju. 11.

ἐκ-χωρέω, ῶ, to depart from, Lu. xxi. 21.*

ἐκ-ψύχω, to expire, Ac. v. 5, 10, xii. 23.*

ἑκών, οῦσα, όν, voluntary, willing; used adverbially, Ro. viii. 20; 1 Cor. ix. 17.*

ἐλαία, ας, ἡ, an olive tree, Ro. xi. 17, 24; its fruit, the olive, Ja. iii. 12; τὸ ὄρος τῶν ἐλαιῶν, the Mount of Olives, Mar. xi. 1.

ἔλαιον, ου, τό, olive oil, Mat xxv. 3; Rev. vi. 6.

ἐλαιών, ῶνος, ὁ, an olive orchard, i.e., the Mount of Olives, Ac. i. 12. (S.)*

Ἐλαμίτης, ου, ὁ, an Elamite, i.e., inhabitant of the province of Elymais, Ac. ii. 9.*

ἐλάσσων or -ττων, ον, compar. of ἐλαχύς for μικρός, less; in excellence, Jn. ii. 10; in age, Ro. ix. 12; in rank, Heb. vii. 7; ἔλαττον, as adv., less, 1 Tim. v. 9.*

ἐλαττονέω, ῶ, to have less, to lack, 2 Cor. viii. 15.*

ἐλαττόω, ῶ, to make less or inferior, Heb. ii. 7, 9; pass., to decrease, Jn. iii. 30.*

ἐλαύνω, perf. part. ἐληλακώς, to drive, Lu. viii. 29; Ja. iii. 4; 2 Pet. ii. 17; to drive a ship, to row, Mar. vi. 48; Jn. vi. 19.*

ἐλαφρία, ας, ἡ, levity, inconstancy, 2 Cor. i. 17.*

ἐλαφρός, ά, όν, light, as a burden, Mat. xi. 30; 2 Cor. iv. 17.*

ἐλάχιστος, η, ον (superl. of ἐλαχύς for μικρός), smallest, least, in size, amount, or importance, Ja. iii. 4; Lu. xvi. 10; 1 Cor. vi. 2.

ἐλαχιστότερος, α, ον, a double comparison, less than the least, Ep. iii. 8. (N. T.)*

ἐλάω, see ἐλαύνω.

Ἐλεάζαρ, ὁ, Eleazar, Mat. i 15.*

ἐλεάω (W. H., Rec. ἐλεέω), Ro. ix. 16; Ju. 22, 23.*

ἐλεγμός, οῦ, ὁ, reproof, 2 Tim iii. 16 (W. H.). (S.)*

ἔλεγξις, εως, ἡ, refutation, rebuke, 2 Pet. ii. 16. (S.)*

ἔλεγχος, ου, ὁ, evident demonstration, proof, Heb. xi. 1; 2 Tim. iii. 16 (not W. H.).*

ἐλέγχω, ξω, to convict, refute, reprove, 1 Cor. xiv. 24; Jn. iii. 20; 1 Tim. v. 20.

ἐλεεινός, ή, όν, pitiable, miserable, 1 Cor. xv. 19; Rev. iii. 17.*

ἐλεέω, ῶ, to have mercy on, succor (acc.), Mat. ix. 27; Lu. xvi. 24; pass., to obtain mercy, Mat. v. 7.

ἐλεημοσύνη, ης, ἡ, mercy, pity; in N. T., alms, sometimes plur., Mat. vi. 4; Lu. xi. 41; Ac. ix. 36.

ἐλεήμων, ον, *full of pity, merci-ful*, Mat. v. 7; Heb. ii. 17.*

ἔλεος, ους, τό (and ον, ὁ, see Gr. § 32 a, Wi. § 9, note 2, Bu. 22), *mercy, pity*, especially on account of misery, Tit. iii. 5; Mat. ix. 13.

ἐλευθερία, ας, ἡ, *liberty, freedom*, from the Mosaic yoke, as 1 Cor. x. 29; Gal. ii. 4; from evil, as Ja. ii. 12; Ro. viii. 21; *license*, 2 Pet. ii. 19.

ἐλεύθερος, α, ον, *free*, as opposed to the condition of a slave; *delivered from obligation* (often with ἐκ, ἀπό); *at liberty to* (inf.); once with dat. of reference, Ro. vi. 20.

ἐλευθερόω, ῶ, *to set free* (generally with acc. and ἀπό); with modal dative, Gal. v. 1.

ἔλευσις, εως, ἡ (ἔρχομαι), *a coming, an advent*, Ac. vii. 52.*

ἐλεφάντινος, η, ον, *made of ivory*, Rev. xviii. 12.*

Ἐλιακείμ, ὁ (Heb.), *Eliakim*, Mat. i. 13; Lu. iii. 30.*

ἕλιγμα, ατος, τό, *a roll*, Jn. xix. 39 (W. H. for Rec. μίγμα).*

Ἐλιέζερ, ὁ (Heb.), *Eliezer*, Lu. iii. 29.*

Ἐλιούδ, ὁ (Heb.), *Eliud*, Mat. i. 14, 15.*

Ἐλισάβετ, ἡ (Heb. *Elisheba*), *Elisabeth*, Lu. i. 5, etc.

Ἐλισσαῖος, ου, ὁ, *Elisha*, Lu. iv. 27.*

ἑλίσσω, ίξω, as εἱλίσσω, *to roll up*, Heb. i. 12; Rev. vi. 14 (W. H.).*

ἕλκος, ους, τό, *a wound, an ulcer, a sore*, Lu. xvi. 21; Rev. xvi. 2, 11.*

ἑλκόω, ῶ, *to make a sore*; pass., *to be full of sores*, Lu. xvi. 20.*

ἑλκύω, σω, *to drag*, Ac. xvi. 19; *to draw*, a net, Jn. xxi. 6, 11; a sword, Jn. xviii. 10; *to draw over, to persuade*, Jn. vi. 44, xii. 32.* Syn.: σύρω *always* means to drag *by force*; ἑλκύω only *sometimes* involves force, often not.

ἕλκω (old form of foregoing), impf. εἷλκον, Ja. ii. 6; Ac. xxi. 30.*

Ἑλλάς, άδος, ἡ, *Hellas, Greece*, = Ἀχαΐα, Ac. xx. 2.*

Ἕλλην, ηνος, ὁ, *a Greek*, as distinguished (1) from βάρβαρος, *barbarian*, Ro. i. 14, and (2)

from Ἰουδαῖος, *Jew*, as Jn. vii. 35. Used for Greek proselytes to Judaism, Jn. xii. 20; Ac. xvii. 4.

Ἑλληνικός, ή, όν, *Grecian*, Lu. xxiii. 38 (W. H. omit); Rev. ix. 11.*

Ἑλληνίς, ίδος, ἡ, *a Greek* or *Gentile woman*, Mar. vii. 26; Ac. xvii. 12.*

Ἑλληνιστής, οῦ, ὁ (ἑλληνίζω, *to Hellenize*, or *adopt Greek manners and language*), *a Hellenist, Grecian Jew* (R. V.); a Jew by parentage and religion, but born in a Gentile country and speaking Greek, Ac. vi. 1, ix. 29, xi. 20.*

Ἑλληνιστί, adv., *in the Greek language*, Jn. xix. 20; Ac. xxi. 37.*

ἐλ-λογέω (ἐν; W. H. -άω), *to charge to, to put to one's account*, Ro. v. 13; Philem. 18. (N. T.)*

Ἐλμωδάμ (W. H. -μα-), ὁ, *Elmodam*, Lu. iii. 28.*

ἐλπίζω, att. fut. ἐλπιῶ, 1st aor. ἤλπισα, *to expect* (acc. or inf., or ὅτι); *to hope for* (acc.); *to trust in* (ἐπί, dat.; ἐν, once dat. only); *to direct hope towards* (εἰς, ἐπί, acc.).

ἐλπίς, ίδος, ἡ, *expectation, hope*; especially of the Christian *hope*. Met., (1) *the author*, as 1 Tim. i. 1; (2) *the object of hope*, as Tit. ii. 13 (in Ro. viii. 20 W. H. read ἐφ' ἐλπίδι).

Ἐλύμας, α, ὁ (from Aram.), *Elymas*, Ac. xiii. 8.*

ἐλωΐ (prob. Aram. = Heb. ἠλί), *my God!* Mar. xv. 34; Mat. xxvii. 46 (W. H.); see ἠλί. (N. T.)*

ἐμαυτοῦ, ῆς, οῦ, *of myself*, a reflexive pron., found only in the gen., dat., and acc. cases; ἀπ' ἐμαυτοῦ, *from myself*, Jn. v. 30.

ἐμ-βαίνω, 2d aor. ἐνέβην, part. ἐμβάς, *to go upon, into* (εἰς), always of entering a ship except Jn. v. 4 (W. H. omit).

ἐμ-βάλλω, *to cast into*, Lu. xii. 5.*

ἐμ-βάπτω, *to dip into*, Mat. xxvi. 23; Mar. xiv. 20; Jn. xiii. 26 (W. H. βάπτω).*

ἐμ-βατεύω, *to enter, to intrude, to pry into*, Col. ii. 18.*

ἐμ-βιβάζω, *to cause to enter, to put on board*, Ac. xxvii. 6.*

ἐμ-βλέπω, *to direct the eyes to anything, to look fixedly, to consider, to know by inspection* (acc., dat., or εἰς), Mar. viii. 25; Mat. xix. 26; Ac. xxii. 11.

ἐμ-βριμάομαι, ῶμαι, dep., *to snort, to be very angry*, Mar. xiv. 5; Jn. xi. 33, 38; *to charge sternly* (dat.), Mat. ix. 30; Mar. i. 43.*

ἐμέω, ῶ, 1st aor. inf. ἐμέσαι, *to vomit forth*, Rev. iii. 16.*

ἐμ-μαίνομαι, *to rage against* (dat.), Ac. xxvi. 11.*

Ἐμμανουήλ, ὁ (Heb. *God with us*), *Immanuel*, a name of Christ, Mat. i. 23. (S.)*

Ἐμμαούς, ἡ, *Emmaus*, a village a short distance from Jerusalem, Lu. xxiv. 13.*

ἐμ-μένω, *to remain* or *persevere in* (dat. or ἐν), Ac. xxviii. 30 (W. H.); Gal. iii. 10.

Ἐμμόρ, ὁ, *Emmor*, or *Hamor*, Ac. vii. 16.*

ἐμός, ή, όν, *mine*, denoting possession, power over, authorship, right, etc. See Gr. § 336, Wi. § 22, 7, Bu. 115 sq.

ἐμπαιγμονή, ῆς, ἡ, *mockery*, 2 Pet. iii. 3 (W. H.). (N. T.)*

ἐμπαιγμός, οῦ, ὁ, *a mocking, scoffing*, Heb. xi. 36. (S.)*

ἐμ-παίζω, ξω, *to mock* (abs. or dat.), Mar. x. 34, xv. 20; *to delude*, Mat. ii. 16.

ἐμπαίκτης, ον, ὁ, *a mocker*, 2 Pet. iii. 13; Ju. 18. (S.)*

ἐμ-περιπατέω, ῶ, ήσω, *to walk about in* (ἐν), 2 Cor. vi. 16. (S.)*

ἐμ-πίπλημι and -πλάω, ἐμπλήσω, ἐνέπλησα, part. pres. ἐμπιπλῶν, *to fill up, to satisfy*, as with food, etc. (gen.), Lu. i. 53; Ro. xv. 24.

ἐμ-πίπτω, *to fall into* or *among* (εἰς), Lu. x. 36; fig., *to incur*, as condemnation or punishment, 1 Tim. iii. 6; Heb. x. 31.

ἐμ-πλέκω, 2d aor. pass. ἐνεπλάκην, *to entangle, involve in*, 2 Tim. ii. 4; 2 Pet. ii. 20 (dat. of thing).*

ἐμ-πλοκή, ῆς, ἡ, *a plaiting, braiding*, of hair, 1 Pet. iii. 3.*

ἐμ-πνέω (W. H. ἐνπ-), *to breathe in, inhale* (gen.), Ac. ix. 1.*

ἐμ-πορεύομαι, dep., *to go about;* hence, *to trade, to traffic,* abs., Ja. iv. 13; *to use for gain* (acc.), 2 Pet. ii. 3.*

ἐμ-πορία, as, ἡ, *trade, merchandise,* Mat. xxii. 5.*

ἐμ-πόριον, ου, τό, *emporium, a place for trading,* Jn. ii. 16.*

ἔμ-πορος, ου, ὁ, *a traveler, merchant, trader,* Mat. xiii. 45; Rev. xviii. 3, 11, 15, 23.*

ἐμ-πρήθω, σω, *to set on fire, to burn,* Mat. xxii. 7.*

ἔμ-προσθεν, adv., *before* (ἔμπροσθεν καὶ ὄπισθεν, *in front and behind,* Rev. iv. 6); as prep. (gen.), *before,* in presence of, Mat. x. 32; *before,* in rank, Jn. i. 15, 30.

ἐμ-πτύω, σω, *to spit upon* (dat. or εἰς), Mat. xxvii. 30; Mar. x. 34.

ἐμ-φανής, ές, *manifest* (dat.), Ac. x. 40; Ro. x. 20.*

ἐμφανίζω, ισω, *to make manifest* (acc. and dat.), Jn. xiv. 22; Heb. ix. 24; *to disclose, make known* (ὅτι, or prepp. πρός, περί, etc.), Heb. xi. 14; Ac. xxv. 15.

ἔμ-φοβος, ον, *terrified, afraid,* Ac. x. 4, xxiv. 25.

ἐμ-φυσάω, ῶ, *to breathe upon,* acc., Jn. xx. 22.*

ἔμ-φυτος, ον, *implanted,* Ja. i. 21.*

ἐν, prep. gov. dat., *in,* generally as being or resting in; *within, among.* See Gr. § 295, Wi. § 48 *a,* Bu. 328 sq. ἐν- in composition has the force of *in, upon, into.* It is changed before γ, κ, ξ, and χ, into ἐγ-; before β, π, φ, ψ, and μ, into ἐμ-; and before λ, into ἐλ- (but W. H. prefer the unassimilated forms). The ν is, however, restored before the augment in verbs.

ἐν-αγκαλίζομαι, *to take into the arms,* Mar. ix. 36, x. 16.*

ἐν-άλιος, ον (ἅλς), *marine,* plur., *marine* animals, Ja. iii. 7.*

ἔν-αντι, adv., as prep. with gen., *in the presence of, before,* Lu. i. 8; Ac. viii. 21 (W. H.). (S.)*

ἐν-αντίος, α, ον, *over against, contrary,* of the wind, as Ac. xxvii. 4; *adverse, hostile,* as Ac. xxvi. 9; ἐξ ἐναντίας, *over against,* Mar. xv. 39. Neut., ἐναντίον, adv. as prep. with

gen., *in the presence of,* as Lu. xx. 26; Ac. vii. 10.

ἐν-άρχομαι, *to begin,* Gal. iii. 3; Phil. i. 6.*

ἔνατος, see ἔννατος.

ἐν-δεής, ές, *in want, destitute,* Ac. iv. 34.*

ἔν-δειγμα, ατος, τό, *proof, token,* 2 Th. i. 5.*

ἐν-δείκνυμι, N. T. mid., *to show, to manifest,* Ro. ix. 22; 2 Tim. iv. 14.

ἔνδειξις, εως, ἡ, *a proof, manifestation,* Ro. iii. 25, 26; 2 Cor. viii. 24; *a sign, token,* Phil. i. 28.*

ἔν-δεκα, οἱ, αἱ, τά, *eleven;* οἱ ἔνδεκα, *the eleven, i.e.,* apostles, Mat. xxviii. 16; Ac. i. 26.

ἐν-δέκατος, η, ον, *eleventh,* Mat. xx. 6, 9; Rev. xxi. 20.*

ἐν-δέχομαι, dep., *to allow;* only impersonally, οὐκ ἐνδέχεται, *it is not admissible* or *possible,* Lu. xiii. 33.*

ἐν-δημέω, ῶ, *to be at home,* 2 Cor. v. 6, 8, 9.*

ἐν-διδύσκω, *to put on, clothe,* Mar. xv. 17 (W. H.); mid., *to clothe one's self with* (acc.), Lu. viii. 27 (not W. H.), xvi. 19; Mar. xv. 17 (W. H.); see ἐνδύνω. (S.)*

ἔν-δικος, ον, *righteous, just,* Ro. iii. 8; Heb. ii. 2.*

ἐν-δόμησις, εως, ἡ, *the material of a building, a structure,* Rev. xxi. 18.*

ἐν-δοξάζω, σω, N. T. pass., *to be glorified in,* 2 Th. i. 10, 12. (S.)*

ἔν-δοξος, ον, *highly esteemed,* 1 Cor. iv. 10; *splendid, glorious,* Lu. xiii. 17; *of external appearance, splendid,* Lu. vii. 25; fig., *free from sin,* Ep. v. 27.*

ἔνδυμα, ατος, τό, *a garment, raiment,* Mat. iii. 4, xxviii. 3. (S.)

ἐν-δυναμόω, ῶ, *to strengthen,* Phil. iv. 13; 1 Tim. i. 12; pass., *to acquire strength, be strengthened,* Ac. ix. 22; Ro. iv. 20. (S.)

ἐν-δύνω (2 Tim. iii. 6) and ἐνδύω, *to clothe* or *to invest with* (two accs.); mid., *to enter, insinuate one's self into* (2 Tim. iii. 6), *to put on, clothe one's self with* (acc.); often fig., *to invest with.*

ἔν-δυσις, εως, ἡ, *a putting on of clothing,* 1 Pet. iii. 3.*

ἐν-έδρα, ας, ἡ, *an ambush,* Ac. xxiii. 16 (W. H.), xxv. 3.*

ἐν-εδρεύω, *to lie in ambush for* (acc.), Lu. xi. 54; Ac. xxiii. 21.*

ἐν-ειλέω, ῶ, 1st aor. ἐνείλησα, *to roll up, wrap in* (acc. and dat.), Mar. xv. 46.*

ἔν-ειμι, *to be in,* Lu. xi. 41, τὰ ἐνόντα, *such things as are in* (the platter, ver. 39), or *the things within your power.* For ἔνεστι, impers., see ἔνι.*

ἕνεκα or ἕνεκεν, sometimes εἵνεκεν, prep. with gen., *because of, by reason of, on account of;* οὗ ἕνεκεν, *because,* Lu. iv. 18; τίνος ἕνεκεν, *for what cause?* Ac. xix. 32.

ἐν-έργεια, ας, ἡ, *working, efficiency,* Ep. i. 19, 20, iv. 16; 2 Th. ii. 9.

ἐν-εργέω, ῶ, *to be operative, to work,* as Gal. ii. 8; trans., *to accomplish,* as 1 Cor. xii. 11; mid., *to work, to display activity,* 2 Cor. i. 6; 1 Th. ii. 13; part., ἐνεργουμένη, Ja. v. 16 (see R. V.).

ἐν-έργημα, ατος, τό, *working, effect;* plur., 1 Cor. xii. 6, 10.*

ἐν-εργής, ές, *active, effectual,* 1 Cor. xvi. 9; Heb. iv. 12; Philem. 6.*

ἐν-εστώς, perf. participle of ἐνίστημι.

ἐν-ευ-λογέω, ῶ, *to bless, to confer benefits on,* Ac. iii. 25 (W. H. εὐλ-); Gal. iii. 8. (S.)*

ἐν-έχω, (1) *to hold in, entangle,* only in pass. (dat.), Gal. v. 1; (2) *to set one's self against* (dat.), Mar. vi. 19; Lu. xi. 53.*

ἐνθά-δε, adv., *here,* Lu. xxiv. 41; Ac. xvii. 6; *hither,* Jn. iv. 15; Ac. xxv. 17.

ἐν-θυμέομαι, οῦμαι, dep. pass., *to revolve in mind, to think upon,* Mat. i. 20, ix. 4; Ac. x. 19 (W. H. διεν-).*

ἐν-θύμησις, εως, ἡ, *thought, reflection,* Mat. ix. 4, xii. 25; Ac. xvii. 29; Heb. iv. 12.*

ἔνι, perhaps contracted from ἔνεστι, impers., *there is in, is present,* 1 Cor. vi. 5 (W. H.); Gal. iii. 28; Col. iii. 11; Ja. i. 17.*

ἐνιαυτός, οῦ, ὁ, *a year,* Ac. xi. 26; Ja. iv. 13.

ἐν-ίστημι, to place in; in pf.,
plpf., and 2d aor., to be at
hand, to threaten, 2 Th. ii. 2;
2 Tim. iii. 1; perf. part. ἐνε-
στηκώς, sync. ἐνεστώς, im-
pending, or present, 1 Cor.
vii. 26; Gal. i. 4; Heb. ix. 9;
τὰ ἐνεστῶτα, present things,
opp. to τὰ μέλλοντα, things
to come, Ro. viii. 38; 1 Cor.
iii. 22.*

ἐν-ισχύω, to invigorate, to
strengthen, Lu. xxii. 43 (W.
H. omit); Ac. ix. 19 (see W.
H.).*

ἔννατος, η, ον (W. H. ἔνατος),
ninth, Lu. xxiii. 44; Rev.
xxi. 20.

ἐννέα, οἱ, αἱ, τά, nine, Lu. xvii.
17.*

ἐννενήκοντα-εννέα (W. H. as
two words), ninety-nine, Mat.
xviii. 12, 13; Lu. xv. 4, 7.
(N. T.)*

ἐννεός, ά, όν (W. H. ἐνεός), dumb,
speechless, as with amazement, Ac. ix. 7.*

ἐν-νεύω, to signify by a nod or
sign (dat.), Lu. i. 62.*

ἔν-νοια, ας, ἡ (νοῦς), way of
thinking, purpose, Heb. iv.
12; 1 Pet. iv. 1.*

ἔν-νομος, ον, bound by the law,
1 Cor. ix. 21; lawful, regular,
Ac. xix. 39.*

ἔν-νυχος, ον (νύξ), in the night,
neut. as adv., Mar. i. 35 (W.
H. ἔννυχα).

ἐν-οικέω, ῶ, ήσω, to dwell in
(ἐν), Ro. viii. 11; Col. iii.
16.

ἑνότης, τητος, ἡ (εἷς), unity, una-
nimity, Ep. iv. 3, 13.*

ἐν-οχλέω, ῶ, to disturb, to occasion tumult, Heb. xii. 15;
Lu. vi. 18 (W. H.).*

ἔν-οχος, ον, guilty of (gen. of
the crime, or of that which
is violated), 1 Cor. xi. 27;
Mar. iii. 29; liable to (dat. of
court, gen. of punishment,
εἰς of the place of punishment), Mat. v. 21, 22; Mar.
xiv. 64.

ἔν-ταλμα, ατος, τό, a precept,
Mat. xv. 9; Mar. vii. 7; Col.
ii. 22. (S.)*

ἐν-ταφιάζω, to prepare for burial, as by washing, swath-
ing, adorning, anointing the
body, Mat. xxvi. 12; Jn. xix.
40.*

ἐνταφιασμός, οῦ, ὁ, preparation

of a body for burial, Mar. xiv.
8; Jn. xii. 7. (N. T.)*

ἐν-τέλλω, in N. T. only mid.
and pass.; fut. mid., ἐντελοῦ-
μαι; perf., ἐντέταλμαι, to
command, to enjoin (dat. of
pers., or πρός with acc.), Ac.
i. 2; Heb. ix 20.

ἐντεῦθεν, adv., hence; from this
place or cause; repeated Jn.
xix. 18, on this side and that.

ἔν-τευξις, εως, ἡ, prayer, inter-
cession, 1 Tim. ii. 1, iv. 5.*
Syn.: see αἴτημα.

ἔν-τιμος, ον, held in honor; precious, highly esteemed, Lu.
vii. 2, xiv. 8; Phil. ii. 29; 1
Pet. ii. 4, 6.*

ἐντολή, ῆς, ἡ, a command or
prohibition: of God's commands, 1 Cor. vii. 19; Christ's
precepts or teachings, 1 Cor.
xiv. 37; 1 Tim. vi. 14; tradi-
tions of the Rabbis, Tit. i.
14; αἱ ἐντολαί, the command-
ments, i.e., the ten.

ἐν-τόπιος, ου, ὁ (prop. adj.), a
resident, Ac. xxi. 12.*

ἐντός, adv. as prep., with gen.,
within, Lu. xvii. 21; τὸ ἐντός,
the inside, Mat. xxiii. 26.*

ἐν-τρέπω, ψω, 2d fut. pass., ἐν-
τραπήσομαι; 2d aor. pass.,
ἐνετράπην; to put to shame,
as 1 Cor. iv. 14; Tit. ii. 8;
mid., to reverence, as Mat.
xxi. 37.

ἐν-τρέφω, to nourish in (dat.);
pass., fig., to be educated in,
1 Tim. iv. 6.*

ἔν-τρομος, ον, trembling through
fear, Ac. vii. 32, xvi. 29;
Heb. xii. 21.*

ἐν-τροπή, ῆς, ἡ, shame, 1 Cor.
vi. 5, xv. 34.* Syn.: see
αἰδώς.

ἐν-τρυφάω, ῶ, to live luxuriously, to revel (with ἐν), 2 Pet.
ii. 13.*

ἐν-τυγχάνω, to meet with, to address, Ac. xxv. 24; with ὑπέρ
(gen.), to intercede for, Ro.
viii. 27, 34; Heb. vii. 25;
with κατά (gen.), to plead
against, Ro. xi. 2.*

ἐν-τυλίσσω, ξω, to wrap in, to
wrap up, Mat. xxvii. 59; Lu.
xxiii. 53; Jn. xx. 7.*

ἐν-τυπόω, ῶ, to engrave, 2 Cor.
iii. 7.*

ἐν-υβρίζω, σω, to treat contempt-
uously, Heb. x. 29.*

ἐν-υπνιάζομαι, dep. pass., to

dream (cognate acc.), Ac.
ii. 17; to conceive impure
thoughts, Ju. 8.*

ἐν-ύπνιον, ου, τό, a dream, Ac.
ii. 17.*

ἐνώπιον (neut. of ἐνώπιος, from
ἐν ὠπί, in view), as prep.,
with gen., before, in sight or
presence of, Lu. i. 17; Rev.
iii. 9; ἐνώπιον τοῦ θεοῦ, in the
sight of God, Ro. xiv. 22;
used in adjuration, 1 Tim. v.
21; χάρις ἐνώπιον τοῦ θεοῦ
(Ac. vii. 4), favor with God.

Ἐνώς, ὁ, Enos, Lu. iii. 38.*

ἐν-ωτίζομαι, dep. mid. (ἐν ὠτίοις,
in the ears), to listen to, Ac.
ii. 14. (S.)*

Ἐνώχ, ὁ, Enoch, Lu. iii. 37;
Ju. 14.*

ἐξ, prep., see ἐκ.

ἐξ-αγγέλλω, to declare abroad,
celebrate, 1 Pet. ii. 9.*

ἐξ-αγοράζω, to redeem, Gal. iii.
13 (ἐκ), iv. 5; τὸν καιρόν, to
buy up, redeem the opportunity from being lost, Ep. v. 16;
Col. iv. 5.*

ἐξ-άγω, 2d aor. ἐξήγαγον, to
lead out (with ἔξω, ἐκ, εἰς).

ἐξ-αιρέω, ῶ (see Gr. § 103, 1,
Wi. § 15, Bu. 53), to take out,
pluck out, Mat. v. 29, xviii.
9; mid., to rescue, deliver,
Ac. vii. 10, 34, xii. 11, xxiii.
27, xxvi. 17; Gal. i. 4.*

ἐξ-αίρω (see Gr. § 92), to lift up;
to remove, 1 Cor. v. 2 (W. H.
αἴρω), 13.*

ἐξ-αιτέω, ῶ, N. T., mid., to demand of; to ask for, Lu.
xxii. 31.*

ἐξ-αίφνης (W. H. ἐξέφ-, except
in Ac. xxii. 6), adv., suddenly, unexpectedly, Mar. xiii. 36.

ἐξ-ακολουθέω, ῶ, to follow after,
to imitate, 2 Pet. i. 16, ii. 2,
15.*

ἑξακόσιοι, αι, α, six hundred,
Rev. xiii. 18, xiv. 20.*

ἐξ-αλείφω, to wipe out, obliterate,
Rev. iii. 5; Col. ii. 14; Ac.
iii. 19; to wipe away (ἀπό or
ἐκ), Rev. vii. 17, xxi. 4.*

ἐξ-άλλομαι, to leap up, Ac. iii. 8.*

ἐξ-ανά-στασις, εως, ἡ, a resurrection, Phil. iii. 11 (followed
by ἐκ, W. H.).*

ἐξ-ανα-τέλλω, to spring up, as
plants or corn, Mat. xiii. 5
Mar. iv. 5.*

ἐξ-αν-ίστημι, (1) trans., to rais-

36

up offspring, Mar. xii. 19; Lu xx. 28; (2) 2d aor. intrans., *to rise up*, Ac. xv. 5.*

ἐξ-απατάω, ῶ, *to deceive thoroughly*, Ro. vii. 11 ; 2 Th. ii. 3.

ἐξάπινα, adv. (= ἐξαίφνης), *suddenly*, Mar. ix. 8. (S.)*

ἐξ-απορέομαι, οῦμαι, dep., *to be utterly without resource, to be in despair*, 2 Cor. i. 8, iv. 8.*

ἐξ-απο-στέλλω, *to send forth, send away*, Ac. vii. 12, xi. 12, xvii. 14.

ἐξαρτίζω, (1) *to completely furnish* (πρός, acc.), 2 Tim. iii. 17; (2) *to complete*, Ac. xxi. 5.*

ἐξαστράπτω, *to shine*, as lightning; of raiment, Lu. ix. 29. (S.)*

ἐξ-αυτῆς, adv. (sc. ὥρας), *from that very time, instantly*, as Mar. vi. 25 ; Ac. x. 33.

ἐξ-εγείρω, *to raise up*, Ro. ix. 17 ; 1 Cor. vi. 14.*

ἔξ-ειμι (εἶμι, see Gr. § 111, Bu. 50), *to go out*, Ac. xiii. 42, xvii. 15, xx. 7, xxvii. 43.*

ἔξ-ειμι (εἰμί), see ἔξεστι.

ἐξ-ελέγχω, *to convict, to rebuke sternly, to punish*, Ju. 15 (W. H. ἐλέγχω).*

ἐξ-έλκω, *to draw out* from the right way, Ja. i. 14.*

ἐξ-έραμα, ατος, τό, *vomit*, 2 Pet. ii. 22.*

ἐξερευνάω (W. H. -ραυ-), ῶ, *to search diligently*, 1 Pet. i. 10.*

ἐξ-έρχομαι (see Gr. § 103, 2, Wi. p. 33, § 15, Bu. 58), *to go* or *to come out of* (with gen. or ἐκ, ἀπό, ἔξω, παρά) : *to go away, to depart, to issue* or *to spring from ; to go forth ;* of a rumor, *to be divulged* or *spread abroad; to emanate*, as thoughts from the heart, healing power from the Savior; *to go out, i.e.,* vanish, as expiring hope, Ac. xvi. 19.

ἔξ-εστι, part. neut. ἐξόν (impers. from ἔξειμι), *it is lawful*, as Mat. xiv. 4; *it is becoming*, as Ac. xvi. 21 ; *it is possible*, as Mat. xx. 15. The part. is used in the same sense, with or without subst. verb, Mat. xii. 4; 2 Cor. xii. 4 (dat. and inf.).

ἐξ-ετάζω, *to search out, to examine strictly*, Mat. ii. 8, x. 11 ; Jn. xxi. 12.*

ἐξ-ηγέομαι, οῦμαι, dep. mid., *to narrate fully*, as Lu. xxiv. 35; *to declare*, as a teacher, as Jn. i. 18.

ἑξήκοντα, οἱ, αἱ, τά, *sixty*.

ἑξῆς, adv. (ἔχω), *next in order*, only in the phrase τῇ ἑξῆς (sc. ἡμέρᾳ), *on the next day* (ἡμέρᾳ is expressed, Lu. ix. 37).

ἐξ-ηχέω, ῶ, N. T. only in pass., *to be sounded forth, promulgated widely*, 1 Th. i. 8.*

ἕξις, εως, ἡ (ἔχω), *habit, use*, Heb. v. 14.*

ἐξ-ίστημι, -ιστάω and -ιστάνω (see Gr. § 107, Wi. § 14, 1, Bu. 44 sq.), *to displace;* (1) trans., *to astonish*, Lu. xxiv. 22; Ac. viii. 9, 11 ; (2) 2d aor., perf. and mid., intrans., *to be astonished*, Mat. xii. 23 ; *to be insane*, 2 Cor. v. 13.

ἐξ-ισχύω, *to be perfectly able*, Ep. iii. 18.*

ἔξ-οδος, ου, ἡ, *an exit, departure*, Heb. xi. 22 ; *departure*, as from life, Lu. ix. 31 ; 2 Pet. i. 15.*

ἐξ-ολοθρεύω, *to destroy utterly*, Ac. iii. 23. (S.)*

ἐξ-ομολογέω, ῶ, *to confess fully, to make acknowledgment of*, as of sins, etc.; in mid., *to acknowledge benefits conferred, to praise* (with dat.). Once, *to promise*, Lu. xxii. 6. (S.)

ἐξ-ορκίζω, *to adjure, put to oath*, Mat. xxvi. 63.*

ἐξ-ορκιστής, οῦ, ὁ, *an exorcist*, one who expels demons by conjuration, Ac. xix. 13.*

ἐξ-ορύσσω, ξω, *to dig out*, Gal. iv. 15; *to dig through*, Mar. ii. 4.*

ἐξ-ουδενέω=ἐξουθενέω, ῶ (οὐδείς), Mar. ix. 12 (W. H.).*

ἐξ-ουδενόω, ῶ = preceding, Mar. ix. 12 (Rec.).*

ἐξουθενέω, ῶ, *to make of no account, to despise utterly*, Lu. xviii. 9; Gal. iv. 14; perf. pass. part. ἐξουθενημένος, *contemned, despised*, 1 Cor. i. 28, vi. 4. (S.)

ἐξουσία, ας, ἡ (ἔξεστι), (1) *power, ability*, as Jn. xix. 11 ; (2) *liberty, license, privilege, right*, as Ro. ix. 21 ; (3) *commission, authority*, as Mat. xxi. 23; (4) αἱ ἐξουσίαι, *the powers, i.e., rulers, magis-*

trates, Lu. xii. 11 ; *angels*, good and bad, Ep. i. 21, vi. 12. In 1 Cor. xi. 10, ἐξουσίαν, *a sign of the authority of a husband over his wife, i.e., the veil.*

ἐξ-ουσιάζω, *to exercise authority over* (gen.), Lu. xxii. 25 ; 1 Cor. vii. 4; pass., *to be under the power of* (ὑπό), 1 Cor. vi. 12.*

ἐξ-οχή, ῆς, ἡ, *eminence, distinction;* only in the phrase κατ' ἐξοχήν, *by way of distinction*, Ac. xxv. 23 (Gr. § 300β, 5).*

ἐξ-υπνίζω, σω, *to wake from sleep*, Jn. xi. 11. (S.)*

ἔξ-υπνος, ον, *roused out of sleep*, Ac. xvi. 27.*

ἔξω, adv., abs., or as prep. with gen., *without, outside ;* οἱ ἔξω, *those without*, as Mar. iv. 11 ; 1 Cor. v. 12, 13. Used often after verbs of motion compounded with ἐκ.

ἔξωθεν, adv. of place, *from without;* τὸ ἔξωθεν, *the outside*, as Lu. xi. 39; οἱ ἔξωθεν, *those from without*, as 1 Tim. iii. 7; as prep. gen., Mar. vii. 15; Rev. xi. 2.

ἐξ-ωθέω, ῶ, *to drive out, expel*, Ac. vii. 45; *to propel*, as a vessel, Ac. xxvii. 39 (not W. H. text).*

ἐξώτερος, α, ον (comp. of ἔξω), *outer*, in the phrase "outer darkness," Mat. viii. 12, xxii. 13, xxv. 30. (S.)*

ἔοικα, see εἴκω.

ἑορτάζω, *to keep* or *celebrate a feast*, 1 Cor. v. 8.*

ἑορτή, ῆς, ἡ, *a feast, a festival;* used of Jewish feasts, especially of the Passover, as Lu. ii. 41, xxii. 1.

ἐπ-αγγελία, ας, ἡ, (1) *a promise*, as 2 Cor. i. 20; Ac. xxiii. 21, generally plur. ; *the promises*, specially, *e.g.*, to Abraham, or those of the Gospel, as 2 Tim. i. 1 ; (2) met., *the thing promised*, as Ac. ii. 33; Heb. xi. 13, 33, 39.

ἐπ-αγγέλλω, mid. in N. T., except pass., Gal. iii. 19, (1) *to promise*, with dat., or acc. and dat., or inf., once cognate acc., 1 Jn. ii. 25; (2) *to make profession* or *avowal of* (acc.), 1 Tim. ii. 10, vi. 21.

ἐπ-άγγελμα, ατος, τό, a promise,
2 Pet. i. 4, iii. 13.*

ἐπ-άγω, to bring upon, Ac. v.
28; 2 Pet. ii. 1, 5.*

ἐπ-αγωνίζομαι, to contend earnestly for (dat.), Ju. 3.*

ἐπ-αθροίζω, pass., to gather together, Lu. xi. 29.*

Ἐπ-αίνετος, ου, ὁ, Epænetus,
Ro. xvi. 5.*

ἐπ-αινέω, ῶ, ἔσω, 1st aor. ἐπῄ-
νεσα, to commend, to praise,
Lu. xvi. 8; Ro. xv. 11; 1 Cor.
xi. 2, 17, 22.*

ἔπ-αινος, ου, ὁ, commendation,
praise, Ro. ii. 29; Ep. i. 6,
12, 14; Phil. i. 11.

ἐπ-αίρω (see Gr. § 92), to raise
up, as hoisting a sail, Ac.
xxvii. 40; to lift up, as the
eyes, the hands in prayer,
the head in courage, the
heel against, or in opposition; pass., to be lifted up
2 Cor. xi. 20, of the ascen
sion of Christ, Ac. i. 9.

ἐπ-αισχύνομαι, to be ashamed,
abs., 2 Tim. i. 12; to be a-
shamed of (acc. or ἐπί, dat.),
Mar. viii. 38; Ro. vi. 21.

ἐπ-αιτέω, ῶ, to beg, to ask alms,
Lu. xvi. 3, xviii. 35 (W. H.).*

ἐπ-ακολουθέω, ῶ, to follow after
(dat.); fig., 1 Tim. v. 10, 24;
1 Pet. ii. 21; Mar. xvi. 20
(see W. H.).*

ἐπ-ακούω, to hearken to favor-
ably (gen. pers.), 2 Cor. vi.
2.*

ἐπ-ακροάομαι, ῶμαι, to hear,
listen to (gen. pers.), Ac. xvi.
25.*

ἐπάν, conj. (ἐπεὶ ἄν), after, when
(subj.), Mat. ii. 8; Lu. xi. 22,
34.*

ἐπ-άναγκες, adv., necessarily
(with art.), Ac. xv. 28.*

ἐπ-αν-άγω, trans., to put a vessel
out to sea, Lu. v. 3, 4; intrans., to return, Mat. xxi.
18.*

ἐν-ανα-μιμνήσκω, to remind one
again (acc.), Ro. xv. 15.*

ἐπ-ανα-παύομαι, to rest upon
(ἐπί, acc.), Lu. x. 6; to rely,
to trust in (dat.), Ro. ii. 17.
(S.)*

ἐπ-αν-έρχομαι, to come back
again, Lu. x. 35, xix. 15.*

ἐπ-αν-ίστημι, N. T. mid., to rise
up against (ἐπί, acc.), Mat.
x. 21; Mar. xiii. 12.*

ἐπ-αν-όρθωσις, εως, ἡ, correction, reformation, 2 Tim. iii.
16.*

ἐπ-άνω, adv., also used as prep.
gen., above, upon; more than,
in price or number; superior
to, in authority.

ἐπ-άρατος, ον, accursed, Jn. vii.
49 (W. H.).*

ἐπ-αρκέω, ῶ, ἔσω, to aid, to re-
lieve (dat.), 1 Tim. v. 10, 16.*

ἐπ-αρχία, ας, ἡ, a province, a
region subject to a prefect,
Ac. xxiii. 34, xxv. 1.*

ἔπ-αυλις, εως, ἡ, a dwelling, Ac.
i. 20.*

ἐπ-αύριον, adv., on the morrow,
τῇ ἐπαύριον (ἡμέρᾳ), on the
next day, Mar. xi. 12. (S.)

ἐπ-αυτο-φώρῳ = ἐπ᾽ αὐτό-φώρῳ.

Ἐπαφρᾶς, ᾶ, ὁ, Epaphras of
Colossæ, Col. i. 7, iv. 12;
Philem. 23.*

ἐπ-αφρίζω, to foam up or out
(acc.), Ju. 13.*

Ἐπαφρόδιτος, ου, ὁ, Epaphro-
ditus, a Macedonian, Phil. ii.
25, iv. 18.*

ἐπ-εγείρω, to raise up, to excite
against (ἐπί, acc., or κατά,
gen.), Ac. xiii. 50, xiv. 2.*

ἐπεί, conj., (1) of time, after,
only Lu. vii. 1 (W. H. ἐπειδή);
(2) of reason, since, because,
seeing that, Lu. i. 34; Jn. xiii.
29.

ἐπει-δή, conj., since, inasmuch
as, Lu. xi. 6; Phil. ii. 26; of
time, after that, only Lu. vii.
1 (W. H.).

ἐπει-δή-περ, conj., since verily,
forasmuch as, Lu. i. 1.*

ἐπ-εῖδον, see ἐφοράω.

ἔπ-ειμι (εἶμι, Gr. § 111, Bu. 50),
to come after, to follow; only
in part., ἐπιών, οὖσα, όν, following, Ac. vii. 26, xxiii. 11;
τῇ ἐπιούσῃ (sc. ἡμέρᾳ), on the
following day, Ac. xvi. 11,
xx. 15, xxi. 18.*

ἐπεί-περ, conj., since indeed,
Ro. iii. 30 (W. H. εἴπερ).*

ἐπ-εισ-αγωγή, ῆς, ἡ, a bringing
in besides, Heb. vii. 19.*

ἔπ-ειτα, adv., thereupon, there-
after; marking succession of
time, as Gal. i. 18; also of
order, as 1 Cor. xv. 46; 1
Th. iv. 17.

ἐπ-έκεινα (sc. μέρη), adv. with
gen., beyond, Ac. vii. 43.*

ἐπ-εκ-τείνω, in mid., to stretch
forward to (dat.), Phil. iii.
14.*

ἐπενδύτης, ου, ὁ, an upper garment, Jn. xxi. 7.*

ἐπ-εν-δύω, in mid., to put on
over, as an upper garment,
2 Cor. v. 2, 4.*

ἐπ-έρχομαι, to come on, approach,
overtake, impend, Ep. ii. 7;
Ac. viii. 24; to attack, Lu. xi.
22; τὰ ἐπερχόμενα, the things
that are coming on (dat.), Lu.
xxi. 26.

ἐπ-ερωτάω, ῶ, (1) to interrogate,
to question (two accs., or acc.
and περί, gen., or with εἰ,
τίς, etc.), Mat. xii. 10; Lu.
ii. 46; Ac. xxiii. 34; to inquire after God, Ro. x. 20;
(2) to demand of (acc. and
inf.), Mat. xvi. 1.

ἐπ-ερώτημα, ατος, τό, probably
inquiry, or earnest desire, 1
Pet. iii. 21; see R. V.*

ἐπ-έχω, (1) to apply (the mind)
to (dat.), give attention to, Lu.
xiv. 7; Ac. iii. 5; 1 Tim. iv.
16; (2) to hold out, to exhibit,
Phil. ii. 16; (3) to delay, tarry,
Ac. xix. 22.*

ἐπηρεάζω, to insult, to treat
abusively, Mat. v. 44 (not W.
H.); Lu. vi. 28; to accuse
falsely (acc. of charge), 1 Pet.
iii. 16.*

ἐπί, a preposition governing
gen., dat., or acc.; general
signification, upon. For its
various applications, see Gr.
§ 305, Wi. §§ 47g, 48c, 49l,
52, 4, 7), Bu. 336 sq. ἐπί-,
in composition, signifies motion upon, towards, or against;
rest on, over, or at; addition,
succession, repetition, renewal; and it is often intensive.

ἐπι-βαίνω, to go upon a ship, to
mount a horse or ass, to come
to or into a country (ἐπί, acc.,
εἰς, or simple dat.), Mat. xxi.
5; Ac. xx. 18, xxi. 2, 4 (W.
H.), 6 (W. H. ἐμβ-), xxv. 1,
xxvii. 2.*

ἐπι-βάλλω, (1) trans., to cast
upon, as Mar. xi. 7; to put
on, as a patch on a garment,
Lu. v. 36; to lay upon, Lu.
xx. 19; Jn. vii. 30; (2) intrans., to rush upon, Mar. iv
37; to fix the mind steadfastly
on (dat.), Mar. xiv. 72; (3)
part., ἐπιβάλλων, falling to
his share, Lu. xv. 12.

ἐπι-βαρέω, ῶ, to burden; fig., 2

Cor. ii. 5; 1 Th. ii. 9; 2 Th.
iii. 8.*

ἐπι-βιβάζω, to cause to mount,
to place upon, Lu. x. 34, xix.
35; Ac. xxiii. 24.*

ἐπι-βλέπω, to look upon with
favor (with ἐπί), Lu. i. 48,
ix. 38; Ja. ii. 3.*

ἐπί-βλημα, ατος, τό, a patch on
a garment, Mat. ix. 16; Mar.
ii. 21; Lu. v. 36.*

ἐπι-βοάω, ῶ, to cry out, Ac. xxv.
24 (W. H. βοάω).*

ἐπι-βουλή, ῆς, ἡ, a design a-
gainst, a plot, Ac. ix. 24, xx.
3, 19 (plur.), xxiii. 30.*

ἐπι-γαμβρεύω, to marry a de-
ceased brother's wife (acc.),
Mat. xxii. 24. (S.)*

ἐπί-γειος, ον, earthly, belonging
to the earth, 2 Cor. v. 1; Phil.
ii. 10; τὰ ἐπίγεια, earthly
things, Phil. iii. 19.

ἐπι-γίνομαι, to arise, spring up,
as a wind, Ac. xxviii. 13.*

ἐπι-γινώσκω, (1) to know clearly, understand, discern; (2)
to acknowledge; (3) to recognize; (4) to learn (ὅτι), become acquainted with (acc.).

ἐπί-γνωσις, εως, ἡ, accurate
knowledge, Ro. x. 2; Ep. i.
17; Heb. x. 26. Syn.: see
γνῶσις.

ἐπι-γραφή, ῆς, ἡ, an inscription,
a title, as Lu. xx. 24, xxiii. 38.

ἐπι-γράφω, ψω, to inscribe, write
upon, as Mar. xv. 26; Rev.
xxi. 12.

ἐπι-δείκνυμι (see Gr. § 114, Bu.
45), (1) to show, exhibit, Mat.
xxiv. 1; Lu. xvii. 14; (2) to
demonstrate, prove by argument, Ac. xviii. 28; Heb. vi.
17.

ἐπι-δέχομαι, to receive hospitably, 3 Jn. 10; to accept, admit, 3 Jn. 9.*

ἐπι-δημέω, ῶ, to sojourn, as
foreigners in a country, Ac.
ii. 10, xvii. 21.*

ἐπι-δια-τάσσομαι, to ordain besides, Gal. iii. 15. (N. T.)*

ἐπι-δίδωμι, to deliver, to give
up (acc. and dat.), as Mat.
vii. 9; Ac. xv. 30; to give
way to the wind, Ac. xxvii.
15.

ἐπι-δι-ορθόω, to set in order besides, Tit. i. 5.*

ἐπι-δύω, to set, as the sun, Ep.
iv. 26.*

ἐπιείκεια, ας, ἡ, clemency, gen-

tleness, Ac. xxiv. 4; 2 Cor.
x. 1.*

ἐπι-εικής, ές, gentle, mild, Phil.
iv. 5; 1 Tim. iii. 3; Tit. iii.
2; Ja. iii. 17; 1 Pet. ii.
18.*

ἐπι-ζητέω, ῶ, to seek for, search
for, Ac. xii. 19; to desire,
Mat. vi. 32; Ac. xiii. 7; to
demand, Mat. xii. 39, xvi.
4.

ἐπι-θανάτιος, ον, condemned to
death, 1 Cor. iv. 9.*

ἐπί-θεσις, εως, ἡ, a laying on of
hands, Ac. viii. 18; 1 Tim.
iv. 14; 2 Tim. i. 6; Heb. vi.
2.*

ἐπι-θυμέω, ῶ, to long for, to
covet, to lust after, Ja. iv. 2;
Ro. vii. 7; Ac. xx. 33. (On
Lu. xxii. 15, see Gr. § 280b,
Wi. § 54, 3, Bu. 184.)

ἐπι-θυμητής, οῦ, ὁ, an eager de-
sirer of, 1 Cor. x. 6.*

ἐπι-θυμία, ας, ἡ, desire, eagerness for, 1 Th. ii. 17; generally in a bad sense, inordi-
nate desire, lust, cupidity, Ja.
i. 14, 15; 2 Pet. ii. 10.

ἐπι-καθίζω, to sit upon, Mat.
xxi. 7.*

ἐπι-καλέω, ῶ, έσω, to call upon,
to call by name, to invoke in
prayer, Ac. vii. 59 (abs.);
Ro. x. 12, 14 (acc.); mid.,
to appeal to (acc.), Ac. xxv.
11; pass., to be called or sur-
named, Lu. xxii. 3; Ac. xv.
17.

ἐπι-κάλυμμα, ατος, τό, a covering, a cloak, a pretext, 1 Pet.
ii. 16.*

ἐπι-καλύπτω, to cover over, of
sins, i.e., to pardon, Ro. iv.
7 (from S.).*

ἐπι-κατ-άρατος, ον, accursed,
doomed to punishment or destruction, Jn. vii. 49 (W. H.
ἐπάρατος); Gal. iii. 10, 13
(from S.).*

ἐπί-κειμαι, to lie upon (dat.),
Jn. xi. 38, xxi. 9; so to press
upon, as the multitude upon
Christ, Lu. v. 1; as a tempest on a ship, Ac. xxvii. 20;
fig., to be laid on, as necessity,
1 Cor. ix. 16; to be laid or
imposed upon, as by a law,
Heb. ix. 10; to be urgent with
entreaties, Lu. xxiii. 23.*

Ἐπικούρειος, ου, ὁ, an Epicu-
rean, a follower of Epicurus,
Ac. xvii. 18.*

ἐπι-κουρία, ας, ἡ (κοῦρος, help),
help, aid, Ac. xxvi. 22.*

ἐπι-κρίνω, to decree, to give sentence (acc. and inf.), Lu.
xxiii. 24.*

ἐπι-λαμβάνω, N. T. mid., to
take hold of (gen.), in kindness, as Lu. ix. 47; Ac. ix.
27; Heb. ii. 16; to seize, as a
prisoner, Ac. xxi. 30, 33;
met., to lay hold of, so as to
possess, 1 Tim. vi. 12, 19.

ἐπι-λανθάνομαι, dep., to forget,
neglect (inf., gen. or acc.),
Mat. xvi. 5; Heb. vi. 10;
part. perf. pass., ἐπιλελησμέ-
νος, forgotten, Lu. xii. 6.

ἐπι-λέγω, in pass., to be named,
Jn. v. 2; mid., to choose, Ac.
xv. 40.*

ἐπι-λείπω, λείψω, not to suffice,
to fail, Heb. xi. 32.*

ἐπι-λείχω, to lick over, Lu. xvi.
21 (W. H.). (N. T.)*

ἐπι-λησμονή, ῆς, ἡ, forgetfulness, Ja. i. 25; see Gr. § 257.
(Ap.)*

ἐπί-λοιπος, ον, remaining over,
1 Pet. iv. 2.*

ἐπί-λυσις, εως, ἡ, an unloosing,
interpretation, 2 Pet. i. 20.
(See ἴδιος.)*

ἐπι-λύω, to explain, interpret,
Mar. iv. 34; to decide, as a de-
bated question, Ac. xix. 39.*

ἐπι-μαρτυρέω, ῶ, to testify earnestly, 1 Pet. v. 12.*

ἐπι-μέλεια, ας, ἡ, care, attention,
Ac. xxvii. 3.*

ἐπι-μέλομαι and έομαι, οῦμαι,
fut. ήσομαι, to take care of
(gen.), Lu. x. 34, 35; 1 Tim
iii. 5.*

ἐπι-μελῶς, adv., carefully, dili
gently, Lu. xv. 8.*

ἐπι-μένω, μενῶ, (1) to remain.
continue, 1 Cor. xvi. 8; Gal.
i. 18; (2) met., to be constant,
to persevere (dat.), Ro. vi. 1;
1 Tim. iv. 16.

ἐπι-νεύω, to nod to, to assent,
Ac. xviii. 20.*

ἐπί-νοια, ας, ἡ, thought, purpose,
Ac. viii. 22.*

ἐπι-ορκέω, ῶ, ήσω, to swear
falsely, Mat. v. 33.*

ἐπί-ορκος, ον, perjured, 1 Tim.
i. 10.*

ἐπιούσιος, ον, probably from
ἐπιοῦσα (ἔπειμι), for the morrow, i.e., necessary or sufficient, Mat. vi. 11; Lu. xi. 3.
(N. T.)*

ἐπι-πίπτω, *to fall upon* (ἐπί, acc.), *rush upon*, Mar. iii. 10 (dat.); fig., *to come upon* (dat., or ἐπί, acc. or dat.), as an emotion, etc., Lu. i. 12; Ac. viii. 16.

ἐπι-πλήσσω, *to rebuke, to chide*, 1 Tim. v. 1.*

ἐπι-ποθέω, ῶ, *to desire earnestly, to long for* or *after* (inf. or acc.), as 2 Cor v. 2; *to lust*, abs., Ja. iv. 5.

ἐπι-πόθησις, εως, ἡ, *longing*, 2 Cor. vii. 7, 11. (N. T.)*

ἐπι-πόθητος, ον, *longed for*, Phil. iv. 1. (N. T.)*

ἐπι-ποθία, ας, ἡ, like ἐπιπόθησις, *longing*, Ro. xv. 23. (N. T.)*

ἐπι-πορεύομαι, dep., mid., *to journey to* (πρός), Lu. viii. 4.*

ἐπι-ρράπτω, *to sew to*, or *upon*, Mar. ii. 21 (ἐπί, dat.). (N. T.)*

ἐπι-ρρίπτω, *to cast*, or *throw upon*, Lu. xix. 35; of care *cast upon* God, 1 Pet. v. 7 (ἐπί, acc.).*

ἐπί-σημος, ον, *remarkable, distinguished*, in either a bad or good sense, Mat. xxvii. 16; Ro. xvi. 7.*

ἐπι-σιτισμός, οῦ, ὁ, *food, provisions*, Lu. ix. 12.*

ἐπι-σκέπτομαι, σκέψομαι, dep., *to look upon, to visit*, as Ac. vii. 23; Mat. xxv. 36, 43; of God, Ac. xv. 14; *to look out, to select*, Ac. vi. 3.

ἐπι-σκευάζομαι, see ἀποσκ-.

ἐπι-σκηνόω, ῶ, *to fix a tent upon, to dwell*, or *remain on* (ἐπί, acc.), 2 Cor. xii. 9.*

ἐπι-σκιάζω, άσω, *to overshadow* (acc. or dat.), Mat. xvii. 5; Mar. ix. 7; Lu. i. 35, ix. 34; Ac. v. 15.*

ἐπι-σκοπέω, ῶ, to act as ἐπίσκοπος, *to oversee, to care for*, 1 Pet. v. 2 (W. H. omit); μή, *lest*, Heb. xii. 15.*

ἐπι-σκοπή, ῆς, ἡ, (1) *visitation* for kind and gracious purposes, Lu. xix. 44; 1 Pet. ii. 12; (2) *office, charge*, Ac. i. 20 (from S.); (3) *the office of a bishop*, 1 Tim. iii. 1. (S.)*

ἐπί-σκοπος, ον, ὁ, (1) *one who inspects*, or *superintends*, of Christ, 1 Pet. ii. 25; (2) *an overseer of a church*, bishop, Ac. xx. 28; Phil. i. 1; 1 Tim. iii. 2; Tit. i. 7.*

ἐπι-σπάω, ῶ, *to become uncircumcised*, 1 Cor. vii. 18.*

ἐπι-σπείρω, *to sow in addition*, Mat. xiii. 25 (W. H.).*

ἐπί-ίσταμαι, dep., *to know well, to understand* (acc.), *to know*, with ὅτι, ὡς, etc.

ἐπί-στασις, εως, ἡ (W. H.), *approach, onset*, Ac. xxiv. 12; 2 Cor. xi. 28.*

ἐπι-στάτης, ου, ὁ, *superintendent, master;* only in Lu., in voc., ἐπιστάτα, addressed to Jesus, *Master*, v. 5, viii. 24, 45, ix. 33, 49, xvii. 13.*

ἐπι-στέλλω, *to send by letter to, to write*, Ac. xv. 20, xxi. 25 (W. H. ἀποστ-); Heb. xiii. 22.*

ἐπι-στήμων, ον, *skillful, experienced*, Ja. iii. 13.*

ἐπι-στηρίζω, *to establish besides, confirm*, Ac. xiv. 22, xv. 32, 41, xviii. 23 (not W. H.).*

ἐπι-στολή, ῆς, ἡ, *an epistle, a letter*, Ac. xv. 30; 2 Cor. x. 10.

ἐπι-στομίζω, *to stop the mouth of*, Tit. i. 11.*

ἐπι-στρέφω, ψω, (1) trans., *to cause to turn* (acc. and ἐπί), as to God, or to the worship of God, Ac. ix. 35; (2) intrans., *to return, to turn back*, either to good or evil, Ac. xxvi. 18; 2 Pet. ii. 21; *to return upon*, as a refused salutation, Mat. x. 13 (ἐπί, εἰς, πρός).

ἐπι-στροφή, ῆς, ἡ, *a turning, conversion*, Ac. xv. 3.*

ἐπι-συν-άγω, ξω, *to gather together*, into one place, as Mat. xxiii. 37.

ἐπι-συν-αγωγή, ῆς, ἡ, *a gathering together*, in one place, 2 Th. ii. 1; Heb. x. 25. (Ap.)*

ἐπι-συν-τρέχω, *to run together besides*, Mar. ix. 25. (N. T.)*

ἐπι-σύ-στασις, εως, ἡ (W. H. ἐπίστασις), (1) *a seditious concourse*, Ac. xxiv. 12; (2) *a troublesome throng*, 2 Cor. xi. 28. (S.)*

ἐπι-σφαλής, ές, *likely to fall, dangerous*, Ac. xxvii. 9.*

ἐπι-ισχύω, *to be more urgent*, Lu. xxiii. 5.*

ἐπι-σωρεύω, εύσω, *to heap up, to obtain a multitude of*, 2 Tim. iv. 3.*

ἐπι-ταγή, ῆς, ἡ, *a command, an injunction*, 2 Cor. viii. 8; Tit. ii. 15.

ἐπι-τάσσω, ξω, *to command* (abs.), Lu. xiv. 22; *enjoin upon* (dat. of pers., thing in acc. or inf.), Mar. ix. 25.

ἐπι-τελέω, ῶ, έσω, *to bring to an end, to perform*, as a service, Heb. ix. 6; mid., *to come to an end, to leave off*, Gal. iii. 3; pass., of sufferings, *to be imposed upon*, 1 Pet. v. 9.

ἐπιτήδειος, a, ον, *fit, needful*, Ja. ii. 16.*

ἐπι-τίθημι, θήσω, *to put, place*, or *lay upon* (with acc. and dat., or ἐπί, acc. or gen.), as the hands (to heal), as stripes, etc.; of gifts, *to load with*, Ac. xxviii. 10; mid., *to rush upon in hostility, to oppose*, Ac. xviii. 10.

ἐπι-τιμάω, ῶ, *to rebuke* (dat.), Lu. xvii. 3; *to admonish* (ἵνα), Mat. xii. 16.

ἐπι-τιμία, ας, ἡ, *punishment*, 2 Cor. ii. 6.*

ἐπι-τρέπω, *to allow, permit*, Mat. viii. 21; Heb. vi. 3.

ἐπι-τροπή, ῆς, ἡ, *commission, full power*, Ac. xxvi. 12.*

ἐπί-τροπος, ον, ὁ, *one who is intrusted with;* (1) *a steward*, Mat. xx. 8; Lu. viii. 3; (2) *a tutor*, Gal. iv. 2.*

ἐπι-τυγχάνω, *to attain, acquire*, (gen. or acc.), Ro. xi. 7; Heb. vi. 15, xi. 33; Ja. iv. 2.*

ἐπι-φαίνω, 1st aor. inf. ἐπιφᾶναι, 2d aor. pass. ἐπεφάνην, (1) *to appear*, as stars, Ac. xxvii. 20; (2) *to shine upon* (dat.), Lu. i. 79; (3) met., *to be clearly known*, Tit. ii. 11, iii. 4.*

ἐπιφάνεια, ας, ἡ, *appearance, the advent* of Christ, past and future, 1 Tim. vi. 14; 2 Tim. i. 10, iv. 1, 8; Tit. ii. 13; *manifestation*, 2 Th. ii. 8.* *Syn.:* see ἀποκάλυψις.

ἐπιφανής, ές, *glorious, illustrious*, Ac. ii. 20.*

ἐπι-φαύω, or -φαύσκω, fut. σω, *to shine upon, give light to* (dat.), Ep. v. 14. (S.)*

ἐπι-φέρω (see Gr. § 103, 6), *to bring to* (ἐπί, acc.), Ac. xix. 12 (not W. H.); *to superadd*, Phil. i. 16; *to bring upon, inflict*, as punishment, Ro. iii. 5; *to bring against*, as an accusation, Ac. xxv. 18 (not W. H.); Ju. 9.*

ἐπι-φωνέω, ῶ, to cry out, to shout, Lu. xxiii. 21; Ac. xii. 22, xxi. 34, xxii. 24 (W. H.).*

ἐπι-φώσκω, to grow light, to dawn, Mat. xxviii. 1; Lu. xxiii. 54.*

ἐπι-χειρέω, ῶ, to take in hand, undertake, Lu. i. 1; Ac. ix. 29, xix. 13.*

ἐπι-χέω, to pour upon, Lu. x. 34.*

ἐπι-χορηγέω, ῶ, to supply, 2 Pet. i. 5; 2 Cor. ix. 10; Gal. iii. 5; pass., to be furnished or supplied, Col. ii. 19; 2 Pet. i. 11.*

ἐπι-χορηγία, ας, ἡ, a supply, Phil. i. 19; Ep. iv. 16. (N. T.)*

ἐπι-χρίω, to spread on, anoint (ἐπί, acc.), Jn. ix. 6 (not W. H.), 11.*

ἐπ-οικοδομέω, ῶ, to build upon (ἐπί, acc. or dat.), fig., 1 Cor. iii. 10–14; Ep. ii. 20; to build up, edify, Ac. xx. 32 (not W. H.); Col. ii. 7; Ju. 20.*

ἐπ-οκέλλω, to force forward, to run (a ship) aground, Ac. xxvii. 41 (ἐπικέλλω, W. H.).*

ἐπ-ονομάζω, to name, or call by a name of honor, pass. only, Ro. ii. 17.*

ἐπ-οπτεύω, to look upon, view attentively, 1 Pet. ii. 12, iii. 2.*

ἐπ-όπτης, ου, ὁ, an eye-witness, 2 Pet. i. 16.*

ἔπος, ους, τό, a word; ὡς ἔπος εἰπεῖν, so to speak, Heb. vii. 9.*

ἐπ-ουράνιος, ον, heavenly, celestial, of God, Mat. xviii. 35 (W. H. οὐράνιος); of intelligent beings, Phil.ii.10; of the starry bodies, 1 Cor. xv. 40; so of kingdom, country, etc.; neut. plur., τὰ ἐπουράνια, heavenly things, or places, Jn. iii. 12; Ep. i. 3, 20, ii. 6, iii. 10; Heb. viii. 5, ix. 23.

ἐπτά, οἱ, αἱ, τά, card. num., seven, Lu. ii. 36; Ac. vi. 3; often symbol. in Revelation; οἱ ἐπτά, the seven deacons, Ac. xxi. 8.

ἐπτάκις, num. adv., seven times, Mat. xviii. 21, 22; Lu. xvii. 4.*

ἐπτακισ-χίλιοι, αι, α, card. num., seven thousand, Ro. xi. 4.*

ἔπω, see εἶπον.

Ἔραστος, ου, ὁ, Erastus, (1) Ac. xix. 22; (2) Ro. xvi. 23. Which is meant in 2 Tim. iv. 20 is uncertain.*

ἐργάζομαι, σομαι, dep., perf. in pass. sense, εἴργασμαι; (1) abs., to work, to trade, Lu.xiii. 14; Mat. xxv. 16; (2) to perform, do, Col. iii. 23; Jn. vi. 28; (3) to practice, as virtues, to commit, as sin, Ac. x. 35; Ja. ii. 9; (4) to acquire by labor, Jn. vi. 27.

ἐργασία, ας, ἡ, (1) a working, performing, Ep. iv. 9; (2) effort, diligent labor, Lu. xii. 58; (3) work, gain by work, Ac. xvi. 16, 19; Ac. xix. 24; (4) occupation, business, Ac. xix. 25.*

ἐργάτης, ου, ὁ, a worker, laborer, Mat. ix. 37; applied to workers in the church, 2 Tim. ii. 15; a doer, of iniquity, Lu. xiii. 27.

ἔργον, ου, τό, work, employment, Mat. xiii. 34; Jn. xvii. 4; 1 Cor. xv. 58; anything accomplished, Ac. vii. 41; Heb. i. 10; an act, deed, in various senses, Jn. ix. 3; Rev. ii. 6; Ja. ii. 14; 1 Pet. i. 17.

ἐρεθίζω, to stimulate, to provoke, 2 Cor. ix. 2; Col. iii. 21.*

ἐρείδω, σω, to stick fast, Ac. xxvii. 41.*

ἐρεύγομαι, ξομαι, to utter, Mat. xiii. 35.*

ἐρευνάω, ῶ, ήσω (W. H. ἐραυνάω), to search diligently, Jn. v. 39; Ro. viii. 27; Rev. ii. 23.

ἐρέω, obsolete, see φημί and εἶπον.

ἐρημία, ας, ἡ, a solitude, a wilderness, Mat. xv. 33; Mar. viii. 4; Heb. xi. 38; 2 Cor. xi. 26.*

ἔρημος, ον, deserted, desolate, waste, Ac. i. 20; Gal. iv. 27; used in the fem., as a subst., for a wilderness, Lu. i. 80· ἔρημος τῆς Ἰουδαίας, the wilderness of Judæa, the tract west of the Dead Sea, Mat. iii. 1; ἡ ἔρημος, the wilderness in which the Israelites wandered, Ac. vii. 30, 36, 38.

ἐρημόω, ῶ, to make desolate, Mat. xii. 25; Lu. xi. 17; to

reduce to naught, Rev. xvii. 16, xviii. 17, 19.*

ἐρήμωσις, εως, ἡ, desolation, Mat. xxiv. 15; Lu. xxi. 20; Mar. xiii. 14. (S.)*

ἐρίζω, ίσω (ἔρις), to contend, dispute, Mat. xii. 19.*

ἐριθεία, ας, ἡ (W. H. ἐριθία), self-seeking, a partisan and factious spirit, Ro. ii. 8; Phil. i. 16, ii. 3; Ja. iii. 14, 16; plur. in 2 Cor. xii. 20; Gal. v. 20.*

ἔριον, ου, τό, wool, Heb. ix. 19; Rev. i. 14.*

ἔρις, ιδος, ἡ, contention, strife, Ro. i. 29; Gal. v. 20.

ἐρίφιον, ου, τό, and **ἔριφος, ου, ὁ,** a goat, kid, Mat. xxv. 32, 33; Lu. xv. 29.*

Ἑρμᾶς, ᾶ, ὁ, Doric for Ἑρμῆς, Hermas, Ro. xvi. 14.*

ἑρμηνεία, ας, ἡ, interpretation 1 Cor. xii. 10, xiv. 26.*

ἑρμηνεύω, to interpret, translate, Jn. i. 38 (not W. H.), 42, ix. 7; Heb. vii. 2.*

Ἑρμῆς, οῦ, ὁ, (1) the Greek deity Hermes (in Latin, Mercury), Ac. xiv. 12; (2) Hermes, Ro. xvi. 14.*

Ἑρμογένης, ους, ὁ, Hermogenes, 2 Tim. i. 15.*

ἑρπετόν, οῦ, τό, a creeping creature, a reptile, Ac. x. 12, xi. 6; Ro. i. 23; Ja. iii. 7.

ἐρυθρός, ά, όν, red; ἡ ἐρυθρὰ θάλασσα, the Red Sea, Ac. vii. 36; Heb. xi. 29.*

ἔρχομαι, ἐλεύσομαι (see Gr. § 103, 2, Wi. § 15, Bu. 58), to come, to go, of persons or of things; ὁ ἐρχόμενος, the coming one, i.e., the Messiah, Mat. xi. 3; Heb. x. 37; Rev. i. 4, 8, iv. 8; to come, after, before, to, against, etc., as determined by the preposition which follows; to come forth, as from the grave, 1 Cor. xv. 35; to come back, as the prodigal, Lu. xv. 30.

ἐρωτάω, ῶ, ήσω, to question, Mat. xxi. 24; to ask, to beseech, Lu. vii. 36; Phil. iv. 3. Syn.: see αἰτέω.

ἐσθής, ῆτος, ἡ (ἔννυμι, 1st aor. ἕσθην), clothing, raiment, Lu. xxiii. 11; Ac. xii. 21.

ἔσθησις, εως, ἡ, clothing, Lu. xxiv. 4 (ἐσθής, W. H.).*

ἐσθίω, 2d aor. ἔφαγον (see Gr. § 103, 3, Wi. § 15, Bu. 58) to eat, to partake of food, used abs. or with acc. of food, or ἐκ, a word like some being understood; with μετά, gen., to eat with; with dat. (as Ro. xiv. 6), to eat to the honor of; met., to devour, to consume, as rust does, Ja. v. 3; or fire, Heb. x. 27.

ϑω (W. H.) = ἐσθίω, Mar. i. 6; Lu. xxii. 30.

Ἐσλί (W. H. -εί), ὁ, Esli, Lu. iii. 25.*

ἔσ-οπτρον, ου, τό, a mirror (of polished metal), Ja. i. 23; 1 Cor. xiii. 12.*

ἑσπέρα, ας, ἡ (prop. adj. with ὥρα), evening, Lu. xxiv. 29; Ac. iv. 3, xxviii. 23.*

Ἐσρώμ, ὁ, Esrom, Mat. i. 3; Lu. iii. 33.*

ἔσχατος, η, ον, (1) the last, remotest, in situation, dignity, or time, τὸ ἔσχατον, τὰ ἔσχατα, as subst., the extremity, last state; (2) used predicatively as an adverb, Mar. xii. 6, 22; absolutely, 1 Cor. xv. 8; (3) the end of what is spoken of, e.g., the feast, Jn. vii. 37; the world, Jn. vi. 39, 40; (4) spec. of the Christian dispensation as the last, or latter (days), Heb. i. 2; (5) the last (day), i.e., the day of judgment; (6) the phrase ὁ πρῶτος καὶ ὁ ἔσχατος, Rev. i. 11, 17, ii. 8, the first and the last, describes the eternity of God.

ἐσχάτως, adv., extremely, ἐσχάτως ἔχει, is at the last extremity, Mar. v. 23.*

ἔσω, adv. of place, within, abs., Mat. xxvi. 58; with gen., Mar. xv. 16; with an article preced., the inner, Ro. vii. 22; οἱ ἔσω, those within the Christian fold, opp. to οἱ ἔξω, 1 Cor. v. 12.

ἔσωθεν, adv. of place, from within, within, Lu. xi. 7; Rev. iv. 8; τὸ ἔσωθεν, the interior, i.e., the mind or soul, Lu. xi. 39.

ἐσώτερος, α, ον (comp. of ἔσω), inner, Ac. xvi. 24; Heb. vi. 19.*

ἑταῖρος, ου, ὁ, a companion, comrade, Mat. xi. 16 (ἕτερος, W. H.); ἑταῖρε, voc., friend, Mat. xx. 13, xxii. 12, xxvi. 50.*

ἑτερό-γλωσσος, ου, ὁ, one of another tongue or language, 1 Cor. xiv. 21.*

ἑτερο-διδασκαλέω, ῶ, to teach a different doctrine, 1 Tim. i. 3, vi. 3. (N. T.)*

ἑτερο-ζυγέω, ῶ, to be unequally yoked, fig., 2 Cor. vi. 14. (N. T.)*

ἕτερος, α, ον, other, another; indefinitely, any other; definitely, the other; diverse, different from. Syn.: see ἄλλος.

ἑτέρως, adv., otherwise, differently, Phil. iii. 15.*

ἔτι, adv., yet, still, even, Lu. i. 15; also, Heb. xi. 36; implying accession or addition, besides.

ἑτοιμάζω, άσω, to prepare, make ready, Lu. xii. 47; Rev. xix. 7.

ἑτοιμασία, ας, ἡ, preparation, readiness, Ep. vi. 15.*

ἕτοιμος, η, ον, and -ος, ον, prepared, ready, of things or persons, Mat. xxii. 4, 8; Lu. xii. 40; ἐν ἑτοίμῳ ἔχειν, to be in readiness, 2 Cor. x. 6.

ἑτοίμως, adv., readily, in readiness, usually with ἔχω, Ac. xxi. 13; 2 Cor. xii. 14; 1 Pet. iv. 5.*

ἔτος, ους, τό, a year, Lu. iv. 25; κατ᾽ ἔτος, yearly, Lu. ii. 41.

εὖ, adv. (old neuter from εὖς), well, Ep. vi. 3; εὖ ποιεῖν (acc.), Mar. xiv. 7, to do good to; εὖ πράσσειν, to fare well, to prosper, Ac. xv. 29; used in commendation, well! well done! Mat. xxv. 21, 23; Lu. xix. 17.*

Εὖα, ας, ἡ, Eve, 2 Cor. xi. 3; 1 Tim. ii. 13.*

εὐ-αγγελίζω, σω, εὐηγγέλισα, εὐηγγέλισμαι, (1) act., to bring glad tidings to (acc. or dat.), Rev. x. 7, xiv. 6; (2) mid., to announce, to publish (acc. of message), to announce the gospel (abs.), to preach to, evangelize (acc. pers.); pass., to be announced, to have glad tidings announced to one. See Mat. xi. 5; Heb. iv. 2.

εὐαγγέλιον, ου, τό, good tidings, the gospel, Mar. i. 15; Ac. xv. 7; Ep. i. 13.

εὐαγγελιστής, οῦ, ὁ, a messenger of good tidings, an evangelist, Ac. xxi. 8; Ep. iv. 11; 2 Tim. iv. 5. (N. T.)*

εὐ-αρεστέω, ῶ, to be well-pleasing to (dat.), Heb. xi. 5, 6; pass., to be pleased with, Heb. xiii. 16.*

εὐ-άρεστος, ον, acceptable, well-pleasing, Ro. xii. 12. (Ap.)

εὐαρέστως, adv., acceptably, Heb. xii. 28.*

Εὔβουλος, ου, ὁ, Eubulus, 2 Tim. iv. 21.*

εὖ-γε, well done! Lu. xix. 17 (W. H.).*

εὐγενής, ές, well-born, noble, noble-minded, Lu. xix. 12; Ac. xvii. 11; 1 Cor. i. 26.*

εὐδία, ας, ἡ (from εὖ and Ζεύς, gen. Διός), fair weather, Mat. xvi. 2.*

εὐ-δοκέω, ῶ, ἥσω, εὐδόκησα and ηὐδόκησα, to think it good, decide, Lu. xii. 32; 1 Th. iii. 1; to be well pleased with, Mat. xvii. 5; 2 Pet. i. 17.

εὐδοκία, ας, ἡ, pleasure, good-will, Phil. ii. 13; 2 Th. i. 11; Mat. xi. 26.

εὐεργεσία, ας, ἡ, a good deed to (gen.), a benefit, Ac. iv. 9; 1 Tim. vi. 2.*

εὐεργετέω, ῶ, to do good, to bestow benefits, Ac. x. 38.*

εὐ-εργέτης, ου, ὁ, a benefactor, Lu. xxii. 25.*

εὔ-θετος, ον, well-placed, fit, useful, Lu. ix. 62, xiv. 35; Heb. vi. 7.*

εὐθέως, adv., immediately, soon, Mat. iv. 20; Gal. i. 16; 3 Jn. 14.

εὐθυ-δρομέω, ῶ, to run in a straight course, Ac. xvi. 11, xxi. 1.*

εὐ-θυμέω, ῶ, to be cheerful, Ac. xxvii. 22, 25; Ja. v. 13.*

εὔ-θυμος, ον, cheerful, having good courage, Ac. xxiv. 10 (Rec.), xxvii. 36.*

εὐθύμως, cheerfully, Ac. xxiv. 10 (W. H.).*

εὐθύνω, to make straight, Jn. i. 23; to guide, to steer, as a ship, Ja. iii. 4.*

εὐθύς, εῖα, ύ, straight; met., right, true; also adv., of time, straight, i.e., immediately, forthwith, as εὐθέως (W. H. often εὐθύς for Rec. εὐθέως).

εὐθύτης, τητος, ἡ, rectitude, uprightness, Heb. i. 8 (from S.).*

εὐ-καιρέω, ῶ, to have leisure or opportunity, Mar. vi. 31; Ac. xvii. 21; 1 Cor. xvi. 12.*

εὐκαιρία, as, ἡ, convenient time, opportunity, Mat. xxvi. 16; Lu. xxii. 6.*

εὔκαιρος, ον, well-timed, opportune, Mar. vi. 21; Heb. iv. 16.*

εὐκαίρως, adv., opportunely, Mar. xiv. 11; opposed to ἀκαίρως, 2 Tim. iv. 2.*

εὔκοπος, ον, easy, neut. comp. only, εὐκοπώτερον, easier, as Mat. ix. 5. (N. T.)

εὐ-λάβεια, as, ἡ, reverence, fear of God, piety, Heb. v. 7, xii. 28.* Syn.: see δειλία.

εὐ-λαβέομαι, οῦμαι, dep. pass., to fear, Ac. xxiii. 10 (W. H. φοβέω); with μή, to take precaution, Heb. xi. 7.*

εὐ-λαβής, ές, cautious, God-fearing, religious, Lu. ii. 25; Ac. ii. 5, viii. 2, xxii. 12 (W. H.).* Syn.: see δεισιδαίμων.

εὐ-λογέω, ῶ, ήσω, to praise, i.e., God, Lu. i. 64; to invoke blessings on, i.e., men, Ro. xii. 14; to bless or to ask blessing on, i.e., food, Lu. ix. 16; so of the Lord's Supper, Mat. xxvi. 26; 1 Cor. x. 16; used of what God does, to bless, to cause to prosper, Ac. iii. 26; hence, perf. pass. part. εὐλογημένος, blessed, favored of God, Mat. xxv. 34.

εὐλογητός, όν (verbal adj. from preced.), worthy of praise, of blessing, used only of God, Mar. xiv. 61; Lu. i. 68; Ro. i. 25, ix. 5; 2 Cor. i. 3, xi. 31; Ep. i. 3; 1 Pet. i. 3. (S.)*

εὐ-λογία, as, ἡ, adulation, flattery, Ro. xvi. 18; blessing, praise, to God, Rev. vii. 12; an invocation of blessings, benediction, Heb. xii. 17; blessing, benefit, 2 Cor. ix. 5; 1 Pet. iii. 9.

εὐ-μετά-δοτος, ον, ready to give, liberal, 1 Tim. vi. 18. (N.T.)*

Εὐνίκη, ης, ἡ, Eunice, 2 Tim. i. 5.*

εὐ-νοέω, ῶ, to be well disposed to, Mat. v. 25.*

εὔ-νοια, as, ἡ, good-will, 1 Cor. vii. 3 (not W. H.); Ep. vi. 7.*

εὐνουχίζω, σω, εὐνουχίσθην, to emasculate, make a eunuch, pass., Mat. xix. 12.*

εὐνοῦχος, ου, ὁ, a eunuch, Mat. xix. 12; Ac. viii. 27-39.*

Εὐοδία, as, ἡ, Euodia, Phil. iv. 2.*

εὐ-οδόω, ῶ, in N. T. pass. only, to be led in a good way, to prosper, Ro. i. 10; 1 Cor. xvi. 2; 3 Jn. 2.*

εὐ-πάρεδρος, ον, see εὐπρόσεδρος. (N. T.)

εὐ-πειθής, ές, easily obeying, compliant, Ja. iii. 17.*

εὐ-περί-στατος, ον, skillfully surrounding, i.e., besetting, Heb. xii. 1.*

εὐ-ποιΐα, as, ἡ, well-doing, beneficence, Heb. xiii. 16.*

εὐ-πορέω, ῶ, mid., to have means, to be prosperous, Ac. xi. 29.*

εὐ-πορία, as, ἡ, wealth, Ac. xix. 25.*

εὐ-πρέπεια, as, ἡ, beauty, gracefulness, Ja. i. 11.*

εὐ-πρόσ-δεκτος, ον, acceptable, Ro. xv. 16, 31; 2 Cor. vi. 2, viii. 12; 1 Pet. ii. 5.*

εὐ-πρόσ-εδρος, ον, assiduous, constantly attending on, 1 Cor. vii. 35 (εὐπάρεδρος, W. H.). (N. T.)*

εὐ-προσωπέω, ῶ, to make a fair appearance, Gal. vi. 12. (N. T.)*

εὐρ-ακύλων, ωνος, ὁ, the Euraquilo, a N.E. wind, Ac. xxvii. 14 (W. H.). (N. T.)*

εὑρίσκω, εὑρήσω, εὕρηκα, εὗρον, εὑρέθην, (1) to find, to discover, Lu. ii. 45; (2) to ascertain, to find by computation, or by examination, as a judge, Ac. xiii. 28; (3) to obtain, Heb. ix. 12; (4) to contrive, find out how, Lu. xix. 48.

εὐρο-κλύδων, ωνος, ὁ (from εὖρος, the S.E. wind, and κλύδων, wave), Euroclydon, a stormy wind, a hurricane, Ac. xxvii. 14. (N. T.)*

εὐρύ-χωρος, ον, broad, spacious, Mat. vii. 13.*

εὐσέβεια, as, ἡ, piety, godliness, Ac. iii. 12; 2 Tim. iii. 5.

εὐσεβέω, ῶ, to show piety, to worship, Ac. xvii. 23; 1 Tim. v. 4.*

εὐ-σεβής, ές, religious, pious, Ac. x. 2, 7, xxii. 12 (W. H. εὐλαβής); 2 Pet. ii. 9.* Syn.: see δεισιδαίμων.

εὐσεβῶς, adv., piously, religiously, 2 Tim. iii. 12; Tit. ii. 12.*

εὔ-σημος, ον, distinct, intelligible, 1 Cor. xiv. 9.*

εὔ-σπλαγχνος, ον, full of pity,

tender-hearted, Ep. iv. 32; 1 Pet. iii. 8.*

εὐ-σχημόνως, adv., in a seemly manner, decently, Ro. xiii. 13; 1 Cor. xiv. 40; 1 Th. iv. 12.*

εὐ-σχημοσύνη, ης, ἡ, decorum, becomingness, 1 Cor. ii. 23.*

εὐ-σχήμων, ον, reputable, decorous, Mar. xv. 43; Ac. xiii. 50, xvii. 12; τὸ εὐσχήμον, seemliness, 1 Cor. vii. 35, xii. 24.*

εὐ-τόνως, adv., vehemently, forcibly, Lu. xxiii. 10; Ac. xviii. 28.*

εὐ-τραπελία, as, ἡ, low jesting, ribaldry, Ep. v. 4.*

Εὔτυχος, ου, ὁ, Eutychus, Ac. xx. 9.*

εὐ-φημία, as, ἡ, commendation, good report, 2 Cor. vi. 8.*

εὔ-φημος, ον, sounding well, spoken in a kindly spirit, Phil. iv. 8.*

εὐ-φορέω, ῶ, to bear plentifully, Lu. xii. 16.*

εὐ-φραίνω, νῶ, εὐφράνθην and ηὐφράνθην, act., to make glad, 2 Cor. ii. 2; pass., to be glad, to rejoice, Lu. xii. 19; Ac. ii. 26; Rev. xviii. 20.

Εὐφράτης, ου, ὁ, the Euphrates, Rev. ix. 14, xvi. 12.*

εὐφροσύνη, ης, ἡ, joy, gladness, Ac. ii. 28, xiv. 17.*

εὐ-χαριστέω, ῶ, to thank, give thanks, Ac. xxvii. 35; Ro. i. 8.

εὐχαριστία, as, ἡ, gratitude, thanksgiving, as 2 Cor. ix. 11, 12. Syn.: see αἴτημα.

εὐ-χάριστος, ον, thankful, grateful, Col. iii. 15.*

εὐχή, ῆς, ἡ, (1) prayer, Ja. v. 15; (2) a vow, Ac. xviii. 18, xxi. 23.* Syn.: see αἴτημα.

εὔχομαι, to pray, Ac. xxvi. 29; 2 Cor. xiii. 7; Ja. v. 16 (for with ὑπέρ or περί, gen.); to wish, Ac. xxvii. 29; Ro. ix. 3; 2 Cor. xiii. 9; 3 Jn. 2.*

εὔ-χρηστος, ον, useful, 2 Tim. ii. 21, iv. 11; Philem. 11.*

εὐ-ψυχέω, ῶ, to be in good spirits, to be cheerful, Phil. ii. 19.*

εὐ-ωδία, as, ἡ, fragrance, good odor, 2 Cor. ii. 15; Ep. v. 2; Phil. iv. 18.*

εὐώνυμος, ον, left, hand, Ac. xxi. 3; foot, Rev. x. 2; ἐξ εὐωνύμων (neut. plur.), on the left, Mat. xx. 21, 23.

43

4

ἐφ-άλλομαι, *to leap upon*, ἐπί, acc., Ac. xix. 16.*

ἐφ-άπαξ, adv., *once for all*, Ro. vi. 10; Heb. vii. 27, ix. 12, x. 10; *at once*, 1 Cor. xv. 6.*

Ἐφεσῖνος, η, ον, *Ephesian, i.e.*, church, Rev. ii. 1 (not W. H.).*

Ἐφέσιος, α, ον, *Ephesian, belonging to Ephesus*, Ac. xix. 28, 34, 35, xxi. 29.*

Ἔφεσος, ου, ἡ, *Ephesus*, Ac. xviii. 19, 21, 24.

ἐφ-ευρετής, οῦ, ὁ, *an inventor, contriver*, Ro. i. 30.*

ἐφ-ημερία, ας, ἡ, *a course*, a division of priests for interchange of service, Lu. i. 5, 8. (S.)*

ἐφ-ήμερος, ον, *daily*, Ja. ii. 15.*

ἐφ-ικνέομαι, dep., 2d aor. inf. ἐφικέσθαι, *to come to, reach*, ἄχρι or εἰς, 2 Cor. x. 13, 14.*

ἐφ-ίστημι, 2d aor. ἐπέστην; perf. part. ἐφεστώς; always intrans. or mid. in N. T., (1) *to stand by*, Lu. ii. 38; Ac. xii. 7; (2) *to be urgent*, 2 Tim. iv. 2; (3) *to befall one*, as evil, Lu. xxi. 34; (4) *to be at hand, to impend*, 2 Tim. iv. 6.

ἐφνίδιος, see αἰφνίδιος.

ἐφ-οράω, ῶ, 2d aor. ἐπεῖδον, *to look upon*, Lu. i. 25; Ac. iv. 29.*

Ἐφραΐμ, ὁ, *Ephraim*, a city, Jn. xi. 54.*

ἐφφαθά, an Aramaic verb, imperative, *be thou opened*, Mar. vii. 34. (N.T.)*

ἐχθές, see χθές.

ἔχθρα, ας, ἡ, *enmity*, Gal. v. 20; Ep. ii. 15, 16.

ἐχθρός, ά, όν, *hated*, Ro. xi. 28; *hostile*, 1 Cor. xv. 25; used as subst., *an enemy*, Mat. x. 36; ὁ ἐχθρός, Lu. x. 19, *the enemy, i.e.*, Satan.

ἔχιδνα, ης, ἡ, *a viper*, lit., Ac. xxviii. 3; fig., as Mat. iii. 7.

ἔχω, ἕξω, impf. εἶχον, 2d aor. ἔσχον, perf. ἔσχηκα; (1) *to have* or *possess*, in general, physically or mentally, temporarily or permanently; μὴ ἔχειν, *to lack, to be poor*, Lu. viii. 6; 1 Cor. xi. 22; (2) *to be able*, Mar. xiv. 8; Heb. vi. 13; 2 Pet. i. 15; (3) with adverbs, or adverbial phrases, elliptically, "to have

(one's self) in any manner," *to be*, as κακῶς ἔχειν, *to be ill;* ἐσχάτως ἔχειν, *to be at the last extremity;* (4) *to hold*, 1 Tim. iii. 9; 2 Tim. i. 13; *to esteem*, Mat. xiv. 5; Phil. ii. 29; (5) mid., ἔχομαι, *to be near* or *next to*, Mar. i. 38; used of time, Ac. xxi. 26, *the day coming, the next day;* τὰ ἐχόμενα σωτηρίας, *things joined to* or *pertaining to salvation*, Heb. vi. 9.

ἕως, conj. and adv., (1) of time, *till, until*, used also as prep. with gen. ἕως οὗ, or ἕως ὅτου, *until when*, Lu. xiii. 8; (2) of place, *up to*, or *as far as*, also with gen., sometimes with εἰς or πρός (acc.), Mat. xxvi. 58; Lu. xxiv. 50; Ac. xxvi. 11; (3) spoken of a limit or term to anything, *up to the point of*, Mat. xxvi. 38; Lu. xxii. 51; Ro. ii. 12; (4) with particles, ἕως ἄρτι, ἕως τοῦ νῦν, *until now;* ἕως ὧδε, *to this place;* ἕως πότε; *how long?;* ἕως ἑπτάκις, *until seven times;* ἕως ἄνω, *up to the brim*, etc.

Z

Z, ζ, ζῆτα, *zeta, z*, the sixth letter, orig. of a mixed or compound sound, as if δς, now generally pronounced *z* or *ts*. As a numeral, ζʹ = 7; ͵ζ = 7000.

Ζαβουλών, ὁ (Heb.), *Zebulon*, Mat. iv. 13, 15; Rev. vii. 8.*

Ζακχαῖος, ου, ὁ, *Zacchæus*, Lu. xix. 2, 5, 8.*

Ζαρά, ὁ (Heb.), *Zara* or *Zerah*, Mat. i. 3.*

Ζαχαρίας, ου, ὁ, *Zacharias* or *Zachariah*, (1) the father of John the Baptist, Lu. i.; (2) the son of Barachiah, slain in the temple, Mat. xxiii. 35; Lu. xi. 51 (in 2 Chron. xxiv. 20 the son of Jehoiada).*

ζάω, ῶ, ζῇς, ζῇ, inf. ζῆν (W. H. ζῆν), fut. ζήσω or -ομαι, 1st aor. ἔζησα, *to live*, as (1) *to be alive;* part. ὁ ζῶν, *the Living One*, a description of God, as Mat. xvi. 16; (2) *to receive* or *regain life*, Jn. iv. 50; Mar. xvi. 11; (3) *to spend life* in any way, Gal. ii. 14; 2 Tim. iii. 12; (4) *to live*, in

the highest sense, to possess spiritual and eternal life, Lu. x. 28; Heb. x. 38; (5) met., as of water, *living* or *fresh*, opposed to stagnant, as Jn. iv. 10.

Ζεβεδαῖος, ου, ὁ, *Zebedee*, Mat. iv. 21, x. 2.

ζεστός, ή, όν (ζέω), *boiling, hot*, fig., Rev. iii. 15, 16.*

ζεῦγος, ους, τό, (1) *a yoke* (ζεύγνυμι, *to join*), Lu. xiv. 19; (2) *a pair*, Lu. ii. 24.*

ζευκτηρία, ας, ἡ, *a band, a fastening*, Ac. xxvii. 40. (N.T.)*

Ζεύς, Διός, acc. Δία, *Zeus* (Lat. *Jupiter*), the chief of the heathen deities, Ac. xiv. 12, 13.*

ζέω, part. ζέων, *to boil;* fig., *to be fervent*, Ac. xviii. 25; Ro. xii. 11.*

ζηλεύω, *to be zealous*, Rev. iii. 19 (W. H.).*

ζῆλος, ου, ὁ, (1) *fervor, zeal*, Jn. ii. 17; (2) *rivalry, jealousy*, Ac. v. 17, xiii. 45; *fierceness*, Heb. x. 27.

ζηλόω, ῶ, ώσω, (1) *to have zeal for, to desire earnestly* (acc.), 1 Cor. xii. 31; 2 Cor. xi. 2; Gal. iv. 17; (2) *to be envious* or *jealous*, Ac. vii. 9; 1 Cor. xiii. 4; Ja. iv. 2.

ζηλωτής, οῦ, ὁ, (1) *one very zealous for* (gen.), Ac. xxi. 20; (2) *a Zealot*, one of a class of Jews very zealous for the Mosaic law, only Lu. vi. 15; Ac. i. 13. See Κανανίτης.

ζημία, ας, ἡ, *damage, loss*, Ac. xxvii. 10, 21; Phil. iii. 7, 8.*

ζημιόω, ῶ, pass., *to be damaged, to suffer loss of* (acc.), Mat. xvi. 26; Phil. iii. 8.

Ζηνᾶς, ᾶ, ὁ, *Zenas*, Tit. iii. 13.*

ζητέω, ῶ, ήσω, (1) *to seek*, absolutely, as Mat. vii. 7; (2) *to seek for* (acc.), Mat. vi. 33; Jn. v. 30; (3) *to desire, to wish for*, Mat. xii. 46; Col. iii. 1; *to inquire into*, Lu. xii. 29; Jn. xvi. 19.

ζήτημα, ατος, τό, *a question, dispute* (gen., or περί, gen.); Ac. xv. 2, xviii. 15, xxiii. 29, xxv. 19, xxvi. 3.*

ζήτησις, εως, ἡ, *question, debate, controversy*, Jn. iii. 25; Ac. xxv. 20.

ζιζάνιον, ου, τό (perh. Syriac), *zizanium, darnel*, a kind of

bastard wheat, Mat. xiii. 25–
40. (N. T.)*

Ζοροβάβελ, ὁ (Heb.), *Zerub-
babel*, Mat. i. 12, 13; Lu. iii.
27.*

ζόφος, ου, ὁ, *darkness, thick
gloom*, 2 Pet. ii. 4, 17; Ju. 6,
13; Heb. xii. 18 (W. H.).*

ζυγός, οῦ, ὁ, *a yoke*, (1) met.,
of servitude, 1 Tim. vi. 1;
(2) fig., of any imposition
by authority, Mat. xi. 29, 30;
Ac. xv. 10; Gal. v. 1; (3) *a
balance, pair of scales*, Rev.
vi. 5.*

ζύμη, ης, ἡ, *leaven*, Mat. xvi. 6;
fig., *corruptness*, 1 Cor. v. 6,
7, 8.

ζυμόω, ῶ, *to ferment, to leaven*,
Mat. xiii. 33; Lu. xiii. 21;
1 Cor. v. 6; Gal. v. 9.*

ζωγρέω, ῶ (ζωός, ἀγρέω), *to take
alive, to catch, capture*, Lu.
v. 10; 2 Tim. ii. 26.*

ζωή, ῆς, ἡ (ζάω), *life*, literal,
spiritual, eternal; ζωὴ αἰώνιος, *eternal life*, used of
Christ, as *the source of life*,
Jn. v. 26. *Syn.:* see βίος.

ζώνη, ης, ἡ, *a girdle*, Ac. xxi.
11; used as *a purse*, Mar.
vi. 8.

ζώννυμι or -ννύω, see Gr. § 114,
Bu. 45, *to gird*, Jn. xxi. 18;
Ac. xii. 8 (W. H.).*

ζωο-γονέω, ῶ, ήσω, *to preserve
alive*, Lu. xvii. 33; Ac. vii.
19; *to give life to*, 1 Tim. vi.
13 (W. H.).*

ζῶον, ου, τό, *a living creature,
animal*, Heb. xiii. 11; 2 Pet.
ii. 12.

ζωο-ποιέω, ῶ, ήσω, *to make alive,
to give life to*, Jn. v. 21, vi.
63; 1 Cor. xv. 22, 36, 45;
2 Cor. iii. 6; Gal. iii. 21;
Ro. iv. 17, viii. 11; 1 Pet.
iii. 18.*

H

H, η, ῆτα, *eta, e*, the seventh
letter. As a numeral, η' = 8;
‚η = 8000.

ἤ, a particle, disjunctive, *or;*
interrogative, *whether* (see
Gr. § 405, Wi. § 57, 1 b, Bu.
249); or comparative, *than*
(see Gr. § 320, Wi. § 35, 1,
2, Bu. 360). With other particles, ἀλλ' ἤ, *except;* ἤ καί,
or else; ἤπερ, *than at all*, Jn.
xii. 43; ἤτοι ... ἤ, *whether*

... *or* (excluding any other
alternative), Ro. vi. 16.

ἤ, affirmative particle with μήν,
surely, Heb. vi. 14 (W. H.
el).*

ἡγεμονεύω, *to be governor*, as
proconsul, Lu. ii. 2; procurator, Lu. iii. 1.*

ἡγεμονία, ας, ἡ, *rule*, as of an
emperor, Lu. iii. 1.*

ἡγεμών, όνος, ὁ, *governor*, as the
head of a district, Mat. x.
18; especially the procurator
of Judæa, as Pilate, Felix,
Festus, Lu. xx. 20; *a chief
town*, Mat. ii. 6.

ἡγέομαι, οῦμαι, dep. mid., (1) *to
be leader*, in N. T. only part.,
ὁ ἡγούμενος, *the leader* or
chief (gen.), as Ac. xiv. 12;
Heb. xiii. 7, 17, 24; (2) *to
consider, reckon, count*, as
Phil. iii. 7, 8.

ἡδέως, adv. (ἡδύς, *sweet*) *gladly*,
Mar. vi. 20, xii. 37; 2 Cor.
xi. 19.*

ἤδη, adv. of time, *now, already*,
as Mat. iii. 10; of the im-
mediate future, Ro. i. 10.

ἥδιστα, adv., *most gladly*, 2
Cor. xii. 9, 15.*

ἡδονή, ῆς, ἡ, *pleasure, i.e.*, sensual, *lust, strong desire*, Lu.
viii. 14; Tit. iii. 3; Ja. iv. 3;
2 Pet. ii. 13; *lust*, Ja. iv. 1.*

ἡδύ-οσμον, ου, τό (ἡδύς, ὀσμή),
mint, Mat. xxiii. 23; Lu. xi.
42.*

ἦθος, ους, τό, as ἔθος, *manner,
custom;* plur. ἤθη, *morals*,
1 Cor. xv. 33.*

ἥκω, ξω (perf. ἧκα, only Mar.
viii. 3), *to have come, to be
present* (see Gr. § 361 d, note,
Wi. § 40, 4 b, Bu. 203).

Ἡλί, ὁ (Heb.), *Heli*, Lu. iii. 23.*

ἠλί (W. H. ἐλωί), (Heb.), *my
God*, Mat. xxvii. 46 (from
Ps. xxii. 2). (N. T.)*

Ἠλίας, ου, ὁ, *Elias, i.e., Elijah*,
Mat. xi. 14, xvi. 14.

ἡλικία, ας, ἡ, (1) *age, adult age;*
ἡλικίαν ἔχει, *he is of age*, Jn.
ix. 21; so, prob., Mat. vi. 27
(R. V. mrg.); (2) *stature,
size*, Lu. xix. 3.

ἡλίκος, η, ον, *how great, how
small*, Col. ii. 1; Ja. iii. 5.*

ἥλιος, ου, ὁ, *the sun, the light of
the sun*, Mat. v. 45; Ac. xiii.
11.

ἧλος, ου, ὁ, *a nail*, Jn. xx.
25.*

ἡμεῖς, gen. ἡμῶν, dat. ἡμῖν, acc
ἡμᾶς, plur. of ἐγώ.

ἡμέρα, ας, ἡ, *a day, i.e.*, from
sunrise to sunset, Lu. xviii.
7; Ac. ix. 24; *a day* of twenty-
four hours, Mat. vi. 34; fig.
in various senses.

ἡμέτερος, α, ον, *our, our own*,
Ac. ii. 11, xxvi. 5.

ἡμιθανής, ές, *half dead*, Lu. x.
30.*

ἥμισυς, εια, υ, gen., ἡμίσους,
half; in neut. only, *half* of,
(gen.) plur. (ἡμίση, W. H.
ἡμίσια), Lu. xix. 8; sing.,
Mar. vi. 23; Rev. xi. 9, 11,
xii. 14.*

ἡμιώριον, ου, τό, *a half-hour*,
Rev. viii. 1.*

ἡνίκα, adv., *when, whenever*,
2 Cor. iii. 15, 16.*

ἤπερ, see ἤ.

ἤπιος, α, ον, *placid, gentle*, 1
Th. ii. 7 (W. H. νήπιος); 2
Tim. ii. 24.*

Ἤρ, ὁ (Heb.), *Er*, Lu. iii. 28.*

ἤρεμος, ον, *quiet, tranquil*, 1
Tim. ii. 2.*

Ἡρώδης (W. H. -ῴ-), ου, ὁ,
Herod. Four of the name
are mentioned: (1) *Herod
the Great*, Mat. ii. 1; (2)
Herod Antipas, or *H. the
tetrarch*, Mat. xiv. 1, 3, 6;
Lu. xxiii.; (3) *H. Agrippa*,
Ac. xii.; (4) *H. Agrippa* the
younger, called only *Agrippa*,
Ac. xxv.

Ἡρωδιανοί (W. H. -ῳ-), ῶν, οἱ,
Herodians, partisans of He-
rod Antipas, Mat. xxii. 16;
Mar. iii. 6, xii. 13.*

Ἡρωδιάς (W. H. -ῳ-), άδος, ἡ,
Herodias, Mat. xiv. 3, 6.*

Ἡρωδίων (W. H. -ῳ-), ωνος, ὁ,
Herodion, Ro. xvi. 11.*

Ἡσαΐας, ου, ὁ, *Esaias, i.e.,
Isaiah*, Mat. iii. 3, iv. 14.

Ἠσαῦ, ὁ, *Esau*, Ro. ix. 13;
Heb. xi. 20, 16.*

ἡσυχάζω, σω, (1) *to rest from
work*, Lu. xxiii. 56; (2) *to
cease from altercation, to be
silent*, Lu. xiv. 4; Ac. xi. 18,
xxi. 4; (3) *to live quietly*, 1
Th. iv. 11.*

ἡσυχία, ας, ἡ, (1) *silence*, Ac.
xxii. 2; 1 Tim. ii. 11; (2)
tranquillity, quietness, 2 Th.
iii. 12.*

ἡσύχιος, α, ον, *quiet, tranquil*,
1 Tim. ii. 2; 1 Pet. iii. 4.*

ἤτοι, see ἤ.

ἡττάομαι, pass., (1) *to be made inferior* (abs.), 2 Cor. xii. 13; (2) *to be overcome by* (dat.), 2 Pet. ii. 19, 20.*

ἥττημα, ατος, τό, *inferiority, diminution,* Ro. xi. 12; *loss,* 1 Cor. vi. 7. (S.)* *Syn.:* see ἀγνόημα.

ἥττων or ἥσσων (W. H.), ον, compar. of κακός, *inferior,* neut. as adv., 2 Cor. xii. 15; τὸ ἧττον, as subst., *the worse,* 1 Cor. xi. 17.*

ἠχέω, ῶ, *to sound,* as the sea, Lu. xxi. 25 (not W. H.); as brass, 1 Cor. xiii. 1.*

ἦχος, ου, ὁ, and ους, τό, *sound, noise,* Lu. xxi. 25 (W. H.); Heb. xii. 19; Ac. ii. 2; *rumor, report,* Lu. iv. 37.*

Θ

Θ, θ, θῆτα, *theta, th,* the eighth letter. As a numeral, θ′ = 9; ⸋θ = 9000.

Θαδδαῖος, ου, ὁ, *Thaddæus,* a surname of the apostle Jude (also called *Lebbæus*), Mat. x. 3; Mar. iii. 18.*

θάλασσα, ης, ἡ, (1) *the sea,* Ro. ix. 27; (2) *sea,* as the Mediterranean, the Red Sea, Ac. vii. 36, x. 6, 32; (3) Hebraistically, for the *lake* Gennesaret, Mat. viii. 24.

θάλπω, *to cherish, nourish,* Ep. v. 29; 1 Th. ii. 7.*

Θάμαρ, ἡ, *Tamar,* Mat. i. 3.*

θαμβέω, ῶ, *to be astonished, amazed,* Ac. ix. 6 (W. H. omit); so pass., Mar. i. 27, x. 32; with ἐπί (dat.), Mar. x. 24.*

θάμβος, ους, τό, *amazement,* Lu. iv. 36, v. 9; Ac. iii. 10.*

θανάσιμος, ον, *deadly, mortal,* Mar. xvi. 18.*

θανατη-φόρος, ον, *death-bringing,* Ja. iii. 8.*

θάνατος, ου, ὁ, *death,* lit. or fig., Jn. xi. 4; 2 Cor. iii. 7; Ro. i. 32; *the cause of death,* Ro. vii. 13.

θανατόω, ῶ, ώσω, *to put to death,* pass., *to be in danger of death,* Ro. viii. 36; fig., *to destroy, subdue,* as evil passions, Ro. viii. 13; pass., *to become dead to* (dat.), Ro. vii. 4.

θάπτω, ψω, 2d aor. ἔταφον, *to bury,* Mat. viii. 21, 22.

Θάρα, ὁ, *Terah,* Lu. iii. 34.*

θαρρέω, ῶ, ήσω, *to be of good courage, to have confidence,* εἰς or ἐν, 2 Cor. v. 6, 8, x. 1. In imperative, forms from θαρσέω are used, θάρσει, θαρσεῖτε, *take courage.*

θάρσος, ους, τό, *courage,* Ac. xxviii. 15.*

θαῦμα, ατος, τό, *a wonder,* 2 Cor. xi. 14 (W. H.); *wonder, amazement,* Rev. xvii. 6.*

θαυμάζω, σω, or σομαι, *to wonder,* abs., with διά, acc., ἐπί, dat., περί, gen., or ὅτι, εἰ; *to wonder at, admire,* acc.; pass., *to be admired* or *honored.*

θαυμάσιος, α, ον, *wonderful,* Mat. xxi. 15.*

θαυμαστός, ή, όν, *wonderful, marvelous,* Mat. xxi. 42; Mar. xii. 11; Jn. ix. 30; 2 Cor. xi. 14 (Rec.); 1 Pet. ii. 9; Rev. xv. 1, 3.*

θεά, ᾶς, ἡ, *a goddess,* Ac. xix. 27, and Rec. in 35, 37.*

θεάομαι, ῶμαι, pass. ἐθεάθην, *to behold, to contemplate, to visit,* Mat. xi. 7; Ro. xv. 24.

θεατρίζω, *to make a spectacle of, expose to contempt,* Heb. x. 33. (N. T.)*

θέατρον, ου, τό, (1) *a place for public shows, a theatre,* Ac. xix. 29, 31; (2) *a spectacle,* 1 Cor. iv. 9.*

θεῖον, ου, τό, *sulphur* (from the following, *a divine incense*), Rev. ix. 17, 18.

θεῖος, εία, εῖον, *divine,* 2 Pet. i. 3, 4; τὸ θεῖον, *the deity,* Ac. xvii. 29.*

θειότης, τητος, ἡ, *deity, divine nature,* Ro. i. 20.* *Syn.:* θειότης is deity, *abstractly;* θεότης, *personally.*

θειώδης, ες, *sulphurous,* Rev. ix. 17. (N. T.)*

θέλημα, ατος, τό, *will,* Lu. xii. 47; Ep. i. 9; plur., *commands,* Ac. xiii. 22; *desire,* Ep. ii. 3.

θέλησις, εως, ἡ, *a willing, will,* Heb. ii. 4. (S.)*

θέλω, impf. ἤθελον, 1st aor. ἠθέλησα (ἐθέλω is not found in N. T.), *to wish, delight in, prefer, to will,* in the sense of assent, determination, or requirement.

θεμέλιος, ον, *belonging to a foundation;* hence, masc. (sc. λίθος), *a foundation,* or τὸ θεμέλιον (Lu.), in the same

sense, 2 Tim. ii. 9; Lu. vi. 49; fig., for the elements of doctrine or life, 1 Cor. iii. 10, 12; Heb. vi. 1.

θεμελιόω, ῶ, ώσω, *to lay a foundation, to found,* Heb. i. 10; fig., *to make stable,* Col. i. 23.

θεο-δίδακτος, ον, *taught of God,* 1 Th. iv. 9. (N. T.)*

θεο-λόγος, ου, ὁ, *one who treats of divine things,* of the apostle John in the title to Rev. (W. H. omit).*

θεο-μαχέω, ῶ, *to fight against God,* Ac. xxiii. 9 (W. H. omit).*

θεο-μάχος, ου, ὁ, *a fighter against God,* Ac. v. 39.*

θεό-πνευστος, ον (πνέω), *God-breathed, inspired by God,* 2 Tim. iii. 16.*

θεός, οῦ, ὁ, voc. once θεέ, Mat. xxvii. 46; (1) *a god,* generically, Ac. vii. 43, xii. 22; 2 Cor. iv. 4; Phil. iii. 19; Jn. x. 34 (quoted from S.); (2) *God;* ὁ θεός, *the revealed God,* Jn. i. 1; Ac. xvii. 24, etc.; (3) applied to Christ, Jn. i. 1, xx. 28.

θεο-σέβεια, ας, ἡ, *fear of God, piety,* 1 Tim. ii. 10.*

θεο-σεβής, ές, *God-worshipping, pious,* Jn. ix. 31.* *Syn.:* see δεισιδαίμων.

θεο-στυγής, ές, *hateful to God,* Ro. i. 30.*

θεότης, τητος, ἡ, *deity, Godhead,* Col. ii. 9.* *Syn.:* see θειότης.

Θεό-φιλος, ου, ὁ, *Theophilus,* Lu. i. 3; Ac. i. 1.*

θεραπεία, ας, ἡ, (1) *service;* hence (abs. for concrete), *servants, household,* Lu. xii. 42; Mat. xxiv. 45 (not W. H.); (2) *medical service, healing,* Lu. ix. 11; Rev. xxii. 2.*

θεραπεύω, εύσω, (1) *to serve, minister to,* only Ac. xvii. 25; (2) *to heal,* acc. of pers., and ἀπό or acc. of disease, Mat. xii. 10; Mar. vi. 5.

θεράπων, οντος, ὁ, *a servant, an attendant,* Heb. iii. 5.*

θερίζω, ίσω, *to reap* or *gather,* as grain, lit. or fig., Mat. vi. 26; Jn. iv. 37, 38.

θερισμός, οῦ, ὁ, *harvest,* lit. or fig., Jn. iv. 35; Lu. x. 2.

θεριστής, οῦ, ὁ, *a reaper,* Mat. xiii. 30, 39.*

θερμαίνω, ανῶ, only mid. in N. T., *to warm one's self,* Mar.

xiv. 54, 67; Jn. xviii. 18, 25; Ja. ii. 16.*

θέρμη, ης, ἡ, *heat*, Ac. xxviii. 3.*

θέρος, ους, τό, *summer*, Mat. xxiv. 32; Mar. xiii. 28; Lu. xxi. 30.*

Θεσσαλονικεύς, έως, ὁ, *a Thessalonian*, Ac. xx. 4.

Θεσσαλονίκη, ης, ἡ, *Thessalonica*, Ac. xvii. 1, 11, 13.

Θευδᾶς, ᾶ, ὁ, *Theudas*, Ac. v. 36.*

θεωρέω, ῶ, *to be a spectator of, to behold, to see, to know by seeing, to experience;* abs., or with acc. or obj. clause.

θεωρία, ας, ἡ, *a sight, a spectacle*, Lu. xxiii. 48.*

θήκη, ης, ἡ (τίθημι), *a receptacle,* as a scabbard, Jn. xviii. 11.*

θηλάζω, (1) *to give suck,* Mat. xxiv. 19; (2) *to suck,* Mat. xxi. 16.

θῆλυς, εια, υ, *female,* fem., Ro. i. 26, 27; neut., Mat. xix. 4; Mar. x. 6; Gal. iii. 28.*

θήρα, ας, ἡ, *hunting,* hence, *a trap,* Ro. xi. 9.*

θηρεύω, σω, *to hunt, to catch,* Lu. xi. 54.*

θηριο-μαχέω, ῶ, *to fight with wild beasts,* 1 Cor. xv. 32.*

θηρίον, ου, τό (prop. *a little beast*), *a wild beast,* as Ac. xi. 6; freq. in Rev.

θησαυρίζω, σω, *to store up, reserve,* lit. and fig., Lu. xii. 21; 2 Pet. iii. 7.

θησαυρός, οῦ, ὁ, *a treasure receptacle, treasure,* Lu. xii. 33, 34.

θιγγάνω, 2d aor. ἔθιγον, *to touch, handle,* abs., Col. ii. 21; with gen., Heb. xii. 20; *to injure,* Heb. xi. 28.* *Syn.:* see ἅπτω.

θλίβω, ψω, *to press upon,* Mar. iii. 9; fig., *to afflict,* 2 Cor. i. 6; pass. perf. part. τεθλιμμένος, *contracted, narrow,* Mat. vii. 14.

θλῖψις, εως, ἡ, *pressure, affliction, tribulation,* Ac. vii. 11; 2 Th. i. 6.

θνήσκω, 2d aor. ἔθανον, *to die;* in N. T. only perf. τέθνηκα, *to be dead,* Lu. viii. 49; 1 Tim. v. 6.

θνητός, ή, όν, *liable to death, mortal,* Ro. vi. 12, viii. 11; 1 Cor. xv. 53, 54; 2 Cor. iv. 11, v. 4.*

θορυβάζω, *to disturb, trouble,* Lu. x. 41 (W. H.). (N. T.)*

θορυβέω, ῶ, *to disturb,* Ac. xvii. 5; pass., *to be troubled, to wail,* Mat. ix. 23; Mar. v. 39; Ac. xx. 10.*

θόρυβος, ου, ὁ, *noise, uproar,* Mar. v. 38; Ac. xx. 1.

θραύω, σω, *to break, shatter,* Lu. iv. 18.*

θρέμμα, ατος, το (τρέφω), *the young of cattle, sheep,* etc., Jn. iv. 12.*

θρηνέω, ῶ, ήσω, abs., *to wail, lament,* Mat. xi. 17; Lu. vii. 32; Jn. xvi. 20; *to bewail,* acc., Lu. xxiii. 27.*

θρῆνος, ου, ὁ, *a wailing,* Mat. ii. 18 (not W. H.).*

θρησκεία, ας, ἡ, *external worship, religious worship,* Ac. xxvi. 5; Col. ii. 18; Ja. i. 26, 27.*

θρῆσκος, ου, ὁ (prop. adj.), *a devotee, religious person,* Ja. i. 26. (N. T.)* *Syn.:* see δεισιδαίμων.

θριαμβεύω, σω, *to triumph over, to lead in triumph,* 2 Cor. ii. 14; Col. ii. 15.*

θρίξ, τριχός, dat. plur. θριξί, ἡ, *a hair,* human or animal, Jn. xi. 2; Rev. ix. 8.

θροέω, ῶ, *to disturb, terrify by clamor;* only pass. in N. T., Mat. xxiv. 6; Mar. xiii. 7; 2 Th. ii. 2.*

θρόμβος, ου, ὁ, *a clot, large drop,* as of blood, Lu. xxii. 44.*

θρόνος, ου, ὁ, *a seat,* as of judgment, Mat. xix. 28; *a throne,* or seat of power, Rev. iii. 21; met., of *kingly power,* Rev. xiii. 2; concrete, of *the ruler,* or occupant of the throne, Col. i. 16.

Θυάτειρα, ων, τά, *Thyatira,* Ac. xvi. 14; Rev. i. 11, ii. 18, 24.*

θυγάτηρ, τρός, ἡ, *a daughter,* Mat. ix. 18; *a female descendant,* Lu. xiii. 16; met., of the inhabitants of a place, collectively, Mat. xxi. 5.

θυγάτριον, ου, τό (dim. of θυγάτηρ), *a little daughter,* Mar. v. 23, vii. 25.*

θύελλα, ης, ἡ, *a tempest,* Heb. xii. 18.*

θύϊνος, η, ον, *made of the citrus tree,* a strongly aromatic tree of Africa, Rev. xviii. 12.*

θυμίαμα, ατος, τό, *incense,* Lu.

i. 10, 11; Rev. v. 8, viii. 3, 4, xviii. 13.*

θυμιατήριον, ου, τό, *a censer,* or *an altar of incense,* Heb. ix. 4.*

θυμιάω, ῶ, *to burn incense,* Lu. i. 9.*

θυμομαχέω, ῶ, *to be very angry with* (dat.), Ac. xii. 20.*

θυμός, οῦ, ὁ, *passion, great anger, wrath,* Lu. iv. 28; Rev. xiv. 19. *Syn.:* θυμός is *impulsive, turbulent* anger; ὀργή is anger as a *settled habit,* both may be right or wrong; παροργισμός is the bitterness of anger, always wrong.

θυμόω, ῶ, *to provoke to great anger;* pass., *to be very angry with,* Mat. ii. 16.*

θύρα, ας, ἡ, *a door,* Lu. xi. 7; Mat. xxvii. 60; met., Jn. x. 7, 9.

θυρεός, οῦ, ὁ, *a large* (door shaped) *shield,* Ep. vi. 16.*

θυρίς, ίδος, ἡ (prop. *a little door*), *a window,* Ac. xx. 9; 2 Cor. xi. 33.*

θυρωρός, οῦ, ὁ, ἡ, *a door-keeper, porter,* Mar. xiii. 34; Jn. x. 3, xviii. 16, 17.*

θυσία, ας, ἡ, *a sacrifice,* lit. and fig., Ep. v. 2; 1 Pet. ii. 5.

θυσιαστήριον, ου, τό, *an altar,* for sacrifices, Lu. i. 11, ii. 51; Ja. ii. 21. (S.) *Syn.:* see βωμός.

θύω, σω, (1) *to slay in sacrifice,* Ac. xiv. 13; (2) *to kill animals,* for feasting, Mat. xxii. 4; (3) *to slay,* generally, Jn. x. 10.

Θωμᾶς, ᾶ, ὁ (from Heb. = δίδυμος), *Thomas,* Mat. x. 3.

θώραξ, ακος, ὁ, *a breast-plate,* Ep. vi. 14; 1 Th. v. 8; Rev. ix. 9, 17.*

I

Ι, ι, ἰῶτα, *iota, i,* the ninth letter. As a numeral, ι' = 10; ͵ι = 10,000.

Ἰάειρος, ου, ὁ, *Jairus,* Mar. v. 22; Lu. viii. 41.*

Ἰακώβ, ὁ (Heb.), *Jacob,* (1) the patriarch, Ac. vii. 8; (2) the father-in-law of Mary, Mat. i. 15.

Ἰάκωβος, ου, ὁ, Greek form of preced., *James,* (1) the son of Zebedee, Mat. iv. 21; (2)

the son of Alphæus, Mat. x.
3; (3) the Lord's brother,
Mat. xiii. 55. Some identify
(2) and (3).

ἴαμα, ατος, τό, *healing, cure*,
plur., 1 Cor. xii. 9, 28, 30.*

Ἰαμβρῆς, ὁ, *Jambres*, 2 Tim.
iii. 8.*

Ἰαννά, ὁ (W. H. -αί), (Heb.),
Jannai, Lu. iii. 24.*

Ἰαννῆς, ὁ, *Jannes*, 2 Tim. iii.
8.*

ἰάομαι, ῶμαι, ἰάσομαι, dep., mid.
aor., but passive in aor.,
perf. and fut., *to heal, to
restore to health*, of body or
mind; with ἀπό, of malady,
Mar. v. 29; Jn. xii. 40.

Ἰαρέδ, ὁ (Heb.), *Jared*, Lu. iii.
37.*

ἴασις, εως, ἡ, *a cure, healing*,
Lu. xiii. 32; Ac. iv. 22, 30.*

ἴασπις, ιδος, ἡ, *jasper*, a precious stone, Rev. iv. 3, xxi.
11, 18, 19.*

Ἰάσων, ονος, ὁ, *Jason*, Ac. xvii.
5, 6, 7, 9; Ro. xvi. 21; perhaps two persons.*

ἰατρός, οῦ, ὁ, *a physician*, Lu.
iv. 23; Col. iv. 14.

ἴδε, or ἰδέ (εἶδον), imper. act.
as interj., *behold!* often followed by nominative.

ἰδέα (W. H. εἰ-), ας, ἡ, *form,
outward appearance*, Mat.
xxviii. 3.* *Syn.*: see Trench,
§ lxx.

ἴδιος, α, ον, (1) *one's own*, denoting ownership, Mat. xxii.
5; Jn. x. 12; also what is
peculiar to, Ac. i. 19 (W. H.
omit); hence, τὰ ἴδια, *one's
own things, home, nation*
or *people, business* or *duty;*
οἱ ἴδιοι, *one's own people,
friends, companions*, neut.
and masc. contrasted in Jn.
i. 11; (2) *that which specially
pertains to, and is proper for*,
as 1 Cor. iii. 8; Gal. vi. 9;
(3) adverbially, κατ' ἴδιαν,
privately; ἰδίᾳ, *individually*.

ἰδιώτης, ου, ὁ, *a private person,
one unskilled in anything*,
Ac. iv. 13; 1 Cor. xiv. 16, 23,
24; 2 Cor. xi. 6.* *Syn.*: see
ἀγράμματος.

ἰδού (see ἴδε), imper. mid. as
interj., *lo! behold!* used to
call attention not only to
that which may be seen, but
also heard, or apprehended
in any way.

Ἰδουμαία, ας, ἡ, *Idumæa*, the
O. T. Edom, Mar. iii. 8.*

ἰδρώς, ῶτος, ὁ, *sweat*, Lu. xxii.
44.*

Ἰεζαβήλ, ἡ (Heb.), *Jezebel*, sym-
bolically used, Rev. ii. 20.*

Ἱεράπολις, εως, ἡ, *Hierapolis*,
in Phrygia, Col. iv. 13.*

ἱερατεία (W. H. -τία), ας, ἡ, *the
office of a priest, priesthood*,
Lu. i. 9; Heb. vii. 5.*

ἱεράτευμα, ατος, τό, *the order
of priests, priesthood*, applied
to Christians, 1 Pet. ii. 5, 9.
(S.)*

ἱερατεύω, σω, *to officiate as a
priest*, Lu. i. 8.*

Ἱερεμίας, ου, ὁ, *Jeremiah*, Mat.
ii. 17, xvi. 14, xxvii. 9 (this
quotation is from *Zecha-
riah*).*

ἱερεύς, έως, ὁ, *a priest*, Mat. viii.
4; sometimes *the High Priest*,
Ac. v. 24 (not W. H.); of
Christ, Heb. v. 6 (Ps. cx. 4);
of Christians generally, Rev.
i. 6, v. 10.

Ἱεριχώ, ἡ (Heb.), *Jericho*, Lu.
x. 30.

ἱερόθυτος, ον, *offered in sacrifice*,
1 Cor. x. 28 (W. H.).*

ἱερόν, οῦ, τό (prop. neut. of
ἱερός), *a temple*, used of a
heathen temple, as Ac. xix.
27; of the temple at Jerusalem, as Mat. xxiv. 1; and
of parts of the temple, as
Mat. xii. 5. *Syn.*: ἱερόν is
the whole sacred enclosure;
ναός, the *shrine* itself, the
holy place and the holy of
holies.

ἱεροπρεπής, ές, *suitable to a
sacred character* (*reverent*,
R. V.), Tit. ii. 3.*

ἱερός, ά, όν, *sacred, holy*, of the
Scriptures, 2 Tim. iii. 15;
τὰ ἱερά, *sacred things*, 1 Cor.
ix. 13.* *Syn.*: see ἅγιος.

Ἱεροσόλυμα (W. H. Ἱ-), ων,
τά, the usual form in Mat.,
Mar., and Jn.; see Ἱερου-
σαλήμ.

Ἱεροσολυμίτης, ου, ὁ, *one of
Jerusalem*, Mar. i. 5; Jn. vii.
25.*

ἱεροσυλέω, ῶ, *to commit sacri-
lege*, Ro. ii. 22.*

ἱερόσυλος, ον, *robbing temples,
sacrilegious*, Ac. xix. 37.*

ἱερουργέω, ῶ (ἱερός, ἔργον), *to
minister in holy things*, Ro.
xv. 16.*

Ἱερουσαλήμ (W. H. Ἱ-), ἡ
(Heb.), (for form, see Gr.
§ 156, Wi. § 10, 2, Bu. 6, 16,
18, 21), *Jerusalem*, (1) the
city; (2) the inhabitants.
In Gal. iv. 25, 26, ἡ νῦν Ἱ.
is the *Jewish dispensation*,
and is contrasted with ἡ
ἄνω Ἱ., the ideal *Christian
community;* also called Ἱ.
ἐπουράνιος, Heb. xii. 22; ἡ
καινὴ Ἱ., Rev. iii. 12, xxi. 2.

ἱερωσύνη, ης, ἡ, *the priestly
office*, Heb. vii. 11, 12, 14
(not W. H.), 24.*

Ἰεσσαί, ὁ (Heb.), *Jesse*, Mat. i.
5, 6.

Ἰεφθάε, ὁ (Heb.), *Jephthah*,
Heb. xi. 32.*

Ἰεχονίας, ου, ὁ, *Jechoniah*, or
Jehoiachin, Mat. i. 11, 12.*

Ἰησοῦς, οῦ, ὁ (Heb.), (see Gr.
§ 25, Wi. § 10, 1, Bu. 21),
(1) *Jesus*, the Savior, Mat.
i. 21, 25; (2) *Joshua*, Ac. vii.
45; Heb. iv. 8; (3) *a fellow-
laborer of Paul*, so named,
Col. iv. 11; (4) *Barabbas* is
so named in some early
MSS., Mat. xxvii. 16; (5)
an ancestor of Joseph, Lu. iii.
29 (W. H.).

ἱκανός, ή, όν, (1) *sufficient, competent* to, inf., πρός (acc.) or
ἵνα; (2) *many, much*, of
number or time.

ἱκανότης, τητος, ἡ, *sufficiency,
ability*, 2 Cor. iii. 5.*

ἱκανόω, ῶ, *to make competent*,
2 Cor. iii. 6; Col. i. 12. (S.)*

ἱκετηρία, ας, ἡ, *supplication*,
Heb. v. 7.* *Syn.*: see αἴτημα.

ἰκμάς, άδος, ἡ, *moisture*, Lu.
viii. 6.*

Ἰκόνιον, ου, τό, *Iconium*, Ac.
xiv. 1, 19, 21.

ἱλαρός, ά, όν, *joyous, cheerful*,
2 Cor. ix. 7.*

ἱλαρότης, τητος, ἡ, *cheerfulness*,
Ro. xii. 8. (S.)*

ἱλάσκομαι, άσομαι, 1st aor. ἱλά-
σθην, (1) *to be propitious to*,
dat., Lu. xviii. 13; (2) *to
make atonement for, expiate*,
acc., Heb. ii. 17.*

ἱλασμός, οῦ, ὁ, *a propitiation,
atoning sacrifice*, 1 Jn. ii. 2,
iv. 10. (S.)* *Syn.*: see ἀπο-
λύτρωσις.

ἱλαστήριος, α, ον, *atoning*, neut.,
propitiation, Ro. iii. 25; (sc.
ἐπίθεμα, *covering*), *the mercy-
seat*, Heb. ix. 5. (S.)*

ἵλεως, ων (Attic for ἵλαος), *propitious, merciful*, Heb. viii. 12; ἵλεώς σοι, (God be) merciful to thee! *God forbid!* Mat. xvi. 22.*

Ἰλλυρικόν, οῦ, τό, *Illyricum*, Ro. xv. 19.*

ἱμάς, άντος, ὁ, *a thong* for scourging, Ac. xxii. 25; *thong, latchet* of a shoe, Mar. i. 7; Lu. iii. 16; Jn. i. 27.*

ἱματίζω, perf. pass. part. ἱματισμένος, *to clothe*, Mar. v. 15; Lu. viii. 35. (N. T.)*

ἱμάτιον, ου, τό (dim. of ἶμα = εἶμα, from ἕννυμι), (1) *clothing*, Mat. ix. 16; (2) *the outer garment*, worn over the χιτών, Jn. xix. 2. *Syn.:* see Trench, § l.

ἱματισμός, οῦ, ὁ, *clothing, raiment*, Lu. vii. 25. *Syn.:* see ἱμάτιον.

ἱμείρομαι, *to long for, to love earnestly*, 1 Th. ii. 8 (W. H. ὁμείρομαι).*

ἵνα, conj., *that, to the end that; ἵνα μή, that not, lest.* See Gr. § 384, Wi. § 53, 9, Bu. 229 sq.

ἱνα-τί, or ἵνα τί (W. H.), conj., *in order that what* (may happen? sc. γένηται), *to what end?*

Ἰόππη, ης, ἡ, *Joppa*, Ac. xi. 5, 13.

Ἰορδάνης, ου, ὁ, *the Jordan*, Mar. i. 5, 9.

ἰός, οῦ, ὁ, (1) *poison*, Ro. iii. 13; Ja. iii. 8; (2) *rust*, Ja. v. 3.*

Ἰουδαία, ας, ἡ (really adj., fem., sc. γῆ), *Judæa*, Mat. ii. 1; including all Palestine, Lu. vii. 17.

Ἰουδαΐζω (from Heb.), *to conform to Jewish practice*, to "Judaize," in life or ritual, Gal. ii. 14. (S.)*

Ἰουδαϊκός, ή, όν (from Heb.), *Jewish*, or *Judaical*, Tit. i. 14.*

Ἰουδαϊκῶς, adv., *Jewishly*, in Jewish style, Gal. ii. 14.*

Ἰουδαῖος, αία, αῖον, *Jewish*, Jn. iv. 9; Ac. x. 28. Often in plur., with subst. understood, οἱ Ἰουδαῖοι, *the Jews. Syn.:* see Ἑβραῖος.

Ἰουδαισμός, οῦ, ὁ (from Heb.), *Judaism, the religion of the Jews*, Gal. i. 13, 14. (Ap.)*

Ἰούδας, α, ὁ, and Ἰούδα, ὁ,

indecl., *Judah*, (1) son of Jacob; (2, 3) other unknown ancestors of Christ, Lu. iii. 26, 30; (4) *Jude*, an apostle; (5) *Judas* Iscariot; (6) *Judas* Barsabas, Ac. xv. 22; (7) *Judas*, a Jew living in Damascus, Ac. ix. 11; (8) *Judas*, a leader of sedition, Ac. v. 37; (9) *Judas*, a brother of our Lord, Mat. xiii. 55. See Ἰάκωβος.

Ἰουλία, ας, ἡ, *Julia*, Ro. xvi. 15.*

Ἰούλιος, ου, ὁ, *Julius*, Ac. xxvii. 1, 3.*

Ἰουνίας, α, ὁ, *Junias*, Ro. xvi. 7.*

Ἰοῦστος, ου, ὁ, *Justus*. Three of the name are mentioned, Ac. i. 23, xviii. 7; Col. iv. 11.*

ἱππεύς, έως, ὁ, *a horseman*, Ac. xxiii. 23, 32.*

ἱππικόν (prop. neut. adj.), οῦ, τό, *cavalry*, Rev. ix. 16.*

ἵππος, ου, ὁ, *a horse*, Ja. iii. 3.

ἶρις, ιδος, ἡ, *a rainbow*, Rev. iv. 3, x. 1.*

Ἰσαάκ, ὁ (Heb.), *Isaac*, Ro. ix. 7, 10.

ἰσ-άγγελος, ον, *like angels*, Lu. xx. 36. (N. T.)*

ἴσασι, see οἶδα.

Ἰσαχάρ, or Ἰσασχάρ, or Ἰσσαχάρ (W.H.), (Heb.), *Issachar*, Rev. vii. 7.*

Ἰσκαριώτης, ου, ὁ, *a man of Kerioth*, Mat. xxvi. 14, 25. See Josh. xv. 25.

ἴσος, η, ον (or ἶσος), *equal* (dat.), Mat. xx. 12; Lu. vi. 34; Jn. v. 18; Ac. xi. 17; *alike, consistent*, as truthful witnesses, Mar. xiv. 56, 59; ἶσα, adverbially, *on an equality* Phil. ii. 6; Rev. xxi. 16.*

ἰσότης, τητος, ἡ, *equality*, 2 Cor. viii. 13, 14; *equity*, Col. iv. 1.*

ἰσό-τιμος, ον, *equally precious*, 2 Pet. i. 1.*

ἰσό-ψυχος, ον *like-minded*, Phil. ii. 20.*

Ἰσραήλ, ὁ (Heb.), *Israel*, Ac. vii. 42, met., for the whole nation of the Israelites, Ro. xi. 2, 7, 26.

Ἰσραηλίτης, ου, ὁ, *an Israelite*, Ro. ix. 4. *Syn.:* see Ἑβραῖος.

ἴστε, see οἶδα.

ἵστημι (in Ro. iii. 31, Rec. has ἱστάω, W. H. ἱστάνω, see

Gr. § 107, Wi. § 15, Bu. 44), trans. in pres., imperf., fut., 1st aor.; *to cause to stand, to set up, to place, to fix* a time, *to confirm, to establish, to put in the balance, to weigh;* intrans. in perf., plup., and 2d aor., *to stand, to stand still* or *firm, to endure, to be confirmed* or *established, to come to a stand, to cease.*

ἱστορέω, ῶ, *to become personally acquainted with*, Gal. i. 18.*

ἰσχυρός, ά, όν, *strong, mighty, powerful, vehement*, Mar. iii. 27; 1 Cor. i. 25; Rev. xix. 6.

ἰσχύς, ύος, ἡ, *strength, power*, 2 Pet. ii. 11; Ep. i. 19.

ἰσχύω, ύσω, *to be strong, sound, to prevail, to be able* (inf.), *to have ability for* (acc.), Mar. ii. 17; Rev. xii. 8.

ἴσως (ἴσος), adv., *perhaps*, Lu. xx. 13.*

Ἰταλία, ας, ἡ, *Italy*, Ac. xviii. 2.

Ἰταλικός, ή, όν, *Italian*, Ac. x. 1.*

Ἰτουραία, ας, ἡ, *Iturœa*, Lu. iii. 1.*

ἰχθύδιον, ου, τό (dim. of ἰχθύς), *a little fish*, Mat. xv. 34; Mar. viii. 7.*

ἰχθύς, ύος, ὁ, *a fish*, Lu. v. 6; Jn. xxi. 11.

ἴχνος, ους, τό, *a footstep*, fig., Ro. iv. 12; 2 Cor. xii. 18; 1 Pet. ii. 21.*

Ἰωάθαμ, ὁ (Heb.), *Jotham*, Mat i. 9.*

Ἰωάννα, ης, ἡ, *Joanna*, Lu. viii. 3, xxiv. 10.*

Ἰωαννᾶς, ᾶ, ὁ, *Joannas*, Lu. iii. 27.*

Ἰωάννης, ου, ὁ, *John*, (1) the Baptist; (2) the apostle; (3) a member of the Sanhedrin, Ac. iv. 6; (4) John Mark, Ac. xii. 12.

Ἰώβ, ὁ (Heb.), *Job*, Ja. v. 11.*

Ἰωβήδ, ὁ Ὠβήδ.

Ἰωήλ, ὁ (Heb.), *Joel*, the prophet, Ac. ii. 16.*

Ἰωνάν, ὁ (Heb.), *Jonan*, Lu. iii. 30.*

Ἰωνᾶς, ᾶ, ὁ, *Jonas*, or *Jonah*, (1) the prophet, Mat. xii. 39–41; (2) the father of Peter, Jn. i. 42.

Ἰωράμ, ὁ (Heb.), *Joram*, or *Jehoram*, son of Jehoshaphat, Mat. i. 8.*

Ἰωρείμ, ὁ (Heb.), *Jorim*, Lu. iii. 29.*

Ἰωσαφάτ, ὁ (Heb.), *Jehoshaphat*, Mat. i. 8.*

Ἰωσῆς, ῆ (or ῆτος, W. H.), ὁ, *Joses.* Four are mentioned: (1) Lu. iii. 29 (W. H. Ἰησοῦ); (2) Mar. vi. 3; Mat. xiii. 55 (W. H. Ἰωσήφ); (3) Mat. xxvii. 56 (W. H. mrg.), Mar. xv. 40, 47; (4) Ac. iv. 36 (W. H. Ἰωσήφ). Some think (2) and (3) identical.*

Ἰωσήφ, ὁ (Heb.), *Joseph*, (1) the patriarch, Jn. iv. 5; (2, 3, 4) three among the ancestors of Jesus, Lu. iii. 24, 26 (W. H. Ἰωσήχ), 30; (5) the husband of Mary, the mother of Jesus, Mat. ii. 13, 19; (6) Joseph of Arimathæa, Mar. xv. 43, 45; (7) Joseph, called also Barsabas, Ac. i. 23. See also under Ἰωσῆς.

Ἰωσίας, ου, ὁ, *Josiah*, Mat. i. 10, 11.*

ἰῶτα, τό, *iota, yod*, the smallest letter of the Hebrew alphabet, Mat. v. 18.*

Κ

Κ, κ, κάππα, *kappa, k*, the tenth letter. As a numeral, κ´ = 20; ͵κ = 20,000.

κἀγώ (κἀμοί, κἀμέ), contr. for καὶ ἐγώ (καὶ ἐμοί, καὶ ἐμέ), *and I, I also, even I.*

καθά, adv., contr. from καθ᾽ ἅ, *according as*, Mat. xxvii. 10.*

καθ-αίρεσις, εως, ἡ, *demolition, destruction* (opp. to οἰκοδομή, which see), 2 Cor. x. 4, 8, xiii. 10.*

καθ-αιρέω, καθελῶ, καθεῖλον, (1) *to take down*, Ac. xiii. 29; (2) *to demolish, destroy*, lit., Lu. xii. 18, or fig., 2 Cor. x. 5.

καθαίρω, αρῶ, *to cleanse, to prune*, Jn. xv. 2; Heb. x. 2 (W. H. καθαρίζω).*

καθ-άπερ, adv., *even as, just as*, 1 Th. ii. 11.

καθ-άπτω, άψω, *to fasten on*, intrans., Ac. xxviii. 3 (gen.).*

καθαρίζω, att. fut. καθαριῶ, *to cleanse*, lit., Lu. xi. 39; a leper, by healing his disease, Mat. viii. 2, 3; from moral pollution, Heb. ix. 22, 23; *to declare clean, i.e.*, from ceremonial pollution, Ac. x. 15.

καθαρισμός, οῦ, ὁ, *cleansing*, physical, moral, or ceremonial, Mar. i. 44; Lu. ii. 22, v. 14; Jn. ii. 6, iii. 25; Heb. i. 3; 2 Pet. i. 9. (S.)*

καθαρός, ά, όν, *clean, pure*, physically, morally, or ceremonially, Mat. xxiii. 26; Tit. i. 15; Ro. xiv. 20.

καθαρότης, τητος, ἡ, *purity, i.e.*, ceremonial, Heb. ix. 13.*

καθ-έδρα, ας, ἡ, *a seat*, lit., Mat. xxi. 12; Mar. xi. 15; met., *a chair* of authority, Mat. xxiii. 2.*

καθ-έζομαι, *to sit down*, ἐν or ἐπί, dat., Lu. ii. 46; Jn. iv. 6.

καθ-εῖς (W. H. καθ᾽ εἷς), adv. (see Gr. § 300β, 4, Wi. § 37, 3, Bu. 30), *one by one*, Jn. viii. 9.

καθ-εξῆς, adv. (see Gr. § 126 d), *in orderly succession*, Lu. i. 3; Ac. xi. 4, xviii. 23. With art., Lu. viii. 1, ἐν τῷ κ., *soon afterwards;* Ac. iii. 24, οἱ κ., *those that come after.*

καθ-εύδω, *to sleep*, lit., Mat. viii. 24; fig., 1 Th. v. 6.

καθηγητής, οῦ, ὁ, *a guide, master*, Mat. xxiii. 8 (not W. H.), 10.*

καθ-ήκω, used only impers., *it is fit, it is becoming* (acc., inf.), Ac. xxii. 22; τὸ καθῆκον, *the becoming*, Ro. i. 28.*

κάθ-ημαι, 2d pers. κάθῃ for κάθησαι, imper., κάθου (see Gr. § 367, Wi. § 15, 4, Bu. 49), *to be seated, to sit down, to sit, to be settled, to abide;* with εἰς, ἐν, ἐπί (gen., dat., acc.).

καθ-ημερινός, ή, όν, *daily*, Ac. vi. 1.*

καθ-ίζω, ίσω, (1) trans., *to cause to sit down, to set;* (2) intrans., *to seat one's self*, preps. as κάθημαι; *to sit down, to be sitting, to tarry;* mid. in Mat. xix. 28; Lu. xxii. 30.

καθ-ίημι, 1st aor. καθῆκα (see Gr. § 112, Bu. 46), *to send or let down*, Lu. v. 19; Ac. ix. 25, x. 11, xi. 5.*

καθ-ίστημι (and καθιστάω or -ανω), *to appoint, constitute, make, ordain, to conduct*, Ac. xvii. 15; *to appoint as ruler* over (ἐπί, gen., dat., acc.).

καθ-ό, adv. (for καθ᾽ ὅ), *as, according as*, Ro. viii. 26; 2

Cor. viii. 12; 1 Pet. iv. 13.*

καθολικός, ή, όν, *general, universal* (found in the inscriptions of the seven Epistles of James, Peter, John and Jude, but omitted by W. H.).*

καθ-όλου, adv., *entirely;* καθόλου μή, Ac. iv. 18, *not at all.**

καθ-οπλίζω, *to arm fully*, pass., Lu. xi. 21.*

καθ-οράω, ῶ, *to see clearly*, pass., Ro. i. 20.*

καθ-ότι, adv., *as, according as*, Ac. ii. 45, iv. 35; *because that, for*, Lu. i. 7, xix. 9; Ac. ii. 24, xvii. 31 (W. H.).*

καθ-ώς, adv., *according as, even as.*

καθώσ-περ, adv., *just as*, Heb. v. 4 (W. H.).*

καί, conj., *and, also, even.* For the various uses of this conjunction, see Gr. § 403, Wi. § 53, 1–4, Bu. 360 sq.

Καϊάφας, α, ὁ, *Caiaphas*, Jn. xi. 49.

Κάϊν, ὁ (Heb.), *Cain*, Heb. xi. 4.

Καϊνάν, ὁ (Heb.), *Cainan*. Two are mentioned, Lu. iii. 36, 37.*

καινός, ή, όν, *new*, Lu. v. 38; Ac. xvii. 19. *Syn.:* νέος is new under the aspect of *time;* καινός, new in quality, of different character.

καινότης, τητος, ἡ, *newness* (moral and spiritual), Ro. vi. 4, vii. 6.*

καί-περ, conj., *although*, Phil. iii. 4; Heb. v. 8.

καιρός, οῦ, ὁ, *a fixed time, season, opportunity*, Lu. viii. 13; Heb. xi. 15; Ac. xiv. 17; Ro. viii. 18. *Syn.:* χρόνος is time in general, viewed simply as such; καιρός, definite, suitable time, the time of some decisive event, *crisis, opportunity.*

Καῖσαρ, αρος, ὁ, *Cæsar*, a title assumed by Roman emperors, after Julius Cæsar, as Lu. ii. 1, xx. 22; Ac. xvii. 7; Phil. iv. 22.

Καισάρεια, ας, ἡ, *Cæsarea.* Two cities of Palestine, one in Galilee (*Cæsarea Philippi*), Mat. xvi. 13; the other on the coast of the Mediterranean, Ac. viii. 40.

καί-τοι, conj., *and yet, although,* Heb. iv. 3; so καίτοιγε.

καίω, perf. pass. κέκαυμαι, *to kindle, light,* Mat. v. 15; pass., *to burn,* Lu. xii. 35; *to burn, consume,* Jn. xv. 6; fig., Lu. xxiv. 32.

κἀκεῖ (καὶ ἐκεῖ), *and there,* Ac. xiv. 7.

κἀκεῖθεν (καὶ ἐκεῖθεν), *and thence,* Ac. vii. 4, xx. 15.

κἀκεῖνος, η, ο (καὶ ἐκεῖνος), *and he, she, it,* Lu. xi. 7; Ac. xv. 11.

κακία, ας, ἡ, *badness,* (1) of character, *wickedness,* Ac. viii. 22; (2) of disposition, *malice, ill-will,* Col. iii. 8; (3) of condition, *affliction, evil,* Mat. vi. 34.

κακο-ήθεια, ας, ἡ, *malignity,* Ro. i. 29.*

κακο-λογέω, ῶ, *to speak evil of* (acc.), Mar. ix. 39; Ac. xix. 9; *to curse,* Mat. xv. 4; Mar. vii. 10.*

κακο-πάθεια, ας, ἡ, *a suffering of evil, affliction,* Ja. v. 10.*

κακο-παθέω, ῶ, *to suffer evil, to endure affliction,* 2 Tim. ii. 3 (W. H. συνκακ-), 9, iv. 5; Ja. v. 13.*

κακοποιέω, ῶ, abs., *to do harm,* Mar. iii. 4; Lu. vi. 9; *to do wrong,* 1 Pet. iii. 17; 3 Jn. 11.*

κακο-ποιός, όν, as subst., *an evil-doer,* Jn. xviii. 30 (not W. H.); 1 Pet. ii. 12, 14, iii. 16 (W. H. omit), iv. 15.*

κακός, ή, όν, *evil, wicked;* τὸ κακόν, *wickedness,* Mat. xxvii. 23; also *affliction,* Lu. xvi. 35.

κακ-οῦργος, ον, as subst., *a malefactor,* Lu. xxiii. 32, 33, 39; 2 Tim. ii. 9.*

κακ-ουχέω, ῶ, only in pass., part., *treated ill, harassed,* Heb. xi. 37, xiii. 3.*

κακόω, ῶ, ώσω, *to ill-treat, oppress,* Ac. vii. 6, 19, xii. 1, xviii. 10; 1 Pet. iii. 13; *to embitter,* Ac. xiv. 2.*

κακῶς, adv., *badly, wickedly,* Jn. xviii. 23; κακῶς ἔχειν, *to be sick,* or *in trouble,* Mat. iv. 24; Lu. v. 31.

κάκωσις, εως, ἡ, *affliction, ill-treatment,* Ac. vii. 34.*

καλάμη, ης, ἡ, *stubble,* 1 Cor. iii. 12.*

κάλαμος, ου, ὁ, *a stalk,* as (1) *a reed,* growing, Mat. xi. 7; (2) *a reed,* as a mock sceptre, Mat. xxvii. 29; (3) *a pen,* 3 Jn. 13; (4) *a measuring-rod,* Rev. xxi. 15.

καλέω, ῶ, έσω, κέκληκα, *to call;* hence, (1) *to summon,* Lu. xix. 13; (2) *to name,* Mat. i. 21, x. 25; (3) *to invite,* Jn. ii. 2; (4) *to appoint,* or *select,* for an office, Heb. v. 4; (5) pass., *to be called,* or *accounted, i.e., to be,* Mat. v. 9, 19; Ja. ii. 23.

καλλι-έλαιος, ου, ἡ, *a cultivated olive tree,* Ro. xi. 24.*

καλλίων (compar. of καλός), *better;* adv., κάλλιον, Ac. xxv. 10.*

καλο-διδάσκαλος, ου, ὁ, ἡ, *a teacher of what is good,* Tit. ii. 3. (N. T.)*

Καλοὶ Λιμένες, *Fair Havens,* a harbor in the island of Crete, Ac. xxvii. 8.*

καλο-ποιέω, ῶ, *to act uprightly,* 2 Th. iii. 13. (S.)*

καλός, ή, όν, *beautiful;* (1) physically, Lu. xxi. 25; (2) morally beautiful, *good, noble,* Mat. v. 16; Heb. xiii. 18; (3) *excellent, advantageous,* Lu. 43; 1 Cor. vii. 1.

κάλυμμα, ατος, τό, *a covering, veil,* 2 Cor. iii. 13–16.*

καλύπτω, ψω, *to cover, veil,* Lu. xxiii. 30; 2 Cor. iv. 3.

καλῶς, adv., *well, rightly, nobly,* Jn. iv. 17; 1 Cor. xiv. 17.

κἀμέ, see κἀγώ.

κάμηλος, ου, ὁ, ἡ, *a camel,* Mar. i. 6, x. 25.

κάμινος, ου, ἡ, *a furnace,* Mat. xiii. 42, 50; Rev. i. 15, ix. 2.*

καμ-μύω (κατά and μύω), *to shut, close the eyes,* Mat. xiii. 15; Ac. xxviii. 27.*

κάμνω, καμῶ, perf. κέκμηκα, *to be weary, to be sick,* Heb. xii. 3; Ja. v. 15; Rev. ii. 3 (W. H. omit).*

κἀμοί, see κἀγώ.

κάμπτω, ψω, *to bend the knee, bow,* Ro. xi. 4, xiv. 11; Ep. iii. 14; Phil. ii. 10.*

κἄν (καὶ ἐάν), *and if,* Lu. xiii. 9; *even if, though,* Mat. xxvi. 35; *if even,* Heb. xii. 20; elliptically, *if only,* Mar. v. 28; Ac. v. 15.

Κανᾶ, ἡ, *Cana,* Jn. ii. 1, 11.

Κανανίτης, ου, ὁ, *a Zealot* (from

the Aramaic, meaning the same as ζηλωτής), Mat. x. 4; Mar. iii. 18 (W. H. read Καναναῖος, which has the same meaning). (N. T.)*

Κανδάκη, ης, ἡ, *Candace,* Ac. viii. 27.*

κανών, όνος, ὁ, prop. *a rod;* hence, (1) *a rule of conduct,* Gal. vi. 16; Phil. iii. 16 (W. H. omit); (2) *a limit* or *sphere of duty, province* (R. V.), 2 Cor. x. 13, 15, 16.*

Καπερ-ναούμ, or Καφαρ-ναούμ (W. H.), ἡ (Heb.), *Capernaum,* Jn. vi. 17, 24.

καπηλεύω, *to be a petty trader;* hence (with acc.), *to make merchandise of,* or *adulterate, corrupt,* 2 Cor. ii. 17.*

καπνός, οῦ, ὁ, *smoke,* Ac. ii. 19; Rev. viii. 4.

Καππαδοκία, ας, ἡ, *Cappadocia,* Ac. ii. 9; 1 Pet. i. 1.*

καρδία, ας, ἡ, *the heart,* met., as the seat of the affections, but chiefly of the understanding; fig., *the heart* of the earth, Mat. xii. 40.

καρδιο-γνώστης, ου, ὁ, *a knower of hearts,* Ac. i. 24, xv. 8. (N. T.)*

καρπός, οῦ, ὁ, *fruit, produce,* Lu. xii. 17; met., for *children,* Ac. ii. 30; *deeds, conduct,* the fruit of the hands, Mat. iii. 8; *effect, result,* Ro. vi. 21. Praise is called *the fruit of the lips,* Heb. xiii. 15.

Κάρπος, ου, ὁ, *Carpus,* 2 Tim. iv. 13.*

καρποφορέω, ῶ, ήσω, *to bring forth fruit,* Mar. iv. 28; mid., *to bear fruit of one's self,* Col. i. 6.

καρπο-φόρος, ον, *fruitful,* Ac. xiv. 17.*

καρτερέω, ῶ, ήσω, *to be strong, steadfast,* Heb. xi. 27.*

κάρφος, ους, τό, *a dry twig, a straw,* Mat. vii. 3, 4, 5; Lu. vi. 41, 42.*

κατά, prep., gov. the gen. and acc. cases, *down;* hence, gen., *down from, against,* etc.; acc., *according to, against,* etc. (see Gr. §§ 124, 147 a, Wi. §§ 47 k, 49 d, Bu. 334 sq.). In composition, κατά may import *descent, subjection, opposition, distribution,* and with certain verbs (as of destruction, diminution, and the like) is *inten-sive* = "utterly."

κατα-βαίνω, βήσομαι, βέβηκα, 2ό aor. κατέβην, *to go* or *come down, descend*, used of persons and of things, as gifts from heaven, of the clouds, storms, lightnings; also of anything that falls, Lu. xxii. 44; Rev. xvi. 21.

κατα-βάλλω, 1st aor. pass. κατεβλήθην, *to cast down*, Rev. xii. 10 (W. H. βάλλω); 2 Cor. iv. 9 mid., *to lay*, as a foundation, Heb. vi. 1.*

κατα-βαρέω, ῶ, *to weigh down, to burden*, 2 Cor. xii. 16.*

κατα-βαρύνω=καταβαρέω,Mar. xiv. 40 (W. H.).*

κατά-βασις, εως, ἡ, *descent, place of descent*, Lu. xix. 37.*

κατα-βιβάζω, *to bring down, cast down*, Mat. xi. 23 (W. H. καταβαίνω), Lu. x. 15 (Rec., W. H. mrg.).*

κατα-βολή, ῆς, ἡ, *a founding, laying the foundation of*, Mat. xiii. 35; Heb. xi. 11.

κατα-βραβεύω, *to give judgment against as umpire of the games, to deprive of reward*, Col. ii. 18.*

κατ-αγγελεύς, έως, ὁ, *a proclaimer, a herald*, Ac. xvii. 18. (N.T.)*

κατ-αγγέλλω, *to declare openly, to proclaim, to preach*, Ac. xiii. 5, xv. 36.

κατα-γελάω, ῶ, *to laugh at, deride*, gen., Mat. ix. 24; Mar. v. 40; Lu. viii. 53.*

κατα-γινώσκω, *to condemn, blame*, gen. of persons, Gal. ii. 11; 1 Jn. iii. 20, 21.*

κατ-άγνυμι, fut. κατεάξω, *to break down, to break in pieces*, Mat. xii. 20; Jn. xix. 31–33.*

κατ-άγω, *to bring down*, as Ac. ix. 30; Ro. x. 6; as a nautical term, *to bring to land*, Lu. v. 11; pass., *to come to land*, Ac. xxvii. 3, xxviii. 12.

κατ-αγωνίζομαι, dep., *to contend against, subdue* (acc.), Heb. xi. 33.*

κατα-δέω, ῶ, *to bind up*, as wounds, Lu. x. 34.*

κατά-δηλος, ον, *thoroughly evident*, Heb. vii. 15.*

κατα-δικάζω, *to condemn, to pronounce sentence against*, Mat. xii. 7, 37; Lu. vi. 37; Ja. v. 6.*

κατα-δίκη, ης, ἡ, *a sentence of condemnation*, Ac. xxv. 15 (W. H.).*

κατα-διώκω, *to follow closely*, Mar. i. 36.*

κατα-δουλόω, ῶ, ώσω, *to enslave*, 2 Cor. xi. 20; Gal. ii. 4.*

κατα-δυναστεύω, *to exercise power over, to oppress*, Ac. x. 38; Ja. ii. 6.*

κατά-θεμα, W. H. for κατανάθεμα, Rev. xxii. 3. (N T.)*

κατα-θεματίζω, W. H. for καταναθ-, Mat. xxvi. 74. (N. T.)*

κατ-αισχύνω, *to make ashamed*, 1 Cor. i. 27; *to dishonor*, 1 Cor. xi. 4, 5; *to shame*, as with disappointed expectation, 1 Pet. ii. 6; pass., *to be ashamed*, as Lu. xiii. 17.

κατα-καίω, αύσω, *to burn up, to consume entirely*, as Mat. iii. 12; Heb. xiii. 11.

κατα-καλύπτω, in mid., *to wear a veil*, 1 Cor. xi. 6, 7.*

κατα-καυχάομαι, ῶμαι, *to rejoice against, to glory over* (gen.), Ro. xi. 18; Ja. ii. 13, iii. 14. (S.)*

κατά-κειμαι, *to lie down*, as the sick, Mar. i. 30; *to recline* at table, Mar. xiv. 3.

κατα-κλάω, ῶ, *to break in pieces*, Mar. vi. 41; Lu. ix. 16.*

κατα-κλείω, *to shut up, confine*, Lu. iii. 20; Ac. xxvi. 10.*

κατα-κληρο-δοτέω, ῶ, *to distribute by lot*, Ac. xiii. 19 (W. H. read the following). (S.)*

κατα-κληρο-νομέω, ῶ, *to distribute by lot*, Ac. xiii. 19 (W. H.). (S.)*

κατα-κλίνω, νῶ, *to cause to recline* at table, Lu. ix. 14, 15 (W. H.); mid., *to recline* at table, Lu. vii. 36 (W. H.), xiv. 8, xxiv. 30.*

κατα-κλύζω, σω, *to inundate, deluge*, pass., 2 Pet. iii. 6.*

κατα-κλυσμός, οῦ, ὁ, *a deluge, flood*, Mat. xxiv. 38, 39; Lu. xvii. 27; 2 Pet. ii. 5.*

κατ-ακολουθέω, ῶ, *to follow after* (abs. or dat.), Lu. xxiii. 55; Ac. xvi. 17.*

κατα-κόπτω, ψω, *to wound*, Mar. v. 5.*

κατα-κρημνίζω, σω, *to cast down headlong*, Lu. iv. 29.*

κατά-κριμα, ατος, τό, *con-demnation*, Ro. v. 16, 18, viii. 1.*

κατα-κρίνω, νῶ, *to judge worthy of punishment* (gen. and dat.), *to condemn*, as Mat. xx. 18; Ro. ii. 1, viii. 3; in a more general sense, Lu. xi. 31, 32.

κατά-κρισις, εως, ἡ, *the act of condemnation*, 2 Cor. iii. 9, vii. 3. (N. T.)*

κατα-κυριεύω, *to exercise authority over*, Mat. xx. 25; Mar. x. 42; 1 Pet. v. 3; *to get the mastery of*, Ac. xix. 16 (gen.).

κατα-λαλέω, ῶ, *to speak against* (gen.), Ja. iv. 11; 1 Pet. ii. 12, iii. 16.*

κατα-λαλιά, ᾶς, ἡ, *evil-speaking, defamation*, 2 Cor. xii. 20, 1 Pet. ii. 1. (N. T.)*

κατά-λαλος, ον, ὁ, ἡ, *an evil-speaker, a defamer*, Ro. i. 30. (N. T.)*

κατα-λαμβάνω, λήψομαι, *to seize* or *lay hold of*, as Mar. ix. 18; *to grasp, to obtain*, as the prize in public games, Phil. iii. 12, 13; *to overtake*, 1 Th. v. 4; mid., *to comprehend, to perceive*, ὅτι, or acc. and inf., Ep. iii. 18.

κατα-λέγω, *to register, to enrol*, pass., 1 Tim. v. 9.*

κατά-λειμμα, ατος, τό, *a remnant, a residue*, Ro. ix. 27 (W. H. ὑπόλιμμα). (S.)*

κατα-λείπω, ψω, *to leave utterly, to forsake*, Mar. x. 7; *to depart from*, Heb. xi. 27; *to leave remaining, to reserve*, Ro. xi. 4.

κατα-λιθάζω, σω, *to stone, to destroy by stoning*, Lu. xx. 6. (N. T.)*

καταλλαγή, ῆς, ἡ, *reconciliation*, Ro. v. 11, xi. 15; 2 Cor. v. 18, 19.* *Syn.:* see ἀπολύτρωσις.

κατ-αλλάσσω, ξω, *to reconcile* (acc. and dat.), Ro. v. 10; 1 Cor. vii. 11; 2 Cor. v. 18, 19, 20.*

κατά-λοιπος, ον, plur., *the rest, the residue*, Ac. xv. 17.*

κατάλυμα, ατος, τό, *a lodging-place, an inn*, Lu. ii. 7; *a guest-chamber*, Mar. xiv. 14; Lu. xxii. 11.*

κατα-λύω, ύσω, *to unloose*, (1. lit., of a building, *to destroy*, Mar. xiv. 58; (2) fig., of law or command, *to render void*, Mat. v. 17; (3) *to pass the night, to lodge*, Lu. ix. 12, xix. 7.

κατα-μανθάνω, 2d aor. κατέμαθον, *to consider carefully*, Mat. vi. 28.*

κατα-μαρτυρέω, ῶ, *to bear testimony against* (acc. of thing, gen. of pers.), Mat. xxvi. 62, xxvii. 13; Mar. xiv. 60, xv. 4 (not W. H.).*

κατα-μένω, *to remain, abide*, Ac. i. 13.*

κατα-μόνας (W. H. κατὰ μόνας), adv., *privately, alone*, Mar. iv. 10; Lu. ix. 18.*

κατ-ανά-θεμα, ατος, τό, *a curse*, Rev. xxii. 3; see κατάθεμα. (N. T.)*

κατ-ανα-θεματίζω, *to curse, devote to destruction*, Mat. xxvi. 74; see καταθεματίζω. (N. T.)*

κατ-αν-αλίσκω, *to consume*, as fire, Heb. xii. 29.*

κατα-ναρκάω, ῶ, ήσω, *to be burdensome to* (gen.), 2 Cor. xi. 9, xii. 13, 14.*

κατα-νεύω, *to nod, to make signs to*, dat., Lu. v. 7.*

κατα-νοέω, ῶ, (1) *to observe carefully, perceive*, Lu. vi. 41; (2) *to consider* (acc.), Ac. xi. 6.

κατ-αντάω, ῶ, *to come to, to arrive at*, with εἰς, as Ac. xvi. 1; once with ἀντικρύ, Ac. xx. 15; met., *to attain to*, Phil. iii. 11.

κατάνυξις, εως, ἡ, *stupor*, Ro. xi. 8. (S.)*

κατα-νύσσω, ξω, 2d aor., pass. κατενύγην, *to prick through, to agitate greatly*, pass., Ac. ii. 37. (S.)*

κατ-αξιόω, ῶ, ώσω, *to judge worthy of* (gen.), pass., Lu. xx. 35, xxi. 36; Ac. v. 41; 2 Th. i. 5.*

κατα-πατέω, ῶ, *to trample on, to tread under foot* (acc.), as Lu. viii. 5.

κατάπαυσις, εως, ἡ, *a resting, rest*, Ac. vii. 49; Heb. iii. 11, 18, iv. 1, 3, 5, 10, 11.*

κατα-παύω, (1) trans., *to restrain*, acc. (also τοῦ μή, and inf.), Ac. xiv. 18; *to give rest*, Heb. iv. 8; (2) intrans., *to rest*, ἀπό, Heb. iv. 4, 10.*

κατα-πέτασμα(πεταννυμι),ατος, τό, *a veil, curtain*, separating the holy place and the holy of holies, as Lu. xxiii. 45. (S.)

κατα-πίνω, 2d aor. κατέπιον, 1st aor. pass. κατεπόθην, *to drink down, swallow*, Mat. xxiii. 24; Rev. xii. 16; fig., *to devour, destroy*, 1 Cor. xv. 54; 2 Cor. ii. 7, v. 4; Heb. xi. 29; 1 Pet. v. 8.*

κατα-πίπτω, 2d aor. κατέπεσον, *to fall down*, Lu. viii. 6 (W. H.); Ac. xxvi. 14, xxviii. 6.*

κατα-πλέω, εύσομαι, 1st aor. κατέπλευσα, *to sail* to land, Lu. viii. 26.*

κατα-πονέω, ῶ, in pass., *to be oppressed, distressed*, Ac. vii. 24; 2 Pet. ii. 7.*

κατα-ποντίζω, pass., *to sink down*, Mat. xiv. 30; *to be drowned*, Mat. xviii. 6.*

κατ-άρα, ας, ἡ, *a curse, cursing*, Gal. iii. 10, 13; Heb. vi. 8; 2 Pet. ii. 14; Ja. iii. 10.*

κατ-αράομαι, ῶμαι, *to curse*, Mat. v. 44 (W. H. omit); Mar. xi. 21; Lu. vi. 28; Ro. xii. 14; Ja. iii. 9; pass., perf. part., *accursed*, Mat. xxv. 41.*

κατ-αργέω, ῶ, ήσω, *to render useless*, Lu. xiii. 7; *to cause to cease, abolish*, as Ro. iii. 3, 31, and frequently in Paul; *to sever* from (ἀπό), Ro. vii. 2; Gal. v. 4.

κατ-αριθμέω, ῶ, *to number among*, Ac. i. 17.*

κατ-αρτίζω, ἴσω, *to refit, to repair*, Mat. iv. 21; *to restore* from error or sin, Gal. vi. 1; *to perfect, to complete*, 1 Th. iii. 10; 1 Pet. v. 10; pass., *to be restored* to harmony, 1 Cor. i. 10.

κατάρτισις, εως, ἡ, *a perfecting*, 2 Cor. xiii. 9.*

καταρτισμός, οῦ, ὁ, *a perfecting*, Ep. iv. 12. (N. T.)*

κατα-σείω, σω, *to shake* the hand, *to beckon*, Ac. xii. 17, xiii. 16, xix. 33, xxi. 40.*

κατα-σκάπτω, ψω, *to dig under, to demolish*, Ro. xi. 3; perf. part., pass., *ruins*, Ac. xv. 16 (not W. H.).*

κατα-σκευάζω, άσω, *to prepare, to build, to equip*, as Mat. xi. 10; Lu. i. 17; Heb. iii. 3, 4.

κατα-σκηνόω, ῶ, ώσω, *to pitch one's tent, to dwell*, Mat. xiii.

32; Mar. iv. 32; Lu. xiii. 19; Ac. ii. 26.*

κατα-σκήνωσις, εως, ἡ, *a dwelling-place, a haunt*, as of birds, Mat. viii. 20; Lu. ix. 58.*

κατα-σκιάζω, σω, *to overshadow*, Heb. ix. 5.*

κατα-σκοπέω, ῶ, *to spy out, to plot against*, Gal. ii. 4.*

κατά-σκοπος, ου, ὁ, *a spy*, Heb. xi. 31.*

κατα-σοφίζομαι, σομαι, *to deal deceitfully with*, Ac. vii. 19.*

κατα-στέλλω, λῶ, 1st aor. κατέστειλα, *to appease, restrain*, Ac. xix. 35, 36.*

κατά-στημα, ατος, τό, *behavior, conduct*, Tit. ii. 3.*

κατα-στολή, ῆς, ἡ, *dress, attire*, 1 Tim. ii. 9.*

κατα-στρέφω, ψω, *to overthrow*, Mat. xxi. 12; Mar. xi. 15; Ac. xv. 16 (W. H.).*

κατα-στρηνιάω, ῶ, άσω, *to grow wanton* to the loss of (gen.), 1 Tim. v. 11. (N. T.)*

κατα-στροφή, ῆς, ἡ, *overthrow, destruction*, 2 Tim. ii. 14; 2 Pet. ii. 6 (W. H. omit).*

κατα-στρώννυμι, στρώσω, *to prostrate, slay*, 1 Cor. x. 5.*

κατα-σύρω, *to drag along* by force, Lu. xii. 58.*

κατα-σφάζω, ξω, *to slay*, Lu. xix. 27.*

κατα-σφραγίζω, σω, *to seal up*, as a book, Rev. v. 1.*

κατά-σχεσις, εως, ἡ, *a possession*, Ac. vii. 5, 45. (S.)*

κατα-τίθημι, θήσω, 1st aor. κατέθηκα, *to deposit*, as a body in a tomb, Mar. xv. 46 (W. H. τίθημι); mid. κατατίθεσθαι χάριν, *to gain favor* with (dat.), Ac. xxiv. 27 xxv. 9.*

κατα-τομή, ῆς, ἡ, *mutilation* paronomasia with περιτομή Phil. iii. 2.*

κατα-τοξεύω, *to transfix*, Heb xii. 20 (W. H. omit).*

κατα-τρέχω, 2d aor. κατέδραμον, *to run down* (ἐπί, acc.), Ac. xxi. 32.*

κατα-φάγω, see κατεσθίω.

κατα-φέρω, κατοίσω, 1st aor. κατήνεγκα, pass. κατηνέχθην, *to cast down*, as an adverse vote, Ac. xxv. 7, xxvi. 10 (W. H.); pass., *to be borne down, to be overcome*, Ac. xx. 9.*

κατα-φεύγω, 2d aor. κατέφυγον, to flee for refuge, with εἰς, Ac. xiv. 6; with inf., Heb. vi. 18.*

κατα-φθείρω, pass., perf. κατέφθαρμαι, 2d aor. κατεφθάρην, to corrupt, 2 Tim. iii. 8; to destroy, 2 Pet. ii. 12 (W. H. φθείρω).*

κατα-φιλέω, ῶ, to kiss affectionately, or repeatedly (acc.), as Mat. xxvi. 49; Lu. xv. 20.

κατα-φρονέω, ῶ, ήσω, to despise (gen.), as Mat. vi. 24.

καταφρονητής, οῦ, ὁ, a despiser, Ac. xiii. 41. (S.)*

κατα-χέω, εύσω, 1st aor. κατέχεα, to pour down upon, Mat. xxvi. 7; Mar. xiv. 3.*

κατα-χθόνιος, ον, subterranean, Phil. ii. 10.*

κατα-χράομαι, ῶμαι, to use fully, 1 Cor. vii. 31, ix. 18 (dat.).*

κατα-ψύχω, to cool, to refresh, Lu. xvi. 24.*

κατ-είδωλος, ον, full of idols (R. V.), Ac. xvii. 16. (N.T.)*

κατ-έναντι, adv., or as prep. with gen., over against, before, in presence or in sight of.

κατ-ενώπιον, adv., in the presence of (gen.). (S.)

κατ-εξουσιάζω, to exercise authority over (gen.), Mat. xx. 25; Mar. x. 42. (N.T.)*

κατ-εργάζομαι, άσομαι, with mid. and pass. aor. (augm. εἰ-), to accomplish, achieve, Ro. xv. 18; Ep. vi. 13; to work out, result in, Ro. iv. 15, vii. 8.

κατ-έρχομαι, 2d aor. κατῆλθον, to come down, Lu. iv. 31, ix. 37.

κατ-εσθίω and -έσθω (Mar. xii. 40, W. H.), fut. καταφάγομαι (Jn. ii. 17, W. H.), 2d aor. κατέφαγον, to eat up, to devour entirely, lit. or fig., Mat. xiii. 4; Jn. ii. 17; Gal. v. 15.

κατ-ευθύνω, νῶ, to direct, to guide, Lu. i. 79; 1 Th. iii. 11; 2 Th. iii. 5.*

κατ-ευλογέω, to bless greatly, Mar. x. 16 (W. H.).*

κατ-εφ-ίστημι, 2d aor. κατεπέστην, to rise up against, Ac. xviii. 12. (N.T.)*

κατ-έχω, κατασχήσω, to seize on, to hold fast, to retain, possess, to prevent from doing

a thing (τοῦ μή, with inf.), to repress, Ro. i. 18; τὸ κατέχον, the hindrance, 2 Th. ii. 6; κατεῖχον εἰς τὸν αἰγιαλόν, they held for the shore, Ac. xxvii. 40.

κατ-ηγορέω, ῶ, ήσω, to accuse, to speak against, abs., or with person in gen.; charge in gen. alone or after περὶ or κατά; pass., to be accused; with ὑπό or παρά, of the accuser.

κατηγορία, ας, ἡ, an accusation, a charge, pers. in gen. alone, or after κατά; charge also in gen., 1 Tim. v. 19; Tit. i. 6.

κατήγορος, ου, ὁ, an accuser, Ac. xxiii. 30, 35.

κατήγωρ, ὁ (Heb.?), an accuser, Rev. xii. 10 (W. H.). (N.T.)*

κατήφεια, ας, ἡ, dejection, gloom, Ja. iv. 9.*

κατ-ηχέω, ῶ, ήσω, perf., pass. κατήχημαι (ῆχος), to instruct orally, to teach, inform, Lu. i. 4; Ac. xviii. 25, xxi. 21, 24; Ro. ii. 18; 1 Cor. xiv. 19; Gal. vi. 6.*

κατ' ἰδίαν, separately, privately, by one's self (see ἰδίος).

κατ-ιόω, ῶ (ἰός), to cover with rust, Ja. v. 3. (Ap.)*

κατ-ισχύω, to prevail against, overpower (gen.), Mat. xvi. 18; Lu. xxi. 36 (W. H.), xxiii. 23.*

κατ-οικέω, ῶ, (1) intrans., to dwell, with ἐν, εἰς (const. praeg.), ἐπί, gen., or adverbs of place, Ac. i. 20, vii. 4; fig., of qualities or attributes, to abide, Col. ii. 9; (2) trans., to dwell in, to inhabit (acc.), Mat. xxiii. 21; Ac. i. 19.

κατοίκησις, εως, ἡ, a dwelling, habitation, Mar. v. 3.*

κατοικητήριον, ου, τό, a dwelling-place, Ep. ii. 22; Rev. xviii. 2. (S.)*

κατοικία, ας, ἡ, a dwelling, habitation, Ac. xvii. 26.*

κατ-οικίζω, to cause to dwell, Ja. iv. 5 (W. H.).*

κατοπτρίζω, mid., to behold, as in a mirror, 2 Cor. iii. 18.*

κατ-όρθωμα, ατος, τό, an honorable or successful achievement, Ac. xxiv. 2 (W. H. διόρθωμα).*

κάτω, adv., downwards, down,

Mat. iv. 6, beneath, Mar. xiv. 66; of age, comp., κατωτέρω, under, Mat. ii. 16.

κατώτερος, α, ον (κάτω), lower, Ep. iv. 9 (on which see Gr. § 259, Wi. § 11, 2 c, Bu. 28).*

καῦμα, ατος, τό (καίω), heat, scorching heat, Rev. vii. 16, xvi. 9.*

καυματίζω, σω, to scorch, burn, Mat. xiii. 6; Mar. iv. 6; Rev. xvi. 8, 9.*

καῦσις, εως, ἡ, a burning, burning up, Heb. vi. 8.*

καυσόω, ῶ, to burn up, pass., 2 Pet. iii. 10, 12. (N.T.)*

καύσων, ωνος, ὁ, scorching heat; perhaps a hot wind from the E., Mat. xx. 12; Lu. xii. 55; Ja. i. 11 (see Hos. xii. 1, etc.). (S.)*

καυτηριάζω (W. H. καυστ-), to brand, as with a hot iron; fig., pass., 1 Tim. iv. 2.*

καυχάομαι, ῶμαι, 2d pers. καυχᾶσαι, fut. ήσομαι, to glory, to boast, both in a good sense and in a bad, 1 Cor. i. 29; Ep. ii. 9; followed with prep., ἐν, περί, gen.; ὑπέρ, gen.; ἐπί, gen.

καύχημα, ατος, τό, the ground of glorying, as Ro. iv. 2; a glorying, 1 Cor. v. 6.

καύχησις, εως, ἡ, the act of boasting, glorying, Ro. xv. 17; Ja. iv. 16. (S.)

Καφαρναούμ (see Καπερναούμ), Capernaum.

Κεγχρεαί, ῶν, αἱ, Cenchreæ, a port of Corinth, Ac. xviii. 18; Ro. xvi. 1.*

κέδρος, ου, ἡ, a cedar, Jn. xviii. 1; perhaps a mistaken reading for following.*

Κεδρών, ὁ (Heb. dark or turbid), Cedron, a turbid brook between the Mount of Olives and Jerusalem, a variant reading in Jn. xviii. 1.*

κεῖμαι, σαι, ται; impf. ἐκείμην, σο, το; to lie, to recline, to be laid, Lu. xxiii. 53; 1 Jn. v. 19; met., to be enacted, as laws, 1 Tim. i. 9.

κειρία, ας, ἡ, a band or bandage of linen, Jn. xi. 44.*

κείρω, κερῶ, to shear, as sheep, Ac. viii. 32; mid., to have the head shorn, Ac. xviii. 18; 1 Cor. xi. 6.*

κέλευσμα, ατος, τό, a command, a loud cry, 1 Th. iv. 16.*

κελεύω, σω, *to command, to order*, Ac. iv. 15, v. 34.

κενοδοξία, ας, ἡ, *vainglory, empty pride*, Phil. ii. 3.*

κενό-δοξος, ον, *vainglorious*, Gal. v. 26.*

κενός, ή, όν, *empty, vain*, Ep. v. 6; Col. ii. 8; *empty-handed*, Lu. i. 53; Ja. ii. 20; *fruitless, ineffectual*, 1 Cor. xv. 10, 58. *Syn.*: κενός, *empty*, refers to the contents; μάταιος, *aimless, purposeless*, to the result.

κενο-φωνία, ας, ἡ, *empty disputing, useless babbling*, 1 Tim. vi. 20; 2 Tim. ii. 16. (N. T.)*

κενόω, ῶ, ώσω, with ἑαυτόν, *to empty one's self, divest one's self of rightful dignity*, Phil. ii. 7; *to make useless* or *false*, Ro. iv. 14; 1 Cor. i. 17, ix. 15; 2 Cor. ix. 3.*

κέντρον, ου, τό, *a sting*, Rev. ix. 10; 1 Cor. xv. 55, 56; *a goad*, Ac. ix. 5 (W. H. omit), xxvi. 14.*

κεντυρίων, ωνος, ὁ, Latin (see Gr. § 154c), *a centurion*, the commander of a hundred foot-soldiers, Mar. xv. 39, 44, 45.*

κενῶς, adv., *in vain*, Ja. iv. 5.*

κεραία, or κερέα (W. H.), ας, ἡ, *a little horn* (the small projecting stroke by which certain similar Hebrew letters are distinguished, as ר and ד); met., *the minutest part*, Mat. v. 18; Lu. xvi. 17.*

κεραμεύς, έως, ὁ, *a potter*, Mat. xxvii. 7, 10; Ro. ix. 21.*

κεραμικός, ή, όν, *made of clay, earthen*, Rev. ii. 27.*

κεράμιον, ου, τό, *an earthen vessel, a pitcher*, Mar. xiv. 13; Lu. xxii. 10.*

κέραμος, ου, ὁ, *a roofing tile*, Lu. v. 19.*

κεράννυμι (see Gr. §§ 113, 114, Wi. § 15, Bu. 60), *to mix, to pour out for drinking*, Rev. xiv. 10, xviii. 6.*

κέρας, ατος, τό, *a horn*, as Rev. v. 6; fig., for *strength*, only Lu. i. 69; *a projecting point, horn* of the altar, only Rev. ix. 13.

κεράτιον, ου, τό, *a little horn*, the name of the fruit of the *carob tree*, Lu. xv. 16.*

κερδαίνω, ανῶ, 1st aor. ἐκέρδησα,

to gain, acquire, Mat. xxv. 16 (W. H.), 22; Ja. iv. 13; *to gain, win*, Phil. iii. 8; *to gain over* to a cause, 1 Cor. ix. 19–22.

κέρδος, ους, τό, *gain, advantage*, Phil. i. 21, iii. 7; Tit. i. 11.*

κέρμα, ατος, τό (κείρω), *a small piece of money*, Jn. ii. 15.*

κερματιστής, οῦ, ὁ, *a money-changer*, Jn. ii. 14.*

κεφάλαιον, ου, τό, *a sum of money*, Ac. xxii. 28; *the sum, main point* of an argument, Heb. viii. 1 (see R. V. and mrg.).*

κεφαλαιόω (W. H. -λιόω), ῶ, ώσω, *to smite on the head*, Mar. xii. 4.*

κεφαλή, ῆς, ἡ, *the head*, of human beings or animals; for the whole person, Ac. xviii. 6; *the head* of a corner (with γωνία), *corner-stone*, Lu. xx. 17; met., implying authority, *head, lord*, 1 Cor. xi. 3; Ep. i. 22; Col. i. 18.

κεφαλίς, ίδος, ἡ (prop. *top*), *a roll, a volume*, Heb. x. 7.*

κημόω, *to muzzle*, 1 Cor. ix. 9 (W. H. mrg.).*

κῆνσος, ου, ὁ, Latin (Gr. § 154d, Bu. 16), *a tax, a poll-tax*, Mat. xvii. 25, xxii. 17, 19; Mar. xii. 14.*

κῆπος, ου, ὁ, *a garden*, Lu. xiii. 19; Jn. xviii. 1, 26, xix. 41.*

κηπ-ουρός, οῦ, ὁ, *a gardener*, Jn. xx. 15.*

κηρίον, ου, τό, *a honeycomb*, Lu. xxiv. 42 (W. H. omit).*

κήρυγμα, ατος, τό, *a proclaiming, preaching*, as Mat. xii. 41; 1 Cor. i. 21; 2 Tim. iv. 17.

κῆρυξ, υκος, ὁ, *a herald, a preacher*, 1 Tim. ii. 7; 2 Tim. i. 11; 2 Pet. ii. 5.*

κηρύσσω, ξω, (1) *to proclaim, to publish*, Mar. vii. 36; (2) specially, *to preach the Gospel*, abs., or acc. and dat., Mar. i. 38; Lu. xii. 3; 1 Pet. iii. 19.

κῆτος, ους, τό, *a sea monster, a whale*, Mat. xii. 40.*

Κηφᾶς, ᾶ, ὁ (Aramaic, *a rock*), *Cephas, i.e.*, Peter, 1 Cor. i. 12, iii. 22.

κιβωτός, οῦ, ἡ, *a wooden chest*, used of the ark of the covenant, Heb. ix. 4; Rev. xi. 19;

of Noah's ark, Lu. xvii. 27; Heb. xi. 7.

κιθάρα, ας, ἡ, *a harp*, 1 Cor. xiv. 7; Rev. xv. 2.

κιθαρίζω, *to play upon a harp*, 1 Cor. xiv. 7; Rev. xiv. 2.*

κιθαρ-ῳδός, οῦ, ὁ, *a harper, singer to the harp*, Rev. xiv. 2, xviii. 22.*

Κιλικία, ας, ἡ, *Cilicia*, Ac. vi. 9, xxi. 39.

κινάμωμον (W. H. κιννά-), ου, τό, *cinnamon*, Rev. xviii. 13.*

κινδυνεύω, σω, *to be in danger*, Lu. viii. 23; Ac. xix. 27, 40; 1 Cor. xv. 30.*

κίνδυνος, ου, ὁ, *danger, peril*, Ro. viii. 35; 2 Cor. xi. 26.*

κινέω, ῶ, ήσω, *to move, to stir*, Mat. xxiii. 4; Ac. xvii. 28; *to shake* the head in mockery, Mat. xxvii. 39; Mar. xv. 29; *to remove*, Rev. ii. 5, vi. 14; *to excite*, Ac. xvii. 28, xxi. 30, xxiv. 5.*

κίνησις, εως, ἡ, *a moving, agitation*, Jn. v. 3 (W. H. omit).*

Κίς (W. H. Κείς), ὁ (Heb.), *Kish*, father of Saul, Ac. xiii. 21.*

κίχρημι, *to lend*, Lu. xi. 5.*

κλάδος, ου, ὁ, *a branch*, as Mat. xiii. 32; met., Ro. xi. 16–19.

κλαίω, αύσω, (1) abs., *to wail, to lament*, Lu. xix. 41; (2) trans., *to weep for* (acc.), Mat. ii. 18.

κλάσις, εως, ἡ, *a breaking*, Lu. xxiv. 35; Ac. ii. 42.*

κλάσμα, ατος, τό, *a broken piece, a fragment*, as Mat. xiv. 20.

Κλαύδη (W. H. Καῦδα), ης, ἡ, *Clauda* or *Cauda*, a small island near Crete, Ac. xxvii. 16.*

Κλαυδία, ας, ἡ, *Claudia*, 2 Tim. iv. 21.*

Κλαύδιος, ου, ὁ, *Claudius*, the Roman emperor, Ac. xi. 28, xviii. 2; a military tribune (Lysias), Ac. xxiii. 26.*

κλαυθμός, οῦ, ὁ (κλαίω), *weeping, lamentation*, as Mat. ii. 18.

κλάω, άσω, only with ἄρτον, *to break* bread, in the ordinary meal, Mat. xiv. 19; or in the Lord's Supper, xxvi. 26; fig., of the body of Christ, 1 Cor. xi. 24 (W. H. omit).

κλείς, κλειδός, acc. sing. κλεῖδα

or κλεῖν, acc. plur. κλεῖδας or κλεῖς, ἡ, a key, as a symbol of power and authority, Mat. xvi. 19; Rev. i. 18, iii. 7, ix. 1, xx. 1; met., Lu. xi. 52.*

κλείω, σω, to shut, shut up, Mat. vi. 6; Lu. iv. 25.

κλέμμα, ατος, τό,(κλέπτω), theft, Rev. xi. 21.*

Κλεόπας, α, ὁ, Cleopas, Lu. xxiv. 18.*

κλέος, ους, τό, glory, praise, 1 Pet. ii. 20.*

κλέπτης, ου, ὁ, a thief, as Mat. vi. 19; met., of false teachers, Jn. x. 8. Syn.: κλέπτης, a thief, who steals secretly; λῃστής, a robber, who plunders openly, by violence.

κλέπτω, ψω, to steal, abs., Mat. xix. 18; or trans. (acc.), Mat. xxvii. 64.

κλῆμα, ατος, τό (κλάω), a tender branch, a shoot, of a vine, etc., Jn. xv. 2, 4, 5, 6.*

Κλήμης, εντος, ὁ, Clement, Phil. iv. 3.*

κληρονομέω, ῶ, ήσω, to inherit, Gal. iv. 30; to obtain, generally, Lu. x. 25.

κληρονομία, ας, ἡ, an inheritance, Lu. xii. 13; a possession, Gal. iii. 18.

κληρο-νόμος, ου, ὁ, an heir, Mat. xxi. 38; applied to Christ, Heb. i. 2; in general, one who obtains a possession, Heb. vi. 17.

κλῆρος, ου, ὁ, (1) a lot, Mat. xxvii. 35; hence, (2) that which is allotted, a portion, Ac. i. 17, 25, viii. 21, xxvi. 18; Col. i. 12; plur., persons assigned to one's care, 1 Pet. v. 3.*

κληρόω, ῶ, to make a heritage, Ep. i. 11.*

κλῆσις, εως, ἡ, a calling, invitation, in N. T. always of the divine call, as Ro. xi. 29; Ep. iv. 4.

κλητός, ή, όν, verb. adj. (καλέω), called, invited, Mat. xxii. 14; of Christians, the called, Ro. i. 6, 7, viii. 28; called to an office, Ro. i. 1; 1 Cor. i. 1.

κλίβανος, ου, ὁ, an oven, a furnace, Mat. vi. 30; Lu. xii. 28.*

κλίμα, ατος, τό, a tract of country, a region, Ro. xv. 23; 2 Cor. xi. 10; Gal. i. 21.*

κλινάριον, ου, τό, a small bed, Ac. v. 15 (W. H.).*

κλίνη, ης, ἡ, a bed, Mar. vii. 30; a portable bed, Mat. ix. 2, 6; a couch for reclining at meals, Mar. iv. 21.

κλινίδιον, ου, τό (dim.), a small bed, a couch, Lu. v. 19, 24.*

κλίνω, νῶ, perf. κέκλικα, (1) trans., to bow, in reverence, Lu. xxiv. 5; in death, Jn. xix. 30; to recline the head for rest, Mat. viii. 20; to turn to flight, Heb. xi. 34; (2) intrans., to decline, as the day, Lu. ix. 12.

κλισία, ας, ἡ, a company reclining at a meal, Lu. ix. 14.*

κλοπή, ῆς, ἡ, theft, Mat. xv. 19; Mar. vii. 21.*

κλύδων, ωνος, ὁ, a violent agitation of the sea, a wave, Lu. viii. 24; Ja. i. 6.*

κλυδωνίζομαι, to be agitated, as waves by the wind, Ep. iv. 14. (S.)*

Κλωπᾶς, ᾶ, ὁ, Clopas, Jn. xix. 25.*

κνήθω, to tickle; pass., to be tickled, to itch, 2 Tim. iv. 3.*

Κνίδος, ου, ἡ, Cnidus, Ac. xxvii. 7.*

κοδράντης, ου, ὁ, Lat. (see Gr. § 154a, Bu. 17), a quadrans, farthing, the fourth part of the Roman as, Mat. v. 26; Mar. xii. 42. (N. T.)*

κοιλία, ας, ἡ, (1) the belly, Mat. xv. 17; (2) the womb, Mat. xix. 12; (3) fig., the inner man, the heart, Jn. vii. 38.

κοιμάω, ῶ, pass., to fall asleep, Lu. xxii. 45; met., to die, Jn. xi. 12.

κοίμησις, εως, ἡ, repose, taking rest, Jn. xi. 13.*

κοινός, ή, όν, common, i.e., shared by many, Ac. iv. 32; unclean, ceremonially, Ac. x. 15; Heb. x. 29.

κοινόω, ῶ, ώσω, to make common or unclean, to profane, Mat. xv. 11; Ac. xxi. 28.

κοινωνέω, ῶ, ήσω, to have common share in, to partake in, Ro. xv. 27; to be associated in, Gal. vi. 6.

κοινωνία, ας, ἡ, participation, communion, fellowship, as 1 Cor. x. 16; 2 Cor. xiii. 13; 1 Jn. i. 3, 6, 7; a contribution, Ro. xv. 26; Heb. xiii. 16.

κοινωνικός, ή, όν, ready to communicate, liberal, 1 Tim. vi. 18.*

κοινωνός, ή, όν, as subst., a partner, Lu. v. 10; a sharer with, gen. obj., 2 Cor. i. 7.

κοίτη, ης, ἡ, a bed, Lu. xi. 7; met., marriage bed, Heb. xiii. 4; sexual intercourse (as illicit), Ro. xiii. 13; κοίτην ἔχειν, to conceive, Ro. ix. 10.*

κοιτών, ῶνος, ὁ, a bed-chamber, Ac. xii. 20.*

κόκκινος, η, ον, dyed from the κόκκος, crimson, Heb. ix. 19; Rev. xvii. 4. (S.)

κόκκος, ου, ὁ, a kernel, a grain, Lu. xiii. 19, xvii. 6.

κολάζω, σω, mid., to chastise, to punish, Ac. iv. 21; pass., 2 Pet. ii. 9.*

κολακεία (W. H. -κία), ας, ἡ, flattery, 1 Th. ii. 5.*

κόλασις, εως, ἡ, chastisement, punishment, Mat. xxv. 46; 1 Jn. iv. 18.*

Κολασσαί, ῶν, αἱ, see Κολοσσαί.

κολαφίζω, σω, to strike with the fist, to maltreat, Mar. xiv. 65. (N. T.)

κολλάω, ῶ, ήσω, pass., to cleave to, to join one's self to, Lu. x. 11; Ac. viii. 29.

κολλούριον, or κολλύριον, ου, τό, collyrium, eye-salve, Rev. iii. 18.*

κολλυβιστής, οῦ, ὁ (κόλλυβος, small coin), a money-changer, Mat. xxi. 12; Mar. xi. 15; Jn. ii. 15.*

κολοβόω, ῶ, ώσω, to cut off, to shorten, Mat. xxiv. 22; Mar. xiii. 20.*

Κολοσσαεύς, έως, ὁ, plur. Κολοσσαεῖς (W. H. Κολασσαεῖς), Colossians, only in the heading and subscription (Rec.) to the Epistle.

Κολοσσαί, or Κολασσαί, ῶν, αἱ, Colossæ, Col. i. 2.*

κόλπος, ου, ὁ, the bosom, the chest, (1) of the body; ἐν τῷ κόλπῳ (or τοῖς κόλποις) εἶναι, ἀνακεῖσθαι, to be in the bosom of, i.e., recline next to, at table; Lu. xvi. 22, 23 (of the heavenly banquet); Jn. xiii. 23; the phrase in Jn. i. 18 implies a still closer fellowship; (2) of the dress, used as a bag or pocket, Lu. vi.

38; (3) *a bay, a gulf of the sea*, Ac. xxvii. 39.*

κολυμβάω, ῶ, ήσω, *to swim*, Ac. xxvii. 43.*

κολυμβήθρα, ας, ή, *a swimming-place, a pool*, Jn. v. 2, 4 (Rec.), 7, ix. 7, 11 (Rec.).*

κολώνια, or κολωνία (W. H.), ας, ή (Lat.), *a colony;* Philippi is so called, Ac. xvi. 12. (N. T.)*

κομάω, ῶ, *to wear the hair long*, 1 Cor. xi. 14, 15.*

κόμη, ης, ή, *hair* of the head, 1 Cor. xi. 15.*

κομίζω, σω, mid. fut. κομίσομαι or κομιοῦμαι, *to bear, to bring*, Lu. vii. 37; mid., *to bring for one's self, i.e., to obtain*, Heb. x. 36; *to receive again, to recover*, Heb. xi. 19.

κομψότερον (comp. of κομψός), *better*, of convalescence, adverbially with ἔχω, Jn. iv. 52.*

κονιάω, ῶ, *to whitewash*, Mat. xxiii. 27; pass., Ac. xxiii. 3.*

κονι-ορτός, οῦ, ὁ (ὄρνυμι), *dust*, Mat. x. 14.

κοπάζω, σω, *to grow weary, to cease*, of the wind, Mat. xiv. 32; Mar. iv. 39, vi. 51.*

κοπετός, οῦ, ὁ (κόπτω), *vehement lamentation*, Ac. viii. 2.*

κοπή, ῆς, ἡ, *cutting, slaughter*, Heb. vii. 1.*

κοπιάω, ῶ, άσω, *to be weary*, Mat. xi. 28; *to labor, to toil*, Lu. v. 5; in the Gospel, Ro. xvi. 6, 12; 1 Cor. xv. 10.

κόπος, ου, ὁ, *labor, toil, trouble*, Lu. xi. 7; 2 Th. iii. 8.

κοπρία, ας, ἡ, *dung, manure*, Lu. xiii. 8 (not W. H.), xiv. 35.*

κόπριον, ου, τό, *dung*, Lu. xiii. 8 (W. H.).*

κόπτω, mid. fut. κόψομαι, *to cut off*, as branches, trees, etc., Mat. xxi. 8; mid., *to beat or cut one's self in grief, to bewail*, as Mat. xi. 17.

κόραξ, ακος, ὁ, *a raven*, Lu. xii. 24.*

κοράσιον, ον, τό (prop. dim. from κόρη), *a girl*, as Mar. vi. 22, 28.

κορβάν (W. H. κορβάν), (indecl.), and κορβανᾶς, ᾶ, ὁ (from Heb.), (1) *a gift, an offering* to God, Mar. vii. 11; (2) *the sacred treasury*, Mat. xxvii. 6.*

Κορέ, ὁ (Heb.), *Korah*, Ju. 11.*

κορέννυμι, έσω, pass. perf. κεκόρεσμαι, *to satiate, satisfy*, Ac. xxvii. 38; 1 Cor. iv. 8.*

Κορίνθιος, ου, ὁ, *a Corinthian*, Ac. xviii. 8; 2 Cor. vi. 11.*

Κόρινθος, ου, ἡ, *Corinth*, Ac. xviii. 1, xix. 1.

Κορνήλιος, ου, ὁ, *Cornelius*, Ac. x.*

κόρος, ου, ὁ (from Heb.), *a cor*, the largest dry measure, equal to ten βάτοι, or ten Attic medimni, Lu. xvi. 7. (S.)*

κοσμέω, ῶ, ήσω, *to put in order, to prepare*, Mat. xxv. 7; *to adorn*, Mat. xxiii. 29; 1 Tim. ii. 9; met., with honor, Tit. ii. 10; 1 Pet. iii. 5.

κοσμικός, ή, όν, (1) *earthly*, opp. to ἐπουράνιος, Heb. ix. 1; (2) *worldly, i.e., corrupt*, Tit. ii. 12.*

κόσμιος, ον, *orderly, modest*, 1 Tim. ii. 9, iii. 2.*

κοσμο-κράτωρ, ορος, ὁ, *lord of this world, world-ruler* (R. V.), Ep. vi. 12.*

κόσμος, ου, ὁ, (1) *ornament, decoration*, only 1 Pet. iii. 3; hence, (2) *the material universe*, Lu. xi. 50, as well ordered and beautiful; (3) *the world*, Jn. xi. 9; *worldly affairs*, Gal. vi. 14; (4) *the inhabitants of the world*, 1 Cor. iv. 9; as opposed to God, Jn. viii. 23; (5) *a vast collection*, of anything, Ja. iii. 6. *Syn.:* see αἰών.

Κούαρτος, ου, ὁ (Latin, see Gr. § 159), *Quartus*, Ro. xvi. 23.*

κοῦμι (a Hebrew imperative fem.), *arise*, Mar. v. 41 (W. H. read κούμ, the masculine form). (N. T.)*

κουστωδία, ας, ἡ (Latin, see Gr. § 154 c, Bu. 17), *a guard*, Mat. xxvii. 65, 66, xxviii. 11. (N. T.)*

κουφίζω, *to lighten*, as a ship, Ac. xxvii. 38.*

κόφινος, ου, ὁ, *a basket*, as Mat. xiv. 20.

κράββατος (W. H. κράβαττος), ου, ὁ, *a couch, a light bed*, as Mar. ii. 12.

κράζω, ξω, *to cry out*, hoarsely, or urgently, or in anguish, Mar. v. 5; Ac. xix. 32.

κραιπάλη, ης, ἡ, *surfeiting*,

caused by excessive drinking, Lu. xxi. 34.*

κρανίον, ου, τό, *a skull*, Lu. xxiii. 33; Κρανίου Τόπος, Greek for Γολγοθά, which see, Mat. xxiii. 33; Mar. xv. 22; Jn. xix. 17.*

κράσπεδον, ου, τό, *the fringe, tassel*, of a garment, as Mat. xxiii. 5.

κραταιός, ά, όν, *strong, mighty*, 1 Pet. v. 6.*

κραταιόω, ῶ, in pass. only, *to be strong, to grow strong*, Lu. i. 80, ii. 40; 1 Cor. xvi. 13; Ep. iii. 16. (S.)*

κρατέω, ῶ, ήσω, with acc., or gen., or acc. and gen. (see Gr. § 264, Wi. § 30, 8 d, Bu. 161), *to get possession of, obtain*, Ac. xxvii. 13; *to take hold of*, Mar. i. 31; Ac. iii. 11; *to seize*, Mat. xiv. 3; *to hold*, Rev. ii. 1; *to hold fast*, Rev. ii. 25, iii. 11; *to retain*, of sins, Jn. xx. 23.

κράτιστος, η, ον (prop. superlative of κρατύς, see κράτος), *most excellent, most noble*, a title of honor, Lu. i. 3; Ac. xxiii. 26, xxiv. 3, xxvi. 25.*

κράτος, ους, τό, *strength, power, dominion*, Ep. i. 19; 1 Pet. iv. 11; Heb. ii. 14; κατὰ κράτος, Ac. xix. 20, *greatly, mightily.*

κραυγάζω, σω, *to cry out, to shout*, as Mat. xii. 19.

κραυγή, ῆς, ἡ, *a crying, outcry*, as Heb. v. 7.

κρέας (ατος, αος, contr. κρέως), τό, plur. κρέατα, κρέα, *flesh, flesh-meat*, Ro. xiv. 21; 1 Cor. viii. 13.*

κρείσσων (or -ττ-), ον (prop. compar. of κρατύς, see κράτος), *stronger, more excellent*, as Heb. vii. 7, xii. 24.

κρεμάννυμι, or κρεμάω, ῶ, fut. άσω, *to hang up*, trans., Ac. v. 30; mid., *to be suspended, to hang*, Mat. xxii. 40; Ac. xxviii. 4.

κρημνός, οῦ, ὁ (κρεμάννυμι), *a precipice*, from its overhanging, Mat. viii. 32; Mar. v. 13; Lu. viii. 33.*

Κρής, ητός, ὁ, *a Cretan*, Ac. ii. 11; Tit. i. 12.*

Κρήσκης, ου (Latin), *Crescens*, 2 Tim. iv. 10.*

Κρήτη, ης, ἡ, *Crete*, now Candia, Ac. xxvii. 7.

κριθή, ῆς, ἡ, barley, Rev. vi. 6.*

κρίθινος, η, ον, made of barley; ἄρτοι κρίθινοι, barley loaves, Jn. vi. 9, 13.*

κρίμα, ατος, τό, a judgment, a sentence, condemnation, as 1 Cor. xi. 29.

κρίνον, ου, τό, a lily, Mat. vi. 28; Lu. xii. 27.*

κρίνω, νῶ, κέκρικα, 1st aor. pass. ἐκρίθην, (1) to have an opinion, to think, Ac. xiii. 46, xv. 19; (2) to approve, prefer, Ro. xiv. 5; (3) to resolve, determine, 1 Cor. vii. 37; Tit. iii. 12; (4) to try, to sit in judgment on, Jn. xviii. 31; pass. and mid., to appeal to trial, i.e., to have a lawsuit, 1 Cor. vi. 6.

κρίσις, εως, ἡ, (1) opinion, formed and expressed, Jn. viii. 16; Ju. 9; (2) judgment, the act or result of, Ja. ii. 13; Lu. x. 14; (3) condemnation and punishment, Heb. x. 27; Rev. xviii. 10; (4) a tribunal, Mat. v. 21, 22; (5) justice, Mat. xxiii. 23.

Κρίσπος, ου, ὁ, Crispus, Ac. xviii. 8; 1 Cor. i. 14.*

κριτήριον, ου, τό, (1) a tribunal, a court of justice, 1 Cor. vi. 2, 4 (see R. V.); Ja. ii. 6.*

κριτής, οῦ, ὁ, a judge, Mat. v. 25; Ac. xviii. 15; of the O. T. "Judges," Ac. xiii. 20.

κριτικός, ή, όν, skilled in judging, gen. obj., Heb. iv. 12.*

κρούω, σω, to knock at a door, Lu. xiii. 25.

κρύπτη, ης, ἡ, a cellar, a vault, Lu. xi. 33.*

κρυπτός, ή, όν, verbal adj. (κρύπτω), hidden, secret, Mat. x. 26; Ro. ii. 16.

κρύπτω, ψω, 2d aor. pass. ἐκρύβην, to hide, conceal, to lay up, as Col. iii. 3.

κρυσταλλίζω, to be clear, like crystal, Rev. xxi. 11. (N.T.)*

κρύσταλλος, ου, ὁ, crystal, Rev. iv. 6, xxii. 1.*

κρυφαῖος, α, ον, hidden, secret, Mat. vi. 18 (W. H.).*

κρυφῇ (W. H. -ῆ), adv., in secret, secretly, Ep. v. 12.*

κτάομαι, ῶμαι, fut. ἤσομαι, ἐκτησάμην, dep., to acquire, procure (price, gen., or ἐκ), (see Gr. § 273, Wi. §§ 38, 7,

40, 4 b), Mat. x. 9; Lu. xviii. 12, xxi. 19; Ac. i. 18, viii. 20, xxii. 28; 1 Th. iv. 4.*

κτῆμα, ατος, τό, anything acquired, a possession, Mat. xix. 22; Mar. x. 22; Ac. ii. 45, v. 1.

κτῆνος, ους, τό, a beast of burden (as representing property), Lu. x. 34; Ac. xxiii. 24; 1 Cor. xv. 39; Rev. xviii. 13.*

κτήτωρ, ορος, ὁ, a possessor, Ac. iv. 34.*

κτίζω, σω, perf. pass. ἔκτισμαι, to create, form, shape, physically or spiritually, as Ro. i. 25; Ep. ii. 10.

κτίσις, εως, ἡ, creation, (1) the act, Ro. i. 20; (2) the thing created, creature, Ro. i. 25; creation, generally, Ro. viii. 19–22; (3) met., an ordinance, 1 Pet. ii. 13.

κτίσμα, ατος, τό, a thing created, a creature, 1 Tim. iv. 4; Ja. i. 18; Rev. v. 13, viii. 9.*

κτίστης, ου, ὁ, a founder; a creator, 1 Pet. iv. 19.*

κυβεία, ας, ἡ, dice-playing, fraud, Ep. iv. 14.*

κυβέρνησις, εως, ἡ, governing, direction, 1 Cor. xii. 28.*

κυβερνήτης, ου, ὁ, a steersman, a pilot, Ac. xxvii. 11; Rev. xviii. 17.*

κυκλεύω, to encircle, surround, Rev. xx. 9 (W. H.).*

κυκλόθεν, adv. (κύκλος), round about, gen., Rev. iv. 3, 4, 8, v. 11 (not W. H.).*

κύκλος, ου, ὁ, a circle; only in dat., κύκλῳ, as adv., abs., or with gen., round about, around, Mar. iii. 34; vi. 6.

κυκλόω, ῶ, to encircle, surround, besiege, Lu. xxi. 20; Jn. x. 24; Ac. xiv. 20; Heb. xi. 30; Rev. xx. 9 (Rec.).*

κύλισμα, ατος, τό, a place for wallowing, 2 Pet. ii. 22 (not W. H.). (N.T.)*

κυλισμός, οῦ, ὁ, a rolling, wallowing, 2 Pet. ii. 22 (W. H.).*

κυλίω (for κυλίνδω), pass., to be rolled, to wallow, Mar. ix. 20.*

κυλλός, ή, όν, crippled, lame, especially in the hands, Mat. xv. 30 (not W. H.), 31 (not W. H.), xviii. 8; Mar. ix. 43.*

κῦμα, ατος, τό, a wave, as Mat. viii. 24; Mar. iv. 37; Ju. 13.

κύμβαλον, ου, τό (κύμβος, hollow), a cymbal, 1 Cor. xiii. 1.*

κύμινον, ου, τό (from Heb.), cumin, Mat. xxiii. 23.*

κυνάριον, ου, τό (dim. of κύων), a little dog, Mat. xv. 26, 27; Mar. vii. 27, 28.*

Κύπριος, ου, ὁ, a Cyprian or Cypriote, Ac. iv. 36.

Κύπρος, ου, ἡ, Cyprus, Ac. xi. 19, xiii. 4.

κύπτω, ψω, to bend, to stoop down, Mar. i. 7; Jn. viii. 6, 8 (W. H. omit).

Κυρηναῖος, ου, ὁ, a Cyrenæan, Ac. vi. 9, xi. 20.

Κυρήνη, ης, ἡ, Cyrene, a city of Africa, Ac. ii. 10.*

Κυρήνιος, ου, ὁ, Cyrenius or Quirinius, Lu. ii. 2.*

κυρία, ας, ἡ, a lady, 2 Jn. i. 5 (some read Κυρία, Cyria, a proper name).*

κυριακός, ή, όν, of or pertaining to the Lord, as the supper, 1 Cor. xi. 20; the day, Rev. i. 10.*

κυριεύω, εύσω, to have authority, abs., 1 Tim. vi. 15; to rule over (gen.), Lu. xxii. 25.

κύριος, ου, ὁ, (1) lord, master, Lu. xx. 15; Ac. xvi. 16; a title of honor, Mat. xiii. 27, xvi. 22; (2) the Lord, applied to God, Mar. v. 19; Ac. vii. 33; (3) the Lord, employed in the Epp. constantly of Christ (see Gr. § 217 b, Wi. § 19, 1 a, p. 124, Bu. 89), Ac. ix. 1; Ro. xiv. 8. Syn.: see δεσπότης.

κυριότης, τητος, ἡ, lordship, dominion; collective concr., lords, Ep. i. 21; Col. i. 16; 2 Pet. ii. 10; Ju. 8. (N.T.)*

κυρόω, ῶ, to confirm, ratify, 2 Cor. ii. 8; Gal. iii. 15.*

κύων, κυνός, ὁ, ἡ, a dog, Lu. xvi. 21; fig., of shameless persons, Phil. iii. 2.

κῶλον, ου, τό, a limb, a carcase, N.T. plur. only, Heb. iii. 17.*

κωλύω, σω, to restrain, forbid, hinder, Mar. ix. 38.

κώμη, ης, ἡ, a village, unwalled, Mat. ix. 35.

κωμό-πολις, εως, ἡ, a large, city-like village, without walls, Mar. i. 38.*

κῶμος, ου, ὁ, a feasting, revel-

ing, Ro. xiii. 13; Gal. v. 21; 1 Pet. iv. 3.*

κώνωψ, ωπος, ὁ, *a gnat*, Mat. xxiii. 24.*

Κῶς, ῶ, ἡ, *Cos*, Ac. xxi. 1.*

Κωσάμ, ὁ (Heb.), *Cosam*, Lu. iii. 28.*

κωφός, ή, όν (κόπτω, lit., *blunted*), *dumb*, Mat. ix. 32, 33; *deaf*, Mat. xi. 5.

Λ

Δ, λ, λάμβδα, *lambda*, *l*, the eleventh letter. As a numeral, λ´ = 30; ͵λ = 30,000.

λαγχάνω, 2d aor. ἔλαχον, trans., *to obtain by lot, to obtain*, acc. or gen., Lu. i. 9; Ac. i. 17; 2 Pet. i. 1; abs., *to cast lots*, περί, gen., Jn. xix. 24.*

Λάζαρος, ου, ὁ, *Lazarus*, (1) of Bethany, Jn. xi. 1, 2; (2) in the parable, Lu. xvi. 20–25.

λάθρα (W. H. λάθρᾳ), (λανθάνω), adv., *secretly*, Jn. xi. 28.

λαῖλαψ, απος, ἡ, *a whirlwind, a violent storm*, Mar. iv. 37; Lu. viii. 23; 2 Pet. ii. 17.*

λακτίζω (λάξ, adv., *with the heel*), *to kick*, Ac. ix. 5 (W. H. omit), xxvi. 14.*

λαλέω, ῶ, ήσω, (1) *to utter a sound, to speak*, absolutely, Rev. x. 4; Heb. xii. 24; Ja. ii. 12; (2) *to speak, to talk*, with acc. of thing spoken, also with modal dat. and dat. of person addressed. Hence, according to the nature of the case, met., *to declare*, by other methods than *vivâ voce*, as Ro. vii. 1; *to preach, to publish, to announce*. *Syn.*: λέγω has reference to the *thought* uttered; λαλέω simply to the *fact* of utterance.

λαλιά, ᾶς, ἡ, (1) *speech, report*, Jn. iv. 42; (2) *manner of speech, dialect*, Mat. xxvi. 73; Mar. xiv. 70 (W. H. omit); Jn. viii. 43.*

λαμά, or λαμμᾶ (perh. Heb.), and λεμά (Aram.), *why*, Mat. xxvii. 46; Mar. xv. 34 (Ps. xxii. 1). (N. T.)*

λαμβάνω, λήψομαι (W. H. λήμψομαι), εἴληφα, ἔλαβον, (1) *to take*, as in the hand, Mat. xiv. 19; hence, (2) *to claim, procure*, Lu. xix. 12; (3) *to*

take by force, seize, Mat. xxi. 35; (4) *to take away*, by violence or fraud, Mat. v. 40; (5) *to choose*, Ac. xv. 14; (6) *to receive, accept, obtain*, Jn. xvi. 24; Ja. iii. 1; Rev. xviii. 4; (7) in certain periphrastic expressions — λαμβάνειν ἀρχήν, *to begin;* λ. λήθην, *to forget;* λ. ὑπόμνησιν, *to remember;* λ. πεῖραν, *to experience;* λ. πρόσωπον, " *to accept the person*," *i.e., to be partial.* The preposition "from," after this verb, is expressed by ἐκ, ἀπό, παρά (ὑπό, 2 Cor. xi. 24).

Λάμεχ, ὁ (Heb.), *Lamech*, Lu. iii. 36.*

λαμπάς, άδος, ἡ, prop. *a torch*, Rev. iv. 5, viii. 10; also *a lamp*, Jn. xviii. 3. *Syn.*: φῶς is light in general; φέγγος, radiance; φωστήρ, a heavenly body, luminary; λαμπάς, a torch; λύχνος, a lamp.

λαμπρός, ά, όν, *shining, magnificent*, Rev. xxii. 16; Lu. xxiii. 11.

λαμπρότης, τητος, ἡ, *splendor, brightness*, Ac. xxvi. 13.*

λαμπρῶς, adv., *magnificently*, Lu. xvi. 19.*

λάμπω, ψω, *to shine*, Mat. v. 15, 16, xvii. 2.

λανθάνω, 2d aor. ἔλαθον, (1) *to be hidden*, abs., Mar. vii. 24; Lu. viii. 47; (2) *to be hidden from* (acc.), Ac. xxvi. 26; 2 Pet. iii. 5, 8; (3) for part. constr., see Gr. § 394, 2, Wi. § 54, 4, Bu. 299; Heb. xiii. 2.*

λαξευτός, ή, όν, *hewn out of a rock*, Lu. xxiii. 53. (S.)*

Λαοδικεία, ας, ἡ, *Laodicea*, Col. ii. 1, iv. 13.

Λαοδικεύς, έως, ὁ, *a Laodicean*, Col. iv. 16; Rev. iii. 14 (not W. H.).*

λαός, οῦ, ὁ, (1) *a people*, spec. of *the people* of God, Lu. ii. 31; Ac. iv. 10; (2) *the common people*, Mat. xxvi. 5.

λάρυγξ, υγγος, ὁ, *the throat*, Ro. iii. 13.*

Λασαία (W. H. Λασέα), ας, ἡ, *Lasæa*, Ac. xxvii. 8.*

λάσκω, 1st aor. ἐλάκησα, *to burst asunder*, Ac. i. 18.*

λατομέω, ῶ, *to hew stones, to cut stones*, Mat. xxvii. 60; Mar. xv. 46. (S.)*

λατρεία, ας, ἡ, *worship, service rendered to God*, Jn. xvi. 2; Ro. ix. 4, xii. 1; Heb. ix. 1, 6.*

λατρεύω, σω, (1) *to worship, to serve*, Ac. vii. 7; (2) *to officiate as a priest*, Heb. xiii. 10. *Syn.*: λατρεύω is to worship God, as any one may do; λειτουργέω, to serve him in a special office or ministry.

λάχανον, ου, τό, *an herb, a garden plant*, Mat. xiii. 32.

Λεββαῖος, ου, ὁ, *Lebbæus*, Mat. x. 3 (not W. H.). See Θαδδαῖος.*

λεγεών (W. H. λεγιών), ῶνος, ὁ (Lat., see Gr. § 154*c*, Bu. 16), *a legion*, Mat. xxvi. 53; Mar. v. 9, 15; Lu. viii. 30; in N.T. times containing probably 6826 men. (N. T.)*

λέγω, only pres. and impf. in N. T., (1) *to speak, to say*, Ac. xiii. 15; Jn. i. 29; used also of writings, as Jn. xix. 37; (2) *to relate, to tell*, Lu. xi. 31, xviii. 1; (3) *to call*, pass., *to be called* or *named;* (4) pass., *to be chosen* or *appointed*. Dat. of person addressed. *Syn.*: see λαλέω.

λεῖμμα, ατος, τό (λείπω), *a remnant*, Ro. xi. 5.*

λεῖος, εία, εῖον, *smooth, level*, Lu. iii. 5 (from S.).*

λείπω, ψω, *to leave, to be wanting*, Lu. xviii. 22; Tit. i. 5, iii. 13; pass., *to be lacking, to be destitute of*, Ja. i. 4, 5, ii. 15.*

λειτουργέω, ῶ, (1) *to serve publicly in sacred things*, Ac. xiii. 2; Heb. x. 11; (2) *to minister to charitably*, Ro. xv. 27.* *Syn.*: see λατρεύω.

λειτουργία, ας, ἡ, (1) *a public ministration or service*, Lu. i. 23; Phil. ii. 17; Heb. viii. 6, ix. 21; (2) *a charitable gift*, Phil. ii. 30; 2 Cor. ix. 12.*

λειτουργικός, ή, όν, *employed in ministering*, Heb. i. 14 (S.)*

λειτουργός, οῦ, ὁ, *a minister* or *servant to*, gen. obj., Ro. xiii. 6, xv. 16; Phil. ii. 25; Heb. i. 7, viii. 2.*

λέντιον, ου, τό (Lat., see Gr. § 154*e*), *a towel, apron*, Jn. xiii. 4, 5. (N. T.)*

λεπίς, ίδος, ἡ, a scale, Ac. ix. 18.*

λέπρα, ας, ἡ, the leprosy, Mat. viii. 3; Mar. i. 42; Lu. v. 12, 13.*

λεπρός, οῦ, ὁ, a leper, Lu. iv. 27, vii. 22.

λεπτόν, οῦ, τό, prop. verb. adj. (sc. νόμισμα), from λέπω (to strip off, pare down), a mite, a small brass coin, one eighth of an as, the smallest Jewish coin, Mar. xii. 42; Lu. xii. 59, xxi. 2.*

Λευΐ, or Λευΐς (W. H. Λευείς), gen. Λευΐ, ὁ, Levi. Four are mentioned: (1) son of Jacob, ancestor of the priestly tribe; (2, 3) ancestors of Jesus, Lu. iii. 24, 29; (4) the apostle, also called Matthew, Lu. v. 27, 29.

Λευΐτης, ου, ὁ, a Levite, Lu. x. 32; Jn. i. 19; Ac. iv. 36.*

Λευϊτικός, ή, όν, Levitical, Heb. vii. 11.*

λευκαίνω, ανῶ, 1st aor. ἐλεύκανα, to make white, Mar. ix. 3; Rev. vii. 14.*

λευκός, ή, όν, (1) white, as Mat. v. 36; Jn. iv. 35; (2) bright, as Mat. xvii. 2.

λέων, οντος, ὁ, a lion, Heb. xi. 33; fig., 2 Tim. iv. 17; of Christ, Rev. v. 5.

λήθη, ης, ἡ, forgetfulness, 2 Pet. i. 9.*

ληνός, οῦ, ὁ, ἡ, a wine-press, Mat. xxi. 33; fig. in Rev. xiv. 19, 20, xix. 15.*

λῆρος, ου, ὁ, idle talk, Lu. xxiv. 11.*

λῃστής, οῦ, ὁ, a robber, Mar. xi. 17; Jn. x. 1, 8. Syn.: see κλέπτης.

λῆψις (W. H. λῆμψις), εως, ἡ Λαμβάνω), a receiving, Phil. iv. 15.*

λίαν, adv., very much; with adj. or adv., very, Mat. iv. 8; Mar. xvi. 2.

λίβανος, ου, ὁ, frankincense, Mat. ii. 11; Rev. xviii. 13.*

λιβανωτός, οῦ, ὁ, a censer for burning frankincense, Rev. viii. 3, 5.*

λιβερτῖνος, ου, ὁ (Lat. libertinus), a freedman, Ac. vi. 9. Probably Jews who had been slaves at Rome under Pompey, and afterwards freed.*

Λιβύη, ης, ἡ, Libya, Ac. ii. 10.*

λιθάζω, σω, to stone, Jn. xi. 8; Ac. xiv. 19.

λίθινος, η, ον, made of stone, Jn. ii. 6; 2 Cor. iii. 3; Rev. ix. 20.*

λιθο-βολέω, ῶ, ήσω, to throw stones at, to stone, Mat. xxiii. 37; Mar. xii. 4 (W. H. omit). (S.)

λίθος, ου, ὁ, a stone, i.e., (1) loose and lying about, Mat. iv. 3, 6; (2) built into a wall, etc., Mar. xiii. 2; (3) a precious stone, Rev. iv. 3, xvii. 4; (4) a statue or idol of stone, Ac. xvii. 29.

λιθό-στρωτον, ου, τό (prop. adj., spread with stones), a mosaic pavement, as name of a place near the prætorium or palace at Jerusalem, Jn. xix. 13.*

λικμάω, ῶ, ήσω, to scatter, as grain in winnowing, to grind to powder that may be scattered, Mat. xxi. 44; Lu. xx. 18.*

λιμήν, ένος, ὁ, a harbor, Ac. xxvii. 8, 12.*

λίμνη, ης, ἡ, a lake, e.g., Gennesaret, Lu. v. 1.

λιμός, οῦ, ὁ, (1) hunger, 2 Cor. xi. 27; (2) a famine, Mat. xxiv. 7.

λίνον, ου, τό, flax, linen made of flax, Rev. xv. 6 (W. H. λίθος); a lamp-wick, Mat. xii. 20.*

Λῖνος (W. H. Λίνος), ου, ὁ, Linus, 2 Tim. iv. 21.*

λιπαρός, ά, όν, fat, dainty, Rev. xviii. 14.*

λίτρα, ας, ἡ, a pound, a weight of twelve ounces, Jn. xii. 3, xix. 39.*

λίψ, λιβός, ὁ, the S.W. wind; used for the S.W. quarter of the heavens, Ac. xxvii. 12.*

λογία, ας, ἡ, a collection, i.e., of money, 1 Cor. xvi. 1, 2. (N. T.)*

λογίζομαι, σομαι, dep. with mid. and pass., (1) to reckon; (2) to place to the account of, to charge with, acc. and dat., or with εἰς (see Gr. § 298, 6, Wi. § 32, 4 b, Bu. 151); (3) to reason, argue, to infer, conclude, from reasoning; (4) to think, suppose.

λογικός, ή, όν, rational, i.e., belonging to the sphere of

the reason, Ro. xii. 1; 1 Pet. ii. 2.*

λόγιον, ου, τό, something spoken, in N. T., a divine communication, e.g., the Old Testament, Ac. vii. 38; Ro. iii. 2; and the doctrines of Christ, Heb. v. 12; 1 Pet. iv. 11.*

λόγιος, ον, eloquent, Ac. xviii. 24.*

λογισμός, οῦ, ὁ, a reasoning, decision, Ro. ii. 15; 2 Cor. x. 5.*

λογο-μαχέω, ῶ, to contend about words, 2 Tim. ii. 14. (N.T.)*

λογομαχία, ας, ἡ, contention about words, 1 Tim. vi 4. (N. T.)*

λόγος, ου, ὁ, (1) a speaking, a saying, a word, as the expression of thought (whereas ἔπος, ὄνομα, ῥῆμα refer to words in their outward form, as parts of speech), Mat. viii. 8; (2) the thing spoken, Mat. vii. 24, 26 — whether doctrine, 1 Tim. iv. 6; prophecy, 2 Pet. i. 19; question, Mat. xxi. 24; a common saying or proverb, Jn. iv. 37; a precept, a command, Jn. viii. 55; the truth, Mar. viii. 38; conversation, Lu. xxiv. 17; teaching, 1 Cor. ii. 4; a narrative, Ac. i. 1; a public rumor, Mat. xxviii. 15; an argument, Ac. ii. 40; a charge or accusation, Ac. xix. 38; (3) reason, Ac. xviii. 14; (4) account, reckoning, Heb. iv. 13; Ac. xx. 24; Mat. xviii. 23; Ac. x. 29; λόγος is used by John as a name of Christ, the Word of God, i.e., the expression or manifestation of his thoughts to man, Jn. i. 1, etc.

λόγχη, ης, ἡ, a lance, a spear, Jn. xix. 34.*

λοιδορέω, ῶ, to rail at, revile, Jn. ix. 28; Ac. xxiii. 4; 1 Cor. iv. 12; 1 Pet. ii. 23.*

λοιδορία, ας, ἡ, reviling, 1 Tim. v. 14; 1 Pet. iii. 9.*

λοίδορος, ου, ὁ, a reviler, 1 Cor. v. 11, vi. 10.*

λοιμός, οῦ, ὁ, a pestilence, Mat. xxiv. 7 (W. H. omit), Lu. xxi. 11; Paul so called, Ac. xxiv. 5.*

λοιπός, ή, όν, remaining, the rest, Mat. xxv. 11; adv. τὸ λοιπόν, as for the rest, more-

over, finally, henceforth, 1
Cor. i. 16; Heb. x. 13; τοῦ
λοιποῦ, *from henceforth,* Gal.
vi. 17.

Λουκᾶς, â, ὁ (from Λουκανός,
see Gr. § 159*d*, Wi. § 16, 4,
note 1, Bu. 20), *Luke,* Ac.
xvi. 10, xx. 5.

Λούκιος, ου, ὁ (Lat.), *Lucius,*
Ac. xiii. 1; Ro. xvi. 21.*

λουτρόν, οῦ, τό, *a bath;* in N.T.
baptism, Ep. v. 26; Tit. iii.
5.*

λούω, σω, *to bathe, to wash,* Ac.
ix. 37, xvi. 33; *to cleanse, to
purify,* Rev. i. 5 (W. H. λύω).
Syn.: πλύνω is to wash *inanimate things;* λούω, to
bathe *the whole body;* νίπτω,
to wash a *part* of the body.

Λύδδα, ης, ἡ, also Λύδδα, ων,
τά (W. H.), *Lydda,* Ac. ix.
32, 35, 38.*

Λυδία, as, ἡ, *Lydia,* Ac. xvi. 14,
40.*

Λυκαονία, as, ἡ, *Lycaonia,* Ac.
xiv. 6.*

Λυκαονιστί, adv., *in the speech
of Lycaonia,* Ac. xiv. 11.*

Λυκία, as, ἡ, *Lycia,* Ac. xxvii. 5.*

λύκος, ου, ὁ, *a wolf,* Jn. x. 12;
fig., Ac. xx. 29.

λυμαίνομαι, *to ravage, to de-
vastate,* Ac. viii. 3.*

λυπέω, ῶ, *to grieve,* a general
word, 2 Cor. ii. 2, 5; pass.,
to be grieved, saddened, Mat.
xxvi. 22, 37; 1 Pet. i. 6; *to
aggrieve* or *offend,* Ro. xiv.
15; Ep. iv. 30.

λύπη, ης, ἡ, *grief, sorrow,* 2
Cor. ix. 7; *cause of grief,
annoyance,* 1 Pet. ii. 19.

Λυσανίας, ου, ὁ, *Lysanias,* Lu.
iii. 1.*

Λυσίας, ου, ὁ, *Lysias,* Ac. xxiii.
26.

λύσις, εως, ἡ, *a loosing, divorce,*
1 Cor. vii. 27.*

λυσι-τελέω, ῶ (lit., *to pay taxes*),
impers., -εῖ, *it is profitable* or
preferable (dat. and ἤ), Lu.
xvii. 2.*

Λύστρα, as, ἡ, or ων, τά, *Lystra,*
Ac. xiv. 6, 8.

λύτρον, ου, τό, *a ransom,* Mat.
xx. 28; Mar. x. 45.*

λυτρόω, ῶ, ώσω, in N. T. only
mid. and pass., *to ransom, to
deliver* by paying a ransom,
Lu. xxiv. 21; Tit. ii. 14; 1
Pet. i. 18 (acc., pers.; dat.,
price, and ἀπό or ἐκ).*

λύτρωσις, εως, ἡ, *deliverance,
redemption,* Lu. i. 68, ii. 38;
Heb. ix. 12.*

λυτρωτής, οῦ, ὁ, *a redeemer, a
deliverer,* Ac. vii. 35.*

λυχνία, as, ἡ, *a lampstand,*
Mat. v. 15; fig., of a church,
Rev. ii. 1, 5; of a Christian
teacher, Rev. xi. 4.

λύχνος, ου, ὁ, *a lamp,* Mat. v.
15, vi. 22; used of John
the Baptist, Jn. v. 35; of
Christ, Rev. xxi. 23. *Syn.:*
see λαμπάς.

λύω, σω, *to loose,* as (1) lit., *to
unbind,* Mar. i. 7; Rev. v. 2;
(2) *to set at liberty,* Jn. xi. 44;
Ac. xxii. 30; (3) *to pronounce
not binding, e.g.,* a law, Mat.
xviii. 18; (4) *to disobey* or
nullify the divine word, Jn.
vii. 23, x. 35; (5) *to destroy,
e.g.,* the temple, Jn. ii. 19;
(6) *to dismiss, i.e.,* an assembly, Ac. xiii. 43.

Λωΐς, ΐδος, ἡ, *Lois,* 2 Tim. i.
5.*

Λώτ, ὁ (Heb.), *Lot,* Lu. xvii.
28–32; 2 Pet. ii. 7.*

M

M, μ, μῦ, *mu, m,* the twelfth
letter. As a numeral, μ′ = 40;
,μ = 40,000.

Μαάθ, ὁ (Heb.), *Maath,* Lu. iii.
26.*

Μαγδαλά, ἡ (Heb.), *Magdala,*
Mat. xv. 39 (W. H. and R.V.
Μαγαδάν).*

Μαγδαληνή, ῆς, ἡ, *Magdalene,
i.e.,* a woman of Magdala, as
Mat. xxvii. 56, 61.

μαγεία (W. H. μαγία), as, ἡ,
magic, plur., *magical arts,*
Ac. viii. 11.*

μαγεύω, σω, *to practice magical
arts,* Ac. viii. 9.*

μάγος, ου, ὁ, (1) *a magus,* a
Persian astrologer, Mat. ii.
1, 7, 16; (2) *a sorcerer,* Ac.
xiii. 6, 8.*

Μαγώγ, ὁ (Heb.), *Magog,* Rev.
xx. 8; see Γώγ.*

Μαδιάμ, ἡ (Heb.), *Midian,* Ac.
vii. 29.*

μαθητεύω, σω, (1) trans., *to
make a disciple of* (acc.), *to
instruct,* Mat. xiii. 52, xxviii.
19; Ac. xiv. 21; (2) intrans.,
to be a disciple, Mat. xxvii.
57 (Rec., W. H. read pass.,
W. H. with active in mrg.).*

μαθητής, οῦ, ὁ (μανθάνω), *a disciple,* Mat. ix. 14, x. 24, xxii.
16; οἱ μαθηταί, specially, *the
twelve,* Mat. ix. 19.

μαθήτρια, as, ἡ, *a female disciple,* Ac. ix. 36.*

Μαθουσάλα, ὁ (Heb.), *Methu-
selah,* Lu. iii. 37.*

Μαϊνάν, ὁ (W. H. Μεννά),
(Heb.), *Mainan* or *Menna,*
Lu. iii. 31.*

μαίνομαι, dep., *to be mad, to
rave,* Jn. x. 20; Ac. xii. 15,
xxvi. 24, 25; 1 Cor. xiv.
23.*

μακαρίζω, fut. ιῶ, *to pronounce
happy* or *blessed,* Lu. i. 48;
Ja. v. 11.*

μακάριος, α, ον, *happy, blessed,*
Mat. v. 3–11; Lu. i. 45, vi.
20; 1 Cor. vii. 40.

μακαρισμός, οῦ, ὁ, *a declaring
blessed, a pronouncing happy,*
Ro. iv. 6, 9; Gal. iv. 15.*

Μακεδονία, as, ἡ, *Macedonia,*
Ac. xvi. 9, 10, 12.

Μακεδών, όνος, ὁ, *a Macedonian,*
Ac. xix. 29, xxvii. 2.

μάκελλον, ου, τό (Lat.), *a meat-
market,* 1 Cor. x. 25.*

μακράν, adv. (acc. of μακρός,
sc. ὁδόν), *afar, afar off,* Lu.
xv. 20; εἰς preceding, Ac. ii.
39; ἀπό following, Ac. xvii.
27.

μακρόθεν, adv., *from afar,* Mar.
viii. 3; with ἀπό, as Mat.
xxvii. 55.

μακρο-θυμέω, ῶ, ήσω, *to suffer
long, to have patience, to be
forbearing,* 1 Cor. xiii. 4; *to
delay,* Lu. xviii. 7; *to wait
patiently,* Heb. vi. 15. (S.)

μακρο-θυμία, as, ἡ, *forbearance, long-suffering, patience,*
Ro. ii. 4, ix. 22. *Syn.:* see
ἀνοχή.

μακρο-θύμως, adv., *patiently,*
Ac. xxvi. 3. (N. T.)*

μακρός, ά, όν, *long;* of place,
distant, Lu. xv. 13, xix. 12;
of time, *long,* only in the
phrase μακρὰ προσεύχεσθαι,
to make long prayers, Mat.
xxiii. 14 (W. H. omit); Mar.
xii. 40; Lu. xx. 47.*

μακρο-χρόνιος, ον, *long-lived,*
Ep. vi. 3.*

μαλακία, as, ἡ, *weakness, infirmity,* Mat. iv. 23, ix. 35,
x. 1.*

μαλακός, ή, όν, *soft,* of garments, Mat. xi. 8; Lu. vii

25; *disgracefully effeminate,*
1 Cor. vi. 9.*

Μαλελεήλ, ὁ (Heb.), *Maleleel*
or *Mahalaleel,* Lu. iii. 37.*

μάλιστα, adv. (superl. of μάλα,
very), *most of all, especially,*
Gal. vi. 10; 2 Tim. iv. 13.

μᾶλλον, adv. (comp. of μάλα),
more, rather; πολλῷ μᾶλλον,
much more, Mat. vi. 30; πόσῳ μᾶλλον, *how much more,*
Mat. vii. 11; μᾶλλον ἤ, *more
than,* Mat. xviii. 13; μᾶλλον
is often of intensive force,
e.g., Mat. xxvii. 24; Ro. viii.
34. See Gr. § 321, Wi. §§ 35,
1, 65, 2, Bu. 83.

Μάλχος, ου, ὁ (Heb.), *Malchus,*
Jn. xviii. 10.*

μάμμη, ης, ἡ, *a grandmother,*
2 Tim. i. 5.*

μαμμωνᾶς (W. H. μαμωνᾶς), ᾶ,
ὁ (Aram.), *mammon, gain,
wealth,* Mat. vi. 24; Lu. xvi.
9, 11, 13. (N. T.)*

Μαναήν, ὁ (Heb.), *Manaen,*
Ac. xiii. 1.*

Μανασσῆς, gen. and acc. ῆ, ὁ,
Manasseh, (1) son of Joseph,
Rev. vii. 6; (2) Mat. i. 10.*

μανθάνω, μαθήσομαι, 2d aor.
ἔμαθον, perf. μεμάθηκα, *to
learn, to understand, to know,
to be informed, to comprehend.* Used abs., or with
acc. (ἀπό or παρά with gen.
of the teacher, ἐν with example, 1 Cor. iv. 6).

μανία, ας, ἡ, *madness,* Ac. xxvi.
24.*

μάννα, τό (Heb., deriv. uncertain), *manna,* the food of
the Israelites in the desert,
Jn. vi. 31, 49; Heb. ix. 4. (S.)

μαντεύομαι, dep., *to utter re-
sponses, practice divination,*
Ac. xvi. 16.*

μαραίνω, ανῶ, fut. pass. μαραν-
θήσομαι, *to wither, to fade
away,* Ja. i. 11.*

μαρὰν ἀθά (two Aram. words),
our Lord cometh (R.V. mrg.),
1 Cor. xvi. 22. (N. T.)*

μαργαρίτης, ου, ὁ, *a pearl,* Mat.
xiii. 45, 46.

Μάρθα, ας, ἡ, *Martha,* Lu. x.
38, 40, 41.

Μαρία, ας, or Μαριάμ, indecl.
(Heb. *Miriam*), ἡ, *Mary.*
Six of the name are men-
tioned: (1) the mother of
Jesus, Lu. i. 27; (2) the
Magdalene, Mar. xv. 40, 47;

(3) the sister of Martha and
Lazarus, Lu. x. 39, 42; (4)
the wife of Cleopas, Mat.
xxvii. 56, 61; (5) the mother
of John Mark, Ac. xii. 12;
(6) a Christian woman in
Rome, Ro. xvi. 6.

Μάρκος, ου, ὁ, *Mark,* Ac. xii.
12, 25.

μάρμαρος, ου, ὁ, ἡ, *marble,* Rev.
xviii. 12.*

μαρτυρέω, ῶ, ήσω, *to be a witness,* abs., *to testify* (περί,
gen.), *to give testimony* (*to,*
dat. of pers. or thing), *to
commend;* pass., *to be at-
tested, i.e., honorably, to be
of good report.*

μαρτυρία, ας, ἡ, *testimony, i.e.,*
legal, Mar. xiv. 56, 59; or
general, Jn. v. 34; with obj.
gen., as Rev. xix. 10.

μαρτύριον, ου, τό, *testimony,*
Mat. viii. 4 (*to,* dat.; *against,*
ἐπί, acc.).

μαρτύρομαι, dep., *to call to
witness,* Ac. xx. 26; Gal. v.
3; *to exhort solemnly,* Ac.
xxvi. 22 (W. H.); Ep. iv. 17;
1 Th. ii. 11 (W. H.).*

μάρτυς, υρος, dat. plur. μάρτυσι,
ὁ, *a witness, i.e.,* judicially,
Mat. xviii. 16; *one who tes-
tifies* from what he has seen
or experienced, 1 Th. ii. 10,
Lu. xxiv. 48; *a martyr,* wit-
nessing by his death, Ac.
xxii. 20; Rev. ii. 13, xvii. 6.

μασσάομαι (W. H. -ασά-), ῶμαι,
to bite, to gnaw, Rev. xvi. 10.*

μαστιγόω, ῶ, ώσω, *to scourge,*
Mat. x. 17; fig., Heb. xii. 6.

μαστίζω, *to scourge,* Ac. xxii.
25.*

μάστιξ, ιγος, ἡ, *a whip, a
scourge,* Ac. xxii. 24; Heb.
xi. 36; fig., *calamity, disease,*
Mar. iii. 10, v. 29, 34; Lu.
vii. 21.*

μαστός, οῦ, ὁ, *the breast,* pl.,
Lu. xi. 27, xxiii. 29; Rev. i.
13.*

ματαιολογία, ας, ἡ, *vain, fruitless talk,* 1 Tim. i. 6.*

ματαιο-λόγος, ου, ὁ, *a vain,
empty talker,* Tit. i. 10.*

μάταιος (αία), αιον, *vain, useless, empty,* 1 Cor. xv. 17;
Ja. i. 26; τὰ μάταια, *vanities,*
spec. of heathen deities, Ac.
xiv. 15 (and O. T.). *Syn.:* see
κενός.

ματαιότης, τητος, ἡ, (1) *vanity,*

2 Pet. ii. 18; (2) *perverseness,* Ep. iv. 17; (3) *frailty,*
Ro. viii. 20.*

ματαιόω, ῶ, *to make vain* or
foolish; pass., Ro. i. 21.
(S.)*

μάτην, adv., *in vain, fruitless-
ly,* Mat. xv. 9; Mar. vii. 7.*

Ματθαῖος (W. H. Μαθθαῖος), ου,
ὁ, *Matthew,* the apostle and
evangelist, Mat. ix. 9, 10;
also called Λευΐ.

Ματθάν (W. H. Μαθθάν), ὁ
(Heb.), *Matthan,* Mat. i. 15.*

Ματθάτ, ὁ (Heb.), *Matthat,* Lu.
iii. 24, 29 (W. H. Μαθθάτ).*

Ματθίας (W. H. Μαθθίας), α, ὁ,
Matthias, Ac. i. 23, 26.*

Ματταθά, ὁ (Heb.), *Mattatha,*
Lu. iii. 31.*

Ματταθίας, ου, ὁ, *Mattathias,*
Lu. iii. 25, 26.*

μάχαιρα, ας and ης, ἡ, *a sword,*
Jn. xviii. 10, 11; met., for
strife, Mat. x. 34; fig., of
spiritual weapons, Ep. vi. 17.

μάχη, ης, ἡ, *battle; contention,
strife,* 2 Cor. vii. 5; 2 Tim.
ii. 23; Tit. iii. 9; Ja. iv. 1.*

μάχομαι, *to fight, contend, dispute,* Jn. vi. 52; Ac. vii. 26;
2 Tim. ii. 24; Ja. iv. 2.*

μεγαλ-αυχέω, ῶ, *to boast great
things, to be arrogant,* Ja. iii.
5 (W. H. μεγάλα αὐχεῖ).*

μεγαλεῖος, εία, εῖον, *grand, magnificent,* Lu. i. 49 (W. H. μεγάλα); Ac. ii. 11.*

μεγαλειότης, τητος, ἡ, *majesty,
magnificence,* Lu. ix. 43; Ac.
xix. 27; 2 Pet. i. 16.*

μεγαλο-πρεπής, ές, gen. οῦς, *fitting for a great man, magnificent, majestic,* 2 Pet. i. 17.*

μεγαλύνω, νῶ, (1) *to make great,*
Mat. xxiii. 5; (2) *to magnify,
extol, celebrate with praise,*
Lu. i. 46; Ac. v. 13.

μεγάλως, adv., *greatly,* Phil. iv.
10.*

μεγαλωσύνη, ης, ἡ, *majesty,*
Heb. i. 3, viii. 1; Ju. 25.
(S.)*

μέγας, μεγάλη, μέγα (see Gr.
§ 39), comp. μείζων, sup. μέ-
γιστος, *great,* in size, *full-
grown, intense,* Mat. ii. 10,
xxviii. 8; *wonderful,* 2 Cor.
xi. 15; *noble, of high rank,*
Rev. xi. 18, xiii. 16; applied
to age, ὁ μείζων, *the elder,*
Ro. ix. 12; μέγας indicates
the *size* of things, their *meas-*

ure, number, cost, and *estimation;* μεγάλη ἡμέρα, *a solemn, sacred day,* Jn. xix. 31.

μέγεθος, ους, τό, *greatness,* Ep. i. 19.*

μεγιστᾶνες, άνων, οἱ (sing. μεγιστάν, only in Ap., Sirach iv. 7), *princes, great men, nobles,* Mar. vi. 21; Rev. vi. 15, xviii. 23. (S.)*

μεθ-ερμηνεύω, *to translate, to interpret,* pass. only, Mar. v. 41; Jn. i. 41.

μέθη, ης, ἡ, *drunkenness,* Lu. xxi. 34; Ro. xiii. 13; Gal. v. 21.*

μεθ-ίστημι (and μεθιστάνω, 1 Cor. xiii. 2), μετασπήσω, 1st aor., pass., μετεστάθην, lit., *to change the place of;* hence, *to remove,* 1 Cor. xiii. 2; Col. i. 13; *to lead astray,* Ac. xix. 26; *to remove* from life, Ac. xiii. 22; *to remove* from office, Lu. xvi. 4.*

μεθ-οδεία (-οδία, W. H.), ας, ἡ, *a fraudulent artifice, a trick,* Ep. iv. 14, vi. 11. (N.T.)*

μεθ-όριος, α, ον, *bordering on;* τὰ μεθόρια, *borders, frontiers,* Mar. vii. 24 (W. H. ὅρια).*

μεθύσκω, *to make drunk;* pass., *to be drunk,* Lu. xii. 45; Jn. ii. 10; Ep. v. 18; 1 Th. v. 7.*

μέθυσος, ου, ὁ (prop. adj.), *a drunkard,* 1 Cor. v. 11, vi. 10.*

μεθύω, *to be drunken,* Mat. xxiv. 49; Ac. ii. 15; met., Rev. xvii. 6.

μείζων, comp. of μέγας, which see. It has itself a comparative, μειζότερος, 3 Jn. 4 (see Gr. § 47, Wi. § 11, 2 b, Bu. 28).

μέλαν, ανος, τό (μέλας), *ink,* 2 Cor. iii. 3; 2 Jn. 12; 3 Jn. 13.*

μέλας, αινα, αν, *black,* Mat. v. 36; Rev. vi. 5, 12.*

Μελεᾶς, ᾶ, ὁ, *Melea,* Lu. iii. 31.*

μέλει, impers. (see Gr. § 101, Wi. § 30, 10 d, Bu. 164), *it concerns,* dat. of pers., with gen. of object, as 1 Cor. ix. 9; or περί, as Jn. x. 13; or ὅτι, as Mar. iv. 38.

μελετάω, ῶ, ήσω, *to practice,* 1 Tim. iv. 15; *to devise,* Ac. iv.

25; *to meditate,* Mar. xiii. 11 (not W. H.).*

μέλι, ιτος, τό, *honey,* Mat. iii. 4; Mar. i. 6; Rev. x. 9, 10.*

μελίσσιος, α, ον, *made by bees,* Lu. xxiv. 42 (W. H. omit). (N. T.)*

Μελίτη, ης, ἡ, *Melita,* now Malta, Ac. xxviii. 1 (W. H. Μελιτήνη).*

μέλλω, ήσω, *to be about to do, to be on the point of doing,* with infin., generally the present infin., rarely aor.; the fut. infin. (the regular classical use) occurs only in the phrase μέλλειν ἔσεσθαι (only in Ac.); the verb may often be adequately rendered by our auxiliaries, *will, shall, must; to delay,* only Ac. xxii. 16. The participle is used absolutely: τὸ μέλλον, *the future,* Lu. xiii. 9; τὰ μέλλοντα, *things to come,* Ro. viii. 38. See Gr. § 363f, Wi. § 44, 7 c, Bu. 259.

μέλος, ους, τό, *a member* of the body, *a limb,* as Mat. v. 29, 30; Ro. xii. 4; fig., 1 Cor. vi. 15.

Μελχί (W. H. -εί), ὁ (Heb.), *Melchi.* Two are mentioned, Lu. iii. 24, 28.*

Μελχισεδέκ, ὁ (Heb. *king of righteousness*), *Melchizedek,* Heb. v., vi., vii.*

μεμβράνα, ης, ἡ (Lat.), *parchment,* 2 Tim. iv. 13. (N.T.)*

μέμφομαι, ψομαι, dep., *to blame, to censure,* abs., Mar. vii. 2 (W. H. omit); Ro. ix. 19; abs. or dat., Heb. viii. 8 (W. H. acc., with dat. mrg.).*

μεμψί-μοιρος, ον, *discontented, complaining,* Ju. 16.*

μέν, antithetic particle, *truly, indeed* (see Gr. § 136, Wi. § 53, 7 b), Bu. 364 sq.).

μεν-οῦν, conj., *moreover, therefore, but.*

μεν-οῦν-γε, conj., *nay rather, nay truly,* Lu. xi. 28 (W. H. μενοῦν); Ro. ix. 20, x. 18; Phil. iii. 8 (W. H. μὲν οὖν γε). See Gr. § 406, Wi. § 61, 6, Bu. 370 sq.*

μέν-τοι, conj., *yet truly, nevertheless, however,* Jn. iv. 27.

μένω, μενῶ, ἔμεινα, (1) intrans., *to remain, to abide;* so (a) of place, *to dwell,* Mat. x. 11; *to lodge,* Lu. xix. 5; (b) of

state, as Ac. v. 4; *to continue firm* and *constant in,* Jn. xv. 4; *to endure, to last, to be permanent,* 1 Cor. iii. 14; (2) trans., *to await, wait for,* only Ac. xx. 5, 23.

μερίζω, σω, (1) *to divide, separate,* mid., *to share* (μετά, gen.), Lu. xii. 13; pass., *to be divided, to be at variance,* Mat. xii. 25, 26; 1 Cor. i. 13; (2) *to distribute,* Mar. vi. 41, acc. and dat.

μέριμνα, ης, ἡ, *care, anxiety,* as dividing, distracting the mind, Mat. xiii. 22; Lu. viii. 14.

μεριμνάω, ῶ, ήσω, *to be anxious, distracted, to care for;* abs., with dat., περί (gen.), acc. The various constructions may be illustrated from Mat. vi.: abs., vers. 27, 31; acc., ver. 34 (Rec.; see also 1 Cor. vii. 32–34); gen., ver. 34 (W. H.); dat., ver. 25; εἰς, ver. 34; περί, ver. 28.

μερίς, ίδος, ἡ, *a part* or *division* of a country, Ac. xvi. 12; *a share, portion,* Lu. x. 42; Ac. viii. 21; 2 Cor. vi. 15; Col. i. 12.*

μερισμός, οῦ, ὁ, *a dividing* or *division,* Heb. iv. 12; *distribution, gifts distributed,* Heb. ii. 4.*

μεριστής, οῦ, ὁ, *a divider,* Lu. xii. 14. (N.T.)*

μέρος, ους, τό, *a part;* hence, (1) *a share,* Rev. xxii. 19; *fellowship,* Jn. xiii. 8; *a business* or *calling,* Ac. xix. 27; (2) *a part,* as the result of division, Jn. xix. 23. In adverbial phrases, μέρος τι, *partly, in some part;* ἀνὰ μέρος, *alternately;* ἀπὸ μέρους, *partly;* ἐκ μέρους, *individually,* of persons, *partially, imperfectly,* of things; κατὰ μέρος, *particularly, in detail,* Heb. ix. 5.

μεσημβρία, ας, ἡ, *midday, noon,* Ac. xxii. 6; *the south,* Ac. viii. 26.

μεσιτεύω, σω, *to mediate, to give surety,* Heb. vi. 17.*

μεσίτης, ου, ὁ, *a mediator, i.e.,* one who interposes between parties and reconciles them, Gal. iii. 19, 20; 1 Tim. ii. 5; in the phrase μεσίτης διαθήκης, *mediator of a covenant,* Heb. viii. 6, ix. 15, xii. 24.*

μεσο-νύκτιον, ου, τό, midnight, as Lu. xi. 5.

Μεσο-ποταμία, as, ἡ, Mesopotamia, the region between the Euphrates and the Tigris, Ac. ii. 9, vii. 2.*

μέσος, η, ον, middle, of time or place, in the midst of (gen.), as Mat. xxv. 6; Jn. i. 26, xix. 18; Ac. i. 18, xxvi. 13; neut., τὸ μέσον, the middle part, used chiefly in adverbial phrases, with prepositions (art. generally omit.), ἐκ μέσου, from among, away; ἐν μέσῳ, among; ἀνὰ μέσον, through the midst, among, between; also with διά and εἰς.

μεσό-τοιχον, ου, τό, a partition-wall, Ep. ii. 14. (N. T.)*

μεσ-ουράνημα, ατος, τό, mid-heaven, Rev. viii. 13, xiv. 6, xix. 17.*

μεσόω, ῶ, to be in the middle, Jn. vii. 14.*

Μεσσίας, ου, ὁ (from Heb. anointed), Messiah, the same as Greek Χριστός, Jn. i. 41, iv. 25. (N. T.)*

μεστός, ή, όν, full, gen., Jn. xix. 29; Ro. i. 29.

μεστόω, ῶ, to fill, gen., Ac. ii. 13.*

μετά (akin to μέσος), prep., gov. the gen. and acc.; gen., with, among; acc., after (see Gr. § 301, Wi. §§ 47 h, 49 f, 52, 4, 10), Bu. 338 sq.). In composition, μετά denotes participation, nearness, change, or succession (often like the Latin prefix trans-, as in the words transfer, translate).

μετα-βαίνω, βήσομαι, to pass over, to depart, Lu. x. 7; Mat. xi. 1.

μετα-βάλλω, in mid., to change one's mind, Ac. xxviii. 6.*

μετ-άγω, to turn about, to direct, as horses, ships, Ja. iii. 3, 4.*

μετα-δίδωμι, to share with, to impart, Lu. iii. 11; Ro. i. 11; 1 Th. ii. 8; Ep. iv. 28; ὁ μεταδιδούς, a distributor of alms, Ro. xii. 8.*

μετά-θεσις, εως, ἡ, (1) a transfer, a translation, Heb. xi. 5; a removal, Heb. xii. 27; (2) a change, Heb. vii. 12.*

μετ-αίρω, to remove, intrans., to depart, Mat. xiii. 53, xix. 1.*

μετα-καλέω, ῶ, in mid., to call to one's self, to send for, Ac. vii. 14, x. 32, xx. 17, xxiv. 25.*

μετα-κινέω, ῶ, to move away, pass., to be moved away, Col. i. 23.*

μετα-λαμβάνω, to take a share of, Ac. ii. 46; partake, gen., 2 Tim. ii. 6; to obtain (acc.), Ac. xxiv. 25.

μετά-λημψις (W. H.-λημψις), εως, ἡ, participation; εἰς μ., to be received, 1 Tim. iv. 3.*

μετ-αλλάσσω, to change one thing (acc.) for (ἐν, εἰς) another, Ro. i. 25, 26.*

μετα-μέλομαι, μελήσομαι, 1st aor. μετεμελήθην, dep., pass., to change one's mind, Mat. xxi. 30, 32; Heb. vii. 21; to repent, to feel sorrow for, regret, Mat. xxvii. 3; 2 Cor. vii. 8. Syn.: μετανοέω is the nobler word, the regular expression for thorough repentance; μεταμέλομαι is more loosely used, generally expressing sorrow, regret or remorse.

μετα-μορφόω, ῶ, to change the form, to transform, Mat. xvii. 2; Mar. ix. 2; 2 Cor. iii. 18; Ro. xii. 2.*

μετα-νοέω, ῶ, ήσω, to change one's views and purpose, to repent, as Mat. iii. 2; Ac. viii. 22. Syn.: see μεταμέλομαι.

μετάνοια, as, ἡ, change of mind, repentance, as Mat. iii. 8, 11.

μετα-ξύ (σύν or ξύν), adv. of time, meanwhile, Jn. iv. 31; afterwards, perh., Ac. xiii. 42 (see Gr. § 298, 7 b); as prep. with gen., between, of place, Mat. xxiii. 35.

μετα-πέμπω, in mid., to send for to one's self, to summon, Ac. x. 5, 22, 29, xi. 13, xxiv. 24, 26, xxv. 3; pass., x. 29.*

μετα-στρέφω (with 2d fut. and 2d aor. pass.), to turn about, to change, Ja. iv. 9; Ac. ii. 20; to pervert, to corrupt, Gal. i. 7.*

μετα-σχηματίζω, ίσω, to change the figure of, transfigure, Phil. iii. 21; mid., to assume the appearance of any one, 2 Cor. xi. 13, 14, 15; fig., to transfer, i.e., to speak by way of illustration, 1 Cor. iv. 6.*

μετα-τίθημι, to transpose, to transfer, Ac. vii. 16; Heb. xi. 5; to change, Heb. vii. 12; mid., to transfer one's self, i.e., to fall away, to desert, Gal. i. 6; to pervert, Ju. 4.*

μετ-έπειτα, adv., afterwards, Heb. xii. 17.*

μετ-έχω, μετασχήσω, 2d aor. μετέσχον, to be partaker of, to share in, 1 Cor. ix. 10, 12, x. 17, 21, 30; Heb. ii. 14, v. 13, vii. 13.*

μετεωρίζω, in pass., to be troubled with anxiety, to be in suspense, Lu. xii. 29.*

μετ-οικεσία, as, ἡ, change of abode, migration (of the Babylonian exile), Mat. i. 11, 12, 17.*

μετ-οικίζω, ιῶ, to cause to change one's habitation, to cause to migrate, Ac. vii. 4, 43.*

μετοχή, ῆς, ἡ, a sharing, a fellowship, 2 Cor. vi. 14.*

μέτοχος, ου, ὁ (prop. adj.), a partaker, Heb. iii. 1, 14, vi. 4, xii. 8; a partner, an associate, Heb. i. 9; Lu. v. 7.*

μετρέω, ῶ, to measure, Rev. xi. 2; Lu. vi. 38; met., to estimate, to judge of, 2 Cor. x. 12.

μετρητής, οῦ, ὁ, prop. a measurer; an amphora, a liquid measure containing 72 sextarii, or somewhat less than 9 English gallons, Jn. ii. 6.*

μετριο-παθέω, ῶ, to treat with moderation, bear gently with (R. V.), Heb. v. 2.*

μετρίως, adv., moderately, Ac. xx. 12.*

μέτρον, ου, τό, a measure, Mat. xxiii. 32; Mar. iv. 24; a measuring-rod, Rev. xxi. 15; a definite portion or measure, Ro. xii. 3; Ep. iv. 16; adv. phrases, ἐκ μέτρου, by measure, sparingly, Jn. iii. 34; ἐν μέτρῳ, in due measure, Ep. iv. 16.

μέτωπον, ου, τό (ὤψ), the forehead, Rev. vii. 3, ix. 4 (only in Rev.).

μέχρι, or μέχρις, adv., as prep. with gen., unto, time, Mat. xiii. 30; Mar. xiii. 30; place, Ro. xv. 19; degree, 2 Tim. ii 9; Heb. xii. 4; as conj., until, Ep. iv. 13.

μή, a negative particle, not; for

distinction between μή and
οὐ, see Gr. § 401, Wi. § 55,
1, Bu. 351; elliptically, *lest*,
see Gr. § 384, Wi. § 56, 2*b*,
Bu. 241 sq.; interrogatively,
see Gr. § 369, Wi. § 57, 3*b*,
Bu. 248; for the combina-
tion οὐ μή, see Gr. § 377,
Wi. § 57, 3*b*, Bu. 211 sq.

μή-γε, in the phrase εἰ δὲ μήγε,
but if not, emphatic.

μηδαμῶς, adv., *by no means*,
Ac. x. 14, xi. 8.*

μηδέ, compare οὐδέ, and see
Gr. § 401, Wi. § 55, 6, Bu.
366 sq.; *not even*, Mar. ii. 2;
1 Cor. v. 11; generally used
after a preceding μή, *and
not, neither, but not, nor yet*,
as Mat. vi. 25, vii. 6.

μηδείς, μηδεμία, μηδέν (εἷς), differing from οὐδείς as μή from
οὐ (see Gr. § 401, Wi. § 55,
1, Bu. 351); *not one, no one,
no person* or *thing, nothing*,
Mat. viii. 4; Mar. v. 26; Gal.
vi. 3.

μηδέ-ποτε, adv., *never*, 2 Tim.
iii. 7.*

μηδέ-πω, adv., *not yet*, Heb.
xi. 7.*

Μῆδος, ου, ὁ, *a Mede*, Ac. ii. 9.*

μηκέτι, adv. (ἔτι), *no more, no
longer*, Mar. ix. 25, xi. 14;
Ac. iv. 17.

μῆκος, ους, τό, *length*, Ep. iii.
18; Rev. xxi. 16.*

μηκύνω, *to make long;* pass., *to
grow up*, as plants, Mar. iv.
27.*

μηλωτή, ῆς, ἡ, *a sheepskin*, Heb.
xi. 37.*

μήν, a part. of strong affirma-
tion, N. T. only in the com-
bination ἦ μήν, *assuredly,
certainly*, Heb. vi. 14 (W. H.
εἰ μήν).*

μήν, μηνός, ὁ, (1) *a month*, as
Ac. vii. 20; (2) *the new moon*,
as a festival, Gal. iv. 10.

μηνύω, *to show, declare*, Lu. xx.
37; Jn. xi. 57; Ac. xxiii. 30;
1 Cor. x. 28.*

μὴ οὐκ, an interrogative formula, expecting the answer
"yes," Ro. x. 18, 19; 1 Cor.
ix. 4, 5.

μή-ποτε, adv., *never*, Heb. ix.
17; as conj., *lest ever, lest
perhaps, lest at any time*, Lu.
xii. 58; Ac. v. 39; interrog.
part., *whether indeed,* Jn. vii.
26; Lu. iii. 15.

μή που, *lest anywhere*, Ac.
xxvii. 29 (W. H., for Rec.
μήπως).

μή-πω, adv., *not yet*, Ro. ix. 11;
Heb. ix. 8.*

μή-πως, conj., *lest in any way,
lest perhaps*, as Ac. xxvii.
29 (W. H. μή που), 1 Th.
iii. 5.

μηρός, οῦ, ὁ, *the thigh*, Rev. xix.
16.*

μήτε, conj., differing from οὔτε
as μή from οὐ (see Gr. § 401);
and not, used after a preceding μή or μήτε, *neither ...
nor;* in Mar. iii. 20, *not even*,
W. H. read μηδέ.

μήτηρ, τρός, ἡ, *a mother*, Mat.
i. 18, ii. 11; met., *a mother
city*, Gal. iv. 26.

μήτι, adv., interrogatively used,
is it? whether at all? generally expecting a negative
answer; μήτιγε (W. H., Rec.
μήτι γε), *not to say then?* 1
Cor. vi. 3.

μήτις (W. H. μή τις), pron.
interrog., *has* or *is any one?
whether any one?* Jn. iv. 33.*

μήτρα, ας, ἡ, *the womb*, Lu. ii.
23; Ro. iv. 19.*

μητρ-αλῴας (W. H. -ολῴας), ου,
ὁ, *a matricide*, 1 Tim. i. 9.*

μία, fem. of εἷς, *one*.

μιαίνω, ανῶ, perf. pass. μεμί-
ασμαι, *to stain, pollute, defile*,
Jn. xviii. 28; Tit. i. 15; Heb.
xii. 15; Ju. 8.*

μίασμα, ατος, τό, *pollution, defilement*, 2 Pet. ii. 20.*

μιασμός, οῦ, ὁ, *the act of defilement, pollution*, 2 Pet. ii.
10.*

μίγμα, ατος, τό, *a mixture*, Jn.
xix. 39 (W. H. text ἕλιγμα).*

μίγνυμι, μίξω, ἔμιξα, perf. pass.
μέμιγμαι, *to mix, to mingle*,
Mat. xxvii. 34; Lu. xiii. 1;
Rev. viii. 7, xv. 2.*

μικρός, ά, όν, *little, small, i.e.*,
in size, Mat. xiii. 32; quantity, 1 Cor. v. 6; number, Lu.
xii. 32; time, Jn. vii. 33;
dignity, Mat. x. 42; age,
Mat. xviii. 6, 10, 14.

Μίλητος, ου, ἡ, *Miletus*, Ac. xx.
15, 17; 2 Tim. iv. 20.*

μίλιον, ου, τό (Lat. *miliarium*),
a mile (somewhat less than
our mile), Mat. v. 41.*

μιμέομαι, οῦμαι, dep. mid., *to
imitate*, 2 Th. iii. 7, 9; Heb.
xiii. 7; 3 Jn. 11.*

μιμητής, οῦ, ὁ, *an imitator*, as
1 Cor. iv. 16.

μιμνήσκω (μνα-), mid., with fut.
in pass. form μνησθήσομαι,
1st aor. ἐμνήσθην, perf. μέμ-
νημαι, *to call to mind, to remember*, gen. pers. or thing,
Mat. xxvi. 75; Lu. xxiii. 42;
pass., *to be remembered, to be
had in mind*, only Ac. x. 31;
Rev. xvi. 16.

μισέω, ῶ, ήσω, *to hate, to detest*,
Mat. v. 43; Jn. vii. 7; Ro.
ix. 13.

μισθ-απο-δοσία, ας, ἡ, *recompense*, as (1) *reward*, Heb. x.
35, xi. 26; (2) *punishment*,
Heb. ii. 2. (N. T.)*

μισθ-απο-δότης, ου, ὁ, *a re-
warder*, Heb. xi. 6. (N. T.)*

μίσθιος, α, ον, *hired*, as subst.,
a hired servant, Lu. xv. 17,
19, 21 (W. H. in br.).*

μισθός, οῦ, ὁ, *hire, wages, recompense*, Mat. xx. 8; used
of *reward*, Mat. v. 12, 46; of
punishment, 2 Pet. ii. 13.

μισθόω, ῶ, ώσω, mid., *to hire*,
Mat. xx. 1, 7.*

μίσθωμα, ατος, τό, *hire, rent;
anything rented*, as a house,
Ac. xxviii. 30.*

μισθωτός, οῦ, ὁ, *a hired servant*,
Mar. i. 20; Jn. x. 12, 13.*

Μιτυλήνη, ης, ἡ, *Mitylene*, the
capital of Lesbos, Ac. xx.
14.*

Μιχαήλ, ὁ (Heb. *who is like
God?*), *Michael*, an archangel, Ju. 9; Rev. xii. 7.*

μνᾶ, ᾶς, ἡ, *a mina*, silver money
= 100 δραχμαί, or about sixteen or seventeen dollars,
Lu. xix. 13–25.*

μνάομαι, see μιμνήσκω.

Μνάσων, ωνος, ὁ, *Mnason*, Ac.
xxi. 16.*

μνεία, ας, ἡ, *remembrance, recollection*, Phil. i. 3; 1 Th.
iii. 6; μνείαν ποιεῖσθαι, *to
mention*, Ro. i. 9.

μνῆμα, ατος, τό, *a monument
a tomb*, Mar. v. 5; Lu. xxiii.
53; less frequent than the
following.

μνημεῖον, ου, τό, *a tomb, a sepulchre*, Mat. viii. 28; Jn.
xi. 31.

μνήμη, ης, ἡ, *remembrance,
mention;* μνήμην ποιεῖσθαι,
to make mention, 2 Pet. i.
15.*

μνημονεύω, *to remember* (ὅτι),

recollect, call to mind (gen. or acc.), Mat. xvi. 9; Ac. xx. 31; to be mindful of, Heb. xi. 15; to make mention of (περί, gen.), Heb. xi. 22.

μνημόσυνον, ου, τό, a memorial, honorable remembrance, Mat. xxvi. 13; Mar. xiv. 9; Ac. x. 4.*

μνηστεύω, to ask in marriage; pass., to be betrothed, Mat. i. 18; Lu. i. 27, ii. 5.*

μογι-λάλος, ου, ὁ (prop. adj.), one speaking with difficulty, a stammerer, Mar. vii. 32.*

μόγις, adv., with difficulty, hardly, Lu. ix. 39 (W. H. μόλις).*

μόδιος, ου, ὁ (Lat.), a dry measure (16 sextarii), containing about a peck; a modius, Mat. v. 15; Mar. iv. 21; Lu. xi. 33. (N. T.)*

μοιχαλίς, ίδος, ἡ, an adulteress, Ro. vii. 3; fig., for departure from God, Mat. xvi. 4; Ja. iv. 4. (S.)

μοιχάομαι, ῶμαι, to commit adultery, Mat. v. 32.

μοιχεία, ας, ἡ, adultery, Mat. xv. 19.

μοιχεύω, σω, to commit adultery, abs. (acc., Mat. v. 28); fig., of forsaking God, Rev. ii. 22.

μοιχός, οῦ, ὁ, an adulterer, Lu. xviii. 11; 1 Cor. vi. 9; Heb. xiii. 4; Ja. iv. 4 (not W. H.).*

μόλις, adv., with difficulty, hardly, Lu. xv. 39 (W. H.); Ac. xiv. 18, xxvii. 7, 8, 16; Ro. v. 7; 1 Pet. iv. 18.*

Μολόχ, ὁ (Heb.), Moloch, Ac. vii. 43 (from S.).*

μολύνω, υνῶ, to pollute, to defile, 1 Cor. viii. 7; Rev. iii. 4, xiv. 4.*

μολυσμός, οῦ, ὁ, pollution, defilement, 2 Cor. vii. 1. (S.)*

μομφή, ῆς, ἡ, complaint, ground of complaint, Col. iii. 13.*

μονή, ῆς, ἡ, an abode, a dwelling-place, Jn. xiv. 2, 23.*

μονο-γενής, ές, gen. οῦς, only begotten, Lu. vii. 12, viii. 42, ix. 38; Heb. xi. 17; of Christ, Jn. i. 14, 18, iii. 16, 18; 1 Jn. iv. 9.*

μόνος, η, ον, only, alone, single, Lu. xxiv. 18; solitary, without company, Mar. vi. 47; forsaken, desolate, Jn. viii. 29; adv., μόνον, only.

μον-όφθαλμος, ον, having but one eye, Mat. xviii. 9; Mar. ix. 47.*

μονόω, ῶ, to leave alone; pass., to be left alone or desolate, 1 Tim. v. 5.*

μορφή, ῆς, ἡ, outward appearance, form, shape, Mar. xvi. 12; Phil. ii. 6, 7.* Syn.: see ἰδέα.

μορφόω, ῶ, ώσω, to form, to fashion, Gal. iv. 19.*

μόρφωσις, εως, ἡ, form, semblance, 2 Tim. iii. 5; form, system, Ro. ii. 20.*

μοσχο-ποιέω, ῶ, to make an image of a calf, Ac. vii. 41. (N. T.)*

μόσχος, ου, ὁ, ἡ, a calf, a young bullock, Lu. xv. 23, 27, 30; Heb. ix. 12, 19; Rev. iv. 7.*

μουσικός, ή, όν, skilled in music, a musician, Rev. xviii. 22.*

μόχθος, ου, ὁ, wearisome labor, toil, 2 Cor. xi. 27; 1 Th. ii. 9; 2 Th. iii. 8.*

μυελός, οῦ, ὁ, marrow, Heb. iv. 12.*

μυέω, ῶ, to initiate into, to instruct, Phil. iv. 12.*

μῦθος, ου, ὁ, a word; hence, a fiction, a fable, a falsehood, 1 Tim. i. 4, iv. 7; 2 Tim. iv. 4; Tit. i. 14; 2 Pet. i. 16.*

μυκάομαι, ῶμαι, to bellow, to roar, as a lion, Rev. x. 3.*

μυκτηρίζω, to turn up the nose; to mock, deride, Gal. vi. 7.*

μυλικός, ή, όν, pertaining to a mill; with λίθος, millstone, Mar. ix. 42 (not W. H.); Lu. xvii. 2 (W. H.). (N. T.)*

μύλινος, η, ον, in sense of foregoing, Rev. xviii. 21 (W. H.).*

μύλος, ου, ὁ, a millstone, as Mat. xviii. 6.

μυλών, ῶνος, ὁ, a mill-house, the place where grain was ground, Mat. xxiv. 41 (W. H. μύλος).

Μύρα (W. H. Μύρρα), ων, τά, Myra, a city near the coast of Lycia, Ac. xxvii. 5.*

μυριάς, άδος, ἡ, a myriad, ten thousand, Ac. xix. 19; a vast multitude, Lu. xii. 1; Ac. xxi. 20; Heb. xii. 22; Ju. 14; Rev. v. 11, ix. 16.*

μυρίζω, σω, to anoint, Mar. xiv. 8.*

μυρίοι, ιαι, ια, innumerable, 1 Cor. iv. 15, xiv. 19; μύριοι,

ιαι, ια, ten thousand, Mat. xviii. 24.*

μύρον, ου, τό, ointment, Mat. xxvi. 7.

Μυσία, ας, ἡ, Mysia, Ac. xvi. 7, 8.*

μυστήριον, ου, τό, a mystery, anything hidden, a secret, Mat. xiii. 11; Ro. xi. 25. In classical Greek, τὰ μυστήρια are hidden religious rites and knowledge, revealed only to the initiated; hence, the word is used in N. T. of the truths of the Gospel as mysteries partly hidden, partly revealed, Ep. iii. 9; Col. i. 26, iv. 3; 1 Tim. iii. 16; a hidden meaning, Ep. v. 32; Rev. i. 20.

μυωπάζω, to see dimly, 2 Pet. i. 9.*

μώλωψ, ωπος, ὁ, a bruise, a stripe, 1 Pet. ii. 24.*

μωμάομαι, ῶμαι, dep., aor. mid. and pass., to blame, to find fault with, 2 Cor. vi. 3, viii. 20.*

μῶμος, ου, ὁ, a blemish; met., disgrace, 2 Pet. ii. 13.*

μωραίνω, ανῶ, to make foolish, 1 Cor. i. 20; pass., to become foolish, Ro. i. 22; to become insipid, tasteless, like spoiled salt, Mat. v. 13; Lu. xiv. 34.*

μωρία, ας, ἡ, folly, absurdity, 1 Cor. i. 18, 21, 23, ii. 14, iii. 19.*

μωρο-λογία, ας, ἡ, foolish talking, Ep. v. 4.*

μωρός, ά, όν, stupid, foolish, Mat. vii. 26, xxiii. 17, 19, (on Mat. v. 22, see Gr. § 153, ii.); τὸ μωρόν, foolishness, 1 Cor. i. 25, 27.

Μωσῆς (W. H. Μωυσῆς), έως, dat. εῖ or ῇ; acc. ῆν (once έα, Lu. xvi. 29), ὁ, Moses, met., the books of Moses, the Pentateuch, Lu. xvi. 29; 2 Cor. iii. 15.

N

N, ν, νῦ, nu, n, the thirteenth letter. As a numeral, ν΄ = 50; ͵ν = 50,000.

Ναασσών, ὁ (Heb.), Naasson, Mat. i. 4; Lu. iii. 32.*

Ναγγαί, ὁ (Heb.), Naggai, Lu. iii. 25.*

Ναζαρέτ, -ρέθ or -ρά (W. H.

have all the forms), ἡ, *Naza-reth*, Mat. ii. 23; Lu. ii. 4, 39, 51.

Ναζαρηνός, οῦ, ὁ, *a Nazarene*, as Mar. i. 24.

Ναζωραῖος, ου, ὁ, *a Nazarene*, an appellation of Christ, Mat. ii. 23, xxvi. 71; Christians are called οἱ Ναζωραῖοι, Ac. xxiv. 5.

Ναθάν (W. H. -άμ), ὁ (Heb.), *Nathan*, Lu. iii. 31.*

Ναθαναήλ, ὁ, *Nathanael*, perhaps the same as *Bartholomew*, Jn. i. 45–49, xxi. 2.*

ναί, adv., affirming, *yes*, Mat. ix. 28; *even so*, Mat. xi. 26; Lu. x. 21; Rev. xxii. 20; *yea*, strongly affirming, Lu. vii. 26.

Ναΐν, ἡ, *Nain*, Lu. vii. 11.*

ναός, οῦ, ὁ (ναίω), *a temple, a shrine*, in general, Ac. xix. 24; *the temple*, Mat. xxiii. 16; met., used of Jesus Christ, Jn. ii. 19, 20; of Christians generally, 1 Cor. iii. 16; 2 Cor. vi. 16. *Syn.:* see ἱερόν.

Ναούμ, ὁ (Heb.), *Nahum*, Lu. iii. 25 (not the prophet).*

νάρδος, ου, ἡ, *nard, oil* or *ointment*, Mar. xiv. 3; Jn. xii. 3.*

Νάρκισσος, ου, ὁ, *Narcissus*, Ro. xvi. 11.*

ναναγέω, ῶ (ἄγνυμι), *to suffer shipwreck*, 2 Cor. xi. 25; fig., 1 Tim. i. 19.*

ναύ-κληρος, ου, ὁ, *a ship-master*, or *owner*, Ac. xxvii. 11.*

ναῦς, acc. ναῦν, ἡ, *a ship*, Ac. xxvii. 41.*

ναύτης, ου, ὁ, *a sailor*, Ac. xxvii. 27, 30; Rev. xviii. 17.*

Ναχώρ, ὁ (Heb.), *Nachor*, Lu. iii. 34.*

νεανίας, ου, ὁ, *a young man, a youth*, Ac. vii. 58, xx. 9, xxiii. 17, 18, 22 (not W.H.).*

νεανίσκος, ου, ὁ, *a young man*, Mat. xix. 20; plur., of soldiers, Mar. xiv. 51; 1 Jn. ii. 13, 14; *an attendant*, Ac. v. 10.

Νεάπολις, εως, ἡ, *Neapolis*, Ac. xvi. 11.*

Νεεμάν (W. H. Ναιμάν), ὁ (Heb.), *Naaman*, Lu. iv. 27.*

νεκρός, ά, όν, *dead*, (1) lit., as Mat. xi. 5; οἱ νεκροί, *the dead*, generally, 1 Pet. iv. 6; (2) fig., *dead*, spiritually, Ep. ii. 1; *dead* to (dat.), Ro. vi. 11;

inactive, inoperative, Ro. vii. 8.

νεκρόω, ῶ, *to put to death;* fig., *to deprive of power, to render weak* and *impotent*, Ro. iv. 19; Col. iii. 5; Heb. xi. 12.*

νέκρωσις, εως, ἡ, *death, a being put to death*, 2 Cor. iv. 10; *deadness, impotency*, Ro. iv. 19.*

νεο-μηνία, see νουμηνία.

νέος, α, ον, (1) *new, fresh*, Mat. ix. 17; 1 Cor. v. 7; Col. iii. 10; (2) *young*, of persons, Tit. ii. 4. *Syn.:* see καινός.

νεοσσός (W. H. νοσσός), οῦ, ὁ, *a young bird*, Lu. ii. 24.*

νεότης, τητος, ἡ, *youth*, Lu. xviii. 21; 1 Tim. iv. 12.

νεό-φυτος, ον, *newly planted;* fig., *a recent convert*, 1 Tim. iii. 6.*

Νέρων, ωνος, ὁ, *Nero*, the Roman emperor, 2 Tim. iv. 23 (Rec.).*

νεύω, σω, *to nod;* so, *to beckon, to signify*, Jn. xiii. 24; Ac. xxiv. 10.*

νεφέλη, ης, ἡ, *a cloud*, Mar. ix. 7, xiii. 26.

Νεφθαλείμ, ὁ (Heb.), *Naphtali*, Mat. iv. 13, 15; Rev. vii. 6.*

νέφος, ους, τό, *a cloud;* met., *a multitude, a great company*, Heb. xii. 1.*

νεφρός, οῦ, ὁ, *a kidney*, plur., *the kidneys, the loins*, used (as Heb.) for the secret thoughts, desires, and purposes, Rev. ii. 23.*

νεω-κόρος, ου, ὁ, ἡ (ναός and κορέω, *to sweep*), *a temple-keeper*, a designation of the people of Ephesus, Ac. xix. 35.*

νεωτερικός, ή, όν, *youthful, juvenile*, 2 Tim. ii. 22.*

νεώτερος, α, ον (comp. of νέος, which see), *younger, inferior in rank*, Lu. xv. 12, 13, xxii. 26; 1 Tim. v. 11, 14.

νή, adv., of affirmative swearing, *by*, with acc., 1 Cor. xv. 31.*

νήθω, *to spin*, Mat. vi. 28; Lu. xii. 27.*

νηπιάζω, *to be an infant*, 1 Cor. xiv. 20.*

νήπιος, α, ον, *infantile;* as subst., *an infant, a babe*, Mat. xxi. 16; 1 Cor. xiii. 11; used of an age below manhood, Gal. iv. 1; fig., of *un-*

learned, unenlightened persons, Mat. xi. 25; Ro. ii. 20; 1 Th. ii. 7 (W. H.).

Νηρεύς, έως, ὁ, *Nereus*, Ro. xvi. 15.*

Νηρί, ὁ (Heb.), *Neri*, Lu. iii. 27.*

νησίον, ου, τό (dim. of νῆσος), *a small island*, Ac. xxvii. 16.*

νῆσος, ου, ἡ (νέω, *to swim*), *an island*, Ac. xiii. 6, xxvii. 26.

νηστεία, ας, ἡ, *a fasting, a fast*, Mat. xvii. 21 (W. H. omit); Ac. xiv. 23; *the day of atonement, the chief Jewish fast-day*, Ac. xxvii. 9; *want of food*, 2 Cor. vi. 5, xi. 27.

νηστεύω, σω, *to abstain from food, to fast*, Mat. iv. 2, vi. 16–18.

νῆστις, ιος, plur. νήστεις, ὁ, ἡ, *fasting*, Mat. xv. 32; Mar. viii. 3.*

νηφάλιος or -λεος, ον, *sober, temperate*, 1 Tim. iii. 2, 11; Tit. ii. 2.*

νήφω, ψω, *to be sober, temperate*, fig., 1 Th. v. 6, 8.

Νίγερ, ὁ (Lat.), *Niger*, Ac. xiii. 1.*

Νικάνωρ, ορος, ὁ, *Nicanor*, Ac. vi. 5.*

νικάω, ῶ, ήσω, *to be victorious*, abs., Rev. iii. 21; *to conquer, overcome* (acc.), Lu. xi. 22; Jn. xvi. 33.

νίκη, ης, ἡ, *victory*, 1 Jn. v. 4.*

Νικό-δημος, ου, ὁ, *Nicodemus*, Jn. iii. 1.

Νικολαΐτης, ου, ὁ, *a follower of Nicolaus* (probably a Greek equivalent for *Balaam*), *a Nicolaitan*, Rev. ii. 6, 15.*

Νικό-λαος, ου, ὁ, *Nicolaus*, Ac. vi. 5 (not to be confounded with preced.).*

Νικό-πολις, εως, ἡ, *Nicopolis*, Tit. iii. 12. Several cities of the name existed; this was probably on the promontory of Epirus.*

νῖκος, ους, τό, *victory*, 1 Cor. xv. 55, 57; εἰς νῖκος, from S., *to a victorious consummation, utterly*, Mat. xii. 20; 1 Cor. xv. 54.*

Νινευΐ, ἡ (Heb.), *Nineveh*, Lu. xi. 32 (W. H. read following).*

Νινευΐτης (W. H. -είτης), ου, ὁ, *a Ninevite*, Mat. xii. 41; Lu. xi. 30, 32 (W. H.).*

νιπτήρ, ῆρος, ὁ, a basin, for washing hands and feet, Jn. xiii. 5. (N. T.)*

νίπτω, ψω, to wash (acc.), Jn. xiii. 8; mid., to wash one's self, acc. of part, as Mar. vii. 3. Syn.: see λούω.

νοέω, ῶ, ήσω, to understand, to consider, abs., or with acc., or ὅτι, Jn. xii. 40; Ep. iii. 4; Mar. xiii. 14.

νόημα, ατος, τό, (1) a thought, purpose, device, 2 Cor. ii. 11, x. 5; Phil. iv. 7; (2) the mind, i.e., the understanding or intellect, 2 Cor. iii. 14, iv. 4, xi. 3.*

νόθος, η, ον, illegitimate, bastard, Heb. xii. 8.*

νομή, ῆς, ἡ (νέμω, to pasture), (1) pasturage, Jn. x. 9; (2) met., growth, increase, as of a gangrene, 2 Tim. ii. 17.*

νομίζω, σω (νόμος), (1) to think, to suppose, to expect, as the result of thinking, Mat. v. 17, xx. 10; (2) pass., to be customary, only Ac. xvi. 13 (but see W. H. and R. V.).

νομικός, ή, όν, pertaining to (the) law, Tit. iii. 9; as subst., a person learned in or teacher of the Mosaic law, Mat. xxii. 35; Tit. iii. 13.

νομίμως, adv., lawfully, 1 Tim. i. 8; 2 Tim. ii. 5.*

νόμισμα, ατος, τό, (lawful) money, coin, Mat. xxii. 19.*

νομο-διδάσκαλος, ου, ὁ, a teacher and interpreter of the Mosaic law, Lu. v. 17; Ac. v. 34; 1 Tim. i. 7. (N. T.)*

νομο-θεσία, ας, ἡ, lawgiving, legislation, Ro. ix. 4.*

νομο-θετέω, ῶ, to enact laws; pass., to be enacted, Heb. viii. 6; to be furnished with laws, Heb. vii. 11.*

νομο-θέτης, ου, ὁ (τίθημι), a lawgiver, legislator, Ja. iv. 12.*

νόμος, ου, ὁ (νέμω, to apportion), a law, an edict, a statute, Lu. ii. 22; a standard of acting or judging, Ro. iii. 27; a written law, Ro. ii. 14; the Mosaic economy, Mat. v. 18; Ro. x. 4; the Christian dispensation or doctrines, Gal. vi. 2; Ro. xiii. 8; met., for the books containing the Mosaic law, i.e., the five books of Moses, Mat. xii. 5;

and for the Old Testament generally, Jn. x. 34. On the article with νόμος, see Gr. § 234, Wi. § 19, 1 a, Bu. 89.

νόος, see νοῦς.

νοσέω, ῶ, to be sick; fig., to have a diseased appetite or craving for, περί (acc.), 1 Tim. vi. 4.*

νόσημα, ατος, τό, disease, sickness, Jn. v. 4 (W. H. omit).*

νόσος, ου, ἡ, disease, sickness, Mat. iv. 23, 24.

νοσσιά, ᾶς, ἡ, a brood of young birds, Lu. xiii. 34. (S.)*

νοσσίον, ου, τό, a brood of young birds, Mat. xxiii. 37.*

νοσσός, see νεοσσός.

νοσφίζω, in mid., to remove for one's self, to purloin, Ac. v. 2, 3; Tit. ii. 10.*

νότος, ου, ὁ, the south wind, Lu. xii. 55; the South, Lu. xi. 31.

νου-θεσία, ας, ἡ, admonition, counsel, 1 Cor. x. 11; Ep. vi. 4; Tit. iii. 10.*

νου-θετέω, ῶ, to admonish, to counsel, Ac. xx. 31.

νου-μηνία (W. H. νεο-), ας, ἡ, the new moon, as a festival, Col. ii. 16.*

νουν-εχῶς, adv., wisely, judiciously, Mar. xii. 34.*

νοῦς (orig. νόος), νοός, νοΐ, νοῦν, ὁ, the mind, i.e., the understanding or intellect, Lu.xxiv. 45; Phil. iv. 7; the reason, Ro. vii. 25, xii. 2; hence, any affection of the mind — as modes of thought — inclinations or dispositions, Ro. xiv. 5; 1 Cor. i. 10.

Νυμφᾶς, ᾶ, ὁ, Nymphas, Col. iv. 15.*

νύμφη, ης, ἡ, a betrothed woman, a bride, Rev. xviii. 23; a daughter-in-law, Mat. x. 35.

νυμφίος, ου, ὁ, a bridegroom, Jn. iii. 29.

νυμφών, ῶνος, ὁ, a bridal chamber; οἱ υἱοὶ τοῦ νυμφῶνος, the sons of the bridal chamber, friends of the bridegroom, Mat. ix. 15; Mar. ii. 19; Lu. v. 34; a room in which the marriage ceremonies were held, Mat. xxii. 10 (W. H.). (Ap.)*

νῦν and νυνί, adv., (1) of time, now, i.e., the actually present; now, in relation to time

just past, just now, even now; now, in relation to future time, just at hand, even now, immediately; ὁ, ἡ, τὸ νῦν, the present, with subst. or (neut.) without; (2) of logical connection, now, 2 Cor. vii. 9; now then, i.e., implying the rise of one thing from another, 1 Cor. xiv. 6; (3) in commands and appeals, νῦν is emphatic, at this instant, Mat. xxvii. 42; Ja. iv. 13.

νύξ, νυκτός, ἡ, the night, night-time, lit., Ac. xvi. 33; often fig., a time of darkness and ignorance, Ro. xiii. 12; 1 Th. v. 5; death, Jn. ix. 4.

νύσσω, ξω, to stab, to pierce, Jn xix. 34.*

νυστάζω, ξω, to nod in sleep, to be drowsy, Mat. xxv. 5; fig., to delay, 2 Pet. ii. 3.*

νυχθ-ήμερον, ου, τό, a night and a day, twenty-four hours, 2 Cor. xi. 25.*

Νῶε, ὁ (Heb.), Noah, Lu. iii. 36, xvii. 26, 27.

νωθρός, ά, όν, sluggish, dull, stupid, Heb. v. 11, vi. 12.*

νῶτος, ου, ὁ, the back of men or animals, Ro. xi. 10.*

Ξ

Ξ, ξ, ξῖ, xi, the double letter x (= γς, κς, or χς), the fourteenth letter of the alphabet. As numeral, ξʹ = 60; ͵ξ = 60,000.

ξενία, ας, ἡ, hospitality; a lodging, Ac. xxviii. 23; Philem. 22.*

ξενίζω, σω, (1) to receive as a guest (acc.), Ac. x. 23, xxviii. 7; Heb. xiii. 2; pass., to be entertained, to lodge, Ac. x. 6, 18, 32, xxi. 16; (2) to astonish by strangeness, Ac. xvii. 20; pass., to think strangely of, to be surprised at (dat.), 1 Pet. iv. 4, 12.*

ξενο-δοχέω, ῶ, to entertain guests, to practice hospitality, 1 Tim. v. 10.*

ξένος, η, ον, masc., a guest-friend; as subst.. a stranger, foreigner, Mat. xxv. 35, 38, 43, 44; a host, Ro. xvi. 23; alien, Ep. ii. 12; new, novel, Heb. xiii. 9; 1 Pet. iv. 12.

ξέστης, ου, ὁ (the Latin sextarius), a sextarius, a vessel

for measuring liquids, holding about a pint; *a pitcher*, of any size, Mar. vii. 4, 8 (W. H. omit).*

ξηραίνω, ανῶ, 1st aor., act., ἐξήρανα, 1st aor., pass., ἐξηράνθην, perf., pass., ἐξήραμμαι (3 s., ἐξήρανται, Mar. xi. 21), *to make dry, to wither*, Ja. i. 11; pass., *to become dry, be withered*, Mat. xiii. 6; *to be dried up*, Rev. xvi. 12; *to be ripened*, as corn, Rev. xiv. 15; *to pine away*, Mar. ix. 18.

ξηρός, ά, όν, *dry, withered*, of a tree, Lu. xxiii. 31; of a useless limb, Mat. xii. 10; Mar. iii. 3 (W. H.); Lu. vi. 6, 8; Jn. v. 3; of land, Heb. xi. 29; ἡ ξηρά (sc. γῆ), *dry land*, Mat. xxiii. 15.*

ξύλινος, ίνη, ινον, *wooden*, 2 Tim. ii. 20; Rev. ix. 20.*

ξύλον, ου, τό, *wood, e.g., timber* in building, 1 Cor. iii. 12; *anything made of wood, e.g., the stocks*, Ac. xvi. 24; *a staff*, Mat. xxvi. 47, 55; *a cross*, Ac. xiii. 29; Gal. iii. 13; *a living tree*, Rev. ii. 7.

ξυράω, ῶ, ήσω, perf. pass. ἐξύρημαι, *to shave*, Ac. xxi. 24; 1 Cor. xi. 5, 6.*

O

Ο, ο, ὃ μικρόν, *omicron*, short *o*, the fifteenth letter. As a numeral, ὀʹ = 70; ͵ο = 70,000.

ὁ, ἡ, τό, the definite article, *the*, originally demonstrative. For its uses, see Gr. §§ 193–234, Wi. §§ 17–20, Bu. 85–103.

ὀγδοήκοντα, num., indeclin., *eighty*, Lu. ii. 37, xvi. 7.*

ὄγδοος, η, ον, ord., *eighth*; on 2 Pet. ii. 5, see Gr. § 331, Wi. § 37, 2, Bu. 30.

ὄγκος, ον, ὁ, *a weight, an encumbrance*, Heb. xii. 1.*

ὅδε, ἥδε, τόδε, demon. pron., *this, that* (here). See Gr. § 339, Wi. § 23, 5, Bu. 103.

ὁδεύω, *to pass along a way, to journey*, Lu. x. 33.*

ὁδηγέω, ῶ, ήσω, *to lead along a way, to conduct, to guide*, Mat. xv. 14; Lu. vi. 39; Jn. xvi. 13; Ac. viii. 31; Rev. vii. 17.*

ὁδ-ηγός, οῦ, ὁ, *a leader, a guide*,

Ac. i. 16; fig., of instructors, Mat. xv. 14, xxiii. 16, 24; Ro. ii. 19.*

ὁδοι-πορέω, ῶ, *to travel, to pursue a way*, Ac. x. 9.*

ὁδοι-πορία, ας, ἡ, *a journey, a journeying*, Jn. iv. 6; 2 Cor. xi. 26.*

ὁδός, οῦ, ἡ, (1) *a way, a road*, Mat. ii. 12; (2) *a going, a progress*, Mar. vi. 8; (3) *a journey*, a day's or a Sabbath day's, Lu. ii. 44; Ac. i. 12; (4) fig., *manner of action, method of proceeding*, Ac. xiii. 10; Mat. xxi. 32; especially (5) *the Christian way*, Ac. ix. 2; 2 Pet. ii. 2; (6) used of Christ himself, *the Way*, Jn. xiv. 6.

ὀδούς, ὀδόντος, ὁ, *a tooth*, Mat. v. 38.

ὀδυνάω, ῶ, in mid. and pass., *to be tormented, to be greatly distressed*, Lu. ii. 48, xvi. 24, 25; Ac. xx. 38.*

ὀδύνη, ης, ἡ, *pain, distress*, of body or mind, Ro. ix. 2; 1 Tim. vi. 10.*

ὀδυρμός, οῦ, ὁ, *lamentation, wailing*, Mat. ii. 18; 2 Cor. vii. 7.*

Ὀζίας, ου, ὁ, *Uzziah*, Mat. i. 8, 9.*

ὄζω, *to stink, be offensive*, Jn. xi. 39.*

ὅθεν, adv., *whence*, of place, source, or cause, Mat. xii. 44; 1 Jn. ii. 18; Heb. ii. 17.

ὀθόνη, ης, ἡ, *a linen cloth*; hence, *a sheet*, Ac. x. 11, xi. 5.*

ὀθόνιον, ου, τό (dim. of ὀθόνη), *a linen bandage*, Jn. xix. 40.

οἶδα, plur. οἴδαμεν (for Attic ἴσμεν), οἴδατε (and Attic ἴστε, Heb. xii. 17), οἴδασι (and Attic ἴσασι, only Ac. xxvi. 4), *I know* (see Gr. § 103, 4, Wi. § 40, 4 b).

οἰκειακός, ή, όν, see οἰκιακός.

οἰκεῖος, α, ον, *domestic, belonging to a household*, Gal. vi. 10; Ep. ii. 19; 1 Tim. v. 8.*

οἰκέτεια, ας, ἡ, *household, body of servants*, Mat. xxiv. 45 (W. H.).*

οἰκέτης, ου, ὁ, *a domestic, a household servant*, Lu. xvi. 13; Ac. x. 7; Ro. xiv. 4; 1 Pet. ii. 18.

οἰκέω, ῶ, ήσω, trans., *to inhabit*, 1 Tim. vi. 16; intrans., *to*

dwell, Ro. viii. 9; 1 Cor. vii. 12, 13.

οἴκημα, ατος, τό, *a dwelling*, used of *a prison*, Ac. xii. 7.*

οἰκητήριον, ου, τό, *a dwelling-place, a habitation*, 2 Cor. v. 2; Ju. 6.*

οἰκία, ας, ἡ, (1) *a house*, Lu. xv. 8; (2) met., *a household, a family, goods, i.e.*, a house and all that is in it, Jn. iv. 53; Mar. xii. 40.

οἰκιακός, οῦ, ὁ, *one of a family*, whether child, or servant, Mat. x. 25, 36.*

οἰκοδεσποτέω, ῶ, *to manage a household*, 1 Tim. v. 14.*

οἰκο-δεσπότης, ου, ὁ, *a householder, a master of a house*, Mat. x. 25.

οἰκοδομέω, ῶ, *to erect a building, build*, Lu. xiv. 30; fig., of the building up of character, *to build up, edify*, 1 Cor. x. 23; *to encourage*, 1 Cor. viii. 10.

οἰκο-δομή, ῆς, ἡ (δέμω), *the act of building; a building*, lit., Mat. xxiv. 1; of the spiritual body, 2 Cor. v. 1; of the church, Ep. ii. 21; met., *edification, spiritual advancement*, Ro. xiv. 19, xv. 2.

οἰκοδομία, ας, ἡ, *edification*, 1 Tim. i. 4 (W. H. οἰκονομία).*

οἰκο-δόμος, ου, ὁ, *a builder*, Ac. iv. 11 (W. H.).*

οἰκονομέω, ῶ, *to be a steward*, Lu. xvi. 2.*

οἰκονομία, ας, ἡ, *management of household affairs, stewardship*, Lu. xvi. 2–4; *a dispensation*, 1 Cor. x. 17.

οἰκο-νόμος, ου, ὁ (νέμω), *a house-manager, a steward*, Lu. xvi. 1, 3, 8; of the Christian stewardship, 1 Cor. iv. 1; 1 Pet. iv. 10; Tit. i. 7.

οἶκος, ου, ὁ, *a house, a building*, for any purpose (gen.); met., *a family resident in one house, a family* perpetuated by succession; *the house* of God, *i.e.*, the temple; *the family* of God, *i.e.*, the church.

οἰκουμένη, ης, ἡ, pres. part. pass. fem. of οἰκέω (sc. γῆ), *the inhabited land*, or *world*; (1) *the Roman empire*, Lu. ii. 1; (2) *the world at large*, Lu. iv. 5, xxi. 26; (3) met., *the inhabitants of the world*

69

Ac. xvii. 6, 31 ; (4) *the universe*, Heb. ii. 5.

οἰκ-ουρός, οῦ, ὁ, ἡ (οὖρος, *keeper*), *attending to household affairs, domestic*, Tit. ii. 5 (W. H. οἰκουργός, with same meaning).*

οἰκτείρω, ήσω, *to pity, to have compassion on*, Ro. ix. 15 (from S.).*

οἰκτιρμός, οῦ, ὁ, *compassion, pity*, Ro. xii. 1 ; 2 Cor. i. 3 ; Phil. ii. 1 ; Col. iii. 12 ; Heb. x. 28.*

οἰκτίρμων, ον, *pitiful, merciful*, Lu. vi. 36 ; Ja. v. 11.*

οἶμαι, see οἴομαι.

οἰνο-πότης, ου, ὁ, *one given to wine-drinking*, Mat. xi. 19 ; Lu. vii. 34.*

οἶνος, ου, ὁ, *wine*, Mar. ii. 22 ; met., *a vine*, Rev. vi. 6 ; fig., of that which excites or inflames, Rev. xiv. 10, xvii. 2.

οἰνο-φλυγία, ας, ἡ (φλύω, *to overflow*), *drunkenness*, 1 Pet. iv. 3.*

οἴομαι and οἶμαι, *to think, to suppose*, acc. and inf., or ὅτι, Jn. xxi. 25 ; Phil. i. 16 ; Ja. i. 7.*

οἷος, α, ον, rel. pron., correl. to τοιοῦτος, *of what kind, such as.*

οἴσω, see φέρω.

ὀκνέω, ῶ, ήσω, *to be slothful, to delay, to hesitate*, Ac. ix. 38.*

ὀκνηρός, ά, όν, *slothful, backward*, Mat. xxv. 26 ; Ro. xii. 11 ; Phil. iii. 1.*

ὀκτα-ήμερος, ον, *of or belonging to the eighth day*, Phil. iii. 5.*

ὀκτώ, num., indecl., *eight*, Lu. ii. 21.

ὄλεθρος, ου, ὁ, *destruction, perdition*, 1 Cor. v. 5 ; 1 Th. v. 3 ; 2 Th. i. 9 ; 1 Tim. vi. 9.*

ὀλιγο-πιστία, ας, ἡ, *little faith*, Mat. xvii. 20 (W. H.). (N. T.)*

ὀλιγό-πιστος, ον, *of little faith*, Mat. vi. 30. (N. T.)

ὀλίγος, η, ον, (1) *little, small, brief*, Lu. x. 2 ; Ac. xiv. 28 ; (2) in plur., *few*, sometimes with gen., Mat. vii. 14 ; Ac. xvii. 4 ; (3) neut. as adv., ὀλίγον, of time, *soon*, Lu. v. 3 ; of space, *a little way*, Mar. vi. 31 ; (4) with prepositions preced. in various phrases,

as ἐν ὀλίγῳ, *with little trouble*, Ac. xxvi. 28.

ὀλιγό-ψυχος, ον, *faint-hearted*, 1 Th. v. 14. (S.)*

ὀλιγωρέω, ῶ, *to care little for, to despise* (gen.), Heb. xii. 5 (from S.).*

ὀλίγως, adv., *a little, scarcely*, 2 Pet. ii. 18 (W. H.).*

ὀλοθρευτής, οῦ, ὁ, *a destroyer*, 1 Cor. x. 10. (N. T.)*

ὀλοθρεύω, *to destroy*, Heb. xi. 28.*

ὁλο-καύτωμα, ατος, τό (καίω), *a whole burnt-offering*, the whole being consumed, Mar. xii. 33 ; Heb. x. 6, 8. (S.)*

ὁλοκληρία, ας, ἡ, *perfect soundness*, Ac. iii. 16. (S.)*

ὁλό-κληρος, ον, *complete in every part, sound, perfect*, 1 Th. v. 23 ; Ja. i. 4. *Syn.:* see ἄρτιος.

ὀλολύζω, as from the cry ολ-ολ, *to howl, to lament aloud*, Ja. v. 1.*

ὅλος, η, ον, *all, the whole* (see Gr. § 225, Wi. § 20, 1 *b*, *a*, Bu. 94), Jn. vii. 23 ; Ja. iii. 2 ; Jn. v. 19.

ὁλο-τελής, ές, *perfect, complete*, 1 Th. v. 23.*

Ὀλυμπᾶς, ᾶ, ὁ, *Olympas*, Ro. xvi. 15.*

ὄλυνθος, ου, ὁ, *an unripe fig*, one which, not ripening in due time, grows through the winter and falls off in the spring, Rev. vi. 13.*

ὅλως (ὅλος), adv., *wholly, altogether*, 1 Cor. v. 1, vi. 7 ; with neg., *not at all*, Mat. v. 34 ; 1 Cor. xv. 29.*

ὄμβρος, ου, ὁ, *a violent rain*, Lu. xii. 54.*

ὁμείρομαι, *to long for*, 1 Th. ii. 8 (W. H., Rec. ἱμείρομαι).*

ὁμιλέω, ῶ, ήσω, *to associate with* (dat.), *to talk with* (πρός, acc.), Lu. xxiv. 14, 15 ; Ac. xx. 11, xxiv. 26.*

ὁμιλία, ας, ἡ, *intercourse, companionship*, 1 Cor. xv. 33.*

ὅμιλος, ου, ὁ, *a crowd, company*, Rev. xviii. 17 (not W. H.).*

ὁμίχλη, ης, ἡ, *a mist*, 2 Pet. ii. 17 (W. H.).*

ὄμμα, ατος, τό, *an eye*, Mat. xx. 34 (W. H.) ; Mar. viii. 23.*

ὄμνυμι and ὀμνύω, ὀμόσω (see Gr. § 116, 3, Wi. § 15, Bu.

45), *to swear, to take an oath*, Mar. xiv. 71 ; *to promise with an oath*, Mar. vi. 23.

ὁμο-θυμαδόν, adv., *with one mind, unanimously*, only in Ac. and Ro. xv. 6.

ὁμοιάζω, σω, *to be like*, Mat. xxiii. 27 (W. H. mrg.) ; Mar. xiv. 70 (not W. H.). (N. T.)*

ὁμοιο-παθής, ές, *being affected like another* (dat.), *having like passions or feelings*, Ac. xiv. 15 ; Ja. v. 17.*

ὅμοιος, οία, οιον, *like, similar to, resembling* (dat.), Jn. ix. 9 ; Rev. iv. 3 ; *of equal rank*, Mat. xxii. 39.

ὁμοιότης, τητος, ἡ, *likeness*, Heb. iv. 15, vii. 15.*

ὁμοιόω, ῶ, ώσω, (1) *to make like*; pass., *to be like*, or *to resemble*, Mat. vi. 8, xiii. 24 ; Ac. xiv. 11 ; (2) *to liken, to compare*, Mat. vii. 24 ; Mar. iv. 30 ; with acc. and dat.

ὁμοίωμα, ατος, τό, *likeness, similitude*, Ro. i. 23, v. 14, vi. 5, viii. 3 ; Phil. ii. 7 ; Rev. ix. 7.* *Syn.:* see εἰκών.

ὁμοίως, adv., *in like manner*, Lu. iii. 11 ; Jn. v. 19.

ὁμοίωσις, εως, ἡ, *likeness*, Ja. iii. 9.* *Syn.:* see εἰκών.

ὁμο-λογέω, ῶ, ήσω, 1st aor. ὡμολόγησα, *to speak the same thing;* hence, (1) *to confess*, in the sense of conceding or admitting, generally with ὅτι, Mat. xiv. 7 ; Heb. xi. 13 ; (2) *to profess*, or *acknowledge openly*, acc., or with ἐν, Mat. x. 32 ; Lu. xii. 8 ; Jn. ix. 22 ; (3) as ἐξομολογέω, *to praise* (dat.), Heb. xiii. 15.

ὁμολογία, ας, ἡ, *a profession, or a confession*, 2 Cor. ix. 13 ; 1 Tim. vi. 12, 13 ; Heb. iii. 1, iv. 14, x. 23.*

ὁμολογουμένως, adv., *confessedly, by assent of all*, 1 Tim. iii. 16.*

ὁμό-τεχνος, ον, *of the same trade or craft*, Ac. xviii. 3.*

ὁμοῦ, adv., *together, at the same place or time*, Jn. iv. 36.

ὁμό-φρων, ον (φρήν), *of one mind*, 1 Pet. iii. 8.*

ὁμόω, see ὄμνυμι.

ὅμως, adv., *yet*, 1 Cor. xiv. 7 ; Gal. iii. 15 ; with μέντοι, *nevertheless*, Jn. xii. 42.*

ὄναρ, τό, indecl., *a dream;*
κατ᾽ ὄναρ, *in a dream,* Mat.
i. 20, ii. 12, 13, 19, 22, xxvii.
19.*

ὀνάριον, ου, τό (dim. of ὄνος),
a young ass, Jn. xii. 14.*

ὀνειδίζω, σω, *to reproach, revile,
upbraid,* Mat. xi. 20; Mar.
xvi. 14; Lu. vi. 22.

ὀνειδισμός, οῦ, ὁ, *reproach, reviling,* Ro. xv. 3; 1 Tim. iii.
7; Heb. x. 33, xi. 26, xiii. 13.
(S.)*

ὄνειδος, ους, τό, *reproach, disgrace,* Lu. i. 25.*

Ὀνήσιμος, ου, ὁ (*profitable*),
Onesimus, Col. iv. 9; Philem.
10.*

Ὀνησί-φορος, ου, ὁ, *Onesi-
phorus,* 2 Tim. i. 16, iv.
19.*

ὀνικός, ή, όν, *pertaining to an
ass;* μύλος ὀνικός, *a millstone
turned by an ass, i.e.,* the
large upper millstone, Mat.
xviii. 6; Lu. xvii. 2 (not W.
H.); Mar. ix. 42 (W. H.).
(N. T.)*

ὀνίνημι, *to be useful, to help;*
mid. aor., opt., ὀναίμην, *may
I have help* or *joy from,*
Philem. 20.*

ὄνομα, ατος, τό, *a name,* almost
always of persons; in N. T.,
as in O. T., the *name* of a
person is a mark of what
he himself is, the name expresses the character, Mat.
i. 21; Mar. iii. 16, v. 9; Lu.
i. 31; hence the expressions
ποιεῖν τι ἐπὶ τῷ ὀνόματι, ἐν
τῷ ὀνόματι, διὰ τοῦ ὀνόματος;
the name is often introduced
by ὀνόματι, *by name,* once
by τοὔνομα (τὸ ὄνομα), Mat.
xxvii. 57; *fame, reputation,*
Ep. i. 21; Phil. ii. 9.

ὀνομάζω, σω, *to give a name to,*
Lu. vi. 13, 14; *to mention,*
Ep. v. 3; *to call upon the
name of,* 2 Tim. ii. 19.

ὄνος, ου, ὁ, ἡ, *an ass,* Mat. xxi.
2, 7; Lu. xiii. 15.

ὄντως, adv. (ὄν, neut. part. of
εἰμί), *really, truly,* 1 Cor. xiv.
25; 1 Tim. v. 3, 5.

ὄξος, ους, τό, *vinegar;* in N. T.,
sour wine, mixed with water,
a common drink of Roman
soldiers, Jn. xix. 29, 30.

ὀξύς, εῖα, ύ, (1) *sharp,* as a
weapon, Rev. i. 16, ii. 12;
(2) *swift, eager,* Ro. iii. 15.

ὀπή, ῆς, ἡ, *an opening, a cavern,*
Ja. iii. 11; Heb. xi. 38.*

ὄπισθεν, adv. of place, *from
behind, after,* Mat. ix. 20,
xv. 23.

ὀπίσω, adv., *behind, after,* of
place, Lu. vii. 38; of time,
Mat. iii. 11; abs., or with
gen.; τὰ ὀπίσω, *those things
that are behind,* Phil. iii. 14;
εἰς τὰ ὀπίσω, *backward,* Jn.
xviii. 6.

ὁπλίζω, σω, N. T., mid., *to arm
one's self* with, acc., fig., 1
Pet. iv. 1.*

ὅπλον, ου, τό, *an instrument,*
Ro. vi. 13; hence, plur.,
arms, weapons, Jn. xviii. 3;
Ro. xiii. 12; 2 Cor. vi. 7,
x. 4.*

ὁποῖος, οία, οῖον, relat. pron.,
of what kind or *manner,*
correl. to τοιοῦτος, Ac. xxvi.
29; 1 Cor. iii. 13; Gal. ii. 6;
1 Th. i. 9; Ja. i. 24.*

ὁπότε, adv. of time, *when,* Lu.
vi. 3 (W. H. ὅτε).*

ὅπου, adv. of place, *where,
whither; where,* referring to
state, Col. iii. 11; *in case
that,* 1 Cor. iii. 3.

ὀπτάνω, *to behold;* in pass., *to
appear,* Ac. i. 3; see ὁράω.
(S.)*

ὀπτασία, ας, ἡ, *a vision, a super-
natural appearance,* Lu. i. 22,
xxiv. 23; Ac. xxvi. 19; 2 Cor.
xii. 1.*

ὀπτός, ή, όν, *roasted, broiled,*
Lu. xxiv. 42.*

ὄπτω, ὄπτομαι, see ὁράω.

ὀπώρα, ας, ἡ, *autumn, autumnal
fruits,* Rev. xviii. 14.*

ὅπως, rel. adv., *how,* Lu. xxiv.
20; as conj., *in order that,
so that;* with ἄν, Ac. iii. 19
(see Gr. § 384, 2, Wi. § 42,
6, Bu. 234); after verbs of
beseeching, and the like, *that,*
Mat. ix. 38; Mar. iii. 10.

ὅραμα, ατος, τό, (1) *a spectacle,*
Ac. vii. 31; (2) *a vision,* Ac.
ix. 10, 12.

ὅρασις, εως, ἡ, *appearance,* Rev.
iv. 3; *a vision,* Ac. ii. 17;
Rev. ix. 17.

ὁρατός, ή, όν, *visible,* plur., neut.,
Col. i. 16.*

ὁράω, ῶ, ὄψομαι, ἑώρακα, εἶδον
(see Gr. § 103, 4, Wi. § 15,
Bu. 64), (1) *to see,* generally;
(2) *to look upon* or *contemplate;* (3) *to see,* and so *to*

participate in, Lu. xvii. 22;
Jn. iii. 36; (4) *to take heed,*
Heb. viii. 5; Mat. viii. 4;
with μή or equiv., *to beware,*
Mat. xvi. 6; (5) pass., *to be
seen, to appear to, to present
one's self to* (dat.).

ὀργή, ῆς, ἡ, *anger, indignation,*
Ep. iv. 31; often of the
wrath of God, and its manifestation, Ro. i. 18. *Syn.:*
see θυμός.

ὀργίζω, σω, *to irritate, to provoke;* pass., *to be angry,* abs.,
Mat. xviii. 34; *to be enraged
with,* dat., or ἐπί, dat., Mat.
v. 22; Rev. xii. 17.

ὀργίλος, η, ον, *prone to anger,*
Tit. i. 7.*

ὀργυιά, ᾶς, ἡ, *a fathom,* about
five or six feet, Ac. xxvii.
28.*

ὀρέγω, *to stretch forth;* mid., *to
reach after, to desire* or *long
eagerly for,* gen., 1 Tim. iii.
1, vi. 10; Heb. xi. 16.*

ὀρεινός, ή, όν, *mountainous,
hilly* (sc. χώρα), Lu. i. 39, 65.*

ὄρεξις, εως, ἡ, *strong desire, lust,*
Ro. i. 27.*

ὀρθο-ποδέω, ῶ, *to walk in a
straight course,* fig., *to act
uprightly,* Gal. ii. 14. (N.T.)*

ὀρθός, ή, όν, *upright,* Ac. xiv.
10; *straight,* Heb. xii. 13.*

ὀρθο-τομέω, ῶ (τέμνω), *to cut
straight;* met., *to handle
rightly, i.e., to teach correctly,*
2 Tim. ii. 15. (S.)*

ὀρθρίζω, *to rise early in the
morning, to come early in
the morning,* Lu. xxi. 38.
(S.)*

ὀρθρινός, ή, όν, *early in the
morning,* Lu. xxiv. 22 (W.
H.); Rev. xxii. 16 (not W.
H.).*

ὄρθριος, α, ον, *early in the
morning,* Lu. xxiv. 22 (W.
H. read preceding).*

ὄρθρος, ου, ὁ, *early dawn, day-
break,* Lu. xxiv. 1; Jn. viii.
2 (W. H. omit); Ac. v. 21.*

ὀρθῶς, adv., *rightly,* Mar. vii.
35; Lu. vii. 43, x. 28, xx.
21.*

ὁρίζω, σω, *to define; to determine,*
Ac. xvii. 26; Heb. iv. 7; *to
appoint, to decree,* Ac. x. 42,
xi. 29; pass., perf. part.,
ὡρισμένος, *decreed,* Ac. ii. 23;
neut., *decree,* Lu. xxii. 22.

ὅριον, ου, τό, plur., *the bound*

71

aries of a place; hence, *districts, territory*, Mat. ii. 6, iv. 13.

ὁρκίζω, *to adjure by, to charge solemnly by*, with double acc., Mar. v. 7; Ac. xix. 13; 1 Th. v. 27 (W. H. ἐνορκίζω).*

ὅρκος, ου, ὁ, *an oath*, Mat. xiv. 7, 9; *a promise with an oath, a vow*, Mat. v. 33.

ὁρκωμοσία, ας, ἡ, *the taking of an oath, an oath*, Heb. vii. 20, 21, 28. (S.)*

ὁρμάω, ῶ, ἥσω, N. T., intrans., *to rush*, Mat. viii. 32; Ac. vii. 57 (εἰς, or ἐπί, acc.).

ὁρμή, ῆς, ἡ, *a rush, a violent assault*, Ac. xiv. 5; Ja. iii. 4.*

ὅρμημα, ατος, τό, *a rushing on, impulse*, Rev. xviii. 21.*

ὄρνεον, ου, τό, *a bird*, Rev. xviii. 2, xix. 17, 21.*

ὄρνις, ιθος, ὁ, ἡ, *a bird, a hen*, Mat. xxiii. 37; Lu. xiii. 34.*

ὁρο-θεσία, ας, ἡ, *a setting of boundaries, a definite limit*, Ac. xvii. 26. (N. T.)*

ὄρος, ους, τό, *a mountain*, Lu. iii. 5, ix. 28.

ὀρύσσω, ξω, *to dig, to dig out*, Mat. xxi. 33, xxv. 18; Mar. xii. 1.*

ὀρφανός, ή, όν, *bereaved, an orphan*, Jn. xiv. 18; as subst., Ja. i. 27.*

ὀρχέομαι, οῦμαι, ήσομαι, dep., mid., *to dance*, Mat. xi. 17, xiv. 6; Mar. vi. 22; Lu. vii. 32.*

ὅς, ἥ, ὅ, relative pronoun, *who, which* (see Gr. §§ 58, 343–348, Wi. § 24, Bu. 281 sq.; for ὅς ἄν, ὅς ἐάν, *whoever*, see Gr. § 380, Wi. § 42, 3, Bu. 288) ; as demonst. in the phrase, ὅς μέν ... ὅς δέ, *that one ... this one*, as 2 Cor. ii. 16.

ὁσάκις, rel. adv., *as often as*, always with ἄν or ἐάν, 1 Cor. xi. 25, 26; Rev. xi. 6.*

ὅσιος (a), ον, *holy, pious*, of human beings, of Christ, and of God; τὰ ὅσια, *the holy promises*, Ac. xiii. 34. *Syn.:* see ἅγιος.

ὁσιότης, τητος, ἡ, *holiness, godliness*, Lu. i. 75; Ep. iv. 24.*

ὁσίως, adv., *holily*, 1 Th. ii. 10.*

ὀσμή, ῆς, ἡ, *a smell, an odor*, lit., Jn. xii. 3; fig., 2 Cor. ii. 14, 16; Ep. v. 2; Phil. iv. 18.*

ὅσος, η, ον, relat. pron., *how much, how great*, (1) of time, *how long, as long as*, Ro. vii. 1; repeated, the meaning is intensified, Heb. x. 37: ἔτι μικρὸν ὅσον ὅσον, *yet a little, a very, very little;* (2) of quantity, of number, *how much*, plur., *how many*, Mar. iii. 8; Jn. vi. 11; Ac. ix. 13; *as many as*, Mat. xiv. 36; with ἄν, ἐάν, *as many as, whatsoever*, Mat. vii. 12, xxi. 22; (3) of measure, degree, Heb. vii. 20.

ὅσ-περ, ἥ-περ, ὅ-περ, *the very one who*, Mar. xv. 6 (not W. H.).*

ὀστέον, contr. ὀστοῦν, οῦ, τό, *a bone*, Jn. xix. 36.

ὅσ-τις, ἥ-τις, ὅ, τι, compound relat., *whosoever, whichsoever, whatsoever* (see Gr. §§ 58c, 349, Wi. § 42, 3, Bu. 115); the addition of ἄν, ἐάν, gives indefiniteness.

ὀστράκινος, η, ον, *made of earth, earthen*, 2 Cor. iv. 7; 2 Tim. ii. 20.*

ὄσφρησις, εως, ἡ, *the sense of smell, smelling*, 1 Cor. xii. 17.*

ὀσφύς, ύος, ἡ, *the loins*, Mat. iii. 4; Lu. xii. 35; Ac. ii. 30; 1 Pet. i. 13.

ὅταν (ὅτε, ἄν), rel. adv., *when, whensoever ;* always with subj. except Mar. iii. 11, xi. 19 (W. H.), 25 (W. H.); Rev. iv. 9, viii. 1 (W. H.).

ὅτε, rel. adv., *when*, Mar. xiv. 12.

ὅτι, conj., (1) *that*, after verbs of declaring, etc., introducing the object-sentence; sometimes as a mere quotation mark, Mat. ii. 23; (2) *because* (see Gr. § 136, 6, Wi. § 53, 8b, Bu. 357 sq.).

ὅτου (gen. of ὅστις), ἕως ὅτου, *until*, Lu. xxii. 16.

οὗ, adv. (gen. of ὅς), *where, whither ;* οὗ ἐάν, *whithersoever ;* also used of time, *when*, in the phrases, ἀφ' οὗ, *since*, ἄχρις, ἕως, μέχρις οὗ, *until*.

οὐ (οὐκ before a vowel, οὐχ if the vowel is aspirated), *no,*

not (see Gr. §§ 134, 401, Wi. §§ 55, 56, Bu. 344 sq.).

οὐά, interj., *ah! aha!* derisive, Mar. xv. 29. (N. T.)*

οὐαί, interj., *woe! alas!* uttered in grief or denunciation, Mat. xi. 21; 1 Cor. ix. 16; ἡ οὐαί, as subst., Rev. ix. 12, *the woe, the calamity*. (S.)

οὐδαμῶς, adv., *by no means*, Mat. ii. 6.*

οὐ-δέ, conj., disj. neg., *but not, nor yet* (cf. μηδέ), *neither, nor, not even* (see Gr. § 401, Wi. § 55, 6, Bu. 366 sq.).

οὐδ-είς, οὐδεμία, οὐδέν (οὐδὲ εἷς), neg. adj., *not one, no one, none, nothing, of no moment, of no value, vain.*

οὐδέ-ποτε, adv., *never*, 1 Cor. xiii. 8; Mat. vii. 23.

οὐδέ-πω, adv., *not yet, never*, Jn. xix. 41.

οὐθείς, οὐθέν (οὔτε εἷς), *no one, nothing*, Ac. xxvi. 26 (W. H.); 1 Cor. xiii. 2, 2 Cor. xi. 8 (W. H.).*

οὐκ-έτι, adv., *no further, no more, no longer.*

οὐκ-οῦν, adv., *not therefore;* hence, in ordinary classic usage, an affirmative adverb. *therefore* (whereas οὔκουν retains its negative force, *not therefore*), Jn. xviii. 37.*

οὐ μή, an emphatic negative (see Gr. § 377, Wi. § 56, 3, Bu. 211 sq.).

οὖν, conj., *therefore, then*, Mat. xii. 12; employed espec. (1) in arguing, 1 Cor. iv. 16; (2) in exhortation, Mat. xxii. 9, 17, 21; (3) in interrogation, Mat. xiii. 27; Gal. iii. 19, 21; (4) to resume an interrupted subject, Mar. iii. 31; Jn. xi. 6; (5) to indicate mere transition from one point to another, most frequently in John, as viii. 13.

οὔ-πω, adv., *not yet.*

οὐρά, ᾶς, ἡ, *a tail* of an animal, Rev. ix. 10, 19, xii. 4.*

οὐράνιος, ον, *heavenly, in or pertaining to heaven*, as Lu. ii. 13; Ac. xxvi. 19.

οὐρανόθεν, adv., *from heaven*, Ac. xiv. 17, xxvi. 13.*

οὐρανός, οῦ, ὁ, *heaven*, (1) *the visible heavens* (both sing. and plural), through their whole extent, *the atmosphere, the sky, the starry heavens ;*

(2) *the spiritual heavens*, the abode of God and holy beings, Mat. vi. 10; 2 Cor. xii. 2; "the third heaven," above the atmospheric and the sidereal; met., for the inhabitants of heaven, Rev. xviii. 20; especially for God, Lu. xv. 18.

Οὐρβανός, οῦ, ὁ, *Urbanus*, Ro. xvi. 9.*

Οὐρίας, ου, ὁ, *Uriah*, Mat. i. 6.*

οὖς, ὠτός, τό, (1) *the ear*, Mat. x. 27; (2) met., *the faculty of perception*, Mat. xi. 15.

οὐσία, ας, ἡ (ὤν, part. εἰμί), *property, wealth*, Lu. xv. 12, 13.*

οὔ-τε, conj., *and not; neither, nor*, with a negative preced.; οὔτε ... οὔτε, *neither ... nor.* (The readings often vary between οὔτε and οὐδέ.)

εὗτος, αὕτη, τοῦτο, demonstr. pron., *this* (near), appl. to persons and things, sometimes emphatic, Mat. v. 19; sometimes comtemptuous, *this fellow*, Mat. xiii. 55 (see Gr. §§ 338–342, Wi. § 23, Bu. 103 sq.; also ἐκεῖνος and ὅδε).

οὕτως (and before a consonant sometimes οὕτω), adv., *thus, in this wise, so,* (1) in reference to antecedent or following statement; (2) correlative with ὡς or καθώς, *so ... as*; (3) qualifying adjectives, adverbs, or verbs, *so*, Heb. xii. 21; Mat. ix. 33; οὕτως ... οὕτως, 1 Cor. vii. 7, *in this manner ... in that.*

οὐχί, adv., (1) an intensive form of οὐ, Jn. xiii. 10, *by no means, not at all,* (2) mostly interrog., as Mat. v. 46, expecting an affirmative answer.

ὀφειλέτης, ου, ὁ, *a debtor*, Mat. xviii. 24; *one bound to some duty, e.g.*, obedience to the law, Gal. v. 3; *a delinquent, sinner*, Lu. xiii. 4.

ὀφειλή, ῆς, ἡ, *a debt, a duty*, Mat. xviii. 32; Ro. xiii. 7; 1 Cor. vii. 3 (W. H.). (N. T.)*

ὀφείλημα, ατος, τό, *a debt, what is justly due*, Ro. iv. 4; fig., *an offense, a sin*, Mat. vi. 12.*

ὀφείλω, (1) *to owe* money (acc.

and dat.), Mat. xviii. 28; τὸ ὀφειλόμενον, *the due*, Mat. xviii. 30; (2) *to be under obligation*, Mat. xxiii. 16; *to sin against*, Lu. xi. 4.

ὄφελον (see Gr. § 378, Wi. § 41 *b*, 5, note 2, Bu. 214 sq.), interjection, *O that! I wish! would that!* followed by indicative, 1 Cor. iv. 8; 2 Cor. xi. 1; Gal. v. 12; Rev. iii. 15.*

ὄφελος, ους, τό (ὀφέλλω, *to increase*), *profit, advantage*, 1 Cor. xv. 32; Ja. ii. 14, 16.*

ὀφθαλμο-δουλεία, ας, ἡ, *eyeservice*, Ep. vi. 6; Col. iii. 22. (N. T.)*

ὀφθαλμός, οῦ, ὁ, *an eye*; fig., of the eye as the receptive channel into mind and heart, Mat. vi. 23 (see Mar. vii. 22; Mat. xx. 15); fig., *the eye of the mind, i.e., the understanding*, Ac. xxvi. 18.

ὄφις, εως, ὁ, *a serpent*, Mat. vii. 10; an emblem of wisdom, Mat. x. 16; of cunning, Mat. xxiii. 33; used symbol. for Satan, Rev. xii. 9, 14.

ὀφρύς, ύος, ἡ, *the eyebrow; the brow* of a mountain or hill, Lu. iv. 29.*

ὀχλέω, ῶ, *to disturb, to vex*, only in pass., Lu. vi. 18 (W. H. ἐνοχλέω), Ac. v. 16.*

ὀχλο-ποιέω, ῶ, *to gather a crowd*, Ac. xvii. 5. (N. T.)*

ὄχλος, ου, ὁ, *a crowd, an unorganized multitude*, Mat. ix. 23, 25; *the multitude, the common people*, Mar. xii. 12.

ὀχύρωμα, ατος, τό, *a fortress, a strong defense*, 2 Cor. x. 4.*

ὀψάριον, ου, τό (a relish with bread), *a little fish*, Jn. vi. 9, 11, xxi. 9, 10, 13. (N. T.)*

ὀψέ, adv., *late, in the evening*, Mar. xi. 11 (W. H.), 19, xiii. 35; *late in*, gen., Mat. xxviii. 1.*

ὄψιμος, ον, *latter*, of the rain, Ja. v. 7.*

ὄψιος, α, ον, *late*, Mar. xi. 11 (not W. H., see mrg.); as subst., ἡ ὀψία, *evening*, either the former of the two evenings reckoned among the Jews, Mat. viii. 16; or the latter, Mat. xiv. 23; see ver. 15.

ὄψις, εως, ἡ, *sight; the countenance*, Jn. xi. 44; Rev. i.

16; *external appearance*, Jn vii. 24.*

ὀψώνιον, ου, τό, lit., *relish, sauce*, like ὀψάριον, (1) plur., the *rations* of soldiers, their *wages*, Lu. iii. 14; 1 Cor. ix. 7; hence, (2) *wages*, generally, Ro. vi. 23; 2 Cor. xi. 8.*

Π

Π, π, πῖ, *pi*, *p*, the sixteenth letter. As a numeral, π′ = 80; ‚π = 80,000.

παγιδεύω, σω, *to ensnare, to entrap*, fig., Mat. xxii. 15. (S.)*

παγίς, ίδος, ἡ, *a snare, a trap*, Lu. xxi. 35; fig., Ro. xi. 9; 1 Tim. iii. 7, vi. 9; 2 Tim. ii. 26.*

πάγος, ου, ὁ, *a hill*; only with the adj. Ἄρειος, *Mars' Hill, Areopagus*, Ac. xvii. 19, 22.*

πάθημα, ατος, τό, (1) *suffering, affliction*, Ro. viii. 18; (2) *affection of mind, passion*, Ro. vii. 5; Gal. v. 24; (3) *an undergoing, an enduring*, Heb. ii. 9.

παθητός, ή, όν, *destined to suffer*, Ac. xxvi. 23.*

πάθος, ους, τό, *suffering, emotion*, in N.T., of an evil kind, *depraved passion, lust*, Ro. i. 26; 1 Th. iv. 5; Col. iii. 5.*

παιδ-αγωγός, οῦ, ὁ, *a boys' guardian* or *tutor*, " pædagogue," a slave who had the charge of the life and morals of the boys of a family, not strictly a teacher, 1 Cor. iv. 15; Gal. iii. 24, 25.*

παιδάριον, ου, τό (dim. of παῖς), *a little boy, a lad*, Mat. xi. 16 (W. H. παιδίον); Jn. vi. 9.*

παιδεία, ας, ἡ, *training and education* of children, Ep. vi. 4; hence, *instruction*, 2 Tim. iii. 16; *chastisement, correction*, Heb. xii. 5–11.*

παιδευτής, οῦ, ὁ, (1) *an instructor*, Ro. ii. 20; (2) *a chastiser*, Heb. xii. 9.*

παιδεύω, σω, *to train a child*, Ac. xxii. 3; hence, (1) *to instruct*, 1 Tim. i. 20, (2) *to correct, to chasten*, 2 Tim. ii. 25; Heb. xii. 7.

παιδιόθεν, adv., *from childhood*, Mar. ix. 21. (N. T.)*

παιδίον, ου, τό (dim. of παῖς),

a little child, an infant, Mat. ii. 8; *a child* more advanced, Mat. xiv. 21; fig., 1 Cor. xiv. 20.

παιδίσκη, ης, ἡ (fem. dim. of παῖς), *a young girl; a young female slave*, Lu. xii. 45, xxii. 56.

παίζω, *to play*, as a child, *to sport, to jest*, 1 Cor. x. 7.*

παῖς, παιδός, ὁ, ἡ, (1) *a child, a boy or girl*, Lu. ii. 43, viii. 51, 54; (2) *a servant, a slave*, as Mat. viii. 6, 8; ὁ παῖς τοῦ θεοῦ, *the servant of God*, used of any servant, Lu. i. 69; *of the Messiah*, Mat. xii. 18.

παίω, σω, *to strike, to smite*, with the fist, Mat. xxvi. 68; Lu. xxii. 64; with a sword, Mar. xiv. 47; Jn. xviii. 10; as a scorpion with its sting, Rev. ix. 5.*

Πακατιανή, ῆς, ἡ, *Pacatiana*, a part of Phrygia, 1 Tim. vi. 22 (Rec.).*

πάλαι, adv., *of old*, Heb. i. 1; *long ago*, Mat. xi. 21.

παλαιός, ά, όν, (1) *old, ancient*, 2 Cor. iii. 14; ὁ παλαιὸς ἄνθρωπος, *the old or former man*, i.e., man in his old, un-renewed nature, Ro. vi. 6; (2) *worn out*, as a garment, Mat. ix. 16.

παλαιότης, τητος, ἡ, *oldness, obsoleteness*, Ro. vii. 6.*

παλαιόω, ῶ, *to make old, to declare obsolete*, Heb. viii. 13; pass., *to grow old, to become obsolete*, Lu. xii. 33; Heb. i. 11, viii. 13.*

πάλη, ης, ἡ, *a wrestling*, Ep. vi. 12.*

παλιγ-γενεσία (W. H. παλιν-γ-), ας, ἡ, *a new birth, regeneration*, Tit. iii. 5; *a renovation* of all things, Mat. xix. 28.* *Syn.*: see ἀνακαίνωσις.

πάλιν, adv., *again, back*, used of place or of time; a particle of continuation, *again, once more, further;* and of antithesis, as 2 Cor. x. 7, *on the other hand.*

παμ-πληθεί, adv., *all at once, all together*, Lu. xxiii. 18. (N. T.)*

πάμ-πολυς, παμπόλλη, πάμπολυ, *very great*, Mar. viii. 1 (not W. H.).*

Παμφυλία, ας, ἡ, *Pamphylia*, Ac. xiii. 13.

παν-δοχεῖον, ου, τό, *a khan*, or Eastern *inn*, Lu. x. 34.*

παν-δοχεύς, έως, ὁ (δέχομαι), *the keeper of a khan, a host*, Lu. x. 35.*

παν-ήγυρις, εως, ἡ (ἀγείρω), *a general festal assembly*, Heb. xii. 23.* *Syn.*: see ἐκκλησία.

παν-οικί, adv., *with one's whole household* or *family*, Ac. xvi. 34.*

παν-οπλία, ας, ἡ, *complete armor*, Lu. xi. 22; Ep. vi. 11, 13.*

πανουργία, ας, ἡ, *shrewdness, skill;* hence, *cunning, craftiness*, Lu. xx. 23, 1 Cor. iii. 19; 2 Cor. iv. 2, xi. 3; Ep. iv. 14.*

παν-οῦργος, ον (ἔργον), *doing everything; cunning, crafty*, 2 Cor. xii. 16.*

πανταχῇ, adv., *everywhere*, Ac. xxi. 28 (W. H.).*

πανταχόθεν, adv., *from all sides*, Mar. i. 45 (W. H. πάν-τοθεν).*

πανταχοῦ, adv., *everywhere*, Mar. xvi. 20; Lu. ix. 6.

παντελής, ές, *complete;* εἰς τὸ παντελές, *completely, perfectly*, Heb. vii. 25; the same phrase, with μή, *not at all*, Lu. xiii. 11.*

πάντη, adv., *in every way*, Ac. xxiv. 3.*

πάντοθεν, adv., *from all sides*, Mar. i. 45 (W. H.); Lu. xix. 43; Heb. ix. 4.*

παντο-κράτωρ, ορος, ὁ, *the almighty*, used of God, Rev. i. 8, iv. 8.

πάντοτε, adv., *always, at all times*, Mat. xxvi. 11.

πάντως, adv., *wholly, entirely*, 1 Cor. v. 10; *in every way, by all means*, Ro. iii. 9; *assuredly, certainly*, Ac. xxi. 22.

παρά, prep., gov. the gen., the dat., and accus., *beside;* with a gen. (of person), it indicates *source* or *origin;* with a dat., it denotes *presence with;* with an accus., it indicates motion *towards*, or *alongside*, and is employed in comparisons, *beyond;* for details see Gr. § 306, Wi. §§ 47 b, 48 d, 49 g, Bu. 339 sq. In composition, παρά retains its general meaning, *besides*, sometimes denoting *nearness*, sometimes *motion by* or

past, so as to miss or fail; occasionally also *stealthiness* (*by the way*), as in παρει-σάγω.

παρα-βαίνω, 2d aor. παρέβην, *to transgress*, Mat. xv. 2, 3; 2 Jn. 9 (W. H. προάγω); *to depart, desert*, Ac. i. 25.*

παρα-βάλλω, (1) *to compare*, Mar. iv. 30 (not W. H.); (2) *to betake one's self, arrive*, Ac. xx. 15.*

παρά-βασις, εως, ἡ, *a transgression*, Ro. ii. 23. *Syn.*: see ἀγνόημα.

παρα-βάτης, ου, ὁ, *a transgressor*, Ro. ii. 25, 27; Gal. ii. 18; Ja. ii. 9, 11.*

παρα-βιάζομαι, *to constrain by entreaties*, Lu. xxiv. 29; Ac. xvi. 15.*

παρα-βολεύομαι, *to expose one's self to peril, to be venturesome*, Phil. ii. 30 (W. H.). (N. T.)*

παρα-βολή, ῆς, ἡ, (1) *a comparison*, Heb. ix. 9; (2) *a parable*, often of those uttered by our Lord, Mar. iv. 2, 10; (3) *a proverb, an adage*, Lu. iv. 23; (4) perhaps in Heb. xi. 19, *a venture, a risk* (see παραβολεύομαι).

παραβουλεύομαι, *to consult amiss, be reckless*, Phil. ii. 30 (Rec.). (N. T.)*

παραγγελία, ας, ἡ, *a command, a charge*, Ac. v. 28, xvi. 24; 1 Th. iv. 2; 1 Tim. i. 5, 18.*

παρ-αγγέλλω, *to notify, to command, to charge*, Lu. viii. 29; 2 Th. iii. 4; dat. of person, acc. of thing, or ὅτι, ἵνα or inf., 1 Tim. vi. 13.

παρα-γίνομαι, *to come near, come forth, come against* (ἐπί, πρός), Lu. xii. 51, xxii. 52; Jn. iii. 23; Heb. ix. 11.

παρ-άγω, *to pass by*, Mat. xx. 30; *to depart*, Mat. ix. 27; *to pass away*, act., 1 Cor. vii. 31; pass., only 1 Jn. ii. 8, 17.

παρα-δειγματίζω, *to make a public example of, to expose to disgrace*, Mat. i. 19 (W. H. δειγματίζω); Heb. vi. 6.*

παράδεισος, ου, ὁ (probably a Persian word, "garden," "park"), *Paradise*, Lu. xxiii. 43; 2 Cor. xii. 4; Rev. ii. 7.*

παρα-δέχομαι, dep., mid., *to receive, accept, acknowledge*, Mar. iv. 20; Ac. xv. 4 (W

H.), xvi. 21, xxii. 18; 1 Tim.
v. 19; Heb. xii. 6.*

παρα-δια-τριβή, ῆs, ἡ, useless
occupation, 1 Tim. vi. 5 (W.
H. διαπαρατριβή). (N. T.)*

παρα-δίδωμι, acc. and dat., (1)
to deliver over, as to prison,
judgment, or punishment,
Mat. iv. 12; to betray, spec.
of the betrayal by Judas;
(2) to surrender, abandon
one's self, Ep. iv. 19; (3) to
hand over, entrust, commit,
deliver, as Mat. xxv. 14; Lu.
i. 2; Ac. vi. 14; (4) to commend to kindness, Ac. xiv.
26; (5) to give or prescribe,
as laws, etc., Ac. vi. 14; (6)
prob. to permit, in Mar. iv.
29, when the fruit permits
or allows.

παρά-δοξος, ον, strange, wonderful, Lu. v. 26.*

παρά-δοσις, εως, ἡ, an instruction, or tradition, Mat. xv. 2;
1 Cor. xi. 2; 2 Th. ii. 15,
iii. 6.

παρα-ζηλόω, ῶ, ώσω, to provoke to rivalry, Ro. xi. 11,
14; to jealousy, Ro. x. 19; to
anger, 1 Cor. x. 22. (S.)*

παρα-θαλάσσιος, a, ον, by the
sea, Mat. iv. 13.*

παρα-θεωρέω, ῶ, to overlook,
neglect, Ac. vi. 1.*

παρα-θήκη, ης, ἡ, a deposit,
anything committed to one's
charge, 1 Tim. vi. 20 (W.H.);
2 Tim. i. 12, 14 (W. H.).*

παρ-αινέω, ῶ, to exhort, admonish, Ac. xxvii. 9, 22.*

παρ-αιτέομαι, οῦμαι, dep., mid.,
to entreat for, to beg off,
make excuse, refuse, reject,
Mar. xv. 6 (W. H.); Lu.
xiv. 18, 19; Ac. xxv. 11;
1 Tim. iv. 7, v. 11; 2 Tim.
ii. 23; Tit. iii. 10; Heb. xii.
19, 25.*

παρα-καθέζομαι, to seat one's
self, Lu. x. 39 (W. H.).*

παρα-καθίζω, intrans., to sit
down beside, Lu. x. 39 (Rec.).*

παρα-καλέω, ῶ, έσω, (1) to send
for, summon, Ac. xxviii. 20;
(2) to beseech, entreat, Mar.
i. 40; (3) to exhort, admonish,
Ac. xv. 32; 1 Tim. vi. 2;
(4) to comfort, 2 Cor. i. 4;
pass., to be comforted, Lu.
xvi. 25.

παρα-καλύπτω, to hide, to conceal, Lu. ix. 45.*

παρα-κατα-θήκη, ης, ἡ, a trust,
a deposit, 1 Tim. vi. 20; 2
Tim. i. 14 (in both passages
W. H. read παραθήκη).*

παρά-κειμαι, to be at hand, be
present with (dat.), Ro. vii.
18, 21.*

παρά-κλησις, εως, ἡ, a calling
for, a summons; hence, (1)
exhortation, Heb. xii. 5; (2)
entreaty, 2 Cor. viii. 4; (3) en-
couragement, Phil. ii. 1; (4)
consolation, comfort, Ro. xv.
4; met., of the Consoler, Lu.
ii. 25; (5) generally, of the
power of imparting all these,
Ac. iv. 36.

παρά-κλητος, ου, ὁ, (1) an ad-
vocate, intercessor, 1 Jn. ii.
1; (2) a consoler, comforter,
helper, of the Holy Spirit,
Jn. xiv. 16, 26, xv. 26, xvi.
7.*

παρ-ακοή, ῆς, ἡ, disobedience,
Ro. v. 19; 2 Cor. x. 6; Heb.
ii. 2.* Syn.: see ἀγνόημα.

παρ-ακολουθέω, ῶ, ήσω, to follow closely, to accompany
(dat.), Mar. xvi. 17 (not W.
H., see mrg.); to follow so
as to trace out, to examine,
Lu. i. 3; to follow teaching,
1 Tim. iv. 6; 2 Tim. iii. 10.*

παρ-ακούω, to hear negligently,
to disregard, Mat. xviii. 17;
Mar. v. 36 (W. H.).*

παρα-κύπτω, ψω, to stoop, Lu.
xxiv. 12; Jn. xx. 5, 11; fig.,
with εἰς, to search into, Ja. i.
25; 1 Pet. i. 12.*

παρα-λαμβάνω, λήψομαι (W. H.
-λήμψ-), (1) to take to one's self,
to take with one, Lu. ix. 10,
28, xi. 26; to lead off a prisoner, Jn. xix. 16; Ac. xxiii.
18; (2) to receive by trans-
mission, Col. iv. 17; Heb.
xii. 28; fig., to receive by instruction, Mar. vii. 4.

παρα-λέγω, N.T. in mid., to lay
one's course near, in sailing,
to coast along, Ac. xxvii. 8,
13.*

παρ-άλιος, ον, adjacent to the
sea, on the coast, Lu. vi.
17.*

παρ-αλλαγή, ῆς, ἡ, change, variation, Ja. i. 17.*

παρα-λογίζομαι, dep., to impose
upon, to delude, acc., Col. ii.
4; Ja. i. 22.*

παρα-λυτικός, ή, όν, afflicted
with paralysis, in the whole

or a part of the body, Mat.
iv. 24, viii. 6. (N. T.)

παρα-λύω, to relax, to enfeeble,
only perf. part., pass., παρα-
λελυμένος, paralyzed, enfee-
bled.

παρα-μένω, μενῶ, to remain by
(dat., or πρός, acc.), to abide
with, 1 Cor. xvi. 6 (W. H.
καταμένω); Phil. i. 25 (W.H.);
to continue, Ja. i. 25; Heb.
vii. 23.*

παρα-μυθέομαι, οῦμαι, to speak
to, to cheer, to comfort, Jn.
xi. 19, 31; 1 Th. ii. 11, v.
14.*

παρα-μυθία, ας, ἡ, encourage-
ment, comfort, 1 Cor. xiv.
3.*

παρα-μύθιον, ου, τό, comfort,
Phil. ii. 1.*

παρα-νομέω, ῶ, to act contrary
to law, Ac. xxiii. 3.*

παρα-νομία, ας, ἡ, violation of
law, transgression, 2 Pet. ii.
16.* Syn.: see ἀγνόημα.

παρα-πικραίνω, ανῶ, 1st aor.
παρεπίκρανα, to provoke God
to anger, Heb. iii. 16. (S.)*

παρα-πικρασμός, οῦ, ὁ, provocation of God, Heb. iii. 8, 15.
(S.)*

παρα-πίπτω, 2d aor. παρέπεσον,
to fall away, Heb. vi. 6.*

παρα-πλέω, ῶ. εύσομαι, to sail
past, acc., Ac. xx. 16.*

παρα-πλήσιον, adv., near to
(gen.), Phil. ii. 27.*

παραπλησίως, adv., similarly,
in like manner, Heb. ii. 14.*

παρα-πορεύομαι, dep., mid., to
pass by, to pass along by, Mar.
xi. 20, xv. 29.

παρά-πτωμα, ατος, τό (παρα-
πίπτω), a falling away or
aside, a sin, Ep. i. 7, ii. 1, 5.
Syn.: see ἀγνόημα.

παρα-ρρέω, 2d aor., pass., παρερ-
ρύην, pass., to be carried
past, to lose, Heb. ii. 1.*

παρά-σημος, ον, marked with
(dat.), Ac. xxviii. 11.*

παρα-σκευάζω, σω, to prepare,
Ac. x. 10; mid., to prepare
one's self, 1 Cor. xiv. 8;
pass., to be in readiness, 2
Cor. ix. 2, 3.*

παρα-σκευή, ῆς, ἡ, a preparation, i.e., the day immediately before a sabbath or
other festival, Mat. xxvii.
62; Mar. xv. 42; Lu. xxiii.
54; Jn. xix. 14, 31, 42.*

παρα-τείνω, to extend, to pro-
long, Ac. xx. 7.*

παρα-τηρέω, ῶ, ήσω, (1) to
watch, Mar. iii. 2; (2) to observe scrupulously, Gal. iv.
10.

παρα-τήρησις, εως, ή, observa-
tion, Lu. xvii. 20.*

παρα-τίθημι, θήσω (see Gr.
§ 107), (1) to place near or
by the side of, as food, Lu.
xi. 6; (2) to set or lay before,
as instruction, used of a parable, Mat. xiii. 24; mid., to
give in charge to, to entrust,
Lu. xii. 48 · to commend, to
recommend (acc. and dat., or
εἰς), Ac. xiv. 23.

παρα-τυγχάνω, to fall in with,
chance to meet, Ac. xvii.
17.*

παρ-αυτίκα, adv., for the moment, 2 Cor. iv. 17.*

παρα-φέρω (see Gr. § 103, 6,
Wi. § 52, 4, 11)), to remove
(acc. and ἀπό), Mar. xiv. 36;
Lu. xxii. 42; pass., to be led
aside, carried away, Heb.
xiii. 9 (W. H.); Ju. 12 (W.
H.).*

παρα-φρονέω, ῶ, to be beside
one's self, 2 Cor. xi. 23.*

παρα-φρονία, ας, ή, being besid-
one's self, madness, folly, 2
Pet. ii. 16. (N. T.)*

παρα-χειμάζω, άσω, to pass the
winter, Ac. xxvii. 12, xxviii
11; 1 Cor. xvi. 6; Tit. iii.
12.*

παρα-χειμασία, ας, ή, a passing
the winter, Ac. xxvii. 12.*

παρα-χρῆμα, adv., instantly, immediately, Lu. i. 64, iv. 39.

πάρδαλις, εως, ή, a leopard, a
panther, Rev. xiii. 2.*

παρ-εδρεύω, to wait upon, to attend to (dat.), 1 Cor. ix. 13
(W. H.).*

πάρ-ειμι (εἰμί), to be near, to be
present; part., παρών, present; τὸ παρὸν, the present
time; τὰ παρόντα, posses-
sions.

παρ-εισ-άγω, ξω, to bring in
secretly, 2 Pet. ii. 1.*

παρ-είσ-ακτος, ον, brought in
secretly, surreptitious, Gal. ii.
4.*

παρ-εισ-δύω, or -ύνω, ύσω, to
come in by stealth, to enter
secretly, Ju. 4.*

παρ-εισ-έρχομαι (see Gr. § 103,
2), (1) to enter secretly, Gal.

ii. 4; (2) to enter in addition,
Ro. v. 20.*

παρ-εισ-φέρω, to contribute besides, 2 Pet. i. 5.*

παρ-εκτός, adv., besides; τὰ
παρεκτός, the things that occur besides, 2 Cor. xi. 28 (see
R.V. mrg.); prep. with gen.,
except, Mat. v. 32; Ac. xxvi.
29; also Mat. xix. 9, W. H.
mrg.*

παρ-εμ-βάλλω, βαλῶ, to cast up
a bank about a city, Lu. xix.
43 (W. H.).*

παρ-εμ-βολή, ῆς, ή, (1) a camp,
Heb. xiii. 11, 13; (2) soldiers'
barracks, Ac. xxi. 34, 37;
(3) an army in battle array,
Heb. xi. 34.

παρ-εν-οχλέω, ῶ, to cause disturbance to, to disquiet (dat.),
Ac. xv. 19.*

παρ-επί-δημος, ον, residing in a
strange country; as subst.,
a stranger, foreigner, Heb.
xi. 13; 1 Pet. i. 1, ii. 11.*

παρ-έρχομαι, ελεύσομαι (see Gr.
§ 103, 2, Wi. § 52, 4, 11)),
(1) to pass by, with acc. of
person or place; (2) to pass,
elapse, as time; (3) to pass
away or perish; (4) to pass
from any one; (5) to pass
carelessly, i.e., to disregard,
neglect.

πάρ-εσις, εως, ή (ἵημι), passing
over, prætermission, Ro. iii.
25.* Syn.: see ἄφεσις.

παρ-έχω, έξω, 2d aor. παρέσχον
(dat. and acc.), (1) to offer, to
supply, Lu. vi. 29; Ac. xxii.
2; espec. the phrase παρέχω
κόπους, to cause trouble, Mat.
xxvi. 10; (2) in mid., to present, manifest, Tit. ii. 7; to
bestow, Col. iv. 1.

παρ-ηγορία, ας, ή, solace, Col.
iv. 11.*

παρθενία, ας, ή, virginity, Lu.
ii. 36.*

παρθένος, ου, ή, a virgin, a maid,
Mat. xxv. 1, 7, 11; hence
one who is chaste, Rev.
xiv. 4, applied to the male
sex.

Πάρθος, ου, ό, a Parthian, Ac.
ii. 9.*

παρ-ίημι, to pass by or over,
to relax; pass., perf. part.,
παρειμένος, weary, Heb. xii.
12.*

παρ-ίστημι, or παριστάνω (Ro.
vi. 13, 16; see Gr. § 107),

στήσω, (1) trans. in act.,
pres., imp., fut., and 1st aor.,
to place near or at hand, to
provide, Ac. xxiii. 24; to present, to offer, Ro. vi. 13, 16;
specially, to dedicate, to consecrate, Lu. ii. 22; to cause
to appear, to demonstrate, Ac.
xxiv. 13; (2) intrans., perf.,
plup., 2d aor., and mid., to
stand by, Mar. xiv. 47, 69,
70; Lu. xix. 24; to have
come, Mar. iv. 29; to stand
by, i.e., for aid or support,
Ro. xvi. 2; to stand in hostile
array, Ac. iv. 26.

Παρμενᾶς, acc. ᾶν, ό, Parmenas,
Ac. vi. 5.*

πάρ-οδος, ου, ή, a passing by or
through, 1 Cor. xvi. 7.*

παρ-οικέω, ῶ, to dwell in (ἐν
or εἰς, const. præg.) as a
stranger, Lu. xxiv. 18; Heb.
xi. 9.*

παρ-οικία, ας, ή, a sojourning,
a dwelling in a strange land,
Ac. xiii. 17; 1 Pet. i. 17.
(S.)*

πάρ-οικος, ον, generally as sub-
stantive, a stranger, a foreigner, Ac. vii. 6, 29; Ep. ii.
19; 1 Pet. ii. 11.*

παρ-οιμία, ας, ή (οἶμος, a way),
(1) a current or trite saying,
a proverb, 2 Pet. ii. 22; (2)
an obscure saying, a symbolic
saying, Jn. xvi. 25, 29; (3) a
comparative discourse, an al-
legory, Jn. x. 6.

πάρ-οινος, ον, given to wine,
drunken, 1 Tim. iii. 3; Tit.
i. 7.*

παρ-οίχομαι, to pass away, of
time, Ac. xiv. 16.*

παρ-ομοιάζω, to resemble, Mat.
xxiii. 27. (N. T.)*

παρ-όμοιος, ον, similar, Mar.
vii. 8 (W. H. omit), 13.*

παρ-οξύνω, to provoke, to irritate, in pass., Ac. xvii. 16; 1
Cor. xiii. 5.*

παρ-οξυσμός, οῦ, ό, (1) incite-
ment, Heb. x. 24; (2) contention, irritation, Ac. xv.
39.*

παρ-οργίζω, ιῶ, to provoke greatly, exasperate, Ro. x. 19; Ep.
vi. 4.*

παρ-οργισμός, οῦ, ό, exaspera-
tion, wrath, Ep. iv. 26. (S.)*
Syn.: see θυμός.

παρ-οτρύνω, to stir up, to incite,
Ac. xiii. 50.*

παρ-ουσία, ας, ἡ (εἰμί), (1) *presence*, 2 Cor. x. 10; Phil. ii. 20; (2) *a coming, an arrival, advent*, often of the second coming of Christ, 2 Cor. vii. 6, 7; 1 Th. iii. 13.

παρ-οψίς, ίδος, ἡ, *a dish for delicacies*, Mat. xxiii. 25, 26.*

παρρησία, ας, ἡ, *freedom, openness*, especially in speaking, *boldness, confidence*, Ac. iv. 13; Heb. x. 19; παρρησίᾳ, ἐν παρρησίᾳ, or μετὰ παρρησίας, *boldly, openly*.

παρρησιάζομαι, dep., mid., 1st aor. ἐπαρρησιασάμην, *to speak freely, boldly, to be confident*, Ac. xviii. 26, xxvi. 26.

πᾶς, πᾶσα, πᾶν (see Gr. § 37), *all, the whole, every kind of* (see Gr. § 224, Wi. § 18, 4, Bu. 119 sq., and for negative in phrases, Gr. § 328, iii., Wi. § 26, 1, Bu. 121 sq.); adverbial phrases are διαπαντός (which see), *always; ἐν παντί, ἐν πᾶσιν, in everything*; and πάντα (neut. plur. acc.), *altogether*.

πάσχα, τό (Aram.), *the paschal lamb*, Mar. xiv. 12; applied to Christ, 1 Cor. v. 7; *the paschal supper*, Mar. xiv. 16; *the passover feast*, Mat. xxvi. 2. (S.)

πάσχω (παθ-, see Gr. § 94, i. 7), *to be affected with* anything, good or bad; so, *to enjoy good*, Gal. iii. 4; more commonly, *to endure suffering*, Mat. xvii. 15; *to suffer* (acc. of that suffered, ἀπό or ὑπό, gen., of person inflicting).

Πάταρα, ἄρων, τά, *Patara*, Ac. xxi. 1.*

πατάσσω, ξω, *to smite, to strike, to smite to death, to afflict*, Mat. xxvi. 31; Ac. xii. 23.

πατέω, ῶ, ήσω, *to tread upon*, Lu. x. 19; *to press by treading*, as grapes, Rev. xiv. 20, xix. 15; fig., *to tread down, to trample upon*, Lu. xxi. 24; Rev. xi. 2.*

πατήρ, τρός, ὁ (see Gr. § 30, ii., Wi. §§ 19, 1 a, 30, 3, Bu. 94), *a father*; often of God as the father of men, Mat. v. 16, 45; as the father of the Lord Jesus Christ, Mat. vii. 21; as the first person in the Trinity, Mat. xxviii. 19; as the source of manifold bless-

ings, 2 Cor. i. 3. Secondary meanings are: (1) *a founder of a race, an ancestor;* (2) *a senior, a father in age*, 1 Jn. ii. 13, 14; (3) *the author*, or *cause*, or *source of anything*, Jn. viii. 44; Heb. xii. 9; (4) *a spiritual father*, or means of converting any one to Christ, 1 Cor. iv. 15; (5) *one to whom resemblance is borne*, Jn. viii. 38, 41, 44.

Πάτμος, ου, ἡ, *Patmos*, Rev. i. 9.*

πατρ-αλῴας (W. H. -ολῴας), ου, ὁ, *a parricide*, 1 Tim. i. 9.*

πατριά, ᾶς, ἡ, *a family* (in O. T. a division between the tribe and the household), Lu. ii. 4; Ac. iii. 25; Ep. iii. 15 (on which see Gr. § 224).*

πατρι-άρχης, ου, ὁ, *head* or *founder of a family, a patriarch*, Ac. ii. 29, vii. 8, 9; Heb. vii. 4. (S.)*

πατρικός, ή, όν, *paternal, ancestral*, Gal. i. 14.*

πατρίς, ίδος, ἡ, *one's native place, fatherland*, Heb. xi. 14; *one's native place, i.e., city*, Mat. xiii. 54, 57.

Πατρόβας, acc. αν, ὁ, *Patrobas*, Ro. xvi. 14.*

πατρο-παρά-δοτος, ον, *handed down from ancestors*, 1 Pet. i. 18.*

πατρῷος, α, ον, *received from the fathers, hereditary*, Ac. xxii. 3, xxiv. 14, xxviii. 17.*

Παῦλος, ου, ὁ, *Paul*, (1) Sergius Paulus, Ac. xiii. 7; (2) the apostle of the Gentiles, Ac. xxi. 40 (see Gr. § 159c, Wi. § 18, 6).

παύω, σω, *to cause to cease, to restrain*, 1 Pet. iii. 10; generally mid., *to cease, desist*, Lu. v. 4, viii. 24.

Πάφος, ου, ἡ, *Paphos*, Ac. xiii. 6, 13.*

παχύνω (παχύς), *to make fat, to fatten*; pass., fig., *to become stupid*, Mat. xiii. 15; Ac. xxviii. 27.*

πέδη, ης, ἡ, *a shackle, a fetter for the feet*, Mar. v. 4; Lu. viii. 29.*

πεδινός, ή, όν, *level*, Lu. vi. 17.*

πεζεύω (πεζός), *to travel on foot* or *by land*, Ac. xx. 13.*

πεζῇ, adv., *on foot*, or *by land*, Mat. xiv. 13; Mar. vi. 33.*

πειθ-αρχέω, ῶ, (1) *to obey a ruler* or *one in authority*, Ac. v. 29, 32; Tit. iii. 1; (2) *to obey*, or *conform to advice*, Ac. xxvii. 21.*

πειθός (W. H. πιθός), ή, όν, *persuasive*, 1 Cor. ii. 4. (N.T.)*

πείθω, πείσω, *to persuade*, Ac. xviii. 4; *to influence by persuasion*, Mat. xxvii. 20; *to seek to please, to conciliate*, Ac. xiv. 29; 2 Cor. v. 11; *to appease, to render tranquil*, 1 Jn. iii. 19; *to conciliate, to aspire to the favor of*, Gal. i. 10; pass., *to yield to persuasion, to assent, to listen to, to obey*, Ac. v. 36, 37; the 2d perf., πέποιθα, is intrans., *to trust, to rely on, to have confidence in*, Mat. xxvii. 43; Ro. ii. 19.

πεινάω, ῶ, inf. πεινᾶν, άσω, (1) *to be hungry*, Mat. iv. 2, xii. 1, 3; hence, (2) *to be needy*, Lu. i. 53; (3) *to desire earnestly, to long for*, acc., Mat. v. 6.

πεῖρα, ας, ἡ, *trial, experiment;* with λαμβάνω, *to make trial of, to experience*, Heb. xi. 29, 36.*

πειράζω, σω, (1) *to attempt* (inf.), Ac. xvi. 7; (2) *to make trial of, to test* (acc.), Jn. vi. 6; (3) *to tempt to sin*, Ja. i. 13, 14; ὁ πειράζων, *the tempter, i.e., the devil*, Mat. iv. 3. *Syn.*: see δοκιμάζω.

πειρασμός, οῦ, ὁ, *a trying, proving*, 1 Pet. iv. 12; Heb. iii. 8; *a tempting to sin*, Mat. vi. 13; *calamity, adversity*, as trying men, Ac. xx. 19. (S.)

πειράω, ῶ, only in mid., *to attempt*, Ac. ix. 26 (W. H. πειράζω), xxvi. 21.*

πεισμονή, ῆς, ἡ, *persuasion, conviction*, Gal. v. 8. (N.T.)*

πέλαγος, ους, τό, *the sea, the deep*, Mat. xviii. 6; Ac. xxvii. 5.*

πελεκίζω (πέλεκυς, *an axe*), *to behead*, Rev. xx. 4.*

πέμπτος, η, ον, ord. num., *the fifth*, Rev. vi. 9.

πέμπω, ψω, (1) *to send*, of persons, *to send forth*, spoken of teachers, as John Baptist, Jn. i. 33; of Jesus, Jn. iv. 34; of the Spirit, Jn. xiv. 26; of apostles, Jn. xiii. 20; (2) *to send*, of things, *to transmit*, Rev. xi. 10; *to send among* or *upon*, 2 Th. ii. 11; *to thrust in* the sickle, Rev. xiv. 15, 18.

πένης, ητος, ὁ, *poor*, 2 Cor. ix. 9.* *Syn.:* πτωχός implies utter destitution, usually beggary; πένης, simply poverty, scanty livelihood.

πενθερά, ᾶς, ἡ, *a mother-in-law*, a wife's mother, Mar. i. 30.

πενθερός, οῦ, ὁ, *a father-in-law*, a wife's father, Jn. xviii. 13.*

πενθέω, ῶ, ήσω, (1) *to mourn*, intrans., Ja. iv. 9; (2) *to mourn passionately for*, *to lament*, trans., 2 Cor. xii. 21.

πένθος, ους, τό, *mourning*, Ja. iv. 9; Rev. xviii. 7, 8, xxi. 4.*

πενιχρός, ά, όν, *poor, needy*, Lu. xxi. 2.*

πεντάκις, num. adv., *five times*, 2 Cor. xi. 24.*

πεντακισ-χίλιοι, αι, α, num., *five thousand*, Mat. xiv. 21.

πεντακόσιοι, αι, α, num., *five hundred*, Lu. vii. 41; 1 Cor. xv. 6.*

πέντε, οἱ, αἱ, τά, num. indecl., *five*, Mat. xiv. 17.

πεντε-και-δέκατος, η, ον, ord. num., *fifteenth*, Lu. iii. 1. (S.)*

πεντήκοντα, οἱ, αἱ, τά, num. indecl., *fifty*, Lu. vii. 41.

πεντηκοστή, ῆς, ἡ (lit. *fiftieth*), *Pentecost*, the feast beginning the fiftieth day after the second day of the Passover, *i.e.*, from the sixteenth day of the month Nisan, Ac. ii. 1, xx. 16; 1 Cor. xvi. 8.*

πέποιθα, see πείθω.

πεποίθησις, εως, ἡ, *trust, confidence*, with εἰς or ἐν, 2 Cor. viii. 22; Phil. iii. 4. (S.)

πέρ, an enclitic particle, cognate with περί, only found joined to pronouns or particles for intensity of meaning, as ἑάνπερ, εἴπερ, *if indeed*; ἐπείπερ, *since indeed*; καίπερ, *and really*; ὅσπερ, *the very one who*.

περαιτέρω (πέρα), adv., *further, besides*, Ac. xix. 39 (W. H.).*

πέραν, adv., *over, on the other side, beyond*, with article prefixed or genitive following, Mat. viii. 18, 28, xix. 1.

πέρας, ατος. τό, *a limit, the ex-*

tremity, in space, as Mat. xii. 42; or time, Heb. vi. 16.

Πέργαμος, ου, ἡ, *Pergamus* or *Pergamum*, Rev. i. 11, ii. 12.*

Πέργη, ης, ἡ, *Perga*, Ac. xiii. 13.

περί, a prep., governing the gen. and acc.; with gen., *about*, *i.e.*, concerning or respecting a thing; with acc., *about, around*, in reference to (see Gr. § 302, Wi. §§ 47 *e*, 49 *i*, Bu. 335). In composition, περί denotes *round about, on account of, above, beyond*.

περι-άγω, trans., *to lead* or *take about*, 1 Cor. ix. 5; intrans., *to go about* (acc. of place), Mat. iv. 23, ix. 35, xxiii. 15; Mar. vi. 6;⸰ Ac. xiii. 11.*

περι-αιρέω, ῶ (see Gr. § 103, 2, Wi. § 15, Bu. 53), *to take from around, take entirely away*, lit., Ac. xxvii. 40 (*to cast off* anchors, R. V.); fig., of the removal of sin, Heb. x. 11.

περι-άπτω, *to kindle*, Lu. xxii. 55 (W. H.).*

περι-αστράπτω, *to lighten around, to flash around* (acc., or περί, acc.), Ac. ix. 3, xxii. 6. (Ap.)*

περι-βάλλω, βαλῶ, βέβληκα, *to cast around* (acc. and dat.), Lu. xix. 43; *to clothe*, Mat. xxv. 36; for const., see Gr. § 284, Wi. § 53, 4, 12), Bu. 149; mid., *to clothe one's self, to be clothed*, Mat. vi. 29.

περι-βλέπω, N. T., in mid., *to look around*, abs., Mar. v. 32, ix. 8, x. 23; *to look round upon*, acc., Mar. iii. 5, 34, xi. 11; Lu. vi. 10.*

περι-βόλαιον, ου, τό, (1) *a mantle*, Heb. i. 12; (2) *a veil*, 1 Cor. xi. 15.*

περι-δέω, *to bind round about*, pass., plup., Jn. xi. 44.*

περι-δρέμω, see περιτρέχω.

περι-εργάζομαι, *to overdo, to be a busybody*, 2 Th. iii. 11.*

περί-εργος, ον, act., *overdoing, intermeddling*, 1 Tim. v. 13; pass., τὰ περίεργα, *superfluous arts, sorcery*, Ac. xix. 19.*

περι-έρχομαι (see Gr. § 103, 2, Wi. § 53, 4, 12)), *to go about*,

Ac. xix. 13; 1 Tim. v. 13; Heb. xi. 37; *to tack*, as a ship, Ac. xxviii. 13 (not W. H.).*

περι-έχω, *to encompass;* so, *to contain*, as a writing, Ac. xxiii. 25 (W. H. ἔχω); intrans., *to be contained*, 1 Pet. ii. 6; *to seize*, as astonishment, Lu. v. 9.*

περι-ζώννυμι, or -ζωννύω (see Gr. § 114, Wi. § 53, 4, 12), Bu. 191), *to gird one's self around*, mid. or pass., Ep. vi. 14; Lu. xii. 35, 37.

περί-θεσις, εως, ἡ, *a putting around*, as ornaments, 1 Pet. iii. 3. (N. T.)*

περι-ΐστημι (see Gr. § 107, Wi. § 14, 1), in intrans. tenses of act., *to stand around*, Jn. xi. 42; Ac. xxv. 7; mid., *to avoid, shun* (acc.), 2 Tim. ii. 16; Tit. iii. 9.*

περι-κάθαρμα, ατος, τό, *refuse, offscouring*, 1 Cor. iv. 13. (S.)*

περι-καλύπτω, *to cover round about, to cover up*, as the face, Mar. xiv. 65; Lu. xxii. 64; Heb. ix. 4.*

περί-κειμαι, *to lie about, surround*, dat., or περί, acc., Mar. ix. 42; Lu. xvii. 2; Heb. xii. 1; *to be encompassed* or *surrounded with*, acc., Ac. xxviii. 20; Heb. v. 2.*

περι-κεφαλαία, ας, ἡ, *a helmet*, Ep. vi. 17; 1 Th. v. 8.*

περι-κρατής, ές, *having full power over* (gen.), Ac. xxvii. 16. (Ap.)*

περι-κρύπτω, *to hide entirely*, Lu. i. 24. (N. T.)*

περι-κυκλόω, ῶ, ώσω, *to encircle, surround*, Lu. xix. 43.*

περι-λάμπω, *to shine around*, Lu. ii. 9; Ac. xxvi. 13.*

περι-λείπω, *to leave remaining;* pass., *to be left*, 1 Th. iv. 15, 17.*

περί-λυπος, ον, *very sorrowful*, Mat. xxvi. 38; Mar. vi. 26, xiv. 34; Lu. xviii. 23, 24 (W. H. omit).*

περι-μένω, *to wait for* (acc.), Ac. i. 4.*

πέριξ, adv., *round about*, Ac. v. 16.*

περι-οικέω, ῶ, *to dwell around, to be neighboring to* (acc.), Lu. i. 65.*

περί-οικος, ον, *dwelling around, a neighbor,* Lu. i. 58.*

περι-ούσιος, ον, *costly, treasured, select;* hence, *specially chosen,* Tit. ii. 14 (S.). (S.)*

περι-οχή, ῆς, ἡ (περιέχω), *a section* or *passage* of Scripture, Ac. viii. 32.*

περι-πατέω, ῶ, ἥσω, *to walk, to walk about;* fig., as Hebrew, *to pass one's life, to conduct one's self* (adv. or nom. pred.), *to live according to* (ἐν, dat.; κατά, acc.).

περι-πείρω, *to pierce through,* fig., 1 Tim. vi. 10.*

περι-πίπτω, *to fall into the midst of* (dat.), robbers, Lu. x. 30; temptations, Ja. i. 2; *to happen upon* a place, Ac. xxvii. 41.*

περι-ποιέω, ῶ, N. T. in mid., *to preserve for one's self,* Lu. xvii. 33 (W. H.); *to get for one's self, purchase,* Ac. xx. 28; 1 Tim. iii. 13.*

περι-ποίησις, εως, ἡ, (1) *a preserving,* Heb. x. 39; (2) *an obtaining, a possessing,* 1 Th. v. 9; 2 Th. ii. 14; (3) *a possession,* Ep. i. 14; 1 Pet. ii. 9.

περι-ρρήγνυμι, *to tear off,* as garments, Ac. xvi. 22.*

περι-σπάω, ῶ, *to drag around;* hence, fig., pass., *to be distracted in mind,* Lu. x. 40.*

περισσεία, ας, ἡ, *abundance, superfluity,* Ro. v. 17; 2 Cor. viii. 2; Ja. i. 21; εἰς περισσείαν, as adv., *abundantly,* 2 Cor. x. 15.*

περίσσευμα, ατος, τό, *abundance,* Mat. xii. 34; Lu. vi. 45; 2 Cor. viii. 14; pl. *a residue,* Mar. viii. 8.*

περισσεύω, εύσω, *to be more than enough, to remain over, to be in abundance,* Lu. xii. 15; Jn. vi. 12; τὸ περισσεῦον, *the residue,* Mat. xiv. 20; *to redound to,* εἰς, 2 Cor. viii. 2; *to make to abound,* Mat. xiii. 12; 2 Cor. iv. 15.

περισσός, ή, όν, *abundant, more than is necessary,* Mat. v. 37; Mar. vii. 36; *superior,* Mat. v. 47; τὸ περισσόν, *excellence, pre-eminence,* Ro. iii. 1.

περισσοτέρως, adv. (compar. of περισσῶς), *more abundantly, more earnestly,* 2 Cor. vii. 13, 15.

περισσῶς, adv., *greatly, exceedingly,* Mar. x. 26.

περιστερά, ᾶς, ἡ, *a dove,* Mat. iii. 16, x. 16.

περι-τέμνω, *to cut around, to circumcise,* Lu. i. 59; pass. and mid., *to undergo circumcision, to cause one's self to be circumcised,* 1 Cor. vii. 18.

περι-τίθημι, *to place,* or *put about* or *around* (dat. and acc.), Mat. xxi. 33; fig., *to bestow, to confer,* 1 Cor. xii. 23.

περι-τομή, ῆς, ἡ, *circumcision,* the act, the custom, or state, Jn. v. 22, 23; Gal. v. 6; with art., *the circumcision, i.e.,* the Jews, Ro. iii. 30, iv. 9, 12; fig., for *spiritual purity,* Ro. ii. 29; Col. ii. 11. (S.)

περι-τρέπω, *to turn about, to turn* into (εἰς) *madness,* Ac. xxvi. 24.*

περι-τρέχω, 2d aor. περιέδραμον, *to run around* (acc.), Mar. vi. 55.*

περι-φέρω, *to bear* or *carry around,* Mar. vi. 55; 2 Cor. iv. 10; pass., fig., *to be carried about, carried away* by false teaching, Ep. iv. 14; Heb. xiii. 9; Ju. 12 (W. H., in last two, παραφέρω).

περι-φρονέω, ῶ, *to look down upon, to despise,* Tit. ii. 15.*

περί-χωρος, ον, *lying round about:* only as subst., ἡ περίχωρος (sc. γῆ), *the region round about,* Lu. iii. 3, iv. 14; *the inhabitants of such a region,* Mat. iii. 5.

περί-ψημα, ατος, τό, *scrapings, offscourings,* 1 Cor. iv. 13.*

περπερεύομαι, dep., intrans., *to boast,* 1 Cor. xiii. 4.*

Περσίς, ίδος, ἡ, *Persis,* Ro. xvi. 12.*

πέρυσι, adv., *last year; ἀπὸ πέρυσι, a year ago,* 2 Cor. viii. 10, ix. 2.*

πετάομαι, ῶμαι, or πέτομαι (W. H.), *to fly,* as a bird, Rev.*

πετεινόν, οῦ, τό, *a bird;* only in plur., *birds,* Mat. vi. 26, xiii. 4.

πέτομαι, see πετάομαι.

πέτρα, ας, ἡ, *a rock, a ledge, cliff,* Mat. vii. 24, 25, xxvii. 51; with art. *the rock, i.e.,* the rocky substratum of the soil, Lu. viii. 6, 13; *a large* detached *rock,* fig., Ro. ix. 33; see also Mat. xvi. 18.

Πέτρος, ου, ὁ, *Peter* (prop., a rock = Κηφᾶς), Lu. iv. 38; Jn. i. 42.

πετρώδης, ες, *rocky, stony,* Mat. xiii. 5, 20; Mar. iv. 5, 16.*

πήγανον, ου, τό, *rue,* Lu. xi. 42.*

πηγή, ῆς, ἡ, *a fountain, spring,* Jn. iv. 14; Ja. iii. 11; fig., Rev. vii. 17; *a flow* of blood, Mar. v. 29.

πήγνυμι, πήξω, *to fasten, to pitch* a tent, Heb. viii. 2.*

πηδάλιον, ου, τό, *the rudder* of a ship, Ac. xxvii. 40; Ja. iii. 4.*

πηλίκος, η, ον, *how large,* Gal. vi. 11 (see γράμμα); *how distinguished,* Heb. vii. 4.*

πηλός, οῦ, ὁ, *clay, mud,* Jn. ix. 6–15; Ro. ix. 21.*

πήρα, ας, ἡ, *a sack, a wallet,* for carrying provisions, Mat. x. 10; Mar. vi. 8; Lu. ix. 3, x. 4, xxii. 35, 36.*

πῆχυς, εως, ὁ, *a cubit,* the length from the elbow to the tip of the middle finger, *about a foot and a half,* Mat. vi. 27; Lu. xii. 25; Jn. xxi. 8; Rev. xxi. 17.*

πιάζω, σω, *to lay hold of,* Ac. iii. 7; *to take,* as in fishing or in hunting, Jn. xxi. 3, 10; Rev. xix. 20; *to arrest,* Jn. vii. 30.

πιέζω, *to press together,* as in a measure, Lu. vi. 38.*

πιθανο-λογία, ας, ἡ, *persuasive* or *plausible speech,* Col. ii. 4.*

πικραίνω, ανῶ, *to render bitter,* lit., Rev. viii. 11, x. 9, 10; *to embitter,* fig., Col. iii. 19.*

πικρία, ας, ἡ, *bitterness,* fig., Ac. viii. 23; Ro. iii. 14; Ep. iv. 31; Heb. xii. 15.*

πικρός, ά, όν, *bitter, acrid, malignant,* Ja. iii. 11, 14.*

πικρῶς, adv., *bitterly,* of weeping, Mat. xxvi. 75; Lu. xxii. 12.*

Πιλᾶτος, or Πιλᾶτος (W. H. Πειλᾶτος), ου, ὁ (Lat. *pilatus,* "armed with a javelin"), *Pilate,* Mar. xv. 1, 2.

πίμπλημι, πλήσω, 1st aorist pass., ἐπλήσθην, (1) *to fill* with (gen.), Mat. xxvii. 48; fig., of emotions, Lu. iv. 28; or of the Holy Spirit, Ac. ii

4; (2) pass., *to be fulfilled* or *completed*, of time, Lu. i. 23, 57.

πίμπρημι (πρα-), and πιμπράω, pass., inf., πίμπρασθαι, *to be inflamed, to swell*, Ac. xxviii. 6.*

πινακίδιον, ου, τό (dim. of πίναξ), *a tablet for writing*, Lu. i. 63.*

πίναξ, ακος, ὁ, *a plate, platter*, Lu. xi. 39.

πίνω, fut. πίομαι, perf. πέπωκα, 2d aor. ἔπιον (inf. πεῖν, W. H.), *to drink*, abs., or with acc. of thing drunk (sometimes ἐκ or ἀπό), Lu. xii. 19, 29; *to imbibe*, as the earth imbibes rain, Heb. vi. 7; fig., *to receive into the soul, to partake of*, Jn. vii. 37.

πιότης, τητος, ἡ, *fatness*, as of the olive, Ro. xi. 17.*

πιπράσκω (πρα-), perf. πέπρακα, 1st aor. pass. ἐπράθην, perf. pass. πέπραμαι, *to sell*, Mat. xiii. 46; pass., with ὑπό, *to be sold under, to be a slave to*, Ro. vii. 14.

πίπτω (πετ-, see Gr. § 94, i. 8 d, Wi. § 13, 1 a, Bu. 167), πεσοῦμαι, (1) *to fall* (whence, by ἀπό or ἐκ; whither, by ἐπί or εἰς, acc.), Mat. xv. 27; Mar. iv. 5, 7, 8; hence, (2) *to fall prostrate*, as of persons, *to die, to perish*, Jn. xviii. 6; Rev. i. 17; of structures, *to fall in ruins*, Mat. vii. 25, 27; of institutions, *to fail*; (3) *to fall to*, as a lot, Ac. i. 26; (4) *to fall into* or *under*, as condemnation.

Πισιδία, ας, ἡ, *Pisidia*, Ac. xiv. 24, xiii. 14, where W. H. have adj. form.*

πιστεύω (see Gr. § 74, Wi. §§ 31, 5, 32, 5, 33 d, 39, 1 a, Bu. 173 sq., 337), εύσω, *to believe, be persuaded* of a thing (acc. or ὅτι); *to give credit to*, dat.; *to have confidence in, to trust, believe*, dat., εἰς, ἐν, ἐπί (dat.) or ἐπί (acc.), often of Christian faith, in God, in Christ; *to entrust* something (acc.) to any one (dat.); pass., *to be entrusted with* (acc.).

πιστικός, ή, όν, *genuine, pure*, of ointment, Mar. xiv. 3; Jn. xii. 3.*

πίστις, εως, ἡ, (1) *faith*, generally, as 2 Th. ii. 13; Heb. xi.

1; the object of the faith is expressed by obj. gen., or by εἰς, ἐν, πρός (acc.); (2) *fidelity, good faith*, Ro. iii. 3; 2 Tim. ii. 22; (3) *a pledge, a promise given*, 2 Tim. iv. 7; (4) met., for the whole of the *Christian character*, and (generally with art.) for the *Christian religion*.

πιστός, ή, όν, (1) *trustworthy, faithful*, in any relation or to any promise, of things or (generally) persons; (2) *believing*, abs., as οἱ πιστοί, the followers of Christ, or with dat.

πιστόω, ῶ, *to make faithful*; N. T., only in pass., *to be assured of*, 2 Tim. iii. 14.*

πλανάω, ῶ, ήσω, *to lead astray, to cause to wander*, Heb. xi. 38; fig., *to deceive*, Jn. vii. 12; pass., *to be misled, to err*, Mar. xii. 24, 27; Lu. xxi. 8.

πλάνη, ης, ἡ, *a wandering*; only fig., *deceit, delusion, error*, Mat. xxvii. 64; Ep. iv. 14.

πλανήτης, ου, ὁ, *a wanderer*; ἀστὴρ πλανήτης, *a wandering star*, Ju. 13.*

πλάνος, ον, *causing to wander, misleading*, 1 Tim. iv. 1; as subst., *a deceiver*, Mat. xxvii. 63; 2 Cor. vi. 8; 2 Jn. 7.*

πλάξ, ακός, ἡ, *a tablet* to write on, 2 Cor. iii. 3; Heb. ix. 4.*

πλάσμα, ατος, τό, *a thing formed* or *fashioned*, Ro. ix. 20.*

πλάσσω, άσω, *to form, mould*, as a potter his clay, Ro. ix. 20; 1 Tim. ii. 13.*

πλαστός, ή, όν, *formed, moulded*; fig., *feigned*, 2 Pet. ii. 3.*

πλατεῖα, ας, ἡ, (fem. of πλατύς, broad, sc. ὁδός), *a street*, Mat. vi. 5, xii. 19.

πλάτος, ους, τό, *breadth*, Ep. iii. 18; Rev. xx. 9, xxi. 16.*

πλατύνω, *to make broad, to enlarge*, Mat. xxiii. 5; pass., fig., *to be enlarged*, in mind or heart, 2 Cor. vi. 11, 13.*

πλατύς, εῖα, ύ, *broad*, Mat. vii. 13.*

πλέγμα, ατος, τό (πλέκω), *anything interwoven, braided hair*, 1 Tim. ii. 9.*

πλεῖστος, η, ον, superl. of πολύς,

the greatest, the most, very great; τὸ πλεῖστον, adv., mostly, at most, 1 Cor. xiv. 27.

πλείων, εῖον (for declension see Gr. § 44, Bu. 127), compar. of πολύς, *more, greater*, in number, magnitude, comparison; οἱ πλείονες, οἱ πλείους, *the more, the most, the many*, majority, 2 Cor. ii. 6; πλεῖον or πλέον, as adv., *more*, Jn. xxi. 15; ἐπὶ πλεῖον, *further, longer*, Ac. iv. 17.

πλέκω, ξω, *to weave together, to plait*, Mat. xxvii. 29; Mar. xv. 17; Jn. xix. 2.*

πλέον, see πλείων.

πλεονάζω, σω, intrans., *to have more than enough*, 2 Cor. viii. 15; *to abound, to increase*, Ro. v. 20; 2 Cor. iv. 15; trans., *to cause to increase*, 1 Th. iii. 12.

πλεονεκτέω, ῶ, *to have more than another*; hence, *to overreach, take advantage of* (R. V.), 2 Cor. vii. 2, xii. 17, 18; 1 Th. iv. 6; pass., 2 Cor. ii. 11.*

πλεον-έκτης, ου, ὁ, *a covetous* or *avaricious person*, 1 Cor. v. 10, 11, vi. 10; Ep. v. 5.*

πλεονεξία, ας, ἡ, *covetousness, avarice*, Lu. xii. 15; 2 Pet. ii. 3. *Syn.*: πλεονεξία is more active, seeking to grasp the things it has not; φιλαργυρία, more passive, seeking to retain and multiply what it has.

πλευρά, ᾶς, ἡ, *the side* of the body, Jn. xix. 34.

πλέω, see πίμπλημι.

πλέω, impf. ἔπλεον, *to sail*, Lu. viii. 23; Ac. xxi. 3, xxvii. 6, 24; Rev. xviii. 17 (W. H.); with acc. of direction, Ac. xxvii. 2 (but W. H. read εἰς).*

πληγή, ῆς, ἡ (πλήσσω), *a blow, a stripe, a wound*, Ac. xvi. 33; Rev. xiii. 14; *an affliction*, Rev. ix. 20.

πλῆθος, ους, τό, *a multitude, a great number*, Mar. iii. 7, 8; Heb. xi. 12; with art., *the multitude, the whole number, the assemblage*, Ac. xiv. 4; *a quantity*, Ac. xxviii. 3.

πληθύνω, νῶ, (1) intrans., *to increase*, Ac. vi. 1; (2) trans., *to multiply, augment*, 2 Cor.

ix. 10; pass., *to be increased*, Mat. xxiv. 12.

πλήθω, see πίμπλημι.

πλήκτης, ου, ὁ, *a striker, a contentious person,* 1 Tim. iii. 3; Tit. i. 7.*

πλημμύρα, as (W. H. ης), ἡ, *a flood*, Lu. vi. 48.*

πλήν, adv. (akin to πλέον, hence it *adds* a thought, generally adversative, sometimes partly confirmatory), *besides, but, nevertheless, of a truth,* Mat. xi. 22, xviii. 7, xxvi. 39, 64; πλὴν ὅτι, *except that,* Ac. xx. 23; as prep. with gen., *besides, excepting,* Mar. xii. 32; Ac. viii. 1.

πλήρης, ες, (1) *full,* abs., Mar. iv. 28; (2) *full of* (gen.), *abounding in,* Mar. viii. 19; Lu. iv. 1.

πληρο-φορέω, ῶ (φέρω), *to bring to the full, to fulfill,* 2 Tim. iv. 5, 17; pass., of things, *to be fully accomplished,* Lu. i. 1; of persons, *to be fully convinced,* Ro. iv. 21, xiv. 5; Col. iv. 12 (W. H.).*

πληρο-φορία, as, ἡ, *fullness, entire possession, full assurance,* Col. ii. 2; 1 Th. i. 5; Heb. vi. 11, x. 22. (N. T.)*

πληρόω, ῶ, ώσω, *to fill* with (gen.), *to fill up, to pervade, to complete,* either time or number; *to bestow abundantly, to furnish liberally,* Phil. iv. 18; Ep. iii. 19; *to accomplish, to perform fully,* as prophecies, etc.; pass., *to be full of,* 2 Cor. vii. 4; Ep. v. 18; *to be made full, complete,* or *perfect,* Jn. iii. 29; Col. iv. 12 (W. H. read πληροφορέω).

πλήρωμα, ατος, τό, *fullness, plenitude, i.e.,* that which fills, 1 Cor. x. 26, 28; so, *the full number,* Ro. xi. 25; *the completion, i.e.,* that which makes full, *the fulfillment,* Mat. ix. 16; Ro. xiii. 10; *the fullness of time,* Gal. iv. 4, is the completion of an era; *the fullness of Christ,* Ep. i. 23, that which is filled by Christ, *i.e.,* the Church; *the fullness of the Godhead,* Col. ii. 9, all divine attributes.

πλησίον, adv., *near, near by,* with gen., Jn. iv. 5; with the art., ὁ πλησίον, *a neighbor,* Ac. vii. 27.

πλησμονή, ῆς, ἡ, *full satisfying, indulgence,* Col. ii. 23.*

πλήσσω, 2d aor. pass. ἐπλήγην, *to smite,* Rev. viii. 12.*

πλοιάριον, ου, τό (dim. of πλοῖον), *a small vessel, a boat,* Mar. iii. 9; Jn. xxi. 8.

πλοῖον, ου, τό, *a ship, a vessel,* Mat. iv. 21, 22; Mar. i. 19.

πλόος, οῦς, gen. οῦ or οός, ὁ, *a voyage,* Ac. xxi. 7, xxvii. 9, 10.*

πλούσιος, a, ον, *rich, abounding in* (ἐν), Lu. xii. 16; Ep. ii. 4.

πλουσίως, adv., *richly, abundantly,* Col. iii. 16.

πλουτέω, ῶ, ήσω, *to become rich, to be rich, to abound in,* Lu. i. 53; Ro. x. 12; Rev. xviii. 15.

πλουτίζω, *to make rich, to cause to abound in,* 1 Cor. i. 5; 2 Cor. vi. 10, ix. 11.*

πλοῦτος, ου, ὁ (see Gr. § 32 a, Wi. § 9 e, note 2, Bu. 22), *riches, wealth, abundance,* Ja. v. 2; Col. i. 27; spiritually, *enrichment,* Ro. xi. 12.

πλύνω, νῶ, *to wash,* Lu. v. 2 (W. H.); Rev. vii. 14, xxii. 14 (W. H.). *Syn.:* see λούω.

πνεῦμα, ατος, τό, (1) properly, *the wind,* or *the air in motion,* Jn. iii. 8; hence, (2) *the human spirit,* dist. from σῶμα and ψυχή, 1 Th. v. 23; (3) *a temper* or *disposition* of the soul, Lu. ix. 55; Ro. viii. 15; (4) *any intelligent, incorporeal being,* as (a) *the human spirit,* separated from the body, *the undying soul;* (b) *angels,* good and bad; (c) *God,* Jn. iv. 24; (d) *the Holy Spirit,* the third person of the Trinity (see Gr. § 217 f, Wi. § 19, 1 a, Bu. 89), in relation to Jesus, Lu. iv. 1; Ac. x. 38; in relation to prophets and apostles, Ac. xxi. 11; Jn. xx. 22; and in relation to saints generally, Gal. iii. 2.

πνευματικός, ή, όν, *spiritual,* relating to the human spirit, or belonging to a spirit, or imparted by the divine Spirit, 1 Cor. ii. 13 (see Gr. § 316, Wi. § 64, 5), 15, xv. 44; τὰ πνευματικά, *spiritual things,* Ro. xv. 27; *spiritual gifts,* 1 Cor. xii. 1.

πνευματικῶς, adv., *spiritually, i.e.,* by the aid of the Holy Spirit, 1 Cor. ii. 14; in a mystical sense, Rev. xi. 8. (N. T.)*

πνέω, εύσω, *to blow,* as the wind, Mat. vii. 25, 27.

πνίγω, *to choke, to seize by the throat,* Mat. xviii. 28; Mar. v. 13.*

πνικτός, ή, όν, *strangled,* Ac. xv. 20, 29; xxi. 25.

πνοή, ῆς, ἡ, (1) *breath,* Ac. xvii. 25; (2) *wind,* Ac. ii. 2.*

ποδήρης, ες, *reaching to the feet;* as subst. (sc. χιτών or ἐσθής), *a long robe,* Rev. i. 13.* *Syn.:* see ἱμάτιον.

πόθεν, adv., interrog., *whence?* of place, Mat. xv. 33; *from what source?* Mat. xiii. 27; of cause, *how?* Lu. i. 43; Mar. xii. 37.

ποία, as, ἡ, *grass, herbage,* according to some, in Ja. iv. 14; but more probably the word here is the fem. of ποῖος, *of what sort?* *

ποιέω, ῶ, ήσω, (1) *to make, i.e., to form, to bring about, to cause;* spoken of religious festivals, etc., *to observe, to celebrate;* of trees and plants, *to germinate, to produce; to cause to be* or *to become,* Mat. xxi. 13; *to declare to be,* Jn. viii. 53; *to assume,* Mat. xii. 33; (2) *to do, generally; to do, i.e., habitually, to perform, to execute, to exercise, to practice, i.e., to pursue a course of action, to be active, to work, to spend, to pass, i.e.,* time or life, Ac. xv. 33. *Syn.:* see Trench, § xcvi.

ποίημα, ατος, τό, *a thing made, a work,* Ro. i. 20; Ep. ii. 10.*

ποίησις, εως, ἡ, *a doing,* Ja. i. 25.*

ποιητής, οῦ, ὁ, (1) *a doer, performer,* Ro. ii. 13; Ja. i. 22, 23, 25, iv. 11; (2) *a poet,* Ac. xvii. 28.*

ποικίλος, η, ον, *various, of different colors, diverse,* Lu. iv. 40.

ποιμαίνω, ανῶ, (1) *to feed a flock,* Lu. xvii. 7; 1 Cor. ix. 7; hence, fig., (2) *to be shepherd of, to tend, to cherish,* Mat. ii. 6; Jn. xxi. 16; Ac. xx. 28; 1 Pet. v. 2; Ju. 12;

Rev. vii. 17; (3) *to rule,
govern*, Rev. ii. 27, xii. 5,
xix. 15.* *Syn.:* see βόσκω.

ποιμήν, ένος, ὁ, (1) *a shepherd,*
Mat. ix. 36, xxv. 32; (2) fig.,
of Christ as the *Shepherd,*
Heb. xiii. 20; 1 Pet. ii. 25;
and of his ministers as *pastors,* Ep. iv. 11

ποίμνη, ης, ἡ, (1) *a flock* of
sheep or goats, Lu. ii. 8; 1
Cor. ix. 7; (2) fig., of Christ's
followers, Mat. xxvi. 31; Jn.
x. 16.*

ποίμνιον, ου, τό (= ποίμνη), *a
flock;* only fig., Lu. xii. 32;
Ac. xx. 28, 29; 1 Pet. v. 2,
3.*

ποῖος, ποία, ποῖον, an interrog.
pronoun corresponding to
οἶος and τοῖος, *of what kind,
sort, species? what? what
one?* In Lu. v. 19, sc. ὁδοῦ.

πολεμέω, ῶ, ήσω, *to make war,
to contend* with (μετά, gen.),
Rev. ii. 16, xiii. 4.

πόλεμος, ου, ὁ, (1) *war, a war,*
Lu. xiv. 31; (2) *a battle,* Rev.
ix. 7, 9; (3) *strife,* Ja. iv. 1.

πόλις, εως, ἡ, *a city,* Ac. v. 16;
met., *the inhabitants of a
city,* Mar. i. 33; with art., *the
city Jerusalem, the heavenly
city,* of which Jerusalem was
a symbol, Heb. xiii. 14; Rev.
iii. 12.

πολιτ-άρχης, ου, ὁ, *a ruler of a
city, a city magistrate,* Ac.
xvii. 6, 8.*

πολιτεία, ας, ἡ, (1) *citizenship,*
Ac. xxii. 28; (2) *a state, commonwealth,* Ep. ii. 12.*

πολίτευμα, ατος, τό, *a state,
a commonwealth,* Phil. iii.
20.*

πολιτεύω, in mid., *to behave as
a citizen;* hence, *to live, i.e.,
to order one's life,* Ac. xxiii.
1; Phil. i. 27.*

πολίτης, ου, ὁ, *a citizen,* Lu. xv.
15; Ac. xxi. 39; with gen.,
αὐτοῦ, *a fellow-citizen,* Lu.
xix. 14; Heb. viii. 11 (W.
H.).*

πολλάκις, adv., *many times,
often,* Mar. v. 4, ix. 22.

πολλα-πλασίων, ον, gen. ονος,
manifold, many times more,
Mat. xix. 29 (W. H.); Lu.
xviii. 30.*

πολυ-λογία, ας, ἡ, *much speaking,* Mat. vi. 7.*

πολυ-μερῶς, adv., *in many*

parts, by many portions,
Heb. i. 1.*

πολυ-ποίκιλος, ον, *much varied,
manifold,* Ep. iii. 10.*

πολύς, πολλή, πολύ (see Gr.
§ 39, 2), *many, numerous;*
πολύ, *much, greatly,* as adv.;
πολλοί, *many,* often with
partitive genitive, or ἐκ; οἱ
πολλοί, *the many* (see Gr.
§ 227, Wi. § 18, 3); πολλά,
in like manner, *much, very
much, often, many times;*
πολλῷ, *by much,* joined with
comparatives; ἐπὶ πολύ, *for
a great while,* Ac. xxviii. 6;
ἐν πολλῷ, *altogether,* Ac. xxvi.
29 (not W. H.).

πολύ-σπλαγχνος, ον, *very compassionate, of great mercy,*
Ja. v. 11. (N. T.)*

πολυ-τελής, ές, *very costly, very
precious,* Mar. xiv. 3; 1 Tim.
ii. 9; 1 Pet. iii. 4.*

πολύ-τιμος, ον, *of great value,
very costly,* Mat. xiii. 46; Jn.
xii. 3; compar., 1 Pet. i. 7
(W. H.).*

πολυ-τρόπως, adv., *in many
ways,* Heb. i. 1.*

πόμα, ατος, τό, *drink,* 1 Cor. x.
4; Heb. ix. 10.*

πονηρία, ας, ἡ, *evil disposition,
wickedness,* Mat. xxii. 18;
Lu. xi. 39; Ro. i. 29; 1 Cor.
v. 8; Ep. vi. 12; plur., *malignant passions, iniquities,*
Mar. vii. 22; Ac. iii. 26.*

πονηρός, ά, όν (πόνος), *evil, bad,*
actively, of things or persons; *wicked, depraved,* spec.
malignant, opp. to ἀγαθός;
ὁ πονηρός *the wicked one, i.e.,
Satan;* τὸ πονηρόν, *evil.*

πόνος, ου, ὁ, (1) *labor,* Col. iv.
13 (W. H.); (2) *pain, anguish,* Rev. xvi. 10, 11, xxi.
4.*

Ποντικός, ή, όν, *belonging to
Pontus,* Ac. xviii. 2.*

Πόντιος, ου, ὁ, *Pontius,* the
praenomen of Pilate, Lu.
iii. 1.

Πόντος, ου, ὁ, *Pontus,* Ac. ii.
9; 1 Pet. i. 1.*

Πόπλιος, ου, ὁ, *Publius,* Ac.
xxviii. 7, 8.*

πορεία, ας, ἡ, *a journey,* Lu.
xiii. 22; *a pursuit, undertaking,* Ja. i. 11.*

πορεύομαι, σομαι, dep., with
pass. aor., ἐπορεύθην, *to go, to
go away, to depart, to journey,*

to travel, often (as Hebrew)
to take a course in life.

πορθέω, ήσω, *to lay waste, to
destroy,* Ac. ix. 21; Gal. i.
13, 23.*

πορισμός, οῦ, ὁ, *a source of
gain,* 1 Tim. vi. 5, 6.*

Πόρκιος, ου, ὁ, *Porcius,* the
praenomen of *Festus,* Ac.
xxiv. 27.*

πορνεία, ας, ἡ, *fornication,* Ac.
xv. 20, 29; fig. in Rev., *idolatry,* xiv. 8, xvii. 2, 4.

πορνεύω, σω, *to commit fornication,* 1 Cor. vi. 18; fig. in
Rev., *to worship idols,* xviii.
3, 9.

πόρνη, ης, ἡ, *a harlot, a prostitute,* Mat. xxi. 31, 32; fig.
in Rev., *an idolatrous community,* xvii. 1, 5.

πόρνος, ου, ὁ, *a man who prostitutes himself; a fornicator,*
Ep. v. 5.

πόρρω, adv., *far, far off,* Mat.
xv. 8; Mar. vii. 6; Lu. xiv.
32; comp., πορρωτέρω (or
-τερον, W. H.), Lu. xxiv. 28.*

πόρρωθεν, adv., *from afar, far
off,* Lu. xvii. 12; Heb. xi.
13.*

πορφύρα, ας, ἡ, *a purple garment,* indicating wealth or
rank, Mar. xv. 17, 20; Lu.
xvi. 19; Rev. xvii. 4 (W. H.
read following), xviii. 12.*

πορφύρεος, οῦς, ᾶ, οῦν, *purple,*
Jn. xix. 2, 5; Rev. xvii. 4
(W. H.), xviii. 16.*

πορφυρό-πωλις, ιδος, ἡ, *a female
seller of purple cloth,* Ac.
xvi. 14. (N. T.)*

ποσάκις, interrog. adv., *how
often?* Mat. xviii. 21, xxiii.
37; Lu. xiii. 34.*

πόσις, εως, ἡ, *drink,* Jn. vi. 55;
Ro. xiv. 17; Col. ii. 16.*

πόσος, η, ον, *how much? how
great?* plur., *how many?*
πόσῳ, as adv. with comparatives, *by how much?*

ποταμός, οῦ, ὁ, *a river, a torrent,*
Mar. i. 5; Lu. vi. 48, 49.

ποταμο-φόρητος, ον, *carried
away by a stream,* Rev. xii.
15. (N. T.)*

ποταπός, ή, όν, interrog. adj.,
of what kind? of what manner? Lu. i. 29, vii. 39.

πότε, interrog. adv., *when? at
what time?* with ἕως, *how
long?*

ποτέ, enclitic particle, *at some*

time, at one time or other
(see Gr. § 129, Wi. § 57, 2).

πότερος, α, ον, which of two?
N. T. neut. as adv., whether,
correlating with ἤ, or, Jn. vii.
17.*

ποτήριον, ου, τό, a drinking-
cup, Mar. vii. 4, xiv. 23; the
contents of the cup, 1 Cor. xi.
25; fig., the portion which
God allots, whether of good
or ill, commonly of the latter, Mat. xx. 22, 23, xxvi. 39.

ποτίζω, σω, to cause to drink
(two accs.); to give drink to
(acc.); fig., 1 Cor. iii. 2; to
water or irrigate, as plants,
1 Cor. iii. 6–8.

Ποτίολοι, ων, οἱ, Puteoli, Ac.
xxviii. 13.*

πότος, ου, ὁ (πίνω), a drinking,
carousing, 1 Pet. iv. 3.*

ποῦ, interrog. adv., where?
whither? Mat. ii. 4; Jn. vii.
35.

πού, an enclitic particle of
place or degree, somewhere,
somewhere about, Heb. ii. 6,
16 (W. H., see δήπου), iv. 4;
Ro. iv. 19 (see Gr. § 129, Bu.
71).*

Πούδης, δεντος, ὁ, Pudens, 2
Tim. iv. 21.*

πούς, ποδός, ὁ, the foot, Lu. i.
79; ὑπὸ τοὺς πόδας, under
the feet, i.e., entirely subdued,
as Ro. xvi. 20.

πρᾶγμα, ατος, τό, a thing done,
a fact, a thing, a business, a
suit, as at law, Lu. i. 1; 1 Th.
iv. 6; Ro. xvi. 2; Heb. x. 1.

πραγματεία (W. H. -τία), ας, ἡ,
a business, occupation, 2 Tim.
ii. 4.*

πραγματεύομαι, σομαι, dep., to
transact business, to trade,
Lu. xix. 13.*

πραιτώριον, ου, τό (Lat. prætorium), the palace at Jerusalem occupied by the Ro-
man governor, Mat. xxvii.
27; Mar. xv. 16; Jn. xviii.
28, 33, xix. 9; so at Cæsarea,
Ac. xxiii. 35; the quarters of
the prætorian army in Rome,
Phil. i. 13.*

πράκτωρ, ορος, ὁ, an officer employed to execute judicial sen-
tences, Lu. xii. 58.*

πρᾶξις, εως, ἡ, (1) a doing,
action, mode of action, Mat.
xvi. 27; Lu. xxiii. 51; plur.,
deeds, acts, Ac. xix. 18; Ro.

viii. 13; Col. iii. 9; and in
inscription to the Acts of
the Apostles; (2) function,
business, Ro. xii. 4.*

πρᾷος, α, ον, Rec. in Mat. xi.
29 for πραΰς (W. H.).*

πρᾳότης, τητος, ἡ, Rec. for
πραΰτης (W. H.) in 1 Cor.
iv. 21; 2 Cor. x. 1; Gal. v.
23, vi. 1; Ep. iv. 2; Col. iii.
12; 1 Tim. vi. 11 (W. H.
πραϋπάθια); 2 Tim. ii. 25;
Tit. iii. 2.*

πρασιά, ᾶς, ἡ, a company
formed into divisions like
garden-beds, Mar. vi. 40.*
For constr., see Gr. § 242,
Wi. § 37, 3, Bu. 30, 139.

πράσσω, or πράττω, ξω, pf.
πέπραχα, πέπραγμαι, (1) to
do, perform, accomplish, with
acc., 1 Th. iv. 11; 2 Cor. v.
10; (2) with advs., to be in
any condition, i.e., to fare,
Ac. xv. 29; Ep. vi. 21; (3) to
exact, to require, Lu. iii. 13.
Syn.: see ποιέω.

πραϋ-πάθεια (or ία), ας, ἡ (W.
H.), mildness, 1 Tim. vi. 11.*

πραΰς, εῖα, ΰ, pl. εῖς, mild, gentle,
Mat. v. 5, xi. 29 (see πρᾷος),
xxi. 5; 1 Pet. iii. 4.*

πραΰτης, τητος, ἡ, mildness,
gentleness, Ja. i. 21, iii. 13;
1 Pet. iii. 15; and W. H.
(πραΰτης) in the passages
quoted under πρᾳότης.*

πρέπω, to become, be fitting to
(dat.), 1 Tim. ii. 10; Tit. ii.
1; Heb. vii. 26; impers. (see
Gr. § 101, Bu. 278), it becomes, it is fitting to, Mat. iii.
15; 1 Cor. xi. 13; Ep. v. 3;
Heb. ii. 10.*

πρεσβεία, ας, ἡ, an embassy,
ambassadors, Lu. xiv. 32,
xix. 14.*

πρεσβεύω, from πρέσβυς (lit.,
to be aged), old men being
usually chosen for the office), to act as ambassador,
2 Cor. v. 20; Ep. vi. 20.*

πρεσβυτέριον, ου, τό, an assembly of elders, the Sanhedrin,
Lu. xxii. 66; Ac. xxii. 5;
officers of the church assembled, presbytery, 1 Tim. iv.
14.*

πρεσβύτερος, τέρα, τερον (compar. of πρέσβυς, old), generally used as subst., elder,
(1) in age, Ac. ii. 17; 1 Tim.

v. 1; plur., often, ancestors,
as Heb. xi. 2; (2) as subst.,
an elder, in dignity and office, a member of the Jewish
Sanhedrin, Mat. xvi. 21; an
elder of a Christian church,
Ac. xx. 17, 28; in Rev., of
the twenty-four members of
the heavenly Sanhedrin, iv.
4, 10.

πρεσβύτης, ου, ὁ, an old man,
Lu. i. 18; Tit. ii. 2; Philem.
9.*

πρεσβῦτις, ιδος, ἡ, an old woman,
Tit. ii. 3.*

πρηνής, ές, falling headlong,
Ac i. 18.*

πρίζω, or πρίω, 1st aor. pass.
ἐπρίσθην, to saw, to saw
asunder, Heb. xi. 37.*

πρίν, adv., of time, formerly;
as conj. in N. T., with or
without ἤ, before that; generally with acc. and inf.,
Mat. xxvi. 34; but after a
negative we find πρὶν ἄν
with subj. where the principal verb is in a primary
tense, Lu. ii. 26; πρίν with
opt. where it is in a histor-
ical tense, Ac. xxv. 16.

Πρίσκα, ης, ἡ, and dim. Πρισ-
κίλλα, ης, ἡ, a proper name,
Prisca or Priscilla, Ro. xvi.
3; 2 Tim. iv. 19.

πρό, prep. with gen., before, i.e.,
of place, time, or superiority
(see Gr. § 294, Wi. § 47 d,
Bu. 153). In composition,
it retains the same mean-
ings.

προ-άγω, άξω, to bring out, Ac.
xvi. 30; gen. intrans., to go
before, to lead the way, to
precede, in place, Mat. ii. 9;
in time, Mar. vi. 45; part.
προάγων, preceding, previous,
1 Tim. i. 18; Heb. vii. 18.

προ-αιρέω, ῶ, N. T., in mid., to
propose to one's self, to purpose, 2 Cor. ix. 7.*

προ-αιτιάομαι, ῶμαι, to lay to
one's charge beforehand, Ro.
iii. 9. (N. T.)*

προ-ακούω, to hear before, Col.
i. 5.*

προ-αμαρτάνω, to sin before, 2
Cor xii. 21, xiii. 2. (N. T.)*

προ-αύλιον, ου, τό, a court before a building, a porch, Mar.
xiv. 68.*

προ-βαίνω, to go forward, Mat.
iv. 21; Mar. i. 19; pf. part

προβεβηκὼς ἐν ἡμέραις, advanced in age, Lu. i. 7, 18, ii. 36.*

προ-βάλλω, to put forth, as trees their leaves, Lu. xxi. 30; to thrust forward, Ac. xix. 33.*

προβατικός, ή, όν, pertaining to sheep, Jn. v. 2.*

προβάτιον, ου, τό, dim. of following, a little sheep, a lamb, Jn. xxi. 16, 17 (W. H.).*

πρόβατον, ου, τό (προβαίνω), a sheep, Mat. vii. 15; fig., a follower of Christ, Jn. x. 7, 8.

προ-βιβάζω, σω, to drag forward, to urge forward, Mat. xiv. 8; Ac. xix. 33 (not W. H.).*

προ-βλέπω, N. T., in mid., to foresee or provide, Heb. xi. 40. (S.)*

προ-γίνομαι, to happen before, Ro. iii. 25.*

προ-γινώσκω, to know beforehand, Ac. xxvi. 5; 2 Pet. iii. 17; of the divine foreknowledge, Ro. viii. 29, xi. 2; 1 Pet. i. 20.*

πρόγνωσις, εως, ή, foreknowledge, Ac. ii. 23; 1 Pet. i. 2.*

πρό-γονος, ου, ὁ, a progenitor, plur., ancestors, 1 Tim. v. 4; 2 Tim. i. 3.*

προ-γράφω, ψω, to write before, in time, Ro. xv. 4; Ep. iii. 3; to depict or portray openly, Gal. iii. 1; to designate beforehand, Ju. 4.*

πρό-δηλος, ον, manifest to all, evident, 1 Tim. v. 24, 25; Heb. vii. 14.*

προ-δίδωμι, (1) to give before, Ro. xi. 35; (2) to give forth, betray; see following word.*

προδότης, ου, ὁ, a betrayer, Lu. vi. 16; Ac. vii. 52; 2 Tim. - iii. 4.*

πρό-δρομος, ου, ὁ, ἡ (προτρέχω), a precursor, a forerunner, Heb. vi. 20.*

προ-εῖδον, 2d aor. of προοράω.

προ-εῖπον, 2d aor. of πρόφημι, perf. προείρηκα.

προ-ελπίζω, to hope before, Ep. i. 12.*

προ-εν-άρχομαι, to begin before, 2 Cor. viii. 6, 10. (N. T.)*

προ-επ-αγγέλλω, in mid., to promise before, Ro. i. 2; 2 Cor. ix. 5 (W. H.). (N. T.)*

προ-έρχομαι (see Gr. § 103, 2,

Bu. 144), (1) to go forward, advance, Ac. xii. 10; (2) to go before, precede, in time or place (gen. or acc.), Lu. xxii. 47; 2 Cor. ix. 5.

προ-ετοιμάζω, σω, to prepare beforehand, to predestine, Ro. ix. 23; Ep. ii. 10.*

προ-ευ-αγγελίζομαι, to foretell good tidings, preach the gospel beforehand, Gal. iii. 8.*

προ-έχω, in mid., to hold one's self before, to be superior, Ro. iii. 9 (see Gr. § 358, Wi. § 39, 3, note 3).*

προ-ηγέομαι, οῦμαι, to lead onward by example, Ro. xii. 10.*

πρόθεσις, εως, ἡ (προτίθημι), (1) a setting forth; οἱ ἄρτοι τῆς προθέσεως, the loaves of the presentation, or the showbread, Mat. xii. 4, compare Heb. ix. 2; (2) a predetermination, purpose, Ac. xi. 23.

προ-θέσμιος, α, ον, set beforehand, appointed before, Gal. iv. 2.*

προ-θυμία, ας, ἡ, inclination, readiness, Ac. xvii. 11; 2 Cor. viii. 11, 12, 19, ix. 2.*

πρό-θυμος, ον, eager, ready, willing, Mat. xxvi. 41; Mar. xiv. 38; τὸ πρόθυμον, readiness, Ro. i. 15.*

προθύμως, adv., readily, with alacrity, 1 Pet. v. 2.*

πρόϊμος, W. H., for πρώϊμος.

προ-ίστημι, N.T. only intrans., act., 2d aor. and perf., and mid., (1) to preside over, to rule, gen., Ro. xii. 8; 1 Th. v. 12; 1 Tim. iii. 4, 5, 12, v. 17; (2) to give attention to, gen., Tit. iii. 8.*

προ-καλέω, ῶ, in mid., to provoke, stimulate, Gal. v. 26.*

προ-κατ-αγγέλλω to announce beforehand, to promise, Ac. iii. 18, 24 (not W.H.), vii. 52; 2 Cor. ix. 5 (not W.H.).*

προ-κατ-αρτίζω, to prepare beforehand, 2 Cor. ix. 5.*

πρό-κειμαι, to lie or be placed before, to be appointed, as duty, example, reward, etc., Heb. vi. 18, xii. 1, 2; Ju. 7; to be at hand, to be present, 2 Cor. viii. 12.*

προ-κηρύσσω, ξω, to announce or preach beforehand, Ac. iii. 20 (not W. H.), xiii. 24.*

προ-κοπή, ῆς, ἡ, progress, advancement, Phil. i. 12, 25; 1 Tim. iv. 15.*

προ-κόπτω, to make progress in (dat. or ἐν), Lu. ii. 52; to advance to (ἐπί, acc.), 2 Tim. iii. 9; of time, to be advanced or far spent, Ro. xiii. 12.

πρό-κριμα, ατος, τό, a prejudgment, a prejudice, 1 Tim. v 21. (N. T.)*

προ-κυρόω, ῶ, to establish or ratify before, Gal. iii. 17. (N. T.)*

προ-λαμβάνω, to take before, anticipate, Mar. xiv. 8 ("she hath anticipated the anointing," i.e., hath anointed beforehand); 1 Cor. xi. 21; pass., to be overtaken or caught, Gal. vi. 1.*

προ-λέγω, to tell beforehand. forewarn, 2 Cor. xiii. 2; Gal. v. 21; 1 Th. iii. 4.*

προ-μαρτύρομαι, to testify beforehand, to predict, 1 Pet. i. 11. (N. T.)*

προ-μελετάω, ῶ, to meditate beforehand, Lu. xxi. 14.*

προ-μεριμνάω, ῶ, to be anxious beforehand, Mar. xiii. 11. (N. T.)*

προ-νοέω, ῶ, to perceive beforehand, to provide for, gen., 1 Tim. v. 8; in mid., to take thought for, acc., Ro. xii. 17; 2 Cor. viii. 21.*

πρό-νοια, ας, ἡ, forethought, Ac. xxiv. 3; provision for (gen.), Ro. xiii. 14.*

προ-οράω, ῶ, 2d aor. προεῖδον, to see beforehand, Ac. ii. 31, xxi. 29; Gal. iii. 8; mid., to have before one's eyes, Ac. ii. 25 (S.).*

προ-ορίζω, to predetermine, to foreordain, Ac. iv. 28; Ro. viii. 29, 30; 1 Cor. ii. 7; Ep. i. 5, 11. (N. T.)*

προ-πάσχω, to suffer beforehand, 1 Th. ii. 2.*

προ-πάτωρ, ορος, ὁ, a forefather, Ro. iv. 1 (W. H.).*

προ-πέμπω, to send forward, to accompany, Ro. xv. 24; to equip for a journey, Tit. iii. 13.

προ-πετής, ές (πίπτω), precipitate, rash, Ac. xix. 36; 2 Tim. iii. 4.*

προ-πορεύομαι, σομαι, in mid., to precede, to pass on before (gen.), Lu. i. 76; Ac. vii. 40.*

πρός (see Gr. § 307, Wi. §§ 47 f,

48 e, 49 h, Bu. 340), prep.,
gov. gen., dat., and accus.
cases, general signif., towards. In composition, it
denotes motion, direction,
reference, nearness, addition.

προ-σάββατον, ου, τό, the day
before the sabbath, Mar. xv.
42. (S.)*

προσ-αγορεύω, to address by
name, to designate, Heb. v.
10.*

προσ-άγω, (1) trans., to bring
to, to bring near, Mat. xviii.
24 (W. H.); Lu. ix. 41; Ac.
xii. 6 (W. H.), xvi. 20; 1 Pet.
iii. 18; (2) intrans., to come to
or towards, to approach, Ac.
xxvii. 27.*

προσ-αγωγή, ῆς, ἡ, approach,
access (εἰς, πρός, acc.), Ro. v.
2; Ep. ii. 18, iii. 12.*

προσ-αιτέω, ῶ, to beg, to ask
earnestly, Mar. x. 46 (not
W. H.); Lu. xviii. 35 (not
W. H.); Jn. ix. 8.*

προσαίτης, ου, ὁ, a beggar, Mar.
x. 46 (W. H.); Jn. ix. 8 (W.
H.).*

προσ-ανα-βαίνω, to go up far-
ther, Lu. xiv. 10.*

προσ-αναλίσκω, to spend in addition, Lu. viii. 43 (W. H.
omit).*

προσ-ανα-πληρόω, ῶ, to fill up
by adding to, to supply, 2 Cor.
ix. 12, xi. 9.*

προσ-ανα-τίθημι, to lay up in
addition; in mid., (1) to communicate or impart (acc.
and dat.), Gal. ii. 6; (2) to
consult with (dat.), Gal. i.
16.*

προσ-απειλέω, ῶ, to utter additional threats, Ac. iv. 21.*

προσ-δαπανάω, ῶ, ήσω, to spend
in addition, Lu. x. 35.*

προσ-δέομαι, to want more, to
need in addition (gen.), Ac.
xvii. 25.*

προσ-δέχομαι, dep. mid., (1) to
receive to companionship, Lu.
xv. 2; (2) to admit, accept,
Heb. xi. 35; (3) to await, to
expect (acc.), Mar. xv. 43.

προσ-δοκάω, ῶ, to look for, expect, anticipate, whether with
hope or fear, Lu. iii. 15, vii.
19, 20.

προσδοκία, ας, ἡ, a looking for,
expectation, Lu. xxi. 26; Ac.
xii. 11.*

προσ-εάω, ῶ, to permit one to
approach, Ac. xxvii. 7. (N.
T.)*

προσ-εγγίζω, to approach, to
come near to (dat.), Mar. ii.
4 (not W. H.).*

προσεδρεύω, to wait upon, to
minister to (dat.), 1 Cor. ix.
13 (W. H. παρεδρεύω).*

προσ-εργάζομαι, dep. mid., to
gain by labor in addition, Lu.
xix. 16.*

προσ-έρχομαι (see Gr. § 103,
2, Wi. § 52, 3, 4, 14)), (1)
generally, to come or to go to,
to approach, abs., or dat. of
place or person, Mat. iv. 11,
ix. 20, xxiv. 1; (2) specially,
to approach, to draw near to,
God or Christ, Heb. vii. 25;
(3) to assent to, concur in, 1
Tim. vi. 3.

προσ-ευχή, ῆς, ἡ, (1) prayer to
God, 1 Cor. vii. 5; Col. iv.
2; (2) a place where prayer
is offered, only Ac. xvi. 13,
16 (see Gr. § 268, note). Syn.:
see αἴτημα.

προσ-εύχομαι, dep. mid., to
pray to God (dat.), to offer
prayer, to pray for (acc. of
thing, ὑπέρ or περί, of person, ἵνα or ὅπως, of object,
occasionally inf.).

προσ-έχω, to apply, with νοῦν
expressed or understood, to
apply the mind, to attend to,
dat.; with ἀπό, to beware of;
also, to give heed to, inf. with
μή.

προσ-ηλόω, ῶ, to fasten with
nails, nail to, Col. ii. 14.*

προσ-ήλυτος, ου, ὁ (from προσ-
έρχομαι, orig. adj.), a new-
comer; a convert to Judaism,
a proselyte, Mat. xxiii. 15;
Ac. ii. 10, vi. 5, xiii. 43. (S.)*

πρόσ-καιρος, ον, for a season,
temporary, Mat. xiii. 21; Mar.
iv. 17; 2 Cor. iv. 18; Heb.
xi. 25.*

προσ-καλέω, ῶ, N. T., mid., to
call to one's self, to call for,
to summon, Mar. iii. 13, 23,
vi. 7; fig., to call to an office,
to call to the Christian faith,
Ac. ii. 39, xiii. 2.

προσ-καρτερέω, ῶ, ήσω, to persevere in, to continue steadfast
in (dat.), Ac. i. 14, ii. 42; to
wait upon (dat.), Mar. iii. 9;
Ac. x. 7.

προσ-καρτέρησις, εως, ἡ, per-

severance, Ep. vi. 18. (N.
T.)*

προσ-κεφάλαιον, ου, τό, a cush-
ion for the head, a pillow,
Mar. iv. 38.*

προσ-κληρόω, ῶ, to assign by
lot, to allot; pass. (dat.), Ac.
xvii. 4.*

προσ-κλίνω, to incline towards,
Ac. v. 36 (W. H.).*

πρόσκλισις, εως, ἡ, an inclination towards, partiality, 1
Tim. v. 21.*

προσ-κολλάω, ῶ, pass., to join
one's self to (dat.), as a companion, Ac. v. 36 (W. H.
προσκλίνω); to cleave to (πρός,
acc.), as husband to wife,
Mat. xix. 5 (W. H. κολλάω);
Mar. x. 7; Ep. v. 31.*

πρόσ-κομμα, ατος, τό, a stumbling-block, an occasion of
falling, Ro. xiv. 13, 20; 1
Cor. viii. 9; with λίθος, a
stone of stumbling (R. V.), 1
Pet. ii. 8; Ro. ix. 32, 33
(S.)*

προσ-κοπή, ῆς, ἡ, an occasion
of stumbling, 2 Cor. vi. 3.*

προσ-κόπτω, to strike the foot
against, Mat. iv. 6; so, to
stumble, 1 Pet. ii. 8.

προσ-κυλίω, to roll to (dat., or
ἐπί, acc.), Mat. xxvii. 60;
Mar. xv. 46.*

προσ-κυνέω, ῶ, to bow down, to
prostrate one's self to, to worship, God or inferior beings,
to adore (dat. or acc.).

προσ-κυνητής, οῦ, ὁ, a worshipper, Jn. iv. 23.*

προσ-λαλέω, ῶ, to speak to
(dat.), Ac. xiii. 43, xxviii.
20.*

προσ-λαμβάνω, N. T., mid., to
take to one's self, i.e., food,
companions, Ac. xxvii. 33,
xxviii. 2; to receive to fellowship, Ro. xiv. 1.

πρόσ-ληψις (W. H. -λημψις),
εως, ἡ, a taking to one's self,
a receiving, Ro. xi. 15.*

προσ-μένω, to continue with or
in, to adhere to (dat.), to stay
in (ἐν) a place, Mat. xv. 32;
1 Tim. i. 3, v. 5.

προσ-ορμίζω (ὅρμος), mid., to
come to anchor, Mar. vi.
53.*

προσ-οφείλω, to owe besides,
Philem. 19.*

προσ-οχθίζω (ὀχθέω or ὀχθίζω),
to be displeased or offended

with (dat.), Heb. iii. 10, 17 (S.).*

πρόσ-πεινος, ον (πεῖνα), very hungry, Ac. x. 10. (N. T.)*

προσ-πήγνυμι, to fasten to, applied to Christ's being fastened to the cross, Ac. ii. 23.*

προσ-πίπτω, (1) to fall down before (dat., or πρός, acc.), Mar. vii. 25; Lu. v. 8; (2) to beat against (dat.), Mat. vii. 25.

προσ-ποιέω, ῶ, in mid., to conform one's self to; hence, to pretend (inf.), Lu. xxiv. 28; in Jn. viii. 6, perhaps, to regard (W. H. omit).*

προσ-πορεύομαι, to come to, approach (dat.), Mar. x. 35.*

προσ-ρήγνυμι, to dash against, as waves, Lu. vi. 48, 49.*

προσ-τάσσω, ξω, abs., or acc. and inf., to enjoin (acc.) upon (dat.), Lu. v. 14; Ac. x. 33.

προ-στάτις, ιδος, ἡ, a female guardian, a protector, Ro. xvi. 2.*

προσ-τίθημι, to place near or by the side of, to add to (dat., or ἐπί, dat. or acc.), Lu. iii. 20; Ac. xi. 24; mid., with inf., to go on to do a thing, i.e., to do again, Ac. xii. 3; Lu. xx. 11, 12; so 1st aor. pass., part., Lu. xix. 11, προσθεὶς εἶπεν, he spoke again (see Gr. § 399 d, Wi. § 54, 5, Bu. 299 sq.).

προσ-τρέχω, 2d aor. προσέδραμον, to run to, Mar. ix. 15, x. 17; Ac. viii. 30.*

προσ-φάγιον, ου, τό, anything eaten with bread, as fish, meat, etc., Jn. xxi. 5.*

πρόσ-φατος, ον (from σφάζω, to slaughter, just slaughtered), recent, new, Heb. x. 20.*

προσφάτως, adv., recently, Ac. xviii. 2.*

προσ-φέρω, to bring to, dat., Mat. iv. 24, viii. 16; to offer, to present, as money, Ac. viii. 18; specially, to offer sacrifice, Ac. vii. 42; pass., to bear one's self towards, to deal with, Heb. xii. 7.

προσ-φιλής, ές, pleasing, acceptable, Phil. iv. 8.*

προσ-φορά, ᾶς, ἡ, an offering, a sacrifice, Ac. xxi. 26; Heb. x. 18.

προσ-φωνέω, ῶ, to call to (dat.),

Mat. xi. 16; to call to one's self (acc.), Lu. vi. 13.

πρόσ-χυσις, εως, ἡ (προσχέω), an affusion, a sprinkling, Heb. xi. 28. (N. T.)*

προσ-ψαύω, to touch lightly, Lu. xi. 46.*

προσωποληπτέω (W. H. προσωπολημπτέω), ῶ, to respect the person of any one, to show partiality, Ja. ii. 9. (N. T.)*

προσωπο-λήπτης (W. H. προσωπολήμπτης), ου, ὁ, a respecter of persons, a partial one, Ac. x. 34. (N. T.)*

προσωποληψία (W. H. -λημψ-), ας, ἡ, respect of persons, partiality, Ro. ii. 11; Ep. vi. 9; Col. iii. 25; Ja. ii. 1. (N. T.)*

πρόσωπον, ου, τό (ὤψ), (1) the face, the countenance, Ja. i. 23; in antithesis with καρδία, mere appearance, 2 Cor. v. 12; (2) the surface, as of the earth, Lu. xii. 35; of the heaven, Lu. xii. 56.

προ-τάσσω, to appoint before, Ac. xvii. 26 (W. H. προτάσσω).*

προ-τείνω, to stretch out, to tie up for scourging, Ac. xxii. 25.*

πρότερος, ερα, ερον (comparative of πρό), former, Ep. iv. 22; πρότερον or τὸ πρότερον, as adv., before, formerly, Heb. iv. 6.

προ-τίθημι, N. T. mid., to set forth, Ro. iii. 25; to purpose, to design beforehand, Ro. i. 13; Ep. i. 9.*

προ-τρέπω, in mid., to exhort, Ac. xviii. 27.*

προ-τρέχω, 2d aor. προέδραμον, to run before, to outrun, Lu. xix. 4; Jn. xx. 4.*

προ-ϋπ-άρχω, to be previously, with participle, Lu. xxiii. 12; Ac. viii. 9.*

πρό-φασις, εως, ἡ, a pretext, an excuse, 1 Th. ii. 5; dat. adverbially, in appearance, ostensibly, Mar. xii. 40.

προ-φέρω, to bring forth, Lu. vi. 45.*

πρό-φημι, fut. προερῶ, perf. προείρηκα, 2d aor. προεῖπον, to say before, i.e., at an earlier time, Gal. i. 9; in an earlier part of the discourse, 2 Cor. vii. 3; or prophetically, Mar. xiii. 23.

προ-φητεία, ας, ἡ, prophecy, as a gift, or in exercise, Ro. xii. 6; Rev. xix. 10; plur., prophecies, 1 Cor. xiii. 8.

προ-φητεύω, σω, to be a prophet, to prophesy, to forth-tell, or speak of divine things (the meaning foretell is secondary and incidental), Lu. i. 67; Ac. ii. 17, 18; of false prophets, Mat. vii. 22; to divine, used in mockery, Mat. xxvi. 68.

προ-φήτης, ου, ὁ, (1) a prophet, i.e., one who has insight into divine things and speaks them forth to others, Mat. v. 12, xxi. 46; plur., the prophetic books of the O. T., Lu. xxiv. 27, 44; (2) a poet, Tit. i. 12.

προ-φητικός, ή, όν, prophetic, uttered by a prophet, Ro. xvi. 26; 2 Pet. i. 19.*

προ-φῆτις, ιδος, ἡ, a prophetess, Lu. ii. 36; Rev. ii. 20.*

προ-φθάνω, to anticipate, to be beforehand, with participle, Mat. xvii. 25.*

προ-χειρίζομαι, to appoint, to choose, Ac. iii. 20 (W. H.), xxii. 14, xxvi. 16.*

προ-χειρο-τονέω, ῶ, to designate beforehand, Ac. x. 41.*

Πρόχορος, ου, ὁ, Prochorus, Ac. vi. 5.*

πρύμνα, ης, ἡ, the hindmost part of a ship, the stern, Mar. iv. 38; Ac. xxvii. 29, 41.*

πρωΐ, adv., early in the morning, at dawn, Mar. i. 35, xi. 20; with advs., ἅμα πρωΐ, λίαν πρωΐ, very early in the morning, Mat. xx. 1; Mar. xvi. 2.

πρώϊμος (W. H. πρό-), -η, ον, early, of the early rain, Ja. v. 7.*

πρωϊνός, ή, όν, belonging to the morning, of the morning star, Rev. ii. 28, xxii. 16. (S.)*

πρώϊος, α, ον, of the morning; fem. (sc. ὥρα), morning, Mat. xxi. 18 (W. H. πρωΐ), xxvii. 1; Jn. xviii. 28 (W. H. πρωΐ), xxi. 4.*

πρώρα, ας, ἡ, the forward part of a ship, the prow, Ac. xxvii. 30, 41.*

πρωτεύω, to have pre-eminence, to be chief, Col. i. 18.*

πρωτο-καθεδρία, ας, ἡ, a chief
seat, Lu. xi. 43. (N. T.)

πρωτο-κλισία, ας, ἡ, the chief
place at a banquet, Mar. xii.
39. (Ap.)

πρῶτος, η, ον (superlative of
πρό), first, in place, time, or
order; like πρότερος with
following gen., before, only
Jn. i. 15, 30; πρῶτον, as adverb, first, Mar. iv. 28; with
gen., before, Jn. xv. 18; τὸ
πρῶτον, at the first, Jn. x. 40.

πρωτο-στάτης, ου, ὁ, a leader,
a chief, Ac. xxiv. 5.*

πρωτοτόκια, ων, τά, the right of
the first-born, the birthright,
Heb. xii. 16. (S.)*

πρωτό-τοκος, ον, first-born; ὁ
πρωτότοκος, specially a title
of Christ, Lu. ii. 7; plur.,
the first-born, Heb. xii. 23, of
saints already dead.

πρώτως, adv., first, Ac. xi. 26
(W. H.).*

πταίω, σω, to stumble, to fall,
to sin, Ro. xi. 11; 2 Pet. i.
10; Ja. ii. 10, iii. 2.*

πτέρνα, ης, ἡ, the heel, Jn. xiii.
18.*

πτερύγιον, ου, τό (dim. of πτέρυξ), an extremity, as a battle-
ment or parapet, Mat. iv. 5;
Lu. iv. 9.*

πτέρυξ, υγος, ἡ, a wing, Rev.
iv. 8, xii. 14.

πτηνός, ή, όν (πέτομαι), winged,
τὰ πτηνά, birds, 1 Cor. xv.
39.*

πτοέω, ῶ, to terrify, Lu. xxi. 9,
xxiv. 37.*

πτόησις, εως, ἡ, terror, conster-
nation, 1 Pet. iii. 6.*

Πτολεμαΐς, ΐδος, ἡ, Ptolemais,
Ac. xxi. 7.*

πτύον, ου, τό, a winnowing-
shovel, Mat. iii. 12; Lu. iii.
17.*

πτύρω, to frighten, Phil. i. 28.*

πτύσμα, ατος, τό, spittle, Jn. ix.
6.*

πτύσσω, ξω, to fold, to roll up,
as a scroll, Lu. iv. 20.*

πτύω, σω, to spit, Mar. vii. 33,
viii. 23; Jn. ix. 6.*

πτῶμα, ατος, τό (πίπτω), a body
fallen in death, a carcase,
Mat. xxiv. 28.

πτῶσις, εως, ἡ, a falling, a fall,
lit. or fig., Mat. vii. 27; Lu.
ii. 34.*

πτωχεία, ας, ἡ, beggary, poverty,
2 Cor. viii. 2, 9; Rev. ii. 9.*

πτωχεύω, σω, to be in poverty,
2 Cor. viii. 9.*

πτωχός, ή, όν, reduced to beggary, poor, destitute, Lu. xiv.
13, 21, xviii. 22; Ja. ii. 5;
spiritually poor, in a good
sense, Mat. v. 3; in a bad
sense, Rev. iii. 17. Syn.: see
πένης.

πυγμή, ῆς, ἡ (πύξ), the fist, Mar.
vii. 3 (see R. V. and mrg.).*

Πύθων, ωνος, ὁ, Python; in N.T.
a divining spirit; called after
the Pythian serpent said to
have guarded the oracle at
Delphi and been slain by
Apollo, Ac. xvi. 16 (see R.
V.).*

πυκνός, ή, όν, frequent, 1 Tim.
v. 23; neut. plur. πυκνά, as
adverb, often, Lu. v. 33; so
πυκνότερον, more frequently,
Ac. xxiv. 26.*

πυκτεύω (πύκτης), to be a boxer,
to box, 1 Cor. ix. 26.*

πύλη, ης, ἡ, a door or gate;
πύλαι ᾅδου, the gates of
Hades, i.e., the powers of
the unseen world, Mat. xvi.
18.

πυλών, ῶνος, ὁ, a large gate, Ac.
x. 17; a gateway, porch, Mat.
xxvi. 71.

πυνθάνομαι, 2d aor. ἐπυθόμην,
(1) to ask, ask from (παρά,
gen.), to inquire, Mat. ii. 4;
Lu. xv. 26; (2) to ascertain
by inquiry, only Ac. xxiii.
34.

πῦρ, πυρός, τό, fire generally;
of the heat of the sun, Rev.
xvi. 8; of lightning, Lu. ix.
54; God is so called, Heb.
xii. 29; fig. for strife, Lu.
xii. 49; trials, 1 Cor. iii.
13; of the eternal fire, or
future punishment, Mat.
xviii. 8.

πυρά, ᾶς, ἡ, a fire, a pile of
burning fuel, Ac. xxviii. 2,
3.*

πύργος, ου, ὁ, a tower, fortified
structure, Lu. xiii. 4, xiv. 28.

πυρέσσω, to be sick with a fever,
Mat. viii. 14; Mar. i. 30.*

πυρετός, οῦ, ὁ, a fever, Lu. iv.
38, 39.

πύρινος, η, ον, fiery, glittering,
Rev. ix. 17.*

πυρόω, ῶ, N. T., pass., to be set
on fire, to burn, to be inflamed, 2 Pet. iii. 12; 1 Cor.
vii. 9; to glow with heat, as

metal in a furnace, to be
purified by fire, Rev. iii. 18.

πυρράζω, to be fire-colored, to be
red, Mat. xvi. 2, 3 (W. H.
omit both). (S. πυρρίζω.)*

πυρρός, ά, όν, fire-colored, red,
Rev. vi. 4, xii. 3.*

Πύρρος, ου, ὁ, Pyrrhus, Ac. xx.
4 (W. H.).*

πύρωσις, εως, ἡ, a burning, a
conflagration, Rev. xviii. 9,
18; severe trial, as by fire,
1 Pet. iv. 12.*

πώ, an enclitic particle, even,
yet, used only in composition;
see μήπω, μηδέπω, οὔπω, οὐ-
δέπω.

πωλέω, ῶ, ήσω, to sell, Mat. xxi.
12.

πῶλος, ου, ὁ, a colt, a young ass,
as Mat. xxi. 2.

πώ-ποτε, adv., at any time, used
only after a negative, not at
any time, never, Jn. i. 18, v.
37.

πωρόω, ῶ, to harden, to render
callous, fig., Jn. xii. 40; Ro.
xi. 7.

πώρωσις, εως, ἡ, hardness οἱ
heart, obtuseness, Mar. iii. 5;
Ro. xi. 25; Ep. iv. 18.*

πῶς, adv., interrog., how? in
what manner? by what
means? Also in exclama-
tions, as Lu. xii. 50; Jn. xi.
36; with subj. or opt. (ἄν),
implying a strong negative,
Mat. xxvi. 54; Ac. viii. 31;
often (N. T.) in indirect in-
terrogations (classical ὅπως),
Mat. vi. 28, etc.

πώς, an enclitic particle, in a
manner, by any means.

P

P, ρ, ῥῶ, rho, r, and as an
initial always ῥ, rh, the
seventeenth letter. As a numeral, ρ'=100; ‚ρ=100,000.

Ῥαάβ, or Ῥαχάβ, ἡ (Heb.),
Rahab, Heb. xi. 31.

ῥαββί (W. H. ῥαββεί), (Heb.),
Rabbi, my master, a title of
respect in Jewish schools of
learning, often applied to
Christ, Jn. iii. 26, iv. 31.
(N. T.)

ῥαββονί, or ῥαββουνί (W. H.
ῥαββουνεί), (Aram.), similar
to ῥαββί, my master, Mar.
x. 51; Jn. xx. 16. (N. T.)*

ῥαβδίζω, ίσω, to scourge, to beat

with rods, Ac. xvi. 22; 2 Cor. xi. 25.*

ῥάβδος, ου, ἡ, *a rod, staff,* Mat. x. 10; 1 Cor. iv. 21; Rev. xi. 1; *a rod of authority, a sceptre,* Heb. i. 8.

ῥαβδ-οῦχος, ου, ὁ (ἔχω), *a holder of the rods, a lictor,* a Roman officer, Ac. xvi. 35, 38.*

Ῥαγαύ, ὁ (Heb.), *Ragau,* Lu. iii. 35.*

ῥᾳδι-ούργημα, ατος, τό, *a careless action, an act of villainy,* Ac. xviii. 14.*

ῥᾳδι-ουργία, ας, ἡ, *craftiness, villainy,* Ac. xiii. 10.*

ῥακά (Aram.), *an empty, i.e., senseless man,* Mat. v. 22 (see Gr. § 153, ii.). (N. T.)*

ῥάκος, ους, τό (ῥήγνυμι), *a remnant torn off, a piece of cloth,* Mat. ix. 16; Mar. ii. 21.*

Ῥαμᾶ, ἡ (Heb.), *Ramah,* Mat. ii. 18.*

ῥαντίζω, ίσω, *to sprinkle, to cleanse ceremonially* (acc.) *by sprinkling, to purify from* (ἀπό), Mar. vii. 4 (W. H.); Heb. ix. 13, 19, 21, x. 22. (S.)*

ῥαντισμός, οῦ, ὁ, *sprinkling, purification,* Heb. xii. 24; 1 Pet. i. 2. (S.)*

ῥαπίζω, ίσω, *to smite with the hand,* Mat. v. 39, xxvi. 67.*

ῥάπισμα, ατος, τό, *a blow with the open hand,* Mar. xiv. 65; Jn. xviii. 22, xix. 3.*

ῥαφίς, ίδος, ἡ, *a needle,* Mat. xix. 24; Mar. x. 25; Lu. xviii. 25 (W. H. βελόνη).*

Ῥαχάβ, see Ῥαάβ.

Ῥαχήλ, ἡ (Heb.), *Rachel,* Mat. ii. 18.*

Ῥεβέκκα, ης, ἡ, *Rebecca,* Ro. ix. 10.*

ῥέδα, or ῥέδη, ης, ἡ (Gallic), *a chariot,* Rev. xviii. 13. (N. T.)*

Ῥεμφάν, or Ῥεφάν (W. H. Ῥομφά), ὁ (prob. Coptic), *Remphan,* the *Saturn* of later mythology, Ac. vii. 43 (Heb., *Chiun,* Amos v. 26).*

ῥέω, ῥεύσω, *to flow,* Jn. vii. 38.*

ῥέω (see φημί, εἶπον). From this obs. root, *to say,* are derived: act. perf., εἴρηκα; pass., εἴρημαι; 1st aor. pass., ἐρρέθην or ἐρρήθην; part., ῥηθείς: espec. the neut. τὸ ῥηθέν, *that which was spoken* by (ὑπό, gen.).

Ῥήγιον, ου, τό, *Rhegium,* now Reggio, Ac. xxviii. 13.*

ῥῆγμα, ατος, τό (ῥήγνυμι), *what is broken, a ruin,* Lu. vi. 49.*

ῥήγνυμι (or ῥήσσω, as Mar. ix. 18), ῥήξω, *to break, to rend, to burst, to dash down, to break forth,* as into praise, Mat. vii. 6, ix. 17; Mar. ii. 22, ix. 18; Lu. v. 37, ix. 42; Gal. iv. 27.*

ῥῆμα, ατος, τό, *a thing spoken;* (1) *a word* or *saying* of any kind, as *command, report, promise,* Lu. vii. 1, ix. 45; Ro. x. 8; (2) *a thing, a matter, a business,* Lu. ii. 15; 2 Cor. xiii. 1.

Ῥησά, ὁ (Heb.), *Rhesa,* Lu. iii. 27.*

ῥήσσω, see ῥήγνυμι.

ῥήτωρ, ορος, ὁ, *an orator,* Ac. xxiv. 1.*

ῥητῶς, adv., *expressly, in so many words,* 1 Tim. iv. 1.*

ῥίζα, ης, ἡ, (1) *a root of a tree* or *a plant,* Mar. xi. 20; met., *the origin* or *source of anything,* 1 Tim. vi. 10; fig., *constancy, perseverance,* Mat. xiii. 21; (2) *that which comes from the root, a descendant,* Ro. xv. 12; Rev. v. 5.

ῥιζόω, ῶ, *to root;* perf. pass., participle, ἐρριζωμένος, *firmly rooted,* fig., Ep. iii. 17; Col. ii. 7.*

ῥιπή, ῆς, ἡ (ῥίπτω), *a stroke, a twinkle,* as of the eye, 1 Cor. xv. 52.*

ῥιπίζω, *to toss to and fro,* as waves by the wind, Ja. i. 6.*

ῥιπτέω, ῶ, *to throw off* or *away,* Ac. xxii. 23.*

ῥίπτω, ψω, 1st aor. ἔρριψα; part. ῥίψας; *to throw, throw down, throw out, prostrate,* Mat. ix. 36, xv. 30, xxvii. 5; Lu. iv. 35, xvii. 2; Ac. xxvii. 19, 29.*

Ῥοβοάμ, ὁ (Heb.), *Rehoboam,* Mat. i. 7.*

Ῥόδη, ης, ἡ (*rose*), *Rhoda,* Ac. xii. 13.*

Ῥόδος, ου, ἡ, *Rhodes,* Ac. xxi. 1.*

ῥοιζηδόν, adv. (ῥοιζέω), *with a great noise,* 2 Pet. iii. 10.*

ῥομφαία, ας, ἡ, *a large sword,* as Rev. i. 16; fig., *piercing grief,* Lu. ii. 35.

Ῥουβήν, ὁ (Heb.), *Reuben,* Rev. vii. 5.*

Ῥούθ, ἡ (Heb.), *Ruth,* Mat. i. 5.*

Ῥοῦφος, ου, ὁ (Lat.), *Rufus,* Mar. xv. 21; Ro. xvi. 13.*

ῥύμη, ης, ἡ, *a street, a lane,* Mat. vi. 2; Lu. xiv. 21; Ac. ix. 11, xii. 10.*

ῥύομαι, σομαι, dep. mid., 1st aor., pass., ἐρρύσθην, *to draw* or *snatch from danger, to deliver,* 2 Pet. ii. 7; ὁ ῥυόμενος, *the deliverer,* Ro. xi. 26.

ῥυπαίνω, *to defile,* Rev. xxii. 11 (W. H.).*

ῥυπαρεύομαι, *to be filthy,* Rev. xxii. 11 (W. H. mrg.). (N. T.)*

ῥυπαρία, ας, ἡ, *filth, pollution,* Ja. i. 21.*

ῥυπαρός, ά, όν, *filthy, defiled,* Ja. ii. 2; Rev. xxii. 11 (W. H.).*

ῥύπος, ου, ὁ, *filth, filthiness,* 1 Pet. iii. 21.*

ῥυπόω, ῶ, *to be filthy,* Rev. xxii. 11 (not W. H.).*

ῥύσις, εως, ἡ (ῥέω), *a flowing, an issue,* Mar. v. 25; Lu. viii. 43, 44.*

ῥυτίς, ίδος, ἡ, *a wrinkle;* fig., *a spiritual defect,* Ep. v. 27.*

Ῥωμαϊκός, ή, όν, *Roman,* Lu. xxiii. 38 (W. H. omit).*

Ῥωμαῖος, ου, ὁ, *a Roman,* Jn. xi. 48.

Ῥωμαϊστί, adv., *in the Latin language,* Jn. xix. 10.*

Ῥώμη, ης, ἡ, *Rome,* Ac. xviii. 2; 2 Tim. i. 17.

ῥώννυμι, *to strengthen;* only perf., pass., impv. ἔρρωσο, ἔρρωσθε, *farewell,* Ac. xv. 29, xxiii. 30 (W. H. omit).*

Σ

Σ, σ, final ς, *sigma, s,* the eighteenth letter. As a numeral, σ′ = 200; ‚σ = 200,000.

σαβαχθανί (W. H. -εί), (Aram.), *sabachthani, thou hast forsaken me,* Mat. xxvii. 46; Mar. xv. 34; from the Aramaic rendering of Ps. xxii. 1. (N. T.)*

σαβαώθ (Heb.), *sabaoth, hosts, armies,* Ro. ix. 29; Ja. v. 4. (S.)*

σαββατισμός, οῦ, ὁ, *a keeping of sabbath, a sabbath rest* (R. V.), Heb. iv. 9.*

σάββατον, ου, τό (from Heb.),

dat. plur. σάββασι(ν), (1) the sabbath, Mat. xii. 8, xxviii. 1; (2) a period of seven days, a week, Mar. xvi. 2, 9; in both senses the plural is also used. (S.)

σαγήνη, ης, ἡ, a drag-net, Mat. xiii. 47. (S.)* Syn.: see ἀμφίβληστρον.

Σαδδουκαῖος, ου, ὁ, a Sadducee; plur., of the sect in general; prob. derived from the Heb. name Zadok.

Σαδώκ, ὁ (Heb.), Sadok, Mat. i. 13.*

σαίνω, to move, disturb, pass., 1 Th. iii. 3.*

σάκκος, ου, ὁ, hair-cloth, sack-cloth, a sign of mourning, Mat. xi. 21; Lu. x. 13; Rev. vi. 12, xi. 3.*

Σαλά, ὁ (Heb.), Sala, Lu. iii. 35.*

Σαλαθιήλ, ὁ (Heb.), Salathiel, Mat. i. 12; Lu. iii. 27.*

Σαλαμίς, ῖνος, ἡ, Salamis, Ac. xiii. 5.*

Σαλείμ, τό, Salim, Jn. iii. 23.*

σαλεύω, σω, to shake, to cause to shake, as Mat. xi. 7; Heb. xii. 27; so, to excite, as the populace, Ac. xvii. 13; to disturb in mind, 2 Th. ii. 2.

Σαλήμ, ἡ (Heb.), Salem, Heb. vii. 1.*

Σαλμών, ὁ (Heb.), Salmon, Mat. i. 4, 5, Lu. iii. 32 (W. H. Σαλά).*

Σαλμώνη, ης, ἡ, Salmone, Ac. xxvii. 7.*

σάλος, ου, ὁ, the tossing of the sea in a tempest, Lu. xxi. 25.*

σάλπιγξ, ιγγος, ἡ, a trumpet, 1 Cor. xiv. 8; 1 Th. iv. 16.

σαλπίζω, ίσω (class. ίγξω), to sound a trumpet, Rev. ix. 1, 13; for impers. use, 1 Cor. xv. 52 (see Gr. § 171, Wi. § 58, 9b, β), Bu. 134).

σαλπιστής, οῦ, ὁ (class. -ιγκτής), a trumpeter, Rev. xviii. 22.*

Σαλώμη, ης, ἡ, Salome, wife of Zebedee, Mar. xv. 40, xvi. 1.*

Σαμάρεια, as, ἡ, Samaria, either (1) the district, Lu. xvii. 11; Jn. iv. 4; or (2) the city, afterwards called Sebaste, only Ac. viii. 5 (W. H.).

Σαμαρείτης, ου, ὁ, a Samaritan, Mat. x. 5; Lu. ix. 52.

Σαμαρεῖτις, ιδος, ἡ, a Samaritan woman, Jn. iv. 9.*

Σαμο-θρᾴκη, ης, ἡ, Samothrace, Ac. xvi. 11.*

Σάμος, ου, ἡ, Samos, Ac. xx. 15.*

Σαμουήλ, ὁ (Heb.), Samuel, Ac. iii. 24.

Σαμψών, ὁ (Heb.), Samson, Heb. xi. 32.*

σανδάλιον, ου, τό, a sandal, Mar. vi. 9; Ac. xii. 8.*

σανίς, ίδος, ἡ, a plank, a board, Ac. xxvii. 44.*

Σαούλ, ὁ (Heb.), Saul, (1) the king of Israel, Ac. xiii. 21; (2) the apostle, only in direct address (elsewhere Σαῦλος), Ac. ix. 4, 17.

σαπρός, ά, όν, rotten, hence, useless, Mat. vii. 17, 18; fig., corrupt, Ep. iv. 29.

Σαπφείρη, ης, ἡ, Sapphira, Ac. v. 1.*

σάπφειρος, ου, ἡ, a sapphire, Rev. xxi. 19.*

σαργάνη, ης, ἡ, a basket, generally of twisted cords, 2 Cor. xi. 33.*

Σάρδεις, ων, dat. εσι(ν), αἱ, Sardis, Rev. i. 11, iii. 1, 4.*

σάρδινος, ου, ὁ (Rec. in Rev. iv. 3 for following). (N. T.)*

σάρδιον, ου, τό, a precious stone, sardius or carnelian, Rev. iv. 3 (W. H.), xxi. 20.*

σαρδ-όνυξ, υχος, ὁ, a sardonyx, a precious stone, white streaked with red, Rev. xxi. 20.*

Σάρεπτα, ων, τά, Sarepta, Lu. iv. 26.*

σαρκικός, ή, όν, fleshly, carnal, whether (1) belonging to human nature in its bodily manifestation, or (2) belonging to human nature as sinful, Ro. xv. 27; 1 Cor. iii. 3, ix. 11; 2 Cor. i. 12, x. 4; 1 Pet. ii. 11; for Rec. σαρκικός, W. H. substitute σάρκινος, in. Ro. vii. 14; 1 Cor. iii. 1; Heb. vii. 16; and ἄνθρωπος in 1 Cor. iii. 4.*

σάρκινος, η, ον, (1) fleshy, consisting of flesh, opp. to λίθινος, 2 Cor. iii. 3; (2) fleshy, carnal (W.H. in the passages quoted under σαρκικός).*

σάρξ, σαρκός, ἡ, flesh, sing., Lu. xxiv. 39; plur., Ja. v. 3; the human body, man; the human nature of man as distinguished from his divine nature (πνεῦμα); human nature, as sinful; πᾶσα σάρξ, every man. all men; κατὰ σάρκα, as a man; σὰρξ καὶ αἷμα, flesh and blood, i.e, man as frail and fallible; ζῆν, περιπατεῖν κατὰ σάρκα, to live, to walk after flesh, cf a carnal, unspiritual life. The word also denotes kinship, Ro. xi. 14.

Σαρούχ, ὁ (Heb.), (W. H. Σε ρούχ), Saruch or Serug, Lu iii. 35.*

σαρόω, ῶ, to sweep, to cleans. by sweeping, Mat. xii. 44; Lu. xi. 25, xv. 8.*

Σάρρα, as, ἡ, Sarah, Ro. iv. 19, ix. 9.

Σάρων, ωνος, ὁ, Sharon, Ac. ix. 35.*

σατᾶν, ὁ (Heb.), and σατανᾶς, ᾶ, ὁ, an adversary, i.e., Satan, the Heb. proper name for the devil, διάβολος, Mat. iv 10, 15; Ac. xxvi. 18; met., for one who does the work of Satan, Mat. xvi. 23; Mar. viii. 33. (S.)

σάτον, ου, τό (Aram.), a seah, a measure equal to about a peck and a half, Mat. xiii. 33; Lu. xiii. 21. (S.)*

Σαῦλος, ου, ὁ, Saul, the apostle. generally in this form (see Σαούλ), Ac. vii. 58, viii. 1, 3.

σβέννυμι, σβέσω, (1) to extinguish, to quench, Ep. vi. 16; (2) fig., to suppress, 1 Th. v. 19.

σεατοῦ, ῆς, οῦ (only masc. in N. T.), a reflex. pron., of thyself; dat., σεαυτῷ, to thyself; acc., σεαυτόν, thyself.

σεβάζομαι, dep., pass., to stand in awe of, to worship, Ro. i. 25.*

σέβασμα, ατος, τό, an object of religious worship, Ac. xvii. 23; 2 Th. ii. 4.*

σεβαστός, ή, όν, venerated, august, a title of the Roman emperors (= Lat. augustus), Ac. xxv. 21, 25. Hence, secondarily, Augustan, imperial, Ac. xxvii. 1.*

σέβομαι, dep., to reverence, to worship God, Mar. vii. 7· οἱ σεβόμενοι, the devout, i.e, proselytes of the gate, Ac xvii. 17.

σειρά, ᾶς, ἡ, a chain, 2 Pet. ii. 4 (W. H. read following).*

σειρός, οῦ, ὁ, a pit, 2 Pet. ii. 4 (W. H.).*

σεισμός, οῦ, ὁ, a shaking, as an earthquake, Mat. xxiv. 7; a storm at sea, Mat. viii. 24.

σείω, σω, to shake, Heb. xii. 26; fig., to agitate, Mat. xxi. 10.

Σεκοῦνδος, ου, ὁ (Lat.), Secundus, Ac. xx. 4.*

Σελεύκεια, ας, ἡ, Seleucia, Ac. xiii. 4.*

σελήνη, ης, ἡ, the moon, Mar. xiii. 24.

σεληνιάζομαι, io be epileptic, Mat. iv. 24, xvii. 15. (N.T.)*

Σεμεΐ, ὁ (Heb.), (W. H. Σεμεεῒν), Semei or Semein, Lu. iii. 26.*

σεμίδαλις, acc. ιν, ἡ, the finest wheaten flour, Rev. xviii. 13.*

σεμνός, ἡ, όν, venerable, honorable, of men, 1 Tim. iii. 8, 11; Tit. ii. 2; of acts, Phil. iv. 8.*

σεμνότης, τητος, ἡ, dignity, honor, 1 Tim. ii. 2, iii. 4; Tit. ii. 7.*

Σέργιος, ου, ὁ, Sergius, Ac. xiii. 7.*

Σήθ, ὁ (Heb.), Seth, Lu. iii. 38.*

Σήμ, ὁ (Heb.), Shem, Lu. iii. 36.*

σημαίνω, 1st aor. ἐσήμανα, to signify, indicate, Jn. xii. 33; Ac. xxv. 27.

σημεῖον, ου, τό, a sign, that by which a thing is known, a token, an indication, of divine presence and power, 1 Cor. xiv. 22; Lu. xxi. 7, 11; hence, especially, a miracle, whether real or unreal, Lu. xi. 16, 29; 2 Th. ii. 9. Syn.: see δύναμις.

σημειόω, ῶ, in mid., to mark for one's self, to note, 2 Th. iii. 14.*

σήμερον, adv., to-day, at this time, now, Mat. vi. 11; Lu. ii. 11; ἡ σήμερον (ἡμέρα), this very day, Ac. xix. 40.

σήπω, to make rotten; 2d perf. σέσηπα, to become rotten, perish, Ja. v. 2.*

σηρικός, ἡ, όν (W. H. σιρικός), silken; neut. as subst., sil., Rev. xviii. 12.*

σής, σητός, ὁ, a moth, Mat. vi. 19, 20; Lu. xii. 33.*

σητό-βρωτος, ον, moth-eaten, Ja. v. 2.*

σθενόω, ῶ, to strengthen, 1 Pet. v. 10. (N.T.)*

σιαγών, όνος, ἡ, the jawbone, Mat. v. 39; Lu. vi. 29.*

σιγάω, ῶ, to keep silence, Lu. ix. 36; pass., to be concealed, Ro. xvi. 25.

σιγή, ῆς, ἡ, silence, Ac. xxi. 40; Rev. viii. 1.*

σιδήρεος, έα, εον, contr., οὖς, ᾶ, οῦν, made of iron, Ac. xii. 10; Rev. ii. 27.

σίδηρος, ου, ὁ, iron, Rev. xviii. 12.*

Σιδών, ῶνος, ἡ, Sidon, Mat. xi. 21, 22.

Σιδώνιος, α, ον, Sidonian, inhabitant of Sidon, Lu. iv. 26 (W. H.); Ac. xii. 20.

σικάριος, ου, ὁ (Lat.), an assassin, Ac. xxi. 38.*

σίκερα, τό (Aram.), intoxicating drink, Lu. i. 15. (S.)*

Σίλας, dat. ᾳ, acc. αν, ὁ, Silas, contr. from Σιλουανός, Ac. xv. 22, 27.

Σιλουανός, οῦ, ὁ, Silvanus, 2 Cor. i. 9.

Σιλωάμ, ὁ, Siloam, Lu. xiii. 4; Jn. ix. 7, 11.*

σιμικίνθιον, ου, τό (Lat. semicinctium), an apron, worn by artisans, Ac. xix. 12. (N. T.)*

Σίμων, ωνος, ὁ, Simon; nine persons of the name are mentioned: (1) Peter, the apostle, Mat. xvii. 25; (2) the Zealot, an apostle, Lu. vi. 15; (3) a brother of Jesus, Mar. vi. 3; (4) a certain Cyrenian, Mar. xv. 21; (5) the father of Judas Iscariot, Jn. vi. 71; (6) a certain Pharisee, Lu. vii. 40; (7) a leper, Mat. xxvi. 6; (8) Simon Magus, Ac. viii. 9; (9) a certain tanner, Ac. ix. 43.

Σινᾶ, τό (Heb.), Sinai, Ac. vii. 30, 38; Gal. iv. 24, 25.*

σίναπι, εως, τό, mustard, Lu. xiii. 19, xvii. 6.

σινδών, όνος, ἡ, fine linen, a linen cloth, Mar. xiv. 51, 52, xv. 46.

σινιάζω, to sift, as grain, to prove by trials, Lu. xxii. 31. (N. T.)*

σιρικός, see σηρικός.

σιτευτός, ἡ, όν, fattened, fatted, Lu. xv. 23, 27, 30.*

σιτίον, ου, τό, grain, Ac. vii. 12 (W. H.).*

σιτιστός, ἡ, όν, fattened; τὰ σιτιστά, fatlings, Mat. xxii. 4.*

σιτο-μέτριον, ου, τό, a measured portion of grain or food, Lu. xii. 42. (N. T.)*

σῖτος, ου, ὁ, wheat, grain, Jn. xii. 24; 1 Cor. xv. 37.

Σιχάρ, see Συχάρ.

Σιών, ἡ, τό, Zion, the hill; used for the city of Jerusalem, Ro. xi. 26; fig., for heaven, the spiritual Jerusalem, Heb. xii. 22; Rev. xiv. 1.

σιωπάω, ῶ, ήσω, to be silent, whether voluntarily or from dumbness, Mar. iii. 4; Lu. i. 20; to become still, as the sea, Mar. iv. 39.

σκανδαλίζω, ίσω, to cause to stumble; met., to entice to sin, Mat. xviii. 6, 8, 9; to cause to fall away, Jn. vi. 61; pass., to be indignant, Mat. xv. 12.

σκάνδαλον, ου, τό, a snare, a stumbling-block; fig., a cause of error or sin, Mat. xiii. 41; Ro. xiv. 13. (S.)

σκάπτω, ψω, to dig, Lu. vi. 48, xiii. 8, xvi. 3.*

σκάφη, ης, ἡ, any hollow vessel; a boat, Ac. xxvii. 16, 30, 32.*

σκέλος, ους, τό, the leg, Jn. xix. 31, 32, 33.*

σκέπασμα, ατος, τό, clothing, 1 Tim. vi. 8.*

Σκευᾶς, ᾶ, ὁ, Sceva, Ac. xix. 14.*

σκευή, ῆς, ἡ, furniture, fittings, Ac. xxvii. 19.*

σκεῦος, ους, τό, (1) a vessel, to contain a liquid, or for any other purpose, Heb. ix. 21; 2 Tim. ii. 20; fig., of recipients generally, a vessel of mercy, of wrath, Ro. ix. 22, 23; an instrument by which anything is done; household utensils, plur., Mat. xii. 29; of a ship, the tackling, Ac. xxvii. 17; fig., of God's servants, Ac. ix. 15; 2 Cor. iv. 7.

σκηνή, ῆς, ἡ, a tent, a tabernacle, an abode or dwelling, Mat. xvii. 4; Ac. vii. 43, xv. 16; Heb. viii. 5, xiii. 10.

σκηνο-πηγία, ας, ἡ, the feast of tabernacles, Jn. vii. 2.*

σκηνο-ποιός, οῦ, ὁ, a tent-maker, Ac. xviii. 3. (N. T.)*

σκῆνος, ους, τό, a tent; fig., of

the human body, 2 Cor. v. 1, 4.*

σκηνόω, ῶ, ώσω, *to spread a tent*, Rev. vii. 15; met., *to dwell*, Jn. i. 14; Rev. xii. 12, xiii. 6, xxi. 3.*

σκήνωμα, ατος, τό, *a tent pitched, a dwelling*, Ac. vii. 46; fig., of the body, 2 Pet. i. 13, 14.*

σκιά, ᾶς, ἡ, (1) *a shadow, a thick darkness*, Mat. iv. 16 (S.); (2) *a shadow, an outline*, Col. ii. 17.

σκιρτάω, ῶ, ήσω, *to leap* for joy, Lu. i. 41, 44, vi. 23.*

σκληρο-καρδία, ας, ἡ, *hardness of heart, perverseness*, Mat. xix. 8; Mar. x. 5, xvi. 14. (S.)*

σκληρός, ά, όν, *hard, violent*, as the wind, Ja. iii. 4; fig., *grievous, painful*, Ac. ix. 5 (W. H. omit), xxvi. 14; Ju. 15; *harsh, stern*, Mat. xxv. 24; Jn. vi. 60.*

σκληρότης, τητος, ἡ, fig., *hardness* of heart, *obstinacy*, Ro. ii. 5.*

σκληρο-τράχηλος, ον, *stiffnecked*; fig., *obstinate*, Ac. vii. 51. (S.)*

σκληρύνω, fig., *to make hard, to harden*, as the heart, Ro. ix. 18; Heb. iii. 8, 15, iv. 7; pass., *to be hardened, to become obstinate*, Ac. xix. 9; Heb. iii. 13.*

σκολιός, ά, όν, *crooked*, Lu. iii. 5; fig., *perverse*, Ac. ii. 40; Phil. ii. 15; *unfair*, 1 Pet. ii. 18.*

σκόλοψ, οπος, ὁ, *a stake* or *thorn;* fig., *a sharp infliction*, 2 Cor. xii. 7.*

σκοπέω, ῶ, (1) *to look at, to regard attentively*, Ro. xvi. 17; (2) *to take heed* (acc.), *beware* (μή), Gal. vi. 1.

σκοπός, οῦ, ὁ, *a mark aimed at, a goal; κατὰ σκοπόν, towards the goal, i.e.*, aiming straight at it, Phil. iii. 14.*

σκορπίζω, σω, *to disperse, to scatter abroad*, as frightened sheep, Jn. x. 12; *to distribute alms*, 2 Cor. ix. 9.

σκορπίος, ου, ὁ, *a scorpion*, Lu. x. 19.

σκοτεινός ή, όν, *full of darkness, dark*, Mar. vi. 23; Lu. xi. 34, 36.*

σκοτία, ας, ἡ, *darkness*, Mat. x.

27; fig., *spiritual darkness*, Jn. i. 5, vi. 17.

σκοτίζω, σω, in pass., *to be darkened*, as the sun, Mar. xiii. 24; fig., as the mind, Ro. i. 21.

σκότος, ους, τό (σκότος, ου, ὁ, only in Heb. xii. 18, where W. H. read ϛόφος), *darkness*, physical, Mat. xxvii. 45; moral, Jn. iii. 19.

σκοτόω, ῶ, pass. only, *to be darkened*, Ep. iv. 18 (W. H.); Rev. ix. 2 (W. H.), xvi. 10.*

σκύβαλον, ου, τό, *refuse, dregs*, Phil. iii. 8.*

Σκύθης, ου, ὁ, *a Scythian*, as typical of the uncivilized, Col. iii. 11.*

σκυθρ-ωπός, όν, *sad-countenanced, gloomy*, Mat. vi. 16; Lu. xxiv. 17.*

σκύλλω, pass. perf. part. ἐσκυλμένος, *to flay; to trouble, annoy*, Mat. ix. 36 (W. H.); Mar. v. 35; Lu. vii. 6, viii. 29.*

σκῦλον, ου, τό, *spoil taken from a foe*, Lu. xi. 22.*

σκωληκό-βρωτος, ον, *eaten by worms*, Ac. xii. 23.*

σκώληξ, ηκος, ὁ, *a gnawing worm*, Mar. ix. 44 (W. H. omit)- 46 (W. H. omit), 48.*

σμαράγδινος, η, ον, *made of emerald*, Rev. iv. 3. (N.T.)*

σμάραγδος, ου, ὁ, *an emerald*, Rev. xxi. 19.*

σμύρνα, ης, ἡ, *myrrh*, Mat. ii. 11; Jn. xix. 39.*

Σμύρνα, ης, ἡ, *Smyrna.* Rev. i. 11, ii. 8 (W. H.).*

Σμυρναῖος, ου, ὁ, ἡ, *one of Smyrna, a Smyrnæan*, Rev. ii. 8 (not W. H.).*

σμυρνίζω, *to mingle with myrrh*, Mar. xv. 23. (N. T.)*

Σόδομα, ων, τά, *Sodom*, Mat. x. 15, xi. 23, 24.

Σολομών or -μῶν, ῶντος or ῶνος, ὁ, *Solomon*, Mat. vi. 29, xii. 42.

σορός, οῦ, ἡ, *a bier, an open coffin*, Lu. vii. 14.*

σός, σή, σόν, poss. pron., *thy, thine* (see Gr. §§ 56, 255, Bu. 115).

σουδάριον, ου, τό (Lat.), *a handkerchief*, Lu. xix. 20; Jn. xi. 44. (N. T.)

Σουσάννα, ης, ἡ, *Susanna*, Lu. viii. 3.*

σοφία, ας, ἡ, *wisdom, insight, skill*, human, Lu. xi. 31; or divine, 1 Cor. i. 21, 24. *Syn.:* see γνῶσις.

σοφίζω, *to make wise*, 2 Tim. iii. 15; pass., *to be devised skillfully*, 2 Pet. i. 16.*

σοφός, ή, όν, *wise*, either (1) in action, *expert*, Ro. xvi. 19; (2) in acquirement, *learned, cultivated*, 1 Cor. i. 19, 20; (3) philosophically, *profound*, Ju. 25; (4) practically, Ep. v. 15.

Σπανία, ας, ἡ, *Spain*, Ro. xv. 24, 28.*

σπαράσσω, ξω, *to convulse, to throw into spasms*, Mar. i. 26, ix. 20 (not W. H.), 26; Lu. ix. 39.*

σπαργανόω, ῶ, perf. pass. part. ἐσπαργανωμένος, *to swathe, to wrap in swaddling clothes*, Lu. ii. 7, 12.*

σπαταλάω, ῶ, ήσω, *to live extravagantly* or *luxuriously*, 1 Tim. v. 6; Ja. v. 5.* *Syn.:* The fundamental thought of στρηνιάω is of insolence and voluptuousness which spring from abundance; of τρυφάω, *effeminate* self-indulgence; of σπαταλάω, is effeminacy and wasteful extravagance.

σπάω, ῶ, mid., *to draw*, as a sword, Mar. xiv. 47; Ac. xvi. 27.*

σπεῖρα, ης, ἡ, (1) *a cohort* of soldiers, the tenth part of a legion, Ac. x. 1; (2) *a military guard*, Jn. xviii. 3, 12.

σπείρω, σπερῶ, 1st aor. ἔσπειρα, perf. pass. part. ἐσπαρμένος, 2d aor. pass. ἐσπάρην, *to sow* or *scatter*, as seed, Lu. xii. 24; *to spread* or *scatter*, as the word of God, Mat. xiii. 19; applied to giving alms, 2 Cor. ix. 6; to burial, 1 Cor. xv. 42, 43; and to spiritual effort generally, Gal. vi. 8.

σπεκουλάτωρ, ορος, ὁ (Lat.), *a body-guardsman, a soldier in attendance upon royalty*, Mar. vi. 27 (see Gr. § 154c). (N. T.)*

σπένδω, *to pour out*, as a libation, fig., Phil. ii. 17; 2 Tim. iv. 6.*

σπέρμα, ατος, τό, *seed, produce*, Mat. xiii. 24–38; *children, offspring, posterity*, Jn. vii. 42; *a remnant*, Ro. ix. 29.

7

σπερμο-λόγος, ου, ὁ, *a babbler*, *i.e.*, one who picks up trifles, as birds do seed, Ac. xvii. 18.*

σπεύδω, σω, (1) *to hasten*, intrans., usually adding to another verb the notion of speed, Lu. xix. 5, 6; (2) *to desire earnestly* (acc.), 2 Pet. iii. 12.

σπήλαιον, ου, τό, *a cave, a den*, Heb. xi. 38.*

σπιλάς, άδος, ἡ, *a rock in the sea, a reef;* fig., of false teachers, *a hidden rock* (R. V.), Ju. 12.*

σπίλος, ου, ὁ, *a spot;* fig., *a fault*, Ep. v. 27; 2 Pet. ii. 13.*

σπιλόω, ῶ, *to defile, to spot*, Ja. iii. 6; Ju. 23.*

σπλάγχνα, ων, τά, *bowels*, only Ac. i. 18; elsewhere, fig., *the affections, compassion, the heart*, as Col. iii. 12; 1 Jn. iii. 17.

σπλαγχνίζομαι, dep., with 1st aor. pass. ἐσπλαγχνίσθην, *to feel compassion, to have pity* on (gen., or ἐπί, dat. or acc., once περί, Mat. ix. 36).

σπόγγος, ου, ὁ, *a sponge*, Mat. xxvii. 48; Mar. xv. 36; Jn. xix. 29.*

σποδός, οῦ, ἡ, *ashes*, Mat. xi. 21; Lu. x. 13; Heb. ix. 13.*

σπορά, ᾶς, ἡ, *seed*, 1 Pet. i. 23.*

σπόριμος, όν, *sown;* neut. plur. τὰ σπόριμα, *sown fields*, Mat. xii. 1; Mar. ii. 23; Lu. vi. 1.*

σπόρος, ου, ὁ, *seed*, for sowing, Lu. viii. 5, 11.

σπουδάζω, άσω, *to hasten, to give diligence* (with inf.), Heb. iv. 11; 2 Tim. iv. 9, 21.

σπουδαῖος, αία, αῖον, *diligent, earnest*, 2 Cor. viii. 17, 22; compar. neut. as adv., σπουδαιότερον, 2 Tim. i. 17 (not W. H.).*

σπουδαίως, adv., *diligently, earnestly*, Lu. vii. 4; 2 Tim. i. 17 (W. H.); Tit. iii. 13; *hastily*, compar., Phil. ii. 28.*

σπουδή, ῆς, ἡ, (1) *speed, haste*, Mar. vi. 25; (2) *diligence, earnestness*, Ro. xii. 11.

σπυρίς (W. H. σφυρίς), ίδος, ἡ, *a plaited basket*, Mar. viii. 8, 20.

στάδιον, ου, τό, plur. οἱ στάδιοι, (1) *a stadium*, one eighth of a Roman mile, Jn. xi. 18; (2) *a race-course*, for public games, 1 Cor. ix. 24.

στάμνος, ου, ὁ, ἡ, *a jar* or *vase*, for the manna, Heb. ix. 4.*

στασιαστής, οῦ, ὁ, *an insurgent*, Mar. xv. 7 (W. H.).*

στάσις, εως, ἡ (ἵστημι), *a standing*, lit. only Heb. ix. 8; *an insurrection*, Mar. xv. 7; *dissension*, Ac. xv. 2.

στατήρ, ῆρος, ὁ, *a stater*, a silver coin equal to two of the δίδραχμον (which see), a Jewish shekel, Mat. xvii. 27.*

σταυρός, οῦ, ὁ, *a cross*, Mat. xxvii. 32, 40; met., often of Christ's death, Gal. vi. 14; Ep. ii. 16.

σταυρόω, ῶ, ώσω, *to fix to the cross, to crucify*, Lu. xxiii. 21, 23; fig., *to destroy*, the corrupt nature, Gal. v. 24.

σταφυλή, ῆς, ἡ, *a grape, a cluster of grapes*, Mat. vii. 16; Lu. vi. 44; Rev. xiv. 18.*

στάχυς, υος, ὁ, *an ear of corn*, Mat. xii. 1; Mar. ii. 23, iv. 28; Lu. vi. 1.*

Στάχυς, ῦος, ὁ, *Stachys*, Ro. xvi. 9.*

στέγη, ης, ἡ (lit. *a cover*), *a* flat *roof* of a house, Mat. viii. 8; Mar. ii. 4; Lu. vii. 6.*

στέγω, *to cover, to conceal, to bear with*, 1 Cor. ix. 12, xiii. 7; 1 Th. iii. 1, 5.*

στεῖρος, α, ον, *barren*, Lu. i. 7, 36, xxiii. 29; Gal. iv. 27.*

στέλλω, *to set, arrange;* in mid., *to provide for, take care*, 2 Cor. viii. 20; *to withdraw from* (ἀπό), 2 Th. iii. 6.*

στέμμα, ατος, τό, *a garland*, Ac. xiv. 13.*

στεναγμός, οῦ, ὁ, *a groaning*, Ac. vii. 34; Ro. viii. 26.*

στενάζω, ξω, *to groan*, expressing grief, anger, or desire, Mar. vii. 34; Heb. xiii. 17.

στενός, ή, όν, *narrow*, Mat. vii. 13, 14; Lu. xiii. 24.*

στενο-χωρέω, ῶ, *to be narrow;* in pass., *to be distressed*, 2 Cor. iv. 8, vi. 12.*

στενο-χωρία, ας, ἡ, *a narrow space; great distress*, Ro. ii. 9, viii. 35; 2 Cor. vi. 4, xii. 10.*

στερεός, ά, όν, *solid*, as food,

Heb. v. 12, 14; fig., *firm, steadfast*, 1 Pet. v. 9; 2 Tim. ii. 19.*

στερεόω, ῶ, ώσω, *to strengthen, confirm, establish*, Ac. iii. 7, 16, xvi. 5.*

στερέωμα, ατος, τό, *firmness, steadfastness*, Col. ii. 5.*

Στεφανᾶς, ᾶ, ὁ, *Stephanas*, 1 Cor. i. 16, xvi. 15, 17.

στέφανος, ου, ὁ, *a crown, a garland*, of royalty, of victory in the games, of festal joy, Jn. xix. 2, 5; 1 Cor. ix. 25; often used fig., 2 Tim. iv. 8; Rev. ii. 10. *Syn.:* see διάδημα.

Στέφανος, ου, ὁ, *Stephen*, Ac. vi., vii.

στεφανόω, ῶ, ώσω, *to crown, to adorn*, 2 Tim. ii. 5; Heb. ii. 7, 9.*

στῆθος, ους, τό, *the breast*, Lu. xviii. 13.

στήκω (ἵστημι, ἕστηκα), *to stand*, in the attitude of prayer, Mar. xi. 25; generally, *to stand firm, persevere*, as Ro. xiv. 4; 1 Cor. xvi. 13; Gal. v. 1. (S.)

στηριγμός, οῦ, ὁ, *firmness, steadfastness*, 2 Pet. iii. 17.*

στηρίζω, ίξω or ίσω, pass. perf. ἐστήριγμαι, (1) *to fix, to set firmly*, Lu. ix. 51, xvi. 26; (2) *to strengthen, to confirm, to support*, as Lu. xxii. 32; Ro. i. 11.

στιβάς, see στοιβάς.

στίγμα, ατος, τό, *a mark* or *brand*, used of the traces of the apostle's sufferings for Christ, Gal. vi. 17.*

στιγμή, ῆς, ἡ, *a point of time, an instant*, Lu. iv. 5.*

στίλβω, *to shine, to glisten*, Mar. ix. 3.*

στοά, ᾶς, ἡ, *a colonnade, a portico*, Jn. v. 2, x. 23; Ac. iii. 11, v. 12.*

στοιβάς, άδος, ἡ (W.H. στιβάς), *a bough, a branch of a tree.* Mar. xi. 8.*

στοιχεῖα, ων, τά, *elements, rudiments*, Gal. iv. 3, 9; Col. ii. 8, 20; Heb. v. 12; 2 Pet. iii. 10, 12.*

στοιχέω, ῶ, ήσω, *to walk*, always fig. of conduct; *to walk* in (local dat.), Ac. xxi. 24; Ro. iv. 12; Gal. v. 25, vi. 16; Phil. iii. 16.*

στολή, ῆς, ἡ, *a robe, i.e.*, the

long outer garment which was a mark of distinction, Lu. xv. 22. *Syn.:* see ἱμάτιον.

στόμα, ατος, τό, (1) *the mouth,* generally; hence, (2) *speech, speaking;* used of testimony, Mat. xviii. 16; *eloquence or power in speaking,* Lu. xxi. 15; (3) applied to an opening in the earth, Rev. xii. 16; (4) *the edge or point* of a sword, Lu. xxi. 24.

στόμαχος, ου, ὁ, *the stomach,* 1 Tim. v. 23.*

στρατεία, ας, ἡ, *warfare, military service;* of Christian warfare, 2 Cor. x. 4; 1 Tim. i. 18.*

στράτευμα, ατος, τό, (1) *an army,* Rev. ix. 16; (2) *a detachment of troops,* Ac. xxiii. 10, 27; plur., Lu. xxiii. 11.

στρατεύομαι, dep. mid., *to wage war, to fight,* Lu. iii. 14; fig., of the warring of lusts against the soul, Ja. iv. 1; *to serve as a soldier,* of Christian work, 1 Tim. i. 18; 2 Cor. x. 3.

στρατ-ηγός, οῦ, ὁ (ἄγω), (1) *a leader of an army, a general;* (2) *a magistrate or governor,* Ac. xvi. 20–38; (3) *the captain* of the temple, Lu. xxii. 4, 52; Ac. iv. 1, v. 24, 26.*

στρατιά, ᾶς, ἡ, *an army;* met., *a host* of angels, Lu. ii. 13; *the host* of heaven, *i.e.,* the stars, Ac. vii. 42.*

στρατιώτης, ου, ὁ, *a soldier,* as Mat. viii. 9; fig., of a Christian, 2 Tim. ii. 3.

στρατο-λογέω, ῶ, ήσω, *to collect an army, to enlist troops,* 2 Tim. ii. 4.*

στρατοπεδ-άρχης, ου, ὁ, *the praetorian prefect, i.e.,* commander of the Roman emperor's body-guard, Ac. xxviii. 16 (W. H. omit).*

στρατό-πεδον, ου, τό, *an encamped army,* Lu. xxi. 20.*

στρεβλόω, ῶ, *to rack, to pervert, to twist,* as words from their proper meaning, 2 Pet. iii. 16.*

στρέφω, ψω, 2d aor. pass. ἐστράφην, *to turn,* trans., Mat. v. 39; Rev. xi. 6 (*to change* into, εἰς); intrans., Ac. vii. 42; mostly in pass., *to turn one's self,* Jn. xx. 14; *to be con-*

verted, to be changed in mind and conduct, Mat. xviii. 3.

στρηνιάω, ῶ, άσω, *to live voluptuously,* Rev. xviii. 7, 9.* *Syn.:* see σπαταλάω.

στρῆνος, ους, τό, *profligate luxury, voluptuousness,* Rev. xviii. 3.*

στρουθίον, ου, τό (dim. of στρουθός), *a small bird, a sparrow,* Mat. x. 29, 31; Lu. xii. 6, 7.*

στρωννύω, or -ώννυμι, στρώσω, pass. perf. part. ἐστρωμένος ἔστρωμαι, *to spread,* Mat. xxi. 8; *to make a bed,* Ac. ix. 34; pass., *to be spread with couches,* ἀνάγαιον ἐστρωμένον, *an upper room furnished,* Mar. xiv. 15; Lu. xxii. 12.

στυγητός, όν, *hateful, detestable,* Tit. iii. 3.*

στυγνάζω, άσω, *to be gloomy,* Mar. x. 22; of the sky, Mat. xvi. 3.*

στύλος, ου, ὁ, *a pillar,* Gal. ii. 9; 1 Tim. iii. 15; Rev. iii. 12, x. 1.*

Στωϊκός, ή, όν (στοά, *portico*), *Stoic,* Ac. xvii. 18.*

σύ, σοῦ, σοί, σέ, plur. ὑμεῖς, *thou, ye,* the pers. pron. of second person (see Gr. § 53).

συγγ-. In some words commencing thus, W. H. prefer the unassimilated form συνγ-.

συγ-γένεια, ας, ἡ, *kindred, family,* Lu. i. 61; Ac. vii. 3, 14.*

συγ-γενής, ές, *akin,* as subst., *a relative,* Mar. vi. 4; Lu. xiv. 12; *a fellow-countryman,* Ro. ix. 3.

συγ-γενίς, ίδος, ἡ, *a kinswoman,* Lu. i. 36 (W. H.).*

συγ-γνώμη, ης, ἡ, *permission, indulgence,* 1 Cor. vii. 6.*

συγκ-. In words commencing thus, W. H. prefer the unassimilated form συνκ-.

συγ-κάθημαι, *to sit with* (dat. or μετά, gen.), Mar. xiv. 54; Ac. xxvi. 30.*

συγ-καθίζω, ῶ, (1) *to cause to sit down with,* Ep. ii. 6; (2) *to sit down together,* Lu. xxii. 55.*

συγ-κακο-παθέω, ῶ, *to suffer hardships together with,* 2 Tim. i. 8, ii. 3 (W. H.). (N. T.)*

συγ-κακουχέω, ῶ, pass., *to suffer*

ill-treatment with, Heb. xi 25. (N. T.)*

συγ-καλέω, ῶ, έσω, *to call together,* Lu. xv. 6; mid., *to call together to one's self,* Lu. ix. 1.

συγ-καλύπτω, *to conceal closely, to cover up wholly,* Lu. xii. 2.*

συγ-κάμπτω, ψω, *to bend together; to oppress,* Ro. xi. 10 (S.)*

συγ-κατα-βαίνω, *to go down with* any one, Ac. xxv. 5.*

συγ-κατά-θεσις, εως, ἡ, *assent, agreement,* 2 Cor. vi. 16.*

συγ-κατα-τίθημι, in mid., *to give a vote with, to assent to* (dat.), Lu. xxiii. 51.*

συγ-κατα-ψηφίζω, in pass., *to be voted* or *classed with* (μετά), Ac. i. 26.*

συγ-κεράννυμι, 1st aor. συνεκέρασα, pass. perf. συνκέκραμαι, *to mix with, to unite,* 1 Cor. xii. 24; pass., *to be united with,* Heb. iv. 2.*

συγ-κινέω, ῶ, ήσω, *to move together, stir up,* Ac. vi. 12.*

συγ-κλείω, σω, *to inclose, to shut in,* as fishes in a net, Lu. v. 6; *to shut* one *up* into (εἰς) or under (ὑπό, acc.) something, *to make subject to,* Ro. xi. 32; Gal. iii. 22, 23.*

συγ-κληρο-νόμος, ου, ὁ, ἡ, *a joint heir, a joint participant,* Ro. viii. 17; Ep. iii. 6; Heb. xi. 9; 1 Pet. iii. 7.*

συγ-κοινωνέω, ῶ, *to be a partaker with, have fellowship with,* Ep. v. 11; Phil. iv. 14; Rev. xviii. 4.*

συγ-κοινωνός, ου, ὁ, ἡ, *a partaker with, a co-partner,* Ro. xi. 17. (N. T.)

συγ-κομίζω, *to bear away together,* as in burying a corpse, Ac. viii. 2.*

συγ-κρίνω, *to join together, to combine,* 1 Cor. ii. 13; *to compare* (acc., dat.), 2 Cor. x. 12.*

συγ-κύπτω, *to be bowed together* or *bent double,* Lu. xiii. 11.*

συγ-κυρία, ας, ἡ, *a coincidence, an accident;* κατὰ συγκυρίαν, *by chance,* Lu. x. 31.*

συγ-χαίρω, 2d aor. in pass form συνεχάρην, *to rejoice with* (dat.), Lu. i. 58, xv. 6, 9; 1 Cor. xii. 26, xiii. 6; Phil. ii. 17, 18.*

συγ-χέω, also συγχύνω and

συγχύννω, perf. pass. συγκέχυμαι, to mingle together; (1) to bewilder, Ac. ii. 6, ix. 22 ; (2) to stir up, to throw into confusion, Ac. xix. 32, xxi. 27, 31.*

συγ-χράομαι, ῶμαι, to have dealings with (dat.), Jn. iv. 9.*

σύγ-χυσις, εως, ἡ, confusion, disturbance, Ac. xix. 29.*

συ-ζάω (W. H. συνζ-), ῶ, ήσω, to live together with (dat.), Ro. vi. 8 ; 2 Cor. vii. 3 ; 2 Tim. ii. 11.*

συ-ζεύγνυμι, 1st aor. συνέζευξα, to yoke together; to unite (acc.), as man and wife, Mat. xix. 6; Mar. x. 9.*

συ-ζητέω, ῶ, to seek together, to discuss, dispute, with dat., or πρός, acc., Mar. viii. 11, ix. 16.

συ-ζήτησις, εως, ἡ, mutual questioning, disputation, Ac. xv. 2 (W. H. ζήτησις), 7 (W. H. ζήτησις), xxviii. 29 (W. H. omit).*

συ-ζητητής, οῦ, ὁ, a disputer, as the Greek sophists, 1 Cor. i. 20. (N. T.)*

σύ-ζυγος, ου, ὁ, a yoke-fellow, a colleague, Phil. iv. 3 (prob. a proper name, Syzygus).*

συ-ζωο-ποιέω, ῶ, 1st aor. συνεζωοποίησα, to make alive together with, Ep. ii. 5; Col. ii. 13. (N. T.)*

συκάμινος, ου, ἡ, a sycamine-tree, Lu. xvii. 6.*

συκῆ, ῆς, ἡ (contr. from -έα), a fig-tree, Mar. xi. 13, 20, 21.

συκο-μωραία, ας, ἡ (W. H. -μορέα), a sycamore-tree, Lu. xix. 4.*

σῦκον, ου, τό, a fig, Ja. iii. 12.

συκο-φαντέω, ῶ, ήσω, to accuse falsely, to defraud, Lu. iii. 14, xix. 8 (gen. person, acc. thing).*

συλ-αγωγέω, ῶ, to plunder, Col. ii. 8. (N. T.)*

συλάω, ῶ, to rob, to plunder, 2 Cor. xi. 8.*

συλλ-. In words commencing thus, W. H. prefer the unassimilated form συνλ-.

συλ-λαλέω, 1st aor. συνελάλησα, to talk with (dat.), μετά (gen.), πρός (acc.), Mat. xvii. 3; Mar. ix. 4; Lu. iv. 36, ix. 30, xxii. 4; Ac. xxv. 12.*

συλ-λαμβάνω, συλλήψομαι, συ-

νείληφα, συνέλαβον, (1) to take together, to seize, Mat. xxvi. 55; (2) to conceive, of a woman, Lu. i. 24, 31 ; (3) mid., to apprehend (acc.), to help (dat.), Ac. xxvi. 21 ; Phil. iv. 3.

συλ-λέγω, ξω, to collect, to gather, Mat. xiii. 28, 29, 30.

συλ-λογίζομαι, σομαι, to reckon with one's self, to reason, Lu. xx. 5.*

συλ-λυπέομαι, οῦμαι, pass., to be grieved (ἐπί, dat.), Mar. iii. 5.*

συμβ-, συμμ-, συμπ-, συμφ-. In some words commencing thus, W. H. prefer the unassimilated form συνβ-, συνμ-, συνπ-, συνφ-.

συμ-βαίνω, 2d aor. συνέβην, to happen, to occur, Mar. x. 32; Ac. xx. 19; perf. part. τὸ συμβεβηκός, an event, Lu. xxiv. 14.

συμ-βάλλω, 2d aor. συνέβαλον, to throw together, hence, to ponder, Lu. ii. 19; to come up with, to encounter, with or without hostile intent (dat.), Lu. xiv. 31; Ac. xx. 14; to dispute with, Ac. xvii. 18; mid., to confer, consult with, Ac. iv. 15; to contribute (dat.), Ac. xviii. 27.*

συμ-βασιλεύω, σω, to reign together with, 1 Cor. iv. 8; 2 Tim. ii. 12.*

συμ-βιβάζω, άσω, (1) to unite, or knit together, Col. ii. 2, 19; (2) to put together in reasoning, and so, to conclude, prove, Ac. ix. 22; (3) to teach, instruct, 1 Cor. ii. 16.

συμ-βουλεύω, to give advice (dat.), Jn. xviii. 14; Rev. iii. 18; mid., to take counsel together (ἵνα or inf.), Mat. xxvi. 4; Jn. xi. 53 (W. H. βουλεύομαι); Ac. ix. 23.*

συμ-βούλιον, ου, τό, (1) mutual consultation, counsel; λαμβάνω, ποιέω συμβούλιον, to take counsel together, Mat. xii. 14, xxii. 15, xxvii. 1, 7, xxviii. 12; Mar. iii. 6, xv. 1; (2) a council, a gathering of counselors, Ac. xxv. 12.*

σύμ-βουλος, ου, ὁ, an adviser, a counselor, Ro. xi. 34.*

Συμεών, ὁ (Heb.), Simeon or

Simon (see Σίμων) ; the apostle Peter is so called, Ac. xv. 14; 2 Pet. i. 1; and four others are mentioned: (1) Lu. ii. 25, 34; (2) Lu. iii. 30; (3) Ac. xiii. 1; (4) Rev. vii. 7.*

συμ-μαθητής, οῦ, ὁ, a fellow-disciple, Jn. xi. 16.*

συμ-μαρτυρέω, ῶ, to bear witness together with, Ro. ii. 15, viii. 16, ix. 1; Rev. xxii. 18 (not W. H.).*

συμ-μερίζω, in mid., to divide together with, partake with (dat.), 1 Cor. ix. 13.*

συμ-μέτοχος, ον, jointly partaking, Ep. iii. 6, v. 7.*

συμ-μιμητής, οῦ, ὁ, a joint-imitator, Phil. iii. 17. (N. T.)*

συμ-μορφίζω, see συμμορφόω. (N. T.)

σύμ-μορφος, ον, similar, conformed to, gen., Ro. viii. 29; dat., Phil. iii. 21.*

συμ-μορφόω, ῶ, to bring to the same form with (dat.), Phil. iii. 10 (W. H. συμμορφίζω, in same sense). (N. T.)*

συμ-παθέω, ῶ, to sympathize with, to have compassion on (dat.), Heb. iv. 15, x. 34.*

συμ-παθής, ές, sympathizing, compassionate, 1 Pet. iii. 8.*

συμ-παρα-γίνομαι, to come together to (ἐπί, acc.), Lu. xxiii. 48; to stand by one, to help (dat.), 2 Tim. iv. 16 (W. H. παραγίνομαι).*

συμ-παρα-καλέω, ῶ, in pass., to be strengthened together, Ro. i. 12.*

συμ-παρα-λαμβάνω, 2d aor. συμπαρέλαβον, to take with one's self, as companion, Ac. xii. 25, xv. 37, 38; Gal. ii. 1.*

συμ-παρα-μένω, μενῶ, to remain or continue together with (dat.), Phil. i. 25 (W. H. παραμένω).*

συμ-πάρειμι, to be present together with, Ac. xxv. 24.*

συμ-πάσχω, to suffer together with, Ro. viii. 17; 1 Cor. xii. 26.*

συμ-πέμπω, to send together with, 2 Cor. viii. 18, 22.*

συμ-περι-λαμβάνω, to embrace completely, Ac. xx. 10.*

συμ-πίνω, 2d aor. συνέπιον, to drink together with, Ac. x. 41.*

94

συμ-πίπτω, *to fall together,* Lu. vi. 49 (W. H.).*

συμ-πληρόω, ῶ, *to fill completely,* Lu. viii. 23; pass., *to be completed, to be fully come,* Lu. ix. 51; Ac. ii. 1.*

συμ-πνίγω, *to choke utterly,* as weeds do plants, Mat. xiii. 22; Mar. iv. 7, 19; Lu. viii. 14; *to crowd upon* (acc.), Lu. viii. 42.*

συμ-πολίτης, ου, ὁ, *a fellow-citizen,* Ep. ii. 19.*

συμ-πορεύομαι, (1) *to journey together with* (dat.), Lu. vii. 11, xiv. 25, xxiv. 15; (2) intrans., *to come together, to assemble,* Mar. x. 1.*

συμπόσιον, ου, τό (συμπίνω), *a drinking party, a festive company,* συμπόσια συμπόσια, *by companies,* Mar. vi. 39.*

συμ-πρεσβύτερος, ου, ὁ, *a fellow-elder,* 1 Pet. v. 1. (N. T.)*

συμ-φάγω, see συνεσθίω.

συμ-φέρω, 1st aor. συνήνεγκα, *to bring together, to collect,* only Ac. xix. 19; generally intrans., and often impers., *to conduce to, to be profitable to,* 1 Cor. x. 23; 2 Cor. xii. 1; part. τὸ συμφέρον, *profit, advantage,* 1 Cor. vii. 35.

σύμ-φημι, *to assent to,* Ro. vii. 16.*

σύμ-φορος, ον, *profitable,* 1 Cor. vii. 35, x. 33 (W. H. for Rec. συμφέρον).

συμ-φυλέτης, ου, ὁ, *one of the same tribe, a fellow-countryman,* 1 Th. ii. 14. (N. T.)*

σύμ-φυτος, ον, *grown together, united with* (R. V.), Ro. vi. 5.*

συμ-φύω, 2d aor. pass. part. συμφυείς, pass., *to grow at the same time,* Lu. viii. 7.*

συμ-φωνέω, ῶ, ήσω, *to agree with, agree together, arrange with* (dat., or μετά, gen.), of persons, Mat. xviii. 19, xx. 2, 13; Ac. v. 9; of things, *to be in accord with,* Lu. v. 36; Ac. xv. 15.*

συμ-φώνησις, εως, ἡ, *concord, agreement,* 2 Cor. vi. 15. (N. T.)*

συμ-φωνία, ας, ἡ, *harmony,* of instruments, *music,* Lu. xv. 25.*

σύμ-φωνος, ον, *harmonious, agreeing with;* ἐκ συμφώνου, *by agreement,* 1 Cor. vii. 5.*

συμ-ψηφίζω, *to compute, reckon up,* Ac. xix. 19.*

σύμ-ψυχος, ον, *of one accord,* Phil. ii. 2. (N. T.)*

σύν, a prep. gov. dative, *with* (see Gr. § 296, Wi. § 48 b, Bu. 331). In composition, σύν denotes association with, or is intensive. The final ν changes to γ, λ, or μ, or is dropped, according to the initial letter of the word with which it is compounded (see Gr. § 4 d, 5, Bu. 8); but W. H. usually prefer the unassimilated forms.

συν-άγω, ἄξω, (1) *to bring together, to gather, to assemble,* Lu. xv. 13; Jn. xi. 47; pass., *to be assembled, to come together,* Ac. iv. 5, xiii. 44; (2) *to receive hospitably,* only Mat. xxv. 35, 38, 43.

συναγωγή, ῆς, ἡ, *an assembly, a congregation, synagogue,* either the place, or the people gathered in the place, Lu. xii. 11, xxi. 12. *Syn.:* see ἐκκλησία.

συν-αγωνίζομαι, *to strive together with* another, *to aid* (dat.), Ro. xv. 30.*

συν-αθλέω, ῶ, ήσω, *to strive together for* (dat. of thing), Phil. i. 27; or *with* (dat. of person), Phil. iv. 3.*

συν-αθροίζω, σω, *to gather or collect together,* Ac. xix. 25; pass., *to be assembled together,* Lu. xxiv. 33 (W. H. ἀθροίζω); Ac. xii. 12.*

συν-αίρω, *to reckon together, to make a reckoning with,* Mat. xviii. 23, 24, xxv. 19.*

συν-αιχμάλωτος, ου, ὁ, *a fellow-captive* or *prisoner,* Ro. xvi. 7; Col. iv. 10; Philem. 23. (N. T.)*

συν-ακολουθέω, ῶ, ήσω, *to follow together with, to accompany,* Mar. v. 37, xiv. 51 (W. H.); Lu. xxiii. 49.*

συν-αλίζω, in pass., *to be assembled together with* (dat.), Ac. i. 4.*

συν-αλλάσσω, *to reconcile,* see συνελαύνω.

συν-ανα-βαίνω, *to go up together with* (dat.), Mar. xv. 41; Ac. xiii. 31.*

συν-ανά-κειμαι, *to recline together with,* as at a meal, *to*

feast with (dat.), Mat. ix. 10; part. οἱ συνανακείμενοι, *the guests,* Mar. vi. 22, 26. (Ap.)

συν-ανα-μίγνυμι, pass., *to mingle together with, to keep company with* (dat.), 1 Cor. v. 9, 11; 2 Th. iii. 14.*

συν-ανα-παύομαι, σομαι, *to find rest* or *refreshment together with* (dat.), Ro. xv. 32. (S.)*

συν-αντάω, ῶ, ήσω, (1) *to meet with* (dat.), Lu. ix. 37, xxii. 10; Ac. x. 25; Heb. vii. 1, 10; (2) of things, *to happen to, to befall;* τὰ συναντήσοντα, *the things that shall happen,* Ac. xx. 22.*

συν-άντησις, εως, ἡ, *a meeting with,* Mat. viii. 34 (W. H. ὑπάντησις).*

συν-αντι-λαμβάνω, mid., lit., *to take hold together with; to assist, help* (dat.), Lu. x. 40; Ro. viii. 26.*

συν-απ-άγω, *to lead away along with;* in pass., *to be led* or *carried away in mind,* Ro. xii. 16 (see R. V. mrg.); Gal. ii. 13; 2 Pet. iii. 17.*

συν-απο-θνήσκω, *to die together with* (dat.), Mar. xiv. 31; 2 Cor. vii. 3; 2 Tim. ii. 11.*

συν-απ-όλλυμι, in mid., *to perish together with* (dat.), Heb. xi. 31.*

συν-απο-στέλλω, *to send together with* (acc.), 2 Cor. xii. 18.*

συν-αρμολογέω, ῶ, in pass., *to be framed together,* Ep. ii. 21, iv. 16. (N. T.)*

συν-αρπάζω, σω, *to seize,* or *drag by force* (dat.), Lu. viii. 29; Ac. vi. 12, xix. 29, xxvii. 15.*

συν-αυξάνω, in pass., *to grow together,* Mat. xiii. 30.*

σύν-δεσμος, ου, ὁ, *that which binds together, a band, a bond,* Ac. viii. 23; Ep. iv. 3; Col. ii. 19, iii. 14.*

συν-δέω, in pass., *to be bound together with* any one, as fellow-prisoners, Heb. xiii. 3.*

συν-δοξάζω, *to glorify together with* (σύν), pass., Ro. viii. 17.*

σύν-δουλος, ου, ὁ, *a fellow-slave, a fellow-servant,* Mat. xviii. 28–33; of Christians, *a fellow-worker, a colleague,* Col. i. 7.

συν-δρομή, ῆς, ἡ, *a running together, a concourse*, Ac. xxi. 30.*

συν-εγείρω, 1st aor. συνήγειρα, pass. συνηγέρθην; *to raise together, to raise with*, Ep. ii. 6; Col. ii. 12, iii. 1. (S.)*

συνέδριον, ου, τό, *a council, a tribunal*, Mat. x. 17; specially, *the Sanhedrin*, the Jewish council of seventy-one members, usually presided over by the high priest, Mat. v. 22, xxvi. 59; *the council-hall*, where the Sanhedrin met, Ac. iv. 15.

συν-είδησις, εως, ἡ, *consciousness*, Heb. x. 2; *the conscience*, Ro. ii. 15; 2 Cor. iv. 2, v. 11; 1 Pet. ii. 19.

συν-εῖδον, 2d aor. of obs. pres., *to be conscious* or *aware of*, *to understand*, Ac. xii. 12, xiv. 6; perf. σύνοιδα, part. συνειδώς, *to be privy to* a design, Ac. v. 2; *to be conscious to one's self* (dat.) *of guilt* (acc.), 1 Cor. iv. 4.*

σύν-ειμι, *to be with* (dat.), Lu. ix. 18; Ac. xxii. 11.*

σύν-ειμι (εἶμι), part. συνιών, *to go* or *come with*, *to assemble*, Lu. viii. 4.*

συν-εισ-έρχομαι, *to enter together with* (dat.), Jn. vi. 22, xviii. 15.*

συν-έκδημος, ου, ὁ, ἡ, *a fellow-traveler*, Ac. xix. 29; 2 Cor. viii. 19.*

συν-εκλεκτός, ἡ, όν, *elected together with*, 1 Pet. v. 13. (N. T.)*

συν-ελαύνω, ελάσω, *to compel, to urge* (acc. and εἰς), Ac. vii. 26 (W. H. συναλλάσσω).*

συν-επι-μαρτυρέω, ῶ, *to unite in bearing witness*, Heb. ii. 4.*

συν-επι-τίθημι, mid., *to join in assailing*, Ac. xxiv. 9 (W. H. for συντίθημι).*

συν-έπομαι, *to follow with, to accompany* (dat.), Ac. xx. 4.*

συν-εργέω, ῶ, *to co-operate with* (dat.), *to work together*, 1 Cor. xvi. 16; Ro. viii. 28.

συν-εργός, όν, *co-working, helping;* as a subst., *a companion in work, a fellow-worker*, gen. of person, obj. with εἰς, or dat., or (met.) gen., 2 Cor. i. 24.

συν-έρχομαι (see Gr. § 103, 2, Wi. § 15, Bu. 58), *to come* or

go with, to accompany, Ac. i. 21; *to come together, to assemble*, Ac. i. 6, v. 16; used also of conjugal intercourse, *to come* or *live together*, Mat. i. 18.

συν-εσθίω, 2d aor. συνέφαγον, *to eat with* (dat., or μετά, gen.), Lu. xv. 2; Ac. x. 41, xi. 3; 1 Cor. v. 11; Gal. ii. 12.*

σύνεσις, εως, ἡ (συνίημι), *a putting together*, in mind; hence, *understanding*, Lu. ii. 47; *the understanding*, the source of discernment, Mar. xii. 33.

συνετός, ἡ, όν (συνίημι), *intelligent, prudent, wise*, Mat. xi. 25; Lu. x. 21; Ac. xiii. 7; 1 Cor. i. 19.*

συν-ευδοκέω, ῶ, *to be pleased together with, to approve together* (dat.), Lu. xi. 48; Ac. viii. 1, xxii. 20; *to be of one mind with* (dat.), Ro. i. 32; *to consent, agree to* (inf.), 1 Cor. vii. 12, 13.*

συν-ευωχέω, ῶ, in pass., *to feast sumptuously with*, 2 Pet. ii. 13; Ju. 12.*

συν-εφ-ίστημι, *to rise up together against* (κατά), Ac. xvi. 22.*

συν-έχω, ξω, (1) *to press together, to close*, Ac. vii. 57; (2) *to press on every side, to confine*, Lu. viii. 45; (3) *to hold fast*, Lu. xxii. 63; (4) *to urge, impel*, Lu. xii. 50; 2 Cor. v. 14; (5) in pass., *to be afflicted with* sickness, Lu. iv. 38.

συν-ήδομαι, *to delight inwardly in* (dat.), Ro. vii. 22.*

συν-ήθεια, ας, ἡ, *a custom*, Jn. xviii. 39; 1 Cor. viii. 7 (W. H.), xi. 16.*

συν-ηλικιώτης, ου, ὁ, *one of the same age*, Gal. i. 14.*

συν-θάπτω, 2d aor. pass. συνετάφην, in pass., *to be buried together with*, Ro. vi. 4; Col. ii. 12.*

συν-θλάω, ῶ, fut. pass. συνθλασθήσομαι, *to break, to break in pieces*, Mat. xxi. 44; Lu. xx. 18.*

συν-θλίβω, *to press on all sides, to crowd upon*, Mar. v. 24, 31.*

συν-θρύπτω, *to break in pieces, to crush*, fig., Ac. xxi. 13. (N. T.)*

συν-ίημι, inf. συνιέναι, part. συνιῶν or συνιείς, fut. συνήσω, 1st aor. συνῆκα, *to put together*, in mind; hence, *to consider, understand* (acc.), *to be aware* (ὅτι), *to attend to* (ἐπί, dat.), Mat. xiii. 23, 51, xvi. 12; Mar. vi. 52.

συν-ίστημι, also συνιστάνω and συνιστάω, *to place together; to commend*, 2 Cor. iii. 1, vi. 4; *to prove, exhibit*, Gal. ii. 18; Ro. iii. 5, v. 8; perf. and 2d aor., intrans., *to stand with*, Lu. ix. 32; *to be composed of, to cohere*, Col. i. 17; 2 Pet. iii. 5.

συν-οδεύω, *to journey with, to accompany* (dat.), Ac. ix. 7.*

συν-οδία, ας, ἡ, *a company traveling together, a caravan*, Lu. ii. 44.*

συν-οικέω, ῶ, *to dwell together*, as in marriage, 1 Pet. iii. 7.*

συν-οικοδομέω, ῶ, in pass., *to be built up together*, Ep. ii. 22.*

συν-ομιλέω, ῶ, *to talk with* (dat.), Ac. x. 27.*

συν-ομορέω, ῶ, *to be contiguous to* (dat.), Ac. xviii. 7. (N. T.)*

συν-οχή, ῆς, ἡ, *constraint* of mind; hence, *distress, anguish*, Lu. xxi. 25; 2 Cor. ii. 4.*

συν-τάσσω, ξω, *to arrange with, prescribe, appoint*, Mat. xxi. 6 (W. H.), xxvi. 19, xxvii. 10.*

συν-τέλεια, ας, ἡ, *a completion, a consummation, an end*, Mat. xiii. 39, 40, 49, xxiv. 3, xxviii. 20; Heb. ix. 26.*

συν-τελέω, ῶ, έσω, (1) *to bring completely to an end*, Mat. vii. 28 (W. H. τελέω); Lu. iv. 2, 13; Ac. xxi. 27; (2) *to fulfill, to accomplish*, Ro. ix. 28; Mar. xiii. 4; *to make, to conclude*, Heb. viii. 8.*

συν-τέμνω, *to cut short, to bring to swift accomplishment*, Ro. ix. 28.*

συν-τηρέω, ῶ, (1) *to preserve, to keep safe*, Mat. ix. 17; Mar. vi. 20; Lu. v. 38 (W. H. omit); (2) *to keep in mind*, Lu. ii. 19.*

συν-τίθημι, in mid., *to place together, to make an agreement*, Lu. xxii. 5; Jn. ix. 22; Ac. xxiii. 20; *to assent*, Ac.

xxiv. 9 (W. H. συνεπιτί-
θημι).*

συν-τόμως, adv., concisely, brief-
ly, Ac. xxiv. 4.*

συν-τρέχω, 2d aor. συνέδραμον,
to run together, as a multitude, Mar. vi. 33; Ac. iii.
11; to run with (fig.), 1 Pet.
iv. 4.*

συν-τρίβω, ψω, to break by
crushing, to break in pieces,
Lu. ix. 39; Ro. xvi. 20; perf.
pass. part. συντετριμμένος,
bruised, Mat. xii. 20.

σύν-τριμμα, ατος, τό, crushing;
fig., destruction, Ro. iii. 16.
(S.)*

σύν-τροφος, ου, ὁ, one brought
up with, a foster-brother, Ac.
xiii. 1.*

συν-τυγχάνω, 2d aor. inf. συν-
τυχεῖν, to meet with, come to
(dat.), Lu. viii. 19.*

Συντύχη, acc. ην, ἡ, Syntyche,
Phil. iv. 2.*

συν-υπο-κρίνομαι, dep. pass.,
1st aorist συνυπεκρίθην, to
dissemble with, Gal. ii.
13.*

συν-υπουργέω, ῶ, to help together, 2 Cor. i. 11.*

συν-ωδίνω, to be in travail together, Ro. viii. 22.*

συν-ωμοσία, ας, ἡ, a swearing
together, a conspiracy, Ac.
xxiii. 13.*

Συράκουσαι, ῶν, αἱ, Syracuse,
Ac. xxviii. 12.*

Συρία, ας, ἡ, Syria, Lu. ii. 2.

Σύρος, ου, ὁ, a Syrian, Lu. iv.
27.*

Συρο-φοίνισσα (W. H. Συρο-
φοινίκισσα, mrg., Σύρα Φοινίκισσα), ης, ἡ, an appellative,
a Syrophenician woman, Mar.
vii. 26.*

Σύρτις, εως, acc. ιν, ἡ, (a quick-
sand), the Syrtis major, Ac.
xxvii. 17.*

σύρω, to draw, to drag, Jn. xxi.
8; Ac. viii. 3, xiv. 19, xvii.
6; Rev. xii. 4.* Syn.: see
ἕλκω.

συσ-. In some words com-
mencing thus, W. H. prefer
the uncontracted form συνσ-.

συ-σπαράσσω, ξω, to convulse
completely (acc.), Mar. ix. 20
(W. H.); Lu. ix. 42.*

σύσ-σημον, ου, τό, a concerted
signal, a sign agreed upon,
Mar. xiv. 44.*

σύσ-σωμος (W. H. σύνσωμος),

ον, belonging to the same
body; fig., of Jews and Gentiles, in one church, Ep. iii.
6. (N. T.)*

συ-στασιαστής, οῦ, ὁ, a fellow-
insurgent (W. H. στασιασ-
τής), Mar. xv. 7.*

συ-στατικός, ή, όν, commenda-
tory, 2 Cor. iii. 1.*

συ-σταυρόω, ῶ, to crucify together with (acc. and dat.);
lit., Mat. xxvii. 44; fig., Gal.
ii. 19. (N. T.)

συ-στέλλω, (1) to contract, perf.
pass. part., contracted, short-
ened, 1 Cor. vii. 29; (2) to
wrap round, to swathe, as a
dead body, Ac. v. 6.*

συ-στενάζω, to groan together,
Ro. viii. 22.*

συ-στοιχέω, ῶ, to be in the same
rank with; to answer to, to
correspond to (dat.), Gal. iv.
25.*

συ-στρατιώτης, ου, ὁ, a fellow-
soldier, i.e., in the Christian
service, Phil. ii. 25; Philem.
2.*

συ-στρέφω, ψω, to roll or gather
together, Mat. xvii. 22 (W.
H.); Ac. xxviii. 3.*

συ-στροφή, ῆς, ἡ, a gathering
together, a riotous concourse,
Ac. xix. 40; a conspiracy, Ac.
xxiii. 12.*

συ-σχηματίζω, in pass., to conform one's self, to be assimi-
lated to (dat.), Ro. xii. 2; 1
Pet. i. 14.*

Συχάρ (W. H.), or Σιχάρ, ἡ,
Sychar, Jn. iv. 5.*

Συχέμ, Shechem, (1) ὁ, the
prince, Ac. vii. 16 (Rec., W.
H. the city); (2) ἡ, the city,
Ac. vii. 16.*

σφαγή, ῆς, ἡ, (1) slaughter, Ac.
viii. 32; Ro. viii. 36 (S.); Ja.
v. 5.*

σφάγιον, ου, τό, a slaughtered
victim, Ac. vii. 42.*

σφάζω, ξω, pass., perf. part.
ἐσφαγμένος, 2d aor. ἐσφάγην,
to kill by violence, to slay, 1
Jn. iii. 12; Rev. v. 9, vi. 4.

σφόδρα, adv., exceedingly, greatly, Mat. ii. 10.

σφοδρῶς, adv., exceedingly, Ac.
xxvii. 18.*

σφραγίζω, ίσω, to seal, to set a
seal upon, (1) for security,
Mat. xxvii. 66; (2) for secrecy, Rev. xxii. 10; (3) for
designation, Ep. i. 13; or

(4) for authentication, Ro.
xv. 28.

σφραγίς, ῖδος, ἡ, (1) a seal, a
signet-ring, Rev. vii. 2; (2)
the impression of a seal
whether for security and
secrecy, as Rev. v. 1; or for
designation, Rev. ix. 4; (3)
that which the seal attests,
the proof, 1 Cor. ix. 2.

σφυρίς, see σπυρίς.

σφυρόν (W. H. σφυδρόν), οῦ,
τό, the ankle-bone, Ac. iii.
7.*

σχεδόν, adv., nearly, almost,
Ac. xiii. 44, xix. 26; Heb. ix.
22.*

σχῆμα, ατος, τό, fashion, habit,
1 Cor. vii. 31; form, appearance, Phil. ii. 7.* Syn.: see
ἰδέα.

σχίζω, ίσω, to rend, to divide
asunder, Mat. xxvii. 51;
pass., to be divided into fac-
tions, Ac. xiv. 4.

σχίσμα, ατος, τό, a rent, as in
a garment, Mar. ii. 21; a
division, a dissension, 1 Cor.
i. 10.

σχοινίον, ου, τό (dim. of σχοῖ-
νος, a rush), a cord, a rope,
Jn. ii. 15; Ac. xxvii. 32.*

σχολάζω, άσω, to be at leisure;
to be empty or unoccupied,
Mat. xii. 44; to have leisure
for (dat.), give one's self to,
1 Cor. vii. 5.*

σχολή, ῆς, ἡ, leisure; a place
where there is leisure for
anything, a school, Ac. xix.
9.*

σώζω, σώσω, perf. σέσωκα, pass.
σέσωσμαι, 1st aor. pass. ἐσώ-
θην; (1) to save, from evil or
danger, Mat. viii. 25, xvi.
25; (2) to heal, Mat. ix. 21,
22; Jn. xi. 12; (3) to save,
i.e., from eternal death, 1
Tim. i. 15; part. pass. οἱ σω-
ζόμενοι, those who are being
saved, i.e., who are in the
way of salvation, Ac. ii. 47.

σῶμα, ατος, τό, a body, i.e., (1)
the living body of an animal,
Ja. iii. 3; or of a man, as 1
Cor. xii. 12, espec. as the
medium of human life, and
of human life as sinful; the
body of Christ, as the medium and witness of his hu-
manity; σώματα, Rev. xviii.
13, slaves; (2) a dead body,
a corpse, Ac. ix. 40; (3) fig.,

a community, the church,
the mystic body of Christ,
Col. i. 24; (4) *any material
body*, plants, sun, moon, etc.,
1 Cor. xv. 37, 38, 40; (5) *substance*, opp. to shadow, Col.
ii. 17.

σωματικός, ή, όν, *of* or *pertaining to the body*, 1 Tim. iv. 8;
bodily, corporeal, Lu. iii. 22.*

σωματικῶς, adv., *bodily, corporeally*, Col. ii. 9.*

Σώπατρος, ου, ὁ, *Sopater*, Ac.
xx. 4; (perh. = Σωσίπατρος,
see Ro. xvi. 21).*

σωρεύω, σω, *to heap up, to load*,
Ro. xii. 20; 2 Tim. iii. 16.*

Σωσθένης, ου, ὁ, *Sosthenes*, (1)
Ac. xviii. 17; (2) 1 Cor. i.
1.*

Σωσίπατρος, ου, ὁ, *Sosipater*,
Ro. xvi. 21 (see Ac. xx. 4).*

σωτήρ, ῆρος, ὁ, *a savior, deliverer, preserver;* a name
given to God, Lu. i. 47; 1
Tim. i. 1, ii. 3, iv. 10; Tit. i.
3, ii. 10, iii. 4; Ju. 25; elsewhere always of Christ, Lu.
ii. 11; Jn. iv. 42.

σωτηρία, ας, ἡ, *welfare, prosperity, deliverance, preservation*, from temporal evils,
Ac. vii. 25, xxvii. 34; Heb.
xi. 7; 2 Pet. iii. 15; specially
salvation, i.e., deliverance
from eternal death, viewed
either as present or future,
2 Cor. i. 6; 1 Th. v. 9.

σωτήριος, ον, *saving, bringing
salvation*, Tit. ii. 11; neut.
τὸ σωτήριον, *salvation*, Lu.
ii. 30, iii. 6; Ac. xxviii. 28;
Ep. vi. 17.*

σωφρονέω, ῶ, ήσω, (1) *to be of
sound mind*, Mar. v. 15; (2)
to be sober-minded, Ro. xii.
3; (3) *to exercise self-control*,
Tit. ii. 6.

σωφρονίζω, *to make soberminded, to admonish*, Tit. ii.
4.*

σωφρονισμός, οῦ, ὁ, *self-control*,
or *discipline*, 2 Tim. i. 7.*

σωφρόνως, adv., *soberly, with
moderation*, Tit. ii. 12.*

σωφροσύνη, ης, ἡ, *soundness of
mind, sanity*, Ac. xxvi. 25;
self-control, sobriety, 1 Tim.
ii. 9, 15.*

σώ-φρων, ον (σάος, σῶς, *sound*,
and φρήν), *of sound mind,
self-controlled, temperate*, 1
Tim. iii. 2; Tit. i. 8, ii. 2, 5.*

T

T, τ, ταῦ, *tau, t*, the nineteenth
letter. As a numeral, τ′ =
300; ͵τ = 300,000.

ταβέρναι, ῶν, αἱ (Lat.), *taverns;*
Ac. xxviii. 15, Τρεῖς Ταβέρναι, *Three Taverns*, a place
on the Appian Way. (N.T.)*

Ταβιθά, ἡ (Aram.), *Tabitha*,
Ac. ix. 36, 40.*

τάγμα, ατος, τό, *an order* or
series, a class, 1 Cor. xv.
23.*

τακτός, ή, όν, *appointed, fixed*,
Ac. xii. 21.*

ταλαιπωρέω, ῶ, ήσω, *to be distressed, to be miserable*, Ja.
iv. 9.*

ταλαιπωρία, ας, ἡ, *hardship,
misery*, Ro. iii. 16; Ja. v.
1.*

ταλαί-πωρος, ον, *afflicted, miserable*, Ro. vii. 24; Rev. iii.
17.*

ταλαντιαῖος, αία, αῖον, *of the
weight of a talent*, Rev. xvi.
21.*

τάλαντον, ου, τό, *a talent*, of
silver or gold, Mat. xviii.
24. The N. T. talent is
probably the Syrian silver
talent, worth about 237 dollars, rather than the Attic,
worth about 1000 dollars.

ταλιθά, ἡ (Aram.), *a damsel*,
Mar. v. 41. (N.T.)*

ταμεῖον (or -μεῖ-), **ου, τό,** *a storechamber*, Lu. xii. 24; *a secret
chamber*, Mat. vi. 6, xxiv. 26;
Lu. xii. 3.*

τανῦν, adv. (τὰ νῦν, *the things
that now are*), *as respects the
present, at present, now*, only
in Ac. (W. H. always write
τὰ νῦν).

τάξις, εως, ἡ, *order, i.e.*, (1)
regular arrangement, Col. ii.
5; (2) *appointed succession*,
Lu. i. 8; (3) *position, rank*,
Heb. v. 6.

ταπεινός, ή, όν, *humble, lowly*,
in condition or in spirit; in
N. T. in a good sense, Ja. i.
9, iv. 6.

ταπεινοφροσύνη, ης, ἡ, *lowliness of mind, humility*, real,
as Phil. ii. 3; or affected, as
Col. ii. 18.

ταπεινό-φρων, ον, *humble*, 1 Pet.
iii. 8 (W. H. for φιλόφρων).
(S.)*

ταπεινόω, ῶ, ώσω, *to make* or

bring low, Lu. iii. 5; *to
humble, humiliate*, 2 Cor.
xii. 21; pass., *to be humbled*,
Lu. xviii. 14; pass., in mid.
sense, *to humble one's self*,
Ja. iv. 10.

ταπείνωσις, εως, ἡ, *low condition*, in circumstances, Lu. i.
48; *abasement*, in spirit, Ja.
i. 10.

ταράσσω, ξω, *to agitate*, as
water in a pool, Jn. v. 4
(W. H. omit), 7; *to stir
up, to disturb in mind*, with
fear, grief, anxiety, doubt,
Ac. xviii. 8; 1 Pet. iii.
14.

ταραχή, ῆς, ἡ, *a disturbance*,
Jn. v. 4 (W. H. omit); *a
tumult, sedition*, Mar. xiii. 8
(W. H. omit).*

τάραχος, ου, ὁ, *a disturbance*,
Ac. xix. 23; *commotion*, Ac.
xii. 18.*

Ταρσεύς, έως, ὁ, *one of Tarsus*,
Ac. ix. 11, xxi. 39.*

Ταρσός, οῦ, ἡ, *Tarsus*, Ac. ix.
30.

ταρταρόω, ῶ, ώσω, *to thrust
down to Tartarus (Gehenna)*,
2 Pet. ii. 4. (N.T.)*

τάσσω, ξω, (1) *to assign, arrange*, Ro. xiii. 1; (2) *to determine;* mid., *to appoint*,
Mat. xxviii. 16.

ταῦρος, ου, ὁ, *a bull*, Ac. xiv.
13.

ταυτά, by crasis for τὰ αὐτά,
the same things.

ταῦτα, see οὗτος.

ταφή, ῆς, ἡ (θάπτω), *a burial*,
Mat. xxvii. 7.*

τάφος, ου, ὁ, *a burial-place, a
sepulchre*, as Mat. xxiii. 27.

τάχα, adv., *quickly; perhaps*,
Ro. v. 7; Philem. 15.*

ταχέως, adv. (ταχύς), *soon,
quickly*, Gal. i. 6; *hastily*,
2 Th. ii. 2; 1 Tim. v. 22.

ταχινός, ή, όν, *swift, quick*, 2
Pet. i. 14; ii. 1.*

τάχος, ους, τό, *quickness, speed*,
only in the phrase ἐν τάχει,
quickly, speedily, Lu. xviii.
8.

ταχύς, εῖα, ύ, *quick, swift*, only
Ja. i. 19; ταχύ, compar. τάχιον (W. H. τάχειον), superl.
τάχιστα, adverbially, *swiftly; more, most quickly*.

τέ, conj. of annexation, *and,
both* (see Gr. § 403, Wi. § 53,
2, Bu. 360 sq.).

τεῖχος, ους, τό, *a wall* of a city, Ac. ix. 25.

τεκμήριον, ου, τό, *a sign, a certain proof*, Ac. i. 3.*

τεκνίον, ου, τό (dim. of τέκνον), *a little child*, Jn. xiii. 33; Gal. iv. 19; 1 Jn. ii. 1, 12, 28, iii. 7, 18, iv. 4, v. 21.*

τεκνο-γονέω, ῶ, *to bear children*, 1 Tim. v. 14.*

τεκνο-γονία, ας, ἡ, *child-bearing*, 1 Tim. ii. 15.*

τέκνον, ου, τό (τίκτω), *a child, a descendant; an inhabitant*, Lu. xiii. 34; fig. of various forms of intimate union and relationship, *a disciple, a follower*, Philem. 10; hence, such phrases as τέκνα τῆς σοφίας, τέκνα ὑπακοῆς, τέκνα τοῦ φωτός, *children of wisdom, obedience, the light*, and espec. τέκνα τοῦ θεοῦ, *children of God*, Ro. viii. 16, 17, 21; 1 Jn.

τεκνο-τροφέω, ῶ, *to bring up children*, 1 Tim. v. 10.*

τέκτων, ονος, ὁ, *a carpenter*, Mat. xiii. 55; Mar. vi. 3.*

τέλειος, α, ον, *perfect*, as (1) *complete* in all its parts, Ja. i. 4; (2) *full grown of full age*, Heb. v. 14; (3) specially of the completeness of Christian character, *perfect*, Mat. v. 48. *Syn.:* see ἄρτιος.

τελειότης, τητος, ἡ, *perfectness, perfection*, Col. iii. 14; Heb. vi. 1.*

τελειόω, ῶ, ώσω, (1) *to complete, to finish*, as a course, a race, or the like, Jn. iv. 34; (2) *to accomplish*, as time, or prediction, Lu. ii. 43; Jn. xix. 28; (3) *to make perfect*, Heb. vii. 19; pass., *to be perfected*, Lu. xiii. 32.

τελείως (τέλειος), adv., *perfectly*, 1 Pet. i. 13.*

τελείωσις, εως, ἡ, *completion, fulfillment*, Lu. i. 45; *perfection*, Heb. vii. 11.*

τελειωτής, οῦ, ὁ, *a perfecter*, Heb. xii. 2. (N. T.)*

τελεσ-φορέω, ῶ, *to bring to maturity*, Lu. viii. 14.*

τελευτάω, ῶ, *to end, to finish, e.g.*, life; so, *to die*, Mat. ix. 18; Mar. vii. 10.

τελευτή, ῆς, ἡ, *end* of life, *death*, Mat. ii. 15.*

τελέω, ῶ, έσω, τετέλεκα, τετέ-

λεσμαι, ἐτελέσθην, (1) *to end, to finish*, Rev. xx. 3, 5, 7; (2) *to fulfill, to accomplish*, Lu. ii. 39; Ja. ii. 8; (3) *to pay*, Mat. xvii. 24.

τέλος, ους, τό, (1) *an end*, Lu. i. 33; (2) *event* or *issue*, Mat. xxvi. 58; (3) *the principal end, aim, purpose*, 1 Tim. i. 5; (4) *a tax*, Mat. xvii. 25; Ro. xiii. 7.

τελώνης, ου, ὁ, *a collector of taxes*, Lu. iii. 12, v. 27.

τελώνιον, ου, τό, *a toll-house, a tax-collector's office*, Mat. ix. 9; Mar. ii. 14; Lu. v. 27.*

τέρας, ατος, τό, *a wonder, a portent;* in N. T. only in plur., and joined with σημεῖα, *signs and wonders*, Ac. vii. 36; Jn. iv. 48. *Syn.:* see δύναμις.

Τέρτιος, ου, ὁ (Lat.), *Tertius*, Ro. xvi. 22.*

Τέρτυλλος, ου, ὁ, *Tertullus*, Ac. xxiv. 1, 2.*

τεσσαράκοντα, *forty*, Mat. iv. 2; Mar. i. 13.

τεσσαρακοντα-ετής, ές, *of forty years*, age or time, Ac. vii. 23, xiii. 18.*

τέσσαρες, τέσσαρα, gen. ων, *four*, Lu. ii. 37; Jn. xi. 17.

τέσσαρες-και-δέκατος, η, ον, ord. num., *fourteenth*, Ac. xxvii. 27, 33.*

τεταρταῖος, αία, αῖον, *of the fourth* (day); τεταρταῖός ἐστιν, *he has been dead four days*, Jn. xi. 39.*

τέταρτος, η, ον, ord. num., *fourth*, Mat. xiv. 25.

τετρά-γωνος, ον, *four-cornered, square*, Rev. xxi. 16.*

τετράδιον, ου, τό, *a quaternion*, or *guard of four soldiers*, Ac. xii. 4.*

τετρακισ-χίλιοι, αι, α, *four thousand*, Mar. viii. 9, 20.

τετρακόσιοι, αι, α, *four hundred*, Ac. v. 36.

τετρά-μηνος, ον, *of four months;* sc. χρόνος, *a period of four months*, Jn. iv. 35.*

τετρα-πλόος, οῦς, ῆ, οῦν, *fourfold*, Lu. xix. 8.*

τετρά-πους, ουν, gen. οδος, *four-footed*, Ac. x. 12, xi. 6; Ro. i. 23.*

τετρ-αρχέω (W.H. τετρααρχέω), ῶ, *to rule over as a tetrarch* (gen.), Lu. iii. 1.*

τετρ-άρχης (W. H. τετραάρχης), ου, ὁ, *a ruler over a fourth part of a region, a tetrarch*, applied also to rulers over any small dominion, Mat. xiv. 1.

τεύχω, see τυγχάνω.

τεφρόω, ῶ, ώσω (τέφρα, *ashes*), *to reduce to ashes*, 2 Pet. ii. 6.*

τέχνη, ης, ἡ, (1) *art, skill*, Ac. xvii. 29; (2) *an art, a trade*, Ac. xviii. 3; Rev. xviii. 22.*

τεχνίτης, ου, ὁ, *an artificer, craftsman*, Ac. xix. 24, 38; Rev. xviii. 22; used of God, Heb. xi. 10.* *Syn.:* see δημιουργός.

τήκω, *to make liquid;* pass., *to melt*, 2 Pet. iii. 12.*

τηλ-αυγῶς, adv. (τῆλε, *afar*, αὐγή, *radiance*), *clearly, distinctly*, Mar. viii. 25.*

τηλικ-οῦτος, αύτη, οῦτο, *so great*, 2 Cor. i. 10; Heb. ii. 3; Ja. iii. 4; Rev. xvi. 18.*

τηρέω, ῶ, ήσω, *to watch carefully*, with good or evil design; (1) *to guard*, Mat. xxvii. 36, 54; (2) *to keep* or *reserve*, 1 Cor. vii. 37; (3) *to observe, keep*, enactments or ordinances, Jn. xiv. 15, 21.

τήρησις, εως, ἡ, (1) *a prison*, Ac. iv. 3, v. 18; (2) *observance*, as of precepts, 1 Cor. vii. 19.*

Τιβεριάς, άδος, ἡ, *Tiberias*, Jn. vi. 1, 23, xxi. 1.*

Τιβέριος, ου, ὁ, *Tiberius*, Lu. iii. 1.*

τίθημι, θήσω (see Gr. § 107, Wi. § 14, 1, Bu. 45 sq.), (1) *to place, set, lay, put forth, put down, put away, put aside;* mid., *to cause to put*, or *to put for one's self;* (2) *to constitute, to make, to render;* mid., *to assign, determine.*

τίκτω, τέξομαι, 2d aor. ἔτεκον, 1st aor. pass. ἐτέχθην, *to bear, to bring forth*, of women, Lu. i. 57, ii. 6, 7; *to produce*, of the earth, Heb. vi. 7.

τίλλω, *to pluck, to pluck off*, Mat. xii. 1; Mar. ii. 23; Lu. vi. 1.*

Τιμαῖος, ου, ὁ, *Timæus*, Mar. x. 46.*

τιμάω, ῶ, ήσω, (1) *to estimate, to value at a price*, Mat. xxvii. 9; (2) *to honor, to reverence*, Mar. vii. 6, 10.

τιμή, ῆς, ἡ, (1) a price, Mat. xxvii. 6, 9; (2) honor, Ro. ix. 21; Heb. v. 4; 2 Tim. ii. 20, 21; 1 Pet. ii. 7.

τίμιος, a, ον, of great price, precious, honored, Rev. xvii. 4; Heb. xiii. 4.

τιμιότης, τητος, ἡ, preciousness, costliness, Rev. xviii. 19.*

Τιμό-θεος, ου, ὁ, Timothy, Ac. xvii. 14, 15.

Τίμων, ωνος, ὁ, Timon, Ac. vi. 5.*

τιμωρέω, ῶ, to punish (acc.), Ac. xxii. 5, xxvi. 11.*

τιμωρία, ας, ἡ, punishment, penalty, Heb. x. 29.*

τίνω, τίσω, to pay; with δίκην, to pay penalty, suffer punishment, 2 Th. i. 9.*

τὶς, τί, gen. τινός (enclitic), indef. pron., any one, some one (see Gr. § 352, Wi. § 25, 2, Bu. 85, 93).

τίς, τί, gen. τίνος; interrogative pron., who? which? what? (see Gr. § 350, Wi. § 25, 1, Bu. 115, 138).

Τίτιος, ου, ὁ, Titius, Ac. xviii. 7 (W. H.).*

τίτλος, ου, ὁ (Lat.), a title, an inscription, Jn. xix. 19, 20.*

Τίτος, ου, ὁ, Titus, 2 Cor. vii. 6, 13, 14.

τοι, an enclitic part., truly, indeed; see καιτοίγε, μέντοι, τοιγαροῦν, τοίνυν.

τοι-γαρ-οῦν, consequently, therefore, 1 Th. iv. 8; Heb. xii. 1.*

τοί-γε, although (in καιτοίγε).

τοί-νυν, indeed now, therefore, Lu. xx. 25; 1 Cor. ix. 26; Heb. xiii. 13; Ja. ii. 24 (not W. H.).*

τοιόσ-δε, τοιάδε, τοιόνδε, demonst. pron., of this kind, such, 2 Pet. i. 17.*

τοιοῦτος, τοιαύτη, τοιοῦτο, demonst. denoting quality (as τοσοῦτος denotes quantity, and οὗτος simply determines), of such a kind, such, so, used either with or without a noun, the corresponding relative is οἷος, as, only Mar. xiii. 19; 1 Cor. xv. 48; 2 Cor. x. 11; once ὁποῖος, Ac. xxvi. 29. For τοιοῦτος with the article, see Gr. § 220, Wi. § 18, 4, Bu. 87.

τοῖχος, ου, ὁ, a wall of a house, Ac. xxiii. 3; disting. from τεῖχος, a wall of a city.*

τόκος, ου, ὁ (a bringing forth), interest, usury, Mat. xxv. 27; Lu. xix. 23.*

τολμάω, ῶ, ήσω, (1) to dare (inf.), Mar. xi. 34; (2) to endure, Ro. v. 7; (3) to be bold, 2 Cor. xi. 21.

τολμηρότερον (τολμηρός), neut. compar. as adv., more boldly, Ro. xv. 15 (W. H. τολμηροτέρως).*

τολμητής, οῦ, ὁ, a daring, presumptuous man, 2 Pet. ii. 10.*

τομός, ή, όν, sharp, keen, comp. τομώτερος, Heb. iv. 12.*

τόξον, ου, τό, a bow, Rev. vi. 2.*

τοπάζιον, ου, τό, topaz, Rev. xxi. 20. (N. T.)*

τόπος, ου, ὁ, (1) a place, i.e., a district or region, or a particular spot in a region; (2) the place one occupies, the room, an abode, a seat, a sheath for a sword; (3) a passage in a book; (4) state, condition; (5) opportunity.

τοσοῦτος, τοσαύτη, τοσοῦτο, demonst. pron. denoting quantity (see τοιοῦτος), so great, so much, so long; plur., so many.

τότε, demonst. adv., then.

τοὐναντίον, for τὸ ἐναντίον, on the contrary, 2 Cor. ii. 7; Gal. ii. 7; 1 Pet. iii. 9.*

τοὔνομα, for τὸ ὄνομα, acc. absol., by name, Mat. xxvii. 57.*

τουτέστι, for τοῦτ᾽ ἔστι (W. H. prefer the uncontracted form), that is, Ac. i. 19; Ro. x. 6, 7, 8.

τοῦτο, neut. of οὗτος, which see.

τράγος, ου, ὁ, a he-goat, Heb. ix. 12, 13, 19, x. 4.*

τράπεζα, ης, ἡ, a table, (1) for food and banqueting, Mat. xv. 27; met., food, Ac. xvi. 34; (2) for money-changing or business, Mar. xi. 15.

τραπεζίτης, ου, ὁ, a money-changer, a banker, Mat. xxv. 27.*

τραῦμα, ατος, τό, a wound, Lu. x. 34.*

τραυματίζω, ίσω, to wound, Lu. xx. 12; Ac. xix. 16.*

τραχηλίζω, in pass., to be laid bare, to be laid open, Heb. iv. 13.*

τράχηλος, ου, ὁ, the neck, Lu. xv. 20; Ro. xvi. 4.

τραχύς, εῖα, ύ, rough, as ways, Lu. iii. 5; as rocks in the sea, Ac. xxvii. 29.*

Τραχωνῖτις, ιδος, ἡ, Trachonitis, the N.E. of the territory beyond Jordan, Lu. iii. 1.*

τρεῖς, τρία, three, Mat. xii. 40.

τρέμω, to tremble, Mar. v. 33; Lu. viii. 47; Ac. ix. 6 (W. H. omit); to be afraid, 2 Pet. ii. 10.*

τρέφω, θρέψω, perf. pass. part. τεθραμμένος, to feed, to nourish, Mat. vi. 26; Ac. xii. 20; Ja. v. 5; to bring up, rear, Lu. iv. 16.

τρέχω, 2d aor. ἔδραμον, (1) to run, in general, Lu. xv. 20; (2) to exert one's self, Ro. ix. 16; (3) to make progress, as doctrine, 2 Th. iii. 1.

τρῆμα, ατος, τό, a perforation, the eye of a needle, Mat. xix. 24 (W. H.); Lu. xviii. 25 (W. H.).*

τριάκοντα, οἱ, αἱ, τά, indecl., thirty, Mat. xiii. 8.

τριακόσιοι, αι, α, three hundred, Mar. xiv. 5; Jn. xii. 5.*

τρίβολος, ου, ὁ, a thistle, Mat. vii. 16; Heb. vi. 8.*

τρίβος, ου, ἡ, a worn path, a beaten way, Mat. iii. 3; Mar. i. 3; Lu. iii. 4.*

τρι-ετία, ας, ἡ, a space of three years, Ac. xx. 31.*

τρίζω, to grate, to gnash, as the teeth, Mar. ix. 18.*

τρί-μηνος, ον, of three months, neut. as subst., Heb. xi. 23.*

τρίς, num. adv., thrice, Mat. xxvi. 34, 75.

τρί-στεγος, ον, having three stories; neut., the third story, Ac. xx. 9.*

τρισ-χίλιοι, αι, α, three thousand, Ac. ii. 41.*

τρίτος, η, ον, ord. num., third; neut. τὸ τρίτον, the third part, Rev. viii. 7; the third time, Mar. xiv. 41; ἐκ τρίτου, the third time, Mat. xxvi. 44; τῇ τρίτῃ (sc. ἡμέρᾳ), on the third day, Lu. xiii. 32.

τρίχες, plur. of θρίξ, which see.

τρίχινος, η, ον, made of hair, Rev. vi. 12.*

τρόμος, ου, ὁ, a trembling, from
fear, Mar. xvi. 8.

τροπή, ῆς, ἡ, a turning, Ja. i.
17 (see R.V.).*

τρόπος, ου, ὁ, (1) way, manner;
ὃν τρόπον, in like manner
as, as, Mat. xxiii. 37; (2)
manner of life, character,
Heb. xiii. 5.

τροπο-φορέω, ῶ, ἥσω, to bear
with the disposition or character of others, Ac. xiii. 18
(Rec. W. H., some read ἐτρο-
φοφόρησεν, he bore them as a
nurse). (S.)*

τροφή, ῆς, ἡ, food, nourishment, Mat. iii. 4, vi. 25.

Τρόφιμος, ου, ὁ, Trophimus,
Ac. xx. 4, xxi. 29; 2 Tim. iv.
20.*

τροφός, οῦ, ἡ, a nurse, 1 Th. ii.
7.*

τροφο-φορέω, ῶ, see τροπο-
φορέω.

τροχιά, ᾶς, ἡ, a track of a
wheel, a path, fig., Heb. xii.
13.*

τροχός, οῦ, ὁ, a wheel, Ja. iii.
6.*

τρύβλιον, ου, τό, a deep dish, a
platter, Mat. xxvi. 23; Mar.
xiv. 20.*

τρυγάω, ῶ, ἥσω, to gather, as
the vintage, Lu. vi. 44; Rev.
xiv. 18, 19.*

τρυγών, όνος, ἡ (τρύζω), a turtle-
dove, Lu. ii. 24.*

τρυμαλιά, ᾶς, ἡ, the eye of a
needle, Mar. x. 25; Lu. xviii.
25 (W. H. τρῆμα).*

τρύπημα, ατος, τό, a hole, the
eye of a needle, Mat. xix. 24
(W. H. text τρῆμα).*

Τρύφαινα, ης, ἡ, Tryphæna, Ro.
xvi. 12.*

τρυφάω, ῶ, ἥσω, to live luxuriously and effeminately, Ja. v.
5.* Syn.: see σπαταλάω.

τρυφή, ῆς, ἡ, effeminate luxury,
Lu. vii. 25; 2 Pet. ii. 13.*

Τρυφῶσα, ης, ἡ, Tryphosa, Ro.
xvi. 12.*

Τρῳάς, άδος, ἡ, Troas, a city of
Mysia, properly Alexandria
Troas, Ac. xvi. 8, 11.

Τρωγύλλιον, ου, τό, Trogyllium,
Ac. xx. 15 (W. H. omit).*

τρώγω, to eat, Mat. xxiv. 38;
Jn. vi. 54–58, xiii. 18.*

τυγχάνω, 2d aor. ἔτυχον, perf.
τέτυχα, (1) to obtain, to get
possession of (gen.), Lu. xx.
35; Ac. xxiv. 2; (2) to fall

out, to happen, to happen to
be; εἰ τύχοι, if it should
chance, it may be, perhaps,
1 Cor. xiv. 10; 2d aor., part.,
τυχών, ordinary, common-
place, Ac. xix. 11; neut. τυχόν, it may be, perhaps, 1
Cor. xvi. 6.

τυμπανίζω, to beat to death when
stretched on a wheel, Heb.
xi. 35.*

τυπικῶς, adv., typically, by way
of example, 1 Cor. x. 11 (W.
H.). (N. T.)*

τύπος, ου, ὁ, (1) a mark, an impression, produced by a blow,
Jn. xx. 25; (2) the figure of
a thing, a pattern, Ac. vii.
44; Heb. viii. 5; (3) an emblem, an example, 1 Cor. x.
6; Phil. iii. 17; (4) the form
or contents of a letter, Ac.
xxiii. 25; (5) a type, Ro. v.
14.

τύπτω, ψω, to beat, to strike,
as the breast in grief, Lu.
xviii. 13; to inflict punishment, Ac. xxiii. 3; to wound
or disquiet the conscience, 1
Cor. viii. 12.

Τύραννος, ου, ὁ, Tyrannus, Ac.
xix. 9.*

τυρβάζω, to agitate or disturb
in mind, Lu. x. 41 (W. H.
θορυβάζω).*

Τύριος, ου, ὁ, ἡ (prop. adj.), a
Tyrian, an inhabitant of
Tyre, Ac. xii. 20.*

Τύρος, ου, ἡ, Tyre, a city of
Phœnicia, Mat. xi. 21, 22.

τυφλός, ή, όν, blind, (1) physically, Lu. xiv. 13, 21; (2)
mentally, i.e., stupid, dull of
apprehension, Ro. ii. 19; 2
Pet. i. 9.

τυφλόω, ῶ, ώσω, fig., to make
blind or dull of apprehension, Jn. xii. 40; 2 Cor. iv. 4;
1 Jn. ii. 11.*

τυφόω, ῶ, to raise a smoke;
pass., fig., to be proud, to
be arrogant and conceited,
1 Tim. iii. 6, vi. 4; 2 Tim.
iii. 4.*

τύφω, pres. pass. part. τυφό-
μενος, smoking, Mat. xii.
20.*

τυφωνικός, ή, όν, violent, tempestuous, Ac. xxvii. 14.*

Τυχικός, or Τύχικος (W. H.),
ου, ὁ, Tychichus, 2 Tim. iv.
12.

τυχόν, see τυγχάνω.

Υ

Υ, υ, ὑψῖλον, upsilon, u, the
twentieth letter. As a numeral, υʹ = 400; ͵υ = 400,000.
At the commencement of a
word, υ is always aspirated.

ὑακίνθινος, η, ον, of the color of
hyacinth, dark purple, Rev.
ix. 17.*

ὑάκινθος, ου, ὁ, a precious stone
of the color of hyacinth,
jacinth, Rev. xxi. 20.*

ὑάλινος, η, ον, glassy, transparent, Rev. iv. 6, xv. 2.*

ὕαλος, ου, ὁ, glass, Rev. xxi.
18, 21.*

ὑβρίζω, σω, to treat with insolence, to insult, Mat. xxii.
6; Lu. xi. 45.

ὕβρις, εως, ἡ, (1) insolence, insult, 2 Cor. xii. 10; (2) damage, loss, Ac. xxvii. 10, 21.*

ὑβριστής, οῦ, ὁ, an insolent, in-
sulting man, Ro. i. 30; 1 Tim.
i. 13.*

ὑγιαίνω, to be well, to be in
health, Lu. v. 31, xv. 27;
fig., to be sound, in (ἐν) faith,
doctrine, etc., Tit. i. 13; part.
ὑγιαίνων, healthful, wholesome, of instruction, 1 Tim.
i. 10.

ὑγιής, ές, (1) sound, whole, in
health, Mat. xii. 13; Jn. v.
11, 15; (2) fig., wholesome,
of teaching, Tit. ii. 8.

ὑγρός, ά, όν, moist, green, i.e.,
full of sap, Lu. xxiii. 31.*

ὑδρία, ας, ἡ, a water-pot, Jn. ii.
6, 7, iv. 28.*

ὑδρο-ποτέω, ῶ, to be a water-
drinker, 1 Tim. v. 23.*

ὑδρωπικός, ή, όν, dropsical, Lu.
xiv. 2.*

ὕδωρ, ὕδατος, τό, water; ὕδατα,
waters, streams, Jn. iii. 23;
also a body of water, as Mat.
xiv. 28; ὕδωρ ζῶν, living or
running water; fig., of spiritual truth, Jn. iv. 14.

ὑετός, οῦ, ὁ (ὕω, to rain), rain,
Heb. vi. 7.

υἱο-θεσία, ας, ἡ, adoption as a
son, into the divine family,
Ro. viii. 15, 23, ix. 4: Gal.
iv. 5; Ep. i. 5.*

υἱός, οῦ, ὁ, a son, Mat. x. 37;
a descendant, Lu. xx. 41,
44; the offspring or young
of an animal, Mat. xxi. 5;
an adopted son, Heb. xi. 24 ·
of various forms of close

union and relationship (see τέκνον); *a disciple* or *follower*, Mat. xii. 27; *one who resembles* (gen.), Mat. v. 45; *one who partakes of any quality* or *character*, Lu. x. 6; Jn. xii. 36; ὁ υἱὸς τοῦ ἀνθρώπου, *son of man* (once only without art., Jn. v. 27), very often used by our Lord of himself (only once by another of him, Ac. vii. 56); *sons of men* denote *men* generally, Mar. iii. 28; Ep. iii. 5; υἱὸς τοῦ θεοῦ, *son of God*, used of men, Lu. xx. 36; Heb. ii. 10; usually of Christ, Mat. viii. 29; Jn. ix. 35; see also Gr. § 217 c.

ὕλη, ης, ἡ, *wood, fuel*, Ja. iii. 5.*

ὑμεῖς, plur. of σύ, which see.

Ὑμέναιος, ου, ὁ, *Hymenæus*, 1 Tim. i. 20; 2 Tim. ii. 17.*

ὑμέτερος, α, ον, possess. pron., *your*, as belonging to, or as proceeding from; for the use of the article with the word, see Gr. § 223.

ὑμνέω, ῶ, ήσω, *to sing hymns to* (acc.), Ac. xvi. 25; Heb. ii. 12; *to sing*, Mat. xxvi. 30; Mar. xiv. 26.*

ὕμνος, ου, ὁ, *a hymn, a sacred song*, Ep. v. 19; Col. iii. 16.* *Syn.*: ψαλμός is used of the Psalms of the O. T.; ὕμνος designates a song of *praise to God*; ᾠδή is a general expression for a song.

ὑπ-άγω, *to go away, to depart*, Mar. vi. 31; Jn. vi. 67; imperat., sometimes an expression of aversion, *begone*, Mat. iv. 10; sometimes a farewell only, Mat. viii. 13, 32; *to die*, Mat. xxvi. 24.

ὑπ-ακοή, ῆς, ἡ, *obedience*, Ro. vi. 16. (S.)

ὑπ-ακούω, σω, (1) *to listen*, as at a door, to find who seeks admission, only Ac. xii. 13; (2) *to hearken to*; hence, *to obey* (dat.), Mat. viii. 27; Heb. xi. 8.

ὑπ-ανδρος, ον, *subject to a husband, married*, Ro. vii. 2.*

ὑπ-αντάω, ῶ, ήσω, *to meet* (dat.), Mat. viii. 28.

ὑπ-άντησις, εως, ἡ, *a meeting*, Mat. viii. 34 (W. H.), xxv. 1 (W. H.); Jn. xii. 13. (S.)*

ὕπαρξις, εως, ἡ, *goods, substance*, property, Ac. ii. 45; Heb. x. 34.*

ὑπ-άρχω, *to begin to be; to be originally, to subsist;* hence generally, *to be*, Lu. viii. 41; Ac. xxi. 20; with dat. of pers., *to have, to possess*, Ac. iii. 6, iv. 37; part., neut. pl., τὰ ὑπάρχοντα, *things which one possesses, goods, property*, Mat. xix. 21.

ὑπ-είκω, *to yield, to submit to authority*, Heb. xiii. 17.*

ὑπ-εναντίος, α, ον, *opposite to, adverse*, Col. ii. 14; as subst., *an adversary*, Heb. x. 27.*

ὑπέρ, prep., gov. gen. and acc.: with gen., *over, for, on behalf of;* with acc., *above, superior to* (see Gr. § 303, Wi. § 47 l, Bu. 335); adverbially, *above, more*, 2 Cor. xi. 23. In composition, ὑπέρ denotes *superiority* (above), or *aid* (on behalf of).

ὑπερ-αίρω, in mid., *to lift up one's self, to exalt one's self, to be arrogant*, 2 Cor. xii. 7; 2 Th. ii. 4.*

ὑπέρ-ακμος, ον, *past the bloom of youth*, 1 Cor. vii. 36.*

ὑπερ-άνω, adv. (gen.), *above*, Ep. i. 21, iv. 10; Heb. ix. 5.*

ὑπερ-αυξάνω, *to increase exceedingly*, 2 Th. i. 3.*

ὑπερ-βαίνω, *to go beyond, to overreach, defraud*, 1 Th. iv. 6.*

ὑπερ-βαλλόντως, adv., *beyond measure*, 2 Cor. xi. 23.*

ὑπερ-βάλλω, intrans., *to surpass;* N.T., only pres. part. ὑπερβάλλων, *surpassing, excelling*, 2 Cor. iii. 10, ix. 14; Ep. i. 19, ii. 7, iii. 19.*

ὑπερ-βολή, ῆς, ἡ, *excess, surpassing excellence, pre-eminence*, 2 Cor. iv. 7, xii. 7; καθ' ὑπερβολήν, as adv., *exceedingly*, Ro. vii. 13; 1 Cor. xii. 31; 2 Cor. i. 8; Gal. i. 13; καθ' ὑπερβολὴν εἰς ὑπερβολήν, *more and more exceedingly* (R. V.), 2 Cor. iv. 17.*

ὑπερ-είδον, *to overlook, to take no notice of*, Ac. xvii. 30.*

ὑπερ-έκεινα, adv., *beyond*, 2 Cor. x. 16. (N. T.)*

ὑπερ-εκ-περισσοῦ, adv., *beyond all measure, in the highest degree*, Ep. iii. 20; 1 Th. iii. 10, v. 13.*

ὑπερ-εκ-τείνω, *to stretch out beyond measure*, 2 Cor. x. 14.*

ὑπερ-εκ-χύνω, pass., *to be poured out, to overflow*, Lu. vi. 38.*

ὑπερ-εν-τυγχάνω, *to intercede for*, Ro. viii. 26. (N. T.)*

ὑπερ-έχω, *to excel, to surpass* (gen.), *to be supreme;* N.T. only pres. part., Ro. xiii. 1; Phil. ii. 3, iv. 7; 1 Pet. ii. 13; part. neut. τὸ ὑπερέχον, *excellency, super-eminence*, Phil. iii. 8.*

ὑπερηφανία, ας, ἡ, *pride, arrogance*, Mar. vii. 22.*

ὑπερ-ήφανος, ον, *proud, arrogant*, Ja. iv. 6.

ὑπερ-λίαν, adv., *very much, pre-eminently*, 2 Cor. xi. 5, xii. 11.*

ὑπερ-νικάω, ῶ, *to be more than conqueror*, Ro. viii. 37. (N. T.)*

ὑπέρ-ογκος, ον, *immoderate, boastful*, of language, 2 Pet. ii. 18; Ju. 16.*

ὑπερ-οχή, ῆς, ἡ, *superiority, excellence*, 1 Cor. ii. 1; 1 Tim. ii. 2.*

ὑπερ-περισσεύω, *to superabound*, Ro. v. 20; pass., *to be very abundant in* (dat.), 2 Cor. vii. 4. (N. T.)*

ὑπερ-περισσῶς, adv., *superabundantly, beyond measure*, Mar. vii. 37. (N. T.)*

ὑπερ-πλεονάζω, *to be exceedingly abundant*, 1 Tim. i. 14.*

ὑπερ-υψόω, ῶ, *to highly exalt*, Phil. ii. 9. (S.)*

ὑπερ-φρονέω, ῶ, *to think too highly of one's self*, Ro. xii. 3.*

ὑπερῷον, ου, τό, *the upper part of a house, an upper chamber*, Ac. i. 13, ix. 37, 39, xx. 8.*

ὑπ-έχω, *to submit to, to undergo* (acc.), Ju. 7.*

ὑπ-ήκοος, ον, *listening to, obedient*, Ac. vii. 39; 2 Cor. ii. 9; Phil. ii. 8.*

ὑπηρετέω, ῶ, *to minister to, to serve* (dat.), Ac. xiii. 36, xx. 34, xxiv. 23.*

ὑπηρέτης, ου, ὁ (ἐρέτης, *a rower*), *a servant, attendant*, specially (1) *an officer, a lictor*, Mat. v. 25; (2) *an attendant in a synagogue*, Lu. iv. 20; (3) *a minister of the gospel*, Ac. xxvi. 16.

ὕπνος, ου, ὁ, *sleep*, Lu. ix. 32;

fig., *spiritual sleep*, Ro. xiii. 11.

ὑπό, prep., gov. gen. and acc., *under*: with gen., *by*, generally signifying the agent; with acc., *under, beneath*, of place, of time, or of subjection to authority (see Gr. § 304, Wi. §§ 47*b*, 49*k*, Bu. 340 sq.). In composition, ὑπό denotes *subjection, diminution, concealment*.

ὑπο-βάλλω, *to suborn, to instruct privately*, Ac. vi. 11.*

ὑπο-γραμμός, οῦ, ὁ, *a writing-copy; an example*, 1 Pet. ii. 21.*

ὑπό-δειγμα, ατος, τό, (1) *a figure, copy*, Heb. viii. 5, ix. 23; (2) *an example* for imitation, or for warning, Jn. xiii. 15; Heb. iv. 11; 2 Pet. ii. 6; Ja. v. 10.*

ὑπο-δείκνυμι, δείξω, *to show plainly, to teach, to warn*, Mat. iii. 7; Lu. iii. 7, vi. 47, xii. 5; Ac. ix. 16, xx. 35.*

ὑπο-δέχομαι, *to receive as a guest* (acc.), Lu. x. 38, xix. 6; Ac. xvii. 7, Ja. ii. 25.*

ὑπο-δέω, ῶ, ήσω, in mid., *to bind on one's sandals, be shod with* (acc.), Mar. vi. 9; Ac. xii. 8; Ep. vi. 15 (lit., *shod as to your feet*).*

ὑπόδημα, ατος, τό, *a sandal*, Mat. iii. 11, x. 10.

ὑπό-δικος, ον, *subject to judgment, under penalty to* (dat.), Ro. iii. 19.*

ὑπο-ζύγιον, ου, τό, *an animal under yoke, an ass*, Mat. xxi. 5; 2 Pet. ii. 16.*

ὑπο-ζώννυμι, *to under-gird*, as a ship for strength against the waves, Ac. xxvii. 17.*

ὑπο-κάτω, adv., *underneath* (as prep. with gen.), Rev. v. 3, 13.

ὑπο-κρίνομαι, dep., *to act under a mask, to personate, to feign* (acc., inf.), Lu. xx. 20.*

ὑπό-κρισις, εως, ἡ, lit., *stage playing; hypocrisy, dissembling*, 1 Tim. iv. 2.

ὑπο-κριτής, οῦ, ὁ, lit., *a stage player; a hypocrite, a dissembler*, Mat. vi. 2, 5, 16.

ὑπο-λαμβάνω, 2d aor. ὑπέλαβον, (1) *to take from under, to receive up*, Ac. i. 9; (2) *to take up a discourse, to answer*, Lu. x. 30; (3) *to think, to*

suppose, Lu. vii. 43; Ac. ii. 15; (4) *to receive, welcome*, 3 Jn. 8 (W. H.).*

ὑπό-λειμμα (or -λιμμα), ατος, τό, *a remnant*, Ro. ix. 27 (W. H.).*

ὑπο-λείπω, *to leave behind*, pass., Ro. xi. 3.*

ὑπο-λήνιον, ου, τό (ληνός), *a wine-vat, a pit under the wine-press*, dug in the ground, Mar. xii. 1. (S.)*

ὑπο-λιμπάνω, *to leave behind*, 1 Pet. ii. 21.*

ὑπο-μένω, μενῶ, (1) *to remain, tarry behind*, Lu. ii. 43; (2) *to bear up under, to endure* (acc.), 1 Pet. ii. 20; (3) *to persevere, to remain constant*, Mat. x. 22.

ὑπο-μιμνήσκω, ὑπομνήσω, 1st aor. pass. ὑπεμνήσθην, *to remind* (acc. of pers.), Jn. xiv. 26; mid., *to be reminded, to remember*, only Lu. xxii. 61.

ὑπό-μνησις, εως, ἡ, (1) *remembrance, recollection*, 2 Tim. i. 5; (2) *a putting in mind*, 2 Pet. i. 13, iii. 1.*

ὑπο-μονή, ῆς, ἡ, *a bearing up under, endurance, steadfastness, patient waiting for* (gen.), Lu. viii. 15; 2 Th. iii. 5. *Syn.*: see ἀνοχή.

ὑπο-νοέω, ῶ, *to conjecture, to suppose*, Ac. xiii. 25, xxv. 18, xxvii. 27.*

ὑπό-νοια, ας, ἡ, *a surmising, suspicion*, 1 Tim. vi. 4.*

ὑπο-πλέω, 1st aor. ὑπέπλευσα, *to sail under, i.e.*, to leeward of (acc.), Ac. xxvii. 4, 7.*

ὑπο-πνέω, 1st aor. ὑπέπνευσα, *to blow gently*, of the wind, Ac. xxvii. 13.*

ὑπο-πόδιον, ου, τό, *a footstool*, Lu. xx. 43; Ac. ii. 35.

ὑπό-στασις, εως, ἡ, *that which underlies; hence*, (1) *the substance, the reality* underlying mere appearance, Heb. i. 3; (2) *confidence, assurance*, 2 Cor. ix. 4, xi. 17; Heb. iii. 14, xi. 1.*

ὑπο-στέλλω, 1st aor. ὑπέστειλα, *to draw back*, Gal. ii. 12; mid., *to shrink, to draw one's self back*, Ac. xx. 27; Heb. x. 38; *to withhold, conceal* (acc.), Ac. xx. 20.*

ὑπο-στολή, ῆς, ἡ, *a shrinking, a drawing back*, Heb. x. 39.*

ὑπο-στρέφω, ψω, *to turn back*,

to return, intrans., Lu. ii. 43, viii. 37, 40.

ὑπο-στρώννυμι, or -ωννύω, *to spread under*, Lu. xix. 36. (S.)*

ὑπο-ταγή, ῆς, ἡ, *subjection, submission*, 2 Cor. ix. 13; Gal. ii. 5; 1 Tim. ii. 11, iii. 4.*

ὑπο-τάσσω, ξω, 2d aor. pass. ὑπετάγην, *to place under, to subject*, 1 Cor. xv. 27; mid., *to submit one's self, to be obedient*, Ro. xiii. 5; Ep. v. 21.

ὑπο-τίθημι, *to set* or *put under, to lay down*, Ro. xvi. 4; mid., *to suggest to, put in mind*, 1 Tim. iv. 6.*

ὑπο-τρέχω, 2d aor. ὑπέδραμον, *to run under* lee or shelter of, Ac. xxvii. 16.*

ὑπο-τύπωσις, εως, ἡ, *pattern, example*, 1 Tim. i. 16; 2 Tim. i. 13.*

ὑπο-φέρω, 1st aor. ὑπήνεγκα, *to bear up under, to sustain, to endure*, 1 Cor. x. 13; 2 Tim. iii. 11; 1 Pet. ii. 19.*

ὑπο-χωρέω, ῶ, ήσω, *to withdraw, to retire*, Lu. v. 16, ix. 10.*

ὑπωπιάζω, *to strike under the eye; hence*, (1) *to bruise; fig., to buffet*, 1 Cor. ix. 27; (2) *to weary out*, by repeated application, Lu. xviii. 5.*

ὗς, ὑός, ὁ, ἡ, *a hog, boar* or *sow*, 2 Pet. ii. 22.*

ὕσσωπος, ου, ἡ (from Heb.), *hyssop, a stalk* or *stem of hyssop*, Jn. xix. 29; *a bunch of hyssop* for sprinkling, Heb. ix. 19. (S.)*

ὑστερέω, ῶ, ήσω, *to be behind; abs., to be lacking, to fall short*, Jn. ii. 3; with obj., *to be lacking* in, acc., Mat. xix. 20; gen., Lu. xxii. 35; ἀπό, Heb. xii. 15; *to be lacking*, Mar. x. 21; pass., *to lack, to come short*, 1 Cor i. 7, viii. 8; *to suffer need*, Lu. xv. 14.

ὑστέρημα, ατος, τό, (1) *that which is lacking* from (gen.), Col. i. 24; 1 Th. iii. 10; (2) *poverty, destitution*, Lu. xxi. 4. (S.)

ὑστέρησις, εως, ἡ, *poverty, penury*, Mar. xii. 44; Phil. iv. 11. (N. T.)*

ὕστερος, α, ον, compar., *later*, only 1 Tim. iv. 1 and Mat. xxi. 31 (W. H.); neut. as an adv., *lastly, afterward,* with gen., Mat. xxii. 27; Lu. xx. 32.

ὑφαντός, ή, όν (ὑφαίνω, to weave), woven, Jn. xix. 23.*

ὑψηλός, ή, όν, high, lofty, lit. or fig., τὰ ὑψηλά, things that are high, Ro. xii. 16; ἐν ὑψηλοῖς, on high, Heb. i. 3.

ὑψηλο-φρονέω, ῶ, to be high-minded, proud, Ro. xi. 20 (W. H. ὑψηλὰ φρόνει); 1 Tim. vi. 17. (N. T.)*

ὕψιστος, η, ον (superlat. of ὕψι, highly), highest, most high; neut., plur., the highest places, the heights, i.e., heaven, Lu. ii. 14; ὁ ὕψιστος, the Most High, i.e., God, Ac. vii. 48, xvi. 17; Lu. i. 32, 35, 76.

ὕψος, ους, τό, height, opp. to βάθος, Ep. iii. 18; Rev. xxi. 16; ἐξ ὕψους, from on high, i.e., from heaven, Lu. i. 78, xxiv. 49; so εἰς ὕψος, to heaven, Ep. iv. 8; fig., high station, Ja. i. 9.*

ὑψόω, ῶ, ώσω, (1) to raise on high, to lift up, as the brazen serpent, and Jesus on the cross, Jn. iii. 14, viii. 28; (2) to exalt, to set on high, Ac. ii. 33; Mat. xxiii. 12.

ὕψωμα, ατος, τό, height, Ro. viii. 39; barrier, bulwark (fig.), 2 Cor. x. 5.*

Φ

Φ, φ, φῖ, phi, ph, the twenty-first letter. As a numeral, φ' = 500; ͵φ = 500,000.

φάγος, ου, ὁ, a glutton, Mat. xi. 19; Lu. vii. 34. (N. T.)*

φάγω, only used in fut. φάγομαι, and 2d aor. ἔφαγον; see ἐσθίω.

φαιλόνης, ου, ὁ (W. H. φελόνης), (Lat. pænula), a traveling-cloak, 2 Tim. iv. 13. (N. T.)*

φαίνω, φανῶ, 2d aor. pass. ἐφάνην, (1) trans., to show, in N.T. only mid. or pass., to appear, to be seen, to seem; τὰ φαινόμενα, things which can be seen, Heb. xi. 3; (2) intrans., to shine, to give light, Jn. i. 5, v. 35. Syn.. see δοκέω.

Φάλεκ, ὁ (Heb.), Peleg, Lu. iii. 35.*

φανερός, ά, όν, apparent, manifest, Ac. iv. 16; Gal. v. 19;

ἐν τῷ φανερῷ, as adv., manifestly, openly, Ro. ii. 28.

φανερόω, ῶ, ώσω, to make apparent, to manifest, to disclose, Jn. vii. 4, xxi. 11; pass., to be manifested, made manifest, 1 Tim. iii. 16; 2 Cor. v. 11.

φανερῶς, adv., clearly, Ac. x. 3; openly, Mar. i. 45; Jn. vii. 10.*

φανέρωσις, εως, ή, a manifestation (gen. obj.), 1 Cor. xii. 7; 2 Cor. iv. 2.* Syn.: see ἀποκάλυψις.

φανός, οῦ, ὁ, a torch, a lantern, Jn. xviii. 3.*

Φανουήλ, ὁ (Heb.), Phanuel, Lu. ii. 36.*

φαντάζω, to cause to appear; pass. part. τὸ φανταζόμενον, the appearance, Heb. xii. 21.*

φαντασία, ας, ή, display, pomp, Ac. xxv. 23.*

φάντασμα, ατος, τό, an apparition, a spectre, Mat. xiv. 26; Mar. vi. 49.*

φάραγξ, αγγος, ή, a valley, ravine, Lu. iii. 5.*

Φαραώ, ὁ, Pharaoh, the title of ancient Egyptian kings, Ac. vii. 13, 21.

Φαρές, ὁ (Heb.), Phares, Mat. i. 3; Lu. iii. 33.*

Φαρισαῖος, ου, ὁ (from the Heb. verb, to separate), a Pharisee, one of the Jewish sect so called, Mar. ii. 16, 18, 24. (N. T.)

φαρμακεία (W. H. -κία), ας, ή, magic, sorcery, enchantment, Gal. v. 20; Rev. ix. 21 (W. H. φάρμακον), xviii. 23.*

φαρμακεύς, έως, ὁ, a magician, sorcerer, Rev. xxi. 8 (W. H. read following).*

φάρμακον, ου, τό, a drug; an enchantment, Rev. ix. 21 (W. H.).*

φαρμακός, οῦ, ὁ (prop. adj.), a magician, sorcerer, Rev. xxi. 8 (W. H.), xxii. 15.*

φάσις, εως, ή, report, tidings, Ac. xxi. 31.*

φάσκω (freq. of φημί), to assert, to affirm, to profess, Ac. xxiv. 9, xxv. 19; Ro. i. 22; Rev. ii. 2 (W. H. omit).*

φάτνη, ης, ή, a manger, a crib, Lu. ii. 7, 12, 16, xiii. 15.*

φαῦλος, η, ον, good for nothing, wicked, base, Jn. iii. 20, v. 29; Ro. ix. 11 (W. H.); 2

Cor. v. 10 (W. H.); Tit. ii. 8; Ja. iii. 16.*

φέγγος, ους, τό, brightness, light, Mat. xxiv. 29; Mar. xiii. 24; Lu. xi. 33 (W. H. φῶς). Syn.: see λαμπάς.

φείδομαι, φείσομαι, dep., (1) to spare (gen.), Ac. xx. 29; (2) to abstain (inf.), 2 Cor. xii. 6.

φειδομένως, adv., sparingly, 2 Cor. ix. 6.*

φελόνης, see φαιλόνης.

φέρω, οἴσω, ἤνεγκα, ἠνέχθην (see Gr. § 103, Wi. § 15, Bu. 68), to bear, as (1) to carry, as a burden, Lu. xxiii. 26; (2) to produce fruit, Jn. xii. 24; (3) to bring, Ac. v. 16; (4) to endure, to bear with, Ro. ix. 22; (5) to bring forward, as charges, Jn. xviii. 29; (6) to uphold, Heb. i. 3; (7) pass., as nautical term, to be borne along, Ac. xxvii. 15, 17; (8) mid., to rush (bear itself on), Ac. ii. 2; to go on or advance, in learning, Heb. vi. 1. Syn.: φορέω means to bear something habitually and continuously, while in φέρω it is temporary bearing, and on special occasions.

φεύγω, ξομαι, ἔφυγον, to flee, to escape, to shun (acc. or ἀπό), Mat. viii. 33; 1 Cor. vi. 18; Heb. xii. 34; Rev. xvi. 20.

Φῆλιξ, ικος, ὁ, Felix, Ac. xxv. 14.

φήμη, ης, ή, a report, fame, Mat. ix. 26; Lu. iv. 14.*

φημί, impf. ἔφην (for other tenses, see εἶπον), to say, with ὅτι, dat. of pers., πρός (acc.), with pers., acc. of thing (once acc., inf., Ro. iii. 8).

Φῆστος, ου, ὁ, Festus, Ac. xxv. 1, 4, 9.

φθάνω, φθάσω, perf. ἔφθακα, (1) to be before, to precede, 1 Th. iv. 15; (2) to arrive, attain to (εἰς, ἄχρι, ἐπί), Mat. xii. 28; Lu. xi. 20; Ro. ix. 31; 2 Cor. x. 14; Phil. iii. 16; 1 Th. ii. 16.*

φθαρτός, ή, όν (φθείρω), corruptible, perishable, Ro. i. 23; 1 Cor. ix. 25, xv. 53, 54; 1 Pet. i. 18, 23.*

φθέγγομαι, γξομαι, dep., to speak aloud, to utter, Ac. iv. 18; 2 Pet. ii. 16, 18.*

φθείρω, φθερῶ, 2d aor. pass. ἐφθάρην, to corrupt, physically or morally, to spoil, to destroy, 2 Cor. vii. 2; Rev. xix. 2.

φθιν-οπωρινός, ή, όν, autumnal, Ju. 12.*

φθόγγος, ου, ὁ (φθέγγομαι), a sound, Ro. x. 18; 1 Cor. xiv. 7.*

φθονέω, ῶ, to envy (dat.), Gal. v. 26.*

φθόνος, ου, ὁ, envy, Phil. i. 15; Tit. iii. 3.

φθορά, ᾶς, ἡ (φθείρω), corruption, destruction, physical or moral, 1 Cor. xv. 42; 2 Pet. i. 4.

φιάλη, ης, ἡ, a bowl, broad and flat, Rev. v. 8, xv. 7.

φιλ-άγαθος, ον, loving goodness, Tit. i. 8.*

Φιλαδέλφεια, ας, ἡ, Philadelphia, Rev. i. 11, iii. 7.*

φιλαδελφία, ας, ἡ, brotherly love, love of Christian brethren, Ro. xii. 10; 1 Th. iv. 9; Heb. xiii. 1; 1 Pet. i. 22; 2 Pet. i. 7.*

φιλ-άδελφος, ον, loving the brethren, 1 Pet. iii. 8.*

φίλ-ανδρος, ον, loving one's husband, Tit. ii. 4.*

φιλ-ανθρωπία, ας, ἡ, love of mankind, benevolence, Ac. xxviii. 2; Tit. iii. 4.*

φιλ-ανθρώπως, adv., humanely, kindly, Ac. xxvii. 3.*

φιλαργυρία, ας, ἡ, love of money, avarice, 1 Tim. vi. 10.* Syn.: see πλεονεξία.

φιλ-άργυρος, ον, money-loving, avaricious, Lu. xvi. 14; 2 Tim. iii. 2.*

φίλ-αυτος, ον, self-loving, selfish, 2 Tim. iii. 2.*

φιλέω, ῶ, ήσω, (1) to love, Mat. vi. 5, x. 37; Lu. xx. 46; (2) to kiss, Mat. xxvi. 48. Syn.: see ἀγαπάω.

φίλη, ἡ, see φίλος.

φιλ-ήδονος, ον, pleasure-loving, 2 Tim. iii. 4.*

φίλημα, ατος, τό, a kiss, Lu. vii. 45; Ro. xvi. 16.

Φιλήμων, ονος, ὁ, Philemon, Philem. 1.*

Φίλητος, or Φιλητός, ου, ὁ, Philetus, 2 Tim. ii. 17.*

φιλία, ας, ἡ, friendship, Ja. iv. 4 (gen. obj.).*

Φιλιππήσιος, ου, ὁ, a Philippian, Phil. iv. 15.*

Φίλιπποι, ων, οἱ, Philippi, Ac. xvi. 12, xx. 6.

Φίλιππος, ου, ὁ, Philip. Four of the name are mentioned: (1) Jn. i. 44–47; (2) Ac. vi. 5; (3) Lu. iii. 1; (4) Mat. xiv. 3.

Φιλό-θεος, ον, loving God, 2 Tim. iii. 4.*

Φιλό-λογος, ου, ὁ, Philologus, Ro. xvi. 15.*

φιλονεικία, ας, ἡ, love of dispute, contention, Lu. xxii. 24.*

φιλό-νεικος, ον, strife-loving, contentious, 1 Cor. xi. 16.*

φιλοξενία, ας, ἡ, love to strangers, hospitality, Ro. xii. 13; Heb. xiii. 2.*

φιλό-ξενος, ον, hospitable, 1 Tim. iii. 2; Tit. i. 8; 1 Pet. iv. 9.*

φιλο-πρωτεύω, to love the first place, to desire pre-eminence, 3 Jn. 9. (N.T.)

φίλος, η, ον, friendly; ὁ φίλος, as subst., a friend, Lu. vii. 6, xi. 5; an associate, Mat. xi. 19; ἡ φίλη, a female friend, only Lu. xv. 9.

φιλοσοφία, ας, ἡ, love of wisdom, philosophy, in N.T. of the Jewish traditional theology, Col. ii. 8.*

φιλό-σοφος, ου, ὁ (prop. adj., wisdom-loving), a philosopher, in N.T. of Greek philosophers, Ac. xvii. 18.*

φιλό-στοργος, ον, tenderly loving, kindly affectionate to (εἰς), Ro. xii. 10.*

φιλό-τεκνος, ον, loving one's children, Tit. ii. 4.*

φιλο-τιμέομαι, οῦμαι, dep., to make a thing one's ambition, to desire very strongly (inf.), Ro. xv. 20; 2 Cor. v. 9; 1 Th. iv. 11.*

φιλοφρόνως, adv., in a friendly manner, kindly, Ac. xxviii. 7.*

φιλό-φρων, ον, friendly, kindly, 1 Pet. iii. 8 (W. H. ταπεινόφρων).*

φιμόω, ῶ, ώσω, to muzzle, 1 Cor. ix. 9; to reduce to silence, Mat. xxii. 34; pass., to be reduced to silence, to be silent, Mat. xxii. 12; of a storm, Mar. iv. 39.

Φλέγων, οντος, ὁ, Phlegon, Ro. xvi. 14.*

φλογίζω, to inflame, to fire with passion, Ja. iii. 6.*

φλόξ, φλογός, ἡ, a flame, Lu. xvi. 24.

φλυαρέω, ῶ, to talk idly, to make empty charges against any one (acc.), 3 Jn. 10.*

φλύαρος, ον, prating; talking foolishly, 1 Tim. v. 13.*

φοβερός, ά, όν, fearful, dreadful, Heb. x. 27, 31, xii. 21.*

φοβέω, ῶ, ήσω, to make afraid, to terrify; in N.T. only passive, to be afraid, to be terrified, sometimes with cognate acc., Mar. iv. 41; to fear (acc.), Mat. x. 26; to reverence, Mar. vi. 20; Lu. i. 50.

φόβητρον (W. H. -θρον), ου, τό, a terrible sight, a cause of terror, Lu. xxi 11.*

φόβος, ου, ὁ, (1) fear, terror, alarm, Mat. xiv. 26; (2) the object or cause of fear, Ro. xiii. 3; (3) reverence, respect, 1 Pet. ii. 18; towards God, Ro. iii. 18; 1 Pet. i. 17. Syn.: see δειλία.

Φοίβη, ης, ἡ, Phœbe, Ro. xvi. 1.*

Φοινίκη, ης, ἡ, Phœnice or Phœnicia, Ac. xi. 19, xv. 3, xxi. 2.

φοῖνιξ, ικος, ὁ, a palm-tree, a palm branch, Jn. xii. 13; Rev. vii. 9.*

Φοῖνιξ, ικος, ὁ, a proper name, Phœnice, a city of Crete, Ac. xxvii. 12.*

φονεύς, έως, ὁ, a murderer, Ac. vii. 52, xxviii. 4.

φονεύω, σω, to murder, Mat. xxiii. 31, 35; Ja. iv. 2.

φόνος, ου, ὁ, murder, slaughter, Heb. xi. 37; Rev. ix. 21.

φορέω, ῶ, έσω, to bear about, to wear, Mat. xi. 8; Jn. xix. 5; Ro. xiii. 4; 1 Cor. xv. 49; Ja. ii. 3.* Syn.: see φέρω.

φόρον, ου, τό (Lat.), forum (see Ἄππιος), Ac. xxviii. 15. (N. T.)

φόρος, ου, ὁ (φέρω), a tax, especially on persons, Lu. xx. 22, xxiii. 2; Ro. xiii. 6, 7.*

φορτίζω, perf. pass. part. πεφορτισμένος, to load, to burden, Mat. xi. 28; Lu. xi. 46.*

φορτίον, ου, τό, a burden, Mat. xi. 30; the freight of a ship, Ac. xxvii. 10 (W. H.); the burden of ceremonial observances, Mat. xxiii. 4; Lu. xi. 46; the burden of faults, Gal. vi. 5.*

φόρτος, ου, ὁ, load, a ship's cargo, Ac. xxvii. 10 (W. H. read φορτίον).*

Φορτουνᾶτος, ου, ὁ (Lat.), *Fortunatus*, 1 Cor. xvi. 17.*

φραγέλλιον, ου, τό (Lat.), *a scourge*, Jn. ii. 15. (N. T.)*

φραγελλόω, ῶ (Lat.), *to flagellate, to scourge*, Mat. xxvii. 26; Mar. xv. 15. (N. T.)*

φραγμός, οῦ, ὁ, *a hedge*, Mat. xxi. 33; Mar. xii. 1; Lu. xiv. 23; fig., *partition*, Ep. ii. 14.*

φράζω, άσω, *to declare, explain, interpret*, Mat. xiii. 36 (not W. H.), xv. 15.*

φράσσω, ξω, *to stop, to close up*, Ro. iii. 19; 2 Cor. xi. 10; Heb. xi. 33.*

φρέαρ, φρέατος, τό, *a pit, a well*, Jn. iv. 11, 12.

φρεναπατάω, ῶ, *to deceive the mind, to impose upon* (acc.), Gal. vi. 3. (N. T.)*

φρεν-απάτης, ου, ὁ, *a mind-deceiver*, Tit. i. 10. (N. T.)*

φρήν, φρενός, ἡ (lit. *diaphragm*), plur. αἱ φρένες, *the mind, the intellect*, 1 Cor. xiv. 20.

φρίσσω, *to shudder*, Ja. ii. 19.*

φρονέω, ῶ, ήσω (φρήν), (1) *to think* (abs.), 1 Cor. xiii. 11; (2) *to think, judge* (acc.), Gal. v. 10; (3) *to direct the mind io, to seek for* (acc.), Ro. viii. 5; (4) *to observe*, a time as sacred, Ro. xiv. 6; (5) with ὑπέρ, *to care for*, Phil. iv. 10.

φρόνημα, ατος, τό, *thought, purpose*, Ro. viii. 6, 7, 27.*

φρόνησις, εως, ἡ, *understanding*, Lu. i. 17; Ep. i. 8.* *Syn.*: see γνῶσις.

φρόνιμος, ον, *intelligent, prudent*, Lu. xii. 42; 1 Cor. x. 15.

φρονίμως, adv., *prudently*, Lu. xvi. 8.*

φροντίζω, *to be thoughtful, to be careful*, inf., Tit. iii. 8.*

φρουρέω, ῶ, *to guard, to keep*, as by a military guard, lit., 2 Cor. xi. 32; fig., Gal. iii. 23 (as if in custody); Phil. iv. 7 (in security); 1 Pet. i. 5 (in reserve).*

φρυάσσω, ξω, *to rage*, Ac. iv. 25. (S.)*

φρύγανον, ου, τό, *a dry stick*, for burning, Ac. xxviii. 3.*

Φρυγία, ας, ἡ, *Phrygia*, Ac. ii. 10, xvi. 6, xviii. 23.

Φύγελλος (W. H. -ελος), ου, ὁ, *Phygellus*, 2 Tim. i. 15.*

φυγή, ῆς, ἡ, *flight*, Mat. xxiv. 20; Mar. xiii. 18 (W. H. omit).*

φυλακή, ῆς, ἡ, (1) *a keeping guard, a watching*, Lu. ii. 8; espec. of the four *watches* into which the night was divided, Mat. xiv. 25, Lu. xii. 38; (2) *a guard*, i.e., men on guard, *a watch*, Ac. xii. 10; (3) *a prison*, Mat. v. 25; (4) *an imprisonment*, 2 Cor. vi. 5.

φυλακίζω, *to imprison*, Ac. xxii. 19. (S.)*

φυλακτήρια, ων, τά (plur. of adj.), *a safeguard, an amulet, a phylactery*, a slip of parchment, with Scripture words thereon, worn by the Jews, Mat. xxiii. 5.*

φύλαξ, ακος, ὁ, *a keeper, sentinel*, Ac. v. 23, xii. 6, 19.*

φυλάσσω, ξω, (1) *to keep guard*, or *watch over*, Ac. xii. 4; (2) *to keep in safety*, Lu. xi. 21; (3) *to observe*, as a precept, Gal. vi. 13; (4) mid., *to keep one's self from* (acc. or ἀπό), Lu. xii. 15; Ac. xxi. 25.

φυλή, ῆς, ἡ, (1) *a tribe*, of Israel, Heb. vii. 13, 14; (2) *a race*, or *people*, Rev. xiii. 7, xiv. 6.

φύλλον, ου, τό, *a leaf*, Mar. xi. 13.

φύραμα, ατος, τό, *a mass kneaded, a lump*, as of dough or clay, Ro. ix. 21, xi. 16; 1 Cor. v. 6, 7; Gal. v. 9.*

φυσικός, ή, όν, *natural*, as (1) *according to nature*, Ro. i. 26, 27; (2) *merely animal*. 2 Pet. ii. 12.*

φυσικῶς, adv., *by nature*, Ju. 10.*

φυσιόω, ῶ, *to inflate, to puff up*, 1 Cor. viii. 1; pass., *to be inflated, arrogant*, 1 Cor. iv. 6, 18, 19, v. 2, xiii. 4; Col. ii. 18.*

φύσις, εως, ἡ, generally, *nature*; specially, (1) *natural birth*, Gal. ii. 15; (2) *natural disposition, propensity*, Ep. ii. 3; (3) *native qualities*, or *properties*, Ja. iii. 7; 2 Pet. i. 4.

φυσίωσις, εως, ἡ, *a puffing up, pride*, 2 Cor. xii. 20. (N. T.)*

φυτεία, ας, ἡ, *a plant*, Mat. xv. 13.*

φυτεύω, σω, *to plant*, abs., or with acc., Mat. xxi. 33; 1 Cor. iii. 6, 8.

φύω, σω, 2d aor. pass. ἐφύην, part. φυείς, *to produce*; pass., *to grow*, Lu. viii. 6, 8; intrans., *to spring up*, Heb. xii. 15.*

φωλεός, οῦ, ὁ, *a burrow, a hole*, Mat. viii. 20; Lu. ix. 58.*

φωνέω, ῶ, ήσω, (1) *to sound, to utter a sound* or *cry*, Lu. viii. 8; espec. of cocks, *to crow*, Mar. xiv. 30; (2) *to call to, to invite* (acc.), Mat. xx. 32; Lu. xiv. 12; (3) *to address, to name*, acc. (nom. of title), Jn. xiii. 13.

φωνή, ῆς, ἡ, (1) *a sound*, musical or otherwise, 1 Cor. xiv. 7, 8; Rev. vi. 1, xiv. 2, xix. 1, 6; (2) *an articulate sound, a voice, a cry*, Lu. xvii. 13; Ac. iv. 24; (3) *a language*, 1 Cor. xiv. 10.

φῶς, φωτός, τό (contr. from φάος, from φάω, *to shine*), (1) lit., *light*, Mat. xvii. 2; Jn. xi. 9; *a source of light*, Lu. xxii. 56; Ja. i. 17; *brightness*, Rev. xxii. 5; ἐν τῷ φωτί, *publicly*, Mat. x. 27; (2) fig., *light*, as an appellation of God, 1 Jn. i. 5; as a symbol of truth and purity, espec. the truth of Christ, Jn. iii. 19, 20, 21; used of Christ, Jn. i. 7, 8. *Syn.*: see λαμπάς.

φωστήρ, ῆρος, ὁ, (1) *a luminary*, Phil. ii. 15; (2) *brightness, splendor*, Rev. xxi. 11.* *Syn.*: see λαμπάς.

φωσ-φόρος, ον, *light-bearing, radiant;* the name of the morning star (Lat. *Lucifer*), the planet Venus, 2 Pet. i. 19.*

φωτεινός (W. H. -τινός), ή, όν, *bright, luminous, full of light*, lit., Mat. xvii. 5; fig., Mat. vi. 22; Lu. xi. 34, 36.*

φωτίζω, ίσω, pass. perf. πεφώτισμαι, 1st aor. ἐφωτίσθην, (1) *to light up, illumine*, lit. or fig. (acc., but ἐπί in Rev. xxii. 5), Lu. xi. 36; (2) *to bring to light, make evident*, 1 Cor. iv. 5.

φωτισμός, οῦ, ὁ, *light, lustre, illumination*, 2 Cor. iv. 4, 6. (S.)*

X

Χ, χ, χῖ, *chi, ch,* guttural, the twenty-second letter. As a numeral, χ′ = 600 ; ͺχ = 600,000.

χαίρω, χαρήσομαι, 2d aor. pass. as act. ἐχάρην, *to rejoice, to be glad,* Lu. xv. 5, 32 ; Jn. iii. 29 ; impv. χαῖρε, χαίρετε, *hail!* Mat. xxvi. 49 ; inf. χαίρειν, *greeting,* Ac. xv. 23.

χάλαζα, ης, ἡ, *hail,* Rev. viii. 7, xi. 19, xvi. 21.*

χαλάω, ῶ, άσω, 1st aor. pass. ἐχαλάσθην, *to let down, to lower,* Mar. ii. 4 ; Lu. v. 4, 5 ; Ac. ix. 25, xxvii. 17, 30 ; 2 Cor. xi. 33.*

Χαλδαῖος, ου, ὁ, *a Chaldæan,* Ac. vii. 4.*

χαλεπός, ή, όν, (1) *hard, troublesome,* 2 Tim. iii. 1 ; (2) *harsh, fierce,* Mat. viii. 28.*

χαλιν-αγωγέω, ῶ, *to bridle, to curb,* Ja. i. 26, iii. 2. (N.T.)*

χαλινός, οῦ, ὁ, *a bridle, a curb,* Ja. iii. 3 ; Rev. xiv. 20.*

χάλκεος, οῦς, ῆ, οῦν, *brazen,* Rev. ix. 20.*

χαλκεύς, έως, ὁ, *a worker in brass* or *copper,* 2 Tim. iv. 14.*

χαλκηδών, όνος, ὁ, *chalcedony,* a precious stone, Rev. xxi. 19.*

χαλκίον, ου, τό, *a brazen vessel,* Mar. vii. 4.*

χαλκο-λίβανον, ου, τό (or -νος, ου, ἡ), meaning uncertain, either *some precious metal,* or *frankincense* (λίβανος) *of a yellow color,* Rev. i. 15, ii. 8. (N.T.)*

χαλκός, οῦ, ὁ, *copper, brass, money,* Mar. vi. 8, 1 Cor. xiii. 1.

χαμαί, adv., *on* or *to the ground,* Jn. ix. 6, xviii. 6.*

Χαναάν, ἡ, *Canaan,* Ac. vii. 11, xiii. 19.*

Χαναναῖος, αία, αῖον, *Canaanite, i.e.,* Phœnician, Mat. xv. 22.*

χαρά, ᾶς, ἡ, *joy, gladness,* Gal. v. 22 ; Col. i. 11 ; *a source of joy,* 1 Th. ii. 19, 20.

χάραγμα, ατος, τό, *sculpture, engraving, a stamp, a sign,* Rev. xiv. 9, 11, xvi. 2.

χαρακτήρ, ῆρος, ὁ, *an impres-*

sion, *an exact reproduction,* Heb. i. 3.*

χάραξ, ακος, ὁ, *a palisade, a mound for besieging,* Lu. xix. 43.*

χαρίζομαι, ίσομαι, dep. mid., fut. pass. χαρισθήσομαι, (1) *to show favor to* (dat.), Gal. iii. 18 ; (2) *to forgive* (dat. pers., acc. thing), 2 Cor. xii. 10 ; Ep. iv. 32 ; Col. ii. 13 ; (3) *to give freely, bestow,* Lu. vii. 21 ; 1 Cor. ii. 12.

χάρις, ιτος, acc. χάριν and χάριτα (W. H. in Ac. xxiv. 27 ; Ju. 4), ἡ, (1) objectively, *agreeableness, charm,* Lu. iv. 22 ; (2) subjectively, *inclination towards, favor, kindness, liberality, thanks,* Lu. i. 30, ii. 40, 52 ; Ac. ii. 47, xxiv. 27 ; χάριν ἔχειν, *to thank ;* χάριν ἔχειν πρός, *to be in favor with ;* especially of the undeserved favor of God or Christ, 2 Cor. iv. 15, xii. 9 ; χάριν, used as prep. with gen. (lit., *with inclination towards*), *for the sake of, on account of,* Ep. iii. 14 ; 1 Tim. v. 14 ; Tit. i. 11.

χάρισμα, ατος, τό, *a gift of grace, an undeserved favor* from God to man, Ro. i. 11, v. 15, 16, vi. 23, xi. 29, xii. 6 ; 1 Cor. i. 7, vii. 7, xii. 4, 9, 28, 30, 31 ; 2 Cor. i. 11 ; 1 Tim. iv. 14 ; 2 Tim. i. 6 ; 1 Pet. iv. 10.*

χαριτόω, ῶ, *to favor, bestow freely on* (acc.), Ep. i. 6 ; pass., *to be favored,* Lu. i. 28. (Ap.)*

Χαρράν, ἡ (Heb.), *Charran* or *Haran,* Ac. vii. 2, 4.*

χάρτης, ου, ὁ, *paper,* 2 Jn. 12.*

χάσμα, ατος, τό, *a gap, a gulf,* Lu. xvi. 26.*

χεῖλος, ους, τό, *a lip ;* plur., *mouth,* Mat. xv. 8 ; 1 Cor. xiv. 21 ; fig., *shore,* Heb. xi. 12.

χειμάζω, in pass., *to be storm-beaten,* or *tempest-tossed,* Ac. xxvii. 18.*

χείμαρρος, ου, ὁ, *a storm-brook, a wintry torrent,* Jn. xviii. 1.*

χειμών, ῶνος, ὁ, (1) *a storm, a tempest,* Ac. xxvii. 20 ; (2) *winter, the rainy season,* Mat. xxiv. 20.

χείρ, χειρός, ἡ, *a hand,* Lu. vi. 6 ; 1 Tim. ii. 8 ; met., for any exertion of *power,* Mat. xvii. 22 ; Lu. ix. 44 ; espec. in the phrases *the hand* of God, *the hand* of the Lord, for help, Ac. iv. 30, xi. 21 ; for punishment, Heb. x. 31.

χειραγωγέω, ῶ, *to lead by the hand,* Ac. ix. 8, xxii. 11.*

χειρ-αγωγός, όν, *leading* one *by the hand,* Ac. xiii. 11.*

χειρό-γραφον, ου, τό, *a handwriting, a bond ;* fig., of the Mosaic law, Col. ii. 14.*

χειρο-ποίητος, ον, *done* or *made with hands,* Mar. xiv. 58 ; Ac. vii. 48, xvii. 24 ; Ep. ii. 11 ; Heb. ix. 11, 24.*

χειρο-τονέω, ῶ, *to vote by stretching out the hand, to choose by vote,* 2 Cor. viii. 19 ; *to appoint,* Ac. xiv. 23.*

χείρων, ον, compar. of κακός (which see), *worse,* Mat. xii. 45 ; *worse, more severe,* Heb. x. 29 ; εἰς τὸ χεῖρον, *worse,* Mar. v. 26 ; ἐπὶ τὸ χεῖρον, *worse and worse,* 2 Tim. iii. 13.

χερουβίμ (W. H. Χερουβείν), τά, *cherubim,* the Heb. plural of cherub, the golden figures on the mercy-seat, Heb. ix. 5. (S.)*

χήρα, ας, ἡ, *a widow,* Ac. vi. 1, ix. 39, 41 ; Ja. i. 27.

χθές (W. H. ἐχθές), adv., *yesterday,* Jn. iv. 52 ; Ac. vii. 28 ; Heb. xiii. 8.*

χιλί-αρχος, ου, ὁ, *a commander of a thousand men, a military tribune,* Ac. xxi-xxv.

χιλιάς, άδος, ἡ, *a thousand,* Lu xiv. 31 ; 1 Cor. x. 8.

χίλιοι, αι, α, *a thousand,* 2 Pet iii. 8 ; Rev. xi. 3.

Χίος, ου, ἡ, *Chios,* Ac. xx 15.*

χιτών, ῶνος, ὁ, *a tunic,* an under-garment, Lu. iii. 11, vi. 29 ; *a garment,* Mar. xiv. 63. *Syn.:* see ἱμάτιον.

χιών, όνος, ἡ, *snow,* Mat. xxviii. 3 ; Mar. ix. 3 (W. H. omit) ; Rev. i. 14.*

χλαμύς, ύδος, ἡ, *a short cloak* worn by Roman officers and magistrates, Mat. xxvii. 28 31.* *Syn.:* see ἱμάτιον.

χλευάζω, to mock, scoff (abs.), Ac. ii. 13 (W. H. διαχλευάζω), xvii. 32.*

χλιαρός, ά, όν, lukewarm, Rev. iii. 16.*

Χλόη, ης, ἡ, Chloe, 1 Cor. i. 11.*

χλωρός, ά, όν, (1) green, Mar. vi. 39; Rev. viii. 7, ix. 4; (2) pale, Rev. vi. 8.*

χξϛ', six hundred and sixty-six, Rev. xiii. 18 (W. H. write the numbers in full).*

χοϊκός, ή, όν, earthy, made of earth, 1 Cor. xv. 47–49. (N. T.)*

χοῖνιξ, ικος, ἡ, a chœnix, a measure containing two sextarii (see ξέστης), Rev. vi. 6.*

χοῖρος, ου, ὁ, plur., swine, Lu. viii. 32, 33, xv. 15, 16.

χολάω, ῶ, to be angry (dat.), Jn. vii. 23.*

χολή, ῆς, ἡ, (1) gall, fig., Ac. viii. 23; (2) perh. bitter herbs, such as wormwood, Mat. xxvii. 34.*

χόος, see χοῦς.

Χοραζίν (W. H. Χοραζείν), ἡ, Chorazin, Mat. xi. 21; Lu. x. 13.*

χορ-ηγέω, ῶ, to lead or furnish a chorus; hence, to furnish abundantly, to supply, 2 Cor. ix. 10; 1 Pet. iv. 11.*

χορός, οῦ, ὁ, a dance, dancing, plur., Lu. xv. 25.*

χορτάζω, to feed, to satisfy with (gen. or ἀπό), Mat. v. 6, xv. 33; Mar. viii. 4; Lu. xvi. 21.

χόρτασμα, ατος, τό, food, sustenance, Ac. vii. 11.*

χόρτος, ου, ὁ, grass, herbage, Mat. vi. 30; growing grain, Mat. xiii. 26; hay, 1 Cor. iii. 12.

Χουζᾶς, ᾶ, ὁ, Chuzas, Lu. viii. 3.*

χοῦς, οός, acc. οῦν, ὁ, dust, Mar. vi. 11; Rev. xviii. 19.*

χράομαι, ῶμαι, dep. (prop. mid. of χράω), to use (dat.), to make use of, 1 Cor. ix. 12, 15; 2 Cor. xiii. 10 (dat. om.); to deal with, Ac. xxvii. 3.

χράω, see κίχρημι.

χρεία, ας, ἡ, (1) need, necessity, plur., necessities, Mar. xi. 3; Tit. iii. 14; ἔχω χρείαν, to need, Jn. xiii. 10; (2) business, Ac. vi. 3.

χρεωφειλέτης (W. H. χρεοφιλέτης), ου, ὁ, a debtor, Lu. vii. 41, xvi. 5.*

χρή, impers. (from χράω), it is necessary, it is proper (acc. and inf.), Ja. iii. 10.*

χρῄζω, to have need of, to need (gen.), Lu. xi. 8, xii. 30.

χρῆμα, ατος, τό, a thing of use; money, sing., only Ac. iv. 37; plur., riches, money, Mar. x. 23; Ac. viii. 18, 20.

χρηματίζω, ίσω, to transact business; hence, (1) to utter an oracle, to give a divine warning, Lu. ii. 26; Heb. xii. 25; pass., to receive a divine response, be warned of God, Mat. ii. 12, 22; Ac. x. 22; Heb. viii. 5, xi. 7; (2) to receive a name, to be called, Ac. xi. 26; Ro. vii. 3.*

χρηματισμός, οῦ, ὁ, an oracle, Ro. xi. 4.*

χρήσιμος, η, ον, useful, profitable, 2 Tim. ii. 14.*

χρῆσις, εως, ἡ, use, Ro. i. 26, 27.*

χρηστεύομαι, dep., to be kind, 1 Cor. xiii. 4. (N. T.)*

χρηστο-λογία, ας, ἡ, a kind address; in a bad sense, plausible speaking, Ro. xvi. 18. (N. T.)*

χρηστός, ή, όν, useful, good, 1 Cor. xv. 33; gentle, pleasant, Lu. v. 39; kind, 1 Pet. ii. 3; τὸ χρηστόν, kindness, Ro. ii. 4.

χρηστότης, τητος, ἡ, (1) goodness, generally, Ro. iii. 12; (2) specially, benignity, kindness, Col. iii. 12. Syn.: see ἀγαθωσύνη.

χρῖσμα, ατος, τό, an anointing, 1 Jn. ii. 20, 27.*

Χριστιανός, οῦ, ὁ, a Christian, Ac. xi. 26, xxvi. 28; 1 Pet. iv. 16.*

χριστός, οῦ, ὁ (verbal adj. from χρίω), anointed; as a proper name, the Messiah, the Christ (see Gr. § 217 e, Wi. § 18, 9, note 1, Bu. 89), Mat. xxiii. 10, etc.

χρίω, σω, to anoint, to consecrate by anointing, as Jesus, the Christ, Lu. iv. 18; Ac. iv. 27, x. 38; Heb. i. 9; applied also to Christians, 2 Cor. i. 21. Syn.: see ἀλείφω.

χρονίζω, to delay, to tarry, Mat.

xxiv. 48, xxv. 5; Lu. i. 21, xii. 45; Heb. x. 37.*

χρόνος, ου, ὁ, (1) time, generally, Lu. iv. 5; Gal. iv. 4; (2) a particular time, or season, Mat. ii. 7; Ac. i. 7. Syn.: see καιρός.

χρονο-τριβέω, ῶ, to wear away time, to spend time, Ac. xx. 16.*

χρύσεος, οῦς, ἡ, οῦν, golden, 2 Tim. ii. 20; Heb. ix. 4.

χρυσίον, ου, τό (dim. of χρυσός), a piece of gold, a golden ornament, Ac. iii. 6; 1 Pet. iii. 3.

χρυσο-δακτύλιος, ον, adorned with a gold ring, Ja. ii. 2. (N. T.)*

χρυσό-λιθος, ου, ὁ (a golden stone), a gem of a bright yellow color, a topaz, Rev. xxi. 20. (S.)*

χρυσό-πρασος, ου, ὁ, a gem of a greenish-golden color, a chrysoprase, Rev. xxi. 20. (N. T.)*

χρυσός, οῦ, ὁ, gold, anything made of gold, gold coin, Mat. ii. 11, x. 9; Ja. v. 3.

χρυσόω, ῶ, to adorn with gold, to gild, Rev. xvii. 4, xviii. 16.*

χρώς, χρωτός, ὁ, the skin, Ac. xix. 12.*

χωλός, ή, όν, lame, Ac. iii. 2; deprived of a foot, Mar. ix. 45.

χώρα, ας, ἡ, (1) a country, or region, Jn. xi. 54; (2) the land, opposed to the sea, Ac. xxvii. 27; (3) the country, dist. from town, Lu. ii. 8; (4) plur., fields, Jn. iv. 35.

χωρέω, ῶ, ήσω, lit., to make room; hence, (1) to have room for, receive, contain, Mat. xix. 11, 12; Jn. ii. 6, xxi. 25; 2 Cor. vii. 2; impers., to be room for, Mar. ii. 2; (2) to make room by departing, to go, Mat. xv. 17; to make progress, Jn. viii. 37; to turn one's self, 2 Pet. iii. 9.*

χωρίζω, ίσω, to put apart, to separate, Mat. xix. 6; mid. (1st aor. pass.), to separate one's self, of divorce, 1 Cor. vii. 11, 15; to depart, to go away (ἀπό or ἐκ), Ac. i. 4. xviii. 1.

χωρίον, ου, τό, a place, a field

Mar. xiv. 32; plur., *lands,* Ac. iv. 34; *a farm, estate,* Ac. xxviii. 7.

χωρίς, adv., *separately, by itself,* only Jn. xx. 7; as prep. gov. gen., *apart from, without,* Jn. xv. 5; Ro. iii. 21; *besides, exclusive of,* Mat. xiv. 21.

χῶρος, ου, ὁ (Lat. *Caurus*), *the N.W. wind;* used for the N.W. quarter of the heavens, Ac. xxvii. 12. (N. T.)*

Ψ

Ψ, ψ, ψῖ, *psi, ps,* the twenty-third letter. As a numeral, ψ′ = 700; ͵ψ = 700,000.

ψάλλω, ψαλῶ, *to sing,* accompanied with instruments, *to sing psalms,* Ro. xv. 9; 1 Cor. xiv. 15; Ep. v. 19; Ja. v. 13.*

ψαλμός, οῦ, ὁ, *a psalm, a song of praise,* Ep. v. 19; Col. iii. 16; plur., *the book of Psalms* in the O. T., Lu. xxiv. 44. *Syn.:* see *ὕμνος.*

ψευδ-άδελφος, ου, ὁ, *a false brother, a pretended Christian,* 2 Cor. xi. 26; Gal. ii. 4. (N. T.)*

ψευδ-απόστολος, ου, ὁ, *a false* or *pretended apostle,* 2 Cor. xi. 13. (N. T.)*

ψευδής, ές, *false, deceitful, lying,* Ac. vi. 13; Rev. ii. 2, xxi. 8.*

ψευδο-διδάσκαλος, ου, ὁ, *a false teacher, a teacher of false doctrines,* 2 Pet. ii. 1. (N. T.)*

ψευδο-λόγος, ον, *false-speaking, speaking lies,* 1 Tim. iv. 2.*

ψεύδομαι, dep., 1st aor. ἐψευσάμην, *to deceive, to lie, to speak falsely,* Heb. vi. 18; Rev. iii. 9; *to lie to* (acc.), Ac. v. 3.

ψευδο-μάρτυρ, or -υς, υρος, ὁ, *a false witness,* Mat. xxvi. 60; 1 Cor. xv. 15.*

ψευδο-μαρτυρέω, ῶ, ήσω, *to testify falsely,* Lu. xviii. 20.

ψευδο-μαρτυρία, ας, ἡ, *false testimony,* Mat. xv. 19, xxvi. 59.*

ψευδο-προφήτης, ου, ὁ, *a false prophet,* one who in God's name teaches what is false, Mar. xiii. 22; 2 Pet. ii. 1. (S.)

ψεῦδος, ους, τό, *a falsehood, a lie,* Jn. viii. 44; 2 Th. ii. 11.

ψευδό-χριστος, ου, ὁ, *a false Christ, a pretended Messiah,* Mat. xxiv. 24; Mar. xiii. 22. (N. T.)*

ψευδ-ώνυμος, ον, *falsely named,* 1 Tim. vi. 20.*

ψεῦσμα, ατος, τό, *falsehood, perfidy,* Ro. iii. 7.*

ψεύστης, ου, ὁ, *a liar, a deceiver,* Jn. viii. 44, 55; Ro. iii. 4.

ψηλαφάω, ῶ, *to feel, to touch, to handle* (acc.), Lu. xxiv. 39; Heb. xii. 18; 1 Jn. i. 1; *to feel after, grope for,* fig., Ac. xvii. 27.* *Syn.:* see ἅπτω.

ψηφίζω, ίσω, *to reckon, to compute,* Lu. xiv. 28; Rev. xiii. 18.*

ψῆφος, ου, ἡ, *a small stone, a pebble,* Rev. ii. 17; used for voting, hence, *a vote,* Ac. xxvi. 10.*

ψιθυρισμός, οῦ, ὁ, *a whispering, a secret slandering,* 2 Cor. xii. 20. (S.)*

ψιθυριστής, οῦ, ὁ, *a whisperer, a secret slanderer,* Ro. i. 30.*

ψιχίον, ου, τό, *a crumb,* Mat. xv. 27; Mar. vii. 28; Lu. xvi. 21 (W. H. omit). (N. T.)*

ψυχή, ῆς, ἡ, (1) *the vital breath, the animal life,* of animals, Rev. viii. 9, xvi. 3, elsewhere only of man, Mat. vi. 25; (2) *the human soul,* as distinguished from the body, Mat. x. 28; (3) *the soul* as the seat of the affections, the will, etc., Ac. xiv. 2, 22; (4) *the self* (like Heb.), Mat. x. 39; (5) *a human person, an individual,* Ro. xiii. 1.

ψυχικός, ή, όν, *animal, natural, sensuous,* 1 Cor. ii. 14, xv. 44, 46; Ja. iii. 15; Ju. 19.*

ψῦχος, ους, τό, *cold,* Jn. xviii. 18.

ψυχρός, ά, όν, *cold,* Mat. x. 42 (sc. ὕδατος); fig., *cold-hearted,* Rev. iii. 15, 16.*

ψύχω, 2d fut. pass. ψυγήσομαι, *to cool;* pass., fig., *to be cooled, to grow cold,* Mat. xxiv. 12.*

ψωμίζω, *to feed,* Ro. xii. 20; *to spend in feeding,* 1 Cor. xiii. 3.*

ψωμίον, ου, τό, *a bit, a morsel,* Jn. xiii. 26, 27, 30. (S.)*

ψώχω, *to rub, to rub to pieces,* as ears of corn, Lu. vi. 1.*

Ω

Ω, ω, ὦ μέγα, *omega, o,* the twenty-fourth letter. As a numeral, ω′ = 800; ͵ω = 800,000. τὸ Ὦ Ω, a name of God and Christ (see under A), Rev. i. 8, 11 (W. H. omit), xxi. 6, xxii. 13.*

ὦ, interj., *O,* used before the vocative in address, Ac. i. 1, xviii. 14; in exclamation, of admiration, Mat. xv. 28; Ro. xi. 33; or of reproof, Lu. xxiv. 25.

Ὠβήδ, ὁ, *Obed,* Mat. i. 5 (W. H. 'Ιωβήδ); Lu. iii. 32 (W. H. 'Ιωβήλ).*

ὧδε, adv., of place, *hither, here;* so, *in this life,* Heb. xiii. 14; *herein, in this matter,* Rev. xiii. 10; ὧδε ἤ ὧδε, *here or there,* Mat. xxiv. 23.

ᾠδή, ῆς, ἡ, *an ode, a song,* Rev. v. 9, xv. 3. *Syn.:* see *ὕμνος.*

ὠδίν, ῖνος, ἡ, *the pain of childbirth, acute pain, severe anguish,* Mat. xxiv. 8; Mar. xiii. 8; Ac. ii. 24; 1 Th. v. 3.*

ὠδίνω, *to feel the pains of childbirth, to travail,* Gal. iv. 27; Rev. xii. 2; fig., Gal. iv. 19.*

ὦμος, ου, ὁ, *a shoulder,* Mat. xxiii. 4; Lu. xv. 5.*

ὠνέομαι, οῦμαι, ἡσόμαι, *to buy* (gen. of price), Ac. vii. 16.*

ὠόν (W. H. ᾠόν), οῦ, τό, *an egg,* Lu. xii. 12.*

ὥρα, ας, ἡ, (1) *a definite space of time, a season;* (2) *an hour,* Mar. xiii. 32; Ac. xvi. 33; (3) *the particular time for anything,* Lu. xiv. 17; Mat. xxvi. 45.

ὡραῖος, αία, αῖον, *fair, beautiful,* Mat. xxiii. 27; Ac. iii. 2, 10; Ro. x. 15.*

ὠρύομαι, dep. mid., *to roar, to howl,* as a beast, 1 Pet. v. 8.*

ὡς, an adv. of comparison, *as, like as, about, as it were, according as,* 2 Pet. i. 3; *how,* Lu. viii. 47; *how!* Ro. x. 15; as particle of time,

when, while, as soon as, Lu.
i. 23, xx. 37 ; Ro. xv. 24 ; as
consecutive particle, *so that*
(inf.), Ac. xx. 24 ; ὡς ἔπος
εἰπεῖν, *so to speak*, Heb. vii.
9.

ὡσαννά, interj., *hosanna!* (Heb.,
Ps. cxviii. 25, *save now!*),
Mat. xxi. 9, 15 ; Mar. xi. 9,
10 ; Jn. xii. 13. (N. T.)*

ὡσ-αύτως, adv., *in like manner,
likewise*, Mat. xx. 5, 1 Tim.
ii. 9.

ὡσ-εί, adv., *as if, as though,
like as*, with numerals, *about*,
Ac. ii. 3, 41.

Ὡσηέ, ὁ, *Hosea*, Ro. ix. 25.*

ὥσ-περ, adv., *just as, as*, Mat.
xii. 40 ; 1 Cor. viii. 5.

ὡσ-περ-εί, adv., *just as if, as it
were*, 1 Cor. xv. 8.*

ὥσ-τε, conj., *so that* (inf., see
Gr. § 391, Wi. §§ 41 *b*, 5,
note 1, 44, 1, Bu. 244), *therefore*, Mat. viii. 24 ; Gal. iii.
9, 24.

ὠτάριον, ου, τό (dim. of οὖς, see
παιδάριον), *an ear*, Mar. xiv.
47 (W. H.) ; Jn. xviii. 10
(W. H.).*

ὠτίον, ου, τό (dim. of οὖς, *an
ear*, Mat. xxvi. 51 ;

Lu. xxii. 51 ; Jn. xviii. 26 ;
also in the passages under
ὠτάριον (Rec.).*

ὠφέλεια, ας, ἡ, *usefulness, profit, advantage*, Ro. iii. 1 ; Ju.
16.*

ὠφελέω, ῶ, ήσω, *to be useful,
to profit, to benefit, to help*
(acc., also acc. of defini-
tion), Ro. ii. 25 ; 1 Cor. xiv.
6 ; pass., *to be profited, to be
helped*, Mat. xvi. 26.

ὠφέλιμος, ον, *profitable, bene-
ficial*, dat. of pers., Tit. iii.
8 ; πρός (acc.), of obj., 1
Tim. iv. 8 ; 2 Tim. iii. 16.*

NEW TESTAMENT SYNONYMS.

INTRODUCTION.

A *careful* discrimination between synonyms in the study of any language is a matter of the utmost importance, and also consequently of considerable difficulty. But there are some considerations which make a treatment of the synonyms of the New Testament especially difficult and especially necessary. The Greek language in classical times was one which was admirably adapted for expressing fine shades of meaning, and therefore one which abounded in synonyms. In later Greek, outside of the New Testament, some of these distinctions were changed or modified. The writers of the New Testament were men of Semitic habits of thought and expression. They also had theological and ethical teachings to impart which were far more profound and spiritual than had been conveyed by the Greek language previous to that time. These and other facts affecting the New Testament Greek necessarily modify the meaning of many of the synonyms there used, in some cases effecting a complete transformation.

The object in the present treatment is to consider the New Testament usage. Hence, the distinctions of classical Greek are stated only so far as they are also found in New Testament usage, or are of importance for determining the latter. For a discrimination of the distinctive meanings of New Testament synonyms, three things must usually be considered :

First, the etymological meaning of the words ;
Second, the relations in which the words are found in classical Greek ;
Third, the relations in which they are found in New Testament Greek, the last being often the chief factor.

The use of the words in the Septuagint is also important, for their connection with the Hebrew words which they are used to translate often throws light on their meaning.

The discussions here given aim to be brief, but yet to outline clearly the important and fundamental differences of meaning. Some words which are often given in works on this subject have been omitted, for the reason that the definitions as given in the Lexicon sufficiently indicate the important distinctions. There has been added, however, a consideration of some other words which are not so commonly included.

The chief works from which material and suggestions have been drawn are mentioned in the Introduction to the Lexicon.

The reason is stated in the Introduction to the Lexicon why in some cases the same word is treated both in the synonyms of the Lexicon itself, and also in this place. In every such instance the treatment here is to be regarded as supplementary to that in the Lexicon proper.

The synonyms here discussed do not belong exclusively nor chiefly to any one class of words. Both theological and non-theological terms are included. The aim has been to consider all the synonyms most likely to be confounded with one another, *i.e.*, all those most important, for practical use, to the average student of the New Testament.

INDEX TO SYNONYMS.

This Index includes all the synonyms discussed in any way, even those indicated by simply giving references to literature concerning them, both in the Lexicon itself and in this separate chapter. Where the same word is discussed in both, the treatment in this separate chapter, as previously stated, is to be considered as supplementary to that in the Lexicon proper.

The references BY PAGES *are in every case to the Lexicon itself;* BY SECTIONS, *to this separate chapter.*

§ 1. Holy, sacred, pure.

ἱερός, ὅσιος, ἅγιος, ἁγνός, σεμνός.

None of these words in classical Greek has necessarily any moral significance. Those which now have such a meaning have developed it in Biblical Greek. ἱερός means *sacred*, implying some special relation to God, so that it may not be violated. It refers, however, to formal relation rather than to character. It designates an external relation, which ordinarily is not an internal relation as well. It is used to describe persons or things. This is the commonest word for *holy* in classical Greek, and expresses their usual conception of holiness, but it is rare in the N.T. because it fails to express the fullness of the N.T. conception. ὅσιος, used of persons or things, describes that which is in harmony with the divine constitution of the moral universe. Hence, it is that which is in accordance with the general and instinctively felt idea of right, "what is consecrated and sanctioned by universal law and consent" (Passow), rather than what is in accordance with any system of revealed truth. As contrary to ὅσιος, *i.e.*, as ἀνοσία, the Greeks regarded, *e.g.*, a marriage between brother and sister such as was common in Egypt, or the omission of the rites of sepulture in connection with a relative. ἅγιος has probably as its fundamental meaning *separation*, *i.e.*, from the world to God's service. If not the original meaning, this at any rate is a meaning early in use. This separation, however, is not chiefly external, it is rather a separation from evil and defilement. The moral signification of the word is therefore the prominent one. This word, rare and of neutral meaning in classical Greek, has been developed in meaning, so that it expresses the full N.T. conception of holiness as no other does. ἁγνός is probably related to ἅγιος. It means specifically *pure*. But this may be only in a ceremonial sense, or it may have a moral signification. It sometimes describes freedom from impurities of the flesh. σεμνός is that which inspires *reverence* or *awe*. In classical Greek it was often applied to the gods. But frequently it has the lower idea of that which is humanly venerable, or even refers simply to externals, as to that which is magnificent, grand, or impressive.

§ 2. Sin.

ἁμαρτία, ἁμάρτημα, ἀσέβεια, παρακοή, ἀνομία, παρανομία, παράβασις, παράπτωμα, ἀγνόημα, ἥττημα.

ἁμαρτία meant originally *the missing of a mark*. When applied to moral things the idea is similar, it is missing the true end of life, and so it is used as a general term for *sin*. It means both the act of sinning and the result, the sin itself. ἁμάρτημα means only the sin itself, not the act, in its particular manifestations as separate deeds of disobedience to a divine law. ἀσέβεια is *ungodliness*, positive and active irreligion, a condition of direct opposition to God. παρακοή is strictly *failing to hear*, or hearing carelessly and inattentively. The sin is in this failure to hear when God speaks, and also in the active disobedience which ordinarily follows. ἀνομία is *lawlessness*, contempt of law, a condition or action not simply without law, as the etymology might indicate, but contrary to law. The law is usually by implication the Mosaic law. παρανομία occurs only once, 2 Pet. ii. 16, and is practically equivalent to ἀνομία. παράβασις is *transgression*, the passing beyond some assigned limit. It is the breaking of a distinctly recognized commandment. It consequently means more than ἁμαρτία. παράπτωμα is used in different senses, sometimes in a milder sense, denoting an error, a mistake, a fault; and sometimes meaning a trespass, a willful sin. ἀγνόημα occurs only once, Heb. ix. 7. It indicates *error*, sin which to a certain extent is the result of ignorance. ἥττημα denotes *being worsted, defeated*. In an ethical sense it means *a failure in duty, a fault.* — All these different words may occasionally but not usually be used simply to describe the same act from different points of view. The fundamental meanings of these words may well be summed up in the language of Trench: Sin "may be regarded as the missing of a mark or aim: it is then ἁμαρτία or ἁμάρτημα; the over-passing or transgressing of a line: it is then παράβασις; the disobedience to a voice: in which case it is παρακοή; the falling where one should have stood upright: this will be παράπτωμα; ignorance of what one ought to have known: this will be ἀγνόημα; diminishing of that which should have been rendered in full measure, which is ἥττημα; non-observance of a law, which is ἀνομία or παρανομία."

§ 3. Sincere.

ἁπλοῦς, ἀκέραιος, ἄκακος, ἄδολος.

ἁπλοῦς is literally *spread out without folds*, and hence means single, simple, without complexity of character and motive. In the N.T. this idea of simplicity is always favorable; in classical Greek the word is also occasionally used in an unfavorable sense, denoting foolish simplicity. ἀκέραιος also means *simple*, literally *free from any foreign admixture, unadulterated, free from disturbing elements*. ἄκακος in Heb. vii. 26 means one in whom exists absence of all evil, and so by implication the presence of all good. It passes also through the merely negative meaning of absence of evil, found in S., to the unfavorable meaning of simple, easily deceived, credulous, which is found in Ro. xvi. 18. ἄδολος, occurring only in 1 Pet. ii. 2, means *sincere, unmixed, without guile.*

§ 4. Sins of the tongue.

μωρολογία, αἰσχρολογία, εὐτραπελία.

μωρολογία, used only once in the N.T., is *foolish talking,* but this in the Biblical sense of the word foolish, which implies that it is also sinful. It is conversation which is first insipid, then corrupt. It is random talk, which naturally reveals the vanity and sin of the heart. αἰσχρολογία, also used once, means any kind of disgraceful language, especially abuse of others. In classical Greek it sometimes means distinctively language which leads to lewdness. εὐτραπελία, occurring once, originally meant *versatility in conversation.* It acquires, however, an unfavorable meaning, since polished, refined conversation has a tendency to become evil in many ways. The word denotes, then, a subtle form of evil-speaking, sinful conversation without the coarseness which frequently accompanies it, but not without its malignity.

§ 5. Shame, disgrace.

αἰδώς, αἰσχύνη, ἐντροπή, (σωφροσύνη).

αἰδώς is the feeling of *innate moral repugnance* to doing a dishonorable act. This moral repugnance is not found in αἰσχύνη, which is rather the feeling of *disgrace* which results from doing an unworthy thing, or the fear of such disgrace which serves to prevent its being done. αἰδώς is thus the nobler word, αἰσχύνη having regard chiefly to the opinions of others. αἰδώς is the fear of doing a shameful thing, αἰσχύνη is chiefly the fear of being found out. "αἰδώς would always restrain a good man from an unworthy act, while αἰσχύνη might sometimes restrain a bad one" (Trench). ἐντροπή stands somewhat between the other two words in meaning, but in the N.T. leans to the nobler side, indicating that *wholesome shame* which leads a man to consideration of his condition if it is unworthy, and to a change of conduct for the better. σωφροσύνη, *self-command,* may not seem to have much in common with these three words. As a matter of fact, however, it expresses positively that which αἰδώς expresses negatively.

§ 6. Prayer.

εὐχή, προσευχή, δέησις, ἔντευξις, εὐχαριστία, αἴτημα, ἱκετηρία.

εὐχή, when it means *prayer,* has apparently a general signification. **προσευχή** and **δέησις** are often used together. προσευχή is restricted to prayer to God, while δέησις has no such restriction. δέησις also refers chiefly to prayer *for particular benefits,* while προσευχή is more general. The prominent thought in **ἔντευξις** is that of boldness and freedom in approach to God. **εὐχαριστία** is *thanksgiving,* the grateful acknowledgment of God's mercies, chiefly in prayer. **αἴτημα,** much like δέησις, denotes a specific petition for a particular thing. In **ἱκετηρία** the attitude of humility and deprecation in prayer is specially emphasized. All these words may indicate at times not different kinds of prayer, but the same prayer viewed from different stand-points.

§ 7. To rebuke; rebuke, accusation.

ἐπιτιμάω, ἐλέγχω; αἰτία, ἔλεγχος.

ἐπιτιμάω means simply *to rebuke,* in any sense. It may be justly or unjustly, and, if justly, the rebuke may be heeded or it may not. **ἐλέγχω,** on the other hand, means to rebuke with sufficient cause, and also effectually, so as to bring the one rebuked to a confession or at least a conviction of sin. In other words, it means *to convince.* A similar distinction exists between the nouns **αἰτία** and **ἔλεγχος.** αἰτία is an accusation, whether false or true. ἔλεγχος is a charge which is shown to be true, and often is so confessed by the accused. It has both a judicial and a moral meaning.

§ 8. Boaster, proud, insolent.

ἀλαζών, ὑπερήφανος, ὑβριστής.

ἀλαζών is properly *a boaster,* who tells great things concerning his own prowess and achievements, with the implied idea that many of his claims are false. This word naturally describes a trait which manifests itself in contact with one's fellow-men, not one which exists simply within the heart. **ὑπερήφανος** describes one who thinks too highly of himself, describing a trait which is simply internal, not referring primarily to external manifestation, although this is implied. It means one who is *proud,* the external manifestation when it appears being in the form of *arrogance* in dealing with others. **ὑβριστής** describes one who delights in *insolent wrong-doing* toward others, finds pleasure in such acts. Cruelty and lust are two of the many forms which this quality assumes. These three words occur together in Ro. i. 30. They are never used in a good sense. They may be said to move in a certain sense in an ascending scale of guilt, designating respectively "the boastful *in words*, the proud and overbearing *in thoughts*, the insolent and injurious *in acts*" (Cremer).

§ 9. Incorruptible, unfading.

ἄφθαρτος, ἀμάραντος, ἀμαράντινος.

ἄφθαρτος is properly *incorruptible*, unaffected by corruption and decay. It is applied to God, and to that which is connected with him. **ἀμάραντος** expresses the same idea in another way. It means *unfading*, the root idea being that it is unaffected by the withering which is common in the case of flowers. **ἀμαράντινος,** derived from *ἀμάραντος*, means *composed of amaranths, i.e.,* of unfading flowers.

§ 10. Faultless, unblamed.

ἄμωμος, ἄμεμπτος, ἀνέγκλητος, ἀνεπίληπτος.

ἄμωμος is *faultless, without blemish, free from imperfections*. It refers especially to character. **ἄμεμπτος** is strictly *unblamed*, one with whom no fault is found. This of course refers particularly to the verdict of others upon one. **ἀνέγκλητος** designates one against whom there is no accusation, implying not acquittal of a charge, but that no charge has been made. **ἀνεπίληπτος** means *irreprehensible*, designating one who affords nothing upon which an adversary might seize, in order to make a charge against him.

§ 11. Regeneration, renovation.

παλιγγενεσία, ἀνακαίνωσις.

παλιγγενεσία means *new birth*. In classical Greek it was used in a weakened sense to denote a recovery, restoration, revival. In the N.T. it is used only twice, but in a higher sense. In Tit. iii. 5 it means *new birth, regeneration*, referring to God's act of causing the sinner to pass from the death of sin into spiritual life in Christ. It has a wider meaning in Mat. xix. 28, where it is used of the change which is ultimately to take place in all the universe, its regeneration, which is the full working out of the change involved in the regeneration of the individual. **ἀνακαίνωσις** is *renewal* or *renovation,* denoting a continuous process through which man becomes more fully Christ-like, in which process he is a worker together with God. Some, as *e.g.* Cremer, without sufficient reason, have thought that the early use of παλιγγενεσία as a somewhat technical term, to denote the Pythagorean doctrine of transmigration, gave to the word a permanent eschatological coloring, so that in the N.T. it has the meaning *resurrection,* especially in Mat. xix. 28.

§ 12. Murderer.

φονεύς, ἀνθρωποκτόνος, σικάριος.

Both in derivation and usage, **φονεύς** and **ἀνθρωποκτόνος** are distinguished from each other just as the English *murderer* from *manslayer* or *homicide.* **σικάριος,** used only in Ac. xxi. 38, is the Latin *sicarius,* and means *an assassin,* usually hired for the work, who furtively stabbed his enemy with a short sword, the Latin *sica.* φονεύς is a generic word and may denote a murderer of any kind, σικάριος being one of the specific varieties which it includes.

§ 13. Anti-Christ, false Christ.

ψευδόχριστος, ἀντίχριστος.

ψευδόχριστος means *a false Christ, a pretended Messiah,* who sets himself up instead of Christ, proclaiming that he is Christ. Some have given about the same meaning to **ἀντίχριστος.** But it is much more probable that it means one diametrically opposed to Christ, one who sets himself up against Christ, proclaiming that there is no Christ.

§ 14. Profligacy.

ἀσωτία, ἀσέλγεια.

The fundamental idea of **ἀσωτία** is "wastefulness and riotous excess; of **ἀσέλγεια,** lawless insolence and wanton caprice" (Trench). ἀσωτία means reckless and extravagant expenditure, chiefly for the gratification of one's sensual desires. It denotes a dissolute, profligate course of life. In ἀσέλγεια also there is included the idea of profligacy, often of lasciviousness, but the fundamental thought is the acknowledging of no restraints, the insolent doing of whatever one's caprice may suggest.

§ 15. Covenant-breaker, implacable.

ἀσύνθετος, ἄσπονδος.

These words are quite similar in their effects, but opposite in their conception. ἀσύνθετος, occurring only in Ro. i. 31, is *covenant-breaker*, one who interrupts a state of peace and brings on war by disregarding an agreement by which peace is maintained. ἄσπονδος is *implacable*, one who refuses to agree to any terms or suggestions of peace. It implies a state of war, and a refusal of covenant or even of armistice to end it permanently or temporarily. In the N.T. use both words probably refer not to war in the strict sense so much as to discord and strife.

§ 16. Beautiful, graceful.

ἀστεῖος, ὡραῖος, καλός.

ἀστεῖος is properly one living in a city, urban. It soon acquires the meaning *urbane, polite, elegant.* Then it obtains to a limited extent the meaning *beautiful*, although never in the highest degree. ὡραῖος, from ὥρα, hour, period, means properly *timely*. From that comes the idea of being beautiful, since nearly everything is beautiful in its hour of fullest perfection. καλός is a much higher word. It means *beautiful*, physically or morally. It is, however, distinctly the beauty which comes from harmony, the beauty which arises from a symmetrical adjustment in right proportion, in other words, from the harmonious completeness of the object concerned.

§ 17. Wisdom, knowledge.

σοφία, φρόνησις, γνῶσις, ἐπίγνωσις.

σοφία is certainly the highest word of all these. It is properly *wisdom*. It denotes mental excellence in the highest and fullest sense, expressing an *attitude* as well as an *act* of the mind. It comprehends knowledge and implies goodness, including the striving after the highest ends, as well as the using of the best means for their attainment. It is never ascribed to any one but God and good men, except in a plainly ironical sense. φρόνησις is a middle term, sometimes having a meaning nearly as high as σοφία, sometimes much lower. It means *prudence, intelligence*, a skillful adaptation of the means to the end desired, the end, however, not being necessarily a good one. γνῶσις is *knowledge, cognition*, the understanding of facts or truths, or else *insight, discernment.* ἐπίγνωσις has an intensive meaning as compared with γνῶσις, it is a fuller, clearer, more thorough knowledge. The verb ἐπιγινώσκω has the same intensive force as compared with γινώσκω.

§ 18. Religious.

θεοσεβής, εὐσεβής, εὐλαβής, θρῆσκος, δεισιδαίμων.

θεοσεβής, according to derivation and usage, means *worship of God* (or of the gods), a fulfillment of one's duty towards God. It is a general term, meaning *religious* in a good sense. εὐσεβής is distinguished from θεοσεβής in two ways. It is used to include the fulfillment of obligations of all kinds, both towards God and man. It is thus applied to the fulfillment of the duties involved in human relations, as towards one's parents. Furthermore, when used in the higher sense, it means not any kind of worship, but, as the etymology indicates, the worshipping of God *aright.* εὐλαβής, meaning originally *careful in handling,* in its religious application means careful in handling divine things. It characterizes the anxious and scrupulous worshipper, careful not to change anything that should be observed in worship, and fearful of offending. It means *devout,* and may be applied to an adherent of any religion, being especially appropriate to describe the best of the Jewish worshippers. θρῆσκος is one who is diligent in the performance of the *outward* service of God. It applies especially to ceremonial worship. δεισιδαίμων, in accordance with its derivation, makes prominent the element of *fear.* It emphasizes strongly the ideas of dependence and of anxiety for divine favor. It may be used as practically equivalent to θεοσεβής. Often, however, it implies that the fear which it makes prominent is an unworthy fear, so that it comes to have the meaning *superstitious.* In the N.T. it is used, as is also the noun δεισιδαιμονία, in a purposely neutral sense, meaning simply *religious,* neither conveying the highest meaning, nor plainly implying a lower meaning.

§ 19. Pure.

εἰλικρινής, καθαρός, ἀμίαντος.

εἰλικρινής denotes chiefly that which is pure as being *sincere,* free from foreign admixture. καθαρός is that which is pure as being *clean,* free from soil or stain. The meaning of both in the N.T. is distinctly ethical. ἀμίαντος is *unspotted,* describing that which is far removed from every kind of contamination.

§ 20. Assembly, church.

συναγωγή, ἐκκλησία, πανήγυρις.

Accordĩng to their derivation, **συναγωγή** is simply *an assembly*, a mass of people gathered together ; **ἐκκλησία** is a narrower word, also *an assembly*, but including only those specially *called together out of* a larger multitude, for the transaction of business. *ἐκκλησία* usually denotes a somewhat more select company than *συναγωγή*. A significant use of *ἐκκλησία* in strict harmony with its derivation was common among the Greeks. It was their common word for the lawful assembly in a free Greek city of all those possessing the rights of citizenship, for the transaction of public affairs. They were *summoned out of* the whole population, "a select portion of it, including neither the populace, nor strangers, nor yet those who had for-feited their civic rights" (Trench). *συναγωγή* had been, before N.T. times, appropriated to designate *a synagogue*, a Jewish assembly for worship, dis-tinct from the Temple, in which sense it is used in the N.T. Probably for that reason, and also for its greater inherent etymological fitness, *ἐκκλησία* is the word taken to designate *a Christian church*, a company of believers who meet for worship. Both these words, however, are sometimes used in the N.T. in a non-technical sense. **πανήγυρις,** occurring only in Heb. xii. 23, differs from both, denoting a solemn assembly for festal rejoicing.

§ 21. Humility, gentleness.

ταπεινοφροσύνη, πρᾳότης.

ταπεινοφροσύνη is *humility*, not the making of one's self small when he is really great, but thinking little of one's self, because this is in a sense the right estimate for any human being, however great. **πρᾳότης** is founded upon this idea, and goes beyond it. It is the attitude of mind and behavioɪ which, arising from humility, disposes one to receive with *gentleness* and *meekness* whatever may come to him from others or from God.

§ 22. Gentleness.

πρᾳότης, ἐπιείκεια.

Both words may be translated *gentleness*, yet there are marked differ-ences in meaning. **πρᾳότης** is rather passive, denoting, as has been said above, see § 21, one's attitude toward others in view of their acts, bad ɪ good. ἐπιείκεια is distinctly active, it is seen in one's deeds toward others, and it usually implies the relation of superior to inferior. It is fundamentally a relaxing of strict legal requirements concerning others, yet doing this in order more fully to carry out the real spirit of the law. It is *clemency* in which there is no element of weakness or injustice.

§ 23. Desire, lust.

ἐπιθυμία, πάθος, ὁρμή, ὄρεξις.

ἐπιθυμία is the broadest of these words. Its meaning may be good, but it is usually bad. It denotes any natural desire or appetite, usually with the implication that it is a depraved desire. πάθος has not as broad a meaning as in classical Greek, but denotes evil desire, chiefly, however, as a condition of the soul rather than in active operation. ὁρμή indicates *hostile* motion toward an object, either for seizing or repelling. ὄρεξις is a desire or appetite, especially seeking the object of gratification in order to make it one's own.

§ 24. Affliction.

θλῖψις, στενοχωρία.

θλῖψις according to its derivation means *pressure*. In its figurative sense it is that which presses upon the spirit, *affliction*. στενοχωρία meant originally *a narrow, confined space*. It denotes affliction as arising from cramping circumstances. In use it cannot always be distinguished from θλῖψις, but it is ordinarily a stronger word.

§ 25. Bad, evil.

κακός, πονηρός, φαῦλος.

These words may be used with very little distinction of meaning, but often the difference is marked. κακός frequently means *evil* rather negatively, referring to the absence of the qualities which constitute a person or thing what it should be or what it claims to be. It is also used meaning *evil* in a moral sense. It is a general antithesis to ἀγαθός. πονηρός is a word at once stronger and more active, it means *mischief-making*, delighting in injury, doing evil to others, dangerous, destructive. κακός describes the quality according to its nature, πονηρός, according to its effects. φαῦλος is the bad chiefly as the *worthless*, the good for nothing.

§ 26. Punishment.

τιμωρία, κόλασις.

τιμωρία in classical and N.T. usage denotes especially the vindicative character of punishment, it is the punishment in relation to the *punisher*. κόλασις in classical Greek meant usually punishment which aimed at the reformation of the offender. But sometimes in later Greek, and always in the N.T., the idea of reformation seems to disappear, so that there remains simply the idea of punishment, but viewed in relation to the *punished*.

§ 27. To pollute.

μιαίνω, μολύνω.

μιαίνω meant originally *to stain*, as with color. μολύνω meant originally *to smear over*, as with mud or filth, always having a bad meaning, while the meaning of μιαίνω might be either good or bad. According to classical Greek, μιαίνω has a religious meaning, *to profane*, while μολύνω is simply *to spoil, disgrace*. As ethically applied in the N.T. they have both practically the same meaning, *to pollute, defile*. It is, however, true that μιαίνω, to judge from classical usage, refers chiefly to the effect of the act not on the individual, but on others, on the community.

§ 28. To do.

ποιέω, πράσσω.

These words are often used interchangeably, but in many cases a distinction can be drawn. ποιέω refers more to the object and end of an act, πράσσω rather to the means by which the object is attained. Hence, while ποιέω means *to accomplish*, πράσσω may mean nothing more than merely *to busy one's self about*. ποιέω often means to do a thing once for all, πράσσω, to do continually or repeatedly. From these distinctions it follows that ποιέω, being on the whole the higher word, is more often used of doing good, πράσσω more frequently of doing evil.

§ 29. Fleshly, fleshy, sensual.

σαρκικός, σάρκινος, ψυχικός.

σαρκικός means *fleshly*, that which is controlled by the wrong desires which rule in the flesh, flesh often being understood in its broad sense, see σάρξ. It describes a man who gives the flesh the dominion in his life, a place which does not belong to it by right. It means distinctly opposed to the Spirit of God, anti-spiritual. **σάρκινος** properly means *fleshy,* made of flesh, flesh being the material of which it is composed. When given a bad meaning, however, it is plainly similar to σαρκικός, but according to Trench not so strong, denoting one as unspiritual, undeveloped, rather than anti-spiritual. Others, as Cremer and Thayer, with more probability make σάρκινος the stronger, it describes one who is flesh, wholly given up to the flesh, rooted in the flesh, rather than one who simply acts according to the flesh (σαρκικός). There is much confusion between the two in the N.T. manuscripts. **ψυχικός** has a meaning somewhat similar to σαρκικός. Both are used in contrast with πνευματικός. But ψυχικός has really a distinct meaning, describing the life which is controlled by the ψυχή. It denotes, therefore, that which belongs to the animal life, or that which is controlled simply by the appetites and passions of the sensuous nature.

§ 30. Mercy, compassion.

ἔλεος, οἰκτιρμός.

Both words denote sympathy, fellow-feeling with misery, mercy, compassion. **ἔλεος,** however, manifests itself chiefly in acts rather than words, while **οἰκτιρμός** is used rather of the inward feeling of compassion which abides in the heart. A criminal might ask for ἔλεος, *mercy,* from his judge; but hopeless suffering may be the object of οἰκτιρμός, *compassion.*

§ 31. To love.

ἀγαπάω, φιλέω.

ἀγαπάω, and not **φιλέω,** is the word used of God's love to men, φιλανθροπία is, however, once used with this meaning, Tit. iii. 4. ἀγαπάω is also the word ordinarily used of men's love to God, but φιλέω is once so used, 1 Cor. xvi. 22. ἀγαπάω is the word used of love to one's enemies. The interchange of the words in Jn. xxi. 15–17 is very interesting and instructive.

§ 32. To will, to wish.

βούλομαι, θέλω.

In many cases these two words are used without appreciable distinction, meaning *conscious willing, purpose.* But frequently it is evident that a difference is intended, although there is much difference of opinion as to the exact distinction. Thayer says that βούλομαι "seems to designate the will which follows deliberation," θέλω, "the will which proceeds from inclination." Grimm, on the other hand, says that θέλω gives prominence to the emotive element, βούλομαι to the rational and volitive; θέλω signifies the choice, while βούλομαι marks the choice as deliberate and intelligent. The view of Cremer on the whole seems preferable to any other. According to this view, βούλομαι has the wider range of meaning, but θέλω is the stronger word, θέλω denotes the active resolution, the will urging on to action, see Ro. vii. 15, while βούλομαι is rather to have in thought, to intend, to be determined. βούλομαι sometimes means no more than to have an inclination, see Ac. xxiii. 15. Instructive examples of the use of the two words in close proximity are found in Mar. xv. 9, 15, and especially Mat. i. 19.

§ 33. Schism.

σχίσμα, αἵρεσις.

σχίσμα is *actual division, separation.* αἵρεσις is rather *the separating tendency,* so it is really more fundamental than σχίσμα.

§ 34. Mind, understanding.

νοῦς, διάνοια.

νοῦς is distinctly *the reflective consciousness,* "the organ of moral thinking and knowing, the intellectual organ of moral sentiment" (Cremer). διάνοια meant originally *activity of thinking,* but has borrowed from νοῦς its common meaning of *faculty of thought.* It is more common than νοῦς, and has largely replaced it in its usual meanings.

§ 35. Law.

νόμος, θεσμός, ἐντολή, δόγμα.

νόμος is the common word meaning *law.* It may mean law in general. In the N.T., however, it usually means the law of God, and most frequently the Mosaic law. θεσμός is law considered with special reference to the authority on which it rests. ἐντολή is more specific, being used of a particular command. δόγμα is an authoritative conclusion, a proposition which it is expected that all will recognize as universally binding.

§ 36. Type, image.

τύπος, ἀντίτυπος.

τύπος has many meanings, among the most common being *image, pattern* or *model*, and *type*. In the last sense it means a person or thing prefiguring a future person or thing, *e.g.*, Adam as a type of Christ, Ro. v. 14. ἀντί-τυπος, as used in 1 Pet. iii. 21, is by Thayer and many others thought to correspond to τύπος as its counterpart, in the sense which the English word antitype suggests. By Cremer it is rather given the meaning *image*.

§ 37. To ask.

αἰτέω, ἐρωτάω.

Thayer, as opposed to Trench and others, would make the distinction between these two words to be this: "αἰτέω signifies to ask for something to be given, not done, giving prominence to the thing asked for rather than the person, and hence is rarely used in exhortation. ἐρωτάω, on the other hand, is to request a person to do (rarely to give) something; referring more directly to the person, it is naturally used in exhortation, etc."

§ 38. World, age.

αἰών, κόσμος.

It is only in a part of their meanings that these two words are in any real sense synonymous, and it is that part which is here considered. Both A. V. and R. V. often translate αἰών by *world*, thus obscuring the distinction between it and κόσμος. αἰών is usually better expressed by *age*, it is the world at a given time, a particular period in the world's history. κόσμος has very frequently an unfavorable meaning, denoting the inhabitants of the world, mankind in general, as opposed to God. A similar meaning is often attached to αἰών, it means the spirit of the age, often in an unfavorable sense. See Ep. ii. 2, where both words occur together. An exceptional meaning for the plural of αἰών is found in Heb. i. 2 and xi. 3, where it denotes the worlds, apparently in reference to space rather than time.

§ 39. Rest.

ἀνάπαυσις, ἄνεσις.

Both words in a certain sense mean *rest*, but from different stand-points. ἀνάπαυσις is rest which comes by cessation from labor, which may be simply temporary. ἄνεσις means literally the relaxation of strings which have been drawn tight. Hence, it is used to designate ease, especially that which comes by relaxation of unfavorable conditions of any kind, such as affliction.

§ 40. Wind.

πνεῦμα, πνοή, ἄνεμος, λαῖλαψ, θύελλα.

πνεῦμα when used in its lower meaning to denote wind means simply *an ordinary wind,* a regularly blowing current of air of considerable force. πνοή is distinguished from it as being a gentler motion of the air. ἄνεμος, on the other hand, is more forcible than πνεῦμα, it is the strong, often the tempestuous, wind. λαῖλαψ is the violent fitful wind which accompanies a heavy shower. θύελλα is more violent than any of the others, and often implies a conflict of opposing winds.

§ 41. Old.

παλαιός, ἀρχαῖος.

According to their derivation, παλαιός is that which has been in existence for a long time, ἀρχαῖος that which has been from the beginning. In use, at times no distinction can be drawn. Often, however, ἀρχαῖος does denote distinctively that which has been from the beginning, and so it reaches back to a point of time beyond παλαιός. παλαιός has often the secondary meaning of that which is old and so worn out, having suffered more or less from the injuries and ravages of time, its opposite in this sense being καινός.

§ 42. Harsh, austere.

αὐστηρός, σκληρός.

αὐστηρός has not necessarily an unfavorable meaning. It is well represented by the word *austere,* it means one who is earnest and severe, strict in his ways, opposed to all levity. By implication it may have the unfavorable meaning of harshness or moroseness. σκληρός has always an unfavorable meaning. It indicates one who is uncivil, intractable, rough and harsh. There is in it the implication of inhumanity.

§ 43. Darkness.

σκότος, γνόφος, ζόφος, ἀχλύς.

σκότος is a general word, meaning *darkness* in any sense. γνόφος usually refers to darkness that accompanies a storm. ζόφος meant originally *the gloom* of twilight. It was then applied in classical Greek to the darkness of the underworld, the gloom of a sunless region. The latter meaning seems to be practically the one which the word has in the N.T. ἀχλύς is specifically a misty darkness.

§ 44. People, nation.

λαός, ἔθνος, δῆμος, ὄχλος.

λαός is a word which is usually limited in use to the chosen people, Israel. ἔθνος in the singular is a general term for nation, applied to any nation, even to the Jews. In the plural it ordinarily denotes all mankind aside from the Jews and in contrast with them, the Gentiles. δῆμος is a people, especially organized and convened together, and exercising their rights as citizens. ὄχλος is *a crowd*, an unorganized multitude, especially composed of those who have not the rights and privileges of free citizens.

§ 45. Servant, slave.

δοῦλος, θεράπων, διάκονος, οἰκέτης, ὑπηρέτης.

δοῦλος is the usual word for *slave*, one who is permanently in servitude, in subjection to a master. θεράπων is simply one who renders service at a particular time, sometimes as a slave, more often as a freeman, who renders voluntary service prompted by duty or love. It denotes one who serves, *in his relation to a person*. διάκονος also may designate either a slave or a freeman, it denotes a servant viewed *in relation to his work*. οἰκέτης designates a slave, sometimes being practically equivalent to δοῦλος. Usually, however, as the etymology of the term indicates, it means a slave as a member of the household, not emphasizing the servile idea, but rather the relation which would tend to mitigate the severity of his condition. ὑπηρέτης means literally *an under-rower*, and was used to describe an ordinary rower on a war-galley. It is then used, as in the N.T., to indicate any man, not a slave, who served in a subordinate position under a superior.

§ 46. To adulterate.

καπηλεύω, δολόω.

Both these words mean *to adulterate,* and some maintain that they are practically identical. But it is more probable that **δολόω** means simply to adulterate, while **κατηλεύω** conveys the idea of adulterating for the sake of making an unjust profit by the process.

§ 47. Animal.

ζῶον, θηρίον.

ζῶον is a general term, meaning *living creature,* which may include all living beings, in classical Greek even including man. In the N.T. it means ordinarily *animal.* **θηρίον** is *beast,* usually wild beast. It implies perhaps not necessarily wildness and ferocity, but at least a certain amount of brutality which is wanting in ζῶον. ζῶον emphasizes the qualities in which animals are akin to man, θηρίον, those in which they are inferior.

§ 48. Sea.

θάλασσα, πέλαγος.

θάλασσα is the more general word, indicating *the sea* or *ocean* as contrasted with the land or shore. It may be applied to small bodies of water. **πέλαγος** is *the open sea,* the uninterrupted expanse of water, in contrast with the portions broken by islands or with partly inclosed bays. The prominent thought is said by Trench to be breadth rather than depth. Noteworthy is the distinction between the two words in Mat. xviii. 6.

§ 49. To grieve.

λυπέομαι, πενθέω, θρηνέω, κόπτομαι.

λυπέομαι is the most general word, meaning simply *to grieve,* outwardly or inwardly. **πενθέω** means properly *to lament for the dead.* It is also applied to passionate lamentation of any kind, so great that it cannot be hid. **θρηνέω** is *to give utterance to a dirge* over the dead, either in unstudied words, or in a more elaborate poem. This word is used by S. in describing David's lament over Saul and Jonathan. **κόπτομαι** is *to beat the breast in grief,* ordinarily for the dead.

§ 50. Form, appearance.

ἰδέα, μορφή, σχῆμα.

ἰδέα denotes merely *outward appearance*. Both **μορφή** and **σχῆμα** express something more than that. They too denote outward form, but as including one's habits, activities and modes of action in general. In *μορφή* it is also implied that the outward form expresses the inner essence, an idea which is absent from *σχῆμα*. *μορφή* expresses the form as that which is intrinsic and essential, *σχῆμα* signifies the figure, shape, as that which is more outward and accidental. Both *σχῆμα* and *ἰδέα* therefore deal with externals, *σχῆμα* being more comprehensive than *ἰδέα*, while *μορφή* deals with externals as expressing that which is internal.

§ 51. Clothing.

ἱμάτιον, χιτών, ἱματισμός, χλαμύς, στολή, ποδήρης.

ἱμάτιον is used in a general sense to mean *clothing*, and may thus be applied to any garment when it is not desired to express its exact nature. In a more specific use, however, it denotes the large loose outer garment, *a cloak*, which ordinarily was worn, but in working was laid aside. **χιτών** is best expressed by the word *tunic*. It was a closely fitting under-garment, usually worn next the skin. At times, especially in working, it was the only garment worn. A person clothed only in the *χιτών* was often called *γυμνός* (Jn. xxi. 7). *ἱμάτιον* and *χιτών* are often found associated as the upper and under garment respectively. **ἱματισμός** does not denote a specific garment, but means *clothing*, being used, however, ordinarily only of garments more or less stately or costly. **χλαμύς** is *a robe* or *cloak*, it is a technical expression for a garment of dignity or office. **στολή** is any stately robe, ordinarily long, reaching to the feet or sweeping the ground, often worn by women. **ποδήρης** was originally an adjective meaning *reaching to the feet*. It can hardly be distinguished in use from *στολή*. It occurs only in Rev. i. 13.

§ 52. New.

νέος, καινός.

νέος is *the new* as contemplated under the aspect of time, that which has recently come into existence. **καινός** is *the new* under the aspect of quality, that which has not seen service. *καινός* therefore often means new as contrasted with that which has decayed with age, or is worn out, its opposite then being παλαιός. It sometimes suggests that which is unusual. It often implies praise, the new as superior to the old. Occasionally, on the other hand, it implies the opposite, the new as inferior to that which is old, because the old is familiar or because it has improved with age. Of course it is evident that both νέος and καινός may sometimes be applied to the same object, but from different points of view.

§ 53. Labor.

μόχθος, πόνος, κόπος.

μόχθος is *labor*, hard and often painful. It is the ordinary word for common labor which is the usual lot of humanity. πόνος is *labor* which demands one's whole strength. It is therefore applied to labors of an unusual kind, specially wearing or painful. In classical Greek it was the usual word employed to describe the labors of Hercules. κόπος denotes *the weariness* which results from labor, or labor considered from the stand-point of the resulting weariness.

§ 54. Drunkenness, drinking.

μέθη, πότος, οἰνοφλυγία, κῶμος, κραιπάλη.

μέθη is the ordinary word for *drunkenness*. πότος is rather concrete, *a drinking, carousing*. οἰνοφλυγία is a prolonged condition of drunkenness, *a debauch*. κῶμος includes *riot* and *revelry*, usually as arising from drunkenness. κραιπάλη denotes *the sickness* and *discomfort* resulting from drunkenness.

§ 55. War, battle.

πόλεμος, μάχη.

πόλεμος ordinarily means *war, i.e.*, the whole course of hostilities; μάχη, *battle*, a single engagement. It is also true that μάχη has often the weaker force of *strife* or *contention*, which is very seldom found in πόλεμος.

§ 56. Basket.

σπυρίς, κόφινος.

These words in the N.T. are used with an evident purpose to discriminate between them. The distinction, however, does not seem to have been chiefly one of size, as some have thought, but of use. σπυρίς is usually a basket for food, *a lunch-basket, a hamper*, while κόφινος is a more general term for *basket*. The descriptions of the two miracles of feeding the multitude use always different words in the two cases, see *e.g.* Mar. viii. 19, 20.

§ 57. It is necessary.

δεῖ, ὀφείλει.

δεῖ, the third person of δέω, is commonly used impersonally in classical Greek. This usage is less common, but frequent, in the N.T. δεῖ indicates a necessity in the nature of things rather than a personal obligation, it describes that which *must* be done. ὀφείλει indicates rather the personal obligation, it is that which is proper, something that *ought* to be done.

§ 58. Tax.

φόρος, τέλος, κῆνσος, δίδραχμον.

φόρος indicates *a direct tax* which was levied annually on houses, lands, and persons, and paid usually in produce. τέλος is *an indirect tax* on merchandise, which was collected at piers, harbors, and gates of cities. It was similar to modern import duties. κῆνσος, originally an enrollment of property and persons, came to mean *a poll-tax*, levied annually on individuals by the Roman government. δίδραχμον was the coin used to pay an annual tax levied by the religious leaders of Israel for the purpose of defraying the general expenses of the Temple.

§ 59. Tax-collector.

τελώνης, ἀρχιτελώνης.

The Roman system of collecting taxes, especially the τέλοι, in their provinces, included ordinarily three grades of officials. There was the highest, called in Latin *publicanus*, who paid a sum of money for the taxes of a certain province, and then exacted that and as much more as he could from the province. This man lived in Rome. Then there were the *sub-magistri*, who had charge each of a certain portion of territory, and who lived in the provinces. Then there were the *portitores*, the actual custom-house officers, who did the real work of collecting the taxes. The N.T. word τελώνης is used to describe one of the *portitores*, it is the lowest of these three grades. It does not correspond to the Latin *publicanus*, and the word *publican* used to translate it in A. V. and R. V. is apt to be misleading, *tax collector* would be better. ἀρχιτελώνης, only occurring in Lu. xix. 2, evidently describes a higher official than τελώνης, and is probably one of the *submagistri*, the next higher grade.

§ 60. Child.

τέκνον, υἱός, παῖς, παιδίον, παιδάριον, παιδίσκη.

τέκνον and **υἱός** both point to parentage. **τέκνον**, however, emphasizes the idea of descent, giving prominence to the physical and outward aspects; while *υἱός* emphasizes the idea of relationship, and considers especially the inward, ethical, and legal aspects. **παῖς** as well as τέκνον emphasizes the idea of descent, but gives especial prominence to age, denoting a child as one who is young. παῖς is also often used of a servant. The number of years covered by the term παῖς is quite indefinite. Its diminutives **παιδίον** and **παιδάριον** are used without appreciable difference to denote a young child. (*παιδίσκος* in classical Greek and) **παιδίσκη**, in which the diminutive force is largely lost, cover the years of late childhood and early youth.

§ 61. Tribe, family, household.

φυλή, πατριά, οἶκος.

These words form a series. **φυλή** is sometimes *a race, nation*, but usually *a tribe*, such as one of the twelve tribes of Israel, descended from the twelve sons of Jacob. **πατριά** is a smaller division within the tribe, it is an association of families closely related, in the N.T. generally used of those descended from a particular one of the sons of Jacob's sons. **οἶκος** is yet narrower, *household*, including all the inmates of a single house, being the unit of organization.